Final Dec. 22.
13, 15, 16, 19.

THE BOOK HOUSE
4508 ARMOUR RD
COLUMBUS GA CSU
706 596 9905SP05

THE BOOK HOUSE
4508 ARMOUR RD
COLUMBUS GA CSU
706 596 9905 SU 04

THE BOOK HOUSE
4508 ARMOUR RD
COLUMBUS GA 31904
SU 05 CSU

THE BOOK HOUSE
4508 ARMOUR RD
COLUMBUS GA CSU
706 596 9905 FA 04

THE BOOK HOUSE
4508 ARMOUR RD
COLUMBUS GA CSU
706 596 9905 SU 05

THE BOOK HOUSE
4508 ARMOUR RD
COLUMBUS GA 31904
SU 04 CSU

THE BOOK HOUSE
4508 ARMOUR RD
COLUMBUS GA CSU
706 596 9905 SU 05

Auditing: An Assertions Approach

To the Student: This text will be an important reference source in your future professional career. You should retain it for your personal library.

A Study Guide for this textbook is available through your college bookstore under the title **Study Guide to Accompany Auditing: An Assertions Approach,** Seventh Edition, by **Donald H. Taylor** and **G. William Glezen.** The Study Guide can help you with course material by acting as a tutorial, review, and study aid. If the Study Guide is not in stock, ask the bookstore manager to order one for you.

Auditing: An Assertions Approach

SEVENTH EDITION

SEVENTH EDITION

Auditing:
An Assertions
Approach

DONALD H. TAYLOR, PH.D., C.P.A.
Austin Peay State University, Clarksville

G. WILLIAM GLEZEN, PH.D., C.P.A.
University of Arkansas, Fayetteville

John Wiley & Sons
New York • Chichester • Brisbane • Toronto • Singapore

ACQUISITIONS EDITOR	Susan Elbe
MARKETING MANAGER	Karen Allman
PRODUCTION EDITOR	Edward Winkleman
DESIGNER	Nancy Field
MANUFACTURING COORDINATOR	Mark Cirillo
ILLUSTRATION COORDINATOR	Gene Aiello

This book was set in New Baskerville by Achorn Graphics and printed and bound by Hamilton Printing. The cover was printed by Hamilton Printing.

Library of Congress Cataloging in Publication Data
Taylor, Donald H., 1933–
    Auditing: An Assertions Approach / Donald H. Taylor,
G. William Glezen.—7th ed.
      p. cm.
    Includes index.
    ISBN 0-471-13421-X (alk. paper)
    1. Auditing. 2. Auditing—Data processing. 3. Sampling
(Statistics) I. Glezen, G. William. II. Title.
HF5667.T295 1997
657'.45—dc20
                                                            96-21083
                                                             CIP

Printed in the United States of America

10 9 8 7 6 5 4

To
Rosetta, Michael, Timothy, George, and Ethel

and to
Sylvia, Paul, and John

About the Authors

Donald H. Taylor holds the Harper-Bourne Chair of Excellence at Austin Peay State University. He received a B.S. in accounting from Louisiana Tech University and an M.B.A. and Ph.D. from Louisiana State University. He is a CPA.

Professor Taylor has had several years of public accounting experience with national and local CPA firms. During his academic career, he has taught basic and graduate auditing courses at a number of universities. Much of his practical and academic experience is reflected in this text. Professor Taylor is the author of a number of textbooks including *Principles of Accounting*, which was coauthored by John Cerepak and published by Prentice-Hall, Inc. in 1987.

G. William Glezen is the Walter B. Cole Professor of Accounting at the University of Arkansas. A native of Texas, he received a B.B.A. in accounting from Texas A & M University and an M.B.A. and Ph.D. from the University of Arkansas. He is a CPA and a member of a number of professional accounting organizations. He has published articles on auditing topics in several academic and professional journals.

Many of the concepts, examples, and illustrations in this book are the result of Professor Glezen's 17 years of experience in public accounting with Arthur Andersen LLP. During this period, which included seven years as a partner, he participated at all levels in, and supervised, audit engagements of both large and small enterprises in a broad range of industries.

Acknowledgments

We thank the American Institute of Certified Public Acountants for permission to quote or reproduce material from [1] Statements on Auditing Standards, [2] the AICPA *Code of Professional Conduct,* [3] Statements on Standards for Accounting and Review Services, [4] Statements on Quality Control Standards, [5] questions from uniform CPA examinations, [6] tables from the AICPA statistical sampling volumes, and [7] procedural flowcharts from AICPA booklets on internal control.

We are grateful to The Institute of Internal Auditors for permission to reproduce and quote from [1] Standards for the Professional Practice of Internal Auditing, [2] *The Internal Auditor,* and [3] questions from CIA examinations.

We appreciate the Institute of Certified Management Accountants of the Institute of Management Accountants granting permission to use questions and unofficial answers from past CMA examinations.

We thank Ernst & Young LLP for permission to use several of their case studies as discussion and problem material.

Many users of our book have been very helpful in making suggestions to improve the seventh edition. We especially appreciate the comments of Professors Margaret A. Berezewski (Robert Morris College), Gary D. Burkette (East Tennessee State University), William J. Donnelly (San Jose State University), Michele Huff (Golden Gate University), Joseph D. Kaderabek (Baldwin-Wallace College), Hossein Nouri (Trenton State College), and Robert L. Terrell (University of Central Oklahoma).

Finally, we express appreciation to our editors, Susan Elbe, Linda Muriello, and Edward Winkleman for valuable aid in the production of the book.

D.H.T.
G.W.G.

Preface

The seventh edition of this book maintains the four traditional strengths of the earlier editions: (1) readability; (2) a balanced approach between concepts and procedures; (3) comprehensive end-of-chapter material; and (4) versatility. We have also updated the book for current auditing standards and appropriate real world examples.

Several features have been added that make this edition more readable and create interesting ways to teach auditing. Many chapters contain examples of value-added auditing that show how auditors can improve the efficiency and effectiveness of their clients' operations. Several cases have been placed in the instructor's manual to shorten the text and still give instructors an opportunity to cover them. The last cases in Chapters 1 through 5 have a continuous theme, allowing the instructor to tie together important concepts in the early part of the course. We have added new and challenging discussion questions from the essay section of recent CPA examinations. We have condensed the book by focusing more sharply on important concepts and eliminating duplicate explanations.

Here is a chapter-by-chapter explanation of the material:

Chapter 1 is an overview of auditing and distinguishes between financial statement, operational, and compliance auditing.

Chapter 2 describes services offered by CPA firms and standards used to perform a financial statement audit. The chapter compares in detail the broad attestation standards and the more narrowly focused auditing standards.

Chapter 3 includes discussions of ethics and the AICPA *Code of Professional Conduct*, including new interpretations and rulings. This chapter can be covered at the end of the course, although we prefer to cover it at this early point.

Chapter 4 covers the auditor's legal environment and landmark cases that have changed this environment. Several new cases are integrated into the appropriate sections. This chapter can also be covered at the end of the course, although we again prefer to cover it earlier.

Chapter 5 covers errors and fraud in a very focused way. Our users have given us positive feedback on this separate chapter started in the previous edition.

Chapter 6 is the first chapter on audit planning and documentation. We have a detailed introduction to management assertions that are highlighted in the remainder of the book.

Chapter 7 introduces materiality and audit risk and contains extensive illustrations of the audit risk model.

Chapter 8 is the third chapter on planning and describes in detail the audit planning process.

Chapters 9 through 12 cover internal control. Chapter 9 introduces two audit strategies for obtaining an understanding of internal control and for testing and evaluating it. We use the new COSO model for describing internal control. Chapter 10 illustrates tests of controls, including the use of nonstatistical and statistical sampling. The sections on sampling can either be covered in depth or omitted. Chapters 11 and 12 cover internal control and substantive tests in a computerized environment. These two chapters can be assigned as a unit.

Chapters 13 through 18 cover substantive testing. Chapter 13 discusses the general nature of evidence gathering and demonstrates how assertions are used to derive audit objectives, which are then used to derive audit procedures. Chapter 14 (which may be omitted by instructors) illustrates nonstatistical and statistical sampling techniques applicable to substantive tests. Chapters 15 through 18 contain extensive discussions of audit procedures for substantive tests, many of which are illustrated with microcomputer-generated working papers. Instructors may wish to condense coverage of these chapters. Some coverage is very desirable because the chapters contain practical material on audit techniques.

Chapters 19 through 21 cover the various audit reporting standards. Instructors may prefer to teach Chapter 19 in summary form because of prior coverage of the standard audit report. Chapter 20 should be studied in depth to acquire knowledge of the various forms of qualifications, disclaimers, and adverse opinions. Chapter 21 contains useful illustrations of review, compilation, and other services that CPAs provide.

Chapter 22 covers operational and compliance auditing. This material can be covered earlier at the instructor's preference.

We have the same type of end-of-chapter material that has been a major strength of our book in the previous six editions. Several cases have been added, some have been modified, and others have been placed either in the test bank or instructor's manual. We now have our best balance of questions and cases.

Review questions can be used to learn the chapter material in the sequence in which the material is written. Objective questions (some written by us and some adapted from CPA, CMA, and CIA examinations) relate chapter material to subject matter covered on professional examinations. Discussion/case questions emphasize the highly subjective nature of auditing. We suggest use of all types of questions; each type has a distinct purpose.

This edition is designed to be used for a one-semester coverage of an undergraduate or graduate auditing course. The book does have the versatility to be used in a number of ways:

1. All 22 chapters can be covered if the instructor prefers to teach a broad overview of auditing.

2. All 22 chapters can be briefly covered in a first course. Other chapters can then be covered in depth in a second course.

3. Chapters 1 through 9, 13, and 19–21 can be covered in a first course. Then, Chapters 10 through 12, 14 through 18, and 22 can be covered in a second course. This option is appropriate if the first course is conceptual and the second course is procedural.

Several supplements are available to assist the instructor and student. The instructor's manual contains (a) guides for covering the chapters; (b) a list of illustrations in the text; (c) answers to all of the end-of-chapter materials; (d) a set of transparency masters; and (e) discussion/case questions and answers we extracted from earlier editions of the text. The Computerized Test Bank contains many types of test questions for each chapter, including discussion/case questions extracted from earlier editions of the text. The Study Guide includes chapter-by-chapter highlights and a large variety of questions.

We hope you enjoy this edition of the book.

Donald H. Taylor
G. William Glezen

Contents

CHAPTER 2 *The Public Accounting Profession
and Auditing Standards*   **19**

CHAPTER 5   *The Auditor's Responsibility— Fraudulent Financial Reporting* 128

CHAPTER 8   *Planning the Audit*   208

CHAPTER 11 — *Obtaining an Understanding of Internal Control in a Computer Environment*   321

CHAPTER 12 *Testing Controls and Gathering Evidence in a Computer Environment* **353**

CHAPTER 13 *Evidence of Financial Statement Assertions* **378**

CHAPTER 14   *Sampling for Substantive Tests of Account Balances—Nonstatistical and Statistical*   **422**

CHAPTER 20   *Modifications of the Standard Audit Report*   644

CHAPTER 21   *Other Types of Reports*   675

CHAPTER 22   *Operational and Compliance Auditing*   **710**

The Audit Function

"The aim of the superior man is truth."

CONFUCIUS, *Analects*

LEARNING OBJECTIVES

After reading and studying the material in this chapter, the student should be able to

▶ Write a brief paragraph about why accounting students should study auditing.

▶ Paraphrase the broad definition of auditing.

▶ Distinguish between accounting and auditing by giving brief examples of each term.

▶ Distinguish among financial statement, compliance, and operational auditing by describing each type.

▶ Distinguish among external, internal, and government auditing by describing each type.

▶ Analyze elements of the theoretical framework of auditing by writing brief comments about each element.

▶ Give an example of a business situation containing the four conditions that create a demand for auditing.

▶ Assess why auditors are the logical group to provide creditors and investors with audit opinions.

▶ Write a brief paragraph describing stewardship or agency theory.

▶ Describe why motivational considerations of an audit add value to financial statement information.

▶ State the limitations of an audit.

▶ Analyze the relationship between integrity and the tasks of auditors.

▶ Write a brief history of auditing.

Auditing is truly interdisciplinary in its scope, encompassing business law, ethics, accounting theory, statistical sampling, and computer processing. This interdisciplinary approach to auditing is not followed merely to pull together material taught at earlier points in the business curriculum (although there is some justification for performing this synthesis). The integrated topics are an expression of the fact that practicing auditors, whether public, internal, or governmental, actually are called on to use the entire range of business knowledge. Whether individuals are engaged in auditing functions or are the preparers of audited data, they need to understand the purposes, techniques, and limitations of this subject matter.

In addition, the work of auditors is in the public spotlight. The financial statements on which public accountants express opinions serve as a basis for securities trading and credit extensions. The reports issued by governmental auditors are often a basis for proposed legislation. In today's society, it is imperative that many types of organizations be subjected to an audit. Management, stockholders, credit institutions, regulatory agencies, and legislative and executive branches of federal, state, and local governments require such audits.

The modern auditor must be a talented individual who has the ability to make vital decisions on many important issues, and the courage and depth of character to stand by personal convictions. The auditing function offers individuals an opportunity that is rare in other fields of endeavor—that is, the opportunity, on almost a daily basis, to be responsible for making decisions and judgments as to what is right and what is wrong, and to stand by those decisions and judgments regardless of the pressures that may be brought to bear. This opportunity has attracted many outstanding individuals to the field of auditing and has helped to retain them.

WHY STUDY AUDITING?

√Why should advanced accounting students study auditing?

1. Many accounting students will choose a career in auditing, either in public accounting, private industry, or government. These students need to acquire technical expertise and to understand the theoretical concepts (ethical, legal, and otherwise) underlying the practice of auditing.

2. Most people in the business world rely on the services of auditors. Investors in equity and debt securities rely on financial statements and other financial information that are given enhanced credibility by audits. Business managers rely on auditors to add credibility to the internal information they use to make a wide variety of decisions. Because of this reliance, these individuals need an understanding of the audit function.

3. The study of auditing develops skills that can be used in a number of business and governmental disciplines. Students learn to obtain an understanding of financial controls, assess risk, and evaluate evidence.

4. Auditing is a pervasive part of business and government. Therefore, accounting students who are employed in private industry or with a government agency will likely work with auditors in some capacity. The ability to understand the tasks of auditors will enhance their ability to work with them.

BROAD DEFINITION OF AUDITING

Auditing in a broad sense may be defined as "a systematic process of objectively obtaining and evaluating evidence regarding assertions about economic actions and events to ascertain the degree of correspondence between these assertions and established criteria and communicating the results to interested users.''[1]

The word *assertions* has a special meaning in auditing. It refers to representations by management that are embodied in financial statement components, records, or systems. Here are examples of two assertions of an organization.

1. The financial statements represent fair measurements of the economic events and business transactions that affected the organization during a certain period of time.
2. The computerized accounting system used by the organization is efficient and reliable.

Both assertions are made by the organization through its accounting process, which collects, summarizes, classifies, and reports business data. Each assertion is made through a different part of the organization's accounting process and is audited in a different way.

The first assertion is made through the financial statements. The auditor determines whether these statements meet the established criterion, which in most cases is whether they are fairly presented in conformity with generally accepted accounting principles.

The second assertion is made through the computerized accounting system. The auditor determines whether the characteristics of this system meet the criteria of efficiency and reliability.

▶ **EXAMPLE**

Auditors perform an audit of a company's financial statements. They discover that several significant accounts are not stated in accordance with generally accepted accounting principles. The auditors reject management's assertion that their financial statements are fairly stated.

Auditors assess a company's computerized accounting system. They discover that, because of defective programming, incorrect bills are sent to customers. The auditors reject management's assertion that their computerized accounting system is efficient and reliable.

THE DIFFERENCE BETWEEN ACCOUNTING AND AUDITING

Accounting is a process that generates information in the form of financial statements and other financial data. The accounting function is the responsibility of the company's management. *Auditing* is a process that evaluates this information and produces conclusions with respect to this information according to the criterion used to make the evaluation.

[1] Committee on Basic Auditing Concepts, *A Statement of Basic Auditing Concepts* (Sarasota, Fla.: American Accounting Association, 1973), p. 2.

> ▶ **EXAMPLE**
>
> Accountants compile business data on products shipped to customers, use dollar measurements to record these shipments as credit sales, summarize and classify credit sales, and prepare financial statements reflecting these credit sales.
>
> Auditors do not record, summarize, or classify any of these transactions. They gather and evaluate evidence and draw conclusions as to whether these credit sales have been fairly reflected in the financial statements.

TYPES OF AUDITS—BY OBJECTIVE

Auditing in a narrower sense may be defined by classifying it according to the objective of the auditing function performed.

Financial Statement Audit

A *financial statement audit* is the gathering of evidence on the financial statement assertions of an entity and using such evidence to determine whether the assertion adheres to generally accepted accounting principles or another comprehensive basis of accounting. This type of audit is discussed throughout most of the text and makes use of a process called attestation. As used in financial statement auditing, *attestation* refers to an independent and competent person communicating an opinion or judgment as to whether an entity's financial statement assertions correspond in all significant respects with the established criterion (usually generally accepted accounting principles). An independent CPA's audit of a commercial business's financial statements is an example.

Compliance Audit

The purpose of a *compliance audit* is to determine whether a person or entity has adhered to laws and regulations. The criteria could be a law prohibiting bribes or a code and accompanying regulations (such as the Internal Revenue code and regulations). The audit of an income tax return is a prime example of a compliance audit in which the IRS is determining a person's or an entity's adherence to tax regulations.

Operational Audit

Operational auditing falls within the broad definition of an audit. However, the criteria against which management's assertions are measured differ from the type of audit emphasized in this text. The American Institute of Certified Public Accountants (AICPA) Special Committee on Operational and Management Auditing describes *operational auditing* as "a systematic review of an organization's activities (or a stipulated segment of them) in relation to specified objectives for the purposes of assessing performance, identifying opportunities for improvement, and developing recommendations for improvement or further action." A review of a company's computerized accounting system, assessment of its efficiency and reliability, and recommendations for improving the system would constitute an operational audit.

FIGURE 1.1 **Comparison among Financial Statement, Compliance, and Operational Auditing**

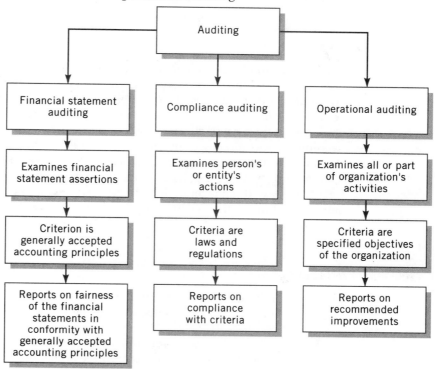

Comparative Illustration

Figure 1.1 shows a comparison among financial statement, compliance, and operational auditing.

Clear distinctions do not always exist among these three classifications of auditing. The major focus of this book is on financial statement auditing; however, auditors offer business advice (a form of operational auditing) during financial statement audits. Examples of such advice will be illustrated in later chapters. Compliance and operational auditing are discussed in Chapter 22.

TYPES OF AUDITS—BY AUDITOR AFFILIATION

Auditing can also be classified according to the affiliation of the individual or group that performs the audit. This classification overlaps the classification by objective.

External Auditors

External auditors are certified public accountants (CPAs) who are independent of the organizations whose assertions or representations are being audited. These independent CPAs offer their audit services on a contractual basis. The majority of audits performed by external auditors are financial statement audits, although this group may perform all audits described in the previous section.

Internal Auditors

Internal auditing is "an independent appraisal function established within an organization to examine and evaluate its activities as a service to the organization."[2] Internal auditors (who may also be CPAs but not independent contractors) are employees of the organizations whose activities they appraise. Measures can be taken, however, to give these auditors some independence. In many companies internal auditors report directly to the audit committee of the board of directors.

Internal auditors perform both compliance and operational audits for their companies and measure the degree to which various functions of their organization adhere to stated managerial policies, laws, or regulations. They also perform operational auditing, such as appraisal of their organization's computerized accounting systems.

Government Auditors

Members of local, state, and federal government units audit various organizational functions for a variety of reasons, such as the following:

1. Local and state government units audit businesses to determine whether sales taxes have been collected and remitted according to stipulated laws or regulations (a type of compliance audit).

2. The Internal Revenue Service audits corporate and individual income tax returns to determine whether income taxes have been calculated according to the applicable laws or interpretations of these laws (another type of compliance audit).

3. The General Accounting Office (GAO), which reports to the U.S. Congress, audits various programs, functions, activities, and organizations of the federal executive branch. Such audits include[3]

   a. Financial audits—that determine whether (1) financial information is presented in accordance with established criteria, (2) the entity has adhered to financial compliance requirements, and (3) the entity's internal control is suitably designed and implemented.

   b. Performance audits (a type of operational audit)—that review for efficiency and economy in the use of resources.

Comparative Illustration

Figure 1.2 shows a comparison among external, internal, and government auditing. Chapter 22 illustrates the work of internal and government auditors.

---

[2] *Standards for the Professional Practice of Internal Auditing* (Alamonte Springs, Fla.: The Institute of Internal Auditors, Inc., 1978), p. 1.
[3] *Government Auditing Standards* (Washington, D.C.: General Accounting Office, 1994).

FIGURE 1.2 Comparison among External, Internal, and Government Auditing

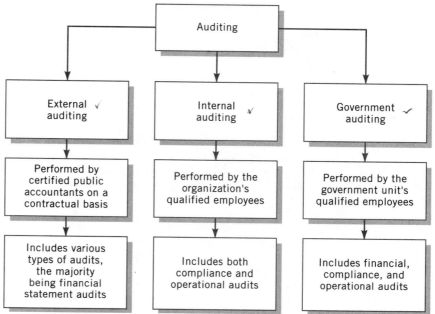

THEORETICAL FRAMEWORK OF AUDITING

The auditing function, regardless of classification, operates within a theoretical framework that has evolved during the last thirty to forty years. The first definitive framework appeared in *The Philosophy of Auditing* by Mautz and Sharaf in 1961. Since then, revisions have been made to the framework to bring it up to date for significant changes in the auditor's accountability to the public. A notable revision is *The Philosophy and Principles of Auditing* by Flint in 1988.

Figure 1.3 on page 8 contains summaries and comments on some of the important elements of a modern-day theoretical framework of auditing.[4] We will discuss auditing standards and procedures in subsequent chapters.

WHY FINANCIAL STATEMENTS ARE AUDITED

Why are financial statement audits performed and who benefits from them? The American Accounting Association has issued *A Statement of Basic Auditing Concepts*, which describes four conditions that create a demand for auditing.

1. There is a potential conflict between those who prepare information (management) and those who use information (owners, investors, creditors, and regulators). This potential conflict can result in biased information.

---

[4] Ideas in this section are from "Towards a Conceptual Framework for Auditing," by Michael J. Pratt and Karen Van Peursem in *Accounting Education*, 1993, pp. 11–32.

FIGURE 1.3   Some Important Elements of the Theoretical Framework of Auditing

Element of the Theoretical Framework of Auditing	Comments
1. The data to be audited can be verified.	An audit requires that the proper quantity and quality of evidence be gathered. Data must exist in a way that it can be substantiated. For example, financial statements consist of account balances and transactions that can be verified.
2. Short-term conflicts may exist between managers who prepare data and auditors who examine the data.	Managers may feel compelled to produce financial data favorable to their needs (temporary high earnings). Auditors should attest to data that is fair, not biased in favor of managers.
3. Auditors must have independence and freedom from managerial constraint.	The credibility of an audit comes from independence. The auditor must gather objective evidence without hindrance from the parties being audited and must report audit results objectively to the groups that need to know these results.
4. An audit benefits the public.	In some cases, the benefit is obvious from cost savings or detection of fraud. In other cases, misstatements, fraud, or misrepresentation is prevented by audits (for example, the lack of an audit could result in financial statements being issued that contain significant misstatement).

2. Information can have substantial economic consequences for a decision maker.
3. Expertise is often required for preparing and verifying information.
4. Users of information frequently are prevented from directly assessing the quality of information.

These four conditions essentially state that a conflict may arise between groups that use financial statements and company managers who prepare them; if so, these financial statements could be biased. Financial statement information is used to help make financial decisions, and the users of financial statements either lack the expertise or are prevented from directly verifying the quality of the financial statement information they use.

▶ **EXAMPLE**

The management of a company is negotiating a badly needed loan from a financial institution. The loan officer of the financial institution wishes to examine the company's most recent financial statements before making a decision on the loan. The loan officer is particularly interested in the company's current ratio and other measures of liquidity (information that will be used to determine whether or not the loan is extended). The manager understands that a high current ratio is necessary to obtain the loan and retain his position as manager (a conflict between the needs of the manager and the loan officer that might result in biased financial statements). The loan officer might require the manager to engage a CPA (required expertise) to conduct an audit of the company's financial statements. An audit will provide the loan officer with reasonable assurance that the financial statements are fairly presented.

Specifically, financial statement audits are performed for the reasons described in the following three subsections.

The Needs of Creditors and Investors

Independent auditors have a duty to provide creditors with unbiased opinions as to whether financial statements are fairly presented. Independent auditors are the logical group to provide these opinions because they (1) have the knowledge and training, (2) are allowed to examine the necessary records, and (3) are not employees of the companies whose financial statements they audit.

Investors also use the work of the independent auditor. Many investors, representing widely disbursed ownership, have little, if any, contact with the operations of the company or management. They, like creditors, regard independent auditors as guardians of the integrity of a company's financial statements.

Comment   The U.S. Supreme Court has stated, "By certifying the public reports that collectively depict a corporation's financial status, the independent auditor assumes a public responsibility transcending any employment relationship with the client. The independent public accountant performing this special function owes ultimate allegiance to the corporation's creditors and stockholders, as well as to the investing public."

Stewardship or Agency Theory

Stewardship or agency theory provides another explanation for the demand for audits.[5] This theory implies that the manager (as well as the owner) wants the credibility an audit adds to the financial statement assertions.

The owner's desires for an audit are reasonably obvious and have been discussed previously. The manager is the agent or steward of the owner, but each party acts in his or her own self-interest and the goals or objectives of each party are different. According to stewardship or agency theory, this situation inevitably creates conflict between the owner and manager. The owner perceives that the manager's goals or objectives may be detrimental to the owner's own goals. Thus, the manager wants financial statement representations audited by an independent party to enhance his or her stewardship of these financial statements and to lessen the owner's mistrust of the manager.

[5] For a summary of agency theory, see Wanda Wallace, *The Economic Role of the Audit in Free and Regulated Markets,* Auditing Monographs (New York: Macmillan, 1985).

► **EXAMPLE**

The owner of a specialty clothing store is interested in long-run profitability, steady growth in market share, and solvency. The manager of the store is interested in maximizing the current-year profit on which her bonus is computed. The owner, concerned that the manager may be using policies to enhance short-term profit at the expense of long-term profit (such as recording revenue before it is earned), considers lowering the amount of the yearly bonus or perhaps eliminating it altogether. An audit conducted by an independent auditor at the request of the manager convinces the owner that the manager is not improperly recording revenue and that the manager's stewardship is satisfactory. As a result, no change is made to the yearly bonus plan.

Motivational Theory

Some people believe that motivational considerations of an audit add value to the information contained in financial statements. According to this theory, preparers of financial statements know that their assertions will be subjected to an audit; thus, financial statements will be brought more in line with accounting standards. The motivational benefits of an audit are difficult to prove conclusively, but some believe that management's knowledge that an audit will be performed mitigates against improper financial statement preparation.

► **EXAMPLE**

The General Accounting Office, an audit agency of the U.S. Congress, made a study of 39 banks that failed in 1988 and 1989, resulting in losses of $9 billion. Four of these banks were never audited, and 23 of them were not audited in the year preceding their failure. We cannot say that recent audits of these 27 banks would have prevented the failures. However, it is possible that knowledge of impending audits might have prompted the banks to present their financial condition more fairly.

LIMITATIONS OF AN AUDIT

An audit is not a guarantee of the exactness or accuracy of assertions in the financial statements. Here are some reasons.

1. Many audit conclusions are made by examining a *sample* of evidence. Often, some dollar representations in the financial statements are supported by thousands, or perhaps millions, of documents (e.g., canceled checks, sales orders, and invoices). Audits are conducted under cost and time constraints, and require an examination of a sample of evidence supporting the dollar representations. Such samples can be scientifically designed to provide a considerable degree of reliance. Nevertheless, conclusions drawn from examining a sample of the available evidence are subject to inherent uncertainties.

2. By necessity, some evidence supporting dollar representations in the financial statements must be obtained by *oral or written representations of management* (e.g., estimates of the collectibility of accounts receivable). Although auditors can obtain evidence that corroborates, or fails to corroborate, management's representations, in some cases it may be necessary to rely heavily on such

representations. If management lacks integrity, auditors might draw incorrect conclusions about the fairness of the financial statements.

3. Human weaknesses, such as *fatigue* and *carelessness,* can cause auditors to overlook pertinent evidence, examine the wrong type of evidence, or draw the wrong conclusions from the evidence examined.

INTEGRITY OF AUDITORS

Auditors must make decisions and judgments that stand the test of right and wrong. To do so, they must have a keen sense of integrity, without which the needs of the accounting profession, and society at large, will not be served.

Integrity is, among other things, an independence of attitude in conducting professional affairs. There is no better test of this type of integrity than the auditor's willingness to withdraw or be fired from the audit of a client who follows accounting practices that are acceptable but highly questionable.

▶ EXAMPLE

A number of years ago, an international accounting firm withdrew from the audit of all savings and loan clients who followed a generally accepted but questionable accounting practice. In the opinion of the accounting firm this practice overstated the capital account.

▶ EXAMPLE

Recently, another international accounting firm insisted that one of its bank audit clients make a controversial adjustment to the accounting records that caused a significant loss in reported quarterly earnings. As a result, the client fired the accounting firm.

COMMENTARY

Auditing is not a sterile subject. Its value to the functioning of the economy in the United States has been firmly established, and the demand for auditing service continues to exist. At the same time, its objectives and techniques are being challenged by various groups that have a financial interest in the quality of this service.

Accounting students need to understand (1) public accounting and the auditing standards it uses, (2) the ethical and legal environment in which auditors function, (3) the responsibilities that an auditor assumes when audits are undertaken, (4) the techniques used to satisfy the audit objectives, and (5) the nature and limitations of the auditor's output. The succeeding chapters are designed to satisfy these needs.

APPENDIX: HISTORY OF AUDITING

We cannot authoritatively assert that the profession of auditing is as old as civilization itself, but we do have historical proof that accounts and records were verified several thousand years ago. In fact, the purposes of auditing throughout history seem to parallel two objectives shown in Figure 1.1: to determine whether assertions are proper and whether others have complied with established criteria.

Primitive auditing   A method of auditing that seemed to be prevalent in ancient Egypt and Babylonia consisted, in part, of two or more officials keeping separate records and checking the accuracy of these records by comparing them with each other. This concept of checks and balances is an acceptable business practice even today. Auditors look for it in evaluating their client's controls.

> Actually, ''audit'' is a Latin word associated with the act of hearing or listening. Hundreds of years ago, most people could not read or write, so auditors who were familiar with the king's possessions listened to the king's servants describe the cattle, sheep, and other assets under their control. Auditors then noted errors or omissions by what they heard or did not hear.

Auditing in Ancient Greece and Rome   Many social and political traditions in Western society have their origins in ancient Greece. One of these traditions was the audit of public accounts. All public officials apparently had to submit their accounts to designated auditors. This requirement probably extended to the highest-ranking members of Greek society.

> If we followed that practice today, we would audit the personal accounts of all individuals in the various branches of the federal government. That aspect of Greek culture has not been copied in modern society.

To many, Roman civilization was the epitome of structure and organization. We should not be surprised to learn, then, that audits of some type were performed in that era. Roman officials, like their Greek counterparts, were required to submit their accounts to a designated person or body when they left office.

Auditing in the Medieval Period   Audits became more sophisticated during the medieval period of British history. High officials accountable to heads of state compared independent tallies of monies collected by sheriffs for the crown. Today, we refer to independent tallies as *controls* and the verification of these tallies by a high official as *auditing*.

> English manors had some of the most sophisticated recordkeeping and auditing of that era. One person would collect revenues from tenants, another person would record these revenues, and yet another—the auditor—would listen to the ''reading of the accounts'' in the presence of the lord of the manor.

Auditing during the Industrial Revolution   The Industrial Revolution produced early examples of English corporations registered with the state. This practice led to laws mandating the preparation of statements by boards of directors and provisions for ''shareholder audits'' of these statements by shareholders of the company. These auditors possessed little or no independence, at least by our modern definition. The only vestige of independence was the requirement that auditors not hold office in the audited company. Auditors were not only allowed to own stock in the audited company, but were required to do so. In later years, this requirement was lifted, and external professionals were hired to perform the audits.

> "Shareholder audits" were referred to by some as a "complete farce." A meeting of shareholders would be called, and, with little notice, designated shareholders would merely compare amounts in the financial statements against amounts in the books of account and ascertain that each payment had a supporting voucher. By today's standards, this type of audit would be inadequate. But auditing had a narrower scope in those days.

Early auditing in the United States American audits in the late nineteenth and early twentieth centuries were patterned after the British model; that is, examinations were made to report on the stewardship of management and to detect fraud. In many cases, all transactions of an entity were audited. Later, cost considerations forced auditors to shift their techniques from detailed examinations to sampling and testing. In addition, early American audits emphasized the balance sheet because the purpose of many of these audits was to secure financing from a bank.

The fair presentation of financial statements became the dominant standard when companies were subjected to more government regulation. In the United States, income taxes were established in the early 1900s. The passage of federal securities acts in 1933 and 1934 mandated audits for companies with publicly traded securities, and the creation of the Securities and Exchange Commission in 1934 provided for federal government oversight of the audits of most large corporations in the country.

Chapter 1 ▶ GLOSSARY OF TERMS

Accounting The process of generating information in the form of financial statements and other financial data. The accounting function is the responsibility of the company's management.

Assertions Representations by management that are embodied in financial statement components, records, or systems.

Attestation An opinion of an independent and competent person as to whether an entity's assertions correspond in all significant respects to an established criterion.

Auditing A systematic process of objectively obtaining and evaluating evidence regarding assertions about economic actions and events to ascertain the degree of correspondence between these assertions and established criteria and communicating the results to interested users.

Certified public accountant (CPA) Accountants who have met the requirements to practice public accounting by passing a uniform examination and meeting other re-

quirements established by individual states that grant the license to practice public accounting.

Compliance audit The gathering of evidence to determine whether a person or entity has adhered to laws and regulations.

External auditing Audits performed by certified public accountants who offer their independent services on a contractual basis.

Financial statement audit The gathering of evidence regarding the financial statement assertions of an entity and using such evidence to ascertain adherence to generally accepted accounting principles or another comprehensive basis of accounting.

Government auditors Auditors representing local, state, and federal government entities.

Internal auditing An objective appraisal function established within an organization to examine and evaluate its activities as a service to the organization.

Operational auditing A systematic review of an organization's activities (or a stipulated segment of them) in rela-

credibility – way goodness(

14

tion to specified objectives for the purposes of assessing performance, identifying opportunities for improvement, and developing recommendations for improvement or further action.

Stewardship or agency theory   An explanation of the demand for audits that implies that the manager of a company wants an audit because of the credibility an audit adds to the financial statement representations.

Chapter 1 ▶ REFERENCES

American Institute of Certified Public Accountants. *Professional Standards*
    AU Section 110 [SAS No. 1]—*Responsibilities and Functions of the Independent Auditor.*
    AU Appendix A—*Historical Background.*

Committee on Basic Auditing Concepts. *A Statement of Basic Auditing Concepts.* Sarasota, Fla.: American Accounting Association, 1973.

Connor, Joseph E. "Enhancing Public Confidence in the Accounting Profession," *Journal of Accountancy* (July 1986), pp. 76–83.

Elliott, Robert K. "The Future of Audits," *Journal of Accountancy* (September 1994), pp. 74–82.

Mednick, Robert. "Our Profession in the Year 2000: A Blueprint of the Future," *Journal of Accountancy* (August 1988), pp. 54–58.

Mednick, Robert. "Reinventing the Audit," *Journal of Accountancy* (August 1991), pp. 71–78.

Palmer, Russell E. "Accounting as a Mature Industry," *Journal of Accountancy* (May 1989), pp. 84–88.

Wallace, Wanda A. *The Economic Role of the Audit in Free and Regulated Markets.* Auditing Monographs. New York: Macmillan, 1985.

Chapter 1 ▶ REVIEW QUESTIONS

1-1   Describe four reasons why auditing should be studied.

1-2   Give examples of two assertions or representations of an organization.

1-3   Explain the difference between accounting and auditing.

1-4   Explain the differences among the following (use Figure 1.1).
   a. Financial statement auditing.
   b. Compliance auditing.
   c. Operational auditing.

1-5   Explain the differences among the following (use Figure 1.2).
   a. External auditors.
   b. Internal auditors.
   c. Government auditors.

1-6   Describe four elements of the theoretical framework of auditing.

1-7   What are four conditions that create a demand for auditing?

1-8   Describe three reasons why independent auditors are the appropriate group to provide the potential investor with an unbiased opinion as to whether the financial statements are fairly presented.

1-9   Explain how stewardship or agency theory helps to explain the demand for audits.

1-10   Explain the motivational effect that an audit has on preparers of financial statements.

1-11   Describe three reasons why an audit is not a guarantee of the exactness or accuracy of the assertions or representations in financial statements.

1-12   What is meant by integrity?

1-13   Answer these questions about the history of auditing.
   a. Describe a method of auditing that seemed to be prevalent in ancient Egypt and Babylonia.
   b. Describe the audit of public accounts in ancient Greece.
   c. Describe the recordkeeping and auditing system used in English manors during the medieval period.
   d. Describe "shareholder audits."
   e. What were the purposes of American audits in the late nineteenth and early twentieth centuries?

Chapter 1 ► OBJECTIVE QUESTIONS

1-14 Which of the following types of audits is performed to determine whether an entity's financial statements are fairly stated in conformity with generally accepted accounting principles?
  a. Operational audit.
  b. Compliance audit.
  c. Financial statement audit.
  d. Performance audit.

1-15 Which of the following types of audit uses as its criteria laws and regulations?
  a. Operational audit.
  b. Compliance audit.
  c. Financial statement audit.
  d. Financial audit.

1-16 Which of the following types of auditing is performed most commonly by CPAs on a contractual basis?
  a. Internal auditing.
  b. Government auditing.
  c. Internal Revenue Service auditing.
  d. External auditing.

1-17 Which of the following statements does not properly describe an element of the theoretical framework of auditing?
  a. The data to be audited can be verified.
  b. Short-term conflicts may exist between managers who prepare data and auditors who examine the data.
  c. Auditors act on behalf of management.
  d. An audit benefits the public.

1-18 Which of the following statements does not describe a condition that creates a demand for auditing?
  a. Conflict between an information preparer and a user can result in biased information.

  b. Information can have substantial economic consequences for a decision maker.
  c. Expertise is often required for information preparation and verification.
  d. Users can directly assess the quality of information.

1-19 Which of the following statements does not properly describe a limitation of an audit?
  a. Many audit conclusions are made on the basis of examining a sample of evidence.
  b. Some evidence supporting dollar representations in the financial statements must be obtained by oral or written representations of management.
  c. Fatigue and carelessness can cause auditors to overlook pertinent evidence.
  d. Many financial statement assertions cannot be audited.

1-20 For each description, list the letter or letters whose term or terms define the description. Each term may be used once, more than once, or not at all.

Description	Term
1. This activity makes use of attestation.	a. Manager/user conflict
2. This activity makes use of internal auditors.	b. Audit limitation
3. This condition creates a demand for auditing.	c. Financial statement auditing
4. Some audit conclusions are made on the basis of a sample of evidence.	d. Stewardship theory
5. Criteria are laws and regulations.	e. Operational auditing
	f. Compliance auditing

Chapter 1 ► DISCUSSION/CASE QUESTIONS

1-21 Reread the broad definition of auditing in the chapter and discuss the meaning of each of the following key words and phrases as they relate to the definition.
  a. Systematic process.
  b. Objectively obtaining and evaluating evidence.
  c. Assertions about economic actions and events.
  d. Degree of correspondence between these assertions and established criteria.
  e. Communicating the results to interested users.

1-22   Reread the definition of operational auditing in the chapter. Select the key words and/or phrases that distinguish this definition from that of financial statement auditing. Discuss the meaning of each of these key words and/or phrases as they relate to the definition of operational auditing.

1-23   Some of the elements of the theoretical framework of auditing are shown in Figure 1.3. For each of these elements, describe the effect on an audit if the element were not true.

1. The data to be audited can be verified.
2. Short-term conflicts may exist between managers who prepare data and auditors who examine the data.
3. Auditors must have independence and freedom from managerial constraint.
4. An audit benefits the public.

1-24   Odom Company is a medium-sized producer of fishing rods with approximately $5 million of annual sales. The company is wholly owned by Mike Odom, who serves as its president and is active in its daily operations. There is no long-term debt, and there are no current plans to incur any. Mr. Odom has no interest in expanding his company's operations in the future because to do so would reduce the amount of time he is able to devote to his favorite pastime, fishing. Some of Mr. Odom's friends who operate businesses of the same size have annual audits of their financial statements.

Required:

a. Give reasons why Mr. Odom should have a financial statement audit performed by an independent CPA.
b. Give reasons why Mr. Odom should not have a financial statement audit performed.

1-25   Ms. Wilson is president of Wilson Company, which operates hamburger restaurants in Houston, New Orleans, Memphis, and Dallas. She believes that her company may be large enough to need an operational audit of its activities. Profits have been good but not as good as expected. Certain accounting records are maintained at each restaurant, and others are maintained centrally. She has estimated the cost of an operational audit and would like to compare the cost with the potential benefits to be gained from such an audit. Ms. Wilson has a sales background.

Required:

a. Describe the general differences between a financial statement and an operational audit.
b. Describe some general benefits Ms. Wilson may derive from an operational audit of her business.

1-26   Explain why each of the following audits would be classified as (1) financial statement, (2) operational, or (3) compliance.
a. Audit of the contract costs of building jet fighter planes. (3)
b. Audit by internal auditors of the efficiency of purchasing operations. (2)
c. Audit by a CPA firm of whether a state government agency operated in accordance with its contract with the federal government. (3)
d. Audit of a tax return by an Internal Revenue Service agent. (3)
e. Audit of a company's financial statements by a CPA firm. (1)

1-27 **(Continuing Case—Part I; Part II in Chapter 2)**

   Members of a single family own the majority of the capital stock of Custom Furniture Company, a small corporation not listed on any stock exchange. The balance of the capital stock is held by a few outside investors.

   Custom Furniture Company sells a limited variety of household furnishings such as chairs, tables, and desks. The majority stockholders are not actively involved in the management of the company, but the minority stockholders try to "keep a close eye" on management's performance, especially profits. Several minority stockholders have tried to sell their stock but were unable to do so at the price they wanted. A few of them blame poor management performance for subpar financial statement results.

   Custom Furniture has a group of approximately 100 customers that order the same type of merchandise each month. Each of them orders the same quantity and in approximately the same time frame. The minority stockholders have tried to persuade the Board of Directors to broaden their customer base and even branch out into other product lines. So far, their efforts have not been successful because of the conservative policies of the majority stockholders.

   A slow but sustained economic recovery has been underway for the past two to three years. Custom Furniture Company is benefiting from increased orders by the select group of reliable customers.

   Custom Furniture Company has 60 full- and part-time employees, including manufacturing, sales, and clerical personnel.

   The Board of Directors, reflecting the attitude of the majority stockholders, has little knowledge of the system that produces the financial statements. Some minority stockholders know enough accounting to make a reasonable analysis of financial statement results, but their lack of knowledge of accounting makes them feel somewhat ignorant about "where the numbers really came from." The Board has consistently refused to hire a CPA firm to perform a financial audit, believing that the close holding of their stock and a personal relationship with their bankers negates any need to have an audit. The minority stockholders disagree, but are always outvoted at meetings of the Board.

   Here are some key figures from the unaudited financial statements as of the last full year of operations, October 31, 19X7.

Sales	$3,963,292
Net income	340,134
Cash balance	112,500
Net Receivables	376,155
Total Assets	2,037,054

   The majority stockholders are satisfied with these amounts and the financial statement results in general. Some minority stockholders believe that the amounts are inflated, although they cannot furnish any proof because the controller and other members of management do not confide in them. Some of the minority stockholders believe that "economic reality" will deflate the amounts sooner or later, forcing them to sell their stock to the majority stockholders at significantly reduced prices.

Required:

Write a short memo (two pages or less) answering the following questions:

a. Give reasons why the Board should hire a CPA firm to perform a financial statement audit. Where applicable, refer to specific paragraphs of the above narrative to support your views.

b. Give reasons why the Board should not hire a CPA firm to perform a financial statement audit. Where applicable, refer to specific paragraphs of the above narrative to support your views.

*marketing
side of business*

c. What parts of the company's activities might be examined in an operational audit? Why? (Make reasonable assumptions about the company's operations.)

d. In what way might stewardship or agency theory play a role in a decision to have a financial statement audit? Where applicable, refer to specific paragraphs in the above narrative.

e. Under what limitations might the auditors be working if a financial statement audit were performed? Where applicable, refer to specific paragraphs in the above narrative.

CHAPTER 2

The Public Accounting Profession and Auditing Standards

"All accountants, including the most proficient, do not necessarily have the inquisitiveness and innate skepticism that mark the good auditor."

WILLIAM D. HALL, *What Does It Take to Be an Auditor?*

LEARNING OBJECTIVES

After reading and studying the material in this chapter, the student should be able to

- ▶ Distinguish among the types of work performed and the general requirements for entry in each of the four career paths in accounting.
- ▶ Describe the requirements for obtaining the CPA certificate.
- ▶ Describe the structure of CPA firms by distinguishing among the forms of organization, sizes, and hierarchy.
- ▶ Provide an example of each type of service provided by CPA firms.
- ▶ Describe how CPA firms implement a system of quality control.
- ▶ Describe the methods used by the accounting profession to enhance self-regulation.
- ▶ Paraphrase the independent auditor's report.
- ▶ Briefly describe the purpose of each paragraph of the independent auditor's report.
- ▶ Analyze the different purposes of the independent auditor's report and the statement of management responsibility for financial statements.
- ▶ Paraphrase the generally accepted auditing standards.
- ▶ Analyze the difference among the four types of audit reports by describing each type.
- ▶ Compare the attestation standards and generally accepted auditing standards by paraphrasing each set of standards, and writing a brief paragraph comparing general, field work, and reporting sections for each set of standards.
- ▶ Describe the organizational structure and purpose of four organizations that affect CPA firms.
- ▶ Describe three events that have affected the expectation gap and changed the practice of public accounting.

In this chapter we discuss the profession of public accounting and the standards auditors use to perform financial statement audits.

DIFFERENT CAREER PATHS IN ACCOUNTING

The term *accountant* describes many occupations such as auditors, preparers of tax returns, consultants, controllers, and accounting educators. In fact, accountants may take at least four general career paths, as shown in Figure 2.1.

FIGURE 2.1   Different Types of Career Paths in Accounting

Career Path	Type of Work Performed	General Requirement for Entry
Public accounting	Independent auditors, tax specialists, and consultants who offer services to the public	Undergraduate or master's degree in accounting
Private accounting	Controllers, treasurers, and accounting employees of nongovernment entities	Undergraduate degree in accounting
Government accounting	Controllers, treasurers, and accounting employees of federal, state, and local governments	Undergraduate degree in accounting
Accounting education	Instructor or professor at a public or private college or university	Master's or doctoral degree in accounting

LICENSING REQUIREMENTS TO PRACTICE PUBLIC ACCOUNTING

Accountants do not need a license to work in private accounting, government accounting, or accounting education. But to protect the public from individuals who are not qualified to express opinions on financial statements, states and territories set minimum standards in the form of *licensing requirements* to practice public accounting.

There are 54 licensing jurisdictions in the United States, including all 50 states, the District of Columbia, and the U.S. territories. Each jurisdiction has a state or territorial board of accounting, which is a government agency empowered by law to regulate the practice of public accounting within that jurisdiction. No federal organization grants a national license to practice public accounting.

The CPA Certificate

The *CPA certificate* is required in most states to perform independent audits, although a few states still allow accountants with other credentials to perform them. Many accountants who obtain the CPA certificate choose not to practice public accounting and instead enter one of the other occupations described in Figure 2.1.

States and territories (which we will call states) have the following three general requirements that an individual must meet to become a *certified public accountant* (*CPA*) and practice public accounting, although specific requirements differ among states.

The Testing Requirement

A uniform CPA examination, developed by the American Institute of Certified Public Accountants, is administered by all states. A passing grade on all parts of the examination is one requirement for obtaining a CPA certificate.

The Education Requirement

Most states require CPA candidates to possess either an undergraduate degree with the equivalent of a major in accounting or 150 hours of college education (generally the equivalent of a master's degree). The 150-hour requirement seems to be the trend nationally.

The Experience Requirement

States have a wide variety of experience requirements, especially as to the type and length of experience. Some states require as many as four years of public accounting experience as an employee of a CPA firm. Other states allow work in industry or government as substitutes for public accounting experience. Still other states accept advanced education as a substitute.

Other Licensing Requirements

Many states automatically grant CPAs a license to practice public accounting. Some states, however, have moved toward two-tier licensing requirements that have these general features:

1. Possession of a CPA certificate.
2. Continuing professional education and certain experience requirements.

Comment   A recent poll taken of readers of *Accounting Today* shows that the vast majority of respondents favored some type of system guaranteeing full interstate reciprocity. This system would allow CPAs licensed by one state to practice in any other state. Reciprocity among states now depends on the laws of each state.

In the remainder of the book we will assume that the practice of public accounting is performed by individual CPAs or CPA firms.

THE STRUCTURE OF CPA FIRMS

Form of Organization of CPA Firms

CPA firms may practice public accounting as sole proprietorships, partnerships, or, in many states, corporations. A sole proprietor may employ others, but he or she is the owner and as such makes all policy decisions. A partnership might have only a few partners, while others might have thousands of partners. A corporation's owners are shareholders; they can transfer their ownership with more ease than a sole proprietor or a partnership and can also obtain some limitation of legal liability. A new form of legal entity, the limited liability partnership (LLP) has recently become popular among CPA firms. Most of the large firms and many of the small firms have adopted this legal form, which provides some protection for the personal assets of the individual partners.

Sizes of CPA Firms

International CPA Firms

The largest CPA firms, in terms of employees and revenues, have operations throughout the world. These firms offer the full range of services and perform financial statement audits of the largest international corporations.

The largest international CPA firms in the United States are known as the Big Six. They are (listed in alphabetical order): Arthur Andersen LLP, Coopers & Lybrand LLP, Deloitte & Touche LLP, Ernst & Young LLP, KPMG Peat Marwick LLP, and Price Waterhouse LLP.

Comment   Here are the 1994 U.S. revenues of the "Big Six" international CPA firms (in millions of dollars).

Arthur Andersen LLP	$3,317
Ernst & Young LLP	2,543
Deloitte & Touche LLP	2,230
KPMG Peat Marwick LLP	1,907
Coopers & Lybrand LLP	1,783
Price Waterhouse LLP	1,570

We can easily see why these firms are the "Big Six." The seventh-ranked firm (Grant Thornton) had revenues of $229 million.

National CPA Firms

Another group of CPA firms are called national firms and have offices throughout the United States as well as offices or affiliates in other countries. Their operations are not as widespread as those of international firms, but still they offer a wide range of services and perform many financial statement audits.

Regional CPA Firms

Still another group of CPA firms are called regional firms and are concentrated largely in certain sections of the United States. These firms perform financial statement audits, but significant amounts of their revenues are earned from other services.

Local CPA Firms

The largest number of CPA firms in the United States are local firms; they normally have one or a few offices, and they conduct their business within the area of a town or city. The ownership of local firms is held by one or a few CPAs. They perform some financial statement audits but generally earn a large percentage of their revenues from other services, such as maintaining accounting records, preparing tax returns, and consulting about tax matters.

Hierarchy of Personnel in CPA Firms

The hierarchy of personnel in CPA firms is not significantly different from that of other organizations, but the titles are different.

1. *Staff accountants* perform detailed audit work under the direct guidance of one or more experienced auditors and have little or no supervisory responsibility.
2. *Seniors* perform more complex audit procedures and supervise the staff accountants.
3. *Supervisors* and *managers* are responsible for supervising several engagements that run concurrently.
4. *Partners* (or *stockholders* if the CPA firm is a corporation) are owners. They review and sign the audit reports, tax returns, and other documents. The owner who has primary responsibility for an office generally is referred to as a managing partner (or stockholder).

SERVICES PROVIDED BY CPA FIRMS

International, national, and some regional CPA firms have the requisite number of personnel that permits development of expertise in many areas; these types of firms offer a wide variety of services. Smaller regional and local CPA firms offer a narrower range and often focus on maintaining accounting records and performing tax services for small clients. CPA firms generally offer the following types of services, the extent of which depends on their size and the needs of their clients.

Auditing

International CPA firms and many national CPA firms devote a large percentage of their time and resources to financial statement auditing. Sometimes, however, other types of audits are performed, for example, the audit of Medicare reports of health care institutions or the audit of campaign expenditures for political candidates. Smaller CPA firms often earn a lower percentage of their total revenues from audits. An increasing number of CPA firms are adding value to their audits by giving their clients valuable business advice. We provide several examples in later chapters.

Review

CPA firms, particularly those serving smaller clients, may receive requests to provide assurance on financial statements that is more limited than that provided by a financial statement audit. This limited assurance is provided by an engagement referred to as a *review*. CPAs confine the scope of a review to asking questions and performing analytical procedures designed to provide limited assurance that the financial statements or other financial data are presented fairly in accordance with stated criteria. Reviews are covered in Chapter 21.

Tax Services

CPA firms perform many *tax services* for their individual and corporate clients, including preparation (using computer software) and review of tax returns, tax litigation (appearance before a court or an administrative body on behalf of their clients), and tax planning (the legitimate avoidance or deferral of taxes).

International, national, and regional firms may spend a larger portion of their time in tax litigation and tax planning than do local firms, which devote much of their resources to preparing tax returns.

Management Consulting Services

Types of Management Consulting Services

A fast-growing area for CPA firms is *management consulting services*, which was formerly known as management advisory services, management information consulting, or administrative services.

▶ EXAMPLE

In a recent survey of local practitioners, respondents indicated that they devote a median of 23 percent of their professional time to management consulting services. Some international, national, and regional firms obtain over 40 percent of their fees from management consulting services, more than double the figure of 17 years ago.

Management consulting services encompass a variety of technical (mostly nonattestation) services performed for clients and can be classified according to six basic activities.

1. *Consultations* are services completed in a short time based on the CPA's existing personal knowledge (e.g., informal advice on the computer system).
2. *Advisory services* usually require studies to develop findings, conclusions, and recommendations for client consideration (e.g., a detailed marketing study).
3. *Implementation services* require the CPA to put into operation a plan the client has accepted (e.g., helping to install a budgeting system).
4. *Transaction services* require the CPA to advise on a specific client transaction that generally involves a third party (e.g., analysis of a merger).
5. *Staff and other support services* occur when a client asks the CPA to supply staff personnel to perform work needed by the client (e.g., computer programming).

6. *Product services* occur when the CPA provides a product or service (e.g., training to operate a computer system).

Management Consulting Services for Audit Clients

Clients of CPA firms sometimes ask for management consulting services before, during, or after financial statement audits are performed. A legitimate question is, "Can CPA firms remain objective when auditing financial statements containing the results of management consulting services provided by them?"

The accounting profession has maintained that independence is not affected when management consulting services are provided to audit clients. Studies by academic accountants, however, have shown that at least the appearance of independence may be affected. Government agencies and public interest groups have continued to question whether management consulting services should be provided to audit clients. Some services, such as merger negotiations and executive recruiting, appear to involve management decisions.

The accounting profession believes that management consulting services are compatible with auditing if the CPA firms performing these services give *advice* to audit clients but do not make *managerial decisions* for them.

Accounting Services

CPA firms, both large and small, perform a variety of accounting services for their clients. These services range from maintaining accounting records to performing compilations, that is, preparing financial statements without providing any assurance on them. Figure 2.2 summarizes the services provided by CPA firms and indicates whether each service requires attestation.

FIGURE 2.2 Summary of Services Provided by CPA Firms

Type of Service	Scope of Service
Audit	Provides positive assurance to third parties by *attesting* to the client's assertions (usually financial statements)
Review	Provides limited assurance to third parties by *attesting* to the client's assertions (usually financial statements)
Tax services	*No attestation*—provides services to clients, such as tax return preparation and tax planning
Management consulting services	*No attestation* in most cases—provides advice to clients, such as systems studies and budgeting suggestions
Accounting services	*No attestation*—provides services to clients, such as preparation of financial statements

QUALITY CONTROL IN CPA FIRMS

A CPA firm's most valuable possession is a reputation for integrity and for performance of quality work. Smaller CPA firms with a few owners and employees can exercise daily control over their practice. This control becomes more difficult, however, as firms become larger, so systems of quality control must be established to ensure quality performance. The AICPA has taken action in recent years to enhance the quality of services offered by CPA firms, as shown in the two following subsections.

System of Quality Control

The *Statement on Quality Control Standards* contains five suggestions on how CPA firms can effectively implement a system of quality control and improve their practices as well as the appearances they project to the public.

Independence, Integrity, and Objectivity

Independence in both fact and appearance should be maintained at all organizational levels.

▶ **EXAMPLE**

CPA firms should keep a record of audit clients and periodically distribute this record to the firm's personnel to ensure that prohibited relationships do not exist. (Audit independence is discussed in Chapter 3.)

Personnel Management

Personnel hired, promoted, and assigned to audit engagements should have the degree of technical training and proficiency required in the circumstances.

▶ **EXAMPLE**

A new staff assistant should not be assigned a task that requires the experience of an audit senior.

Engagement Performance

The performance of work at all organizational levels should meet the firm's standards of quality.

▶ **EXAMPLE**

New staff assistants should not perform highly complicated tasks without continuing on-the-job supervision by seniors, managers, or partners.

Acceptance and Continuance of Clients and Engagements

CPA firms should not accept or retain clients whose managements lack integrity.

▶ **EXAMPLE**

CPA firms should not accept an audit engagement for a company whose management has a history of misstating financial statements, ignoring generally accepted accounting principles, or engaging in illegal acts.

Monitoring

CPA firms should ascertain through monitoring that the elements of quality control are being effectively applied.

▶ **EXAMPLE**

CPA firms should have techniques for documenting, through the use of memoranda, evaluation forms, and the like, that the other elements of quality control are being applied.

The nature and extent of a firm's quality control policies and procedures will depend on the size of the firm, its personnel's operating autonomy, the nature of its practice and organization, and cost-benefit considerations.

Self-Regulation of the Accounting Profession

The AICPA has attempted to enhance self-regulation (and prevent government regulation of the accounting profession) by establishing methods to evaluate a CPA firm's quality control for its accounting and auditing practice. One method is called *peer* (or *quality*) *review*. It consists of periodic reviews of CPA firms' accounting and auditing practices by other CPA firms through visitations, interviews, and review of workpapers.

Peer reviews have been part of a self-regulatory program used by the accounting profession since the late 1970s. The AICPA promoted this program by creating an internal organization called the *Division of CPA Firms*, which has two sections:

1. *The SEC Practice Section,* which consists of CPA firms that audit companies that have issued securities to the public. The CPA firms belonging to this section audit about 90 percent of all public companies.
2. *The Private Companies Practice Section,* which consists of CPA firms that audit companies that have not issued securities to the public.

CPA firms that are members of either section are required to have a peer review performed every three years. The peer review teams observe the activities of these firms and review documentation of their audits, after which the teams communicate their findings to the reviewed CPA firms and prepare written reports that are publicly available.

Membership in the Division of CPA Firms is voluntary; therefore, some CPA firms whose partners and employees already were members of the AICPA did not join the division. But the AICPA wanted these CPA firms involved in the self-regulatory process, so in 1988 the AICPA amended its bylaws. Henceforth, a CPA firm with partners and employees belonging to the AICPA had to participate in an approved practice-monitoring program (which is similar to a peer review program). Otherwise, the CPA firm's partners and employees could not continue as members of the AICPA.

THE AUDIT REPORT

A CPA firm's major service or product is a financial statement audit. An example of a standard audit report is shown in Figure 2.3. It is issued if the auditors follow generally accepted auditing standards and if they conclude that the financial statements are fairly presented, in all material respects, in conformity with generally accepted accounting principles.

Each part of the independent auditor's report is explained below.

1. *The heading* specifies that the report is issued by an independent auditor.
2. The report is *addressed* to the shareholders and board of directors of the client. The shareholders own the company, and the board functions as the shareholders' representative; each group relies on the auditor's attestation.
3. a. *The first sentence of the opening (first) paragraph* specifically identifies the management assertions that were audited, namely, the individual financial statements.
   b. *The second and third sentences of the opening paragraph* clearly delineate the responsibility of management (to generate the financial statements) and

FIGURE 2.3   The Independent Auditor's Report

Independent Auditor's Report

To the Shareholders and Board of Directors of X Company:

    We have audited the accompanying balance sheet of X Company as of December 31, 19X8, and the related statements of income, retained earnings, and cash flows for the year then ended. These financial statements are the responsibility of the Company's management. Our responsibility is to express an opinion on these financial statements based on our audit.

    We conducted our audit in accordance with generally accepted auditing standards. Those standards require that we plan and perform the audit to obtain reasonable assurance about whether the financial statements are free of material misstatement. An audit includes examining, on a test basis, evidence supporting the amounts and disclosures in the financial statements. An audit also includes assessing the accounting principles used and significant estimates made by management, as well as evaluating the overall financial statement presentation. We believe that our audit provides a reasonable basis for our opinion.

    In our opinion, the financial statements referred to above present fairly, in all material respects, the financial position of X Company as of December 31, 19X8, and the results of its operations and its cash flows for the year then ended in conformity with generally accepted accounting principles.

Jones & Jones, CPAs
City, State

March 4, 19X9

---

the responsibility of the auditor (to express an opinion on these financial statements).

4. **a.** *The first sentence of the scope (second) paragraph* states that established standards were followed, namely, generally accepted auditing standards.

 b. *The second sentence of the scope paragraph* defines the scope of the audit by stating that the auditors obtained reasonable (not absolute) assurance about whether the financial statements are free of material (not all) misstatement.

 c. *The third sentence of the scope paragraph* explains a limitation of any financial statement audit, that only a part of the evidence underlying the financial statements was examined.

 d. *The fourth sentence of the scope paragraph* provides additional details about the scope of the audit and emphasizes that significant (not all) estimates were assessed and overall (not every) financial statement presentation was evaluated.

 e. *The fifth sentence of the scope paragraph* points out that the audit process gives the auditor a reasonable basis for an opinion.

5. *The opinion (third) paragraph* states

 a. the auditor's *opinion* (not guarantee)

 b. that all of the financial statements referred to in the opening paragraph are presented *fairly,* in all *material respects* (not necessarily in a completely accurate manner or without minor errors) in conformity with *generally accepted accounting principles* (which are broad concepts, assumptions, and conventions used to formulate financial statements and are the criteria against which management's assertions are compared to determine whether they are fairly presented).

6. *The date of the report* is the last day of any significant work done in the client's place of business.

7. *The signature* is that of the accounting firm.

MANAGEMENT'S RESPONSIBILITIES

Management is responsible for the financial statements. Figure 2.4 on page 30 presents an example of management's acknowledgement of their responsibility for financial statements. The management of Wal-Mart Stores, Inc. takes responsibility for the financial statements, while the auditors of Wal-Mart Stores, Inc. attest to fair presentation of the financial statements.

GENERALLY ACCEPTED AUDITING STANDARDS

The audit report illustrated in Figure 2.3 is the product of a process in which auditing procedures are performed to gather the necessary evidence to attest to the fair presentation of financial statements. Auditing standards are used as guidelines in performing these auditing procedures.

Auditing procedures ''relate to acts to be performed,'' whereas *auditing*

FIGURE 2.4   Statement of Management Responsibility for Financial Statements

Responsibility for Financial Statements/Corporate Information

The financial statements and information of Wal-Mart Stores, Inc. and Subsidiaries presented in this Report have been prepared by management which has responsibility for their integrity and objectivity. These financial statements have been prepared in conformity with generally accepted accounting principles, applying certain estimates and judgments based upon currently available information and management's view of current conditions and circumstances.

Management has developed and maintains a system of accounting and controls, including an extensive internal audit program, designed to provide reasonable assurance that the Company's assets are protected from improper use and that accounting records provide a reliable basis for the preparation of financial statements. This system is continually reviewed, improved and modified in response to changing business conditions and operations and to recommendations made by the independent auditors and the internal auditors. Management believes that the accounting and control systems provide reasonable assurance that assets are safeguarded and financial information is reliable.

The Company has adopted a Statement of Ethics to guide our management in the continued observance of high ethical standards of honesty, integrity and fairness in the conduct of the business and in accordance with the law. Compliance with the guidelines and standards is periodically reviewed and is acknowledged in writing by all management associates.

The Board of Directors, through the activities of its Audit Committee consisting solely of outside Directors, participates in the process of reporting financial information. The duties of the Committee include keeping informed of the financial condition of the Company and reviewing its financial policies and procedures, its internal accounting controls, and the objectivity of its financial reporting. Both the Company's independent auditors and the internal auditors have free access to the Audit Committee and meet with the Committee periodically, with and without management present.

Paul R. Carter

Paul R. Carter
Executive Vice President and
Chief Financial Officer

"deal with measures of the quality of the performance of those acts and the objectives to be attained by the use of the procedures undertaken."[1]

▶ **EXAMPLE**

An auditor requests confirmation of accounts receivable balances directly from customers (an auditing procedure) to obtain competent and sufficient evidence to afford a basis for an opinion (an auditing standard).

The auditing standards used by CPA firms are referred to as *generally accepted*

[1] *AICPA Professional Standards,* Volume 1, AU Section 150.01.

FIGURE 2.5   An Overview of Generally Accepted Auditing Standards

The Three General Standards	*The Three Standards of Fieldwork*	*The Four Standards of Reporting*
These standards address the qualifications of the auditor and the quality of his or her work.	These standards address planning and performing the audit.	These standards describe the nature and contents of the auditor's report.
These standards are discussed in Chapters 3 and 4.	These standards are discussed in Chapters 5–18.	These standards are discussed in Chapters 19–21.

auditing standards (see Figure 2.5) and have been approved and adopted by the membership of the AICPA. The *Auditing Standards Board of the AICPA,* which consists of representatives from CPA firms and the academic community, issues pronouncements on auditing matters that serve as interpretations of these standards. These interpretations are compiled as *Statements on Auditing Standards* and are updated in booklet form each year.

These generally accepted auditing standards are the guidelines used to perform a financial statement audit, which consists of the three following steps or phases, each of which requires a distinct set of auditing standards:

1. Taking steps to assure the quality of the audit.
2. Planning and performing the audit procedures.
3. Reporting the audit results.

The General Standards (Assuring the Quality of the Audit)

The *first general standard* is:

> The audit is to be performed by a person or persons having adequate technical training and proficiency as an auditor (AU Section 210.01).

This technical training and proficiency must be in the field of auditing, no matter how capable a person is in aspects of business and finance.

> **Comment**   Most states have laws requiring that persons possess the CPA certificate before being in charge of independent audits (financial statement audits as independent contractors).

The *second general standard* is:

> In all matters relating to the assignment, an independence in mental attitude is to be maintained by the auditor or auditors (AU Section 220.01).

Independence is the most important standard of all, without which there can be no audit. The auditor in public practice must be without bias with respect to the client (independence in fact) and must be recognized as independent by users of the audit report (independence in appearance). If the auditor has any obligation to or interest in the client, users of the audit report might have the impression that independence is impaired, an impression that is not acceptable.

▶ EXAMPLE

An auditor who owns a client's securities may actually be unbiased in expressing an opinion, but the public may believe the auditor is biased because the auditor appears to have an interest in presenting financial statements that enhance his or her investment.

An auditor who is a director of a client company may be independent in his or her own mind, but the public may believe independence is impaired because the auditor is auditing decisions in which he or she participated.

The *third general standard* is:

Due professional care is to be exercised in the performance of the audit and the preparation of the report (AU Section 230.01).

The purpose of this standard is evident and applies to all the standards of fieldwork and reporting we discuss in the remainder of this section.

The Standards of Fieldwork (Planning and Performing the Audit Procedures)

The *first standard of fieldwork* is:

The work is to be adequately planned, and assistants, if any, are to be properly supervised (AU Section 311.01).

Planning in itself is a generic term, but audit planning requires an overall strategy for assessing risk and performing the audit.

▶ EXAMPLE

The auditor is planning the audit of a manufacturing company. He or she determines that risk of misstatements is high for inventories and accounts payable. The auditor plans additional time and supervision for these two accounts.

The *second standard of fieldwork* is:

A sufficient understanding of internal control is to be obtained to plan the audit and to determine the nature, timing, and extent of tests to be performed (AU Section 319.01).

This standard is discussed in Chapters 9 through 12. Basically, the auditor must acquire an understanding of the processes that generate the financial statement amounts and disclosures before making decisions about the audit tests that will be performed on these amounts and disclosures.

▶ **EXAMPLE**

An auditor plans certain tests of a client's inventory balance. The auditor needs an understanding of records, controls, and transaction processing that generated this inventory balance, so that he or she can determine what tests to perform, when to perform them, and the amount of testing to do.

The *third standard of fieldwork* is:

Sufficient competent evidential matter is to be obtained through inspection, observation, inquiries, and confirmations to afford a reasonable basis for an opinion regarding the financial statements under audit (AU Section 326.01).

The validity of legal evidence is determined by law; the validity of audit evidence, however, is determined by the auditor's judgment. The auditor must exercise this judgment and determine the quantity (sufficiency) and quality (competency) of evidence needed to evaluate management's assertions in the financial statements.

▶ **EXAMPLE**

In some cases, the auditor will examine evidence supporting all transactions in an account balance. In other cases, the auditor will examine evidence supporting only a sample of transactions in an account balance. For some accounts, the auditor will examine only evidence generated by the client's accounting system. For other accounts, the auditor will examine evidence originating from an outside independent source.

The Standards of Reporting (Reporting the Audit Results)

The *first standard of reporting* is:

The report shall state whether the financial statements are presented in accordance with generally accepted accounting principles (AU Section 410.01).

The auditor cannot allow the readers of the audit report to assume that generally accepted accounting principles were followed in presenting the financial statements. The auditor must state this conclusion clearly in his or her report.

▶ **EXAMPLE**

This conclusion is stated in the opinion paragraph of the independent auditor's report by using this wording: "In our opinion, the financial statements referred to above present fairly, in all material respects, . . . in conformity with generally accepted accounting principles."

Other wording (covered in Chapter 20) is used in the report if generally accepted accounting principles are not followed in all material respects.

√ The *second standard of reporting* is:

√ The report shall identify those circumstances in which such principles have not been consistently observed in the current period in relation to the preceding period (AU Section 420.01).

The opinion paragraph of the independent auditor's report shown above implies (does not explicitly state) that the auditor is satisfied that generally accepted accounting principles have been consistently applied between accounting periods. Other wording (see Chapter 20) is used if a change in accounting principles occurs.
√ The *third standard of reporting* is:

√ Informative disclosures in the financial statements are to be regarded as reasonably adequate unless otherwise stated in the report (AU Section 430.01).

The auditor's opinion that the financial statements are in conformity with generally accepted accounting principles implies that adequate disclosures were made in these statements. Other wording (see Chapter 20) is used if the auditor believes that disclosures required by generally accepted accounting principles are omitted in the financial statements.
√ The *fourth standard of reporting* is:

√ The report shall either contain an expression of opinion regarding the financial statements, taken as a whole, or an assertion to the effect that an opinion cannot be expressed. When an overall opinion cannot be expressed, the reasons therefor should be stated. In all cases where an auditor's name is associated with financial statements, the report should contain a clear-cut indication of the character of the auditor's work, if any, and the degree of responsibility the auditor is taking (AU Section 504.01).

Properly worded audit reports indicate this degree of responsibility, as shown in the following four types of reports:

1. A report that expresses an *unqualified opinion* (also referred to as a standard report), an example of which is shown in Figure 2.3. It states that (1) the auditor performed the audit in accordance with generally accepted auditing standards and (2) in the auditor's opinion, the financial statements are presented fairly, in all material respects, in conformity with generally accepted accounting principles.

2. A report that expresses a *qualified opinion*. This report states that, except for the effects of the matter(s) to which the qualification relates, the financial statements are presented fairly, in all material respects, in conformity with generally accepted accounting principles.
    A qualified opinion is issued for two reasons.
    a. Circumstances prevent the auditor from *performing all audit procedures* necessary to comply with generally accepted auditing standards (e.g., failure to observe inventory counts of a client where inventory is material to the financial statements and satisfactory alternative procedures cannot be performed).
    b. The auditor concludes (1) that the financial statements contain a *material departure from generally accepted accounting principles* (e.g., the client records property and equipment above cost by an amount that is material to the

financial statements), or (2) that all *informative disclosures* have not been made in the financial statements (e.g., the client refuses to disclose a pending lawsuit).

3. A report that contains a *disclaimer of opinion,* which states that the auditor does not express an opinion on the financial statements. This report is issued if

   a. The auditor *cannot gather all necessary evidence* because (1) unavoidable circumstances prevent it, or (2) the client imposes restrictions on the evidence the auditor can gather (e.g., the refusal of the client to allow the auditor to observe the inventory at year-end when inventory is material to the financial statements).

   b. The going concern status of an entity might have such a serious potential impact on the financial statements that they may not be meaningful (e.g., the potential loss from a lawsuit could result in bankruptcy).

   A disclaimer of opinion can have a serious impact on the reader's views of the accompanying financial statements. This type of report is rendered only if the auditor is convinced that the inability to perform all necessary audit procedures or the going concern uncertainty is extremely serious.

4. A report that contains an *adverse opinion,* which states that, because of a very material departure from generally accepted accounting principles (GAAP), the auditor's opinion is that the financial statements are not presented fairly in conformity with generally accepted accounting principles (e.g., the refusal of the client to restate property and equipment from appraised value to cost when the amount is very material to the financial statements). An adverse opinion is issued when a qualified opinion is not adequate.

   Figure 2.6 summarizes the opinions discussed here.

FIGURE 2.6   Summary of the Basic Types of Audit Reports

Unqualified opinion if

the audit was performed in accordance with generally accepted auditing standards	and	in the auditor's opinion, the financial statements are fairly presented in all material respects, in conformity with GAAP.
But a qualified opinion if, except for the effects of the failure to perform a significant auditing procedure, the audit was performed in accordance with generally accepted auditing standards.		But a qualified opinion if, except for the effects of a material departure from GAAP, the financial statements are presented fairly, in all material respects, in conformity with GAAP.
Or a disclaimer of opinion if, because of the effects of the failure to perform a very significant auditing procedure, or because the going concern status of the entity has such a serious potential impact that an opinion is not expressed.		Or an adverse opinion if, because of a very material departure from GAAP, the financial statements are not presented in conformity with GAAP.

THE BROAD ATTEST SERVICES— ATTESTATION STANDARDS

Historical Background

Until recently, CPA firms attested only to the fairness of their client's historical financial statements. The range of attest services has now extended into many types of assertions or representations, such as reports on

1. Prospective financial statements.
2. Descriptions of computer software.
3. Compliance with statutory, regulatory, and contractual requirements.
4. Investment performance statistics.
5. Information supplementary to financial statements.

It became more difficult to apply generally accepted auditing standards to this increasing array of attest services. A need arose for a separate and broader set of standards covering the services described above and providing opinions other than those given on historical financial statements.

A set of 11 *attestation standards* were issued in the mid-1980s. They cover many of the same areas as generally accepted auditing standards, although they do not supersede them. The attestation standards are broader in scope simply because they apply to all forms of attestations, while generally accepted auditing standards apply only to audits.

The Attestation Standards

Attest Engagement

The attestation standards apply to the performance of an attest engagement by a certified public accountant who practices public accounting (generally referred to as a practitioner).

An *attest engagement* is one in which a practitioner is engaged to issue or does issue a written communication that expresses a conclusion about the reliability of a written assertion that is the responsibility of another party.[2]

Example of a Written Communication in an Attest Engagement

Figure 2.7 is an illustration of a report that could be written when a practitioner performing an attest engagement expresses a positive opinion about an assertion concerning investment performance statistics.

Differences Between Attestation Standards and Generally Accepted Auditing Standards

In comparing the attestation report shown in Figure 2.7 and the independent auditor's report shown in Figure 2.3, we note several phrases that illustrate fundamental

---

[2] *AICPA Professional Standards*, Volume 1, AT Section 100.01.

FIGURE 2.7　**Example of a Written Communication in an Attest Engagement**

> We have examined the accompanying Statement of Investment Performance Statistics of XYZ Fund for the year ended December 31, 19X1. Our examination was made in accordance with standards established by the American Institute of Certified Public Accountants and, accordingly, included such procedures as we considered necessary in the circumstances.
>
> In our opinion, the Statement of Investment Performance Statistics referred to above presents the investment performance of XYZ Fund for the year ended December 31, 19X1 in conformity with the measurement and disclosure criteria set forth in Note 1.
>
> *Source:* AT Section 100.54.

FIGURE 2.8　**Comparison of Attestation General Standards and Auditing General Standards**

Attestation Standards	*Generally Accepted Auditing Standards*
1. The engagement shall be performed by a practitioner or practitioners having adequate technical training and proficiency in the attest function.	1. The audit is to be performed by a person or persons having adequate technical training and proficiency as an auditor.
2. The engagement shall be performed by a practitioner or practitioners having adequate knowledge of the subject matter of the assertion.	2. In all matters relating to the assignment, an independence in mental attitude is to be maintained by the auditor or auditors.
3. The practitioner shall perform an engagement only if he or she has reason to believe that the following two conditions exist: a. The assertion is capable of evaluation against reasonable criteria that either have been established by a recognized body or are stated in the presentation of the assertion in a sufficiently clear and comprehensive manner for a knowledgeable reader to be able to understand them. b. The assertion is capable of reasonably consistent estimation or measurement using such criteria.	
4. In all matters relating to the engagement, an independence in mental attitude shall be maintained by the practitioner or practitioners.	
5. Due professional care shall be exercised in the performance of the engagement.	3. Due professional care is to be exercised in the performance of the audit and the preparation of the report.

Discussion of Comparison

　The second and third general attestation standards establish boundaries around the attest function because the subject matters of the attestations extend beyond historical financial statements. The boundary of the subject matter of the audit is generally accepted accounting principles. Also, the attestation standards use the term *engagement* because the attest function extends beyond the audit. The balance of the comparative wording is similar.

FiGURE 2.9   Comparison of Attestation Standards of Fieldwork and Auditing Standards of Fieldwork

Attestation Standards	*Generally Accepted Auditing Standards*
1. The work shall be adequately planned, and assistants, if any, shall be properly supervised.	1. The work is to be adequately planned and assistants, if any, are to be properly supervised.
	2. A sufficient understanding of internal control is to be obtained to plan the audit and to determine the nature, timing, and extent of tests to be performed.
2. Sufficient evidence shall be obtained to provide a reasonable basis for the conclusion that is expressed in the report.	3. Sufficient competent evidential matter is to be obtained through inspection, observation, inquiries, and confirmations to afford a reasonable basis for an opinion regarding the financial statements under audit.

Discussion of Comparison

The second auditing standard of fieldwork refers to internal control that may not be relevant for assertions for which attest engagements will be performed. Also, the second attestation standard of fieldwork is broad enough to cover the step of obtaining an understanding of internal control should that step be performed in an attest engagement. The balance of the wording of the standards is similar.

differences between attestation standards and generally accepted auditing standards.

1. The attestation report does not contain a reference to financial statements. Attestation standards extend beyond attesting to historical financial statements.
2. The attestation report refers to an assertion other than historical financial statements. Attestation standards accommodate an expanding number of attest services that have a wide range of assertions.
3. The attestation report refers to criteria other than generally accepted accounting principles. Attestation standards provide for attest services that are structured to the needs of the users, who, in turn, may have participated in establishing the criteria against which the assertions are measured.

Let us now examine the attestation standards themselves and contrast them with the generally accepted auditing standards described earlier. Figures 2.8, 2.9, and 2.10 show general standards, standards of fieldwork, and standards of reporting, respectively.

ORGANIZATIONS THAT AFFECT THE PUBLIC ACCOUNTING PROFESSION

Many organizations affect the practice of public accounting because of the regulatory authority they exert, the standards they set, and other professional activities in which they engage.

FIGURE 2.10   Comparison of Attestation Standards of Reporting and Auditing Standards of Reporting

Attestation Standards	*Generally Accepted Auditing Standards*
1. The report shall identify the assertion being reported on and state the character of the engagement.	1. The report shall state whether the financial statements are presented in accordance with generally accepted accounting principles.
2. The report shall state the practitioner's conclusion about whether the assertion is presented in conformity with the established or stated criteria against which it was measured.	2. The report shall identify those circumstances in which such principles have not been consistently observed in the current period in relation to the preceding period.
	3. Informative disclosures in the financial statements are to be regarded as reasonably adequate unless otherwise stated in the report.
3. The report shall state all of the practitioner's significant reservations about the engagement and the presentation of the assertion.	4. The report shall either contain an expression of opinion regarding the financial statements, taken as a whole, or an assertion to the effect that an opinion cannot be expressed. When an overall opinion cannot be expressed, the reasons therefor should be stated. In all cases where an auditor's name is associated with financial statements, the report should contain a clear-cut indication of the character of the auditor's work, if any, and the degree of responsibility the auditor is taking.
4. The report on an engagement to evaluate an assertion that has been prepared in conformity with agreed-upon criteria or on an engagement to apply agreed-upon procedures should contain a statement limiting its use to the parties who have agreed on such criteria or procedures.	

Discussion of Comparison

The attestation standards of reporting cover a significant expansion of the attest function compared to auditing. Some attest engagements limit the reports to users because the engagements are patterned to the needs of these users. Also, the second standard of reporting of attestation covers the second and third standards of reporting of generally accepted auditing standards.

State Boards of Accounting

State boards of accounting are government agencies that administer public accounting laws in states and territories. Each state board of accounting awards a license to practice public accounting to anyone who satisfies the qualifications imposed by the applicable statutes.

State boards of accounting have ultimate responsibility for discipline in public accounting; they have the power to suspend or revoke the CPA's certificate and/or the CPA's license to practice public accounting in that jurisdiction. Many state boards promote quality within public accounting by enforcing codes of conduct and continuing professional education requirements for CPAs.

State Societies of Certified Public Accountants

The accounting profession also has *state societies of certified public accountants,* which are voluntary organizations of CPAs within states. State societies do not possess statutory authority to grant, suspend, or revoke a CPA's certificate or license to practice public accounting. However, they do encourage quality performance in public accounting by establishing codes of conduct and by providing continuing professional education courses and peer review programs for CPA firms.

CPAs do not have to belong to a state society of certified public accountants. Many CPAs, however, join to support the accounting profession at the state and local levels.

American Institute of Certified Public Accountants

The *American Institute of Certified Public Accountants (AICPA)* is an influential national accounting organization whose objectives are

to unite certified public accountants in the United States; to promote and maintain high professional standards of practice; to assist in the maintenance of standards for entry to the profession; to promote the interests of CPAs; to develop and improve accounting education; and to encourage cordial relations between CPAs and professional accountants in other countries.[3]

These objectives are accomplished partially by issuing a number of publications, such as

1. The *Code of Professional Conduct* (discussed in Chapter 3), which serves as a model for codes of conduct of state societies and state boards.
2. *Statements on Auditing Standards,* which are authoritative interpretations of generally accepted auditing standards.
3. Bulletins that provide guidance to AICPA members on various accounting issues.

Practicing CPAs do not have to join the AICPA, which has no regulatory authority over the practice of public accounting. Nonetheless, a substantial number of CPAs, both in and out of public practice, do join the AICPA because of its prestige and the CPAs' desire to promote the accounting profession. Anyone who has a valid CPA certificate can join the AICPA.

The Securities and Exchange Commission

The *Securities and Exchange Commission (SEC)* is a federal agency that regulates the distribution of securities to the public and the trading of securities on stock exchanges. The SEC was created by an act of the U.S. Congress in 1934 and empow-

[3] *AICPA Professional Standards,* Volume 2, BL Section 101.01.

ered with statutory authority to determine accounting principles for use in the published financial statements of companies that sell securities to the public.

Generally, the SEC has not exercised this authority, preferring to let the accounting profession itself set accounting standards. The SEC, however, does affect the formulation and application of accounting principles through its pronouncements and influence over the Financial Accounting Standards Board (the organization that sets accounting standards in the private sector of the accounting profession).

THE EVOLVING PRACTICE OF PUBLIC ACCOUNTING

Public accounting in the United States has changed considerably since its inception over 100 years ago. Much of that change has occurred because of an *expectation gap,* that is, a gap between the public's and auditors' perception of audit functions and responsibilities. This gap developed partly because of highly publicized financial failures which Congress and some members of the public blamed on poor performance by auditors.

Commission on Auditors' Responsibilities

In the mid-1970s the AICPA attempted to address this gap by appointing an independent group to examine the problems and issues facing CPAs in the role of independent auditor. This group was called the *Commission on Auditors' Responsibilities* (also known as the *Cohen Commission*). The commission issued a set of recommendations to clarify auditors' responsibilities in several critical areas and to restore the public's confidence in auditing services.

Investigations by the U.S. Congress

During the 1970s committees of both houses of Congress conducted investigations of accounting practices and auditing services and issued reports on how each could be improved.

In the 1980s Congressman Dingell held hearings to determine how well auditors of publicly owned companies and the SEC were meeting their responsibilities as auditors and regulators, respectively. Congressman Dingell was particularly critical of the accounting profession's failures to (1) detect fraud, (2) alert the public to potential business failures, and (3) discipline its members for ethics violations.

During the same decade, Congressman Brooks chaired another investigation on the failures of the accounting profession. He cited a report by the General Accounting Office that contained numerous examples of substandard auditing of government entities by CPAs.

The AICPA reacted to these congressional criticisms by revising a large number of auditing standards. State boards of accounting reacted by implementing new enforcement programs.

The Treadway Commission

The accounting profession has acknowledged another accelerating problem in recent years—management-related fraud in financial reporting (i.e., deliberate misstatement of financial statements by management). In 1985 the AICPA established the *Treadway Commission* to study management-related fraud and the role of independent auditors in detecting this type of fraud.

In 1987 the commission issued a report that contained a number of recommendations (the details of which are covered in Chapter 5). The report also contained criticism of auditors in management-related fraud cases. In some cases, auditors had failed to obtain sufficient audit evidence (the third standard of fieldwork) and were not sufficiently skeptical about suspicious situations encountered during the audits.

Throughout the text, we will emphasize the need to adhere to the third standard of fieldwork and to maintain an objective and skeptical attitude.

Chapter 2 ▶ GLOSSARY OF TERMS

Accounting services   Primarily assistance in the preparation of financial statements and other services not involving attestation, tax, or management services.

Adverse opinion   An audit opinion that states that, because of a very material departure from GAAP, in the auditor's opinion, the financial statements are not presented fairly in conformity with GAAP.

Advisory services   Management consulting services that require studies to develop findings, conclusions, and recommendations for client consideration and decision making.

American Institute of Certified Public Accountants   A voluntary national organization of CPAs that issues accounting and auditing standards and promotes the accounting profession.

Attest engagement   An engagement in which a practitioner is engaged to issue or does issue a written communication that expresses a conclusion about the reliability of a written assertion that is the responsibility of another party.

Attestation standards   A broad set of standards used to attest to assertions or representations of a client.

Auditing procedures   Acts to be performed; the gathering of evidence to attest to financial statement fairness.

Auditing standards   Measures of the quality of the performance of audit procedures and the objectives to be attained by the use of the procedures.

Auditing Standards Board   A senior committee of the AICPA that issues pronouncements on auditing matters that serve as interpretations of generally accepted auditing standards.

Certified public accountant   A title held by one who has passed the uniform CPA examination and met appropriate education and experience requirements.

Commission on Auditors' Responsibilities (the Cohen Commission)   An independent group appointed by the AICPA to examine the problems and issues facing the CPA in the role of independent auditor.

Consultations   Management consulting services completed in a short time based on the CPA's existing personal knowledge.

Disclaimer of opinion   An auditor's report in which the auditor does not express an opinion on the financial statements.

Division of CPA Firms   A division of the AICPA created as part of its self-regulatory program; peer reviews are part of this program.

Expectation gap   A gap between the public's and auditors' perception of audit functions and responsibilities.

General standards   The three generally accepted auditing standards that address the qualifications of the auditor and the quality of his or her work.

Generally accepted auditing standards   Auditing standards that have been adopted by the membership of the AICPA and that are used by CPAs to perform financial statement audits.

Government accountants   Accounting employees of a federal, state, or local government entity.

Implementation services   Management consulting services that require the CPA to put into operation a plan the client has accepted.

Independent auditor's report   The audit report issued by an independent auditor to a client.

International CPA firms CPA firms that have operations throughout the world.

Licensing requirements Requirements of states, the District of Columbia, and U.S. territories to practice public accounting.

Local CPA firms CPA firms that normally have one or a few offices and conduct their business within the area of a town or city.

Management consulting services A variety of technical services performed for clients, which involve studies of management problems and recommendations to clients.

National CPA firms CPA firms that have offices throughout the United States.

Opening (first) paragraph of the independent auditor's report The paragraph that names the financial statements and delineates the responsibilities of management and the auditor.

Opinion (third) paragraph of the independent auditor's report The auditor's opinion as to the fair presentation of the financial statements.

Partners (or stockholders) Owners of CPA firms.

Peer (or quality) reviews Periodic reviews of CPA firms' accounting and auditing practices by other CPA firms through visitations, interviews, and review of workpapers.

Private accountants Accounting employees of nongovernment entities other than public accounting firms.

Private Companies Practice Section The section of the Division of CPA Firms which consists of CPA firms that audit companies that are not publicly owned.

Product services Management consulting services in which the CPA provides a product or service.

Public accounting Independent auditors, tax specialists, and consultants who offer services to the public.

Qualified opinion An audit opinion that takes exception to the scope of the audit or the fair presentation of the financial statements in conformity with GAAP.

Quality control Measures taken by CPA firms to ensure the quality of performance of services rendered to clients.

Regional CPA firms CPA firms that have offices concentrated largely in certain sections of the United States.

Review A service in which limited assurance is provided on the financial statements.

Scope (second) paragraph of the independent auditor's report The paragraph that defines the scope of the audit by describing the standards used to perform the audit, the assurance provided, and the general procedures performed.

SEC Practice Section The section of the Division of CPA Firms that consists of CPA firms that audit companies that have publicly-traded securities.

Securities and Exchange Commission (SEC) A federal agency that regulates the distribution of securities to the public and the trading of securities on stock exchanges.

Seniors Employees of CPA firms who perform complex audit procedures and supervise staff accountants.

Staff accountants Employees of public accounting firms who perform detailed audit work under the direct guidance of one or more experienced auditors and have little or no supervisory responsibility.

Staff and other support services Management consulting services in which the CPA is asked by a client to supply one or more staff personnel to perform work needed by the client.

Standards of fieldwork The three generally accepted auditing standards that are concerned with planning and performing the audit.

Standards of reporting The four generally accepted auditing standards that describe the nature and contents of the auditor's report.

State boards of accounting Government agencies that administer public accounting laws in a particular jurisdiction. They award CPA certificates and licenses to practice public accounting, and they have the power to revoke the CPA's certificate and/or CPA's license to practice public accounting in that jurisdiction.

State societies of certified public accountants Voluntary organizations of CPAs within the states.

Supervisors (or managers) Employees of CPA firms who have responsibility for supervising several engagements that run concurrently.

Tax services Services consisting of preparation or review of tax returns, tax litigation, and tax planning.

Transaction services Management consulting services that require the CPA to advise on a specific client transaction involving a third party.

Treadway Commission A commission appointed by the AICPA to study management-related fraud and the role of independent auditors in detecting this type of fraud.

Uniform CPA examination A uniform examination developed by the AICPA, the passing of which is one requirement for obtaining a CPA certificate.

Unqualified opinion An audit opinion that states that the audit was performed in accordance with generally accepted auditing standards and that, in the auditor's opinion, the financial statements are presented fairly, in all material respects, in conformity with generally accepted accounting principles.

Chapter 2 ► REFERENCES

Akresh, Abraham D. "Common Myths about Audits," *Journal of Accountancy* (May 1990), pp. 110–111.

American Institute of Certified Public Accountants. *Professional Standards:*

AT Section 100—*Attestation Standards.*

AU Section 110—*Responsibilities and Functions of the Independent Auditor*

AU Section 150—*Generally Accepted Auditing Standards*

AU Section 161—*The Relationship of Generally Accepted Auditing Standards to Quality Control Standards*

AU Section 201—*Nature of the General Standards*

AU Section 210—*Training and Proficiency of the Independent Auditor*

AU Section 220—*Independence*

AU Section 230—*Due Care in the Performance of Work*

BL Section 100—*Bylaws of the American Institute of Certified Public Accountants*

Statement of Standards for Consulting Services

Barrett, Gene R. "Is Accounting Becoming the First Truly International Profession?" *Journal of Accountancy* (October 1992), pp. 110–113.

Brewer, Peter C., and Mills, Tina Y. "ISO 9000 Standards: An Emerging CPA Service," *Journal of Accountancy* (February 1994), pp. 63–67.

Briloff, Abraham J. "Our Profession's Jurassic Park," *The CPA Journal* (August 1994), pp. 26–31.

Jeffords, Raymond, and Thibadoux, Greg M. "TQM and CPA Firms," *Journal of Accountancy* (July 1993), pp. 59–63.

Kuttner, Monroe S. "CPA Consulting Services: A New Standard," *Journal of Accountancy* (November 1991), pp. 41–42.

Mason, Eli. "Public Accounting—No Longer a Profession," *The CPA Journal* (July 1994), pp. 34–37.

Mingle, J. Curt. "CPA 2000: What's Ahead in Staffing? The Shape of Firms to Come," *Journal of Accountancy* (July 1994), pp. 39–46.

Muns, Roger E., Roussey, Robert S., and Whitmer, William E. "Practical Definitions of Six Consulting Functions," *Journal of Accountancy* (November 1991), pp. 43–45.

Chapter 2 ► REVIEW QUESTIONS

2-1 Describe the type of work performed and the general education requirements needed to enter each of the following career paths in accounting:
   a. Public accounting.
   b. Private accounting.
   c. Government accounting.
   d. Accounting education.

2-2 What are the three general requirements that must be followed to obtain a license to practice public accounting?

2-3 Describe the differences among the following types of CPA firms.
   a. International CPA firms.
   b. National CPA firms.
   c. Regional CPA firms.
   d. Local CPA firms.

2-4 Describe the scope of service of each of the following services offered by CPA firms.
   a. Audit.
   b. Review.
   c. Tax services.
   d. Management consulting services.
   e. Accounting services.

2-5 Under what conditions is it acceptable for a CPA to perform management consulting services for an audit client?

2-6 Describe the five suggestions on how CPA firms can effectively implement a system of quality control.

2-7 Name the two sections of the Division of CPA Firms and describe the purpose of each section.

2-8 Give an explanation of each of the following parts of the independent auditor's report:
   a. The heading.
   b. The addressee.
   c. The first sentence of the opening paragraph.
   d. The second and third sentences of the opening paragraph.
   e. The first sentence of the scope paragraph.
   f. The second sentence of the scope paragraph.
   g. The third sentence of the scope paragraph.
   h. The fourth sentence of the scope paragraph.
   i. The fifth sentence of the scope paragraph.
   j. The opinion paragraph.
   k. The date of the report.
   l. The signature.

2-9 Answer the following questions about generally accepted auditing standards.
   a. What do the general standards address?
   b. What do the standards of fieldwork address?
   c. What is described in the standards of reporting?

2-10 Name the generally accepted auditing standards from which the following phrase or phrases are taken. (For example, the phrase "adequate technical training and proficiency" is taken from the first general standard.)

wystarcza/gu

a. "Due professional care is to be exercised."

b. "Sufficient competent evidential matter is to be obtained."

c. "Informative disclosures in the financial statements."

d. "The work is to be adequately planned."

e. "Are presented in accordance with generally accepted accounting principles."

2-11 Describe the four types of audit opinions.

2-12 Describe three fundamental differences between attestation standards and generally accepted auditing standards.

2-13 Answer the following questions.

a. What is the purpose of the second and third general attestation standards shown in Figure 2.8?

b. In Figure 2.9, why is there no attestation standard of fieldwork referring to internal control?

c. In Figure 2.10, why are there no attestation standards of reporting that refer to consistency and informative disclosures?

2-14 Answer the following questions about organizations that influence operations of CPA firms.

a. What is the purpose of state boards of accounting?

b. What are state societies of certified public accountants?

c. What are the objectives of the American Institute of Certified Public Accountants?

d. What does the Securities and Exchange Commission (SEC) regulate?

2-15 Answer the following questions.

a. Why was the Commission on Auditors' Responsibilities appointed?

b. Why was the Treadway Commission established?

Chapter 2 ▶ OBJECTIVE QUESTIONS

(* = author prepared; ** = CPA examination)

*2-16 Which of the following is a correct statement?

a. All states require only a CPA certificate to obtain a license to practice public accounting.

b. All states require public accounting experience to obtain a license to practice public accounting.

c. Most states require a CPA certificate to practice public accounting.

d. All states require a CPA certificate, a college degree with the equivalent of a major in accounting, and public accounting experience to obtain a license to practice public accounting.

*2-17 Which of the following is a correct statement?

a. An audit provides limited assurance by attesting to the fairness of the client's assertions.

b. A review provides positive assurance by attesting to the reliability of the client's assertions.

c. Management consulting services provide attestation in all cases.

d. Accounting services do not provide attestation.

*2-18 Which of the following is not a quality control standard?

a. Independence in fact and appearance should be maintained at all organizational levels.

b. Personnel should be hired who possess the appropriate characteristics to enable them to perform competently.

c. CPA firms should not accept or continue clients whose managements lack integrity.

d. Due professional care is to be exercised.

*2-19 Which of the following sentences or phrases from the auditor's report is not correctly stated?

a. We have audited the accompanying . . .

b. We conducted our audit in accordance with generally accepted auditing standards.

c. In our opinion, the financial statements referred to above present fairly the financial position . . .

d. . . . in conformity with generally accepted accounting principles.

*2-20 The first general standard of generally accepted auditing standards states that

a. An independence in mental attitude is to be maintained.

b. Due professional care is to be exercised.

c. The audit is to be performed by a person or persons having adequate technical training and proficiency as an auditor.

d. The work is to be adequately planned.

*2-21 When the financial statements contain a material departure from generally accepted accounting principles, the auditor should issue either

a. An unqualified or qualified opinion.

b. A qualified opinion or a disclaimer of opinion.

c. A qualified opinion or an adverse opinion.

d. An adverse opinion or a disclaimer of opinion.

*2-22 Which of the following is not an attestation standard?
a. The engagement shall be performed by a practitioner or practitioners having adequate knowledge in the subject matter of the assertion.
b. Sufficient evidence shall be obtained to provide a reasonable basis for the conclusion that is expressed in the report.
c. The work shall be adequately planned, and assistants, if any, shall be properly supervised.
d. The report shall state whether the financial statements are presented in accordance with generally accepted accounting principles.

**2-23 Which of the following is *not* an attestation standard?
a. Sufficient evidence shall be obtained to provide a reasonable basis for the conclusion that is expressed in the report.
b. The report shall identify the assertion being reported on and state the character of the engagement.
c. The work shall be adequately planned and assistants, if any, shall be properly supervised.
d. A sufficient understanding of internal control shall be obtained to plan the engagement.

**2-24 Which of the following best describes what is meant by the term generally accepted auditing standards?
a. Pronouncements issued by the Auditing Standards Board.
b. Rules acknowledged by the accounting profession because of their universal application.
c. Procedures to be used to gather evidence to support financial statements.
d. Measures of the quality of the auditor's performance.

**2-25 Which of the following is a conceptual difference between the attestation standards and generally accepted auditing standards?
a. The attestation standards provide a framework for the attest function beyond historical financial statements.
b. The requirement that the practitioner be independent in mental attitude is omitted from the attestation standards.
c. The attestation standards do *not* permit an attest engagement to be part of a business acquisition study or a feasibility study.
d. *None* of the standards of fieldwork in generally

accepted auditing standards are included in the attestation standards.

**2-26 The primary purpose of establishing quality control policies and procedures for deciding whether to accept a new client is to
a. Enable the CPA firm to attest to the reliability of the client.
b. Satisfy the CPA firm's duty to the public concerning the acceptance of new clients.
c. Minimize the likelihood of association with clients whose management lacks integrity.
d. Anticipate before performing any field work whether an unqualified opinion can be expressed.

**2-27 Snow, CPA, was engaged by Master Co. to examine and report on management's written assertion about the effectiveness of Master's internal control over financial reporting. Snow's report should state that
a. Because of inherent limitations of internal control, errors or fraud may occur and *not* be detected.
b. Management's assertion is based on criteria established by the American Institute of Certified Public Accountants.
c. The results of Snow's tests will form the basis for Snow's opinion on the fairness of Master's financial statements in conformity with GAAP.
d. The purpose of the engagement is to enable Snow to plan an audit and determine the nature, timing, and extent of tests to be performed.

*2-28 For each description, list the letter or letters of the term or terms that define the description. Each term may be used once, more than once, or not at all.

Description	Term
1. Indicates that personnel should be hired who possess the characteristics to enable them to perform competently.	a. Attestation standards b. Disclaimer of opinion
2. Indicates that generally accepted auditing standards were followed.	c. Generally accepted auditing standards
3. Emphasizes the need for adequate technical training.	d. Quality control standard
4. Emphasizes the need for a sufficient understanding of internal control.	e. Scope paragraph
5. Emphasizes the need for an independence in mental attitude.	

Chapter 2 ▶ DISCUSSION/CASE QUESTIONS

(* = author prepared; ** = CPA examination)

*2-29   You are a supervisor with a midsized regional CPA firm that has offices in several cities throughout the southwestern part of the United States. Your state has two-tier licensing requirements to practice public accounting; a person must have a CPA certificate and 40 hours of continuing professional education per year. Your firm offers a wide variety of services beyond audits, including (1) attestation of assertions other than historical financial statements, (2) preparation of tax returns, (3) reviews, and (4) consultation for installation of computer systems. You have participated in some of these tasks.

Your niece, Claire Comet, is a senior in accounting at the local university. She has an A− grade point average in accounting courses and has aspirations to become a CPA and to practice public accounting. She is interested in employment with a regional firm in your state and one that offers services comparable to your firm. She has written a letter asking what job opportunities are open in a firm like yours and what types of work might she be doing in three years.

Required:
Draft a one-page letter to your niece answering her questions.

*2-30   A business associate makes the following statements.
1. The auditing standards for your profession are too general and provide no real guidelines. It would be very difficult to tell whether or not an audit is substandard.
2. What is the "actual message" being conveyed in an unqualified opinion? Does it mean that the company is a good investment or a good credit risk?
3. A qualified opinion in an audit report is hard to understand. If the financial statements are accurate, why not say so? If they are not accurate, why not indicate the reasons?

Required:
Reply to the business associate's comments. In your replies, describe
a. What specific acts or omissions in an audit could result in violations of which specific auditing standards.
b. The "actual message" in an unqualified opinion.
c. The meaning of a qualified opinion.

*2-31   A graduating senior with a major in accounting is considering the following job offers.
a. From a "Big Six" CPA firm.
b. From a small local CPA firm.
c. From a large corporation with training to become an internal auditor.
d. From the Internal Revenue Service with training to become a revenue agent.

Required:
Discuss the advantages and disadvantages of accepting each job offer.

*2-32   You have been asked by a client to provide professional assurance regarding the operation of a software package developed by your client. Explain how each of the attestation standards would be of assistance in this engagement.

*2-33   After completing his auditing course with a grade of D−, a student was so excited about a career in auditing that he opened an office and began to solicit clients, even though he had

*Public's accoun
need to have
license
requir*

not yet taken the CPA examination. His first client was a small hardware store owned by his father. D. Minus hired several accounting students to assist him in the audit. They spent several days checking the clerical accuracy of the general ledger and found no errors.

Based on this work, D. Minus issued an audit report that stated that the accounting records were accurate. Attached to the report was a trial balance of the accounts.

Required:

Describe the violations of generally accepted auditing standards committed by D. Minus.

*2-34   Several years ago, Prescott Need opened a sporting goods store and invested heavily in a variety of inventory, including fishing rods, golf clubs, and a specialized brand of snow ski. He also secured a large loan from a local bank by using a personal relationship with one of the loan officers and pledging most of his equipment. The loan officer did not require any type of audit for the first note, nor did she specifically indicate that an audit might be necessary to secure additional credit.

Mr. Need leased several hundred square feet of empty, but expensive, space in the middle of the town's most prestigious mall. He spent several thousand dollars the first year on prime-time television advertising and half-page spreads in the local newspaper. He used much of his original cash investment on expensive inventory, equipment that he did not secure on credit, advertising, lease costs, and payroll to hire half a dozen experienced salespeople.

During the first year, revenues were higher than anticipated because many of Mr. Need's friends bought their merchandise from him as personal favors and because economic times were good and numerous customers were planning expensive vacations. But in the second year a recession set in, and potential customers began to spend money for essentials rather than for vacation or recreational purposes. Revenues dropped noticeably, but expenses remained high because of the fixed costs, such as interest, rent expense on the building space, and salaries of the salespeople.

Near the end of the second year, Mr. Need approached Susan Furnish, a local CPA, about hiring her to provide some services for his company.

Required:

a. Discuss five possible services that Ms. Furnish might provide for Mr. Need and the reasons why each one might be beneficial.

After due consideration, Mr. Need decided to hire Ms. Furnish's brother-in-law as his bookkeeper. He told Ms. Furnish that he might engage her as an auditor if any additional bank credit was necessary and the bank required an audit. Anticipating that he might have to extend and increase his bank loan, Mr. Need instructed his bookkeeper to "use whatever acceptable accounting methods are available to show the largest net income, the highest asset base, and the most favorable current ratio possible." The bookkeeper did this by (1) changing from a specific identification method of computing inventory to the first-in first-out (FIFO) method, thus charging to cost of goods sold many old and less expensive items of inventory, (2) changing from accelerated depreciation of equipment to the straight-line method, (3) capitalizing many supply items that had previously been expensed, and (4) reclassifying the bank note as a long-term liability on the assumption that it could be renewed for two more years.

Near the end of the year, Mr. Need asked for an extension of the bank note and an increase in the line of credit. The loan officer stated that an audit of Mr. Need's sporting goods company would be necessary. The audited financial statements should be submitted to the bank before the loan extension could be considered.

Mr. Need asked Ms. Furnish to conduct the audit. Ms. Furnish, who was aware that Mr. Need had changed some of his accounting methods, agreed to consider the request.

Required:

b. Describe the factors Ms. Furnish should consider before accepting the audit. In your discussion, distinguish between the obligations Ms. Furnish would have to (1) her client, Mr. Need, and (2) the bank, which is the third party.

Ms. Furnish decided to perform the audit, but she informed Mr. Need that it would be necessary to take a close look at the accounting methods used to compile the financial statements of the company. During the audit, Ms. Furnish discovered numerous clerical errors, all of which the bookkeeper reluctantly corrected. Many hours were spent arguing the merits of the accounting methods used by Mr. Need, including the classification of the note as a long-term liability. Ms. Furnish neglected to read a provision of the note that specified that if a current ratio of 2 to 1 was not maintained, the bank had the right to demand payment of the note. The audited financial statements that Ms. Furnish gave to the bank, along with her audit report, showed an acceptable current ratio because the note was classified as long term. The note was extended, and Mr. Need was allowed to borrow additional amounts.

Several months later, the sporting goods company declared bankruptcy and filed for protection from creditors under Chapter 11 of the bankruptcy laws.

Required:

c. Should Ms. Furnish have conducted the audit? Give reasons for and against her accepting the audit.

d. What specific auditing standards did Ms. Furnish violate? Give reasons for your answers.

 *2-35 **(Continuing Case—Part II; Part III in Chapter 3)**

The atmosphere was tense as the Board of Directors met in July, 19X8. It was the second meeting since a member of Custom Furniture's original family of owners unexpectedly sold his stock to an outsider. For the first time in the company's history, a majority of stock was held by those outside the family group.

A new president, John Forth, had been selected by the Board at its June 19X8 meeting. The "family," now the minority stockholders, had objected to displacement of the previous president who they believed was following a prudent marketing policy and producing good financial results. They knew that the new president, along with the new majority stockholders, favored an expansion of the customer base and a possible expansion into new product lines.

The new president had been with the company three years as vice president of marketing. Prior to that, he was a marketing manager for an advertising agency. The immediate plans of the Board were to let Mr. Forth continue temporarily as both the president and the person in charge of marketing.

The Board had also appointed a new controller named Genna Gentry. Ms. Gentry had previously been employed as an accounting clerk with a local utility company.

The major item on the Board's agenda was hiring a CPA firm to perform a variety of services. The new minority stockholders (the traditional family group) opposed any expenditures of this type, arguing that the company was doing fine and had no need for any services offered by a CPA firm.

The new majority stockholders were unanimously in favor of expansion. Many of them also believed that "shoddy recordkeeping" had made it difficult to tell "what was really happening in the business." They also argued that an audit at this point would help them secure new capital, both from additional borrowing and possible sale of stock to the public. In addition, Custom had complicated contractual agreements with its salespeople, who had complained about their commissions. The Board asked the new president to contact a CPA firm and pursue the possibility of rendering consulting and auditing services.

John Forth called Bill Locat, an old college friend and the managing partner of Locat and Givet. They met for lunch and Mr. Locat described all the services offered by his firm and the qualifications of each staff member. After lunch, Mr. Forth asked Mr. Locat to send a letter to Custom's Board of Directors detailing all the matters they had discussed.

Required:

Answer the following questions about the content of the letter sent by Mr. Locat to the Board of Directors of Custom Furniture Company. Where applicable, support your answers by referencing one or more paragraphs in the above narrative.

a. What services might be needed by Custom Furniture Company? Why would each one be needed?

b. What specific qualifications are needed by the staff of Locat and Givet to render the services described above?

c. What specific quality control measures should Locat and Givet have in place to perform these services? Why?

The Auditor's ✓ *Ethical Environment*

"Expedients are for the hour, but principles are for the ages."

HENRY WARD BEECHER, *Proverbs from Plymouth Pulpit*

LEARNING OBJECTIVES

After reading and studying the material in this chapter, the student should be able to

▶ Write a paragraph describing the importance of personal ethical standards.

▶ Paraphrase the general model for making ethical decisions.

▶ State clear distinctions among the following parts of the *Code of Professional Conduct:* Principles of Professional Conduct, Rules of Professional Conduct, Interpretations of the Rules, and Ethics Rulings.

▶ Write a brief paragraph describing the seven major areas of the Principles of Professional Conduct.

▶ Paraphrase the purpose of each of the Rules of Professional Conduct.

▶ Describe the effect on independence of direct and indirect financial interests, managerial or employee relationships, joint closely held investments, and loans from clients.

▶ Demonstrate an understanding of the rule on confidential client information by analyzing CPAs' dual responsibility to their clients and the public and assessing the commonality of this rule with similar rules of other professions.

▶ Write a brief paragraph describing and assessing the reason for the rule on contingent fees.

▶ Describe proper and improper forms of advertising activities.

A trademark of professionals is their willingness to accept a set of professional and ethical principles and follow these principles in the conduct of their daily affairs. The acceptance of these principles requires that professionals maintain a higher standard of conduct than is called for by law. Professionals are required to consider carefully the implications of alternative actions and to conduct themselves in a manner that is not only lawful but proper.

In this chapter the following sequence will be used to cover the ethical environment in which CPAs perform their tasks.

1. We will lay a background by discussing ethical principles in general.
2. We will explore the current ethical environment in which auditors and other accounting professionals operate. General ethical principles will be related to the unique tasks of the auditor.
3. To apply 1 and 2, above, to the daily practice of auditing, we will then cover the AICPA *Code of Professional Conduct*, including the Principles of Professional Conduct (general in nature) and the Rules of Professional Conduct (prohibited actions).

ETHICAL TRENDS IN OUR SOCIETY

Ethical conduct by members of professions is highly valued in our society. Codes of conduct, codes of ethics, and canons of law provide ample evidence of these values. Even without codes and canons, professionals should feel a strong obligation to act ethically because it is in the best interests of both themselves and society.

Many observers of the contemporary scene are disturbed by an increasing trend toward unethical behavior in society, and a pronounced increase in the impact that unethical behavior has on daily living.

▶ **EXAMPLE**

A waste disposal firm, once hailed on Wall Street as a spectacular growth stock, misstated its financial statements from its inception in the mid-1980s. The firm's financial statements had showed large profits in its seven-year history when it actually had incurred losses. On at least one occasion, when informed that profits for a given year would fall short of projections, the chief executive officer of the firm told an executive to "find the rest of it."

Improprieties by those who own, manage, or finance business operations can damage the accounting profession's reputation for the integrity of its services.

▶ **EXAMPLE**

The merger of two silver mining companies in a western state resulted in a significant writeup of assets and a substantial increase in the net income of the merged companies. Later, the Securities and Exchange Commission required that the net income be restated to a lower amount. The external auditor took much of the blame for the overstated profits. The auditor had failed to insist that the merged companies follow generally accepted accounting principles, was not sufficiently skeptical, and did not maintain independence because he owned several thousand shares in both companies.

It is vitally important that students be exposed to ethical concepts early; the study of auditing can then be placed in proper context.

GENERAL CONCEPTS OF ETHICS

A partial definition of *ethics* as found in the *American Heritage Dictionary* follows: "The study of the general nature of morals and of the specific moral choices to be made by the individual in his relationship with others." The choices we make determine our ethical values and the image we project to others. We have little difficulty in being ethical about many of the large and conscious decisions we periodically make. Returning money that belongs to someone else is a relatively easy choice for most of us; refusing to accept the legitimacy of false transactions entered on the books by a client is another easy choice. But it is the subtle decision that is difficult and that provides a true test of our integrity. What would most of us do when faced with the choice of remaining with or resigning from an audit engagement for a client that engaged in questionable business practices? Overt cheating would give most of us no moral dilemma, but the situation described previously may be less obviously wrong and probably more difficult to resolve.

Most of us wish to be ethical, and we assume that we are just as ethical as the next person. The operative question is how to translate this desire to be ethical into our daily lives (and specifically for the accounting professional, how to translate this desire into our business affairs).

First, personal ethical standards require an *ethical commitment* on our part, that is, a personal resolve to act ethically. Next, we must have an *ethical awareness,* an ability to perceive the ethical implications of a situation (e.g., the acceptance of a small gift from an audit client involves ethical considerations).

But it may be the need for *ethical competency* that creates our largest hurdle. To make the right choices, we must possess the ability to engage in sound moral reasoning and to develop practical problem-solving strategies. This means that we must cast away a common misconception about ethics—"it's ethical if it's legal."

Take the example of questionable business practices by a client. These practices might not lead to illegal activities, but still they should be disclosed in the financial statements. As professionals knowledgeable of auditing and our client's financial affairs, we should know that such activities are questionable; our sound moral reasoning should tell us to require the disclosure.

A GENERAL MODEL FOR MAKING ETHICAL DECISIONS

CPAs need a structured way to approach the many ethical decisions they encounter when they are performing the variety of professional services described in Chapter 2. Here is a model that could be used by a CPA or anyone who faces critical ethical questions in their work.

1. Gather or identify all the relevant facts about the situation that raises the ethical issue and creates the need for an ethical decision (determine the nature of the proposed questionable activities).

2. Consider the individuals or groups that will be affected (the stakeholders). The questionable business activities may affect management, the CPA, the stockholders, and society as a whole.

3. Consider the alternative courses of action (e.g., do nothing, try to convince the client of the advisability of including the disclosure in the financial statements, resign from the engagement).

4. Consider the possible results or consequences of each course of action (e.g., collect the usual fee but risk subsequent disclosure of your inaction and the possible loss of reputation, lose the client but enhance your reputation for integrity and "feel better" about your sense of ethics).

5. Compare the courses of action with the standards for the ethical question(s) raised (the code of conduct of your profession, your own moral principles that evolve from your training and life's experiences).

6. Select a course of action from among the alternatives.

SUMMARY OF DISCUSSION OF ETHICAL CONCEPTS

Ethical issues faced by CPAs are not always straightforward or easy to resolve. In the remainder of this chapter we discuss many of the difficult ethical issues encountered by CPAs and attempts by the AICPA to resolve them with a code of professional conduct. As the chapter's subjects are covered, consider how each principle, rule, or interpretation of the AICPA's code applies general ethical concepts to the subjects and adapts these concepts to the particular circumstances of the CPA's environment.

THE ACCOUNTING PROFESSION'S CODE OF PROFESSIONAL CONDUCT

Most professions have written codes of professional conduct and there is a general commonality among them.

1. Members of each profession are usually expected to maintain a higher standard of conduct than is required by law.

2. The principles, codes, and canons of each profession usually contain positive admonishments designed to encourage ethical conduct and project a positive image to the public.

3. Professions also expressly prohibit certain acts on the part of their members. These acts are not compatible with the ethical standards that ensure quality work, clients' trust, and a positive public image.

The ethical principles of the accounting profession, embodied in the AICPA's *Code of Professional Conduct,* have these three characteristics and emphasize certain responsibilities to a public that cannot directly assess the quality of services rendered by CPAs.

1. CPAs must possess independence, integrity, and objectivity. As we will discuss in a later section of this chapter, the independence required of CPAs for the attest function is unique.
2. CPAs must have the technical expertise of their profession.
3. CPAs must serve their clients with professional concern and in a manner consistent with their responsibilities to the public (a dual obligation to clients and the public).

State boards of accounting, state CPA societies, and the AICPA all have codes of professional conduct. We discuss the AICPA code because it often is a model for the codes of state boards and state societies. The *Code of Professional Conduct* (Code) replaces an earlier AICPA code and now serves as a model for codes of individual states. Figure 3.1 on page 56 illustrates the structure of the Code.

The Principles of Professional Conduct

The *Principles of Professional Conduct* are worded positively and contain admonitions about the proper behavior of CPAs and the special role of CPAs in our society. The *Principles of Professional Conduct* are made operative through the *Rules of Professional Conduct* and through interpretations of the various senior-level committees of the AICPA mentioned in Figure 3.1.

The *Principles of Professional Conduct* include seven major areas collectively listed and individually discussed:

1. A statement of the purpose of the principles.
2. Responsibilities (Article I).
3. The public interest (Article II).
4. Integrity (Article III).
5. Objectivity and independence (Article IV).
6. Due care (Article V).
7. Scope and nature of services (Article VI).

A Statement of the Purpose of the Principles

Many provisions of the AICPA *Code of Professional Conduct* can be violated without also violating a law or regulation. A major reason for a code of conduct is to encourage members to exercise self-discipline above and beyond laws and regulations.

For example, a CPA would not violate the law if he or she charged an audit client a fee based on the amount of net income shown in that client's audited financial statements. But the CPA is performing an independent audit, and such fees are improper because of the potential effect on the CPA's objectivity. The CPA might be tempted to "overlook" needed adjustments to the financial statements that would decrease audited net income and lower the CPA's fee.

FIGURE 3.1   The Structure of the AICPA *Code of Professional Conduct*

The Structure of the Code of Professional Conduct

The Code of Professional Conduct (Code) was adopted by the membership of the AICPA to provide guidance and rules to all members—those in public practice, industry, government, and education—in the performance of their professional responsibilities. The Code has two sections:

Principles of Professional Conduct—definitive concepts that are the framework of the Code.

Rules of Professional Conduct—rules that govern the performance of professional services by members and identify both acceptable and unacceptable behavior and for which violation by a member could result in some type of sanction by the AICPA against that member.

Compliance with the Code depends on

1. The AICPA members' understanding of the Code and voluntary actions on their part.
2. Reinforcement of the Code by members' peers and by public opinion.
3. Disciplinary proceedings, when necessary, against members who fail to comply with the Code.

Technical Standards Under the Rules of Professional Conduct

Certain senior technical committees of the AICPA are designated to formulate technical standards under the Rules, and members are required to adhere to these standards. These senior technical committees consist of the following: Ethics, Accounting and Auditing, Accounting and Review Services, Taxes, and Management Advisory Services.

Interpretations of the Rules

The AICPA's Professional Ethics Division's Executive Committee issues *Interpretations of the Rules* that serve as guidelines for the scope and application of the Rules. Members of the AICPA are required to justify any departure from these Interpretations.

Ethics Rulings

Ethics Rulings are more specific than Interpretations and summarize the application of the Rules and Interpretations to a particular set of factual circumstances. Again, members of the AICPA must justify departure from the Ethics Rulings.

Applicability of the Rules of Professional Conduct

The Rules apply to all professional services performed except where the wording of the Rules indicates otherwise.

Responsibility for Compliance with the Rules

Members are responsible for compliance with the rules by all persons associated with them in the practice of public accounting.

Members' Responsibility for Others

Certain acts, if carried out by members, would cause them to be in violation of the Rules of Professional Conduct. Members should not permit others to carry out acts of this sort on their behalf, either with or without compensation.

Responsibilities (Article I)

CPAs have responsibilities to (1) their clients (e.g., the independent auditor/client relationship), (2) their employers (e.g., the internal auditor/employer relationship), and (3) the general public.

The Public Interest (Article II)

The CPA's current environment is highly competitive, has few restrictions on advertising, and allows competitive bidding for engagements. In addition, CPAs are offering a wider range of services than in past years.

In the context of this environment this statement best summarizes the CPA's obligation.

When members observe their responsibility to the public, the interests of clients and employers also are best served.

Integrity (Article III)

This section admonishes members to discharge their responsibilities with a sense of integrity. CPAs consistently have access to information about clients' activities. Information about a client's business strategy is a prime example. As professionals, CPAs have an obligation to keep such information private unless the need for disclosure is clearly overriding. We will discuss this issue when we cover the *Rules of Professional Conduct*.

Objectivity and Independence (Article IV)

No other standard in the *Code of Professional Conduct* is more important than *independence,* which is often defined as the ability to act with integrity and objectivity. Independence is such an integral aspect of auditing and other attest services that without it no real attest service can be performed.

Independence precludes certain relationships that may appear to impair objectivity in rendering auditing and other attestation services. For example, a CPA's ownership of a small percentage of an audit client's stock may do nothing to impair the CPA's *independence in fact,* but it would impair the CPA's *independence in appearance.* As a result (and as we will discuss later), no direct ownership of stock of an audit client is allowed.

This section contains this type of guidance about objectivity and independence.

1. A member who provides auditing and other attestation services should be independent in fact (mental attitude) and in appearance (the image projected to the public).
2. In providing all other services, a member should be objective and avoid conflicts of interest (but need not be independent, as required for auditing and other attestation services).

Consider these four situations.

1. A CPA expresses an unqualified opinion on financial statements that are prepared in such a way as to deliberately conceal his or her client's poor business decision. For example, the client made a poor investment that is now worth

less than its cost. Yet, the auditor does not qualify his or her opinion when the investment is stated at cost in the financial statements.

2. The CPA performing what is supposed to be an independent audit is actually an employee of the audit client.

3. The CPA owns a small percentage of the audit client's stock.

4. The CPA's income is derived solely from attest services performed for clients.

Which of these four situations is an impairment of independence? Clearly, the first situation is unacceptable. The second situation, although not as apparent, is also considered an impairment of independence. The third situation may be less damaging than the first two. Still, any direct stock ownership in an audit client might appear to impair independence. What about the fourth situation? Even though the auditor is dependent on his or her clients for income, the auditor/client relationship is considered acceptable and would not impair independence. The general public, when asked about each of the previously listed situations, would probably give a variety of opinions as to which ones are proper and improper. Defining independence, though necessary, also may be difficult.

Due Care (Article V)

CPAs should be competent and diligent in carrying out their responsibilities. In addition, CPAs should know the limitations of their competence and should seek consultation or referral when necessary.

This last admonition is especially important because of the vast array of services now offered by CPAs. For example, a CPA who is performing an audit may be called on to assist the client in deciding on the proper computer software to use in some accounting applications. If the CPA is qualified to give such advice, he or she should feel free to do so. However, if the CPA lacks that qualification and is unable to obtain it, the CPA should consult with someone else or refer the client to someone more knowledgeable in that area.

Scope and Nature of Services (Article VI)

At one time, CPAs rendered mostly audit and tax services, but management consulting services have increased significantly as a percentage of the CPA's total revenues.

Some of these management consulting services are natural extensions of audit services (e.g., advice on budgeting and cost accounting systems). But some types of management consulting services raise questions about conflicts of interest.

▶ **EXAMPLE**

A CPA is asked to install a complete accounting system that is later audited by the same CPA. Will a CPA be as critical as need be of financial statements prepared from records generated from a system he or she installed? Or will a CPA be less critical of these financial statements than he or she would have been if there had been no involvement in the installation of the system?

The Code does not provide answers to these specific questions. Rather, it suggests that members use these guidelines:

1. Practice in firms that have good internal quality control procedures.
2. Give serious consideration as to whether nonaudit services provided to audit clients might create or appear to create conflicts of interest.
3. Think about whether each nonaudit service is consistent with the CPA's role as a professional and is a reasonable extension of existing services offered by the profession.

Rules of Professional Conduct

The *Rules of Professional Conduct* are more specific because they designate actions and relationships in which the CPA should not engage and for which violation of a rule could result in sanction from the AICPA. We provide a framework for discussing the rules in Figure 3.2 (pages 60–61), which contains:

1. The section description for each associated group of rules.
2. The number and name of each rule under that section.
3. The general purpose of each rule.

Section 100—Rule 101. Independence

No rule of professional conduct is more important than the one on independence, which reads as follows.

> A member in public practice shall be independent in the performance of professional services as required by standards promulgated by bodies designated by Council.

Without independence, an audit cannot be performed because the auditor has an inappropriate relationship with his or her client and cannot impartially attest to the fairness of the financial statements. A number of interpretations and ethics rulings have been issued to clarify the many questions that inevitably arise in practice. These interpretations and rulings address:

Certain Financial Relationships, for Example:
1. Direct financial interests
2. Material indirect financial interests
3. Loans from audit clients
4. Client litigation

Certain Managerial or Employee Relationships, for Example:
1. Positions with clients
2. Performing accounting services for audit clients
3. Performing management consulting services for audit clients

Financial Relationships—Direct Financial Interest

Neither members of the AICPA nor their firms can own an investment in their client's securities during the time of a professional engagement or at the time an opinion on the financial statements is issued.

FIGURE 3.2   **Chart of the *Rules of Professional Conduct***

Section Number 100	*Independence, Integrity, and Objectivity*	
Rule Number	*Name of the Rule*	*Purpose of the Rule*
101	Independence	To state that members in public practice must be independent in the performance of designated professional services, and to illustrate situations where independence is impaired
102	Integrity and Objectivity	To emphasize to all members who perform any professional service the obligation to maintain objectivity and integrity, be free of conflicts of interest, and not knowingly misrepresent facts or subordinate their judgment to others
Section Number 200	*General Standards—Accounting Principles*	
Rule Number	*Name of the Rule*	*Purpose of the Rule*
201	General Standards	To establish standards for professional competence, due care, planning and supervision, and sufficient relevant data
202	Compliance with Standards	To establish a member's responsibility for upholding professional standards when performing auditing, review, compilation, management consulting, tax, or other professional services
203	Accounting Principles	To make adherence to generally accepted accounting principles a part of the *Code of Professional Conduct*
Section Number 300	*Responsibilities to Clients*	
Rule Number	*Name of the Rule*	*Purpose of the Rule*
301	Confidential Client Information	To state the obligation of confidentiality borne by members in public practice
302	✓ Contingent Fees	To establish the obligations of members in public practice not to charge fees contingent on findings or results of services when the professional services require independence or tax return preparation

FIGURE 3.2 *(Continued)*

Section Number 400	Responsibilities to Colleagues	
No Rules exist at this time		

Section Number 500	Other Responsibilities and Practices	

Rule Number	Name of the Rule	Purpose of the Rule
501	Acts Discreditable	To emphasize to all members the importance of integrity in all actions
502	Advertising and Other Forms of Solicitation	To prohibit members in public practice from engaging in advertising or other forms of solicitation that are false, misleading, or deceptive, or from using coercion, overreaching, or harassing conduct
503	Commissions and Referral Fees	To prohibit members in public practice from paying or accepting commissions in rendering services to clients when such services require independence
505	Form of Organization and Name	To prohibit members from practicing public accounting in firms with misleading names

---

Comment For purposes of Rule 101, a member or a member's firm includes the following.

1. The accounting firm and all of its owners (proprietors, partners, or shareholders).
2. All professional individuals participating in the engagement.
3. All management personnel located in an office that participates in a significant portion of the engagement.
4. Any entity controlled by persons described in 1 through 3, above.
5. Spouses of the above individuals (whether or not dependent) and dependents (whether or not related).

The amount of the investment is not significant because none is allowed. This prohibition expresses the importance of independence and the image the AICPA wishes to project to the public.

▶ **EXAMPLE**

The appearance of independence is so important that the AICPA believes it might be affected if members have direct financial interests in nonclients that are related in certain ways to a client. *Question:* Is a member's independence impaired if he or she has a direct financial interest in a partnership that invests in a client of the member's firm? *Answer:* Yes, if the member is a general partner in that partnership, which means the member has a direct, vested interest in the financial health of his or her client.

(*Source:* ET 191.158–.159)

▶ **EXAMPLE**

What if a member owns an interest in an investment club that holds shares of stock in the member's client? There is a presumption that the member could significantly influence investments in the client and that the member could influence his or her client's financial position or results of operations. Materiality is not an issue; the member's independence is impaired.

(*Source:* ET 191.071–.072)

Financial Relationships—Indirect Financial Interest

Material indirect financial interests can also give the appearance of loss of independence. A CPA's interest may be impaired if the CPA has too large a financial interest in an entity that has a financial interest in an audit client.

▶ **EXAMPLE**

A member who owns stock in a mutual fund that, in turn, owns stock in a client has a financial interest in the client. If the member has no significant influence over the mutual fund, it is presumed that he or she holds an indirect financial interest in the client. The relationship will not impair independence as long as the indirect financial interest is not material to the member's net worth. If the indirect financial interest becomes material, however, or if the member gains significant influence over the mutual fund, the member's independence is impaired.

(*Source:* ET 191.069–.070)

▶ **EXAMPLE**

Would the member have an indirect financial interest in the client if the member owned stock in a bank from which his or her client borrowed money? Yes, but the stock ownership is acceptable as long as the value of the stock is not material to the member's net worth. (Materiality generally is presumed to be 5 percent of the member's net worth.)

(*Source:* ET 191.025–.026)

Financial Relationships—Loans from Audit Clients

The rule on independence prohibits loans to or from audit clients; however, loans from financial institution clients are acceptable in certain limited circumstances if they are made under "normal lending procedures."

▶ **EXAMPLE**

An auditor has a fully collateralized automobile loan from a bank that is an audit client. Would it be necessary to withdraw from the audit because of this loan? No, if the loan was personal and followed the bank's usual lending procedures, terms, and requirements. Other permitted loans include loans on the cash surrender value of an insurance policy, loans on fully collateralized cash deposits, and credit card balances of $5,000 or less.

► **EXAMPLE**

But assume that the auditor has a home mortgage with the same bank. Independence is impaired, although provision has been made for members who had home mortgages with audit clients before January 1, 1992, to let such mortgages "run their course" as long as they are kept current as to all terms.

(*Source:* ET 101.07, 101–5)

Financial Relationships: Client Litigation

Independence might be impaired if an audit client starts or indicates an intention to start litigation against the CPA performing the audit. Consider two essential features of an audit:

1. Audit clients must be willing to disclose all aspects of their business operations to auditors.
2. Auditors, in turn, must be objective in their appraisal of clients' financial reporting decisions.

Actual or threatened litigation against the auditor would place the auditor and client in adversarial positions (as could actual or threatened litigation by the auditor).

What litigation situations are likely to impair independence and result in the auditor's withdrawal from the engagement?

1. Management of the client starts litigation against the auditor for alleged deficiencies in the audit work.
2. The auditor starts litigation against the management of his or her audit client, the reason being alleged management fraud or deceit.
3. Management announces an intention to start litigation against the auditor for alleged deficiencies in audit work, and the auditor thinks it probable that litigation will begin.

► **EXAMPLE**

What if management initiates litigation because of a dispute between the auditor and the client concerning the results of tax services? If the amount is not material to the auditor's firm or to the client, independence is not impaired because the litigation is not related to an engagement requiring independence.

(*Source:* ET 101.08, 101–6)

Managerial or Employee Relationships—Positions with Clients

Generally, members will not be independent if they are associated with audit clients as employees, officers, directors, or similar positions during the period of their professional engagement or at the time of expressing an opinion. Members can be associated with the financial statements of charitable, religious, or civic organizations if they are only honorary directors or trustees of such organizations, are identified as such in official materials, and do not participate in management functions.

▶ **EXAMPLE**

What is the effect on independence if a client offers an auditor employment while the auditor is participating in the audit of that client? The auditor must consider whether his or her ability to act with integrity and objectivity has been impaired. Overtly, the auditor could settle the issue by immediately rejecting the offer of employment. If the decision is given consideration, however, the auditor should withdraw from participation in the audit until the offer is rejected.

What if the auditor seeks employment with his or her client while participating in the audit? The answer is basically the same: The auditor should withdraw from participation in the audit until he or she is no longer seeking employment with the client.

Acceptance of employment with the audit client impairs independence.

Managerial or Employee Relationships— Accounting Services for Audit Clients

Under certain conditions, members can perform auditing and bookkeeping services for the same client. One rationale for allowing such a relationship is that auditors judge the fairness of presentation of the results of management's operating decisions, not the wisdom of the decisions. Certain conditions must be met, however, for members to provide their audit clients with accounting or bookkeeping services and maintain their independence with regard to these clients.

1. The client must accept responsibility for the financial statements. When necessary, the auditor must assist his or her client in understanding accounting matters sufficiently to take this responsibility.

2. The auditor must not assume the role of employee or management. At a minimum, this means that the auditor should not authorize transactions, have custody of the client's assets, or exercise authority on behalf of the client. The client should prepare source documents, and the auditor should not change basic accounting data without the consent of the client.

3. When auditing financial statements prepared from books he or she has maintained, the auditor should comply with generally accepted auditing standards.

Comment   The Securities and Exchange Commission (SEC) has a different rule on auditors' joint performance of auditing and accounting services for companies that are subject to its jurisdiction. According to SEC regulations, auditors lose their independence when they perform these joint services.

Managerial or Employee Relationships—Auditors' Independence and Management Consulting Services

Do CPAs lose their independence when they perform management consulting services for their audit clients? Unlike an audit, management consulting services do not include an opinion on the fairness of financial statements.

Management consulting services range from functions that have some financial base or relationship, such as the installation of a responsibility accounting system or a computerized billing system, to services further removed from the accounting records, such as merger assistance, actuarial services, executive recruiting, and office layout.

> **Comment** Some members of the accounting profession consider executive recruiting to be the most potentially damaging to independence in appearance, and perhaps independence in fact. The public might not believe an accounting firm could recommend an individual as a client's controller and later be completely objective in its review of the controller's work. The public might believe that the accounting firm would rather overlook certain errors during an audit than suffer the embarrassment of having recommended a less than competent individual.

The AICPA takes the position that no impairment of independence occurs when management consulting services are confined to advice rather than management decisions. Some members of the accounting profession doubt that the AICPA position fully answers the difficult questions. How can CPAs truly conduct an independent audit of a computer system, for example, when they have helped the client design that system? The current consensus is that it can be done if a CPA insists on a proper arrangement of roles. The current trend toward adding value to an audit by giving business advice to the client seems consistent with this consensus.

▶ **EXAMPLE**

Consider these two roles with regard to executive recruiting:

1. During the period of the audit engagement, client personnel are impressed with the auditor's overall business abilities. They ask the auditor to help in a search for a controller—specifically, to recommend a position description and candidate specifications, search for and initially screen candidates, and recommend several qualified candidates for the position. Would this type of consulting impair audit independence? The services, in themselves, would not, because they consist of recommendation and advice.
2. Taking the situation one step further, assume that during the course of the audit engagement, client personnel ask the auditor to recruit and hire a controller for the company. Audit independence is impaired because a management function—hiring—is performed by the auditor.

(*Source:* ET 191.111–.112)

Commentary on independence A special advisory panel of the Public Oversight Board of the American Institute of CPAs recently issued a report on a number of issues important to the accounting profession, including the question of auditor independence.

The advisory panel determined that there are sufficient safeguards regarding the conflict-of-interest aspect of auditor independence (such as the rule on independence). But the panel did recommend that, to ensure greater independence, auditors look to the representatives of the shareholders—the board of directors—as the client, not management of the company being audited.

Section 100—Rule 102. Integrity and Objectivity
This rule is very general, and its text speaks for itself.

> In the performance of any professional service, a member shall maintain objectivity and integrity, shall be free of conflicts of interest, and shall not knowingly misrepresent facts or subordinate his or her judgment to others.

Section 200—Rule 201. General Standards

The following rule establishes general standards as part of the *Code of Professional Conduct.*

A member shall comply with the following standards and with any interpretations thereof.

a. Professional Competence. Undertake only those professional services that the member or the member's firm can reasonably expect to be completed with professional competence.

b. Due Professional Care. Exercise due professional care in the performance of professional services.

c. Planning and Supervision. Adequately plan and supervise the performance of professional services.

d. Sufficient Relevant Data. Obtain sufficient relevant data to afford a reasonable basis for conclusions or recommendations in relation to any professional services performed.

▶ **EXAMPLE**

A CPA is performing management consulting services for a client who needs a new computer system. The CPA engages a systems analyst who specializes in computer systems. To supervise the systems analyst properly, must the CPA be able to perform all the services the systems analyst can perform? No. However, the CPA should be able to define the tasks and evaluate the end-product.

(*Source:* ET 291.017–.018)

Section 200—Rule 202. Compliance with Standards

The following rule establishes the member's responsibilities for upholding the standards associated with auditing and other professional services.

A member who performs auditing, review, compilation, management consulting, tax, or other professional services shall comply with standards promulgated by bodies designated by Council.

The Auditing Standards Board has been designated to issue generally accepted auditing standards. A member who fails to comply with these standards when performing an audit is in violation of the rule.

Section 200—Rule 203. Accounting Principles

Here is another rule that applies to AICPA members who perform audits and certain other services (such as review services discussed in Chapters 2 and 21).

A member shall not (1) express an opinion or state affirmatively that the financial statements or other financial data of any entity are presented in conformity with generally accepted accounting principles or (2) state that he or she is not aware of any material modifications that should be made to such statements or data in order for them to be in conformity with generally accepted accounting principles, if such statements or data contain any departure from an accounting principle promulgated by bodies designated by Council to establish such principles that has a material effect on the statements or data taken as a whole. If, however, the statements or data contain such a departure and the member can demonstrate that due to unusual circumstances the financial statements or data would otherwise have been misleading, the member can comply with the rule by describing the departure, its approximate effects, if practicable, and the reasons why compliance with the principle would result in a misleading statement.

The bodies designated to establish accounting principles are the Financial Accounting Standards Board (FASB) and the Governmental Accounting Standards Board (GASB). Before the establishment of these boards, certain committees of the AICPA issued pronouncements on generally accepted accounting principles. These pronouncements are Accounting Research Bulletins and Accounting Principles Board Opinions; they are authoritative until superseded.

Under limited circumstances, AICPA members may express unqualified opinions on financial statements that utilize accounting principles other than those described previously. To do so, a member must be convinced that the literal application of a pronouncement on accounting principles by an authoritative body would render the financial statements misleading.

Some exceptional circumstances are the following:

1. New legislation.
2. The evolution of a new form of business transaction.

However, the following are not exceptional circumstances:

1. An unusual degree of materiality.
2. The existence of conflicting industry practices.

Section 300—Rule 301. Confidential Client Information

CPAs have a dual responsibility to their clients and to the public. They must have professional concern for their clients' interests and at the same time serve the public by maintaining their independence, integrity, and objectivity.

A good example of this dual responsibility is the CPA's obligation of *confidentiality*. Information about the client's affairs that is acquired during an engagement should be held in confidence. But the CPA should not use this obligation of confidentiality as a reason to accept a client's inadequate disclosures in financial statements. A CPA who can satisfactorily balance these two obligations is successfully serving both the client and the public.

The concept of confidentiality is well illustrated with this rule.

A member in public practice shall not disclose any confidential client information without the specific consent of the client.

This rule is not to be construed to (1) relieve a member of his or her professional obligations under Rules 202 and 203, (2) affect in any way the member's obligation to comply with a validly issued and enforceable subpoena or summons, or to prohibit a member's compliance with applicable laws and government regulations, (3) prohibit review of a member's professional practice under AICPA or state CPA society or Board of Accountancy authorization, or (4) preclude a member from initiating a complaint with, or responding to any inquiry made by, the professional ethics division or trial board of the AICPA or a duly constituted investigative or disciplinary body of a state CPA society or Board of Accountancy.

Members of any of the bodies identified in (4) and members involved with professional practice reviews identified in (3) should not use to their own advantage or disclose any member's confidential client information that comes to their attention in carrying out those activities. This prohibition is not to restrict members' exchange of information in connection with the investigative or disciplinary proceedings described in (4) or the professional practice reviews described in (3).

Although the concept of independence is unique to a CPA's services, the notion of confidentiality is not. Members of all professions are expected to use discretion in disclosing information that they acquire from clients. Lawyers, for example, should not reveal the results of their confidential conversations with civil or criminal clients. Medical doctors are obligated to keep secret any sensitive facts gathered from their patients. Also, certain members of the clergy are sworn to secrecy about facts learned during the course of their duties.

A CPA acquires confidential information during the course of audits, tax return preparations, and management consulting engagements. If this confidence were to be broken, the CPA's credibility would drop and clients would no longer be willing to allow him or her access to the records that are necessary to perform audits. Consider the damage that could result if a CPA revealed details of a firm's payroll or a plan to acquire property for plant expansion.

The CPA's obligation of confidentiality does not extend to incomplete or improper disclosure in the financial statements. If auditors discover that a lawsuit against the client is not disclosed in the financial statements and that its possible consequences are material, the auditors should reveal this finding in their report.

A major problem arises when a CPA learns that a client apparently has broken a law. Assume that a CPA discovers, while performing an audit, that the client has failed to file tax returns for previous years. Is there a "higher" duty to breach the rule of confidentiality and inform the Internal Revenue Service of the omission? According to official guidelines of the AICPA, the answer is "no" unless the client grants permission. However, if the failure to file the tax return materially affected an auditor's opinion regarding the financial statements, the auditor may disclose the matter in his or her report. As a practical matter, CPAs should consider withdrawing from an engagement if they advise their client to go voluntarily to the IRS and the client refuses to do so.

Another potential problem arises when auditors have clients who compete with each other. A client could be damaged if information such as its strategic plan were revealed to a competing client. The current rule on confidentiality permits the simultaneous rendering of audit services to competing clients but prohibits the auditor from revealing confidential information.

▶ **EXAMPLE**

A municipality engages a CPA firm to audit the records of businesses to determine whether the proper amount of personal property tax has been paid on property and equipment. The auditors will examine, among other items, the sales, purchases, and property accounts of the businesses. Managers of competing businesses might object to this arrangement because information could be inadvertently conveyed to competitors. The arrangement is acceptable, however, but information should not be passed from one competing business to another.

(*Source:* ET 391.011–.012)

This ethics ruling may not be the last word on the subject. In the 1980s a jury decided against an auditor and made a large damage award to the auditor's client (Client A) because the auditor did not disclose to them information obtained during the audit of another client (Client B).

Client A had purchased properties from Client B at inflated prices. When Client A declared bankruptcy, its liquidator discovered the magnitude of the prices and successfully sued the auditor for not revealing to Client A the profits earned by Client B on the transaction.[1]

The large damage award in this case might have been avoided if CPAs possessed the protection of *privileged communications*. Professionals who enjoy privileged communications cannot be required to reveal information obtained from a client, even in a court of law. In most states, however, CPAs do not have this protection; they can and have been required to disclose confidential client information in court proceedings.

It is unlikely that privileged communications will be uniformly granted to the accounting profession in the near future. The findings of a recent survey showed that most public accountants are not in favor of privileged communications for auditors because it would affect the appearance of independence. For example, privileged communications might prevent auditors from testifying against a client who had acted improperly.

Section 300—Rule 302. Contingent Fees

CPAs are expected to provide services in a competent manner and are expected to charge fees that are appropriate to these services. But CPAs are not allowed to make their fees contingent on their findings or on the result of their services for any clients for whom the CPA performs audit, review, certain compilation services, examination of prospective financial statements, or preparation of an original or amended tax return or claim for a tax refund. Contingent fee arrangements are permitted with clients for whom none of these services are performed.

All contingent fees used to be completely prohibited, but the Federal Trade Commission (FTC) threatened action in the 1980s against the AICPA for limiting competition. The above rule resulted from negotiations between the AICPA and the FTC. This action illustrates the effect of the economic environment on the accounting profession.

The rule reads as follows:

A member in public practice shall not

(1) Perform for a contingent fee any professional services for, or receive such a fee from, a client for whom the member or the member's firm performs,

    (a) an audit or review of a financial statement; or

    (b) a compilation of a financial statement when the member expects, or reasonably might expect, that a third party will use the financial statement and the member's compilation report does not disclose a lack of independence; or

    (c) an examination of prospective financial information; or

(2) Prepare an original or amended tax return or claim for a tax refund for a contingent fee for any client.

---

[1] For a full account of this case, see S. Douglas Beets, "CPA Confidentiality and the 'Fund of Funds' Case," *The Attorney-CPA*, 1990.

The prohibition in (1) applies during the period in which the member or the member's firm is engaged to perform any of the services listed above and the period covered by any historical financial statements involved in any such listed services. Except as stated in the next sentence, a contingent fee is a fee established for the performance of any service pursuant to an arrangement in which no fee will be charged unless a specified finding or result is attained, or in which the amount of the fee is otherwise dependent upon the finding or result of such service. Solely for purposes of this rule, fees are not regarded as being contingent if fixed by courts or other public authorities, or, in tax matters, if determined based on the results of judicial proceedings or the findings of governmental agencies.

A member's fee may vary depending, for example, on the complexity of services rendered.

The reason why contingent fees are prohibited for audit engagements is evident. A wide variety of net income amounts can be produced in financial statements, depending on which accounting methods are followed. Financial statements belong to the client; still, auditors are in a position to influence the financial results.

▶ EXAMPLE

An auditor arranges with a client to make the fee contingent on net income published in the financial statements and attested to by the auditor (a $10,000 fee for net income of $1 million, $15,000 for net income of $1.5 million, etc.). During the course of the audit, the auditor determines that the allowance for doubtful accounts is understated by a considerable amount. If any adjustment is made to the client's books, reported net income will be reduced, and so, too, will the auditor's fee. One can easily imagine the temptation for the auditor to overlook such an adjustment.

An interpretation of the rule does give examples of circumstances where contingent fees for tax services are permitted because the tax findings are based on the results of judicial proceedings or findings of governmental agencies. For example, a CPA may represent a client in an examination by a revenue agent of the client's federal or state income tax return.

The rule on contingent fees is unique to the accounting profession because of the requirement of auditor independence. Lawyers are allowed to collect a percentage of the amounts gained for their clients in civil suits. But lawyers act as advocates of their clients, whereas auditors are independent and report on the fairness of presentation of financial statements used by third parties.

Section 500—Rule 501. Acts Discreditable

The public should have confidence in the reputations of CPAs. To emphasize this point, the AICPA has adopted the following rule:

A member shall not commit an act discreditable to the Profession.

A member of the AICPA who is convicted of a felony could be charged with violating this rule.

Section 500—Rule 502. Advertising and Other Forms of Solicitation

A rule that has been controversial and that has changed over the years is the one on advertising and other forms of solicitation. Here is the rule in its current form.

> A member in public practice shall not seek to obtain clients by advertising or other forms of solicitation in a manner that is false, misleading, or deceptive. Solicitation by the use of coercion, overreaching, or harassing conduct is prohibited.

In the 1970s the possibility of antitrust action by the U.S. Department of Justice persuaded the AICPA to amend the rule that had been in effect for almost 60 years. The rule stated that advertising and solicitation were not in the public interest and were prohibited. The new rule, as shown above, permits normal types of advertising and solicitation.

As a result of this rule change, any type of advertising media can be used to show the following:

1. Information about the CPA and the CPA's firm, such as names and addresses of partners, services offered by the firm (including hourly rates and fixed fees for such services), and educational and professional attainments by the firm's members.
2. Policy or position statements related to public accounting or matters of public interest (a CPA firm's position on a pending congressional bill, for example).

▶ EXAMPLE

It is acceptable for CPAs to permit their firm's name to be imprinted on a newsletter, tax booklet, or similar publication they did not produce, provided they have a reasonable basis to conclude that the information contained therein is not false, misleading, or deceptive.

(*Source:* ET 591.351–.352)

There are some activities, however, that CPAs might consider to be false, misleading, or deceptive such as those that:

1. Create false or unjustified expectations of favorable results.
2. Imply the ability to influence any court, tribunal, regulatory agency, or similar body or official.
3. Contain a representation that specific professional services in current or future periods will be performed for a stated fee, estimated fee, or fee range when at the time of the representation it was likely that such fees would be substantially increased and the prospective client was not advised of that likelihood.
4. Contain any other representations that would be likely to cause a reasonable person to misunderstand or be deceived.

The previous rule on advertising and solicitation contained specific prohibitions and tended to be general about what actions were permitted. The current rule is general about those acts that are prohibited. Many CPAs are likely to consider the following acts to be false, misleading, or deceptive.

1. A CPA firm advertises that it can obtain a reduced tax liability for tax clients because some of its members are former employees of the Internal Revenue Service.
2. A CPA firm advertises that it has larger clients than its local competition, and this assertion is untrue. (Presumably, a truthful advertisement that a CPA firm has more public clients than local competition is acceptable.)

Section 500—Rule 503. Commissions and Referral Fees

The AICPA passed the following rule as a further attempt to discourage potential conflicts of interest in rendering services to clients.

A. Prohibited commissions

   A member in public practice shall not for a commission recommend or refer to a client any product or service, or for a commission recommend or refer any product or service to be supplied by a client, or receive a commission, when the member or the member's firm also performs for that client

   (a) an audit or review of a financial statement; or
   (b) a compilation of a financial statement when the member expects, or reasonably might expect, that a third party will use the financial statement and the member's compilation report does not disclose a lack of independence; or
   (c) an examination of prospective financial information.

   This prohibition applies during the period in which the member is engaged to perform any of the services listed above and the period covered by any historical financial statements involved in such listed services.

B. Disclosure of permitted commissions

   A member in public practice who is not prohibited by this rule from performing services for or receiving a commission and who is paid or expects to be paid a commission shall disclose that fact to any person or entity to whom the member recommends or refers a product or service to which the commission relates.

C. Referral fees

   Any member who accepts a referral fee for recommending or referring any service of a CPA to any person or entity or who pays a referral fee to obtain a client shall disclose such acceptance or payment to the client.

The current rule is an outgrowth of an earlier rule that prohibited commissions in general by stating that "A member shall not pay a commission to obtain a client, nor shall he accept a commission for a referral to a client of products or services of others." Now, the receipt of commissions is prohibited only in connection with services requiring independence, but is not prohibited in connection with such services as tax. However, the CPA must disclose the fact of the permitted commission to the appropriate parties.

▶ **EXAMPLE**

Assume that a CPA arranged for a client to purchase an interest in a tax shelter. Would it be acceptable for the CPA to accept a commission for this referral? No, if the CPA provided the client with any of the services described in part (A) of the rule. Yes, if the CPA provided only tax services and disclosed to the client the acceptance of the commission.

Section 500—Rule 505. Form of Organization and Name

This last rule addresses the form of practice of CPA firms.

> A member may practice public accounting only in a form of organization permitted by state law or regulation whose characteristics conform to resolutions of Council. A member shall not practice public accounting under a firm name that is misleading. Names of one or more past owners may be included in the firm name of a successor organization. Also, an owner surviving the death or withdrawal of all other owners may continue to practice under a name which includes the name of past owners for up to two years after becoming a sole practitioner.

The *Code of Professional Conduct* allows CPAs to practice in any organizational form allowed by state law. This change in the Code has spawned several new forms of organization such as limited liability companies (LLCs) and limited liability partnerships (LLPs).

An LLC has many characteristics of a corporation. Members of this organizational form can limit their personal liability exposure unless they are part of the wrongdoing that was the cause of the lawsuit against the LLC. The assets of the LCC, itself, are always at risk.

LLPs are general partnerships that provide partners with protection of personal assets if these partners are not involved in wrongdoing. LLPs do not protect assets of the firm or of the firm's partners involved in malpractice.

One purpose of this rule is to apply the *Code of Professional Conduct* to CPAs who offer one or more types of services rendered by public accountants, even if CPAs participate in the operation of a separate business with non-CPAs. The CPA cannot avoid an obligation to obey the Code because the separate business does not refer to itself as a public accounting practice. If the separate business offers public accounting-type services, the CPA must adhere to the provisions of the Code and is also responsible for adherence by non-CPA members of the same business.

▶ **EXAMPLE**

A CPA in public practice forms a separate business to perform centralized billing services for local doctors. In the conduct of this separate business, would the CPA be bound by the AICPA *Code of Professional Conduct?* Yes, because this service constitutes service of a type performed by public accountants, even though it is referred to as a separate business.

(*Source:* ET 591.353–.354)

INTERNATIONAL STANDARDS ON AUDITING—ETHICS

The section of *International Standards on Auditing* that covers ethics is very general and, for the most part, parallels similar provisions of the *Code of Professional Conduct* of the AICPA. The *Guidelines on Ethics for Professional Accountants* issued by the International Federation of Accountants cover the following subjects.

Integrity, Objectivity, and Independence

The auditor should be straightforward and honest in performing professional work. The auditor must be fair and should not allow prejudice or bias or influence of others to override objectivity. The auditor should maintain an impartial attitude and both be and appear to be free of any interest that might be regarded, whatever its actual effect, as being incompatible with integrity, objectivity, and independence. The auditor should be independent in fact and appearance.

Confidentiality

The auditor should "respect the confidentiality of information acquired during the course of performing professional services and should not use or disclose any such information without proper and specific authority or unless there is a legal or professional right or duty to disclose."

Professional Competence, Due Care, and Technical Standards

In agreeing to provide professional services, the auditor implies that a certain level of competence is necessary to perform professional services and that the knowledge, skill, and experience of the auditor will be applied with reasonable care and diligence. Auditors should therefore refrain from performing any services that they are not competent to carry out unless advice and assistance are obtained to ensure that the services are performed in a satisfactory manner. An auditor should perform professional services with due care, competence, and diligence. He or she has a continuing duty to maintain professional knowledge and skill at a level required to ensure that a client or employer receives the advantage of competent professional service based on up-to-date developments in practice, legislation, and techniques.

An auditor should carry out professional services in accordance with the relevant technical and professional standards. Auditors have a duty to carry out, with care and skill, the instructions of the client or employer insofar as they are compatible with the requirements of integrity, objectivity, and independence.

SUMMARY

The *Code of Professional Conduct* has an impact on the way CPAs conduct their professional affairs. The code is enforced through disciplinary action such as suspension or expulsion from the AICPA. Because AICPA membership is voluntary, the AICPA has little effective enforcement power. On the other hand, a state board of accountancy can revoke a CPA's certificate if its code is violated, giving it extremely effective enforcement powers. A positive approach for CPAs is to understand and voluntarily adapt themselves to their special environment and their public obligations.

Here are some guidelines that can be used.

1. CPAs, as well as members of other professions, operate in a special environment; the personal nature of their services makes them subject to special rules.

2. It is not enough for CPAs merely to act "within the law," for many actions that are considered unethical are legal. Contingent fees are an example.

3. In many cases, the guidelines by which CPAs are expected to conduct themselves are not simple and clear-cut, and judgment must be exercised. To illustrate, consider the decision auditors should make in disclosing certain sensitive information in their report. The rule on confidentiality must be balanced against the full disclosure requirement of generally accepted accounting principles.

One impression that should not be given is that CPAs are frequently subjected to disciplinary measures. CPAs can and do avoid most ethical problems by using good professional judgment in their relations with clients, colleagues, and others. If CPAs have any doubt as to the propriety of their actions, they can consult the AICPA, their state society, or their state board and usually receive an answer. If their past actions are discovered to have been improper, immediate corrective measures may be sufficient.

Chapter 3 ▶ GLOSSARY OF TERMS

Code of Professional Conduct Guidance for professional actions.

Commission The acceptance of an amount for a referral (1) to a client of products or services of others or (2) to others the products or services of a client.

Confidentiality Auditors' practice of not disclosing information acquired from clients in professional engagements without the clients' consent.

Contingent fee A professional fee based on a specified finding or an attained result.

Direct financial interest Ownership of an investment in a client.

Ethical awareness An ability to perceive the ethical implications of a situation.

Ethical commitment A personal resolve to act ethically.

Ethical competency The ability to engage in sound moral reasoning and to develop practical problem-solving strategies.

Ethics The study of the general nature of morals and of the specific moral choices to be made by an individual in his or her relationship with others.

Independence The ability to act with integrity and objectivity.

Independence in appearance The appearance of independence projected to the public.

Independence in fact The auditor's mental attitude toward independence.

Indirect financial interest Financial interest in an entity that has a direct financial interest in a client.

Management consulting services Provisions of advice and technical assistance the primary purpose of which is to help the client improve the use of its capabilities and resources to achieve its objectives.

Principles of Professional Conduct The "constitution" of the *Code of Professional Conduct* that provides general, but enforceable, guidance to professional acts.

Privileged communications The right of certain professionals to withhold information received from a client, even in a court of law.

Rules of Professional Conduct Enforceable applications of the *Principles of Professional Conduct.*

Chapter 3 ▶ REFERENCES

Axline, Larry L. "The Bottom Line on Ethics," *Journal of Accountancy* (December 1990), pp. 87–91.

Beets, S. Douglas. "The Revised AICPA Code of Professional Conduct: Current Considerations," *The CPA Journal* (April 1992), pp. 26–32.

Cohen, Jeffery R., Pant, Laurie W., and Sharp, David J. "Culture-Based Ethical Conflicts Confronting Multinational Account-

ing Firms," *Accounting Horizons* (September 1993), pp. 1–13.

Elliott, Robert K., and Jacobson, Peter D. "Audit Independence: Concept and Application," *The CPA Journal* (March 1992), pp. 34–39.

Farmer, Timothy A., Rittenberg, Larry E., and Trompeter, Gregory M. "An Investigation of the Impact of Economic and Organizational Factors on Auditor Independence," *Auditing: A Journal of Practice and Theory* (Fall 1987), pp. 1–14.

Mednick, Robert. "Independence: Let's Get Back to Basics," *Journal of Accountancy* (January 1990), pp. 86–93.

Wixon, John A. "Can a CPA Sell Computer Products and Still Give Unbiased Advice?" *Journal of Accountancy* (July 1991), pp. 83–85.

Chapter 3 ▶ REVIEW QUESTIONS

3-1 Define the following terms:
  a. Ethics.
  b. Ethical commitment.
  c. Ethical awareness.
  d. Ethical competency.

3-2 Describe the six-step model for making ethical decisions.

3-3 Describe three common elements of each profession's code of conduct.

3-4 What is the difference between the two following sections of the *Code of Professional Conduct?*
  a. Principles of Professional Conduct.
  b. Rules of Professional Conduct.

3-5 What is the difference between the two following sections of the Rules of Professional Conduct?
  a. Interpretations of the Rules.
  b. Ethics Rulings.

3-6 Answer the following questions for the cited articles of the Principles of Professional Conduct.
  a. Responsibilities (Article I). To which three groups do CPAs have responsibilities?
  b. The Public Interest (Article II). What statement best summarizes the CPA's obligation to the public?
  c. Integrity (Article III). What obligation does a CPA have concerning information obtained about his or her client?
  d. Objectivity and Independence (Article IV). Describe the two-part guidance about objectivity and independence.
  e. Due Care (Article V). What should a CPA do if he or she lacks the qualification to give advice to a client and is unable to obtain the qualification?
  f. Scope and Nature of Services (Article VI). Describe the three-part guideline that CPAs should use when deciding whether to render management consulting services to audit clients.

3-7 Describe the purpose of each of the following Rules of Professional Conduct.
  a. 101—Independence.
  b. 102—Integrity and Objectivity.
  c. 201—General Standards.
  d. 202—Compliance with Standards.
  e. 203—Accounting Principles.
  f. 301—Confidential Client Information.
  g. 302—Contingent Fees.
  h. 501—Acts Discreditable.
  i. 502—Advertising and Other Forms of Solicitation.
  j. 503—Commissions and Referral Fees.
  k. 505—Form of Organization and Name.

3-8 What two types of relationships between auditors and their clients are prohibited by Interpretations and Ethics Rulings relating to the rule on independence?

3-9 In each of the three following situations, indicate whether the auditor has (1) a direct financial interest in his or her client or (2) an indirect financial interest in his or her client.
  a. The auditor has a direct financial interest in a partnership that invests in the auditor's client.
  b. The auditor owns stock in a bank from which his or her audit client borrowed money.
  c. The auditor owns shares in a mutual fund that, in turn, owns shares of stock in the auditor's client.

3-10 What does the rule on independence state about loans from audit clients?

3-11 Under certain conditions, independence may be impaired if an audit client starts or indicates an intention to start litigation against the CPA conducting the audit. Two essential features of an audit underlie this rule. Describe these two features.

3-12 What should auditors do if they seek employment with their client while participating in the audit?

3-13 Certain conditions must be met for CPAs to provide their audit clients with accounting services and still maintain their independence. Describe these conditions.

3-14 Under what conditions could a CPA perform management consulting services for an audit client and not impair independence?

3-15 State the rule on integrity and objectivity.

3-16 Describe the four standards that are part of the rule on general standards.

3-17 Under limited circumstances, CPAs may express unqualified opinions on financial statements that utilize accounting principles other than those formulated by designated bodies. Give two examples of these circumstances.

3-18 Describe the dual responsibility borne by CPAs.

3-19 What protection is given to professionals who have privileged communications?

3-20 What is a contingent fee?

3-21 To which types of services does the rule on contingent fees apply? Why?

3-22 Describe the advertising of four activities that CPAs might consider to be false, misleading, or deceptive.

3-23 Describe the professional services for which the receipt of commissions is prohibited.

3-24 Describe one purpose of the rule on form of organization and name.

Chapter 3 ▶ OBJECTIVE QUESTIONS

(* = author prepared; ** = CPA examination)

**3-25 A violation of the profession's ethical standards most likely would have occurred when a CPA
  a. Issued an unqualified opinion on the 19X2 financial statements when fees for the 19X1 audit were unpaid.
  b. Recommended a controller's position description and candidate specifications to an audit client.
  c. Purchased a CPA firm's practice of monthly write-ups for a percentage of fees to be received over a three-year period.
  d. Made arrangements with a financial institution to collect notes issued by a client in payment of fees due for the current year's audit.

*3-26 Which of the following is not a general commonality among professions' codes of conduct?
  a. Members of each profession are usually expected to maintain a higher standard of conduct than is required by the law.
  b. Each profession's code of conduct contains positive admonishments designed to encourage ethical conduct.
  c. Each profession's code of conduct contains similar rules on independence.
  d. Professions expressly prohibit certain actions on the part of the members.

*3-27 All of the following are part of the structure of the *Code of Professional Conduct* except
  a. Principles of Professional Conduct.
  b. Concepts.
  c. Rules of Professional Conduct.
  d. Interpretations of rules by senior technical committees of the AICPA.

*3-28 The principles of the AICPA's *Code of Professional Conduct* emphasize certain responsibilities. Which of the following is an incomplete statement of those responsibilities?
  a. CPAs must serve their clients with professional concern.
  b. CPAs must possess independence, integrity, and objectivity.
  c. CPAs must have the technical expertise of their profession.
  d. CPAs must have appropriate professional relationships with their colleagues, even though some colleagues are competitors.

*3-29 Ethical behavior requires an individual to
  a. Act only in accord with the law.
  b. Perceive the ethical implications of a situation only if it involves the possibility of unlawful conduct.
  c. Consider a course of action to be unlawful if it is unethical.
  d. Consider that certain conduct may be lawful but not ethical.

*3-30 In using a general model for making ethical decisions, the CPA should do all of the following except
  a. Gather or identify all the relevant facts about the situation that raises the ethical issue.
  b. Consider the alternative courses of action.
  c. Consider the possible consequences of some of the courses of action.
  d. Select a course of action from among the alternatives.

**3-31 According to the profession's ethical standards, a CPA would be considered independent in which of the following instances?
  a. A client leases part of an office building from the CPA, resulting in a material indirect financial interest to the CPA.
  b. The CPA has a material direct financial interest in a client, but transfers the interest into a blind trust.

c. The CPA owns an office building and the mortgage on the building is guaranteed by a client.

d. The CPA belongs to a country club client in which membership requires the acquisition of a pro rata share of equity.

3-32 The issue of audit independence might be raised by the auditor's participation in management consulting engagements. Which of the following statements is most consistent with the profession's attitude toward this issue?

a. Information obtained as a result of a management consulting engagement is confidential to that specific engagement and should not influence performance of the attest function.

b. The decision as to loss of independence must be made by the client based on the facts of the particular case.

c. The auditor should not make management decisions for an audit client.

d. The auditor who is asked to review management decisions is also competent to make these decisions and can do so without loss of independence.

3-33 May a CPA hire for the CPA's public accounting firm a non-CPA systems analyst who specializes in developing computer systems?

a. Yes, provided the CPA is qualified to perform each of the specialist's tasks.

b. Yes, provided the CPA is able to supervise the specialist and evaluate the specialist's end product.

c. No, because non-CPA professionals are *not* permitted to be associated with CPA firms in public practice.

d. No, because developing computer systems is *not* recognized as a service performed by public accountants.

3-34 According to the AICPA *Code of Professional Conduct,* a CPA who has a financial interest in a partnership that invests in a client is considered to have

a. An indirect financial interest in the client.

b. A direct financial interest in the client.

c. No financial interest in the client.

d. A partial financial interest in the client.

3-35 A violation of the profession's ethical standards most likely would have occurred when a CPA

a. Compiled the financial statements of a client that employed the CPA's spouse as a bookkeeper.

b. Received a fee for referring audit clients to a company that sells limited partnership interests.

c. Purchased the portion of an insurance company that performs actuarial services for employee benefit plans.

d. Arranged with a financial institution to collect notes issued by a client in payment of fees due.

3-36 A CPA discovered irregularities in the tax return of a client and withdrew from the engagement. Which course of action should the CPA take?

a. Take the matter to the Internal Revenue Service.

b. Voluntarily reveal to a successor CPA the reason why the engagement was terminated.

c. If the CPA is contacted by a successor CPA, suggest that the successor ask the client to permit a free discussion of the matter between the predecessor and successor CPAs.

d. If the CPA is contacted by a successor CPA, tell the successor about the situation without suggesting that the client be contacted.

Reason for Correct Answer   *Comments on Other Answers*

3-37 A CPA is an elected legislator in a local government. The city manager is responsible for all administrative functions. Would the CPA's independence be impaired with respect to an audit of the local government?

a. No, because the CPA is an elected legislator, not an appointed official.

b. No, if the city manager is elected rather than appointed by the legislative body.

c. Yes, even if the city manager is elected rather than appointed by the legislative body.

d. No, because the CPA does not perform any administrative functions.

Reason for Correct Answer   *Comments on Other Answers*

3-38 A CPA has been asked to audit a municipal authority. The CPA owns some of the authority's outstanding bonds. The amount is immaterial. Would the CPA's independence be impaired with respect to an audit of the authority?

a. Yes, because the CPA has a loan to a client.

b. No, because the amount of bonds held by the CPA is immaterial.

c. No, because the municipal authority is a not-for-profit enterprise.

d. No, because the CPA has no managerial position with the authority.

Reason for Correct Answer   Comments on Other Answers

*3-39 For each description, list the letter or letters of the term or terms that define the description. Each term may be used once, more than once, or not at all.

Description	Term
1. Does not extend to incomplete or improper disclosure in financial statements.	a. Direct financial interest
2. Protection not granted to most CPAs.	b. Indirect financial interest
3. Ownership of stock in an audit client.	c. Confidentiality
4. Based on the auditor's findings.	d. Privileged communications
5. Owns an interest in an investment club that holds shares in an audit client.	e. Contingent fees
	f. Advertising

Chapter 3 ► DISCUSSION/CASE QUESTIONS

(* = author prepared; ** = CPA examination)

*3-40 Each of the following statements is incorrect. In the spaces provided, write the correct statement and the reason why the original statement is incorrect. [*Hint:* The chapter material is background reading for all parts of this question, but in some cases the text material will not specifically furnish you with the answers, particularly reasons why the statements are incorrect.]

a. Incorrect Statement
Enforcement of the *Code of Professional Conduct* depends totally on disciplinary proceedings.

Correct Statement   Why Original Statement Is Incorrect

b. Incorrect Statement
CPAs must be independent in providing all types of professional services.

Correct Statement   Why Original Statement Is Incorrect

c. Incorrect Statement
A CPA cannot be independent when his or her income is derived solely from attest services performed for clients.

Correct Statement   Why Original Statement Is Incorrect

d. Incorrect Statement

The rule on contingent fees prohibits, for all professional services, fees contingent on findings or results of services.

Correct Statement   Why Original Statement Is Incorrect
_____   _____

e. Incorrect Statement

CPAs are prohibited from having any financial interests in their audit clients.

Correct Statement   Why Original Statement Is Incorrect
_____   _____

f. Incorrect Statement

There is no difference between the AICPA and SEC rules on CPAs' performance of accounting services for audit clients.

Correct Statement   Why Original Statement Is Incorrect
_____   _____

g. Incorrect Statement

Impairment of independence always occurs when CPAs perform management consulting services for audit clients.

Correct Statement   Why Original Statement Is Incorrect
_____   _____

h. Incorrect Statement

If a CPA discovers that a client has failed to file income tax returns for the past five years, he or she should report that client to the Internal Revenue Service.

Correct Statement   Why Original Statement Is Incorrect
_____   _____

i. Incorrect Statement

CPAs are prohibited from seeking clients by using any form of advertising.

Correct Statement   Why Original Statement Is Incorrect
_____   _____

j. Incorrect Statement

A member shall not endeavor to provide a person or entity with a professional service that is currently provided by another public accountant.

Correct Statement   Why Original Statement Is Incorrect
_____   _____

k. Incorrect Statement
Receipt of a commission is improper for any service a CPA performs for a client.

Correct Statement   Why Original Statement Is Incorrect
_____

*3-41 In each of the following cases, indicate whether there is a violation of the rule on independence of the AICPA *Code of Professional Conduct.* Support your answer.

a. A CPA is a director of a charitable organization that serves some audit clients. Part of the directors' responsibilities is to decide who will receive benefits from the charitable organization.

b. A CPA obtained a personal loan from an audit client that represented approximately five percent of her wealth. The amount of collateral and the repayment terms were normal for loans of that type.

c. A CPA recommends controller position descriptions for audit clients, including screening and recommending candidates to the client. All the clients have indicated that they will follow these recommendations. All CPA recommendations have been followed.

d. During an audit, the client indicates an intent to start litigation against the CPA for deficiencies in the prior year's work. The auditor decides to finish the current year's engagement.

e. A CPA audits the financial statements of Sell Company and Buy Company. During the audit, the CPA discovers that Sell Company engaged in price discrimination on products sold to Buy Company. The CPA does not reveal this information to the board of directors of Buy Company, but the CPA does ask the management of Sell Company to record a liability for possible price rebates to certain customers.

f. A CPA has an investment in a bank that has loaned money to an audit client. The investment is about five percent of the CPA's wealth.

g. A CPA is interested in serving the community. She asked the vice-president of her client to help her get an appointment to the board of directors of the United Fund. The CPA received the appointment and has devoted many hours to this activity.

h. A CPA keeps books for his audit client and also decides where his client will invest surplus cash accumulated from time to time.

i. The treasurer of a client pays for two of a CPA's lunches. Only the client's business was discussed at one lunch; no business was discussed at the other lunch.

**3-42 Savage, CPA, has been requested by an audit client to perform a nonrecurring engagement involving the implementation of a computer information and control system. The client requests that in setting up and converting to the new system, Savage do the following:

1. Counsel on potential expansion of business plans.
2. Arrange interviews for potential new personnel.
3. Recruit and hire a systems supervisor for the company.
4. Instruct and oversee the training of client personnel.
5. Supervise the operation of the new system.
6. Monitor and help prepare source documents and make necessary changes in computer-generated data.

Required:

Which of these services may Savage perform and which may Savage not perform and retain independence? Give reasons for your answers.

*3-43   The president of Shambra Products has consulted you in regard to an audit. Shambra, which has never been audited, has been developing a process to convert swamp gas into natural gas. Although developments to date have been encouraging, numerous problems remain to be resolved.

The company has expended substantially all of the funds it has been able to raise to date, and an audit is needed in connection with further attempts to raise money from a stock or debt offering. The company does not have sufficient funds to pay for an audit now, but it will be able to pay if additional financing is acquired. Although the company is small at the present time, it has the potential for becoming one of the largest companies in the nation if it is successful in developing its process.

Should you accept the audit of Shambra Products? If so, why? If not, why not?

*3-44   Judy Hanlon, CPA, performed an audit and prepared the federal income tax return for the Guild Corporation for the year ended December 31, 19X2. This was Ms. Hanlon's first engagement for this client.

Ms. Hanlon found a significant error on the 19X1 return. She reported this error to Guild's controller, the officer responsible for tax returns. The controller stated, "Let the revenue agent find the error." The controller offered to furnish Ms. Hanlon with a letter assuming full responsibility for the error and his refusal to change it.

Required:

Answer the following questions, giving reasons for your answers.

a.   Would Ms. Hanlon have acted properly to accept the letter and take no further action? Explain the reasons for your answer.

b.   Would Ms. Hanlon have acted properly to take this information to the IRS? Explain the reasons for your answer.

c.   What course of action should Ms. Hanlon have taken and why?

*3-45   Meek, CPA, discovers that an audit client has a pending lawsuit against it for a significant sum of money. If the lawsuit is lost, the client's assets will be reduced by a substantial amount. Meek suggests to the client that a contingent liability should be disclosed in the audited financial statements. The client objects for two reasons.

1.   The subject of the lawsuit is highly sensitive. Revealing its contents would be a breach of the auditor's rule on confidential client information.

2.   Disclosure of the liability in the financial statements would provide the plaintiff with evidence of admission of a liability. Disclosure of the liability could damage the client's case in the lawsuit.

Required:

Reply to both of the client's points.

*3-46   During the course of an audit, Fred Curious, the senior, noticed that several employees were paid at a rate less than that required for the federal minimum wage law. He checked into this matter and found that the company was engaged in interstate commerce, which means that all employees are subject to the federal minimum wage law.

He decided to tell the company controller, feeling that the violation was probably an oversight and could be corrected easily. However, the controller was irritated when told of this situation by the senior. She informed Mr. Curious that this matter had nothing to do with the audit and that it should be dropped.

Mr. Curious took his information to the CPA firm's partner in charge of the audit. The partner showed concern for the senior's feelings but was reluctant to do anything about it. He suggested that Mr. Curious make a notation of the underpayment in his working papers and assured Mr. Curious that, as partner, he would take full responsibility.

Required: partner sign notes

    a. If you were Mr. Curious, what position would you take about the partner's suggestions?

    b. What position should the partner have taken when he learned of this situation? What action should he have taken?

    c. Answer this question without regard for the *Code of Professional Conduct.* Do you think that Mr. Curious or the audit partner, or both, should take this matter directly to the applicable federal authorities?

*3-47 During the audit of Park Company, a bottler and distributor of "Marshwater" soft drink, your discussion with the financial vice-president reveals that the company is paying rebates to certain of its larger customers for carrying Marshwater. The financial vice-president is reluctant to discuss the rebates and tells you that information regarding them is confidential and cannot be discussed further. He points out that your *Code of Professional Conduct* requires you to respect confidentiality.

    Discuss what, if any, further action you would take on this matter.

*3-48 Mr. Ambit was employed by Keen & Keen, CPAs, in early June 19X2.

    a. Prior to employment, Mr. Ambit owned considerable stock in several of Keen & Keen's audit clients. Upon employment, he sold all the stock of clients whose financial statements would be audited by him or anyone in the office where he worked. He kept the rest of the stock.

    b. Mr. Ambit is an honorary director of the local United Fund, an audit client of his new firm.

    c. Mr. Ambit has a personal automobile loan with a bank that is an audit client. The terms of the loan are basically the same as the terms of other automobile loans held by the audit client.

    d. Mr. Ambit's brother is an internal auditor of an audit client. Mr. Ambit has been assigned to this audit.

    e. Mr. Ambit's wife works as a part-time salesperson for an audit client to which he has been assigned.

Required:

For each of the five independent situations listed above, indicate whether Mr. Ambit is or is not in violation of the rule on independence of the *Code of Professional Conduct.* Support your answers with reasons.

*3-49 You are a member of the ethics committee of your state society. You are reviewing the work of Mr. Quest, a CPA who practices in your state. In recent years numerous complaints have been made against him by other CPAs in the same locality. During the course of your investigations, you learn the following about Mr. Quest.

    a. Mr. Quest started his business by soliciting interviews with clients of other CPAs in the same city. During the course of the interviews, he indicated that he could perform the same services as his competitors at a lower fee and with the same quality. He was factual about his own background and qualifications and had no intention of subsequently increasing the fee.

    b. Using legitimate means, Mr. Quest managed to learn how much his competitors were charging for audit fees and consistently bid a lower price. He was successful in obtaining some of the audits.

    c. During the audits Mr. Quest continued to keep the books and prepare the financial statements of the new clients. In many cases the owners had never kept books or prepared financial statements and had little understanding of them.

    d. Mr. Quest recommended that the controllers of some new audit clients be discharged and replaced by people whom he knew and considered to be better qualified.

    e. Mr. Quest learned that some of his new audit clients had not filed tax returns for several years. He took this information to the board of directors.

    f. Mr. Quest paid referral fees to obtain some of his audit clients.

    g. Mr. Quest's tax fees were based on the amount of reduction in tax liability he could obtain for his clients; that is, he charged a larger fee if he reduced the taxes of his clients below what he believed the amount would have been if another CPA had prepared the tax return.

    h. Mr. Quest advertised all of his audit, tax, and management consulting services specialties in the local newspaper.

    i. The name of Mr. Quest's firm is "Quest for the Best, CPA."

Required:

    a. Write a report indicating which of these actions you consider to be acceptable and which ones you consider to be violations of the AICPA *Code of Professional Conduct.*

    b. Without regard to the code of professional conduct, write a narrative indicating which actions you consider to be acceptable and unacceptable.

*3-50   For each of the ethical situations listed below, indicate (1) whether or not a rule of professional conduct has been violated and (2) which rule has been violated (if your answer to (1), above, is yes). Give reasons for your answers.

    a. An auditor maintains accounting records for an audit client and estimates the amount of the bad debt expense.

    b. An auditor's client begins litigation against her for deficiencies in audit work; the audit is continued.

    c. An auditor's client has a material investment in a company in which the auditor has a direct financial interest. The investor has the ability to exercise significant influence over operating and financial policies of the investee.

    d. The same as c, above, except that the auditor's financial interest is indirect and is not material.

    e. An auditor has a direct financial interest in a company that is not a client but that has a material investment in a client. The investor company has the ability to exercise significant influence over operating and financial policies of the auditor's client.

    f. A partner in an accounting firm is treasurer of the local United Fund which is an audit client of his firm. This particular auditor does not participate in the audit of the local United Fund.

    g. The spouse of an auditor is employed as a bookkeeper by an audit client. (No management functions are performed by the spouse.)

    h. An auditor is an elected legislator in the city government audited by her firm.

    i. A CPA audits the financial statements of a municipal authority. Other partners in the firm own one percent of the municipal bonded indebtedness of the authority.

    j. A CPA renders actuarial services to an audit client. All significant matters of judgment on the services are determined or approved by the audit client.

    k. A CPA uses an outside service bureau for processing a client's tax returns.

    l. A CPA withdraws from an engagement when irregularities are discovered in his client's tax return. The CPA, without the client's permission, reveals to the successor accountant why the relationship was terminated.

    m. A CPA bases his fee for preparing a tax return on how much in taxes he can save his client.

n. A CPA retains part of her client's records after her client asks for the return of the records. The laws of the state grant her a lien on the client's records as a way of enforcing payment of fees.

o. A CPA in public accounting has an immaterial financial interest in a commercial corporation that performs for the public services of a type performed by public accountants. The CPA is only an investor.

p. A CPA's firm makes arrangements with a bank to collect notes issued by a delinquent client in payment of fees due.

q. A CPA represents himself on his letterhead as both an attorney and a CPA.

r. A CPA arranges for an audit client to furnish another client with supplies at a discount. She increases the fee to the client who furnished the supplies.

s. A CPA in public practice serves as a director of a bank with which the member's audit clients engage in significant transactions.

*3-51 Tucei, CPA, is the auditor of LGS, Inc., a midsized diversified public company with several subsidiaries; one of which sells life insurance.

The chief executive officer of LGS met with Tucei to discuss the upcoming audit. He told Tucei that businesspeople should reciprocate in their business dealings with each other. Because he was buying an audit from Tucei, he said, Tucei should purchase a large life insurance policy from his company. Tucei explained that he did not need additional insurance coverage, but when threatened with the loss of the audit, he agreed to purchase the policy.

The audit proved to be very difficult; many differences of opinion arose between Tucei and his client. Tucei had to work a significant amount of overtime, much of which he did not report on his time sheet because it would have caused a budget overrun.

All problems were resolved to Tucei's and his client's satisfaction, and Tucei issued an unqualified opinion on the financial statements. To show his appreciation, the chief executive officer of LGS, Inc. gave Tucei a new barbecue grill.

Required:

a. Identify the ethical issues raised by the narrative, and identify the stakeholders (people affected by the ethical issues).

b. Describe alternative courses of action Tucei might have taken for each ethical issue, and the consequences of each alternative course.

c. What courses of action should Tucei have taken? Why?

*3-52 **(Continuing Case—Part III; Part IV in Chapter 4)**

Custom Furniture Company enjoyed reasonably good profits during all of its years. But at the beginning of 19X4, the company's new board of directors decided to expand the line of furniture to capture part of an emerging market for highly specialized lounge chairs. The controller reviewed the operations and financial position and issued a report to the board advising them to seek an increase in an existing loan with the local bank rather than seeking a public sale of stock.

The controller's report strongly advised the termination of their present auditor and the hiring of Ms. Hunt, a CPA with a regional firm and a good reputation with bankers in the town and surrounding communities. The board took the controller's advice and asked him to contact Ms. Hunt and to inform Mr. Detach, the present auditor, of the board's decision. The loan officer of the bank reacted positively when the controller informed her of their decision to change auditors.

Ms. Hunt was asked to submit an audit proposal to the board of directors of Custom Furniture. The proposal included per diem rates, the estimated audit fee, and a description of some management consulting services needed by the company. A long, intense conversation was held among Ms. Hunt, the controller, and the head of the newly formed Audit Committee of the board. The following facts emerged during this conversation.

1. Custom Furniture Company had an ongoing dispute with the Internal Revenue Service about the application of the installment sales method of recognizing some of their revenue. An assessment of several thousand dollars was under appeal with the tax court. The controller was confident that the tax court would reverse all or most of the assessment. Ms. Hunt pressed the issue and was told, reluctantly, that Mr. Detach had not agreed with the controller's view and believed that a liability should be recorded on the books for the estimated taxes due. The controller also acknowledged that the bank was not aware of the assessment by the Internal Revenue Service.

2. Ms. Hunt owned stock in the bank to which Custom Furniture Company had applied for an increase in its loan. The current market value of the stock was approximately four percent of Ms. Hunt's net worth, and all indications pointed to increases in the stock's market value in the near future. The controller asked about the propriety of owning this stock. While Ms. Hunt seemed reluctant to dispose of it, she nevertheless said that she would consider the matter.

3. The conversation became contentious when Ms. Hunt asked the controller and the head of the Audit Committee for permission to speak freely with Mr. Detach about all auditing and financial matters pertinent to the years in which Mr. Detach had performed the audit. The controller argued against the consultation because he believed Mr. Detach's "sour attitude" about being fired would prejudice his attitude toward Custom Furniture Company. Ms. Hunt thought the matter over and said that she would consider performing the audit without consulting with Mr. Detach.

4. Ms. Hunt discovered, to her surprise, that a spouse of one of her professional employees worked as a mail clerk for Custom Furniture Company and was being considered for a position as assistant controller. Ms. Hunt asked the controller if it was acceptable to use this professional employee on the audit. The controller had no objection.

5. When pressed by the head of the Audit Committee, Ms. Hunt revealed that she had performed the audit of Elaborate Furniture Company, a competitor of Custom Furniture Company. Ms. Hunt tried to explain that arrangements of this sort were common among auditors, as contrasted with the practice of lawyers. The head of the Audit Committee seemed to be pleased when Ms. Hunt told him that her expertise in auditing furniture companies could be used in the audit of Custom Furniture Company and that comparisons between the companies could help Custom Furniture Company.

6. Ms. Hunt seemed reluctant to agree to some of the management services requested by the controller, particularly a feasibility study of computerizing some financial operations of the company. She asked permission to refer these services to a colleague who specialized in such services. The controller agreed to this arrangement.

7. Under intense pressure by the controller, Ms. Hunt agreed tentatively to reduce her per diem rates to 75 percent of the usual figure. She did not tell the controller that such rates would give her firm an extremely small profit on the audit engagement.

8. The controller wanted the audit fee to be reduced if the adjusted net income for the year under audit was less than expected. Ms. Hunt would not agree, but she did say that the fees would be adjusted downward if the controller believed that they were too high.

9. When Ms. Hunt told the controller who one of her audit assistants would be, the controller replied that they might make this person a job offer if he did well on the audit and "got along with the company personnel." Ms. Hunt did not respond to this comment.

10. Ms. Hunt did not say anything to the controller and the head of the Audit Committee about another audit client who sold materials to Custom Furniture Company. She knew that the markups on such sales were very large and hoped that the board and management of Custom Furniture Company would not discover this fact. She made a mental

note to tell her probable assistant (the spouse of Custom Furniture Company's mail clerk) about the pitfalls of revealing such information.

Required:

a. Assume that Ms. Hunt has asked you, as a partner of her firm, to advise her of all ethical considerations concerning the prospective audit of Custom Furniture Company. Write a one- to two-page memo detailing all the ethical factors Ms. Hunt should consider before accepting the audit and all ethical factors she should consider during the audit, if she accepts the engagement.

b. Should Ms. Hunt accept the audit engagement if Custom Furniture Company refuses permission to allow her to discuss auditing matters with Mr. Detach? Why or why not?

c. If Ms. Hunt declines the engagement, what, in your opinion, would be the most compelling reasons for her decision?

The Auditor's Legal Environment

"The first thing we do, let's kill all the lawyers."

SHAKESPEARE, *Henry VI, Part II, IV, ii*

LEARNING OBJECTIVES

After reading and studying the material in this chapter, the student should be able to

▶ Explain why the expectation gap has caused a significant increase in litigation against auditors.

▶ Write, in one phrase each, definitions of common law, ordinary negligence, gross negligence, fraud, privity relationships, primary beneficiary relationships, foreseen party relationships, and foreseeable party relationships.

▶ Write a brief paragraph analyzing legal relationships under common law by distinguishing between 1) relationships with the auditor and 2) standards of proof.

▶ Paraphrase the facts of the following cases and the significance of each case to the auditors' liability for ordinary negligence under common law: *Ultramares, C.I.T., Rush Factors, Rosenblum,* and *Credit Alliance.*

▶ Compare the burden of proof under common law and the Securities Act of 1933.

▶ Write a brief paragraph distinguishing between auditors' legal liability under the Securities Act of 1933 and the Securities Exchange Act of 1934.

▶ Explain why the *Barchris* case is an application of the Securities Act of 1933 and how the *Hochfelder* case changed the burden of proof under the Securities Exchange Act of 1934.

▶ Write a brief paragraph describing the implications of the following cases to auditors' legal liability: *McKesson & Robbins, Continental Vending, 1136 Tenants' Corporation, Equity Funding, ZZZZ Best,* and *ESM Government Securities.*

▶ Summarize the auditors' present-day legal environment.

▶ Analyze the future of auditor liability.

INTRODUCTION

The Litigation Explosion

In recent years, there has been an explosion of litigation against CPAs in public accounting. A profession that used to draw most of its attention from the business community suddenly has been cast into the public spotlight by business failures, particularly of financial institutions.

> ► **EXAMPLE**
>
> According to an article in *Time,* there are approximately 4,000 liability suits pending against practicing accountants in the United States; more than $15 billion in potential damages are at stake. In 1991 alone the "Big Six" CPA firms paid more than $300 million to settle some of these lawsuits.

Most lawsuits against CPA firms allege neglect or failure to follow professional standards in an audit. But plaintiffs often charge auditors with failure to detect fraud or to inform them of disreputable client activities, many of which might not be discovered by the normal application of generally accepted auditing standards. In some cases, the damage awards have reached astronomical proportions and have stretched the CPA firms' capacity to pay.

> ► **EXAMPLE**
>
> A state court jury in Arizona recently found Price Waterhouse guilty of negligence in connection with that firm's audit of an Arizona bank before it was purchased by another large bank in London. The CPA firm was ordered to pay Standard Chartered PLC a staggering $338 million. This award was later reduced by an appeals court.

> ► **EXAMPLE**
>
> Ernst & Young recently agreed to pay a lesser, but still sizable, sum of $63 million to settle investor fraud claims associated with the infamous Lincoln Savings & Loan Association scandal.

> ► **EXAMPLE**
>
> Coopers & Lybrand was a codefendant in a lawsuit brought by bondholders of the now bankrupt MiniScribe Corp, a former maker of disk drives. A Texas jury awarded the bondholders more than $550 million in damages.

The Expectation Gap

Students might wonder why the public accounting profession is so beset with litigation. The likely answer is that the "expectation gap" (discussed in Chapter 2) still exists; that is, the business community and the public at large still expect more from auditors than auditors believe they can and should provide. For instance:

1. The public assumes that auditors should be among the first to know if a company is failing and, therefore, should be in a position to advise the public of

any impending failure. Auditors, in turn, believe that the public has not made a clear distinction between business failure and audit failure. Business failure occurs because of poor management, competition, bad luck, or some combination of the above. Audit failure occurs when auditors do not follow generally accepted auditing standards.

▶ **EXAMPLE**

An auditor gives an unmodified report on the financial statements of a company that has a significant investment in a shopping center. At the time the report is given, all available evidence examined by the auditor shows that the company should recoup its investment. Because of an unexpected event, such as a severe recession or a competitor's shopping center, the company's investment declines in value and the company is forced into bankruptcy (a form of business failure).

▶ **EXAMPLE**

Assume the same situation as above except that evidence is available to the auditors that the company probably will not recoup its investment. Because of carelessness, the auditor does not examine this evidence and issues an unmodified report, resulting in an audit failure.

2. The public assumes that auditors should be among the first to detect management fraud. Auditors, in turn, reject the assumption that they can detect every type of fraud, especially fraud resulting from collusion by top management. We will explore fraud detection in Chapter 5.

In addition, investors who lose money in a business failure use all available means to regain their investment. Management, boards of directors, and auditors are obvious targets for such actions. CPA firms accept this threat of litigation as an inevitable risk of practicing public accounting, but they reject the notion that they guarantee infallibility of their audit opinion.

THE AUDITOR'S LIABILITY UNDER COMMON LAW

Common law is based on the precedents established from past court cases, sometimes decided centuries ago. Common law has its basis in English law and may be used by certain plaintiffs as a basis for legal action against auditors.

Common law does not require the auditor to ensure or guarantee the infallibility of the audit or the audit opinion. It does require that an audit be performed with due care, that is, with the same degree of skill, judgment, and knowledge possessed by other auditors. Certain plaintiffs using common law will try to prove (often through the expert testimony of other auditors) that the auditor did not practice due care because he or she deviated from generally accepted auditing standards.

▶ **EXAMPLE**

Plaintiffs might attempt to show that the auditor failed to follow the third standard of fieldwork (discussed in Chapter 2) because he or she did not gather independent outside evidence of significant accounts receivable, which later proved to be nonexistent.

Plaintiffs are most likely to be successful in their common law litigation if they were clients of the auditor at the time the audit was performed. A *client* is the entity or person that originally hires the auditor, or the entity or person that "stands in the shoes" of the client by (1) paying the client's losses under fidelity bonds, (2) acting as a trustee in the client's bankruptcy, or (3) acting in other capacities that allow him or her to make the same claim against the auditor that could be made by the original client.

Standards of Proof—Ordinary Negligence

Certain plaintiffs may successfully sue the auditor for ordinary negligence under common law if they can prove that the auditor failed to perform the audit with due care. Ordinary negligence is simple carelessness without any attempt to deceive or commit fraud; for example, an auditor carelessly fails to recognize an important contingent liability that should have been included in the client's financial statements. A more formal definition that relates to auditing is that *ordinary negligence*

> represents a lack of due care in the performance of professional accounting tasks, due care implying the use of the knowledge, skill, and judgment possessed by practitioners in similar practice circumstances.

For plaintiffs to prevail, they must prove, among other things, that the auditor had a duty to the plaintiff to exercise due care in the performance of the audit. It is relatively easy for the auditor's client to prove this duty of due care; the auditor and client have a contract. It is more difficult for nonclients to prove that this duty of due care runs from the auditors to them; no contract exists between the auditor and nonclients.

Generally speaking, there are four potential relationships between plaintiffs and the auditor. These relationships help determine whether plaintiffs will be successful in a lawsuit for negligence under common law.

Privity Relationships

Plaintiffs who are clients of the auditor have a common law relationship described as *privity,* which is

> a contractual relationship between the auditor and the client for the performance of professional services.

Only clients of the auditor can use a privity relationship to successfully sue the auditor for ordinary negligence under common law. The auditor usually has no control over (1) the identity or number of nonclients who rely on the audit report or (2) the magnitude of the risk these nonclients may take in reliance on the audit report. Without some limitation, the auditor's liability might be disproportionate to the size of the audit fee and the magnitude of the auditor's error or carelessness.

Primary Beneficiary Relationships

Nonclient plaintiffs could have a *primary beneficiary* relationship with the auditor that the courts sometimes regard as "near-privity" or "equated with privity." This relationship is defined as one in which the auditor knows the client has specifically engaged him or her to perform an audit for the benefit of an identified third party whose reliance is the aim of the engagement.

Nonclient plaintiffs who can prove a primary beneficiary relationship with the auditor have the same recourse against the auditor as client plaintiffs, that is, action for ordinary negligence under common law. For the nonclient plaintiff to have this recourse, however, two conditions must exist:

1. The nonclient plaintiff must be specifically identified to the auditor.
2. The nonclient plaintiff must be the one who will receive the primary benefit from the audit.

► EXAMPLE

A prospective purchaser of a company asks the owner to hire an auditor to attest to the fairness of the company's financial statements as a condition of the purchase. The prospective purchaser is identified to the auditor, and the auditor is told that the audit is for the benefit of the purchaser in making the decision on acquiring the company. Although the prospective purchaser and the auditor have no contract, a primary beneficiary relationship exists. So the auditor owes the same duty of due care to the prospective purchaser as he or she owes to the client.

Foreseen Party Relationships

Nonclient plaintiffs might also have recourse against the auditor for ordinary negligence under common law if the courts construe them to be *foreseen parties*, which are

parties known to, or reasonably expected to be known to, the auditor and who will rely on the auditor's work in making a particular business decision.

A foreseen party relationship is more remote than a primary beneficiary relationship because foreseen parties are not specifically known to the auditor to be the primary beneficiary of the audit. Foreseen parties are persons or limited classes of persons whose reliance on the audited financial statements is, or should be, foreseen by the auditor. Two keys used by the courts to identify foreseen parties are:

1. The auditor's knowledge of the specific person or limited classes of persons.
2. The auditor's knowledge of the specific transaction or substantially similar transactions.

► EXAMPLE

An auditor accepts an offer to audit Peach Company's financial statements. The auditor knows that the client is negotiating a loan with the First National Bank of Jonesville and that the audited financial statements will be given to this specific bank for its use in evaluating the loan application. The auditor's knowledge of the specific persons (First National Bank of Jonesville) and of the specific transaction (a prospective bank loan to Peach Company) gives First National Bank of Jonesville a foreseen party relationship with the auditor.

► **EXAMPLE**

An auditor accepts an offer to audit Peach Company's financial statements. The auditor knows that Peach Company is negotiating for a loan from one of several banks with which it usually does business and that Peach Company will use the audited financial statements in its loan application with one of these banks. The auditor's knowledge of the limited classes of persons (the group of banks with which Peach Company usually does business) and of the specific transaction (a prospective bank loan to Peach Company) *might* give any of these banks a foreseen party relationship with the auditor, even though the auditor did not know which bank would make the loan when the audit was arranged.

Because common law varies among various states, the precise definition of a foreseen party varies as well. The auditor in the second example above might be a foreseen party in some states where knowledge of the group or groups is sufficient, but the auditor might not be a foreseen party in other states where knowledge of the specific bank is required.

Foreseeable Party Relationships

Foreseeable parties have the most remote relationship to the auditor of any nonclient plaintiffs. *Foreseeable parties* are

users of audited financial statements who are not specifically known or identified to the auditor, or who use the statements for transactions not specifically known to the auditor, but who may reasonably be expected to see the statements and to act or refrain from acting because of reliance on them.

In a few states the courts permit foreseeable parties to sue auditors for ordinary negligence under common law. This opens legal recourse to a wide range of users of audited financial statements, even though the auditor does not know them or the specific transactions for which audited financial statements might be used. Because of the potentially far-reaching liability, the negligence standard is not often applied to foreseeable parties.

Comment   Conceivably, a literal interpretation of the foreseeable party relationship could make it possible for an investor who lost money on stock traded on an exchange to successfully sue an auditor for ordinary negligence under common law. But most of these lawsuits have not been successful.

Standards of Proof—Gross Negligence

Nonclient plaintiffs may successfully sue the auditor if they can prove *gross negligence,* which is

an extreme, flagrant, or reckless departure from the standards of due care and competence in performing professional duties.

Gross negligence is considerably more serious than ordinary negligence, is more than carelessness, and, in the opinion of some courts, represents evidence from which an inference of fraud may be drawn. The auditor's actions, however, would have to be so reckless that they would have no basis to believe in the genuineness of their work. For this reason, nonclient plaintiffs have a heavy burden of proof in their lawsuits for gross negligence.

► **EXAMPLE**

An auditor is hired to audit the financial statements of a company that has significant amounts of accounts receivable and inventory. The auditor totally disregards generally accepted auditing standards by failing to examine any evidence supporting these two assets. Shortly after the auditor issues an unqualified opinion, both accounts are discovered to be grossly overstated, causing the financial statements to be materially misstated. The company is forced into bankruptcy, and its creditors sustain losses. These creditors (as foreseeable parties) may be able to successfully sue the auditor for gross negligence.

Standards of Proof—Fraud

 Auditors may be sued for *fraud,* the elements of which (using the auditor as an example) are

The auditor's false representation of a material fact.
The auditor's deliberate intent to deceive.
The auditor's intent to induce the plaintiff to rely on the false representation.
The plaintiff's justified reliance on the false representation.
Resulting damages suffered by the plaintiff.

The courts have held that auditors have committed fraud when they actually knew of false representations.

► **EXAMPLE**

An auditor gives an unqualified opinion on financial statements knowing that net income is grossly overstated (false representation). The auditor delivers the audited financial statements (to which the unqualified opinion is attached) to the client. He or she knows that the client will give them to a financial institution that, in turn, will rely on them in making a lending decision (deliberate intent to deceive and intent to induce the financial institution to rely on the financial statements). The financial institution, relying on the unqualified opinion, makes a loan to the auditor's client (justifiable reliance). The client declares bankruptcy when it is discovered that net income is grossly overstated, and the financial institution's loan is not repaid (resulting in damages). The financial institution may successfully sue the auditor for fraud.

Summary of Standards of Proof and Relationships of Parties

Figure 4.1 illustrates the common law standards of proof and relationships of parties discussed so far.

FIGURE 4.1   **Summary of Legal Relationships Under Common Law**

Relationship with the Auditor	Standard of Proof	Summary Definition
Clients have recourse against the auditor because of privity.	Ordinary negligence	Lack of due care
Nonclient primary beneficiaries have essentially the same recourse against the auditor because of "near privity."	Ordinary negligence	Lack of due care
Nonclient foreseen parties do not have privity but do have recourse against the auditor in several states (because they are known to or reasonably expected to be known to the auditor).	Ordinary negligence	Lack of due care
Nonclient foreseeable parties do not have privity but do have recourse against the auditor in a very few states (even though they are not specifically known or identified to the auditor).	Ordinary negligence	Lack of due care
Client and nonclient parties have recourse against the auditor.	Gross negligence	Flagrant or reckless disregard of due care
Client and nonclient plaintiffs have recourse against the auditor.	Fraud	Deliberate intent to deceive or without belief in truth of representations

Standards of Proof—Breach of Contract

Client plaintiffs may sue the auditor for breach of contract under common law if they believe the auditor has failed to use due care in performing the audit. The contract would be the agreement between the auditor and the client describing the terms of the audit engagement and the duties and responsibilities of each party.

The contract is usually a written engagement letter (discussed in Chapter 8) indicating the auditor's responsibility to perform an audit in accordance with generally accepted auditing standards or whatever standards are appropriate if a financial statement audit is not performed. The client, in turn, agrees to pay a fee at stipulated rates and to give the auditor access to all necessary books and records.

Nonclient plaintiffs may also sue the auditor for breach of contract on the basis that they are third-party beneficiaries of the contract between the auditor and his or her client. The courts have generally been reluctant to hold the auditor liable to a nonclient for breach of contract.

THE EVOLUTION OF LIABILITY FOR ORDINARY NEGLIGENCE UNDER COMMON LAW

In this section, we will examine the auditor's liability by (1) briefly describing how audits have changed in scope and purpose, (2) summarizing the facts and significance of landmark cases that changed the auditor's legal exposure to nonclients, and (3) commenting on today's divergent views about the rights of nonclients to gain recourse against the auditor for ordinary negligence.

Auditor Responsibilities in the Early Part of the Century

Today, financial statements attract the attention of a wide variety of *third parties* (nonclients of the auditor). Consequently, some of these third parties have acquired legal recourse against the auditor for ordinary negligence under common law. This legal recourse did not exist in the early part of the century. Absentee ownership had not reached today's level, there were no federal securities laws mandating an audit of a public company's financial statements, and the Securities and Exchange Commission had not been created.

In fact, the scope of many audits in the early 1900s was significantly different from what it is today. For example:

1. The management of a company (often the owners as well) hired the auditor, and the audit report was addressed to them rather than to absentee stockholders.

2. The audit tended to be viewed as a type of guarantee or certification as to the correctness of the books. Auditors placed almost complete reliance on evidence originating with or held by the client. It was not standard practice to obtain independent evidence external to the client's accounting system.

3. Auditors concentrated on the company's balance sheet, which, for many companies, showed net income as a single amount added to the retained earnings account. There was no demand for a published income statement because third-party stock ownership had not reached today's level.

4. Accounting and reporting principles were not defined as completely as they are today. There was a widespread impression (as there still is) that the amounts in financial statements represented exactness. Because the auditor was often acting on behalf of management and because management wanted a certificate, it was only natural that the auditor would attest to the "correctness" of the financial statements.

A typical audit report issued in 1915 reflected this limited scope of an audit. (Note the major differences between this report style and the report style shown on page 28 in Chapter 2.)

> We have audited the books and accounts of the ABC Company for the year ended December 31, 1915, and we certify that, in our opinion, the above balance sheet correctly sets forth its position as at the termination of that year, and that the accompanying profit and loss account is correct.

An Emerging Class of Third Parties

In the 1920s companies increased their capital-raising activities by borrowing from and selling stock to the public. A separate group of third parties, consisting of investors and potential investors, began to grow. This group did not have contracts with the auditor, but had a pronounced interest in the company's audited financial statements. These third-party investors began to claim an obligation of due care from the auditor. A triangle of relationships emerged that today forms the core of auditor, client, and third-party relationships. Figure 4.2 illustrates this triangle.

FIGURE 4.2   Auditor, Client, and Third-party Relationships

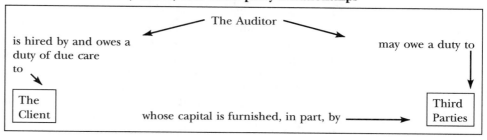

The Ultramares Case—
A Reaffirmation of Privity

Arguably, *Ultramares Corporation v. Touche* has had a more far-reaching effect on auditor/third-party relationships than any other common law case in this century. In this case the judge reaffirmed an existing theory of ordinary negligence (that excluded third parties from privity) and, in the opinion of some, created a new theory of negligence (gross negligence) for third parties.

Facts of the *Ultramares* Case

Touche, Niven & Co. (now merged in Deloitte & Touche) was hired to perform an audit of the balance sheet of Fred Stern & Co. for the year ended December 31, 1923.[1] Touche knew that creditors of their client would use the balance sheet, but they did not know the specific creditor (thus eliminating the creditor as a primary beneficiary of the audit).

Touche issued the following report when the audit was completed. (Note the similarity of this report to the independent auditor's report illustrated above.)

> We have examined the accounts of Fred Stern & Co., Inc. for the year ending December 31, 1923, and hereby certify that the annexed balance sheet is in accordance therewith and with the information and explanations given us. We further certify that, sub-

---

[1] All large CPA firms have been involved in litigation. The naming of specific firms is not an adverse reflection on those firms.

ject to provision for federal taxes on income, the said statement, in our opinion, presents a true and correct view of the financial situation of Fred Stern & Co., Inc. as at December 31, 1923.

The creditor of Fred Stern & Co. relied on the auditors' opinion and loaned the company about $165,000. The audited balance sheet showed total assets of approximately $2.5 million and net worth of approximately $1 million. Unknown to the creditor and overlooked by the auditor was a large fictitious entry to increase sales and accounts receivable, which meant that the net worth of Fred Stern & Co. was virtually zero. The overstatement was discovered when Fred Stern filed for bankruptcy. The creditor sued Touche for both ordinary negligence and fraud.

Touche was negligent in failing to investigate the large fictitious entry. However, remember from Figure 4.1 that to sustain a lawsuit for ordinary negligence under common law, the plaintiff must prove that the auditor had a duty to the plaintiff to exercise due care.

This duty of due care did not reach all the way from the auditor to the unknown third-party creditor at this evolutionary stage of auditor/third-party relationships. The judge in the original trial disallowed both the charge of fraud and ordinary negligence, the negligence charge being disallowed because the creditor had no contract with the auditor and thus had no privity.

The verdict was appealed, but the appeals judge also disallowed the liability for ordinary negligence, with the following justification:

> If liability for negligence exists, a thoughtless slip or blunder, the failure to detect a theft or forgery beneath the cover of deceptive entries, may expose accountants to a liability in an indeterminate amount for an indeterminate time to an indeterminate class.

The appeals judge was following the common law concept of that time, namely, that only a client, because of a contractual relationship and privity, had legal recourse against the auditor for ordinary negligence.

The appeals judge ordered a new trial on the charge of fraud because the facts of the case suggested negligence so serious as to constitute a form of fraud. The appeals judge raised the question of whether the accountants had any basis for a genuine belief in the validity of the balance sheet and made this statement:

> Our holding does not emancipate accountants from the consequences of fraud. It does not relieve them if their audit has been so negligent as to justify a finding that they had no genuine belief in its adequacy, for this again is fraud.

Analysis of the Case

Ultramares Corporation v. Touche was ultimately settled out of court. Nevertheless, the case had important auditing implications, namely, the establishment of the common law relationships shown in Figure 4.3. These common law relationships would last for several decades.

FIGURE 4.3 **Common Law Relationships Established by the *Ultramares* Case**

Auditor's Liability under Common Law	
To the Auditor's Client	*To a Third Party for Gross Negligence*
Auditors are liable to the client for ordinary negligence.	Auditors might be liable to a third party for gross negligence.

The Extension of Auditor's Liability to Primary Beneficiaries

A quarter of a century after the *Ultramares* case, a case entitled *C.I.T. Financial Corporation v. Glover* interpreted the *Ultramares* case to extend the auditor's liability for ordinary negligence under common law to third parties that have a primary beneficiary relationship with the auditor.

The primary beneficiary relationship is historically regarded as "near privity" or the "equivalent of privity," and third parties who can establish this relationship acquire nearly the same legal recourse against auditors as clients, who have a privity relationship.

The Extension of Auditor's Liability to Foreseen Parties

During the 1960s both jurists and public interest groups severely criticized the limits that *Ultramares* had placed on the auditor's liability. One court opinion even included a statement that expressed doubt as to the wisdom of the *Ultramares* case.

The Restatement of the Law of Torts

The auditor's liability for ordinary negligence under common law did widen in 1965 when the American Law Institute published a second *Restatement of the Law of Torts* and extended the liability of professionals to include foreseen parties.[2] The *Restatement,* though not binding on the courts, does provide guidance.

> **Comment**   A liberal definition of foreseen parties could include banks that the auditor knows, or should know, will require an audit report before making or extending a loan, or lenders that typically make loans to the audit client, if the auditor knows, or should know, the audit report will be used to obtain financing. The language of the *Restatement* is general, however, and courts have interpreted its provisions differently.

▶ **EXAMPLE**

A third-party bank sued an auditor for ordinary negligence under common law. The court upheld the lawsuit because the auditor knew and acknowledged the bank's requirements to receive annual audited financial statements of the client.

[2] Henry R. Jaenicke, *The Effect of Litigation on Independent Auditors,* Commission on Auditors' Responsibilities, *Research Study No. 1, 1977,* pp. 11–12.

► **EXAMPLE**

Another court's interpretation extended the auditor's liability only to parties that the auditor "is actually aware will rely upon the information."

Rusch Factors, Inc. v. Levin

A legal case in the late 1960s applied the principles of the *Restatement* to a specific situation and provided an important court precedent for the rights of foreseen parties. Following are some pertinent facts of the case.

In late 1963 and early 1964 a corporation located in Rhode Island borrowed more than $300,000 from the plaintiff, a commercial bank. The plaintiff requested, received, and relied on audited financial statements in making the loan. The Rhode Island corporation later declared bankruptcy, and the bank recovered only part of the loan.

The bank, a third-party creditor of the corporation, sued the auditor for ordinary negligence under common law, charging that reliance had been placed on audited financial statements that contained misrepresentations that the auditor had negligently failed to detect.

The auditor asked that the case be dismissed on the basis that the bank, as a third-party creditor, had no privity with the auditor. But the court refused to dismiss the case and stated that the bank was a party whose reliance was foreseen by the auditor. The court differentiated this case from the *Ultramares* case by indicating that the plaintiff in *Ultramares* was a foreseeable rather than a foreseen party.

The Current Status of Foreseen Parties

In a number of states the courts have endorsed the *Restatement of the Law of Torts* as a standard for legal action taken by third parties against the auditor for ordinary negligence under common law. The reasons for expanding the negligence standard are a reflection of current societal values as contrasted with those in an earlier part of the century.

1. There has been an increase in the scope of liability of other professionals to users of their services who do not have privity with these professionals.
2. Auditors are in a better position to bear the burden of economic loss than users of financial statements (as opposed to the view in the *Ultramares* case that the auditor's liability should be limited to a determinate amount).
3. Expanding the auditor's liability for ordinary negligence to foreseen parties might provide an incentive to improve auditing procedures and obtain liability insurance.
4. Auditors can pass on their added audit costs and increased insurance premiums to clients through higher fees (thereby spreading a particular group's losses to society).

Not all states have adopted the extension of auditor liability to foreseen parties. But the *Restatement of the Law of Torts,* the *Rusch Factors* case, and other court decisions have widened, perhaps permanently, the auditor's exposure to lawsuits by third parties who are not primary beneficiaries.

The Extension of Auditor's Liability to Foreseeable Parties

By the 1980s it had been firmly established that certain third parties could success-fully sue auditors for ordinary negligence under common law. These rights were expanded considerably in a few states that adopted foreseeability, the most expan-sive of the existing standards affecting the liability of auditors to third parties. New Jersey became the first state to adopt the standard of foreseeability when one of its courts ruled in favor of a third-party plaintiff who had neither a primary beneficiary nor a foreseen party relationship with the auditor.

Rosenblum v. Adler

A company purchased Rosenblum's business and issued common stock to Rosen-blum as part payment for the purchase. The value of the common stock was deter-mined by the net income shown in the purchaser's audited financial statements. The auditor did not know Rosenblum, nor was the audit performed for the purpose of determining the value of the common stock.

But the net income in the purchaser's financial statements had been overstated by recording fictitious assets and omitting liabilities, thus inflating the value of the common stock. Rosenblum attempted to regain the loss by filing suit against the auditors of the purchaser's financial statements and charging that the auditors were negligent by failing to detect the overstatement of net income.

The court ruled that the auditors were liable for ordinary negligence and in doing so broke new ground legally by granting recourse to a foreseeable party. The court cited two factors in supporting this ruling. (Note the similarity between these factors and the ones used to support the rights of foreseen parties.)

1. The auditors had insurance to cover the liability risk (an apparent doctrine of "spreading" the liability risk to the public).
2. The auditors had a moral responsibility to serve the interests of those who rely on the audit opinion, even if those individuals are strangers to the auditor.

Implications

Many CPAs object to the court's reasoning that auditors' insurance will cover the liability and that increased audit costs can be passed on to clients in the form of higher fees. CPAs argue that the prohibitive cost of liability insurance might make it unavailable to smaller accounting firms and that increased audit fees are hard to sustain in the face of today's intensive competition (see Chapter 3). At present, the standard of foreseeable parties has not been widely adopted.

The Narrowing of Auditor's Liability for Ordinary Negligence

In the mid-1980s the New York Court of Appeals reversed the trend toward ex-tending the auditor's ordinary negligence liability to foreseen and foreseeable par-ties. In its verdict, this court turned back toward the standard of liability used in the *Ultramares* case by ruling that third parties cannot sustain a legal action against an auditor for ordinary negligence unless they establish with the auditor a privity relationship or one that is "sufficiently intimate to be equated with privity."

Credit Alliance v. Arthur Andersen & Co.

In this 1985 New York case, the court ruled that a third party who relies on errone-ous audited financial statements must satisfy a three-part test to sustain legal action against the auditor for ordinary negligence:

1. The auditor must have been aware that the financial statements were to be used for a particular purpose or purposes.
2. The auditor must have known that the third party would rely on the financial statements.
3. There must be evidence *linking* the auditor with the third party showing that the auditor understood there was a particular purpose for the audited finan-cial statements and acted to further that purpose.

Implications

The *Credit Alliance* case affected later court cases in New York. In *Iselin & Co. v. Mann Judd Landau* in 1988, the New York Supreme Court dismissed a lawsuit against an auditor for ordinary negligence because there was no evidence showing a "link" between the third party and the auditor.

Several states have endorsed this liability standard of "privity or near privity," and the American Institute of Certified Public Accountants has drafted a model statute on negligence suits against CPAs based on the *Credit Alliance* case.

Present-Day Situation on Auditor's Liability for Ordinary Negligence[3]

There is no universal standard of liability that courts apply to third-party lawsuits levied against auditors for ordinary negligence under common law. Instead, one of three standards is currently being used, depending on the state in which the case is tried.

The Conservative States Using the Primary Beneficiary Standard

A few states appear to be offering auditors protection against all third parties except those that qualify as primary beneficiaries.

The Moderate States Using the Foreseen Standard

A large group of states appear to be extending the auditor's liability for ordinary negligence to foreseen parties. Based on court cases in these states, foreseen parties include potential user groups who are known, or who should have been known, to the auditor as users of the report (even though the auditor may not know the pre-cise identity of the user).

The Liberal States Using the Foreseeable Standard

A very small group of states appears to be extending the auditor's liability for ordi-nary negligence to foreseeable parties.

---

[3] A paper prepared by Carole Cheatham and Jacqueline O'Neal, professors at Northeast Louisiana Uni-versity, was very helpful in preparing this section.

THE AUDITOR'S LIABILITY UNDER STATUTORY LAW

Statutory law is based not on court precedents but on law passed by a legislative body. As such, plaintiffs may use statutory law in place of or in addition to common law in situations where such laws are applicable.

▶ **EXAMPLE**

Mr. Eger invests in the stock of a public company and loses the investment when the company declares bankruptcy. He believes the loss was caused by the auditor's negligence in performing the audit and issuing an unqualified opinion on financial statements that were materially misstated. Mr. Eger is reluctant to sue the auditor under common law because he would have to prove gross negligence. But a federal securities law exists that requires him to prove only ordinary negligence, and the law has been used successfully to recover damages from the auditor. Mr. Eger may sue under both common law and the federal statute, but his chances of success are better under the federal statute.

Some statutory law imposes a more stringent standard of performance on the auditor than common law. The Securities Act of 1933 is an example. Examine Figure 4.4, and contrast the plaintiff's burden of proof under common law with the lack of burden of proof under Section 11(a) of the Securities Act of 1933. It is little wonder that plaintiffs will use this federal statute to sue the auditor if the facts of the situation permit its use.

FIGURE 4.4   A Comparison of Burdens of Proof Under Common Law and a Federal Statute

To sustain a lawsuit for ordinary negligence under common law, the plaintiff must prove that	*Under the Securities Act of 1933, the plaintiff may successfully sue the auditor for ordinary negligence if the financial statements contain a material misstatement or omission and the plaintiff can prove a loss; the plaintiff does not have to prove*
1. The auditor had a duty to the plaintiff to exercise due care.	1. Negligence by the auditor (the auditor must prove that he or she was not negligent).
2. The auditor breached that duty by failing to perform in accordance with professional standards.	2. Reliance on the auditor's opinion.
3. The auditor's breach of duty was the primary cause of the plaintiff's injury.	3. A causal relationship between misstatement or omission and the plaintiff's loss.
4. The plaintiff suffered actual loss or damage from the injury.	4. Any contractual relationship between the plaintiff and the auditor.

THE EFFECT OF STATUTORY LAW ON THE AUDITOR'S LIABILITY TO THIRD PARTIES

Certain federal laws have given third parties additional legal recourse beyond what they could obtain using common law standards in their particular states. We will cover two of these federal laws and see how each one has increased the auditor's legal exposure and has created new standards of auditor liability.

The Securities Act of 1933—New Securities Offerings

In the middle of this century's worst depression, Congress passed the *Securities Act of 1933,* the purpose of which is to regulate new security offerings to the public. When a company offers new securities to the public, it must file a registration statement with the appropriate federal agency (the Interstate Commerce Commission in 1933, and starting in 1934 the Securities and Exchange Commission). The registration statement is a lengthy document containing a detailed description of operations of the company offering the new securities, and includes financial statements audited by independent public accountants.

The Securities Act of 1933 was passed to ensure that purchasers of new public offerings of securities have adequate information on which to make investment decisions. It is vital, therefore, that the registration statement, including the financial statements, be free of material misrepresentations or omissions. Certain sections of the act impose stringent standards on auditors of financial statements included in registration statements.

The Securities Act is a federal statute and covers the sale of new securities to the public. Accordingly, Section 11(a) of the act gives third-party investors the right to sue auditors of financial statements included in registration statements. Furthermore, this federal statute allows third parties to sue auditors for ordinary negligence, regardless of the fact that they are not the auditors' clients with a privity relationship or known third parties with a primary beneficiary relationship. Third parties may also sue the auditors under common law, but if they incur losses on investments in new publicly offered securities, they are more likely to recover their losses by using Section 11(a) of the Securities Act of 1933. The loss that may be recovered by a third-party investor is the difference between (1) the amount paid for the securities and (2) either the market price of the securities at the time of the lawsuit or the price at which the investor sold the securities.

Under common law, third parties who are primary beneficiaries or foreseen parties must generally prove that the auditor failed to exercise due care and that this failure caused the third parties' damages or losses. But Section 11(a) of the Securities Act contains the following provisions that impose more difficult standards of responsibility on the auditor:

1. The third parties' prima facie case is an alleged false statement or misleading omission in the audited financial statements. If the financial statements contain a false statement or misleading omission, the third parties have a basis for their lawsuits without having to prove that they relied on these financial statements and the auditor's opinion in making a decision to invest in the securities.

2. The third parties do not have to prove that their investment losses were caused by the false statement or misleading omission in the audited financial state-

ments. Rather, the auditor must prove that the third-party losses were caused by factors other than the false statement or misleading omission in the financial statements and the auditor's negligence in attesting to these financial statements.

► **EXAMPLE**

Company X offers a new issue of common stock to the public and files a registration statement in connection with this offering. Mr. Pearson, a CPA, audits the financial statements that are included in the registration statement. Ms. Mearson buys 500 shares of this common stock and later sells them at half the purchase price. She sues Mr. Pearson, alleging that the financial statements omitted a number of significant liabilities. If the financial statements did omit these liabilities, Ms. Mearson does not have to prove that her loss on the common stock was caused by this omission or Mr. Pearson's negligence in attesting to the financial statements that contained this omission. She can win her lawsuit by establishing the omission and her loss unless Mr. Pearson can prove there was no connection between the two events.

In addition, the auditor's potential liability extends to the effective date of the registration statement, which extends beyond the date of the audit report. The auditor's responsibility is normally limited to the audit report date.

► **EXAMPLE**

A CPA firm audits the financial statements of a company that plans to make a new offering of common stock to the public. These statements cover a period of three years, from January 1, 19X4 to December 31, 19X6.

The auditors complete the audit on February 15, 19X7, and the audit report bears this date. However, because it takes a longer time to prepare the registration statement in which these financial statements are included, the registration statement becomes effective April 15, 19X7.

Suppose the company is sued in March 19X7 for a sum that is quite significant in relation to the company's net income and total assets, but the financial statements included in the registration statement contain no disclosure of this litigation.

If third-party investors buy the common stock and the price drops after knowledge of the litigation becomes public, these third parties may sue the auditors to recover their investment. The February 15, 19X7 date of the audit report is not a defense because the auditor's responsibility for the fairness of the financial statements extends to April 15, 19X7, the effective date of the registration statement in which the financial statements are included. The auditor should have extended certain audit procedures to the effective date of the registration statement.

The auditor bears a large responsibility for the fairness of financial statements that are included in a registration statement and has liability exposure to third parties extending far beyond common law standards. But the auditor does have a defense under the Securities Act of 1933 if he or she can prove any of the following:

1. After making a reasonable investigation of events up to the effective date of the registration (i.e., exercising "due diligence"), the auditor had a reasonable basis to believe, and did believe, that the audited financial statements in the registration statement were true; that is, the auditor was not negligent.

2. The third party incurred the loss on the investment for reasons other than

the auditor's negligence in attesting to financial statements that contained the false statement or misleading omission.

3. The third party knew the auditor's opinion on the financial statements was an improper one when the securities were purchased.

The Barchris Construction Corporation Case—An Application of the Securities Act of 1933

The 1960s ushered in an increasing amount of litigation against auditors by third parties. Through the application of statutory law, the *Barchris* case confirmed the auditor's expanded responsibility to third parties.

Facts of the *Barchris* Case

Barchris Construction Corporation built bowling facilities and, until 1961, financed all its needs without a public sale of its securities. In early 1961, however, Barchris sold convertible bonds to the public, thus subjecting the company to the provisions of the Securities Act of 1933. The company filed a registration statement with the SEC; the statement included financial statements audited by Peat, Marwick, Mitchell & Co. (now KPMG Peat Marwick).

Late in 1962, Barchris declared bankruptcy. The purchasers of the bonds sued the auditor for ordinary negligence and used the Securities Act of 1933 as the basis for the lawsuit. The purchasers claimed that the registration statement contained false statements and material omissions. The auditors tried to use the due diligence defense, but the court rejected this defense partly because it believed the auditors were negligent in their review of events subsequent to the date of the audited balance sheet. (Remember that the auditor's responsibility extended to the effective date of the registration statement.) The case was ultimately settled out of court.

Implications of the *Barchris* Case

The court applied the stringent standards of the Securities Act of 1933 which allow third parties to recover damages from an auditor for ordinary negligence without invoking common law standards.

The Securities Exchange Act of 1934— Continuing Securities Trading

In 1934 Congress passed the *Securities Exchange Act*, which in some respects is companion legislation to the Securities Act of 1933. The Securities Act of 1933 regulates first-time offerings of new securities and requires that a registration statement be filed with the SEC before securities can be sold to the public. Once the securities are sold and trading begins on an exchange, such as the New York Stock Exchange, the company whose securities are traded must comply with the provisions of the Securities Exchange Act. This act regulates public trading of securities. The 1934 act also created the *Securities and Exchange Commission (SEC)*, which serves as the regulatory agency that administers both the 1933 and 1934 acts.

The Securities Exchange Act requires that all public companies file with the

SEC, on a periodic basis, various types of financial information, including financial statements audited by independent public accountants. *Public companies* sell their securities to the public and their securities are traded on a national or over-the-counter exchange. Private companies sell their securities to a limited number of persons in private transactions and are not subject to the 1933 or 1934 acts.

Section 18(a) of the Securities Exchange Act

This section of the Securities Exchange Act imposes liability on any person who makes a materially false or misleading statement in any document filed with the SEC. Auditors of financial statements filed with the SEC are subject to this liability.

Section 18(a) of the Securities Exchange Act, however, has less severe standards of third-party liability than those imposed by Section 11(a) of the Securities Act of 1933. Figure 4.5 shows the significant differences between the standards of liability in these two acts.

For the reasons shown in Figure 4.5, third parties rarely use Section 18(a) of the Securities Exchange Act to sue auditors for recovery of investment losses in public securities.

FIGURE 4.5   **Comparison Between Selected Parts of the Securities Act of 1933 and the Securities Exchange Act of 1934**

Under Section 11(a) of the Securities Act of 1933, third parties who sue the auditor for ordinary negligence do not have to prove that	*Under Section 18(a) of the Securities Exchange Act of 1934, third parties who sue the auditor must prove that*
1. The auditor was guilty of negligence. (The auditor must prove that he or she was not negligent.)	1. The auditor was guilty of *scienter* (a form of fraud).
2. They relied on the financial statements and the auditor's opinion in making an investment decision.	2. They relied on the financial statements and the auditor's opinion in making an investment decision.
3. Their investment losses were caused by the false statement or misleading omission in the audited financial statements.	3. Their investment losses were caused by reliance on the false statement or misleading omissions in the audited financial statements.

Section 10(b) of the Securities Exchange Act

To recover investment losses from auditors, third parties are more likely to use Section 10(b) rather than Section 18(a) of the Securities Exchange Act. The courts have consistently ruled that third parties may use this section of the Securities Exchange Act and an accompanying SEC ruling to sue auditors for damages. Consequently, from the early 1960s to the mid-1970s third parties employed the Securities Exchange Act for an extensive number of lawsuits against auditors.

The *Hochfelder* Case—Limitations on Auditor Liability

For many years, however, it was not clear whether third parties could use Section 10(b) to sue auditors for ordinary negligence or whether fraud had to be proven. In 1976 the U.S. Supreme Court, in *Ernst & Ernst v. Hochfelder,* handed down a decision that settled the issue; third parties would have to prove *scienter* (a deliberate attempt to manipulate, deceive, or defraud) to successfully bring action against auditors under Section 10(b).

The president and majority shareholder of First Securities Company of Chicago, a small brokerage firm, convinced some of the firm's customers to invest in what were represented to be special escrow accounts paying high rates of return. In fact, the escrow accounts were fictitious, and the president made personal use of the money without proper accountability. He covered up the fraud by using a "mail rule" that prohibited anyone but himself from opening incoming mail addressed to the company. Escrow account receipts were not recorded in the accounting records, and the auditors, Ernst & Ernst (now Ernst & Young), failed to detect the fraud.

The fraud was uncovered when the president murdered his wife and committed suicide. The third-party investors sued the auditors for negligence under Section 10(b) of the Securities Exchange Act. The auditors were not accused of participating in a fraud but of "inexcusable negligence" for failing to detect the weakness in controls from the mail rule. The U.S. Supreme Court found for the auditors and ruled that the third-party investors had to prove scienter rather than ordinary negligence.

Actions to Circumvent the *Hochfelder* Case

Subsequently, the SEC has tried to circumvent the *Hochfelder* ruling by using administrative proceedings to sanction auditors believed to be guilty of ordinary negligence. For example, the SEC has sanctioned individual CPAs and CPA firms by denying them the right to accept public companies as clients for a designated period of time.

Figure 4.6 summarizes both securities acts.

FIGURE 4.6   A Comparison of Auditor's Legal Liability Under the Securities Acts

Standard of Liability	The Securities Act of 1933	The Securities Exchange Act of 1934
Ordinary negligence	May be liable to third parties if there is a false statement or misleading omission in the audited financial statements and third parties suffered a loss. (The third party does not have to prove a connection between the two.)	Generally not liable to third parties under the act.
Gross negligence	Liable to third parties.	May be liable to third parties for "recklessness" or lacking a genuine belief in the truth of the statements made.
Fraud	Liable to third parties.	Liable to third parties.

ADDITIONAL CASES THAT CHANGED THE AUDITOR'S LEGAL ENVIRONMENT

All the legal cases discussed so far had a direct bearing on the evolutionary changes in the auditor's liability under common or statutory law. Still other cases, however, have affected the auditor's legal environment and the public's view of the auditor's responsibilities to clients and third parties. The cases in this section are presented in the order in which they occurred, accompanied by commentaries on their lessons and implications.

The McKesson & Robbins Case—A Fraud that Changed Auditing Standards

McKesson & Robbins was a wholesale drug company with securities listed on the New York Stock Exchange and registered under the Securities Exchange Act of 1934. One of the firm's alleged activities was a foreign business conducted through a Canadian subsidiary. This subsidiary reported sizable purchases, sales, and inventories, but, in fact, the transactions were fictitious.

The fraud became known in 1939. In 1940 the Securities and Exchange Commission conducted an investigation in which it was very critical of the scope of audit procedures followed by the entire profession. Although it declined to exercise the full authority granted by Congress, the SEC made several suggestions:

1. In the two important areas of accounts receivable and inventory, the SEC recommended that evidence of existence should be obtained from external and independent sources.
2. The stockholders should elect the auditor.
3. The audit report should be addressed to the stockholders.
4. The auditors should attend stockholder meetings and answer questions from this group.

The AICPA issued a pronouncement requiring auditors to gather independent and external evidence on accounts receivable and inventory, if the amounts are *material.* (An amount is considered material if it would cause an informed reader to view the financial statements differently.) Today, it is routine procedure to seek independent verification of such accounts.

The SEC's suggestions, however, have only been followed in part. Sometimes stockholders ratify the auditors, but this action is often a mere formality because the recommendation for the auditors comes from the board of directors or management. There is no SEC requirement concerning the addressee of the audit report, so the addressee can be the stockholders or the board of directors. Although the auditor's attendance at stockholder meetings is still optional, the SEC does require that the auditor be available to attend such meetings or that management disclose to stockholders that the auditor will not be available.

The Continental Vending Case— Criminal Exposure

Continental Vending Machine Corporation (Continental) and an affiliate named Valley Commercial Corporation (Valley) were dominated by the president, who owned about 25 percent of the stock of Continental. He borrowed sums of money from Valley, which, in turn, borrowed the same amount from Continental. At the balance sheet date, approximately $3.5 million appeared on the books of Continental as a receivable from Valley (in reality, a receivable from the president who was unable to repay it).

Also, Continental discounted notes to a bank through Valley. These notes appeared on the books of Continental as a note payable to Valley (actually a note to the bank). At the balance sheet date, the amount was about $1 million.

The notes to the financial statements contained an explanation that the $3.5 million receivable, less the $1 million payable, was secured on the date of the auditor's report by securities with a market value in excess of the net amount of the receivable. Coopers & Lybrand were aware of the details of these transactions when they issued their report on the financial statements.

The collateral, however, was worth only $2.9 million on the report date, and because the offset of the $1 million payable against the $3.5 million receivable was improper, a shortage of approximately $600,000 resulted (the $3.5 million gross receivable less the $2.9 million of collateral).

The auditors were charged with conspiring and adopting a scheme to violate federal *criminal* statutes by certifying false and misleading financial statements. The court used the following language in stating the case that the government had to prove:

> Not to show that the defendants were wicked men, with designs on anyone's purse, which they obviously were not, but rather that they had certified a statement knowing it to be false.

Three auditors of the CPA firm were found guilty and fined, thus illustrating the legal risk of auditors in the area of criminal conduct.

The 1136 Tenants' Corporation Case—A Misunderstanding Resulting in Negligence

A cooperative apartment corporation hired a CPA to "perform all necessary accounting and auditing services," particularly as they related to the custodianship of the corporation's managing agent.

There was a misunderstanding between the corporation and the accountant as to the nature and extent of the services. No letter explaining the terms of the engagement had been written to the owners of the apartment corporation. The owners apparently thought that an audit would be performed, whereas the CPA apparently understood that the services would be confined to accounting work consisting of maintaining the accounting records and preparing financial statements and related tax returns.

Later, it was determined that the managing agent had stolen funds from the cooperative. When the thefts were discovered, the client sued the accountant under common law for ordinary negligence in failing to uncover the fraud. The CPA, in turn, maintained that he had not been engaged to perform an audit. The court decided that the weight of the argument was in favor of the client; money damages were awarded.

After the verdict, several articles appeared suggesting the use of safeguards to avoid this type of situation in the future. Chief among these safeguards is the realization that the concept of due care exists regardless of the type of work performed by the CPA. Also needed is a clearly worded engagement letter from the CPA to his or her prospective client stating specifically the scope of the proposed work.

The ZZZZ Best Case—A Question of Auditor Disclosure

Auditors have traditionally dealt with suspicions of client fraud by resigning from the audit while obeying Rule 301 of the *Code of Professional Conduct* that requires confidentiality regarding client affairs. The *ZZZZ Best* case, which occurred in 1988, has raised the issue as to whether auditors can continue to react to such circumstances in traditional ways.

Ernst & Whinney (now Ernst & Young) were performing an audit of ZZZZ Best, a company engaged in carpet-cleaning and building restoration. The auditors suspected fraud and resigned but did not disclose the facts of the suspected fraud to the SEC or to the public on a timely basis.

Hearings were conducted by the U.S. Congress during which it was asserted that the auditors had a public duty to notify regulatory authorities of suspected fraud, an action at odds with Rule 301 on confidentiality.

This case raised the question (still unanswered) as to whether auditors' public duty to disclose fraud transcends their duty to maintain confidential relations with their clients.

The ESM Government Securities Case— Ethical Behavior of Auditors

For several years, a partner of Alexander Grant & Co. attested to the fairness of ESM Government Securities' financial statements that he knew to be false. Thus he committed fraud, himself, by allowing a fraud to continue.

The fraud was eventually uncovered and the auditor was convicted of criminal conduct. What followed was increased emphasis by the profession on quality control as well as technical competence to perform a complicated audit. The case damaged the reputation of the profession and forced fresh looks at the ethical environment of the auditor.

THE PRESENT-DAY LEGAL ENVIRONMENT

So where do auditors stand today as the result of 70 years of cases that range from privity protection under *Ultramares* to severe legal exposure under the Securities Act of 1933? Here are some general answers.

1. The auditor's potential liability for ordinary negligence under common law definitely extends to third parties with primary beneficiary relationships, often extends to third parties with foreseen relationships, and sometimes extends to third parties with foreseeable relationships.

2. The auditor's potential liability to third parties has been widened considerably by the passage of the Securities Act of 1933. Specific provisions of this law

can and are used by third parties to recover losses from auditors for ordinary negligence.

3. Auditors continue to be embarrassed by major frauds that they fail to discover. These frauds have changed the public's perception of auditors' effectiveness.

4. Many lawsuits against auditors are levied for *business failures* (bankruptcy caused by management inefficiency, unforeseen circumstances, etc.) rather than *audit failures* (failures to comply with generally accepted auditing standards in the performance of an audit). Auditors have had only limited success in educating the public on the difference between these two concepts.

Responses by Auditors— More Attention and Care

Auditors have responded to this increased litigious environment by (1) reexamining their auditing and quality control standards, (2) periodically updating their knowledge with continuing professional education, and (3) exercising more care in selecting clients and defining the scope of their audit engagements.

Responses by Auditors—The Coalition to Eliminate Abusive Securities Suits

In the early 1990s auditors responded to the litigious environment in a more contentious way. The "Big Six" CPA firms, the AICPA, and leaders of business and industry formed a group called the *Coalition to Eliminate Abusive Securities Suits (CEASS)*. The major purpose of this group is to obtain congressional reform to curb litigation brought under the federal securities acts.

CEASS is seeking reforms in the following areas: (These suggested reforms are restated with the terms used throughout the chapter.)

1. *Proportionate liability.* Establish a liability rule so that auditor/defendants who did not gain from an alleged fraud will be responsible only for their proportionate share of the damages awarded to third parties.

2. *Fee-shifting.* Require third parties who are unsuccessful in their lawsuits against auditors to pay the auditors' attorney fees.

3. *Curb abusive litigation practices.* Prohibit certain abuses such as attorneys paying "bounties" to third parties to encourage them to sue auditors.

4. *Clear and convincing proof standard.* Require third parties to establish a "clear and convincing" standard of proof for alleged fraud against auditors rather than a standard of proof based on simple misstatements in audited financial statements.

5. *Pleading reform.* Require third parties to state in their lawsuits against auditors the specific circumstances of the alleged fraud, so that unwarranted claims of fraud can be dismissed early in the case.

6. *Aiding and abetting liability.* Specify that auditor/defendants are not liable as

"aiders and abettors" of the fraud unless they knowingly intended to assist the fraud for their own direct monetary advantage.[4]

In 1995 Congress passed a law that gives auditors and others some relief from securities lawsuits. Among its provisions are

- A higher standard for allegations during the pleadings stage (i.e., plaintiffs must plead specific facts rather than general allegations).
- Elimination of the joint-and-several liability system (auditors will only be liable for the proportion of a loss for which a judge concludes they were responsible—not for the entire loss).

The law also imposes on auditors a legally required duty to report illegal acts when they find them during audits of public companies. Finally, the law does not contain a broad "loser-pays" provision sought by the accounting profession, but it does impose sanctions against attorneys who file abusive lawsuits.

Comment Auditors may have entered the sixth phase of a "liability cycle," as described by the head of a company that provides liability insurance for professionals. According to this person's analysis:

1. The first phase occurs when auditors experience small legal claims, are embarrassed, and settle out of court.
2. The second phase occurs when a few noteworthy cases break into the public consciousness. The auditors feel guilty and repair their quality control systems.
3. The third phase occurs when lawsuits become so frequent that auditors accept them as a given and do not seem to believe they can "do things right." Auditors react by conducting peer reviews.
4. The fourth phase occurs when auditors become overconfident about their defense, lose their confidence, and settle lawsuits at any cost.
5. The fifth phase occurs when third parties and lawyers go into the business of suing auditors.
6. The sixth and final phase occurs when judges and juries see auditors and their insurance companies as a source of compensation for business failure (which we have defined and distinguished from audit failure).

THE FUTURE OF AUDITOR LIABILITY

Prospects for the Future

We can expect CEASS (or a similar group) to continue to pursue changes in securities laws so that third parties will not automatically sue auditors who attest to the financial statements of companies experiencing business failure.

Auditors will levy more countersuits against audit clients who sue them if the

---

[4] A recent U.S. Supreme Court decision in *Central Bank of Denver v First Interstate Bank of Denver* addressed this issue. The decision ended aider and abettor lawsuits by investors and other parties under Section 10(b) of the Securities Exchange Act of 1934.

auditors believe that the client suits are unwarranted or that the clients committed wrongdoing themselves.

▶ **EXAMPLE**

BDO Seidman won a settlement for a countersuit for fraud filed against an audit client, presumably the first successful settlement of its kind. In 1979 several managers of Cenco, Inc. were convicted of fraudulent financial practices. Cenco sued Seidman for audit malpractice in failing to detect the fraud. Seidman countersued Cenco for fraud, charging that Cenco's management had misled them into issuing an unqualified opinion on Cenco's financial statements. The company that acquired Cenco settled the case out of court.

Auditors will be more careful about clients they accept and retain. Companies that have a history of financial difficulties are more likely to falsify earnings and to hide financial statement disclosures than companies without such difficulties. Auditors will be more cautious about accepting and auditing such clients.

Auditors will take greater care to assure that generally accepted auditing standards are followed. In many of the cases in this chapter, one or more auditing standards were violated. Auditors will be more aware that the quality of their work is subject to intense scrutiny when they are sued by clients or third parties.

Auditors will be more careful to issue engagement letters that set out clearly the scope of the audit and the auditors' responsibility. (Engagement letters were discussed briefly in this chapter and are covered more extensively in Chapter 8.)

Litigation Guidelines

The issuance of litigation guidelines has almost become an industry of its own in response to numerous articles published in recent years advising auditors to take or avoid specific actions to lower the probability of lawsuits. Many steps currently being taken by auditors are the result of litigation. In addition, other recommendations have been made that are applicable to the ever-shifting legal risks to auditors caused by varying laws and court opinions.

1. Follow the reporting standards on any report issued to a client and be precise about responsibilities taken or not taken on the engagement.

▶ **EXAMPLE**

Ernst & Young reviewed the financial statements of ZZZZ Best Co. for a three-month period (recall from Chapter 2 the difference between a review and an audit). The report stated that Ernst & Young had not performed the audit work necessary to form an opinion. ZZZZ Best Co. went bankrupt, and a creditor sued the CPA firm because of alleged reliance on the review report in making a loan. The court ruled that the CPA firm was not liable.

2. Limit the group using the audit report when it is possible to do so. It is difficult to predict the decision of courts even in states that have histories of conservative, moderate, or liberal views on the auditor's liability to third parties. The

courts might assume the audit report is to be widely used unless the auditor specifically restricts it.

▶ **EXAMPLE**

A California court, after decades of expanding the auditor's liability to third parties, ruled that the auditor is not liable to third parties unless (1) the auditor knows the audit is being performed for the specific benefit of a third party (a primary beneficiary relationship) or (2) the auditor engages in fraudulent conduct. The plaintiffs will probably try to establish a primary beneficiary relationship, which they conceivably could do if the auditors did not specifically state who would receive the audit report.

SUMMARY

Auditing in this century has not been a steady succession of court cases. Landmark cases have proved the auditor's fallibility, but for each such case, we know there are thousands of instances where the auditor has insisted on adjustments to misstated financial statements or resigned from the audit. Each audit failure has been matched thousands of times by audits that have given the financial community much-needed reliance on financial statements.

Auditing is not like other tasks; it involves unique risks and it requires unique personal characteristics. In the rest of the chapters, we will explore what it takes to perform an audit.

APPENDIX

Summary of Cases and Their Importance

The Evolution of Auditors' Ordinary Negligence Liability Under Common Law

Name of Case	Importance of Case
Ultramares Corporation v. Touche (255 N.Y. 170, 174 N.E., 441, 1931)	1. Confirmed that auditors are liable to the client for ordinary negligence but not to third parties. 2. Opened the possibility that auditors might be liable to third parties for gross negligence.
C.I.T. Financial Corporation v. Glover (224 F 2nd 44 [2nd Cir. 1955])	Extended the auditor's ordinary negligence liability to third parties with a primary beneficiary relationship.
Rusch Factors, Inc. v. Levin (284 F. Supp. 85 [D.R.I. 1968])	Extended the auditor's ordinary negligence liability to third parties with a foreseen party relationship.
Rosenblum v. Adler (461 A.D.D. 2nd 128 [N.J. 1983])	Extended the auditor's ordinary negligence liability to third parties with a foreseeable party relationship.

Name of Case	Importance of Case
Credit Alliance Corporation v. Arthur Andersen & Co. (493 N.Y. Supp. 2nd 435 [1985])	Reversed the trend toward extending the auditor's ordinary negligence liability to foreseen and foreseeable parties and helped return the third-party burden of proof to near privity by establishing this three-point test. In the absence of a contract, the accountant will be liable to a third party for ordinary negligence only if 1. The accountant knew that the third party would rely on the financial reports. 2. The accountant was aware that the financial reports were to be used for a particular purpose or purposes. 3. There was evidence linking the accountant with the third party showing that the accountant understood that reliance would be placed on the reports.

The Effect of Statutory Law on Auditor's Liability to Third Parties

Name of Case	Importance of Case
Escott v. Barchris Construction Corporation (283 F. Supp. 643, 701 [S.D.N.Y. 1968])	Applied to a set of factual circumstances the standards of the Securities Act of 1933 that allow third parties to sue the auditor for ordinary negligence without invoking common law standards.
Ernst & Ernst v. Hochfelder (425 U.S. 185 [1976])	Changed the burden of proof under the Securities Exchange Act of 1934 by ruling that third parties would have to prove scienter (deliberate attempt to manipulate, deceive, or defraud) to bring action against the auditors under this act.

Additional Cases that Changed the Auditor's Legal Environment

Name of Case	Importance of Case
McKesson & Robbins, Inc.	Created a permanent change in the evidence-gathering techniques (requirement for independent evidence) that the accounting profession uses in audits.

Continental Vending—U.S. v. Simon (425 F. 2nd 796 [1969])	Demonstrated the auditor's risk in the area of criminal law. Broadened the concept of fairness beyond the application of generally accepted accounting principles.
1136 Tenants' Corp. v. Max Rothenberg & Co. (36 A.D. 2nd 804, 319, N.Y.S. 2nd 1007 [1971])	Emphasized that due care must be exercised in nonattest engagements and demonstrated the need for a clearly worded engagement letter from the CPA to his or her prospective client stating specifically the scope of the proposed work.
ZZZZ Best (1988)	Highlighted a growing controversy on whether an auditor's duty to publicly disclose fraud transcends the duty of confidentiality.
ESM Government Securities (1987)	Pointed out the need for the profession to emphasize quality control in its audit activities.

Chapter 4 ▶ GLOSSARY OF TERMS

Audit failure Performance of an audit that is not in conformity with generally accepted auditing standards.

Auditors' due diligence defense A defense that can be used by auditors against charges of ordinary negligence under the Securities Act of 1933. The auditors must have reason to believe that the statements were true as of the effective date of a registration statement.

Auditors' good faith defense A defense that can be used by auditors against charges under the Securities Exchange Act of 1934. The defense is that the auditors performed in good faith and had no knowledge that the financial statements were false or misleading.

Business failure Bankruptcy caused by management inefficiency, competition, unforeseen circumstances, and such.

Common law Law based on the precedents established from past court cases.

Foreseeable parties Users of financial statements who are not specifically identified or who use the statements for transactions not specifically known to the auditor, but who may reasonably be expected to see the statements and to act or refrain from acting because of reliance on them.

Foreseen parties Third parties known to or reasonably expected to be known to the auditor who will rely on the auditor's work in making a particular business decision.

Fraud Knowledge of a false representation consisting of the following elements: false representation, deliberate intent to deceive, expectation of reliance by another, justifiable reliance, and resulting damages.

Gross negligence An extreme, flagrant, or reckless departure from due care in performing professional duties.

Material amount in the financial statements An amount that would cause an informed reader to view the financial statements differently.

Ordinary negligence A lack of due care in the performance of professional accounting tasks, due care implying the use of the knowledge, skill, and judgment usually possessed by practitioners in similar practice circumstances.

Primary beneficiary An identified third party for whose benefit the auditor knows the client has specifically engaged him or her to perform an audit and whose reliance is the aim of the engagement.

Privity A contractual relationship between the auditor and the client for performance of professional services.

Public companies Companies that sell their securities to the public or whose securities are traded on an exchange.

Scienter An intent to manipulate, deceive, or defraud.

Securities and Exchange Commission The federal regulatory agency that regulates the public issuing and trading of securities.

Statutory law Law passed by a legislative body.

Third parties Groups that have a vested interest in a company's financial statements and are not a part of management. Examples are creditors and stockholders.

Chapter 4 ▶ REFERENCES

American Institute of Certified Public Accountants, *Professional Standards:* AU Section 230—*Due Care in the Performance of Work.*

Augenbraun, Barry S. "Liability of Accountants Under the Federal Securities Laws," *The CPA Journal* (December 1994), pp. 34–35.

Gavin, Thomas A., Hicks, Rebecca L., and Scheiner, James H. "Auditor's Common Law Liability: What We Should Be Telling Our Students," *Journal of Accounting Education,* Vol. 5 (1987), pp. 1–12.

Goldwasser, Dan L. "Damage Control for Professional Liability," *The CPA Journal* (July 1991), pp. 16–22.

Hall, William D., and Renner, Arthur J. "Lessons Auditors Ignore

at Their Own Risk: Part II," *Journal of Accountancy* (June 1991), pp. 63–71.

Hanson, Randall K., and Rockness, Joanne W. "Gaining a New Balance in the Courts," *Journal of Accountancy* (August 1994), pp. 40–44.

Murray, Mark F. "How to Respond to a Malpractice Claim," *Journal of Accountancy* (March 1992), pp. 61–64.

Murray, Mark F. "When a Client Is a Liability," *Journal of Accountancy* (September 1992), pp. 54–58.

Simonetti, Gilbert, and Andrews, Andrea R. "A Profession at Risk, A System in Jeopardy," *Journal of Accountancy* (April 1994), pp. 45–54.

Chapter 4 ▶ REVIEW QUESTIONS

4-1 Give two reasons why there is an expectation gap.

4-2 Name and define four legal relationships between plaintiffs and the auditor.

4-3 Name and define four standards of proof.

4-4 What is the difference between statutory law and common law?

4-5 Describe the ways in which the scope of many audits in the early 1900s was significantly different from what it is today.

4-6 Describe the triangle of relationships shown in Figure 4.2.

4-7 Describe the two auditing implications of the *Ultramares* case as shown in Figure 4.3.

4-8 What effect did each of these cases have on auditors' ordinary negligence liability to third parties?
a. *C.I.T. Financial Corporation.*
b. *Rusch Factors, Inc. v. Levin.*
c. *Rosenblum v. Adler.*

4-9 Describe the three-part test established in the *Credit Alliance v. Arthur Andersen & Co.* case.

4-10 Describe the two provisions of Section 11(a) of the Securities Act of 1933 that impose strict standards of responsibility on the auditor.

4-11 What was the significance of the *Barchris* case?

4-12 Explain the significant differences between the standards of liability under Section 11(a) of the Securities Act of 1933 and Section 18(a) of

the Securities Exchange Act of 1934. (Refer to Figure 4.5.)

4-13 In what way did the *Hochfelder* case put limitations on auditor liability under Section 10(b) of the Securities Exchange Act of 1934?

4-14 Describe the four suggestions made by the SEC after an investigation into the *McKesson & Robbins* case.

4-15 Why were criminal charges made against the auditors in the *Continental Vending* case?

4-16 What conflict did the *ZZZZ Best* case cause between the auditor's "public duty" and the *Code of Professional Conduct?*

4-17 What is the relationship between the *ESM Government Securities Case* and the accounting profession's quality control?

4-18 Answer the following questions:
a. What is the auditor's liability for ordinary negligence under common law?
b. How has the auditor's liability to third parties been widened under statutory law?

4-19 What is the difference between business failures and audit failures?

4-20 How have auditors responded to the increasingly litigious environment?

4-21 Describe the reforms being addressed by the Coalition to Eliminate Abusive Securities Suits (CEASS).

4-22 Describe the phases of the liability cycle.

4-23 Describe two litigation guidelines.

Chapter 4 ▶ OBJECTIVE QUESTIONS

4-24 Which of the following is *least* likely to be an example of ordinary negligence?

a. The auditor misinterprets a transaction because he or she did not read the invoice carefully.

b. The auditor reads the minutes of the meetings of the client's board of directors and fails to note an important property acquisition approved by them.

c. The auditor omits the observation of the client's inventory that is material.

d. The auditor misreads an invoice and fails to note that an expenditure charged to an expense account should have been capitalized.

4-25 Which of the following is *most* likely to be an example of fraud?

a. The auditor fails to properly determine the reason why so many of the client's customers complain that they have been overcharged.

b. The auditor allows an important footnote describing a large contingent liability to be omitted from the financial statements.

c. The auditor miscounts the amount in the client's cash funds.

d. The auditor forgets to observe inventory-taking at a client's place of business when inventory is a significant amount in the client's balance sheet.

4-26 Which of the following is an example of a privity relationship?

a. A third party for whom the audit is being primarily conducted is known by the auditor.

b. A third party unknown specifically by the auditor but known to be a person to whom the client might take the audited financial statements and apply for a loan.

c. A third-party creditor unknown to the auditor who relies on the audited financial statements to make a credit decision concerning the auditor's client.

d. The auditor's client for whom the auditor agreed to perform the audit.

4-27 Which of the following is *more* likely to be a foreseen party?

a. The president of the auditor's client.

b. A local bank that might be expected to lend the client money relying, in part, on the audited financial statements.

c. The chairman of the board of directors of the auditor's client.

d. A local bank that has never done business with the client and is unknown to the auditor.

4-28 Which of the following is *more* likely to be a foreseeable party?

a. A member of the general public, unknown to the auditor, who invests in stock of the auditor's client and relies on the audited financial statements for his or her investment decision.

b. The controller of the auditor's client.

c. A company known to the auditor that is interested in buying the client and that asks the client to provide it with audited financial statements.

d. A local credit institution that has consistently done business with the auditor's client over the years and has relied on the audited financial statements in making credit decisions.

4-29 In the *Ultramares* case the plaintiff's charge of negligence

a. Was disallowed because the plaintiff was not a foreseen party.

b. Was disallowed because the plaintiff had a privity relationship with the auditor.

c. Was disallowed because the plaintiff did not have a privity relationship with the auditor.

d. Was allowed.

4-30 The *C.I.T. Financial Corporation* case resulted in extending the auditor's liability to third parties for ordinary negligence under common law to

a. Foreseen parties.

b. Foreseeable parties.

c. Primary beneficiaries.

d. Those with privity relationships.

4-31 The *Rusch Factors* case resulted in extending the auditor's liability to third parties for ordinary negligence under common law to

a. Foreseen parties.

b. Foreseeable parties.

c. Primary beneficiaries.

d. Those with privity relationships.

4-32 The *Rosenblum v. Adler* case extended the auditor's liability for ordinary negligence under common law to

a. Foreseen parties.

b. Foreseeable parties.

c. Primary beneficiaries.

d. Those with privity relationships.

4-33 The three-point test for third-party lawsuits established in the *Credit Alliance* case included all of the following except

a. The accountant must be aware that a financial report will be used for a particular purpose.

b. There must be a written contract between the auditor and the third party.

c. The accountant knows that a third party will rely on his or her report.

d. Evidence linking the accountant with the third party shows that the accountant understands the report will be relied on.

4-34 Which of the following statements about the Securities Act of 1933 is not true?

a. Third parties must prove that the auditor was guilty of negligence.

b. Third parties' prima facie case is an alleged false statement or misleading omission in the audited financial statements.

c. Third parties do not have to prove that their investment losses were caused by the false statement or misleading omission in the audited financial statements.

d. The auditor's potential liability extends to the effective date of the registration statement.

4-35 Which of the following statements about the Securities Exchange Act of 1934 is not true?

a. Third parties must prove that they relied on the financial statements and the auditor's opinion in making an investment decision.

b. Third parties must prove that their investment losses were caused by reliance on the false statement or misleading omission in the audited financial statements.

c. There is no effective date of the registration statement that extends the auditor's liability under this law.

d. Third parties do not have to prove the auditor's guilt.

4-36 In the *Hochfelder* case, all of the following were factors in the case except

a. The Securities Exchange Act of 1934.

b. Violation of federal criminal statutes.

c. Scienter.

d. Negligence.

4-37 For each of the following descriptions, indicate the letter or letters associated with that description. You may use a letter more than once or not at all.

Description	Term
1. Third parties that, in some states, can sue the auditor for ordinary negligence under common law.	a. Foreseen parties
	b. Statutory law
2. The Securities Act of 1933.	c. Foreseeable parties
3. The Securities Exchange Act of 1934.	d. Regulates new offerings of securities to the public
4. Common law.	e. Privity

Chapter 4 ► DISCUSSION/CASE QUESTIONS

4-38 Indicate why each of the following statements is incorrect. Provide the correct statement.

a. Using a foreseen standard for determining ordinary negligence, only clients could sue an auditor for ordinary negligence under common law.

Why Statement Is Incorrect   Correct Statement

b. Using a foreseeable standard for determining ordinary negligence, a third party must be specifically identified to the auditor.

Why Statement Is Incorrect   Correct Statement

c. Auditors commit ordinary negligence when they make a false representation of a material fact.

Why Statement Is Incorrect   Correct Statement

d. The *Rusch Factors* case reaffirmed the ordinary negligence theory of privity.

Why Statement Is Incorrect   Correct Statement

e. The *Hochfelder* case gave third parties the right to sue the auditor for ordinary negligence.

Why Statement Is Incorrect   Correct Statement

4-39 For each of the following scenarios, indicate whether action by the indicated party could be successfully brought against the auditor for (a) ordinary negligence under common law, (b) gross negligence under common law, (c) violation of the Securities Act of 1933, (d) violation of the Securities and Exchange Act of 1934, or (e) violation of federal criminal statutes. Give reasons for your answers. (In some cases more than one might be appropriate.)

1. A company with publicly-traded securities omitted an important footnote to its financial statements. The auditor knew of and accepted the omission. Third parties suffered losses because they relied on the statements in making investment decisions.

2. Company A, a nonpublic company, applied for a loan from a local bank. The bank required an audit of the financial statements of Company A as a basis for making the loan. The auditor knew that the audit was being performed solely for the bank. The auditor did not confirm accounts receivable or observe the taking of inventory. (Each account balance was material.) Company A subsequently defaulted on the loan, and the bank suffered a loss.

3. The same situation as in (2) except that the auditor overlooked material errors while confirming accounts receivable and observing the taking of inventory.

4. An auditor of a nonpublic company aided a client in writing and using fraudulent computer programs. The company subsequently entered bankruptcy, and the stockholders incurred substantial losses.

5. A third-party investor discovered that the investee company (nonpublic) materially understated a contingent liability that was disclosed in its financial statements. The company declared bankruptcy when the actual liability had to be paid. The auditor considered the amount of the contingent liability disclosed in a footnote to be an acceptable amount and the footnote to be a proper disclosure. The company's stockholders incurred substantial losses.

4-40 Susan Jason, CPA, had been auditing the financial statements of Rosfeld Stores, Inc., a large department store, for several years. During the last two years a nationwide economic recession had affected Rosfeld's sales and net income severely. The company, looking for ways to lower operating expenses, constantly asked Jason how the audit fee could be reduced.

One day Rosfeld's president called Jason and suggested a method for saving money on the forthcoming audit. The president suggested that his personnel select the customer accounts to which confirmation letters would be sent. The same personnel would write and mail the confirmation letters. All of these procedures would be performed under the supervision of one of Jason's auditors.

Jason agreed to this procedure. As the auditor watched, two of Rosfeld's employees selected every fifth account, wrote a confirmation letter, and mailed the letters with the CPA firm's return address on the envelope. All of the confirmation letters were returned by the customers directly to the auditor with indications that the amount of accounts receivable on Rosfeld's books was correct. Jason issued a report with an unqualified opinion.

The next year it was discovered that Rosfeld Stores, Inc., had been inflating its sales by creating "dummy" customers, complete with assumed records and files. Rosfeld declared bankruptcy, and its creditors filed suit against Jason for negligence and fraud.

Required:

Answer the following questions.

a. Name the auditing standards that, in your opinion, were violated. Give reasons for your answers.

b. What conditions would have to exist for the creditors to be regarded by the court as primary beneficiaries?

c. What conditions would have to exist for the creditors to be regarded by the court as foreseen parties?

d. What conditions would have to exist for the creditors to be regarded by the court as foreseeable parties?

e. If the creditors were regarded as foreseen parties, would they probably win their negligence case? Give reasons for your answer.

f. Assume that Rosfeld Stores' securities are traded on the New York Stock Exchange. In your opinion, would investors be able to prove that scienter existed? Give reasons for your answer.

4-41   XYZ Oil Co. had been a problem for its auditor, Joe Jones, CPA, for several years. The company's stock was traded in the over-the-counter market, and management was concerned with keeping net income as high as possible to support the stock price. Each year, the controller would refuse to record any of Jones's proposed entries if he could establish that they were not material. Accordingly, each year's net income was generally overstated by 5 to 10 percent, which Jones accepted on the basis that it was not material.

Of particular concern to Jones was a $10 million investment in an oil venture in South America; however, he had been unsuccessful to date in proving to the controller's satisfaction that a loss should be recorded on this investment.

During the current year's audit, Jones discovered a report indicating that the South American oil venture was worthless and had been for two years. When he discussed this report with the controller, the controller suggested that the investment be written off in equal amounts over the next 10 years to prevent a significant effect in any year and to prevent embarrassment or liability to Jones from disclosing that past financial statements were misstated. The controller stated that recognition of the loss in the current year would mean bankruptcy for XYZ Oil Co. and certain liability for Jones.

Required:

Answer the following questions.

a. Assume that the stock is being offered for the first time and the provisions of the Securities Act of 1933 apply. If the investment was written off in 10 installments and the company went bankrupt in one year, what case would investors who lost money have against the auditor?

b. Assume the same situation as in (a) above. How might the auditor prove that the investor losses were caused by other factors?

c. Assume the same situation as in (a) above. In your opinion, would the auditor have a due diligence defense against the charge of ordinary negligence? Give reasons for your answers.

d. Assume that the stock has been on the market for several years and that the provisions of the Securities Exchange Act of 1934 apply. If the investment was written off in 10 installments and the company went bankrupt in two years, what conditions would have to exist for investors who lost money to prove scienter?

    e. Taking the case situation as stated, give reasons why the auditor should accept the controller's solution. What liability does he face if he does accept it? Give reasons why the auditor should not accept the controller's solution. What liability does he face if he does not accept it?

    f. What should the auditor do? Give reasons for your answer.

4-42   Mr. Clyde Neglent, CPA, was engaged to perform an audit of Hidden Records, Inc., a retail department store. Mr. Neglent had investigated the business and its owners before accepting the engagement and had found that Hidden Records, Inc., securities were popular, particularly during the last two years when total assets had risen by 20 percent and earnings by 15 percent. The company appeared to have the characteristics of a solid commercial establishment. But one thing bothered Mr. Neglent. The president and other key officers had unstable records of employment. In addition, Mr. Neglent was puzzled by the sudden rise in profits during a period when retail sales in that region of the country had dropped. Nevertheless, the audit was accepted and work soon commenced.

    The company kept most of its records on computer files. The accounts receivable were maintained on magnetic disk. Mr. Neglent's knowledge of computer systems was minimal (another reason for his hesitation in accepting the engagement). Therefore, he decided to consult with the company's data processing manager to determine the best way to audit the records stored in computer files.

    Ms. Clev, the data processing manager, made several suggestions on the various techniques that could be used to extract audit evidence. Most of them involved printouts of information stored in the computer. These suggestions all appeared to be reasonable and were followed by Mr. Neglent.

    Mr. Neglent wished to send confirmation letters to a sample of the customers whose accounts made up the accounts receivable balance, because this amount represented approximately 20 percent of the total assets. Ms. Clev stated that she had a sampling plan that she used when it was necessary to select customer accounts randomly for various reasons. She offered to make the sample selection for Mr. Neglent and to print confirmation requests. These requests would be given to Mr. Neglent, who, in turn, would mail them to the customers. Mr. Neglent agreed, and this procedure was followed. Replies received from the customers indicated that the account balances were correct.

    All other phases of the audit went smoothly, and the audit report was issued with an unqualified opinion. Several months later, Hidden Records, Inc., declared bankruptcy. The company had inflated its earnings and assets by creating false sales and accounts receivable.

Required:

Answer the following questions.

    a. Would third parties who relied on the financial statements and invested in the company's securities be able to successfully sue the auditor for ordinary negligence under the assumption that the investors constituted foreseen parties? Give reasons for your answer.

    b. Would third-party investors qualify as foreseeable parties? Give reasons for your answer.

    c. Would the investors be able to prove scienter and successfully sue the auditor? Give reasons for your answer.

    d. Name any auditing standards violated by the auditor. Give reasons for your answers.

    e. All things considered, in what ways should the auditor have acted differently in this audit?

4-43   Amy Love gingerly seated herself in the witness chair directly below the gently rotating fan hanging from the top of the high, arched ceiling. Her palms were slightly damp, but she hid this fact by methodically folding them across her lap. She raised her head and looked directly at her defense attorney, as she had been carefully instructed to do.

    The defense attorney, dressed in a gray, vested suit, arose, deliberately checked a few pencil notes laying on the table, and strolled toward the witness box.

DEFENSE ATTORNEY: "Tell us about your professional background, Ms. Love."

MS. LOVE: "I graduated from Sufon University six years ago . . ."

DEFENSE ATTORNEY: "You are a CPA? Is that correct?"

MS. LOVE: "Yes, I am. I passed the examination during my first year at Best and Best."

DEFENSE ATTORNEY: "What is your current position with Best and Best?"

MS. LOVE: "I'm an audit manager."

DEFENSE ATTORNEY: "Tell me about your job ratings since you've been at Best and Best."

MS. LOVE: "Generally, they've been very good."

DEFENSE ATTORNEY: "Were you the manager of the audit engagement for Super Computer, Inc. just before they declared bankruptcy?"

MS. LOVE: "Yes, I was. That was for the calendar year ended December 31, 1996."

DEFENSE ATTORNEY: "And when did they declare bankruptcy?"

MS. LOVE: "Seven months ago, in August 1997."

DEFENSE ATTORNEY: "And what type of audit report did you give them?"

MS. LOVE: "We gave them an unqualified opinion on their financial statements for the year 1996."

DEFENSE ATTORNEY: "Is it possible that you could certify that a profit amount, is say, $100,000 and it turns out to be only $50,000?"

MS. LOVE: "It is possible, but unlikely. That's why we give an opinion rather than a guarantee or certification, and that's why we say in our audit report that we're only giving reasonable assurance. There's always a risk that financial statements that we say are fair will turn out to be significantly misstated."

DEFENSE ATTORNEY: "You allow for that in what you call audit planning?"

MS. LOVE: "Yes, we do. We have to take some risk, just like any other professional."

DEFENSE ATTORNEY: "And didn't the people who ran Super Computer, Inc. hide many things from you?"

MS. LOVE (her face slightly flushed):   "They certainly did."

DEFENSE ATTORNEY: "Perhaps we should start from the beginning. Tell us what you know about Super Computer, Inc."

MS. LOVE (leaning back a little):   "The company started in 1982 as a producer and seller of computer hardware and accompanying software that was compatible with it."

DEFENSE ATTORNEY: "They were very successful, weren't they?"

MS. LOVE: "Yes. For the first few years, their sales were very good. At that time, they had another auditor."

DEFENSE ATTORNEY: "Then what happened?"

MS. LOVE: "In the late 1980s, their domestic sales started to drop, so they picked up some large customers in other countries. Or at least it seemed they did."

DEFENSE ATTORNEY: "What do you mean seemed?"

MS. LOVE: "We know now that most of that business never existed. Many of their customers were fictitious, and much of the merchandise they shipped was old phonograph records."

DEFENSE ATTORNEY: "At the time your firm took over the audit engagement, did any of you have reason to believe that this situation existed?"

MS. LOVE: "No, of course not. We certainly would never have taken on that type of client if we had known what they were."

DEFENSE ATTORNEY: "What about the other CPA firm that performed the audit before your firm took over?"

MS. LOVE: "Roth and Roth? They did the audit from 1983 until 1993 when we took over."

DEFENSE ATTORNEY: "Why did you take over the audit engagement?"

MS. LOVE: "Roth and Roth had a serious disagreement with the client about a significant accounting matter."

DEFENSE ATTORNEY: "And what was the nature of the disagreement?"

MS. LOVE: "The management of Super Computer, Inc. decided to write off several million dollars of special software research cost over a period of several years rather than expensing it in the income statement as the expenditures were incurred."

DEFENSE ATTORNEY: "And what did Roth and Roth do?"

Ms. LOVE: "They told the management of Super Computer, Inc. that they would issue an adverse opinion on the financial statements."

DEFENSE ATTORNEY: "So what happened?"

Ms. LOVE (slightly smiling): "Super Computer, Inc. wrote off all the research costs in the 1989 income statement. Then they fired Roth and Roth and approached us to do the audit."

DEFENSE ATTORNEY: "Why would your firm take on this audit engagement?"

Ms. LOVE (straightening up in her chair): "We did not take the engagement until the company agreed to continue writing off research costs the way Roth and Roth insisted they do."

DEFENSE ATTORNEY: "What was your reaction when you were asked to supervise this audit?"

Ms. LOVE (hesitating): "I did not particularly want the job, but Mr. Best, the managing partner of the office, insisted because of my prior experience auditing computer firms and my reputation for being hard-nosed about audit adjustments."

DEFENSE ATTORNEY: "Did you get along with the personnel at Super Computer, Inc.?"

Ms. LOVE: "For the most part."

DEFENSE ATTORNEY: "When did you first suspect that the sales to foreign countries were fraudulent and no inventory was being sent to those places?"

Ms. LOVE: "In the 1996 audit. Super Computer, Inc. had a very bad year in 1996 when domestic sales went down and they were forced to write off all research costs."

DEFENSE ATTORNEY: "What made you suspicious?"

Ms. LOVE: "Many things. First of all, the sales outside this country were made in bunches at amounts that seemed to support what I thought were inflated amounts of year-end inventory."

DEFENSE ATTORNEY: "Could you be a little less technical?"

Ms. LOVE: "Sorry. What I mean is that we believed that their inventory, that was counted on January 1, 1997, was inflated because of the uncertainty of getting decent prices when they sold it. We were convinced that they couldn't even get their money back in sales from some of the stuff, so we insisted on a large write-down of the inventory in their December 31, 1996 balance sheet."

DEFENSE ATTORNEY: "How did the management of the company react?"

Ms. LOVE: "They didn't like it, but I said we wouldn't give them an unqualified opinion unless they did."

DEFENSE ATTORNEY: "What happened then?"

Ms. LOVE (taking a deep breath): "Right out of the blue, they produced these shipping documents, which showed that a large percentage of the inventory subsequently had been sold in other countries at high prices. They insisted that these sales provided a good reason to value the inventory higher on December 31, 1996."

DEFENSE ATTORNEY: "Did you verify that these sales were real?"

Ms. LOVE: "Yes, I asked our audit senior to send special letters asking the managers of these companies to verify, directly to us, that they received this merchandise. One of the staff assistants inspected bank documents for the overseas accounts that Super Computer, Inc. supposedly set up to collect the money for these sales."

DEFENSE ATTORNEY: "It was all fictitious?"

Ms. LOVE: "We know now that it was. They arranged for people who worked for these overseas companies to dummy up receiving documents, bank records, and reply to our requests for confirmation of the sales."

DEFENSE ATTORNEY: "Were all the top officials in on the scheme?"

Ms. LOVE: "Most of them, including the member of the audit committee that I stayed in touch with through both of the audits in which I participated."

DEFENSE ATTORNEY: "When did you finally believe it was time for Best and Best to disassociate themselves from Super Computer, Inc.?"

Ms. LOVE: "I asked to be taken off the audit in early 1997 before we gave our opinion on the 1996 statements. I couldn't prove it conclusively, but I just felt we were in for trouble."

DEFENSE ATTORNEY: "Did you express these misgivings in a memo you put in the working papers for the 1996 audit?"

Ms. LOVE (hesitating):   "Yes, I did, and I had a long, long discussion with our managing partner. I suggested that we abandon the audit engagement without any opinion on the 1996 statements."

DEFENSE ATTORNEY: "What was his reaction?"

Ms. LOVE: "He was very cool to the idea. He asked me to stay on and insist on the lowest valued inventory I could talk them into."

DEFENSE ATTORNEY: "Do you believe you properly supervised the senior and the staff assistants on the audit for your two years?"

Ms. LOVE: "Absolutely! I instructed the senior to make sure that several boxes of inventory were opened and examined during each inventory count. The senior said that this had been done and noted in the working papers that legitimate inventory had been counted."

DEFENSE ATTORNEY: "Do you believe that your superiors reacted properly to your suggestions?"

Ms. LOVE (hesitating for a few seconds):   "They honestly believed we could perform a proper audit, and we did. We were held back at every turn. Even our own standards don't require us to dig our way through this kind of fraud."

DEFENSE ATTORNEY: "Are you satisfied that the senior and the staff assistants did their jobs properly?"

Ms. LOVE: "Absolutely. The work of the staff assistants was mostly routine. The senior consulted with me on every decision."

Required:

a. Write some questions and answers for the cross-examination of Ms. Love by the attorney of the third party primary beneficiary who is filing a suit for ordinary negligence.

b. Predict the outcome of the trial. Give your reasons.

4-44   **(Continuing Case—Part IV; Part V in Chapter 5)**

Potential conflicts of interest and other ethical matters were resolved between Custom Furniture Company and Ms. Hunt, and she began the audit. The loan officer of the bank was notified and told that the bank would receive a copy of the audited financial statements and Ms. Hunt's opinion as soon as the audit was completed. No copy of the letter to the loan officer was given to Ms. Hunt, and no one at Custom Furniture Company was sure that Ms. Hunt knew the specific bank that would receive the audit report.

The audit proceeded smoothly for the first three weeks. Ms. Hunt's brother-in-law continued to act as mail clerk, and there was very little contact between the two. The major conflict between Ms. Hunt and Custom Furniture Company occurred when receivables were examined for proper valuation. Custom Furniture Company had insisted that gross profits from large installment sales be shown as current revenues, with only a small allowance for doubtful accounts provided in the balance sheet. Ms. Hunt was willing to show these gross profits as current revenues only if a substantial allowance for doubtful accounts was recorded in valuing net receivables.

The financial statement results both with and without an adjustment for uncollectible installment sales are shown below.

	Without an adjustment	With an adjustment
Net income before taxes	$100,000	$ 80,000
Net receivables	520,000	500,000

The conversations became so contentious that Ms. Hunt discontinued the audit for several days. The controller of Custom Furniture Company contended that the loan would be jeopardized by a sharply reduced net income that was too far below what they had told the bank the company would earn. The controller strongly hinted that the company's inability to secure the loan might create problems in paying the audit fee. Ms. Hunt, visibly shaken by this veiled threat, decided to discuss it with her partner who would bear joint responsibility for signing the audit report.

Ms. Hunt's partner insisted that the threat to withhold the audit fee was a form of blackmail that they must not tolerate. He had never been strongly in favor of accepting the audit, and he suggested that a prudent course of action was to resign from the audit and "cut our losses."

Ms. Hunt initially agreed with her partner, but after some reflection believed the relationship could be repaired and the audit completed, at least for that year. She doubled the scope of her audit procedures on net accounts receivable, examining practically every credit file that looked doubtful of collection. By the time she finished these procedures, the budgeted time on the audit had already been exceeded. More discouraging was the resistance she continued to receive when she showed the credit manager evidence of poor collectibility for many of the installment sales. She offered to lower the proposed adjustment by 25 percent, but the controller refused to adjust the books for any more allowance for doubtful accounts than he had previously provided.

A few days later, the controller brought in a large check from one of the installment sales previously regarded as uncollectible. Ms. Hunt was so happy about this turn of events that she accepted the check as legitimate and failed to substantiate its legitimacy. She made some calculations and concluded that she could live with the allowance for doubtful accounts currently on the books.

Later in her office, Ms. Hunt called her partner and gave him the happy news. But her worksheet calculations did not impress her partner, who continued to insist that the unadjusted allowance would make the financial statements materially misstated. After considerable discussion, Ms. Hunt reluctantly concluded that even such a large and unexpected collection would not alter the need for several thousand dollars of adjustment to net receivables.

The next day, both Ms. Hunt and her partner had a lengthy meeting with several of Custom Furniture Company's top officials, including the controller and credit manager. When the meeting ended, everyone agreed that the audit engagement was over and that the appropriate report would be sent from Ms. Hunt to Custom Furniture Company. The loan was turned down by the bank, and Custom Furniture Company contracted its operations.

Required:

a. Write a memo describing the auditors' legal exposure if they had accepted the unadjusted financial statements. Indicate in the memo what legal relationship the court might determine and what standard of proof the court might require.

b. What were the "hero's" reasons for rejecting Ms. Hunt's argument to leave the net receivables unadjusted?

The Auditor's Responsibility— Fraudulent Financial Reporting

"It's a wicked world, and when a clever man turns his brains to crime, it is the worst of all."

A. CONAN DOYLE, *Adventure of the Speckled Band*

LEARNING OBJECTIVES

After reading and studying the material in this chapter, the student should be able to

▶ Describe the three-part definition of errors and write an example of each part.

▶ Describe the three-part definition of fraud and write an example of each part.

▶ Write, in one sentence each, four statements that summarize the auditor's responsibility to detect errors and fraud.

▶ Specify the warning signs that point to the possibility of management fraud.

▶ Compare the consideration of errors and fraud in the audit planning process at both the financial statement and account balance levels.

▶ Analyze the alternative actions auditors might take if errors and fraud are discovered.

▶ Describe the types of fraudulent financial reporting and the reasons why they occur.

▶ Give one example each of indicators of fraudulent financial reporting that relate to condition, motivation, and attitude.

▶ Depict the auditor's responsibility for detection of illegal acts that have a material and direct effect on amounts in the financial statements and illegal acts that have a material but indirect effect on amounts in the financial statements.

INTRODUCTION

Any financial statements examined by auditors could contain improprieties. For example, serious misstatements might have been made in calculating the allowance for doubtful accounts, merchandise might have been stolen, revenues that belong in a future accounting period might have been improperly classified as current period revenues, or a company might have failed to file tax returns.

The auditor bears some responsibility for detecting and reporting all of the above matters. It is appropriate, therefore, to describe how such improprieties might occur and what actions the auditor should take to provide reasonable assurance of detecting them if they do occur.

We begin with broad discussions of errors and fraud, how they occur, and the auditor's responsibility to detect and report them. We continue with explanations of a special form of fraud, fraudulent financial reporting, and the auditor's responsibility for this form of impropriety. We finish the chapter with a discussion of illegal acts and the auditor's responsibility in this area.

ERRORS AND FRAUD IN THE FINANCIAL STATEMENTS

Definition of Errors

Errors can, and sometimes do, occur in management assertions in financial statements because of unintentional misstatements or omissions of amounts or disclosures. Specifically:

1. Entity personnel might make mistakes in gathering or processing accounting data from which financial statements are prepared.

▶ **EXAMPLE**

Sales invoices are recorded improperly, resulting in incorrect amounts posted to the accounts receivable and sales accounts.

▶ **EXAMPLE**

Near the end of the accounting period, some unrecorded vendor invoices are overlooked or misplaced, resulting in understatements of purchases and accounts payable.

2. Entity personnel might overlook or misinterpret facts, causing accounting estimates to be incorrect.

▶ **EXAMPLE**

Management may fail to recognize that some inventory cannot be sold, resulting in an inadequate allowance for inventory obsolescence.

> ▶ **EXAMPLE**
>
> The credit manager may be overly optimistic in evaluating the collection history of several large customers, resulting in an allowance for doubtful accounts that is too small.

   ✗   **3.** Entity personnel might make mistakes in the application of accounting principles relating to amount, classification, manner of presentation, or disclosure.

> ▶ **EXAMPLE**
>
> The controller misinterprets expenditures for equipment repairs as expenditures for additions to equipment, resulting in overstatements of equipment and net income.

> ▶ **EXAMPLE**
>
> The controller overlooks the fact that credit balances in accounts receivable should be classified as current liabilities, resulting in understatement of both current assets and current liabilities.

As we can see, errors distort the financial statements, but they are unintentional and are corrected by entity personnel if they are detected.

Definition of Fraud

Fraud is more serious than errors because it includes intentional misstatements or omissions of amounts or disclosures in financial statements. Fraudulent financial reporting (management fraud) and misappropriation of assets (defalcations) are examples.

Basically, fraud occurs from the following:

1. Manipulation, falsification, or alteration of accounting records or supporting documents from which financial statements are prepared.

> ▶ **EXAMPLE**
>
> Sales invoices are created for fictitious sales, resulting in accounts receivable that do not exist and sales that are deliberately inflated.

2. Misrepresentation or intentional omission of disclosures of events, transactions, or other significant information.

> ▶ **EXAMPLE**
>
> A pending lawsuit likely to have an unfavorable outcome for the entity is not disclosed in the entity's financial statements.

3. Intentional misapplication of accounting principles relating to amounts, classification, manner of presentation, or disclosure.

► **EXAMPLE**

The purchase of another business is deliberately accounted for as a pooling of interests rather than a purchase, even though all evidence supports the classification of the transaction as a purchase.

Sometimes it is easy to distinguish between errors and fraud; at other times, the distinction is more difficult.

► **EXAMPLE**

Sales invoices containing unintentional clerical mistakes are errors; sales invoices for fictitious customers are fraud.

► **EXAMPLE**

On the other hand, a significant understatement of the allowance for doubtful accounts might result from unintentional misinterpretations of customers' debt-paying ability or intentional attempts to increase net income.

Therefore, the auditor's responsibilities to detect errors and fraud in clients' financial statements are basically the same.

The Auditor's Responsibilities to Detect Errors and Fraud

Professional standards provide a description of the auditor's responsibility in these areas.

1. The auditor should *assess* the risk that errors and fraud may cause the financial statements to contain a material (significant) misstatement (misstatements encompass both errors and fraud).
2. Based on that assessment, the auditor should *design and perform* the audit to provide *reasonable assurance* of detecting errors and fraud that are material (significant) to the financial statements.
3. Because the auditor's opinion on the financial statements is based on the concept of reasonable assurance, the auditor is not an *insurer* and his report does not constitute a *guarantee.*
4. Therefore, the subsequent discovery that a material misstatement exists in the financial statements *does not,* in and of itself, evidence inadequate planning, performance, or judgment on the part of the auditor.

These four statements may appear to be inconsistent in that the auditor designs procedures to detect errors and fraud but does not automatically bear responsibility if these designed procedures fail to detect them. These statements are basically consistent, however, and reflect the complexity of financial statement audits.

Warning Signs—''Red Flags''

KPMG Peat Marwick conducted a fraud survey in 1993. A significant number of the respondents indicated that the following warning signs or ''red flags'' point to the possibility of fraud in their companies:

1. Internal controls that were either poor or ignored by management.
2. A large amount of inventory losses.
3. Results of both external and internal audits that were ignored by management.
4. Unusual banking activities.
5. An exceptionally large amount of expenses and purchases.

Activities such as these could cause the auditor to assess certain areas of the audit as ''high risk areas'' and take appropriate measures such as assignment of senior personnel to these areas and/or performance of more than normal audit procedures for the affected accounts.

► EXAMPLE

Internal auditors of a retail department store found it strange that the physical inventory of one department was considerably lower than the perpetual inventory records while all other departments showed only small physical inventory shortages. An investigation of cash register sales revealed that clerks in that department were making ''whole dollar'' sales of merchandise several yards from the department's cash register and not placing the money in the register. The thefts were detected and measures taken to encourage customers to ask for cash register receipts when making purchases.

Planning the Audit to Consider Errors and Fraud

At the financial statement level, the auditor must consider a number of broad-based matters in deciding on the scope of the audit work necessary to provide reasonable assurance of detecting material errors and fraud. Each of these matters taken in isolation might not signal a need to broaden the scope of the audit, but collectively they might indicate a need to do so.

1. Certain management characteristics are clear danger signals, for example, domination by one person, an aggressive attitude toward financial reporting, high management turnover, undue emphasis on meeting earnings projections, and management's poor reputation in the business community.

► EXAMPLE

Mr. Spark makes all key operating and financing decisions for his business. Furthermore, he considers preparation of financial statements to be a ''necessary evil.'' He has hired and fired six controllers in the last five years, and he places increases in quarterly net income above all other considerations. Moreover, he is not well thought of among the auditor's other clients. The auditor must consider whether to retain the client. If the auditor believes the entity can be audited, he or she should expand the scope of the audit to recognize the increased risk that net income is being ''created'' to satisfy the client's singular financial goal.

2. Certain operating and industry characteristics might also present danger signals. The client might be less profitable than other companies in its industry, operating results might fluctuate significantly with general economic conditions, the industry itself might be declining, or the company might have poorly decentralized operating procedures.

► EXAMPLE

One of the auditor's clients is a large department store chain offering traditionally priced merchandise. The store's profits have lagged below industry averages for years, and that type of department store is losing customers to discount retail stores. Each store appears to have little organizational guidance. These operating characteristics may increase the potential for errors (because of inadequate guidance at individual stores) or fraud (because of pressure to show improved performance). The auditor must consider an expansion of audit procedures to account for the increased risk of misstated financial statements.

3. Certain characteristics of the audit engagement might pose danger signals to the auditor. The auditor must work with many difficult accounting issues, some of the client's transactions and account balances are hard to audit, and prior-period audits revealed many errors.

► EXAMPLE

The client is an airline whose liability for frequent flyer awards is difficult to estimate. Many of its planes are acquired in complex lease arrangements that are hard to audit. The auditor must consider an expansion of audit procedures.

At the account balance level, the auditor must consider a number of more narrowly focused matters in deciding on the scope of the audit work. For example:

1. The accounting issues affecting a particular account balance might be complex or contentious.

► EXAMPLE

The auditor's client sells high-fashion clothing that is very popular for limited periods of time. The estimate of inventory obsolescence will be more subjective than usual and may create differences of opinion between the auditor and client, necessitating more audit effort for the inventory account.

2. Significant misstatements have been discovered in certain account balances in prior audits.

► EXAMPLE

An auditor's client habitually understates accounts payable by omitting large-dollar invoices from the list that constitutes the account balance at year-end. The auditor should plan to spend considerable time examining accounts payable because of the risk that the same misstatement will occur in the current year.

3. Determining the account balance might require considerable judgment for the auditor's client.

▶ **EXAMPLE**

An auditor's client sells items that carry extensive warranty contracts that result in sporadic and unpredictable warranty claims. The liability for warranty costs is very difficult to estimate and involves considerable subjectivity, necessitating extensive audit procedures.

The Auditor's Responsibility if Errors and Fraud Are Detected

Discovery of an Error or Fraud

What should the auditor do if the amounts shown in the client's accounting records and the audited amounts differ? The auditor must make judgments as to whether these differences are errors or fraud. Errors generally require adjustment of the client's accounting records, whereas fraud has serious implications that go beyond the monetary effect on the financial statements.

What if the auditor has determined that a difference is, or may be, fraud, but the effect on the financial statements could not be material? The auditor should

1. Refer the matter to an appropriate level of management that is at least one level above those involved.
2. Satisfy himself or herself that the implications of the fraud for other aspects of the audit have been given proper consideration.

▶ **EXAMPLE**

The auditor discovers that the custodian of a small petty cash fund has made unauthorized withdrawals from the fund. The matter should be reported to the custodian's supervisor or a higher level, and consideration should be given to the implications of this fraud. The misappropriation might be an isolated act of a low-level employee, in which case the auditor need not pursue the matter further.

The employee's other duties may include preparing deposit slips for all cash received on account. In addition to reporting the fraud to an appropriate level of management, the auditor should consider that some cash received on account may have been misappropriated.

What if the auditor has determined that the difference is, or may be, fraud and the effect on the financial statements could be material? The auditor should

1. Consider the implications for other aspects of the audit.
2. Discuss the matter with a level of management at least one level above those involved in the fraud.
3. Try to obtain evidence to determine whether the fraud is material and what its effect will be on the financial statements.
4. If appropriate, suggest that the client consult with legal counsel on matters of law.

► EXAMPLE

What if the auditor discovers that the cashier is misappropriating daily cash receipts? This matter is more serious than theft from a petty cash fund because it could materially affect many accounts in the financial statements. The auditor should extend audit procedures on any accounts affected by this misappropriation (cash, accounts receivable, etc.). Discussions should be held with levels of management higher than anyone who might have been involved in the misappropriation, and the client should be strongly advised to consult with legal counsel.

Effect of Fraud on the Audit Report

The auditor's responsibility for material fraud extends to the opinion in the audit report. The financial statements should be revised if necessary or a qualified or adverse opinion issued (see Chapter 2).

► EXAMPLE

The auditor discovers that material amounts of merchandise that have been recorded as sales have been misappropriated instead of being shipped to customers. As a result, material amounts of recorded accounts receivable do not exist. The auditor should insist that revised financial statements be issued showing lower amounts of accounts receivable and sales. If the client refuses to issue revised statements, the auditor should not express an unqualified opinion.

The auditor may not be allowed to or may be unable to perform the necessary auditing procedures to conclude whether possible fraud materially affects the financial statements. In such cases, the auditor should

1. Disclaim an opinion or express a qualified opinion on the financial statements (see Chapter 2).
2. Report the findings on the possible fraud to the audit committee or the board of directors.

The auditor should withdraw from the engagement if the client refuses to accept a disclaimer of opinion or a qualified opinion because of the circumstances described above.

► EXAMPLE

A company officer writes checks to cash, takes the cash, and omits the amounts from the cash disbursements records. The records are inadequate to permit the auditor to perform the necessary auditing procedures to ascertain the extent of the fraud or the effect on the financial statements. A disclaimer or qualified opinion is issued.

FRAUDULENT FINANCIAL REPORTING

Definition and Reasons for Fraudulent Financial Reporting

A special form of fraud, *fraudulent financial reporting,* is defined as

intentional or reckless conduct, whether act or omission, that results in materially misleading financial statements.

Fraudulent financial reporting is not the same as theft or embezzlement of company funds, although this type of reporting may be used to cover thefts or embezzlements.

► **EXAMPLE**

The infamous Lincoln Savings and Loan scandal was (at least in part) a "tax-sharing" agreement in which Lincoln transferred millions of dollars to its parent company to "pay taxes." Lincoln attempted to partially cover this improper transfer of funds by creating a fictitious transaction that gave it a substantial "paper profit."

Fraudulent financial reporting is often used to make a company's financial statements look better than they really are. The National Association of Certified Fraud Examiners lists a number of reasons why fraudulent financial reporting (sometimes called *financial statement fraud*) is committed. Some of these reasons are:

1. To make the company's stock look more attractive and encourage investment.
2. To increase earnings per share and allow for increased dividend payouts.
3. To obtain additional financing or more favorable terms on existing financing.
4. To meet company goals and objectives.
5. To produce bonuses based on financial performance.

The *National Commission on Fraudulent Financial Reporting* (sometimes called the *Treadway Commission*) states that the risk of fraudulent financial reporting will increase substantially if these two situations exist:

1. Pressure on company managers to issue fraudulent financial statements.
2. The perception of an opportunity to commit a fraud without being detected.

► **EXAMPLE**

A company's revenues have decreased as a result of competition or a slumping economy. When the company begins to lose market share, the company's board of directors puts pressure on management to reverse the situation. But the board of directors does not provide proper oversight of financial reporting, and significant estimates by management appear in the financial statements. The conditions are right for management to create favorable earnings by making improper estimates of such accounts as allowance for doubtful accounts, inventory obsolescence, or liability for warranty costs.

► **EXAMPLE**

Each department manager has a bonus plan that depends on monthly departmental net income. Controls are weak, and there is no internal audit staff. The conditions are right for department managers to increase monthly net income on their departmental financial statements by inflating inventories.

Types of Fraudulent Financial Reporting[1]

Recognizing Revenue in an Earlier Accounting Period

Companies may engage in fraudulent financial reporting by improperly recording revenues in an accounting period.

---

[1] Examples are furnished by the National Association of Certified Fraud Examiners.

▶ **EXAMPLE**

A company traditionally recognized sales when the merchandise was shipped and the sales invoice was prepared. In 19X3 the company began recognizing sales when customers sent in orders. The company held title to the merchandise at year-end and overstated its revenue by almost $5 million in less than two years.

▶ **EXAMPLE**

A company began recognizing revenue when it completed the manufacture and factory testing of its telecommunications products and delivered the products to designated sites for further testing. The company retained rights to the products until they were shipped to the customer. In one year net income was overstated by more than $16 million.

Fictitious Sales

Sales can be recorded on the books that either do not exist or are inflations of amounts on sales documents.

▶ **EXAMPLE**

The SEC filed a complaint against a company for improperly recognizing revenue by (1) recording sales on merchandise that had not been delivered to the customers and that the customers had not agreed to buy, (2) recording sales on the basis of a sales prospect list, and (3) simulating the removal of inventory from the company's premises and delivery to customers. During one year this practice of revenue recognition produced a significant understatement of a loss.

Risk Factors Relating to Fraudulent Financial Reporting

Risk factors the auditor can use to assess the probability of fraudulent financial reporting include the following:

Management Characteristics

- Management does not display and communicate an appropriate attitude regarding internal control and the financial reporting process.

▶ **EXAMPLE**

There is little or no board of director or audit committee oversight of management, which is dominated by one person or a few people.

▶ **EXAMPLE**

The accounting staff does not have enough personnel or the existing staff is ineffective.

- Management's compensation is based on unreasonable targets for operating results or financial position.
- Management tries to increase the stock price or earnings trend by using aggressive accounting practices.

- Senior management or board members turn over rapidly.
- Management and its current or predecessor auditor have strained relationships.

▶ **EXAMPLE**

Management frequently argues with the auditor on financial reporting matters and as a result engages in "opinion shopping."

▶ **EXAMPLE**

Management limits or restricts the auditor from obtaining information or communicating with the board of directors or audit committee.

Industry Conditions

- New accounting, statutory, or regulatory requirements impair the financial stability or profitability of the entity.
- A high degree of competition or market saturation causes or accompanies declining margins.
- The client is in a declining industry with frequent business failures.
- The industry experiences rapidly changing customer demand, technology, or product obsolescence.

Operating Characteristics and Financial Stability

- The client is under significant pressure to obtain needed capital for major research or capital expenditures.
- The financial statements are based on subjective estimates that are subject to potential significant change in the near term.
- The financial structure of the client makes it highly vulnerable to changes in interest rates.
- The client is threatened with imminent bankruptcy or foreclosure.
- The client has reported earnings growth, but cannot generate cash flows from operations.
- Unusually complex transactions occur near the end of the year.

Risk Factors Relating to Misappropriation of Assets

Risk factors an auditor can use to assess the probability of misappropriation of assets include the following.

Susceptibility of Assets to Misappropriation

- Large amounts of cash are processed.
- Inventory consists of small high value items.

Employee Relationships or Pressures

- Dissatisfied employees have access to assets.
- Employees exhibit a life style that is beyond their means.
- Employee behavior changes in unusual and unexplained ways.

Controls

- Management fails to provide adequate oversight.
- Job applicants are inadequately screened.
- The accounting system is in disarray.

✓ *The Auditor's Responsibility for Detecting Fraudulent Financial Reporting*

Recommendations by the National Commission on Fraudulent Financial Reporting

The National Commission on Fraudulent Financial Reporting made a number of recommendations in its report entitled *Report of the National Commission on Fraudulent Financial Reporting.* Among the recommendations that affect the role of the auditor are the following.

1. The Auditing Standards Board should revise the independent public accountant's responsibility for detecting fraudulent financial reporting. This revision should require the independent public accountant to

   a. Take positive steps in each audit to assess the potential for fraudulent financial reporting.

   b. Design tests to provide reasonable assurance of detecting fraudulent financial reporting if it should exist.

   The report also recommended that auditors abandon their traditional assumption of management integrity and, instead, approach the audit with *professional skepticism.*

2. Steps should be taken to improve audit quality. One possible step is to require that all firms auditing companies regulated by the SEC belong to a professional organization that requires the review of their professional work (peer review).

3. The Auditing Standards Board should revise the auditor's standard report to state that the audit provides reasonable but not absolute assurance that the audited financial statements are free from material misstatements as a result of fraud or error. (Chapter 19 contains more on this subject.)

4. The AICPA should reorganize the Auditing Standards Board so that there is more participation by non-CPAs who are affected by and understand auditing standards. The report recommended that the size of the Board be expanded without removing auditing standard-setting from the domain of the accounting profession.

Research Findings

Some accounting organizations have performed research on ways for the auditor to assess the risk that clients engage in fraudulent financial reporting. KPMG Peat Marwick developed a research model that estimates the probability of fraudulent financial reporting based on

1. *Conditions.* The degree to which conditions indicate that a material management fraud could be committed.
2. *Motivation.* The degree to which persons in positions of responsibility in the entity have a reason or motivation to commit management fraud.
3. *Attitude.* The degree to which persons in positions of responsibility in the entity have an attitude or set of ethical values such that they would allow themselves (or even seek) to commit management fraud.

The auditor can use this model by assessing the degree to which each of the above requirements exists and by subjectively combining them. All requirements must be present for a positive likelihood of material management fraud to exist.

FIGURE 5.1   A Model of Indicators of Fraudulent Financial Reporting

---

Conditions

Primary Indicators

1. Management decisions are dominated by one person or a few people acting together.
2. The entity is involved in purchase, sale, or merger activities with another entity.
3. The entity has weak controls.

Secondary Indicators

1. Management has high turnover.
2. The entity is a new client that has never been audited.
3. The entity has had rapid growth in recent years.

Motivation

Primary Indicators

1. The entity's industry is in decline, and its net income relative to the industry is low.
2. The entity has significant contractual commitments.

Secondary Indicators

1. Management compensation is based on recorded performance.
2. The entity faces significant losses from lawsuits.

Attitude

Primary Indicators

1. The auditor has detected a degree of management dishonesty.
2. The entity places undue emphasis on meeting earnings projections.
3. The entity has had fraud in prior years.

Secondary Indicators

1. Management has had frequent disputes with the auditor.
2. The company frequently changes auditors.

The model is developed in more detail by primary and secondary indicators of conditions, motivation, and attitude, as shown in Figure 5.1. The degree to which indicators exist indicates the likelihood of fraudulent financial reporting.

▶ **EXAMPLE**

The major functions of Equity Funding were to sell insurance and investments in mutual funds. During the 1960s Equity Funding's earnings grew. But in the late 1960s and early 1970s mutual funds lost some of their glamour, and interest in this type of investment waned. The management of Equity Funding was unwilling to accept a lower net income in the financial statements. Dummy customers were created and false information was stored in computer files.

Equity Funding cleverly concealed the deception by using a set of computer programs to make the transactions appear real. Large-scale collusion occurred between Equity Funding's officers and computer personnel.

Equity Funding convinced other insurance companies to make advances to it on a coinsurance arrangement. Future premiums were to be used to repay these companies in later years. A sizable percentage of the policies never existed, and future premiums never materialized; these insurance companies incurred significant losses.

ILLEGAL ACTS

The accounting profession has also addressed the question of illegal acts by audit clients, which is a topical issue in view of the public's perceptions about this issue. *SAS No. 54* was issued to define the auditor's responsibilities in this area.

The statement defines *illegal acts* as

violations of laws or governmental regulations by the audited entity or its management or employees acting on behalf of the entity.

Nonbusiness personal misconduct by client personnel is not part of the definition of illegal acts.

Although auditors are in a position to detect the possibility of some illegal acts (e.g., a pay rate for certain employees below the minimum wage), a person qualified in the law must make the final determination as to the illegality of the acts.

The auditor's responsibility for illegal acts falls into two categories:

1. Responsibility for detection.
2. Responsibility for reporting.

Responsibility for Detection

Some laws and regulations have a material and *direct* effect on the amounts in the financial statements. For example, tax laws affect expenses; other laws affect revenue accrued under government contracts. Basically, the auditor's responsibility to detect such illegal acts is the same as for errors and fraud, and is as follows:

> The auditor should assess the risk that illegal acts may have a material and direct effect on the financial statements. Based on that assessment, the auditor should design the audit to provide reasonable assurance of detecting such illegal acts.

Other laws and regulations have a material but *indirect* effect on amounts in the financial statements. Laws and regulations relating to occupational safety and environmental protection are examples. Their indirect effect usually results in the need to disclose a contingent liability because of possible losses from fines, penalties, and terminated operations. The auditor may not know such illegal acts exist unless he or she is informed by the client or in other ways.

Nevertheless, the auditor does have the following responsibility to detect these types of illegal acts:

> The auditor should be aware of the possibility that such illegal acts may have occurred. If specific information comes to the auditor's attention that provides evidence concerning the existence of possible illegal acts that could have a material indirect effect on the financial statements, the auditor should apply audit procedures specifically directed to ascertaining whether an illegal act has occurred.

▶ **EXAMPLE**

The auditor should not attempt to monitor the discharge from a client's plant to test for air or water pollution. However, if the auditor learns from inquiry or a review of documents that the client has been cited by the EPA for pollution, he or she should investigate the matter to attempt to determine if an illegal act has occurred.

Responsibility for Reporting

The auditor's reporting responsibilities are the same whether the illegal act has a material and direct or a material and indirect effect. The audit committee, or other groups with equivalent authority and responsibility, should be informed of illegal acts that come to the auditor's attention. *SAS No. 54* states that

> the communication should describe the act, the circumstances of its occurrence, and the effect on the financial statements. . . . The communication may be oral or written. If the communication is oral, the auditor should document it.

If the illegal act has not been properly accounted for or disclosed in the financial statements, the auditor should express a qualified or adverse opinion. If the client prevents the auditor from obtaining enough evidence to properly evaluate whether a material illegal act has occurred, the auditor should generally disclaim an opinion due to a limitation on the scope of the audit. If the client refuses to accept the auditor's properly modified report (qualified opinion, adverse opinion, or disclaimer of opinion), the auditor should consider withdrawing from the engagement and providing written reasons to the audit committee or the board of directors.

A Summary of the Auditor's Detection and Reporting Responsibilities

Figure 5.2 summarizes the auditor's responsibility to detect and report illegal acts.

FIGURE 5.2   Summary of the Auditor's Responsibility to Detect and Report Illegal Acts

Effect on Financial Statements	Responsibility for Detection of Illegal Act	Responsibility for Reporting if Illegal Act Is Detected
Direct and Material (e.g., a violation of federal income tax laws)	Auditor assesses the risk that illegal acts could have occurred that have a material effect on the financial statements, and plans the audit to provide reasonable assurance of detecting such acts.	Bring the illegal act to the attention of the audit committee. If the illegal act is not properly accounted for or disclosed, express a qualified or adverse opinion. If the client prevents the obtaining of sufficient evidence, express a disclaimer. If the client refuses to accept the modified report, consider withdrawal.
Indirect and Material (e.g., violation of safety, health, or environmental laws)	Auditor does not plan specific procedures but should apply applicable audit procedures if specific information comes to his or her attention indicating that a material and indirect illegal act has occurred.	The same as for material and direct effect illegal acts.

Chapter 5 ▶ GLOSSARY OF TERMS

Errors   Unintentional misstatements or omissions of amounts or disclosures in financial statements.

Financial statement fraud   Another name for fraudulent financial reporting.

Fraud   Intentional misstatements or omissions of amounts or disclosures in financial statements.

Fraudulent financial reporting   Intentional or reckless conduct, whether act or omission, that results in materially misleading financial statements.

Illegal acts   Violations of laws or government regulations by the audited entity or its management or employees acting on behalf of the entity.

National Commission on Fraudulent Financial Reporting (Treadway Commission)   An independent commission created to study and make recommendations on how fraudulent financial reporting could be prevented or detected.

Chapter 5 ▶ REFERENCES

American Institute of Certified Public Accountants, Professional Standards
     AU Section 316—*Consideration of Fraud in a Financial Statement Audit*
     AU Section 317—*Illegal Acts by Clients*
Bull, Ivan. "Board of Director Acceptance of Treadway Responsibilities," *Journal of Accountancy* (February 1991), pp. 67–74.
Neebes, Donald L., Guy, Dan M., and Whittington, O. Ray. "Illegal Acts: What Are the Auditor's Responsibilities?" *Journal of Accountancy* (January 1991), pp. 82–93.
Report of the National Commission on Fraudulent Financial Reporting.

Washington, D.C.: National Commission on Fraudulent Financial Reporting, 1987.
Romney, Marshall. "Computer Fraud—What Can Be Done About It?" *The CPA Journal* (May 1995), pp. 30–33.
Seidman, Jack S. "A Case Study of Employee Fraud," *The CPA Journal* (January 1990), pp. 28–35.
Specht, Linda B. "The Auditor, SAS 54, and Environmental Violations," *Journal of Accountancy* (December 1992), pp. 67–72.
Wells, Joseph T. "Six Common Myths About Fraud," *Journal of Accountancy* (February 1990), pp. 82–88.

Chapter 5 ▶ REVIEW QUESTIONS

5-1 Describe three types of acts by entity personnel that represent errors.

5-2 Describe three types of acts that represent fraud.

5-3 Describe the broad framework of the auditor's responsibility to detect errors and fraud.

5-4 Describe the broad-based matters that the auditor must consider at the financial statement level when deciding on the scope of the audit work necessary to provide reasonable assurance of detecting material errors and fraud.

5-5 Describe the narrowly focused matters that the auditor must consider at the account balance level when deciding on the scope of the audit work necessary to provide reasonable assurance of detecting material errors and fraud.

5-6 What two steps should the auditor take if he or she determines that a difference between amounts on the client's accounting records and audited amounts is fraud that could not be material to the financial statements?

5-7 What four steps should the auditor take if he or she determines that a difference between amounts on the client's accounting records and audited amounts is fraud that could be material to the financial statements?

5-8 What type of audit report should the auditor issue if a material fraud is detected and the financial statements are not revised?

5-9 Give five reasons why fraudulent financial reporting is committed.

5-10 Name two situations that will increase the risk of fraudulent financial reporting.

5-11 Describe three risk factors relating to fraudulent financial reporting.

5-12 Describe four recommendations made by the National Commission on Fraudulent Financial Reporting.

5-13 Fraudulent financial reporting has been described as a function of three requirements. Describe these requirements (not the primary or secondary indicators of each requirement).

5-14 Describe the two types of illegal acts.

5-15 Summarize the auditor's detection and reporting responsibilities for each of the two types of illegal acts.

Chapter 5 ▶ OBJECTIVE QUESTIONS

(* = author prepared; ** = CPA examination)

*5-16 Which of the following is not an example of an error?
     a. Entity personnel make mistakes in gathering or processing accounting data from which financial statements are prepared.
     b. Entity personnel alter accounting records from which financial statements are prepared.
     c. Entity personnel overlook or misinterpret facts, causing accounting estimates to be incorrect.

    d. Entity personnel make mistakes in the application of accounting principles.

*5-17 Which of the following is an incorrect statement?

    a. The auditor should assess the risk that errors and fraud may cause the financial statements to contain a material misstatement.

    b. The auditor should design the audit to provide reasonable assurance of detecting errors and fraud that are material to the financial statements.

    c. The auditor is not an insurer, and his or her report does not constitute a guarantee.

    d. The subsequent discovery that a material misstatement exists in the financial statements is evidence of inadequate planning, performance, or judgment on the part of the auditor.

**5-18 Which of the following statements concerning illegal acts by clients is correct?

    a. An auditor's responsibility to detect illegal acts that have a direct and material effect on the financial statements is the same as an auditor's responsibility for errors and fraud.

    b. An audit in accordance with generally accepted auditing standards normally includes audit procedures specifically designed to detect illegal acts that have an indirect but material effect on the financial statements.

    c. An auditor considers illegal acts from the perspective of the reliability of management's representations rather than their relation to audit objectives derived from financial statement assertions.

    d. An auditor has no responsibility to detect illegal acts by clients that have an indirect effect on the financial statements.

**5-19 When an auditor becomes aware of a possible illegal act by a client, the auditor should obtain an understanding of the nature of the act to

    a. Increase the assessed level of control risk.

    b. Recommend remedial actions to the audit committee.

    c. Evaluate the effect on the financial statements.

    d. Determine the reliability of management's representations.

**5-20 What assurance does the auditor provide that errors, fraud, and direct-effect illegal acts that are material to the financial statements will be detected?

    a. Negative.

    b. Limited.

    c. Absolute.

    d. Reasonable.

**5-21 Which of the following statements best describes an auditor's responsibility to detect errors and fraud?

    a. The auditor should study and evaluate the client's internal control, and design the audit to provide reasonable assurance of detecting all errors and fraud.

    b. The auditor should assess the risk that errors and fraud may cause the financial statements to contain material misstatements, and determine whether the necessary internal controls are prescribed and are being followed satisfactorily.

    c. The auditor should consider the types of errors and fraud that could occur, and determine whether the necessary internal controls are prescribed and are being followed.

    d. The auditor should assess the risk that errors and fraud may cause the financial statements to contain material misstatements, and design the audit to provide reasonable assurance of detecting material errors and fraud.

**5-22 Which of the following statements describes why a properly designed and executed audit may *not* detect a material fraud?

    a. Audit procedures that are effective for detecting an unintentional misstatement may be ineffective for an intentional misstatement that is concealed through collusion.

    b. An audit is designed to provide reasonable assurance of detecting material errors, but there is no similar responsibility concerning material fraud.

    c. The factors considered in assessing control risk indicated an increased risk of intentional misstatements, but only a low risk of unintentional errors in the financial statements.

    d. The auditor did not consider factors influencing audit risk for account balances that have pervasive effects on the financial statements taken as a whole.

**5-23 An auditor concludes that a client's illegal act, which has a material effect on the financial statements, has not been properly accounted for or disclosed. Depending on the materiality of the effect on the financial statements, the auditor should express either a(an)

    a. Adverse opinion or a disclaimer of opinion.

    b. Qualified opinion or an adverse opinion.

    c. Disclaimer of opinion or an unqualified opinion with a separate explanatory paragraph.

    d. Unqualified opinion with a separate explanatory paragraph or a qualified opinion.

**5-24 Which of the following characteristics most likely would heighten an auditor's concern about the risk of intentional manipulation of financial statements?

a. Turnover of senior accounting personnel is low.

b. Insiders recently purchased additional shares of the entity's stock.

c. Management places substantial emphasis on meeting earnings projections.

d. The rate of change in the entity's industry is slow.

**5-25 Which of the following statements reflects an auditor's responsibility for detecting errors and fraud?

a. An auditor is responsible for detecting employee errors and simple fraud, but *not* for discovering fraud involving employee collusion or management override.

b. An auditor should plan the audit to detect errors and fraud that are caused by departures from GAAP.

c. An auditor is *not* responsible for detecting errors and fraud unless the application of GAAS would result in such detection.

d. An auditor should design the audit to provide reasonable assurance of detecting errors and fraud that are material to the financial statements.

**5-26 During the annual audit of Ajax Corp., a publicly held company, Jones, CPA, a continuing auditor, determined that illegal political contributions had been made during each of the past seven years, including the year under audit. Jones notified the board of directors about the illegal contributions, but they refused to take any action be-

cause the amounts involved were immaterial to the financial statements.

Jones should reconsider the intended degree of reliance to be placed on the

a. Letter of audit inquiry to the client's attorney.

b. Prior years' audit programs.

c. Management representation letter.

d. Preliminary judgment about materiality levels.

**5-27 Jones, CPA, is auditing the financial statements of XYZ Retailing, Inc. What assurance does Jones provide that direct effect illegal acts that are material to XYZ's financial statements, and illegal acts that have a material, but indirect effect on the financial statements will be detected?

	Direct effect illegal acts	*Indirect effect illegal acts*
a.	Reasonable	None
b.	Reasonable	Reasonable
c.	Limited	None
d.	Limited	Reasonable

**5-28 An auditor concludes that a client has committed an illegal act that has not been properly accounted for or disclosed. The auditor should withdraw from the engagement if the

a. Auditor is precluded from obtaining sufficient competent evidence about the illegal act.

b. Illegal act has an effect on the financial statements that is both material and direct.

c. Auditor cannot reasonably estimate the effect of the illegal act on the financial statements.

d. Client refuses to accept the auditor's report as modified for the illegal act.

Chapter 5 ▶ DISCUSSION/CASE QUESTIONS

(* = author prepared; ** = CPA examination; *** = CMA examination)

*5-29 John Petite was performing his first audit as a senior. His client was a small toy store with a reputation as a solid and expanding merchandiser. John's CPA firm had performed the audit for several years, and very few problems had been encountered. There was no reason to believe this audit would be different.

John arrived at the client's place of business and waited for the office manager to introduce himself. The office manager appeared in a few minutes looking very distraught. He pulled the door shut and asked to speak confidentially to John. As far as John could tell from the fractured conversation, the following events had occurred:

1. The cashier had confessed to theft of sizable amounts of money, taken over a period of several months.

2. No one knew about the theft except the office manager and the clerk who kept the cash receipts journal.

3. The fraud had been discovered when this clerk had been assigned the task of reconciling the bank statement, a task normally assigned to the cashier. It seems that the cashier had been improperly endorsing and keeping customer checks that arrived a day or two before statements were mailed to customers.

4. The fraud had been covered by preparing fictitious deposit slips to compare with the record of cash receipts. By reconciling the bank statement, the underdeposit of cash receipts could be hidden. Customers rarely complained about receiving a statement with no credit for cash payments because they assumed that the next statement would show the proper amount of credit.

The office manager explained what had happened and asked John to begin the audit somewhere other than with cash. He told John that as soon as the matter was resolved and the books corrected, the cash part of the audit could be performed. The office manager also explained to John that nothing about this theft was being reported to upper-level management, and he asked John to refrain from discussing it with any other member of the company.

Required:

a. How should John reply to these requests by the office manager?

b. What should John do? Why?

*5-30 During the audit of Irreg. Company, Betty Bestow was examining the endorsements on payroll checks and comparing the endorsements to the names of the payees on the face of the checks. In prior audits, there had been no comparison of endorsements with authorized signatures of employees kept on file in the personnel office.

Betty noticed that a remarkable number of endorsements looked like the writing of the same person. On a hunch, she checked the signature of the payroll supervisor in the personnel office and discovered that his signature was similar to those on the suspicious checks. Betty traced all of these checks to the personnel files and found that all of them were written to recently terminated employees.

Required:

a. To whom should Betty report this apparent fraud?

b. Betty's first inclination was to show these checks to the payroll supervisor, thinking that the matter could easily be resolved. Should Betty do this? Why or why not?

c. What additional procedures should Betty perform to investigate this matter?

d. How could this fraud affect the fairness of the financial statements?

*5-31 Warren Presit was the senior in charge of the audit of Put-on, Inc., a maker of men's fashion shoes. He had instructed his assistant, Stephie Scent, to examine support for every sales invoice recorded during the last week of the year under audit to determine whether these invoices represented legitimate sales for the year.

Stephie compared each sales invoice with a shipping document, noting whether the shipment took place before or after year-end. During the examination, she noted that several sales invoices had no shipping documents. She asked the personnel in the shipping department about this oddity and received a shrug of the shoulders and a somewhat cool response.

Stephie took the sales invoices to Warren who, in turn, took them to the controller asking for an explanation. The controller, looking rather contrite, explained that their practice was to prepare "advance invoices" for customers who regularly purchased the same type and quantity of merchandise each month. When Warren pressed the issue, the controller explained that sickness among shipping personnel had put the shipping schedule behind and that these particular shipments would be made soon.

Warren suggested that an adjustment should be made reversing the charge to accounts receivable and the credit to sales for the total amount of these invoices. The controller became irritated and asserted that these invoices were legitimate sales and that the company should not be penalized because of sickness among shipping personnel.

Warren tried to be polite but refused to give in to the demand that the revenue be allowed to remain recorded in this year's financial statements. Finally, the controller calmed down and suggested a compromise. An adjustment would be made taking the revenue out of this year's financial statements, but a footnote would be put in the financial statements stating that $100,000 of revenue were deferred to next year because of scheduling problems in shipping the merchandise. Warren considered the proposal for a few minutes and indicated that he would give the controller an answer later.

Required:

a. Was Warren correct in refusing to accept amounts from these sales invoices as revenue of the accounting period under audit? Why or why not?

b. Would it be acceptable for Warren to agree to this footnote in the financial statements? Why or why not?

c. Assuming that Warren agrees to the footnote, indicate what evidence Warren must gather to validate the revenue on the invoices as legitimate revenue of the next accounting period.

d. Write the footnote, assuming Warren accepts a footnote.

*5-32   Smog, Inc. is a manufacturer of equipment designed to limit emissions from the tailpipes of automobiles. An audit of the financial statements of Smog, Inc. was being performed by Clean & Clean, a regional CPA firm.

Felicia Fogg, the senior in charge of the audit, was examining the income tax liability account and tracing items in the account balance to supporting evidence. Near the end of her examination, she noticed several thousand dollars of charges and tax deductions for a resort condo in Florida. She inquired about these charges and was told that they were legitimate tax deductions and would remain as such.

Felicia raised the matter with one of the CPA firm's tax partners who did extensive research in the tax code and concluded that the charges were not tax-deductible. Felicia returned to the client with this opinion from the tax partner but was told bluntly that the charges would remain as a tax deduction.

Meanwhile, Alex Took, an assistant on the audit, accidentally discovered a report by the Environmental Protection Agency questioning the quality of some of Smog, Inc.'s emission equipment. He took this information to Felicia who dismissed it as minor and outside the scope of their audit. Alex dropped the matter and made no mention of it in the audit working papers.

Required:

a. Indicate whether each of the two matters directly or indirectly affects the financial statements. Why?

b. Evaluate Felicia's reaction to each matter.

***5-33   The studies conducted by the Treadway Commission revealed that fraudulent financial reporting usually occurs as the result of certain environmental, institutional, or individual influences and opportune situations. These influences and opportunities, present to some degree in all companies, add pressures and motivate individuals and companies to engage in fraudulent financial reporting. The effective prevention and detection of fraudulent financial reporting requires an understanding of these influences and opportunities, while evalu-

ating the risk of fraudulent financial reporting that these factors can create in a company. The risk factors to be assessed include not only internal ethical and control factors, but also external environmental conditions.

Required:

a. Identify two situational pressures in a public company that would increase the likelihood of fraud.

b. Identify three corporate circumstances (opportune situations) when fraud is easier to commit and when detection is less likely.

c. For the purpose of assessing the risk of fraudulent financial reporting, identify the external environmental factors that should be considered in the company's

    1. Industry.

    2. Business environment.

    3. Legal and regulatory environment.

***5-34 In the last decade, there has been significant growth in the number and size of legal actions against accounting firms. A study of several years' lawsuits suggests that auditors' legal problems arose from five major types of lawsuits, of which two, client fraud and fraud by the auditor, represented 20 percent of all litigation. The public's perception of the role of the independent auditor differs from that of the auditing profession. Many parties believe that the auditors should search diligently for material client errors, fraud, and illegal acts, that is, be the "guarantors" of external financial information, while many auditors contend that management has the responsibility for reported financial information. To clarify the auditor's role, the auditing profession has issued standards that (1) define the auditor's responsibility for detecting errors, fraud, and illegal acts by clients and (2) outline procedures to be followed when an audit suggests that one or more of these conditions may exist.

Required:

a. 1. Define "errors." *un intentional*

    2. Define "fraud." *intentional*

    3. Outline the procedures that external auditors should follow when errors or fraud are suspected.

b. 1. Define "illegal acts."

    2. Identify the circumstances that make "illegal acts" more difficult to detect than "errors" and "fraud."

c. Situational pressures on a company or an individual manager may lead to fraudulent financial reporting. Describe several situational pressures that the auditor should give attention to as potential indicators of fraudulent reporting.

*5-35
(Continuing Case—Part V)

Modern Office Furnishings, Inc. (MOF) is a relatively small public company. Its stock is listed on the NASDAQ national exchange. MOF manufactures and sells a limited variety of office furnishings such as desks, chairs, tables, and lamps, with particular emphasis on furniture that is computer compatible (e.g., desks designed to accommodate computer monitors, keyboards, and printers). The company negotiated a contract this year with Advanced Computer Systems to produce computer surge protectors (i.e., electronic devices that protect computer equipment from surges in electric current). This contract is the company's first attempt at electronics manufacturing. MOF markets its office furnishings through wholesale and discount retail businesses. Its largest customer is Wal-Mart Stores. All of its surge protectors are sold to Advanced Computer Systems.

The company began operations in 1979. At that time it was named Custom Furniture

Company, and it sold household furnishings. In 1992 a group of venture capital investors acquired the company, changed its name and product lines, and sold 20 percent of its outstanding stock in an initial public offering. The initial public offering price was $10 per share. After trading as high as $12 per share, the stock has traded in a range of $6 to $8 per share for the last year. The venture capital group continues to control the company through control of the board of directors.

In the past two years, 1996 and 1997, the economy has been in a long recovery phase after the recession of 1994 and 1995. Gross National Product, the overall gauge of production of goods and services in the U. S. economy, rose by an inflation-adjusted 3 percent in 1997. Inflation, which was low in 1994 and 1995, was 5 percent in 1997, but this increase was not felt in the office furnishings industry. Industry sales tend to be dependent on new business startups, which in turn are affected by interest rates. Long-term interest rates have moved up slightly in the past six months.

A new chief executive officer, John Smith, was selected in February 1997. The previous CEO left because of a disagreement with the Board of Directors over the desirability of expanding into electronics manufacturing. The previous CEO opposed such expansion as too risky, but Smith, who at the time was vice president of marketing, supported the expansion. The expansion plans are presently being implemented. Smith has been with the company for three years. Prior to that he was a marketing manager for an advertising agency. The position of vice president of marketing was not filled because Smith will continue to perform that function. As part of his compensation package Smith was granted options to purchase 20,000 shares of stock at an option price of $9 per share. The option expires in five years. Additionally, Smith is eligible for a cash bonus of 3 percent of the excess of net income before taxes over $3,000,000.

The chief financial officer, Tracy Adamson, has been with the company only a short time. She was hired after the previous CFO resigned with the previous CEO. Prior to this, Adamson was employed as an accounting clerk with a local utility company. As part of her compensation package she was granted options to purchase 8,000 shares of stock at an option price of $9 per share. The option expires in five years.

Charles Pendley, vice president of production, is in charge of plant operations and has been with the company from its inception.

Mary Pinkerton, treasurer, supervises the deposits and disbursements of cash, custody of securities, and reconciliation of bank statements. Pinkerton has been treasurer for two years.

Required:

Refer to Figure 5.1 in the text. Give as many examples as you can of indicators of fraudulent financial reporting. Give reasons for your examples.

Audit Objectives and Audit Documentation

"The very volume of documentation required today and the highly structured system developed to obtain, compile, and review it can lull unwary auditors—and even normally careful ones—into focusing on the road they are traveling rather than on where they are actually going."

HALL AND RENNER, *"Lessons Auditors Ignore at Their Own Risk"*

LEARNING OBJECTIVES

After reading and studying the material in this chapter, the student should be able to

- ► Write in one sentence each, definitions of each of the five general assertions.
- ► Write a brief paragraph assessing the way auditors reason from management assertions to audit objectives to audit procedures.
- ► Describe the difference between control risk assessment procedures and substantive tests.
- ► Describe the differences between tests of details of transactions and balances and analytical procedures.
- ► Provide the general guidelines of working paper content.
- ► Give five examples of permanent audit files.
- ► Analyze the triangle of working papers in current audit files by writing brief descriptions of audit trial balances, lead schedules, and detailed schedules.

In this chapter we discuss the general audit objectives that are applicable to the audits of financial statement account balances. Audit documentation of the results of applying the audit procedures is also presented. Audit objectives and audit documentation are introduced at this point because they will be referred to and used in most of the following chapters.

OVERALL AUDIT OBJECTIVE

(In an ordinary financial statement audit, the *overall audit objective* is the expression of an opinion on the fairness with which the financial statements present financial position, results of operations, and cash flows in conformity with generally accepted accounting principles. The auditor does not express an opinion on individual accounts or footnotes but only on their presentation in the aggregate. Nevertheless, auditors must perform an audit sufficient to satisfy themselves regarding all material account balances and disclosures to serve as a basis for their opinion on the financial statements taken as a whole. 7

ASSERTIONS FOR ACCOUNT BALANCES AND DISCLOSURES

The financial statements, including the individual account balances and disclosures, are the representations of management. Management is responsible for recording, processing, summarizing, and reporting the financial information.[1] When preparing financial statements, management (implicitly or explicitly) makes certain assertions regarding the account balances and related disclosures. The auditor determines the objectives of auditing each account by relating them to management's *assertions,* that is, the *auditor's objectives* are to determine if management's assertions are valid. The five general assertions (which are related to audit objectives) are:

1. **Existence or occurrence.** Management asserts that all assets, liabilities, and equity accounts in the balance sheet *exist* and that all revenues, expenses, gains, and losses in the income statement *occurred* during the period covered by the financial statements. For example, management asserts that inventories physically exist and accounts payable are legal liabilities at a given date and that sales and operating expenses actually occurred during a given period.

2. **Rights and obligations.** Management asserts that the entity *owns* the unimpaired rights to assets and that it *owes* the liabilities shown in the financial statements. For example, management asserts that the entity has unencumbered title to inventories, and accounts payable are actually owed to other parties.

3. **Completeness.** Management asserts that the financial statements include *all* assets, liabilities, equity, revenue, expenses, gains, and losses. For example, management asserts that there are no unrecorded inventories or accounts payable and all sales and operating expenses that occurred are included in the income statement.

4. **Valuation or allocation.** Management asserts that assets, liabilities, equity, revenue, expenses, gains, and losses are presented in the financial statements *at appropriate amounts.* For most general-purpose financial statements, appropriate amounts are those determined in conformity with generally accepted accounting principles. For example, management asserts that inventory is valued at the lower of first-in first-out cost or market, and the allocation of property and equipment cost in the form of depreciation expense is made in the appropriate amounts to the proper periods.

5. **Presentation and disclosure.** Management asserts that financial statement

---

[1] Auditors often participate in drafting the financial statements, but the statements remain the responsibility of management.

amounts are *properly classified* and that *disclosures conform* with those required by generally accepted accounting principles. For example, management asserts that inventory classified as a current asset is expected to be sold within one year or the normal operating cycle and any pledging of inventory to collateralize debt is adequately disclosed.

The auditor's objectives in the audit of each account are to determine whether management's assertions concerning the account are valid. Within this general framework, each individual account may be analyzed to determine specific objectives.

In some cases, the auditor must determine the proper accounting treatment for the financial statement item either by reference to official pronouncements or by a knowledge of the "generally accepted" accounting principle to establish his or her objective. One specific objective in auditing inventory is to ascertain that the amount of inventory shown on the balance sheet is stated at the lower of cost or market, by use of one of the generally accepted pricing methods. This objective, in turn, relates to the assertion of valuation (i.e., determining that the inventory is valued properly).

In other cases, the specific objectives flow naturally from the assertions. Again with inventory as an example, the assertion of existence leads to the specific objective of determining whether the inventory amount on the balance sheet is represented by physical items actually on hand, in transit, or on consignment. By this approach, the auditor can arrive at the following specific objectives for the audit of inventories.

1. Determine whether the inventory amount on the balance sheet is represented by all physical items actually on hand, in transit, or on consignment (existence and completeness).
2. Determine whether the inventory is calculated properly at the lower of cost or market in accordance with generally accepted accounting principles (valuation).
3. Determine whether the inventory belongs to the company and whether any liens on the inventory are disclosed properly (rights and disclosure).
4. Determine whether any excess, slow-moving, or special-purpose items are properly valued and classified (valuation and presentation).

A similar approach may be used to arrive at the audit objectives for other financial statement amounts.

The Assertions Approach to Auditing   Auditors sometimes begin their work by performing commonly applied audit procedures without first considering what they are attempting to accomplish for each account and then determining the most efficient and effective way to proceed. Only by considering the assertions applicable to each account can an auditor know whether appropriate audit procedures have been planned and performed. Similarly, by considering assertions, the auditor can avoid excess work that does not contribute to testing their validity.

OTHER AUDIT ASSERTIONS

In addition to assertions relating to specific accounts, management makes assertions that may apply to several accounts or to the financial statements in general. Examples of the assertions are:

1. The accounting principles used to prepare the financial statements are not materially different from those used in the prior period unless a difference is disclosed. Changes in accounting principles between years can cause changes in financial position and results of operations that are not the result of real economic factors. To alert readers of financial statements to changes in accounting principles, such changes must be described in footnotes to the financial statements and referenced in the auditor's report. Therefore, auditors compare accounting principles used in the current year with those used in the prior year.

2. Transactions summarized in the financial statements occurred between independent parties unless related party transactions are disclosed. Transactions between related parties are not the result of arms-length negotiations and are subject to manipulation by the parties. For this reason, generally accepted accounting principles require the disclosure of related party transactions. Auditors must be alert for such transactions when performing the audit.

3. The entity will continue as a going concern for at least one year from the balance sheet date unless an exception to this assumption is disclosed. A basic assumption underlying the presentation of financial statements of an entity is that it will continue as a going concern. That assumption permits assets to be presented at historical cost (if an entity will not continue as a going concern, liquidating values may be more appropriate) and assets and liabilities to be classified as long and short term (there is no long term if an entity will be in existence for only a few months). As discussed in Chapter 13, auditors have a responsibility to evaluate the going concern status of an entity as part of every audit.

4. The entity has complied with applicable laws and regulations unless material noncompliance together with its effect on the financial statements is disclosed. Failure of an entity to comply with laws and regulations may result in contingent and direct liabilities that should be shown in the financial statements. Auditors perform procedures to test the assertion that management has complied with applicable laws and regulations.

DERIVATION OF AUDIT PROCEDURES
FROM AUDIT OBJECTIVES

After the audit objectives have been determined, the next step is to define the *audit procedures* that will accomplish the specified objectives. Auditors reason from an audit objective to audit procedures that will provide evidence regarding an assertion. No one set or official list of audit procedures can be used on each audit because the nature of the accounts and their risk and materiality vary. For example, the procedures for the audit of inventory existence and valuation of a manufacturer of a complex product with several stages of production and a sophisticated standard cost system would be different from those for a company whose inventory consists of a large pile of coal. Also, if inventory is an immaterial amount in the financial statements, only a few limited procedures may need to be applied to this account.

There is no table in professional standards indicating the percentage of inventory items to be counted or accounts receivable to be confirmed. Some accounting firms have developed structured decision aids to attempt to quantify the effectiveness of the internal controls and the extent of audit procedures. Judgment, however, with a tempering of experience, remains the basis for determining the extent of audit procedures. Exercise of this judgment is one trademark of a professional.

AUDIT PROCEDURES FOR CONTROL RISK ASSESSMENT AND SUBSTANTIVE TESTS

Auditors perform audit procedures to assess control risk and to evaluate the amounts and disclosures in the financial statements. The former are called *control risk assessment procedures,* and the latter are called *substantive tests.* Control risk assessment procedures consist of (1) procedures to obtain an understanding of internal controls and (2) tests of controls on which some reliance will be placed. Substantive tests consist of tests of details of transactions and balances and analytical procedures.

Figure 6.1 shows the general relationship between these types of evidence. Notice that the choices are to

FIGURE 6.1   General Relationship Between Control Risk Assessment Procedures and Substantive Tests

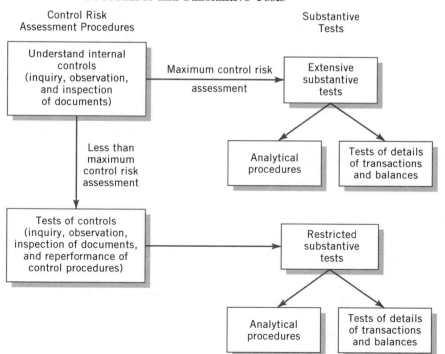

1. Perform *extensive* (many) substantive tests.
2. Perform *restricted* (some) substantive tests.

Control Risk Assessment Procedures

Auditors use control risk assessment procedures to obtain an understanding of internal controls (inquiry, observation, and inspection of documents) and perform *tests of controls* (inquiry, observation, inspection of documents, and reperformance of control procedures). Evidence of the performance of these procedures includes memoranda, flowcharts, questionnaires, and listings of transactions as discussed in Chapter 9.

Tests of Details of Transactions and Balances

These tests are performed to obtain evidence as to whether management's assertions regarding the financial statement balances and disclosures are valid. They include observation of inventory counts, confirmation of accounts receivable balances with customers, inquiry regarding collectibility of accounts receivable, and examination of vendor invoices for operating expenses.

Analytical Procedures

Analytical procedures involve the study and comparison of relationships among data to identify fluctuations that are not expected, the absence of fluctuations that are expected, or other unusual items. The auditor develops expectations based on an understanding of the client's operations and the industry in which it operates. These expectations are then compared with amounts recorded by the client. The expectations may be developed from the following sources:

1. Financial information for prior periods, after giving effect to known changes.
2. Anticipated amounts such as budgets and forecasts.
3. Relationships among elements within the financial statements.
4. Industry averages and standards.
5. Nonfinancial information such as number of units shipped or square feet of shelf space.

All significant variations and fluctuations between auditor expectations and client records should be investigated and resolved.

Because analytical procedures are intended to disclose unusual items, they are *required* to be employed in the planning stage of the audit so that audit programs can be designed to concentrate work in areas that appear unusual. They *may* be employed as substantive tests during the audit to obtain evidence and support or confirm other audit findings. They are *required* to be used in the overall review stage at the end of the audit to see that all unusual items were properly investigated.

Tests with Dual Purposes

In practice, control risk assessment tests and substantive tests often overlap if auditors design procedures to achieve objectives of both types of tests concurrently. For example, when auditors trace a sample of entries from the cash receipts listings to the customer ledger accounts, they may be accomplishing two objectives.

1. They are assessing the control risk that the prescribed posting procedures are not functioning. If too many errors are found, the auditors may conclude that the risk that the procedures are not functioning is high.

2. They are performing a substantive test to help them form a conclusion as to whether accounts receivable exist. If errors are found when the transactions are traced from the receipt listings to the customer ledger accounts, the auditor may conclude that the account balance is in error.

AUDIT DOCUMENTATION

An auditor must document the audit procedures performed to support the understanding, tests, and evaluation of risks and the substantive tests performed directly on the amounts and disclosures shown in the financial statements. This evidence is accumulated in files of audit working papers. Although the term *working papers* suggests paper documents, much audit evidence now exists only in electronic files. A number of accounting firms are now developing paperless auditing systems. Spreadsheets, text, checklists, and other evidence are prepared and saved in an electronic format. Even confirmation letters from outside parties can be electronically scanned into the audit files. The term *working papers* is used here to include all audit documentation, both electronic and paper.

Definition and Purposes of Working Papers

For auditors to conduct their audit properly and provide adequate support for their opinion, they must prepare audit *working papers.*

Working papers are records kept by the auditor of the procedures applied, the tests performed, the information obtained, and the pertinent conclusions reached in the engagement.

Working papers should be sufficient to show that the financial statements or other information on which the auditor is reporting were in agreement with (or reconciled with) the client's records. Listed below are *general* guidelines as to what working papers should include or show.

1. The work has been adequately planned and supervised, indicating observance of the first standard of fieldwork.

2. A sufficient understanding of the internal controls has been obtained to plan the audit and to determine the nature, timing, and extent of tests to be performed, indicating observance of the second standard of fieldwork.

3. The audit evidence obtained, the auditing procedures applied, and the testing performed have provided sufficient competent evidential matter to afford a reasonable basis for an opinion, indicating observance of the third standard of fieldwork.

(In summary, properly prepared working papers are necessary for an auditor to demonstrate compliance with the standards of fieldwork. They should show how the work was planned (e.g., the use of audit programs) and the extent of supervision of assistants (indication of reviews made by the auditor). They should contain sufficient, competent evidence (e.g., control risk checklists, confirmations from creditors, bank reconciliations) on which to base an opinion.)

Comment   If an auditor's performance is challenged, the audit working papers are both a potential strength and a potential vulnerability. Professional standards require an auditor to obtain sufficient audit evidence to afford a reasonable basis for his or her audit opinion. Proof of fulfillment of that standard requires documentation of the audit work. The auditor's ability to defend the audit opinion is likely to depend on the adequacy or inadequacy of the working papers. An audit that was adequate in fact may be inadequate in law because of a failure of proof through lack of documentation.

R. James Gormley, *The Law of Accountants and Auditors*

Ownership of Working Papers

Working papers prepared by an auditor in connection with his or her audit of a client's financial statements are generally the property of the auditor. The client normally has no claim to the working papers, regardless of the fact that he or she paid the auditor to perform the audit for which the working papers are prepared. Working papers generally are not "privileged" in the manner of communications between an attorney and his or her client, and must be surrendered in response to a subpoena or other legal action. This means that information obtained by an auditor during an audit of financial statements could be used against the auditor or the client in a legal proceeding. Even though the working papers belong to the auditor, he or she is required to comply with the confidentiality requirements of Rule 301 of the AICPA *Code of Professional Conduct,* as discussed in Chapter 3.

Importance of Working Papers

Audit working papers constitute the auditor's evidence of the work performed; they may be either helpful or detrimental if problems subsequently arise concerning the audited financial statements. They will become the most important documents involved in any subsequent litigation, and, because they are subject to subpoena, they may provide evidence for the plaintiff or prosecution as well as for the auditor's defense.

It is unfortunate that the term *working papers* is used to describe the evidence that an auditor accumulates during an audit of financial statements. The term connotes an unfinished product such as an accumulation of preliminary notes and calculations on scratch pads. Though only a very imprudent auditor would prepare working papers in such a manner, many auditors are not as careful as they should be. For example, an auditor may spend many hours considering a serious accounting or reporting problem of a client, but make only a brief note of the conclusion once it is reached. Without evidence to show the careful consideration given the problem, it may appear later that only superficial thought was given to it. Even if working papers are complete, inadequate preparation will cast doubt on them. An adversary attorney might use such working papers to attempt to demonstrate a careless approach to the audit. Auditors must keep in mind that they may not be the only ones to read the working papers they prepare, and they must consider the impression others might gain from reading them.

Types of Working Papers

Auditors normally maintain two types of working paper files. One is referred to as a permanent or continuing audit file, and the other often is called the current-year audit file.

Permanent Audit Files

The *permanent audit file* is composed of documents, schedules, and other data that will be of continuing significance to several years' audits. For example, an auditor must obtain a copy or extract of a client's articles of incorporation as evidence of the types (common and preferred), par values, and number of authorized shares of stock that the company may issue, as well as restrictions on payment of dividends, purchase of treasury stock, or other matters requiring disclosure in the financial statements. Rather than obtaining a copy or extract of the same document each year, the auditor places one copy in the permanent file, which is a part of each year's audit evidence. Of course, it is necessary to check each year for any amendment to the articles of incorporation and to indicate any changes on the document in the permanent file. Amendments normally would be detected by the auditor during his or her review of minutes of stockholders' and directors' meetings, because approval generally is required by one or both of these bodies.

Although the organization of permanent files varies, most would contain the following sections:

1. **Historical information regarding the client.** This section usually includes a memorandum describing the company and its operations, major plants and manufacturing processes, and products, distribution facilities, and important customers. An organization chart listing the names and positions of key officers and employees and any recurring audit administrative matters are also shown. This type of information is particularly important to auditors assigned to a client for the first time. It allows them to learn something about the operations of the company in a brief period of time and makes them aware of any unusual matters concerning the audit, such as timing deadlines and reporting requirements. The client is saved the task of acquainting different members of the auditing firm with basic information about the company. A partial example of such a memorandum follows.

X Co.
Company Operation
and
Audit Administration Memo

X Co. was formed in 19X0 by Mr. Fitzgerald and Mr. Hamilton, both of whom remain 50% stockholders. X Co. operates a 40,000 barrel per day refinery near Granville, Arkansas (also the location of its administrative offices), at the intersection of Highways 65 and 71. The President and Plant Manager is Mr. Foote and the Treasurer, with whom we arrange the timing of our work, is Ms. Johnson. The company acquires most of its raw materials (crude oil) in the open market and is subject to the regulations of the Department of Energy (a copy of the DOE regulations is filed behind this memo). The crude oil is refined into premium and regular gasoline, which is sold to a chain of independent gasoline stations. The company reports on a December 31 fiscal year. Our audit report is to be delivered to the shareholders by February 10. In the past we have experienced difficulty and delay in obtaining confirmation of a significant accounts receivable from the chain of independent gasoline stations, so we must be sure to mail the confirmation at the earliest possible date and include sufficient details to. . . .

By reading the memorandum, an auditor who had never worked on the X Company engagement would know where the company is located and what it does, whom to contact at the company, what some of the important reporting and timing requirements are, and that he or she would need a knowledge of DOE regulations in the audit.

2. **A description of the entity's internal controls.** This material might consist of narrative descriptions of the client's control environment, accounting and control procedures, internal control questionnaires, flowcharts, decision tables, or any combination of these items. A chart of accounts and samples of any records or forms that would aid in understanding company procedures may also be included. A brief example of a description of accounting procedures relating to notes payable and long-term debt follows.

X Co.
Procedures for Notes Payable
and
Long-Term Debt

X Co. has outstanding a $5 million issue of 8% bonds due in installments of $500,000 per year beginning in 20X2. All refinery property and equipment is pledged to these bonds. The bond indenture restricts payment of dividends to $200,000 per year. The company also borrows on short-term notes for working capital purposes.

   All borrowings are authorized by the Board of Directors, and the banks or other creditors are specifically mentioned in the minutes. Both the President and the Treasurer must sign any notes that are issued. The Treasurer maintains a schedule showing the due dates of all bond, note, and interest payments. . . .

Internal control questionnaires and flowcharts are shown in Chapter 9.

3. **Legal documents.** In addition to the articles of incorporation, the permanent file normally contains copies or extracts of loan agreements, bond indentures, labor contracts, stock option plans, pension plans, important long-term op-

erating agreements or contracts, and other documents. Because all of these documents could significantly affect the company's operations and its financial statements, the auditor must have evidence of the provisions of these documents and of his or her reviews thereof.

4. **Continuing analyses of certain accounts.** It is often more efficient to maintain cumulative or carry-forward schedules in the permanent files for certain accounts with little activity, or for which comparisons with several prior years are helpful, than to prepare such schedules each year in the current files. Continuing analysis might be used for capital stock, long-term debt, checklists for compliance with loan agreements, net operating loss carry-forward schedule, equity in earnings of subsidiaries, and gross profit ratios by major product class. An illustration of such an analysis is shown in the following table.

X Co.
Analyses of Uncollectible Accounts

For the year	19X5	19X6	19X7	19X8
Sales	$4,365,000	$5,837,000	$5,679,000	$5,928,000
Bad debt provision	54,000	68,000	63,000	71,000
Bad debt charge-offs	54,000	67,000	63,000	91,000
Accounts receivable balance 12-31				
Current	$372,000	$498,000	$501,000	$530,000
30–60 days	31,000	54,000	53,000	57,000
Over 60 days	2,000	19,000	16,000	52,000
Total	$405,000	$571,000	$570,000	$639,000
Allowance for doubtful accounts	$30,000	$35,000	$35,000	$15,000
Ratios—				
Bad debt charge-offs to sales	1.2%	1.1%	1.1%	1.5%
Allowance to total accounts receivable	7.4%	6.1%	6.1%	2.3%
Allowance to accounts receivable over 60 days	15.0	1.8	2.2	0.3
Days' sales in accounts receivable	33.9	35.7	36.6	39.3

This analysis should alert the auditor that there has been a deterioration in accounts receivable during the year, and it should raise a question as to the adequacy of the allowance for doubtful accounts.

5. **Audit planning.** This section would include a master copy of the audit program (often on computer diskettes) that could be revised and copied each year rather than completely rewritten; schedules of plant capacity and volumes of tanks, bins, and other containers (an auditor would be embarrassed to discover, after being satisfied as to inventory, that his or her client did not have the physical capacity to store the amount of inventory shown in the accounting records); and, if certain procedures are performed on a rotating basis, a record of the accounts (cost centers, bank accounts, etc.) or locations (branch offices, subsidiaries, etc.) tested each year to ensure that nothing is overlooked, or that the same account or location is not tested repeatedly year after year, while others are never tested.

The permanent audit file can be a very useful tool of the auditor if it is kept current and used. Occasionally, in his or her haste to complete the current-year audit, an auditor will neglect to review and update the permanent file. When this happens, the file becomes less useful and less used each succeeding year, until it becomes a file of obsolete or superseded data. At that point, it becomes less than useless to the auditor; it becomes a threat because it is evidence of negligent and inadequate work.

Current Audit Files

The *current audit files* for each year contain the evidence gathered and the conclusions reached in the audit for that year. The material in the current files includes schedules and analyses of accounts; memoranda of audit work performed and audit problems considered and resolved; an audit program; correspondence with third parties (banks, customers, creditors, legal counsel, etc.) confirming balances, transactions, and other data; and other documents. Examples of many of these items are provided in this and following chapters. Most of the working paper examples are prepared on a microcomputer because of its extensive use in auditing.

Working papers organized logically improve the efficiency of an audit and the effectiveness of its review. Although an auditor must be aware of the interrelationships among accounts (such as between sales and accounts receivable, or accounts payable, inventory, and cost of sales), and design his or her audit procedures accordingly, a logical approach to the organization of working papers is to begin with the financial statements on which the auditor expresses his or her opinion, which, of course, are the final product of the client's records and accounting system.

Using the financial statements as the apex, the auditor dissects the individual financial statement items to the point at which they are most efficiently and effectively audited. This point varies by company and by account. For example, it would be difficult to perform much effective auditing on the total accounts receivable balance shown in the financial statements. This account must first be broken down into subaccounts, such as customer, notes, officer and employees, interest, and other receivables on a schedule sometimes referred to as a *lead schedule*. Then the more significant of the subaccounts would be analyzed further by customer, note, officer and employee, and so forth to obtain amounts that the auditor can subject to such audit tests as confirmation and aging. Thus, the organization of working papers can be likened to the triangle shown below.

This concept is illustrated later in the discussion of indexing the working papers.

Audit Trial Balances

Although auditors would prefer to use the financial statements as the starting point for their audit, there are often practical reasons why they cannot. Sometimes the financial statements have not been prepared while the audit is in progress. In other cases auditors process adjusting entries as a result of their work, which would change any financial statements that have been prepared. Therefore, auditors normally prepare an audit trial balance, which resembles the financial statements (without footnotes) but contains columns for adjustments and reclassifications proposed as a result of the audit. The adjustments columns are for the posting of adjusting entries proposed by the auditors to correct errors in the accounting records. On many audit engagements auditors have no adjustments, whereas on others, numerous adjustments may be made. The reclassification columns are for the posting of reclassification entries—for example, entries to change the classification of an item for financial statement presentation purposes. When accepted by the client, adjusting entries must always be posted to the accounting records by the client because they are corrections of errors in those records, but reclassification entries are not posted to the accounting records because they are only rearrangements of the ledger accounts for financial statement purposes.

The audit trial balance (asset accounts only) shown in Figure 6.2 contains certain adjusting and reclassifying entries (from Figures 6.3 and 6.4). The column entitled "As Adjusted and Reclassified" should agree with the amounts shown in the client's financial statements. The proposed adjusting and reclassifying entries must be accepted by the client company's management, because the responsibility for the financial statements is theirs. If such entries are proposed by the auditor, the documentation and support for the entries must be included in the working papers. Note that the entries in Figures 6.3 and 6.4 include references to working paper schedules in which the support for the entries can be found.

Lead Schedules

An example of the next level in the triangle, the *lead schedule,* is shown in Figure 6.5. It illustrates the division of the total inventory amount into subgroups by stage of completion. In other cases, the total inventory amount might be divided according to product lines, inventory storage location, or other criteria. The type of breakdown shown on the lead schedule is determined by the classifications used by each client in its accounting records. Thus, in this, as in many other aspects of auditing, no single format is applicable to all engagements; each must be tailored to the particular aspects of each audit.

Detailed Schedules

The base of the working paper triangle symbolizes the detailed audit schedules—myriad schedules and documents, each representing a specific piece of evidence gathered during the audit. Examples of such schedules and documents are shown in the following chapters.

These examples illustrate the concept of the working paper triangle. From the audit trial balance, the accounts are analyzed on the lead schedules, of which, in this case, there would be approximately 15, and then each lead schedule is supported by several detailed audit schedules. Thus, the base expands as accounts are analyzed in greater detail.

Form and Indexing

The examples in this and following chapters illustrate the methods of indicating the performance of audit work and the indexing of working papers.

The actual audit procedure performed can be indicated in several ways. First,

FIGURE 6.2 **Audit Trial Balance**

TB-1

J. Jones
1-20-x9

X Co.
Audit Trial Balance
12-31-X8

	Index	As Adjusted 12-31-X7	Per Books 12-31-X8	Adjustments Dr.	Adjustments Cr.	As Adjusted 12-31-X8	Reclassifications Dr.	Reclassifications Cr.	As Adjusted and Reclassified 12-31-X8
Current Assets									
Cash	A	73,430ⁿ	65,141√			65,141			65,141
Accounts receivable	B	121,189ⁿ	140,767√		②6,000	134,767	(a)18,797		153,564
Inventories	C	276,502ⁿ	243,030√			243,030			243,030
Prepayments	D	11,343ⁿ	12,255√			12,255			12,255
		482,464	461,193			455,193			473,990
Property and Equipment	G	581,750ⁿ	604,988√			604,988			604,988
Less Allowance for depreciation		89,266ⁿ	108,716√			108,716			108,716
		492,484	496,272			496,272			496,272
Other assets	H	17,392ⁿ	16,629√			16,629			16,629
		992,340	974,094			968,094			986,891

ⁿ Traced to prior year audit working papers.
√ Traced to general ledger.

FIGURE 6.3 **Audit Adjusting Entries**

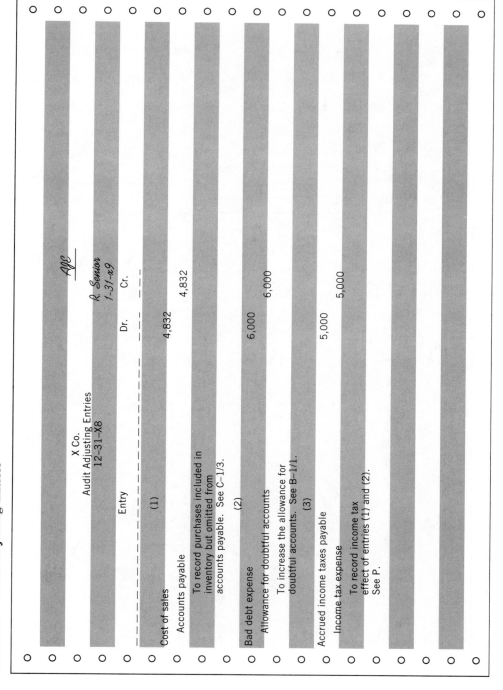

X Co.
Audit Adjusting Entries
12-31-X8

Entry	Dr.	Cr.
(1)		
Cost of sales	4,832	
Accounts payable		4,832
To record purchases included in inventory but omitted from accounts payable. See C–1/3.		
(2)		
Bad debt expense	6,000	
Allowance for doubtful accounts		6,000
To increase the allowance for doubtful accounts. See B–1/1.		
(3)		
Accrued income taxes payable	5,000	
Income tax expense		5,000
To record income tax effect of entries (1) and (2). See P.		

AJE

R. Senior
1-31-x9

FIGURE 6.4   Audit Reclassifying Entries

X Co.
Audit Reclassifying Entries
12-31-X8

RJS
R. Senior
1-31-x9

	Dr.	Cr.
Entry		
(101)		
Long-term debt	50,000	
Notes payable		50,000
To reclassify as a current liability the portion of long-term debt due within one year. See R.		
(102)		
Accounts receivable	18,797	
Accounts payable		18,797
To reclassify credit balances in accounts receivable to accounts payable. See B.		

FIGURE 6.5 Inventory Lead Schedule

X Co.
Inventory Lead Schedule
12-31-X8

C

J. Jones
1-20-x9

	Index	As Adjusted 12-31-X7	Per Books 12-31-X8	Adjustments Dr.	Adjustments Cr.	As Adjusted 12-31-X8
Raw materials	C-1	76,425 ⌐	51,014 √			– – – –
Work in progress	C-2	29,760 ⌐	36,253 √			= = = =
Finished goods	C-3	151,903 ⌐	137,692 √			= = = =
Supplies	C-4	18,414 ⌐	18,071 √			– – – –
		276,502	243,030 ①			= = = =
		= = = =	= = = =			
		TB-1	TB-1			

⌐ Traced to prior year working paper.

√ Traced to general ledger.

① The plant manager stated that the decline in inventory was due to a decline in sales orders during the last quarter of this year. This was confirmed by examination of the sales backlog report as of 12-31-x8.

Figure 6.5 illustrates a narrative documentation of evidence at ①. This inquiry of the plant manager could have been made in connection with an audit procedure to explain unusual variations in inventory balances between years (an analytical procedure). Note that the auditor confirmed the plant manager's explanation by examination of the sales backlog report. A second method of documenting the performance of audit procedures is the use of schedule headings to describe the examination of certain records and documents. For example, "Per Vendor Invoice" denotes the examination of invoices from vendors to obtain the information shown on the schedule. The third method, illustrated in Figure 6.5, is the use of the "tick" mark. In this case, the *tick mark* ✔ shows that the amount was traced to the general ledger. The type of tick mark used does not matter as long as the auditor and anyone reviewing the working papers can understand its meaning. Because these working papers are prepared on the auditor's microcomputer, they are automatically checked for clerical accuracy, so no notation of this check is indicated.

Other aspects of the form of working papers that can be noted from the foregoing illustrations are (1) each schedule has a heading consisting of the client's name, a description of the information shown on the schedule, and the audit date, (2) each schedule is indexed, and (3) each schedule is signed and dated by the auditor performing the work.

To facilitate the organization and review of the working papers, auditors generally use some type of indexing or coding system to identify each schedule. One such indexing system, used in Figures 6.2 through 6.5, is the designation of each balance sheet account with a letter (such as "A" for cash, "B" for accounts receivable, etc.) and each income statement account group with a number (such as "10" for sales, "20" for cost of goods sold, etc.). These designations are modified further with numbers to provide the indexes of the detailed audit schedules.

As shown in the illustrations, each account group listed on the audit trial balance is assigned a single letter that also is the index of the lead schedule for that account group. On the inventory lead schedule in the example, each subaccount is assigned an index consisting of the letter "C" (indicating that it is part of and should be filed in the inventory section) and a number (by type of inventory). Similar indexing would appear on other lead schedules. The schedules showing the detailed audit work performed on each subaccount would be indexed with the subaccount number (indicating that the work relates to a particular subaccount) and an additional number to designate the schedule on which the work was performed. All schedules would be filed first in alphabetical order and then in numerical order. This type of indexing is simple and can be expanded in many ways.

The working paper triangle introduced on page 162 with the indexes of the schedules described is shown in the illustration on page 169.

If a supervisor or other person had reason to review the audit work performed in the example on raw materials inventory, rather than look through what might be hundreds of pages of working papers, he or she would look first at the audit trial balance (Figure 6.2) to find the index of inventory (C).[2] The inventory lead

---

[2] In practice, most firms use a standard index system, and this first step would not be necessary; inventory always would be indexed as "C" or some other designation.

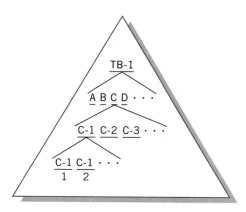

schedule (Figure 6.5) could then be found, and this would locate the index of raw materials (C-1). Considerable time can thus be saved if a logical indexing system is used.

Client Assistance

Clients assist their auditors by preparing certain working papers. This practice can be advantageous to both auditors and clients. From the auditors' standpoint, the time spent on clerical and mechanical tasks is reduced, and more important and significant aspects of the audit can be emphasized. The auditors must test the preparation of all such working papers to the extent necessary to satisfy themselves as to accuracy and credibility, but the time required to do so is normally much less than would be necessary for the initial preparation. From the client's standpoint, any clerical work that can be shifted from the auditor to the client should reduce the total audit fee, which is usually based on the total time required to perform the audit.

Auditors may use the client's internal audit staff to assist in preparing working papers and performing certain audit procedures. Independent auditors should consider the competence and objectivity of the internal auditors and supervise and test their work to the extent they consider necessary. The independent auditor must make all judgments concerning the audit.

Security of Working Papers

Because auditors' working papers represent the support for their professional opinions and contain confidential information regarding their clients' operations, it is important to maintain control of the working papers at all times. On the client's premises, auditors should use a trunk or briefcase that can be locked to secure the working papers (including computer diskettes) at night, during lunch, or any other time they are not in use. Within their office, auditors normally maintain a fireproof safe for the protection and security of their working papers. Cases exist where client employees have gained access to unsecure audit working papers and altered them to cover shortages and fraudulent transactions.

INTERNATIONAL STANDARDS ON AUDITING

International standards on auditing have more specific requirements as to the content of an auditor's working papers (e.g., a list is provided of schedules, analyses, and other working papers that would normally be included) than U.S. standards. U.S. standards are more general, with the form and content of the working papers being left to the auditor's judgment.

Chapter 6 ▶ GLOSSARY OF TERMS

Analytical procedures   A type of substantive test involving the study and comparison of relationships among data.

Assertions   Characteristics of an account or disclosure consisting of its existence, rights, completeness, valuation, and presentation.

Audit objectives   Determination by the auditor of the validity of management's assertions.

Audit procedures   Specific actions taken by the auditor to accomplish the audit objectives.

Control risk assessment procedures   Audit procedures performed to assess control risk.

Current audit files   A file of audit working papers containing evidence pertinent to the current-year audit.

Lead schedule   An audit working paper that summarizes subaccounts of an amount shown in the audit trial balance.

Overall audit objective   The expression of an opinion on the fairness with which the financial statements present financial position, results of operations, and cash flows

in conformity with generally accepted accounting principles.

Permanent audit files   A file of audit working papers containing evidence pertinent to more than one year's audit.

Substantive tests   Audit procedures performed to evaluate amounts and disclosures in the financial statements.

Tests of controls   A control risk assessment procedure used to determine if specific controls are operating effectively.

Tests of transactions and balances   A type of substantive test involving examination of evidence underlying specific transactions and balances.

Tick mark   A symbol used to document the performance of audit work in the working papers.

Working papers   Records kept by the auditor of the procedures applied, the tests performed, the information obtained, and the pertinent conclusions reached in the audit.

Chapter 6 ▶ REFERENCES

American Institute of Certified Public Accountants, *Professional Standards.*
AU Section 326—*Evidential Matter*
AU Section 329—*Analytical Procedures*
AU Section 339—*Working Papers*
Scott, David A., and Wallace, Wanda A. "A Second Look at an Old Tool: Analytical Procedures," *The CPA Journal* (March 1994), pp. 30–35.
Whittington, Ray, Zulinski, Marilyn, and Ledwith, James W. "Completeness—The Elusive Assertion," *Journal of Accountancy* (August 1983), pp. 82–92.

Chapter 6 ▶ REVIEW QUESTIONS

 6-1 What is the auditor's overall objective in an audit of financial statements?

 6-2 How does the auditor determine the objectives of auditing each account?

 6-3 What five general assertions does management make regarding individual account balances and disclosures?

6-4 How do auditors determine what audit procedures to apply to a particular account?

6-5 Provide four examples of control risk assessment procedures.

6-6 What are substantive tests?

6-7 Explain the relation between control risk assessment procedures and substantive tests.

6-8 Provide two examples of tests of details of balances and transactions.

6-9 What are analytical procedures?

6-10 List five sources from which expectations for analytical procedures may be developed.

6-11 In what two stages of an audit are analytical procedures required to be performed?

6-12 What is the significance of the lack of privileged communication between an auditor and his or her client?

6-13 What are the two types of working paper files?

6-14 What is the purpose of the permanent audit file?

6-15 List five types of data found in the current audit files.

6-16 Explain the difference between adjusting and reclassifying entries proposed by the auditor.

6-17 What is a lead schedule?

6-18 Who has the final responsibility for determining whether or not a proposed adjusting entry will be recorded?

6-19 State three ways of indicating the performance of audit work in the working papers.

6-20 What is the purpose of an index system for the working papers? Describe the system illustrated in the text.

Chapter 6 ▶ OBJECTIVE QUESTIONS

(* = author prepared; ** = CPA examination)

 *6-21 An auditor's overall objective in a financial statement audit is to
   a. Determine that all individual accounts and footnotes are fairly presented.
   b. Employ the audit risk model.
   c. Express an opinion on the fair presentation of the financial statements in accordance with generally accepted accounting principles.
   d. Detect all errors and fraud.

*6-22 When auditing individual accounts and disclosures, an auditor's objective is to determine the validity of management's
   a. Calculations.
   b. Recording process.
   c. Assertions.
   d. Internal control.

*6-23 All of the following are general audit objectives for auditing an account or disclosure except
   a. Existence.
   b. Reliability.
   c. Valuation.
   d. Completeness.

*6-24 Recording a sale for goods not shipped and failing to record a sale for goods that are shipped violate the accounts receivable assertions of
   a. Existence and valuation.
   b. Rights and completeness.
   c. Existence and completeness.
   d. Rights and valuation.

*6-25 Management makes all of the following assertions about the financial statements in general except
   a. The entity will continue as a going concern for a period of at least one year from the balance sheet date unless an exception to this assumption is disclosed.
   b. Transactions summarized in the financial statements occurred between independent parties unless related party transactions are disclosed.
   c. The entity has been operated efficiently unless exceptions to this assumption are disclosed.
   d. The accounting principles used are not mate-

rially different from those used in the prior period unless a difference is disclosed.

*6-26 Auditors determine the audit procedures to be performed for a *specific* account by reference to
  a. Audit objectives for that account.
  b. Generally accepted auditing standards.
  c. AICPA sanctioned standards.
  d. SEC approved audit procedures.

*6-27 Control risk assessment procedures include all of the following except
  a. Inspection of documents.
  b. Observation of procedures.
  c. Confirmation of bank balances.
  d. Inquiry of client personnel.

**6-28 A basic premise underlying analytical procedures is that
  a. These procedures *cannot* replace tests of details of balances and transactions.
  b. Statistical tests of financial information may lead to the discovery of material errors in the financial statements.
  c. The study of financial ratios is an acceptable alternative to the investigation of unusual fluctuations.
  d. Plausible relationships among data may reasonably be expected to exist and continue in the absence of known conditions to the contrary.

*6-29 Evidence of the performance of control risk assessment procedures includes all of the following except
  a. Flowcharts.
  b. Lead schedules.
  c. Questionnaires.
  d. Memoranda.

**6-30 Which of the following is ordinarily designed to detect possible material dollar errors in the financial statements?
  a. Control risk assessment procedures.
  b. Analytical procedures.
  c. Computer controls.
  d. Postaudit working paper review.

**6-31 An auditor's working papers should
  a. Not be permitted to serve as a reference source for the client.
  b. Not contain critical comments concerning management.
  c. Show that the accounting records agree or reconcile with the financial statements.
  d. Be considered the primary support for the financial statements being audited.

**6-32 Working papers ordinarily would *not* include

  a. Initials of the in-charge auditor indicating review of the staff assistants' work.
  b. Cut-off bank statements received directly from the banks.
  c. A memo describing the auditor's understanding of the internal controls.
  d. Copies of client inventory count sheets.

**6-33 In connection with a lawsuit, a third party attempts to gain access to the auditor's working papers. The client's defense of privileged communication will be successful only to the extent it is protected by the
  a. Auditor's acquiescence in use of this defense.
  b. Common law.
  c. AICPA *Code of Professional Conduct.*
  d. State law.

**6-34 Which of the following statements ordinarily is correct concerning the content of working papers?
  a. Whenever possible, the auditor's staff should prepare schedules and analyses rather than the entity's employees.
  b. It is preferable to have negative figures indicated in red figures instead of parentheses to emphasize amounts being subtracted.
  c. It is appropriate to use computer printouts with names or explanations on the computer printouts rather than writing separate lists onto working papers.
  d. The analysis of asset accounts and their related expense or income accounts should *not* appear on the same working paper.

**6-35 The permanent file of an auditor's working papers generally would *not* include
  a. Bond indenture agreements.
  b. Lease agreements.
  c. Working trial balance.
  d. Flowchart of the internal control.

**6-36 The audit working paper that reflects the major components of an amount reported in the financial statements is the
  a. Interbank transfer schedule.
  b. Carry-forward schedule.
  c. Supporting schedule.
  d. Lead schedule.

**6-37 An auditor ordinarily uses a working trial balance resembling the financial statements without footnotes, but containing columns for
  a. Cash flow increases and decreases.
  b. Audit objectives and assertions.
  c. Reclassifications and adjustments.
  d. Reconciliations and tick marks.

6-38 During an audit engagement, pertinent data are compiled and included in the audit working papers. The working papers are primarily considered to be

    a. A client-owned record of conclusions reached by the auditors who performed the engagement.

    b. Evidence supporting financial statements.

    c. Support for the auditor's representations as to compliance with generally accepted auditing standards.

    d. A record to be used as a basis for the following year's engagement.

6-39 Match the term or terms with the related description. Each term may be used once, more than once, or not at all.

Description	Term
1. The auditor expresses an opinion on the fairness with which the financial statements present financial position, results of operations, and cash flows in conformity with generally accepted accounting principles.	a. Management assertion
2. The entity owns the unimpaired rights to assets, and it owes the liabilities shown in the financial statements.	b. Working papers
3. The financial statements include all assets, liabilities, equity, revenue, expenses, gains, and losses.	c. Auditor's overall objective
4. The auditor obtains an understanding of the internal control.	d. Substantive tests
5. The auditor performs analytical procedures.	e. Tests of controls
6. The auditor maintains records of the procedures applied, the tests performed, the information obtained, and the pertinent conclusions reached in the engagement.	f. Control risk assessment procedures

Chapter 6 ▶ DISCUSSION/CASE QUESTIONS

(* = author prepared; ** = CPA examination)

6-40 The general audit objectives apply to all financial statement accounts. The general objectives are used to determine specific audit objectives for each account.

    a. Describe the specific audit objective for the valuation assertion for the following accounts:
        (1) Accounts receivable.
        (2) Inventory.
        (3) Property and equipment.
        (4) Goodwill.

    b. Describe the specific audit objective for the presentation and disclosure assertion for each of the following accounts:
        (1) Cash.
        (2) Accounts receivable.
        (3) Inventory.
        (4) Property and equipment.
        (5) Notes payable.

6-41 Indicate the audit objectives that are accomplished by the following audit procedures:

    a. Confirmation of the cash bank balance with the bank.

    b. Analysis of inventory turnover.

    c. Review of a copy of a note payable to determine the due date.

    d. Comparison of sales invoices with shipping documents.

    e. Comparisons of shipping documents with sales invoices.

    f. Confirmation of the collateral of a note payable.

    g. Inquiry regarding compensating balance arrangements.

h. Inquiry regarding collectibility of accounts receivable. *evaluation*
i. Observation of physical inventories. *existence & right valuation*
j. Inspection of marketable securities. *existence*   *rights*

*6-42 Classify the following audit procedures as (1) control risk assessment procedures, (2) tests of details of balances and transactions, or (3) analytical procedures. Give reasons for your classification.

a. Observation of a physical inventory.
b. Observation of the mail clerk opening the mail.
c. Inquiry about the client's organizational structure.
d. Inquiry about obsolete inventory. (2)
e. Comparison of the current-year balance in an account to the prior-year balance. (3)
f. Inspection of canceled checks for dual signatures.
g. Comparison of the recorded cost of a machine to the related vendor's invoice. (2)
h. Inspection of sales invoices to determine if they are prenumbered. (1)
i. Inspection of sales invoices to determine if the revenue account is properly substantiated. (2)

**6-43 Analytical procedures are useful substantive tests.

Required:

a. Explain why analytical procedures are considered substantive tests.
b. Explain how analytical procedures are used in the audit planning stage.
c. Identify the analytical procedures that one might expect a CPA to use during an audit performed in accordance with generally accepted auditing standards.

*6-44 Indicate whether you would expect to find the following documents in the permanent audit file or the current-year audit file.

a. A letter from a customer confirming an account balance. *current*
b. A memorandum describing the auditor's work and conclusions regarding the adequacy of the allowance for doubtful accounts. *permanent*
c. A copy of the client's articles of incorporation. *per*
d. A description of the client's internal controls. *per*
e. A worksheet containing a bank reconciliation. *cur*
f. A worksheet containing an analysis of common stock transactions from inception of the company until the current date. *per*
g. A memorandum describing the auditor's inventory observation. *per (curr)*
h. A computer listing of the client's inventory balances. *curr*
i. A lead schedule. *curr*

*6-45 Using the indexing method described in this chapter, index the following audit working papers.

a. Notes receivable confirmation control schedule.
b. Analysis of allowance for doubtful accounts.
c. Test of calculation of interest receivable.
d. Audit trial balance.
e. Notes receivable confirmations.
f. Officer and employee accounts receivable trial balance.
g. Receivables lead schedule.
h. Accounts receivable confirmations.

i. Trade accounts receivable trial balance.

j. Trade accounts receivable confirmation control schedule.

k. Notes receivable trial balance.

*6-46 Indicate whether the following matters would require (1) an adjusting entry, (2) a reclassification entry, or (3) a footnote disclosure. Give reasons for your answers.

a. An uncollectible account receivable that exceeds the allowance for doubtful accounts. (1)

b. Accounts receivable from related parties. (2)

c. Long-term notes receivable that are included in accounts receivable. (2)

d. Current maturities that are included in long-term debt. (2)

e. An overstatement of inventory due to incorrect pricing. (1)

f. Valuation of inventory on the LIFO basis. (3)

g. A cash balance that is restricted as to future withdrawals. (2)&(3)

h. An unrecorded vendor invoice. (1)

*6-47 Review the following audit working paper and list the deficiencies in its preparation.

Hogeye Ranch Company
Cattle Inventory

Type	Quantity	Average Price	Amount
Bulls	10†	$3,000	$ 30,000
Steers	35†	500*	17,500
Heifers (1)	41†	550*	22,500
Cows	103	800*	82,400
Calves	67†	200*	13,400
			$185,800

*Price tested by auditor. See separate working paper.

†Cattle observed by auditor. See separate working paper.

*6-48 Grace Mature was conducting a training class for new audit staff assistants. She was trying to emphasize the need for them to think about proper auditing procedures rather than merely relying on the audit program and following it in a rote manner.

Ms. Mature used this model to explain how new staff assistants could arrive at appropriate audit procedures.

Auditor's overall objective	To express an opinion on the fairness with which the financial statements present financial position, results of operations, and cash flows in conformity with generally accepted accounting principles.
Auditor's general objectives for each account	To determine whether management's assertions (existence or occurrence, rights and obligations, completeness, valuation or allocation, presentation or disclosure) concerning the account are valid.
Auditor's specific objectives for each account (using certain specific objectives for inventory as an example)	To determine whether the inventory amount on the balance sheet is represented by all physical items on hand, in transit, or on consignment (existence and completeness).

Ms. Mature then asked each member of the group to design an auditor's specific objectives for a different account. Will Start was asked to design specific objectives for cash, Myrna New was asked to design specific objectives for net accounts receivable, and Hyman Begin was asked to design specific objectives for property and equipment. Each person had to include objectives that took into consideration at least three of the five general management assertions.

Required:

Using the model illustrated by Ms. Mature and described in the chapter, perform the assignment for each of the three new audit assistants.

Basic Auditing Concepts

"Take calculated risks. That is quite different from being rash."

GEORGE S. PATTON, *letter to his son, June 6, 1944*

LEARNING OBJECTIVES

After reading and studying the material in this chapter, the student should be able to

▶ Describe when and for what purpose each section of the audit is performed.

▶ Examine the scope and opinion paragraphs of the independent auditor's report and characterize three important concepts that underlie the assurances made by auditors in their report.

▶ Paraphrase the definition of materiality and explain its importance to the auditor.

▶ Analyze the factors the auditor uses in deciding on the level of materiality.

▶ Write brief paragraphs explaining the importance of each risk assessed by the auditor.

▶ Analyze the relationship between financial statement assertions and risks assessed by the auditor.

▶ Compare the two sources of detection risk.

▶ Use the audit risk model to compute various levels of detection risk.

In this chapter we describe the general sections of an audit and discuss the concepts underlying the planning and performance of an audit. Throughout the book, we will use these concepts and explain them in more detail.

THE SECTIONS OF AN AUDIT

CPAs do not enter the offices of their clients, examine some documents, and deliver an audit report. They plan audits carefully, perform a logical sequence of steps, and prepare a proper report. While the requirements of each audit differ, generally they include the following steps:[1]

---

[1] The time frames used in the examples are general and differ for each audit, depending on its scope and complexity.

The Audit Is Planned

The auditor prepares or revises (in the case of continuing clients) a written audit program that describes the audit steps and the sequence in which they will be performed. The auditor must consider the risk that the financial statements contain significant misstatements.

Much of this audit planning is done several months before the end of the year covered by the client's financial statements.

▶ EXAMPLE

For an audit client whose financial statements cover January 1, 19X4 to December 31, 19X4, the auditor might begin planning the audit during the summer of 19X4. The auditor would consider what types of errors, fraud, or illegal acts might occur.

The Internal Control Is Studied and Tested

The auditor examines and evaluates the processes and controls that produce the amounts and disclosures in the financial statements. The auditor assesses the risk that internal control will not prevent or detect errors and/or fraud that significantly misstate the financial statements. A substantial amount of work on understanding and testing internal control can be done weeks or months before the end of the year covered by the client's financial statements.

▶ EXAMPLE

For an audit client whose financial statements cover January 1, 19X4 to December 31, 19X4, the auditor might visit the client's offices in October, 19X4. During that time, the auditor would ask questions, make observations, and examine the records necessary to obtain an understanding of and test internal control. This work in October will help determine the nature, timing, and scope of the audit tests performed in the early part of 19X5.

Substantive Tests Are Performed

The auditor, using the audit plan and the understanding and tests of internal control, examines evidence supporting the account balances and disclosures in the financial statements. Substantive tests are an important part of the audit because they provide the basis for determining whether the client's financial statements are fairly presented in conformity with generally accepted accounting principles. Because many substantive tests are performed on year-end balances and disclosures, the performance of at least some of these tests must be delayed until after the year covered by the client's financial statements.

▶ EXAMPLE

For an audit client whose financial statements cover January 1, 19X4 to December 31, 19X4, the auditor might perform many of the substantive tests in January and February 19X5 after the client has finalized the accounting records for 19X4. The auditor must perform sufficient substantive tests to form an opinion on the fair presentation of the financial statements as of December 31, 19X4 and for the year 19X4. This might take until the end of February 19X5.

The Audit Report Is Issued

The auditor prepares an audit report after considering the type of opinion appropriate for the conclusions formed about the fair presentation of the client's financial statements. The auditor will issue the audit report a short time after the completion of the substantive testing.

► **EXAMPLE**

For an audit client whose financial statements cover January 1, 19X4 to December 31, 19X4, the auditor might complete the substantive tests near the end of February 19X5. Reviews and quality control processes might take a week, and, if no unforeseen problems occur, the audit report might be issued in early March 19X5.

AN EXPLANATION OF ASSURANCES PROVIDED BY AUDITORS

Assurances Provided by the Auditor

Figure 7.1 shows the income statement for the year ended December 31, 19X8, and Figure 7.2 on page 180 shows the balance sheets for the years ended December 31, 19X8 and 19X7. What assurances does the auditor provide in an opinion on the fairness of presentation of financial statements, such as this income statement and these balance sheets? Refer to the scope and opinion paragraphs of the independent auditor's report on page 28.

FIGURE 7.1 **Income Statement**

Begin Company
Income Statement
For the Year Ended December 31, 19X8

Sales		$1,000,000
Cost of goods sold		
Beginning inventory	$300,000	
Purchases	580,000	
Cost of goods available for sale	$880,000	
Less: ending inventory	280,000	600,000
Gross margin		$ 400,000
Operating expenses		300,000
Income before income tax expense		$ 100,000
Income tax expense		30,000
Net income		$ 70,000

FIGURE 7.2   Balance Sheets

Begin Company
Balance Sheets
December 31, 19X8 and 19X7

	December 31	
	19X8	*19X7*
Assets		
Current assets		
Cash	$ 150,000	$ 100,000
Accounts receivable (Net)	220,000	200,000
Inventory	280,000	300,000
Prepaid expenses	20,000	10,000
Total current assets	$ 670,000	$ 610,000
Property and equipment, net of depreciation		
Equipment	$ 280,000	$ 250,000
Buildings	420,000	500,000
Net property and equipment	$ 700,000	$ 750,000
Total assets	$1,370,000	$1,360,000
Liabilities and Stockholders' Equity		
Current liabilities		
Accounts payable	$ 120,000	$ 180,000
Accrued liabilities	220,000	220,000
Total current liabilities	$ 340,000	$ 400,000
Long-term liabilities		
Notes payable	$ 450,000	$ 400,000
Total liabilities	$ 790,000	$ 800,000
Stockholders' equity		
Common stock	$ 200,000	$ 200,000
Retained earnings	380,000	360,000
Total stockholders' equity	$ 580,000	$ 560,000
Total liabilities and stockholders' equity	$1,370,000	$1,360,000

Material Misstatement

The auditor's report contains these phrases:

(Scope Paragraph)

. . . Those standards require that we plan and perform the audit to obtain *reasonable assurance* about whether the financial statements are free of *material misstatement* . . .

(Opinion Paragraph)

. . . In our opinion, the financial statements referred to above present fairly, in all *material respects* . . .

The report contains no guarantee that the financial statements are accurate. Rather, the auditor provides *reasonable assurance* concerning *material misstatement* and an opinion on fairness, in all *material respects.*

To ascertain the difference between (1) guarantee and accurate and (2) reasonable assurance and material, refer to the $200,000 and $220,000 amounts for accounts receivable shown in Figure 7.2. The auditor understands how these amounts were derived and has gathered and evaluated evidence regarding these amounts. But because of cost/benefit constraints the auditor does not examine every transaction that affected accounts receivable. (Even an examination of all transactions would not guarantee accuracy because of the estimates involved in the allowance for doubtful accounts.)

But the auditor does sample enough evidence supporting these accounts receivable amounts to provide reasonable assurance that the financial statements are free of material misstatement and are fairly presented, in all material respects. A key word is *material.* It means that, while the accounts receivable amounts may not be exactly $200,000 and $220,000, they are close enough so that users of the financial statements will not be misled.

Reasonable Assurance

The scope paragraph of the auditor's report contains this sentence:

> Those standards require that we plan and perform the audit to obtain reasonable assurance about whether the financial statements are free of material misstatement.

The term *reasonable assurance* alludes to the concept of *audit risk,* that is, the risk that the auditor may unknowingly issue an unqualified opinion on financial statements that are materially misstated. The auditor cannot avoid this risk; it is implicit in the audit function, and it is implied in the scope paragraph of the independent auditor's report.

Sampling

The scope paragraph also contains this sentence.

> An audit includes examining, on a *test basis,* evidence supporting the amounts and disclosures in the financial statements.

The term *test basis* states explicitly that some sampling is used to gather evidence on financial statement amounts and disclosures. The auditor does not necessarily examine all evidence supporting the $200,000 and $220,000 of accounts receivable in Figure 7.2. In all likelihood, the auditor examines a sample of evidence and, on the basis of this sample, forms a conclusion as to whether these accounts receivable amounts are fairly presented.

Summary of Assurances Provided by the Auditor

Therefore, three important concepts underlie the assurances that the auditor makes to users of the financial statements.

1. On the basis of evidence gathered (which, in all likelihood, includes some *sampling*),
2. the auditor provides reasonable assurance (an implicit *risk* that the overall audit conclusion is not correct)
3. that the financial statements are not *materially misstated* (*materiality*).

The concepts of materiality and risk are so fundamental to the audit function that they are used to establish

1. How much evidence the auditor will obtain.
2. When and how the evidence will be obtained.
3. What type of evidence will be obtained.
4. What criteria will be used to evaluate the evidence.

In the remainder of the chapter, we will discuss these concepts and will use the terms *materiality* and *audit risk* to explain how the auditor plans and performs an audit.

THE USE OF MATERIALITY IN PLANNING AND PERFORMING AN AUDIT

Look again at Figures 7.1 and 7.2 and use these two examples.

1. A few days before the end of 19X8, a $100 expenditure for the repair of equipment was incorrectly charged to the equipment account in the balance sheet rather than to operating expenses in the income statement. As a result (ignoring depreciation), total assets should be stated at $1,369,900 rather than $1,370,000 and income before taxes should be stated at $99,900 instead of $100,000. Are the financial statements fairly presented and not materially misleading?
2. A few days before the end of 19X8, a $50,000 expenditure for the repair of equipment was incorrectly charged to the equipment account rather than to operating expenses. As a result (ignoring depreciation), total assets should be stated at $1,320,000 rather than $1,370,000 and income before taxes should be stated at $50,000 instead of $100,000. Are the financial statements fairly presented and not materially misleading?

The auditors would probably answer the question in the first example "yes" and the second example "no." Why? Because of the application of a concept called *materiality*, which is defined by the Financial Accounting Standards Board as

> the magnitude of an omission or misstatement of accounting information that, in light of surrounding circumstances, makes it probable that the judgment of a reasonable person relying on the information would have been changed or influenced by the omission or misstatement.

The $100 misstatement is not likely to change or influence a reasonable person's judgment in this circumstance, but the $50,000 misstatement is likely to do so. Thus, materiality is a major factor that auditors consider when planning an audit and evaluating the evidence as the audit is conducted. Auditors would have to establish what is called a threshold of materiality by selecting some dollar figure as the amount by which the financial statements would be materially misstated if the total of the misstatements were above that amount.

Materiality Considerations

There is much more to materiality decisions than arbitrarily selecting a single dollar amount for the financial statements. Consideration must be given to

1. Quantitative factors such as the relationship of a misstatement to certain key amounts in the financial statements including (this list is not exhaustive)
   a. Net income.
   b. Net income before taxes.
   c. Revenue.
   d. Total assets.
   e. Current assets.
   f. Stockholders' equity.
2. Qualitative factors such as (again, this list is not exhaustive)
   a. The probability that illegal payments might occur.
   b. The probability that fraud might occur.
   c. Provisions in a client's loan agreement with a bank requiring that certain financial statement ratios be maintained at minimum levels.
   d. An interruption in a trend in earnings.

Quantitative Factors

Refer to Figures 7.1 and 7.2. The auditors may decide that any combination of misstatements that totals more than eight percent of income before taxes will be material, subject to qualitative considerations. If the combination of misstatements is less than three percent of income before taxes, the auditors may consider them to be immaterial, subject to qualitative considerations. Misstatements that total between three and eight percent would require judgment. Therefore, in this example the *materiality borders* for the income statement are

$$\$3,000 \ (\$100,000 \times 3\%) \text{ to } \$8,000 \ (\$100,000 \times 8\%).$$

The auditors may apply a similar methodology to the materiality borders for total assets, current assets, and stockholders' equity in the balance sheet. Assume these materiality borders.

For total assets in the balance sheet:
   $41,100 to $109,600
For current assets in the balance sheet:
   $20,100 to $53,600
For total stockholders' equity in the balance sheet:
   $17,400 to $46,400

Qualitative Factors

Management resistance to adjusting the accounting records for previously discovered errors might cause the auditors to lower the amounts in all of the materiality borders. Any illegal act or fraud that is detected will probably be qualitatively material regardless of the dollar amount involved.

Another qualitative factor is a provision in one of the client's loan agreements that specifies that a minimum current ratio be maintained. Look at Figure 7.2, and assume that the notes payable of $450,000 will become immediately payable if Begin Company does not maintain a current ratio of at least 2 to 1. The current ratio on the December 31, 19X8 balance sheet is barely under 2 to 1 (total current assets of $670,000/total current liabilities of $340,000). Begin Company may be tempted to increase current assets or reduce current liabilities. Therefore, the auditors may lower the materiality borders. (In fact, the auditors may establish a very low materiality level on current assets and current liabilities because of this provision in the loan agreement.)

Preliminary Estimates of Materiality in Planning

Preliminary Estimates in the Total Financial Statements

Auditors use materiality in two ways. The first is in planning the audit and the second is in evaluating the evidence while performing the audit. In planning the auditors need to make preliminary estimates of materiality because

> there is an inverse relationship between the amounts in the financial statements that the auditors consider to be material and the amount of audit work necessary to attest to the fairness of the financial statements.

For example, if the auditor considers $8,000 to be material for the financial statements, a certain amount of time and effort must be spent gathering evidence on the individual accounts. On the other hand, if that materiality threshold is lowered to $3,000, additional time and effort must be expended in gathering the necessary evidence. The reason is that it is more difficult to find a small error than a large error.

> Auditors must give careful consideration to the setting of preliminary estimates of materiality in planning the audit. If the dollar amount of materiality is set too low, unnecessary audit effort will be expended. If the dollar amount of materiality is set too high, the auditors might overlook a significant misstatement and attest to financial statements that are materially misstated.

Even though the materiality borders illustrated on page 183 ($3,000 to $8,000 for the income statement, etc.) may be used to make the final decisions on acceptability of the fairness of the financial statements, the auditors may use the upper borders to set the *preliminary estimate of materiality* for planning purposes. The auditors might consider the following:

1. The financial statements will be materially misstated if the misstatement of income before income taxes exceeds $8,000.
2. The financial statements will be materially misstated if the misstatement of total assets exceeds $109,600.
3. The financial statements will be materially misstated if the misstatement of current assets exceeds $53,600.
4. The financial statements will be materially misstated if the misstatement of stockholders' equity exceeds $46,400.

The auditors should choose $8,000 as their preliminary estimate of materiality for purposes of planning the amount of audit effort. This is the smallest materiality threshold and provides reasonable assurance that the auditors will gather enough evidence to make the following statement:

> There is an acceptably low audit risk that income before income taxes is misstated by more than $8,000.

Why should the auditors select $8,000 as their materiality threshold? Because misstatements in one financial statement are likely to cause misstatements in other financial statements. For example, the failure to accrue an adequate provision for income taxes understates current liabilities and overstates net income. By selecting $8,000 as the materiality threshold, the auditors are extending their audit effort and should also have an *even lower* audit risk that

Total assets are misstated by more than $109,600,
Current assets are misstated by more than $53,600,
Stockholders' equity is misstated by more than $46,400.

Preliminary Estimates for Individual Accounts

Although auditors render an opinion on the financial statements taken as a whole, they must audit individual accounts to gather the necessary evidence to render this opinion. This means that materiality for planning purposes can be assigned to individual financial statement accounts being examined. The portion of materiality allocated to individual accounts is referred to as *tolerable misstatement* for that account. Allocations can be made using such factors as the following:

1. Some accounts may be more important than their dollar balance would imply because of the number of transactions that affect that account. A prime example is inventory, which has a $280,000 balance in Figure 7.2. Even though the inventory balance is approximately 10 percent of the sum of all the account balances under consideration, its special importance might call for assigning it less than 10 percent of the $8,000 of materiality (thus necessitating more audit effort than normal on inventory).
2. Experience in prior-year audits might cause the auditors to believe that certain accounts are more or less likely to contain misstatements than other accounts. Accounts receivable might be a case in point. The absence of detected misstatements in previous years might suggest that a higher than normal amount of materiality be assigned to this account (thus lowering the amount of necessary effort).

3. Cost considerations might dictate that only a minimum amount of audit effort be expended on certain accounts. For example, some prepayments in the balance sheet might not require much audit effort because it is not cost beneficial to spend extensive time auditing an immaterial account balance that has changed little from year to year.

In auditing accounts receivable and inventory, therefore, the auditors might wish to use the following materiality guidelines.

1. Accounts receivable—design audit procedures to provide reasonable assurance of detecting errors of $1,500 or greater.
2. Inventory—design audit procedures to provide reasonable assurance of detecting errors of $1,200 or greater.

It may seem strange to plan to find relatively small errors in accounts with $220,000 and $280,000 balances, but remember these points.

1. Misstatements that affect accounts receivable and inventory will probably affect income before income taxes, and the overall materiality of $8,000 in the financial statements is based on the potential misstatement of income before income taxes.
2. The amounts of $1,500 and $1,200 were assigned to accounts receivable and inventory, respectively, because errors in these accounts must be aggregated with errors in all other accounts and compared with the $8,000 materiality standard for the overall financial statements.

In practice auditors follow widely different approaches to allocating materiality to individual account balances. The approaches range from use of mathematical equations to subjective judgment.

Use of Materiality in Evaluating Audit Evidence

Assume that $2,000 of errors were found in the Inventory account. Would the auditors assume that the financial statements taken as a whole are materially misstated? Not necessarily. The auditors might extend their audit effort on Inventory because of the particular importance of that account or because of the nature of the errors. However, the auditors would aggregate the $2,000 of errors with errors found in other accounts.

To illustrate, consider this hypothetical schedule of errors found during the course of the audit.

Uncorrected errors in Inventory	$2,000
Uncorrected errors in all other accounts	7,000
	$9,000

The auditors may have revised their threshold of materiality upward from the preliminary estimate of $8,000 used for planning to $10,000 used to evaluate audit evidence. Perhaps the preliminary estimate of materiality was based on preliminary financial statement amounts that differed from the amounts shown in the final financial statements, so that 8 percent of net income before tax is now $10,000. The auditors might not consider the financial statements to be materially misstated because the estimate of the total misstatements ($9,000) is less than revised materiality.

On the other hand, the auditors could conclude that the financial statements are not fairly presented because the total uncorrected errors ($9,000) exceed materiality of $8,000. We will discuss in later chapters all of the alternatives available to the auditors, but ''something would have to be done,'' such as (1) convincing the client to correct the errors or (2) considering a modification of the audit report.

What if the estimate of the total misstatements was less than $8,000? The auditors might use the materiality borders on net income ($3,000 to $8,000 from page 183) to help them make a judgment as to whether the financial statements should be accepted as fair and not misleading.

THE USE OF AUDIT RISK IN PLANNING AN AUDIT[2]

√*Audit risk* is defined as

> the risk that the auditor may unknowingly fail to appropriately modify his or her opinion on financial statements that are materially misstated.

Materiality must be coupled with consideration of audit risk in planning an audit. The auditors can then make the following types of statements:

> We will accept, *at a certain risk level,* the financial statements as not materially misstated if
>
> > income before income taxes is not misstated by more than $3,000,
> >
> > total assets are not misstated by more than $41,100,
> >
> > current assets are not misstated by more than $20,100, and
> >
> > stockholders' equity is not misstated by more than $17,400.

Figure 7.3 presents a sequence the auditor might use in applying the concept of audit risk to planning the audit. This sequence might not be formalized in audit practice because there is little guidance in the professional standards for doing so. Nevertheless, these steps are presented as a theoretical approach to the application of audit risk.

The Overall Planned Audit Risk √

The auditors consider the *overall planned audit risk* they are willing to take that they will attest to the fair presentation of the financial statements when, in fact, the financial statements are materially misstated. Considering the importance of this task, surprisingly few definitive guidelines exist on how the level of overall audit

---

[2] See ''Audit Risk—Tracing the Evolution,'' by Janet L. Colbert in *Accounting Horizons* (September 1987), pp. 49–57 for an additional discussion of audit risk.

FIGURE 7.3   Sequence of Steps in Applying the Concepts of Audit Risk

1. Set the *overall planned audit risk.*
2. Consider the *assertions* for each account balance and disclosure in the financial statements.
3. Set *detection risk* for each assertion for each account balance and disclosure by
   a. Setting an *individual audit risk* for each assertion.
   b. Assessing an *inherent risk* for each assertion.
   c. Assessing a *control risk* for each assertion.
   d. Using the audit risk model to determine the *detection risk* for each assertion.

risk should be set. *SAS No. 47* merely states that the audit should be planned so that audit risk will be limited to a low level.

Audit risk may be assessed in either quantitative or qualitative terms. We use a quantitative approach (e.g., a risk of 5 or 10 percent) to illustrate the concepts, although a qualitative approach (e.g., a low or moderate risk) may be more common in practice. In setting a certain overall audit risk, the auditors are also expressing a certain level of confidence. For example, a 5 percent overall audit risk that the auditors will incorrectly accept the financial statements as fairly presented is also a 95 percent confidence level that the financial statements are fairly presented if indeed the auditors state that they are. A 10 percent risk level is a 90 percent confidence level, and so on. Audit risk is the complement of the level of confidence.

By requiring that auditors set overall audit risk at a low level for purposes of planning their audit procedures, *SAS No. 47* implies that caution should be exercised. Remember that there is an inverse relationship between risk levels and the amount of necessary audit effort. (Lower risk levels mean more audit effort, and higher risk levels mean less audit effort.)

For example, auditors could use 5 percent as the overall risk level for planning purposes. (Could most of us "live" with a 95 percent confidence level that our business decisions are correct?) Using materiality amounts from the earlier part of the chapter, the auditors could express their decision guidelines in several ways.

- At an overall risk of 5 percent, the financial statements will be accepted as fairly presented in all material respects if the overall misstatement in income before income taxes is no more than $3,000.

  or

- The financial statements will be accepted as fairly presented in all material respects if there is no more than a 5 percent chance that income before income taxes is misstated by more than $3,000.

  or

- The financial statements will be accepted as fairly presented in all material respects if there is 95 percent confidence that income before income taxes is not misstated by more than $3,000.

Assertions in Financial Statements

All account balances and related disclosures in the financial statements represent expressed or implied assertions of management. These assertions were introduced in Chapter 6 and are used here to illustrate the concept of audit risk.

Consider, for example, the December 31, 19X8 cash balance of $150,000 shown in Figure 7.2. Management asserts that

1. The cash balance actually exists at December 31, 19X8.
2. They own and have unimpaired rights to this asset as of December 31, 19X8.
3. All cash owned at December 31, 19X8 is included in the balance shown.
4. The balance in the cash account as of December 31, 19X8 is properly valued.
5. The balance in the cash account as of December 31, 19X8 is properly classified, and all necessary disclosures conform with those required by generally accepted accounting principles.

The wording of management's assertions differs with each account balance and disclosure. Figure 7.4 provides examples of how the general assertions can be used to develop assertions for individual accounts.

FIGURE 7.4   Examples of General and Specific Account Assertions

| The General Assertions | Specific Assertions on | | |
	Accounts Receivable	Accounts Payable	Revenue and Expense Accounts
Existence or occurrence	Receivables represent amounts due from others.	Payables represent amounts due to others.	All recorded revenues and expenses occurred during the period.
Rights and obligations	Receivables represent amounts owned by the company.	Payables represent amounts owed by the company.	(This assertion is not applicable to these accounts.)
Completeness	All transactions that affected receivables are recorded.	All transactions that affected payables are recorded.	All revenues and expenses applicable to the period are recorded.
Valuation or allocation	Receivables are stated at net realizable value.	Payables are reflected at proper amounts.	Expenses are properly matched with revenues.
Presentation and disclosure	Receivables are properly classified, and disclosures are adequate.	Payables are properly classified, and disclosures are adequate.	Revenues and expenses are properly classified, and disclosures are adequate.

There is a risk that the accounts with which these assertions are associated contain material misstatements that make these assertions invalid. (If there are enough invalid assertions in the account balances, the financial statements could be materially misstated. So a potentially invalid assertion is important.)

▶ **EXAMPLE**

The allowance for doubtful accounts could be so significantly understated that the valuation assertion for accounts receivable described in Figure 7.4 could be invalid. This may result in the entire accounts receivable balance being materially misstated.

Setting Detection Risk for Each Assertion

The auditor cannot prevent a material misstatement in an assertion, but he or she can adjust audit procedures to set an acceptable risk of not detecting these material misstatements. To do so, the auditor uses the following steps.

Decide on an Individual Audit Risk for Each Assertion

The *individual audit risk* for each assertion is

> the risk that the assertion contains material misstatements that, when aggregated with misstatements in other assertions, could make the entire financial statements materially misstated.

There are no official guidelines for setting individual audit risks for each assertion. The auditor decides how much risk he or she is willing to take that an assertion accepted as valid might be invalid because of material misstatements. Auditors are likely to be cautious and initially set individual audit risks at the same low level as the overall planned audit risk.

Assess Inherent Risk for Each Assertion

Every assertion has a "built-in" risk that it might be invalid simply because of the nature of the assertion and the account or disclosure to which it relates. *Inherent risk* is

> the susceptibility of an assertion to a material misstatement, assuming that there are no related internal control policies or procedures.

▶ **EXAMPLE**

The calculation of allowance for doubtful accounts is often complex and is derived from accounting estimates. The complexity and subjectivity of the estimates increase the probability of misstatement. Without regard to control measures (such as firm policies on credit approvals), a risk of material misstatements may be inherent in the account.

Assess Control Risk for Each Assertion

Control risk is

> the risk that a material misstatement that could occur in an assertion will not be prevented or detected on a timely basis by the entity's internal control policies and procedures.

▶ **EXAMPLE**

An accounts payable system is designed and placed in operation to record merchandise received, vendor invoices, and payments to creditors. Still, there is a risk that the system will not detect or prevent unrecorded purchases and accounts payable.

Set Detection Risk for Each Assertion

Detection risk is

> the risk that the auditor will not detect a material misstatement that exists in an assertion.

▶ **EXAMPLE**

To determine the validity of the existence and rights assertions relating to accounts receivable, the auditor sends letters to a sample of the client's customers asking them to respond directly to him or her and to state whether the balance on the client's records is correct. There is a risk that this evidence will not detect falsified receivables or other material errors in the assertions. The sample of letters may not have included the falsified receivables, or the auditor may have misinterpreted some replies from customers whose accounts were in dispute.

Detection risk relates to the nature, timing, and extent of evidence that the auditor gathers to test assertions that relate to account balances and disclosures in the financial statements. Figure 7.5 identifies procedures the auditor uses to test the validity of the existence and completeness assertions associated with the accounts payable balance.

FIGURE 7.5   Examples of Audit Procedures Relating to the Existence and Completeness Accounts Payable Assertions

The General Assertions	Specific Assertions Relating to Accounts Payable	Procedures the Auditor Uses to Establish the Validity of These Assertions
Existence or occurrence	Payables represent amounts owed by the entity.	Compare accounts payable recorded on the books with vendor invoice and receiving report.
Completeness	All transactions that affect accounts payable are recorded.	Send letters to vendors asking them to send directly to the auditor a detailed statement of the amount the client owes the vendors.

Assume that the auditor uses only the procedures described in Figure 7.5 to test the validity of the two specific accounts payable assertions. Further assume that the accounts payable account contains errors and omissions that render these two assertions invalid and result in the material misstatement of accounts payable. For example, (1) material errors were made in compiling the recorded accounts payable from purchase invoices, receiving reports, and so on, and (2) material purchases were omitted from the listings that constitute the recorded accounts payable.

The auditor cannot eliminate the risk that these material misstatements will not be detected by the audit procedures performed to test the validity of the existence or occurrence and completeness assertions. However, the two sources of detection risk can be identified, and each source can be controlled through the auditor's actions.

1. *Nonsampling risk.* Uncertainties still exist even if the auditor examines 100 percent of an account balance. Specifically, the auditor may
    a. Use the incorrect audit procedure.
    b. Misapply an auditing procedure.
    c. Misinterpret an audit result.

Figure 7.6 shows how the auditor could make all three of these mistakes with the procedures described in Figure 7.5.

FIGURE 7.6   **Examples of the Nonsampling Element of Detection Risk**

	Nonsampling Error Made by Auditor		
Audit Procedure	*Use of an Incorrect Audit Procedure*	*Misapplying an Audit Procedure*	*Misinterpreting an Audit Result*
To test the validity of the accounts payable assertions of existence and occurrence, compare accounts payable recorded on the books with purchase orders.	Amounts should have been compared with vendor invoices and receiving reports.		
To test the validity of the accounts payable assertion of completeness, send letters to vendors with large year-end balances asking them to send directly to the auditor a detailed statement of the amount the client owes the vendor.		Letters should have been sent to vendors with significant purchases during the year (where understatements are more likely to exist) rather than to vendors with large balances at year-end.	The auditor should have examined vendors' replies closer to detect invoices not listed on client records.

The nonsampling element of detection risk can be controlled by proper audit training and supervision as well as by the use of quality control measures discussed in Chapter 2.

2. *Sampling risk.* Uncertainties are implicit when the auditor examines less than 100 percent of an account balance. That is, there is a risk that the sample results will not be representative of the account balance. For example, the auditor might correctly compare a sample of recorded accounts payable amounts with vendor invoices and receiving reports, but the sample may not contain amounts with material misstatements. This sampling element of detection risk cannot be eliminated when sampling is used, but it can be controlled by careful attention to proper sampling techniques, as illustrated in Chapters 10 and 14.

The sampling element of detection risk can be specified and quantified by use of an *audit risk model.* This model is used for planning and provides guidelines for establishing the detection risk for each relevant assertion. The level of detection risk for each relevant assertion influences not only the sample size of audit procedures (the scope), but also the types of audit procedures (the nature) and the time at which the auditing procedures will be performed (the timing).

Here is the equation for the audit risk model as derived from concepts illustrated in *SAS No. 47* and *SAS No. 39.*

$$\text{Individual audit risk} = \text{Inherent risk} \times \text{Control risk} \times \text{Detection risk}$$

For our purposes, the model is restated as

$$\text{Detection risk} = \frac{\text{Individual audit risk}}{\text{Inherent risk} \times \text{Control risk}}$$

The model is, in some ways, oversimplified. For example:

1. To reduce detection risk, the auditor performs both analytical procedures and tests of details. Thus, detection risk is sometimes subdivided into the risk that
   a. Analytical procedures will not detect a material misstatement.
   b. Tests of details will not detect a material misstatement.
2. As a practical measure, the auditor sometimes assesses inherent and control risks together because of the difficulty of assessing them separately. It may be difficult, for example, to determine whether the susceptibility of cash to theft is inherent or is caused by weak or nonexistent controls over custody of cash.

Figure 7.7 illustrates the computations and the reasons for selecting the amounts

FIGURE 7.7   Illustration of the Audit Risk Model

Accounts Payable Assertion	*Individual Audit Risk/*	*Inherent Risk*	$\times$	*Control Risk*	$=$	*Detection Risk*
All transactions that affected payables are recorded.	0.05	/ 0.60	$\times$	0.30	$=$	0.28

The above calculation indicates that the auditor plans to accept a 0.28 risk (approximately one chance in four) that substantive tests of the accounts payable assertion of completeness will not detect material misstatements that render the assertion invalid. The scope of audit procedures is set using this risk as a guide. (Note that, although the detection risk is high at 0.28, the overall audit risk is low at 0.05.)

1. Individual audit risk is set at a low 0.05 (5 percent) level for this assertion because of the low overall audit risk.
2. Inherent risk is set at a relatively high 0.60 (60 percent) because of
   a. Economic factors; that is, the client needs a high current ratio to show debt-paying ability on its balance sheet.
   b. A high volume of purchases is made from decentralized locations.
3. Control risk is set at a relatively low 0.30 (30 percent) because accounts payable records are adequate and there is a separation of duties among key personnel.

used in the computations. Given the level of individual audit risk (0.05), Figure 7.8 demonstrates the inverse relationship between detection risk and inherent risk and between detection risk and control risk.

FIGURE 7.8   Inverse Relationships Between Detection Risk and Inherent and Control Risks

---

Assumption   The inherent risk is set at 0.80 rather than 0.60 because the auditor believes there is a higher risk of misstatement that renders the completeness assertion invalid.

$$\text{Individual Audit Risk} / \text{Inherent Risk} \times \text{Control Risk} = \text{Detection Risk}$$
$$0.05 \qquad\qquad /0.80 \qquad\quad \times 0.30 \qquad = 0.20$$

This means that the auditor will *plan* on a *lower* detection risk and will have to *increase* the scope of audit procedures to achieve this lower risk.

Assumption   The control risk is set at 0.20 rather than 0.30 because the auditor believes there is a lower risk that internal controls will not prevent or detect misstatements that render the assertion invalid.

$$\text{Individual Audit Risk} / \text{Inherent Risk} \times \text{Control Risk} = \text{Detection Risk}$$
$$0.05 \qquad\qquad /0.60 \qquad\quad \times 0.20 \qquad = 0.42$$

This means that the auditor will *plan* on a *higher* detection risk and can *decrease* the scope of audit procedures to achieve this higher risk.

Summary of Audit Risk for Planning the Audit

Figure 7.9 shows the relationship between the audit risks discussed here and the parts of the audit described earlier in the chapter.

FIGURE 7.9   Relationship Between Audit Risks and Parts of an Audit

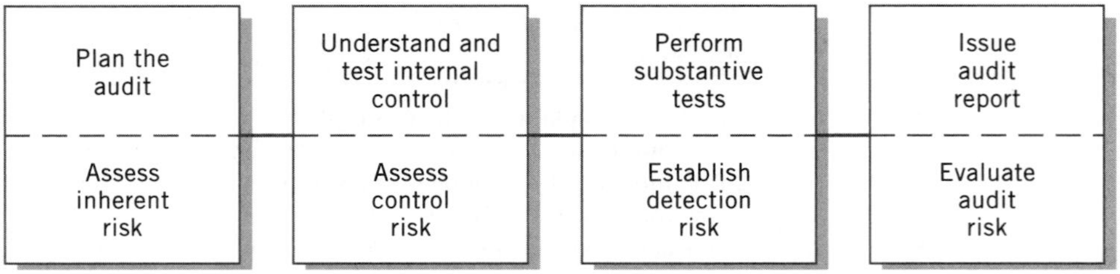

Plan the audit	Understand and test internal control	Perform substantive tests	Issue audit report
Assess inherent risk	Assess control risk	Establish detection risk	Evaluate audit risk

Figure 7.10 illustrates the entire audit risk concept by showing factors the auditor would consider for inherent, control, and detection risk.

THE USE OF AUDIT RISK IN EVALUATING EVIDENCE

The audit risk model discussed in the previous section is a planning model, so it is not normally used in the evaluation of audit evidence. Auditors subjectively aggre-

FIGURE 7.10   Illustration of the Audit Risk Concept

	Examples of Attributes Considered by the Auditor		*Responses by the Auditor*
	Inherent Risk	*Control Risk*	*Detection Risk*

Financial statement level	• Profitability relative to the industry
	• Sensitivity of operating results to economic factors
	• Going concern problems
	• Nature, cause, and amount of known and likely misstatements detected in the prior audit
	• Management turnover
	• Management reputation
	• Management accounting skills
		• Business planning, budgeting, and monitoring of performance
		• Management attitude and actions regarding financial reporting
		• Management consultation with auditors
		• Management concern about external influences
		• Audit committee
		• Internal audit function
		• Personnel policies and procedures
		• Effectiveness of the accounting system
			• Overall audit strategy
			  • Number of locations
			  • Significant balances or transaction classes
			• Degree of professional skepticism
			• Staffing
			• Levels of supervision and review

Account balance or transaction class level (including assessment for individual assertions)	• Difficult to audit accounts or transactions
	• Contentious or difficult accounting issues
	• Susceptibility to misappropriation
	• Complexity of calculations
	• Extent of judgment related to assertions
	• Sensitivity of valuations to economic factors
	• Nature, cause, and amount of known and likely misstatements detected in the prior audit
		• Effectiveness of the accounting system
		• Personnel policies and procedures
		• Adequacy of accounting records
		• Segregation of duties
		• Adequacy of safeguards over assets and records (including software)
		• Independent checks on performance
			• Substantive analytical procedures and tests of details
			  • Nature of tests
			  • Timing of tests
			  • Extent of tests

Source: AICPA, *Audit Guide for Consideration of the Internal Control Structure in a Financial Statement Audit* (1990), p. 210.

gate risk assessments across assertions and accounts. When evaluating audit evidence, however, certain situations (such as unexpected control deficiencies or unexpected errors in the accounts) might make an achieved individual audit risk higher than planned (perhaps 0.20 rather than 0.05). Additional audit effort should be applied to the assertions for which these unexpected situations occurred.

There is also a business risk that the entity will fail because of poor management, unexpected competition, or a combination of events beyond anyone's control. All too often, the general public confuses business and audit risk and tends to place all the blame for a business failure on the auditor.

Chapter 7 ► GLOSSARY OF TERMS

Audit risk   The risk that the auditor may unknowingly fail to appropriately modify his or her opinion on financial statements that are materially misstated.

Audit risk model   A planning model used to provide guidelines for the level at which detection risk will be set.

Control risk   The risk that a material misstatement that could occur in an assertion will not be prevented or detected on a timely basis by the entity's internal control policies and procedures.

Detection risk   The risk that the auditor will not detect a material misstatement that exists in an assertion.

Individual audit risk   The risk that the assertion contains material misstatements that, when aggregated with misstatements in other assertions, could make the financial statements materially misstated.

Inherent risk   The susceptibility of an assertion to material misstatement, assuming that there are no related internal control policies or procedures.

Material misstatement   Errors or fraud whose effect is important enough to cause the financial statements not to be fairly presented in conformity with generally accepted accounting principles.

Materiality   The magnitude of an omission or misstatement of accounting information that, in the light of surrounding circumstances, makes it probable that a reasonable person's judgment would be changed or influenced by the omission or misstatement.

Materiality borders   A range of possible dollar misstatements in the financial statements. Any combination of misstatements that totals more than the upper end of the range is considered material. Any combination of misstatements that totals less than the lower end of the range is considered immaterial. Any combination of misstatements within the range calls for additional judgment by the auditor.

Nonsampling risk   The uncertainties that are implicit when the auditor examines 100 percent of an account balance.

Overall planned audit risk   The risk that auditors are willing to take that they will attest to the fair presentation of financial statements when, in fact, the financial statements are materially misstated.

Preliminary estimates of materiality   Estimates of materiality made during the planning phase of the audit.

Sampling   An examination of less than 100 percent of the items in a population, the results of which are projected to the population.

Sampling risk   The uncertainties that are implicit when the auditor examines less than 100 percent of an account balance.

Tolerable misstatement   The portions of total materiality for the financial statements that are allocated to individual accounts for planning purposes.

Chapter 7 ► REFERENCES

American Institute of Certified Public Accountants. *Professional Standards.*
  AU Section 312 [*SAS No. 47*]—*Audit Risk and Materiality in Conducting an Audit.*
  AU Section 350 [*SAS No. 39*]—*Audit Sampling.*
Alderman, C. Wayne, and Tabor, Richard H. "The Case for Risk Driven Audits," *Journal of Accountancy* (March 1989), pp. 55–61.
Chewning, Gene, Pany, Kurt, and Wheeler, Stephen. "Auditor Reporting Decisions Involving Accounting Principles Changes: Some Evidence on Materiality Thresholds," *Journal of Accounting Research* (Spring 1989), pp. 78–96.

Colbert, Janet L. "Audit Risk—Tracing the Evolution," *Accounting Horizons* (September 1987), pp. 49–57.
Daniel, Shirley J. "Some Empirical Evidence about the Assessment of Audit Risk in Practice," *Auditing: A Journal of Practice and Theory* (Spring 1988), pp. 174–181.
Houghton, Clarence W., and Fogarty, John A. "Inherent Risk," *Auditing: A Journal of Practice and Theory* (Spring 1991), pp. 1–21.
Huss, H. Fenwick, and Jacobs, Fred. "Risk Containment: Exploring Auditor Decisions in the Engagement Process," *Auditing: A Journal of Practice and Theory* (Fall 1991), pp. 16–32.

Chapter 7 ▶ REVIEW QUESTIONS

 7-1 Describe what the auditor does in each of the following sections of an audit.
  a. Planning.
  b. Studying and testing internal control.
  c. Performing substantive tests.
  d. Issuing the audit report.

7-2 Paraphrase the section or sections of the scope and/or opinion paragraphs that refer or allude to the following terms:
  a. Material.
  b. Risk.
  c. Sampling.

 7-3 Describe six quantitative and five qualitative factors auditors may consider when making materiality decisions.

7-4 Why do auditors make preliminary estimates of materiality for the total financial statements?

7-5 Why do auditors make preliminary estimates of materiality for the individual accounts in the financial statements?

7-6 Explain two alternative courses of action that the auditor can follow if the total misstatement in the financial statements is more than materiality for the total financial statements.

7-7 Describe the sequence the auditor might use in applying the concept of audit risk to planning the audit.

7-8 Name the five general assertions in financial statements.

7-9 Describe the four steps the auditor takes to set an acceptable risk of not detecting material misstatements in an assertion.

7-10 Describe the two sources of detection risk that can be identified and controlled by the auditor.

7-11 Give two versions of the audit risk model.

7-12 Demonstrate with percentages the inverse relationship between (1) detection risk and inherent risk and (2) detection risk and control risk.

7-13 Why is the audit risk model not normally used in the evaluation of audit evidence?

7-14 Why is it inappropriate to apply the audit risk model to business risk?

Chapter 7 ▶ OBJECTIVE QUESTIONS

(* = author prepared; ** = CPA examination)

 *7-15 Which of the following parts of the audit is described by this statement? "The auditor examines and evaluates processes that produce the numbers and disclosures in the financial statements."
  a. Planning.
  b. Studying and testing internal control.
  c. Performing substantive tests.
  d. Issuing the audit report.

*7-16 Which of the following parts of the audit is described by this statement? "The auditor examines evidence supporting the account balances and disclosures in the financial statements."
  a. Planning.
  b. Studying and testing internal control.
  c. Performing substantive tests.
  d. Issuing the audit report.

*7-17 Which of the following phrases or sentences in the independent auditor's report is improperly stated?

  a. Those standards require that we plan and perform the audit to obtain assurance about whether the financial statements are free of material misstatement. *reasonable*
  b. An audit includes examining, on a test basis, . . .
  c. In our opinion, the financial statements referred to above present fairly, in all material respects, . . .
  d. We conducted our audit in accordance with generally accepted auditing standards.

 *7-18 The term *testing* alludes to the concept of
  a. A guarantee.
  b. A certificate.
  c. Accuracy.
  d. Sampling.

 *7-19 Which of the following is an incorrect statement?
  a. Financial statements are materially misstated when they contain misstatements whose effect, individually or in the aggregate, is impor-

tant enough to cause the financial statements not to be presented fairly, in all material respects, in conformity with generally accepted accounting principles.

b. Materiality for planning purposes is the largest aggregate level of misstatements that could be considered material to any one of the financial statements.

c. Preliminary judgments about materiality may differ from judgments about materiality used in evaluating the audit findings.

d. If significantly lower materiality levels become appropriate in evaluating audit findings, the auditor should reevaluate the sufficiency of the audit procedures.

*7-20 Which of the following is an incorrect statement?

a. Detection risk is a function of the effectiveness of an auditing procedure and its application.

b. Detection risk arises partly from uncertainties that exist when the auditor does not examine 100 percent of the population.

c. Detection risk arises partly because of other uncertainties that exist even if the auditor were to examine 100 percent of the population.

d. Detection risk exists independently of the audit of the financial statements.

*7-21 Which of the following is an incorrect statement?

a. Detection risk cannot be changed at the auditor's discretion.

b. If individual audit risk remains the same, detection risk bears an inverse relationship to inherent and control risks.

c. The greater the inherent and control risks the auditor believes exist, the less detection risk that can be accepted.

d. The auditor might make separate or combined assessments of inherent risk and control risk.

**7-22 The existence of audit risk is recognized by the statement in the independent auditor's standard report that the auditor

a. Obtains reasonable assurance about whether the financial statements are free of material misstatement.

b. Assesses the accounting principles used and also evaluates the overall financial statement presentation.

c. Realizes some matters, either individually or in the aggregate, are important while other matters are not important.

d. Is responsible for expressing an opinion on the financial statements, which are the responsibility of management.

**7-23 The risk that an auditor will conclude, based on audit tests, that a material misstatement does not exist in an account balance when, in fact, such misstatement does exist is referred to as

a. Sampling risk.

b. Detection risk.

c. Nonsampling risk.

d. Inherent risk.

**7-24 Inherent risk and control risk differ from detection risk in that inherent risk and control risk are

a. Elements of audit risk while detection risk is not.

b. Changed at the auditor's discretion while detection risk is not.

c. Considered at the individual account balance level while detection risk is not.

d. Functions of the client and its environment while detection risk is not.

**7-25 Inherent risk and control risk differ from detection risk in that they

a. Arise from the misapplication of auditing procedures.

b. May be assessed in either quantitative or nonquantitative terms.

c. Exist independently of the financial statement audit.

d. Can be changed at the auditor's discretion.

**7-26 Which of the following statements is *not* correct about materiality?

a. The concept of materiality recognizes that some matters are important for fair presentation of financial statements in conformity with GAAP, while other matters are *not* important.

b. An auditor considers materiality for planning purposes in terms of the largest aggregate level of misstatements that could be material to any one of the financial statements.

c. Materiality judgments are made in light of surrounding circumstances and necessarily involve both quantitative and qualitative judgments.

d. An auditor's consideration of materiality is influenced by the auditor's perception of the needs of a reasonable person who will rely on the financial statements.

**7-27 The acceptable level of detection risk is inversely related to the

a. Assurance provided by substantive tests.

b. Risk of misapplying auditing procedures.

c. Preliminary judgment about materiality levels.

d. Risk of failing to discover material misstatements.

7-28 For each description, list the letter or letters of the term or terms that are identified with the description. Each term may be used once, more than once, or not at all.

Description	Term
1. This term is contained in the scope paragraph of the independent auditor's report.	a. Material
2. This term is contained in the opinion paragraph of the independent auditor's report.	b. Control risk
	c. Detection risk
3. This term is a quantitative consideration in materiality.	d. Net income before taxes
4. This term is an assertion.	e. Existence
5. This term is part of the audit risk model.	

(handwritten answers: 1. a; 2. ?; 3. d; 4. e; 5. b, c)

**7-29 This question consists of 15 items pertaining to an auditor's risk analysis of an entity. Select the *best* answer for each item.

Bond, CPA, is considering audit risk at the financial statement level in planning the audit of Toxic Waste Disposal (TWD) Company's financial statements for the year ended December 31, 19X3. TWD is a privately owned entity that contracts with municipal governments to remove environmental wastes. Audit risk at the financial statement level is influenced by the risk of material misstatements, which may be indicated by a combination of factors related to management, the industry, and the entity.

Required:

Based only on the information below, indicate whether each of the following factors would most likely increase audit risk, decrease audit risk, or have *no* effect on audit risk. Give reasons why.

Company Profile:

a. This was the first year TWD operated at a profit since 19W9 because the municipalities received increased federal and state funding for environmental purposes.

b. TWD's Board of Directors is controlled by Mead, the majority stockholder, who also acts as the chief executive officer.

c. The internal auditor reports to the controller and the controller reports to Mead.

d. The accounting department has experienced a high rate of turnover of key personnel.

e. TWD's bank has a loan officer who meets regularly with TWD's CEO and controller to monitor TWD's financial performance.

f. TWD's employees are paid biweekly.

g. Bond has audited TWD for five years.

Recent Developments:

h. During 19X3, TWD changed its method of preparing its financial statements from the cash basis to generally accepted accounting principles.

i. During 19X3, TWD sold one half of its controlling interest in United Equipment Leasing (UEL) Co. TWD retained a significant interest in UEL.

j. During 19X3, litigation filed against TWD in 19W8 alleging that TWD discharged pollutants into state waterways was dropped by the state. Loss contingency disclosures that TWD included in prior years' financial statements are being removed for the 19X3 financial statements.

k. During December 19X3, TWD signed a contract to lease disposal equipment from an entity owned by Mead's parents. This related party transaction is not disclosed in TWD's notes to its 19X3 financial statements.

l. During December 19X3, TWD completed a barter transaction with a municipality. TWD removed waste from a municipally owned site and acquired title to another contaminated site at below market price. TWD intends to service this new site in 19X4.

m. During December 19X3, TWD increased its casualty insurance coverage on several pieces of sophisticated machinery from historical cost to replacement cost.

n. Inquiries about the substantial increase in revenue TWD recorded in the fourth quarter of 19X3 disclosed a new policy. TWD guaranteed to several municipalities that it would refund the federal and state funding paid to TWD if any municipality fails federal or state site clean-up inspection in 19X4.

o. An initial public offering of TWD's stock is planned for late 19X4.

Chapter 7 ▶ DISCUSSION/CASE QUESTIONS

(* = author prepared; ** = CPA examination)

*7-30 Evaluate the following statement:
There is a 10 percent or less risk that the financial statements are misstated by more than $3,000.

Required:

a. Give the definition of materiality and audit risk.

b. Indicate the way(s) in which materiality and audit risk are incorporated in the preceding statement.

**7-31 Audit risk and materiality should be considered when planning and performing an audit of financial statements in accordance with generally accepted auditing standards. Audit risk and materiality should also be considered together in determining the nature, timing, and extent of auditing procedures and in evaluating the results of those procedures.

Required:

a. 1. Define materiality.

2. Discuss the factors affecting its determination.

3. Describe the relationship between materiality for planning purposes and materiality for evaluation purposes.

b. 1. Define audit risk.

2. Describe its components of inherent risk, control risk, and detection risk.

3. Explain how these components are interrelated.

*7-32 Begin Company was organized in January of 19X7. The company is in the business of taking computer chips from discarded personal computers and making vases and other items that are used to decorate residences.

Begin had managed to raise $200,000 from the sale of capital stock and $400,000 by borrowing on a long-term note. In 19X8, it borrowed another $50,000 on a long-term note. However, certain provisions in the notes give the bank the right to call the notes if the current ratio falls below 2 to 1 in the balance sheet issued at the end of the second year of operations.

By using skillful marketing techniques and holding down expenses, the company was "in the black" by 19X8. However, federal authorities had cited Begin several times for paying its employees less than the required minimum wage.

In late 19X8 Begin engaged a CPA firm to audit its financial statements, parts of which are shown in Figure 7.1 and 7.2. During the planning stages of the audit, the CPA firm decided that the threshold of materiality would be a misstatement of income before income tax expense of $10,000.

Required:

a. Using the amounts in Figures 7.1 and 7.2 assign the materiality of $10,000 to the appropriate accounts in the financial statements. Supply a written justification for the tolerable misstatement assigned to each account. If you did not assign some of the $10,000 to certain accounts, explain why.

b. For each of the accounts to which you assigned some of the $10,000 of materiality, indicate what steps you might take if the misstatements found in the account exceeded, by a small amount, the tolerable misstatement assigned to that account.

c. Assume that, after aggregating the misstatements in each account, the total is $11,000.

What are the possible actions you could take? Indicate the advantages and disadvantages of each possible course of action.

    d. Assume that, after aggregating the misstatements in each account, the total is $15,000. In what way, if any, would your possible courses of action be different from the possible courses of action you might take in situation (c) above?

*7-33 Using the audit risk model, calculate detection risk if the other risks are set at these levels.

    a. Individual audit risk of 5 percent.
        Inherent risk of 50 percent.
        Control risk of 40 percent.

    b. Individual audit risk of 5 percent.
        Inherent risk of 70 percent.
        Control risk of 20 percent.

Why might inherent risk be set at 70 percent rather than at 50 percent?
Why might control risk be set at 20 percent rather than at 40 percent?

*7-34 For the following sets of circumstances, indicate whether the auditor would have a high or low risk of failing to detect these circumstances with appropriate audit procedures. Give reasons for your answers.

    a. When the company took a physical inventory on December 31, 19X6, one out of every ten items was miscounted by an average of 5 to 12 percent of its correct amount.

    b. The allowance for doubtful accounts was stated at 2 percent of accounts receivable. The allowance should have been stated between 6 and 10 percent of accounts receivable. The dollar amount of accounts receivable is ten times as much as net income.

    c. Accounts payable is understated by 3 percent as a result of leaving some accounts off the books at the end of the year. These accounts were not paid until 45 days after the end of the fiscal year. The dollar amount of accounts payable is $30,000, and net income is $20,000.

*7-35 The auditor decided to examine 100 percent of the invoices supporting additions to property and equipment. Several months after the audit was completed and the audit report was issued, significant amounts of expenditures were discovered to have been charged to the property and equipment accounts instead of repairs expense. Explain how the auditor could have overlooked these misclassifications.

**7-36 Green, CPA, is considering audit risk at the financial statement level in planning the audit of National Federal Bank (NFB) Company's financial statements for the year ended December 31, 19X0. Audit risk at the financial statement level is influenced by the risk of material misstatements, which may be indicated by a combination of factors related to management, the industry, and the entity. In assessing such factors Green has gathered the following information concerning NFB's environment.

Company Profile: NFB is a federally insured bank that has been consistently more profitable than the industry average by marketing mortgages on properties in a prosperous rural area, which has experienced considerable growth in recent years. NFB packages its mortgages and sells them to large mortgage investment trusts. Despite recent volatility of interest rates, NFB has been able to continue selling its mortgages as a source of new lendable funds.

    NFB's board of directors is controlled by Smith, the majority stockholder, who also acts as the chief executive officer. Management at the bank's branch offices has authority for directing and controlling NFB's operations and is compensated based on branch profitability. The internal auditor reports directly to Harris, a minority shareholder, who also acts as chairman of the board's audit committee.

The accounting department has experienced little turnover in personnel during the five years Green has audited NFB. NFB's formula consistently underestimates the allowance for loan losses, but its controller has always been receptive to Green's suggestions to increase the allowance during each engagement.

Recent Developments: During 19X0, NFB opened a branch office in a suburban town 30 miles from its principal place of business. Although this branch is not yet profitable due to competition from several well-established regional banks, management believes that the branch will be profitable by 19X2.

Also, during 19X0, NFB increased the efficiency of its accounting operations by installing a new, sophisticated computer system.

Required:

Based only on the information above, describe the factors that would most likely have an effect on the risk of material misstatements. Indicate whether each factor increases or decreases the risk. Use the format illustrated below.

Environmental factor	Effect on risk of material misstatements
Branch manager has authority for directing and controlling operations.	Increase

*7-37   Assume that the audit risk model used to set detection risk contains the following percentages (from the prior-year audit) relating to the valuation assertion for net accounts receivable.

Individual audit risk for this assertion	0.05
Inherent risk for this assertion	0.40
Control risk for this assertion	0.40
Detection risk for this assertion	?

Required:

a. Use the audit risk model to set the detection risk used in the prior-year audit.

b. In your own words, indicate what detection risk means.

c. Answer the following questions:

1. What reason might the auditor have to assess inherent risk for the valuation assertion at less than 0.40 for this year's audit? At more than 0.40 for this year's audit?

2. What reason might the auditor have to assess control risk for the valuation assertion at less than 0.40 for this year's audit? At more than 0.40 for this year's audit?

*7-38   The noise of the huge folder dropping on his desk startled Alan Weisner, a new staff member of Kosner & Kosner. He had recently returned from the firm's staff training school.

"What's this?" inquired Alan as he looked up to Benny Curtz, whose imposing six-foot frame seemed to tower over the small cubicle directly outside the ornate offices of the audit seniors and supervisors.

"It's an audit program for Begin Company, that hardware chain outfit. We're starting the final work this Monday."

"So you want me to look over the program this weekend?"

"Right! Meet me in my office at 8:00 sharp and we'll go over it. That bunch out there at Begin can be pretty cranky, so we need to walk in there as sharp as can be and ready for work."

"Ok," replied Alan sheepishly, "It's just that this weekend I was going to . . ."

"Work in a review of this program," snapped Benny. "Take a long look and make sure you know what we're trying to do out there."

"We're doing the year-end part of the audit, aren't we?"

"This is a lot more messy than anything you saw in training school. These guys have a dozen or more lawsuits against them, and, as usual, they messed up their inventory count and who knows what they're trying to do to make up for it."

Alan stared at his new audit senior. "And I'm assigned to this audit?"

"Yeah. I asked Susan down the hall to give me someone else who's been around a bit."

"And . . ."

"Can't do it. Everyone's tied up. Anyway, you finished first in the training school and Mr. Kosner thought it would be good experience for you."

"Sounds like it," replied Alan. "So I'll look at this program over the weekend and meet you Monday morning."

"Make a list of any questions you have about what you're doing. Begin's controller will spot you as a new auditor the minute you walk in the door. You need to know as much about Begin as possible. I've given you last year's working papers and the permanent file, which includes our proposed audit program. We've already changed it some because of what we found out there last October when we did the internal control work. We'll probably change it some more."

"Ok, Benny, I'll spend a few hours looking at it and make out some questions for you."

At home that weekend, Alan pulled out the section of the working papers that contained a brief history of Begin Company. He read through a description of the company's beginning as a neighborhood hardware store and current situation as a 10-store chain that covered all the metropolitan area. Next, he carefully reviewed last year's working papers, paying particular attention to attorneys' correspondence and the work done on Begin's large inventory. Then, he looked at this year's proposed audit program and the preliminary financial statements for the year ended December 31, 19X8. Finally, Alan turned on his personal computer, created a file, and began typing out questions he would ask Benny Curtz Monday morning. Here are some of his questions.

1. Why did we assess $3,500 as the total materiality for the financial statements? It looks to me like their listed inventory of $280,000 could be misstated by at least that much.

2. In what way will all these pending lawsuits affect our materiality assessment? I learned in my auditing course and in the training school that these types of things had to be considered, but I'm not sure how.

3. I noticed that the audit program uses the audit risk model on each assertion the way I was taught in school. But I have some questions on it.

   a. Why are we using a 5 percent audit risk on each assertion? The problems that Begin has had with its inventory counts and perpetual inventory seem to indicate that most of our work should be in that area.

   b. For Prepaid Expenses, Equipment, and Buildings, you have inherent risk and control risk assessed together. The total dollar amount of these accounts on Begin's 12-31-X8 balance sheet is $720,000 of the total assets of $1,370,000. Isn't there some difference between the two risks for these large accounts?

   c. At the same time, you assign a high inherent risk to cash even though it's only $150,000 of the total assets of $1,370,000. I know hardware stores have many cash registers and open spaces. But why spend so much time on such a relatively small amount that has never been troublesome?

4. I'm a little curious about our sampling plans. For example:

   a. Why are we checking every bank reconciliation for Begin's cash account? Is this a function of the high inherent risk we put on all the assertions for the cash account?

   b. We plan to look at every purchase transaction from December 15, 19X8 to January 15, 19X9. Why such a long period? Cutoff problems fall near the end of December, don't they?

    c. Will the agreement with the bank on its long-term debt be considered in deciding how much work to do on the $450,000 of notes payable? The bank requires that certain ratios be maintained.

    d. Why are we sending out such a large sample of letters to accounts payable creditors?

On Monday morning, Alan met with Benny and presented him with a list of questions, some of which are shown above. Benny looked wide-eyed at the list for a few minutes, but slowly began to answer them, trying, as best he could, to be as practical as possible in his replies.

Required:

Write the answers you would give to Alan if you were Benny.

*7-39 Custom Furniture Company was ready for an audit by a new CPA firm after replacing the previous auditor who had performed the audit for several years. The lawsuit filed by Custom's creditors against the predecessor auditors was still in court, but the billing clerk and cashier who perpetrated last year's fraud had been replaced by experienced and bonded personnel. Several members of the board of directors had been replaced, and Custom Furniture Company had a new group of officers.

    Taught and Tight, CPAs, were hired to be the new auditors after submitting the low bid among a large group of CPA firms. A number of "get acquainted" meetings had been held, and at the present time, relations between Custom Furniture Company and its new auditors seemed to be pleasant.

    Tonnie, an experienced audit senior, and Bill, a new staff assistant, were assigned to perform the audit of the financial statements for the year ended December 31, 19X8. Even though it was early in 19X8, Tonnie and Bill were holding meetings to plan the audit. The initial plan was to obtain an understanding of and test Custom's internal control in October 19X8 and then to return in mid-January 19X9 to perform the remaining work.

    Tonnie and Bill were reviewing Custom's financial statements for the year ended December 31, 19X7, which had been audited by the prior CPA firm and adjusted for the thefts of the billing clerk and cashier. Consultations had been held with the prior CPA firm, and Tonnie and Bill had no reason to believe the 19X7 financial statements were not fairly presented after all adjustments were recorded. Some of the financial statements are shown on the next two pages.

Custom Furniture Company
Statement of Income
Year Ended December 31, 19X7

Sales	$3,963,292	100.00%
Sales returns and allowances	138,715	3.50%
Net sales	$3,824,577	96.50%
Cost of goods sold	2,932,685	74.00%
Gross margin	$891,892	22.50%
Operating expenses:		
Selling expenses	$219,913	5.55%
Administrative expenses	175,548	4.43%
Total expenses	$395,461	9.98%
Operating income	$496,431	12.53%
Other income	29,450	0.74%
	$525,881	13.27%
Interest expense	10,330	0.26%
Income before income taxes	$515,551	13.01%
Income taxes	175,417	4.43%
Net income	$340,134	8.58%
Earnings per share	$1.42	

Custom Furniture Company
Balance Sheet
December 31, 19X7

Assets			
Current assets			
Cash and cash equivalents		$112,500	5.5%
Accounts receivable	387,695		
Allowance for doubtful accounts	11,540	376,155	18.5%
Inventories		513,668	25.2%
Prepaid expenses		13,025	0.6%
Total current assets		$1,015,348	49.8%
Noncurrent assets			
Investments in long-term securities		$75,025	3.7%
Land		125,000	6.1%
Building	265,000		
Less: Accumulated depreciation	29,444	235,556	11.6%
Equipment, furniture, and fixtures	703,350		
Less: Accumulated depreciation	117,225	586,125	28.8%
Total assets		$2,037,054	100.0%

Liabilities and stockholders' equity
Current liabilities

Accounts payable	$692,825	34.0%
Accrued expenses	46,325	2.3%
Income taxes payable	205,055	10.1%
Current portion of long-term debt	4,600	0.2%
Total current liabilities	$948,805	46.6%

Noncurrent liabilities

Long-term debt	$497,158	24.4%
Deferred income taxes	60,850	3.0%
Total noncurrent liabilities	$558,008	27.4%
Total liabilities	$1,506,813	74.0%

Stockholders' equity

Common stock, $1 par value	$240,000	11.8%
Paid-in capital	153,044	7.5%
Retained earnings	137,197	6.7%
Total stockholders' equity	$530,241	26.0%
Total liabilities and stockholders' equity	$2,037,054	100.0%

Custom Furniture Company
Statement of Cash Flows
For the Year Ended December 31, 19X7

Cash flows from operating activities	
Cash received from customers	$3,507,380
Interest and dividends received	28,040
Cash provided by operating activities	3,535,420
Cash paid to suppliers and employees	2,822,960
Interest and taxes paid	174,117
Cash disbursed for operating activities	2,997,077
Net cash flow from operating activities	538,343
Cash flows from investing activities	
Proceeds from sales of marketable securities	35,000
Purchases of plant assets	(153,613)
Net cash used by investing activities	(118,613)
Cash flows from financing activities	
Proceeds from short-term borrowing	100,000
Repayment of short-term debt	(100,000)
Repayment of long-term debt	(117,733)
Dividends paid	(240,000)
Net cash used by financing activities	(357,733)
Net increase (decrease) in cash	$61,997

Tonnie and Bill were trying to put together a preliminary audit program that would be altered appropriately when more planning and more work on internal control had been done. They were concentrating on how estimates of materiality and audit risk would affect their audit of individual accounts and assertions.

Subject to later review, they decided to use the "textbook approach" and do the following:

1. Assess an overall materiality to the financial statements based on the factors relevant to this year's audit and the factors that had caused the prior-year auditors so much trouble (the fraud carried out by the billing clerk and the cashier). Also, some of Custom's prior customers had filed lawsuits against Custom for bodily damage when some of Custom's furniture collapsed while in use.

2. Assign a part of the overall materiality to all or most of the financial statement accounts.

3. Assess an overall audit risk to the financial statements and use that percentage as individual audit risks for each assertion within accounts and disclosures.

4. Use the audit risk model to compute detection risk for each assertion.

Required:

Using the 19X7 financial statements on pages 205–206 and other information discussed in previous pages, do the following:

a. Write a memo describing all the factors Tonnie and Bill should consider in deciding on total materiality for the financial statements. Do not decide on an actual amount.

b. Write a memo describing all the factors Tonnie and Bill should consider in deciding how the total materiality should be assigned to the accounts. Do not decide on actual amounts.

c. Write a memo describing all the factors Tonnie and Bill should consider in deciding on the overall audit risk for the financial statements. Do not decide on an actual percentage.

d. Write a memo describing all the factors Tonnie and Bill should consider in assessing and computing the percentages to derive detection risk for each assertion. Do not decide on actual percentages.

Planning the Audit

"It's a bad plan that can't be changed."

PUBLILIUS SYRUS, *Moral Sayings*

LEARNING OBJECTIVES

After reading and studying the material in this chapter, the student should be able to

▶ Describe the elements of the planning phase of the audit.

▶ Analyze communications between the successor and predecessor auditor and briefly describe the importance of the communications.

▶ Analyze the contents of an engagement letter and write a brief paragraph describing its importance.

▶ Describe the major sources of planning information for an audit.

▶ Describe the composition of the audit team.

▶ Discuss the major sections of an audit program and describe its use.

▶ Assess the reason for the use of the audit risk model in planning the audit.

▶ Discuss when and why each segment of an audit is performed.

This chapter describes the matters an auditor considers in planning an audit. It addresses the first block in the general flowchart of an audit in Figure 8.1 (see next page), including client acquisition and preliminary audit planning. Chapters 9 through 12 cover the understanding and testing of internal control. Chapters 13 through 18 cover the performance of substantive tests, and Chapters 19 through 21 cover audit reporting. Keep in mind that audit plans are continually revised as the work is performed and new or unexpected information comes to light.

The first box in Figure 8.1 is further broken down as shown in Figure 8.2. Each step in the planning phase will be discussed in this chapter.

ACCEPTANCE OF CLIENTS

How do accounting firms obtain clients? The reputation of an accounting firm and its individual members for the performance of quality work is an important source of new clients. Quality audit work may be difficult for clients and others to recog-

FIGURE 8.1 **General Flowchart of an Audit**

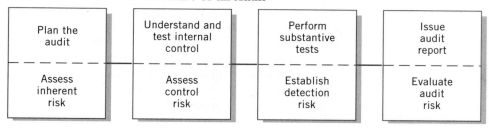

FIGURE 8.2 **Flowchart of the Planning Phase of the Audit**

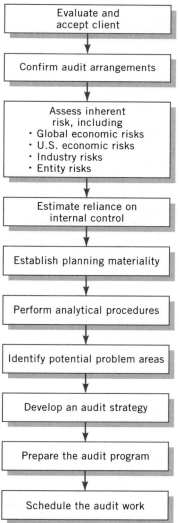

nize, but clients who are satisfied that they have received high levels of professional services at reasonable prices are important contributors to the development of a professional reputation. CPAs seek public exposure to potential clients by participating in leadership capacities in civic and charitable organizations such as the Chamber of Commerce and United Way.

Competition for clients among accounting firms has intensified in recent years. As a result, management of a potential client may select the accounting firm that proposes the lowest audit fee without considering other matters. Here are some examples from *Public Accounting Report* of comments made by management following a change in auditors:

> "We got better service at lower cost," said the VP. Predecessor's fee was between $43,000 and $50,000; successor's was $17,500.

> Management wasn't dissatisfied with the predecessor, but its $35,000 fee was too much. "Dollars make decisions," said the controller. For the current year precedessor bid $25,000; successor bid $20,000.

> Successor's fee is half of predecessor's $50,000, and successor made a three-year commitment. "Predecessor's bid was lower than its last fee," said the president.

> "I was kind of shocked because I thought we were getting a pretty good audit fee, but it's a competitive world out there."

Factors that have been shown to affect the level of audit fees include size of client (measured by total assets or revenues), proportion of assets in inventories and receivables, type of audit report (qualified or unqualified), size of audit firm (Big Six or non-Big Six), and audit firm tenure.

Another factor in the selection of accounting firms that has become significant enough to attract the attention of the Auditing Standards Board and the SEC is the practice of *opinion shopping*. A client wishing to employ an accounting method that is not acceptable to its present auditor may consult a number of other accounting firms until it finds one that will consider the method to be generally accepted. That firm is then hired as the auditor. The client has shopped among the accounting firms until it has found one that will issue an unqualified opinion on financial statements that include the effect of a questionable accounting method. To discourage this practice, the Auditing Standards Board has issued a statement (AU Section 625) requiring an accounting firm that is consulted regarding the acceptability of an accounting principle to consider all relevant facts and to communicate with the existing auditor.

Audit Committees

The *audit committee* of the board of directors is increasingly important in selecting auditors and in maintaining auditor independence. Audit committees have existed at most large and many smaller companies for many years. The New York Stock Exchange and the American Stock Exchange require that all companies listed on those exchanges have audit committees. Also, recommendations for the establishment of audit committees have been made by the AICPA, SEC, and professional and congressional committees.

Members of audit committees should be outside directors. An outside director should not be an officer or employee of the company. Although the duties of audit committees will vary among companies, they often include (1) nominating the independent auditors, (2) reviewing the plan for the audit and related services, (3) reviewing audit results and financial statements, and (4) overseeing the adequacy of the company's internal control. To aid the audit committee in performing these functions, auditors communicate with them regarding a number of matters that are discussed in a subsequent chapter.

Audit committees may increase auditor independence by serving as an arbitrator of unsolved problems between management and the auditor. Because audit commitee members (unlike management) have no direct responsibility for the results of a company's operations, they should be more objective in evaluating any disputes. In addition, if the audit committee selects the auditor, management cannot threaten the auditor with dismissal, thereby substantially reducing pressure on the auditor's independence.

Preacceptance Procedures

Most auditors are eager to obtain new clients, but they should be prudent and follow generally accepted auditing standards by investigating prospective clients before they are accepted.

As a matter of prudence, many auditors discuss the business reputation of a prospective client with their acquaintances in the business community, such as bankers and attorneys. Sometimes auditors use private detectives to investigate potential clients. Any indication of improper conduct by a company or of its officers should cause the auditor to consider rejecting that company as a prospective client.

The matter of acceptance of new clients is included in a *Statement on Quality Control Standard* and AU Section 315. The *Statement* outlines quality control considerations for accounting firms and includes the establishment of policies and procedures for deciding whether to accept or continue a professional relationship with a client to minimize the likelihood of associating with a company whose management lacks integrity. AU Section 315 states the requirements for communications between predecessor and successor auditors when a change of auditors occurs. It places the initiative for the communications with the successor auditor, who is required to make specific inquiry (after obtaining permission from the prospective client) of the predecessor auditor as to such matters as the integrity of management, disagreements with management about accounting principles, auditing standards, and other significant matters, and the reason for the change in auditors. The predecessor auditor should respond promptly and fully; any limitation on the response must be noted. A limited response or one that reflects adversely on the management of a prospective client must be given serious consideration in the decision to accept or reject the client. A flowchart of this process is shown in Figure 8.3 on page 212.

In recent years, auditors have become more selective in their acceptance of clients because lack of management integrity was a major factor in most important lawsuits against auditors (discussed in Chapter 4). Auditors learned a painful lesson from these criminal and civil suits. An early evaluation of management integrity is as important to the assurance of fair financial statements as the time spent in performing audit procedures. The *Equity Funding* and *Continental Vending* cases discussed in Chapter 4 are prime examples.

In addition to investigating the backgrounds of potential clients, auditors should determine whether they are qualified to perform each audit. For example, we know

FIGURE 8.3   **Flowchart of Communication Between Successor and Predecessor Auditor**

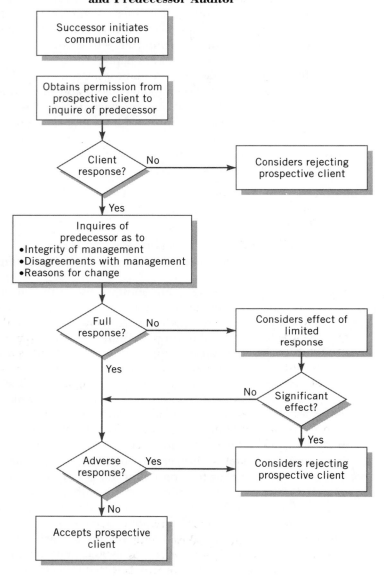

that auditors must be independent of their clients to comply with the second general standard of generally accepted auditing standards.

> In all matters relating to the engagement, an independence in mental attitude is to be maintained by the auditor or auditors.

Auditors should determine that they are independent, as required by the applicable codes of conduct. This process may involve circulation of the identity of the new client to the applicable professional personnel of the firm, so that they can terminate any of the prohibited relationships or investments described in Chapter 3.

Auditors should also consider whether their clients perceive a conflict of interest.

▶ **EXAMPLE**

When Arthur Young (the auditors of Pepsico) merged with Ernst & Whinney (the auditors of Coca Cola), Coca Cola informed Ernst & Young that it must decide which one of the two competing soft-drink companies it would continue to audit. Ernst & Young resigned from the Pepsico audit.

Auditors should also determine if they have adequate staff to perform the work and the expertise to deal with such matters as specialized industry problems, complex computer systems, and unique regulatory requirements of the potential client. Auditors are not prohibited from accepting clients when they lack such expertise, provided they acquire it before completing the audit. In many firms, auditors specialize in audits of particular industries to develop special expertise.

Continuation of Existing Clients

The auditor's evaluation of clients is not a one-time consideration. Clients should be reevaluated each year to be sure that they continue to meet the accounting firm's standards. Actions that raise questions as to management's integrity, numerous disagreements over accounting and auditing matters, and slow payment or nonpayment of fees are some reasons why an existing client relationship might be terminated.

Retention of first-year audit clients should be subjected to particular scrutiny. Auditors should ask themselves, "Would we have accepted this client if we knew then what we know now?" If the answer is "no," consideration should be given to terminating the client relationship.

Engagement Letters

The discussion of the *1136 Tenants' Corporation* case in Chapter 4 illustrates the danger of a misunderstanding between the accountant and the client when each party has a different understanding as to the nature of the engagement. Although not required by professional standards, an *engagement letter* should be prepared for all audit engagements to confirm the CPA's responsibility. These letters, normally addressed to the board of directors or the audit committee, include (1) a confirmation of the audit engagement for the current year, (2) a statement of responsibility for detection of errors and fraud, (3) fee and billing arrangements, and (4) other matters, if applicable, such as reviews of financial statements included in SEC filings or preparation of income tax returns. One form that an audit engagement letter might take is shown in Figure 8.4.

Most accounting firms base their bills to their clients on a per diem basis, that is, at daily rates and fractions thereof. These rates depend on the experience and expertise of the individuals working on the engagement (partners have the highest billing rates and new staff members have the lowest), and the type of work being

FIGURE 8.4   An Audit Engagement Letter

Partner & Co.
100 Main Street
Fayetteville, Arkansas 72701

May 1, 19X8

Mr. Robert K. Luckey
Chairman of the Audit Committee
X Company
122 West Avenue
Center City, Arkansas 70000

Dear Mr. Luckey:

This will confirm our arrangements with you to audit the financial statements of X Company for the year 19X8. The financial statements are the responsibility of the company's management. Our responsibility is to express an opinion on the financial statements based on our audit.

Our work is to consist of an audit of the balance sheet at December 31, 19X8, and the related statements of income, retained earnings, and cash flows for the year then ending in accordance with generally accepted auditing standards. Those standards require that we plan and perform the audit to obtain reasonable assurance about whether the financial statements are free of material misstatement. An audit includes examining, on a test basis, evidence supporting the amounts and disclosures in the financial statements. An audit also includes assessing the accounting principles used and significant estimates made by management, as well as evaluating the overall financial statement presentation.

We intend to assess the company's existing internal control. Primary reliance for the prevention and detection of errors and fraud must be placed on internal control because it is in constant operation and covers all periods and transactions; however, it cannot eliminate the possibility that errors and fraud may occur. Although there can be no guarantee that such errors and fraud will be detected by us, we will plan and perform our audit to provide reasonable assurance of finding errors and fraud that would have a material effect on the financial statements.

The charges for our services will be at our regular per diem rates plus out-of-pocket expenses. An interim billing of $30,000 will be delivered on or about November 30, 19X8, with a final billing on or about March 15, 19X9. We will attempt to minimize our charges by using your staff to prepare certain audit schedules and provide other assistance to us.

If these arrangements are in accordance with your understanding, please sign and return to us the enclosed copy of this letter. We appreciate this opportunity to be of service to you.

Sincerely,
Partner & Co.

Accepted by

_____
Robert K. Luckey

performed (work on a registration statement requiring knowledge of SEC rules and regulations may be billed at a higher rate than regular audit work).

The Planning Process

The first standard of fieldwork of generally accepted auditing standards states:

> The work is to be adequately planned and assistants, if any, are to be properly supervised.

Planning is essential to the efficient conduct of an audit, regardless of its size. An audit should be planned with an attitude of *professional skepticism* (i.e., the auditor assumes that management is neither honest nor dishonest). Throughout the planning process the auditor should consider the fraud risk factors described in Chapter 5. In planning an audit, an auditor should also consider the following matters:

1. Inherent risk based on general economic and industry conditions and peculiarities of the client.
2. Anticipated reliance on internal control.
3. Preliminary judgment about materiality.
4. Potential problem areas in the financial statements.
5. The type of audit report anticipated.

Inherent Risk

Inherent risk is the susceptibility of an account balance to misstatement. Inherent risk also exists at the financial statement level. That is, financial statements may be more susceptible to misstatements under certain economic conditions, in certain industries, or in certain entities.

Global Economic Risks

In the past there has been a tendency to think of the U.S. economy when considering general economic conditions. Today, however, auditors must consider many global economic and financial aspects. Some clients will have operations in foreign countries, other clients will export products to foreign countries, and most clients will compete with goods and services from foreign countries. Fluctuations in foreign exchange rates, restrictive international trade agreements, and political instability will create audit risks for many U.S. clients. Changes in foreign exchange rates may increase the cost of a client's exports, decrease the cost of competitors' imports, or create losses on repatriation of earnings from some foreign countries. Restrictive international trade agreements may restrict or impose tariffs on imports or exports. Political instability may jeopardize foreign markets. All of these factors create risks that should be considered when planning the audit. For example, the imposition of a tariff on a U.S. product may reduce the export sales of that product and increase the risk of excess inventory. The auditor may plan extended tests of the inventory valuation assertion in this case.

U.S. Economic Risks

The auditor should also be sensitive to the overall state of the U.S. economy and its impact on the client's industry and particularly on the client. Such factors as inflation rates, interest rates, and position of the economy in the business cycle (i.e., whether in a period of economic growth or recession) will affect most clients. Changes in these factors will change the risks the auditor faces and will affect the planning of the audit. For example, the risks of uncollectible receivables and obsolete inventories are generally higher during an economic recession than during an economic expansion. Auditors will plan extended audit procedures to address the increased risks.

Industry Risks

Industry conditions often determine the environment in which a client operates. Many risks are generated at the industry level. Two important industry factors are stability of operations and rate of technological change. Generally, the more stable the operations and the slower the rate of technological change in the industry, the lower the risk the auditor faces. These factors, however, may be subject to rapid change.

▶ EXAMPLE

At one time the savings and loan industry was considered a stable and low-risk industry, but with deregulation the policy of borrowing on a short-term basis and lending on a long-term basis led to disaster. As short-term interest rates rose, the savings and loan companies were forced to seek investments with higher yields and higher risks (such as speculative real estate loans). Many of these loans ultimately proved uncollectible. This industry characteristic increased the risk that the allowance for uncollectible loans would be inadequate. Auditors who understood the savings and loan industry planned additional audit procedures for loan losses during this period to compensate for the additional risks. Unfortunately, some auditors did not.

A high rate of technological change increases risk because of potential obsolescence of inventory, property, and equipment and loss of market share to competitors. Some developers of microcomputers and microcomputer software failed to adjust in that rapidly changing market, with fatal consequences. Another example of an event with industrywide effects is the decline of the price of oil because of overproduction by OPEC countries. Auditors of oil companies should have recognized increased risk in inventory (the potential for market price to decline below cost) and property (the potential for the value of oil reserves to decline below the cost of the related oil properties). Other examples of industry characteristics and related risks are shown in Figure 8.5.

Entity Risks

Each entity has characteristics that affect the risk that its financial statements may be misstated. Some of these characteristics result from conscious management decisions such as operating style, personnel turnover, extent of planning, integrity of personnel, attitude toward financial policies and financial reporting, and so forth. Characteristics controlled directly by management constitute the control environment, which in turn is part of internal control. Internal control and related risks are discussed in Chapter 9.

FIGURE 8.5 **Examples of Industry Characteristics and Related Risks**

Industry Characteristic	*Risk (and Effect on Audit Procedures)*
1. Labor intensive (e.g., genetic engineering)	1. Misstated labor costs. (Shift audit emphasis from purchasing and production to payroll.)
2. Highly competitive (e.g., automobile companies)	2. Unrecorded rebates, refunds, and incentives. (Plan extended audit procedures for revenue and accounts receivable.)
3. Difficult to audit transactions (e.g., frequent flyer awards)	3. Unrecorded or improperly recorded transactions. (Plan extended audit procedures for these transactions.)
4. Significant accounts requiring estimates (e.g., percentage-of-completion construction contracts)	4. Improper or biased estimates. (Plan extended audit procedures for these estimates.)

Some entity characteristics cannot be controlled directly by management. These include such matters as customer characteristics (e.g., a few large customers or many moderate-sized ones), legal constraints (e.g., patent or antitrust injunctions), and financial viability (e.g., strong or weak financial position). Generally, an entity with few customers, a contentious legal environment, and a weak financial position is considered a high-risk client. The auditor responds to this risk by assigning more experienced staff to the engagement and increasing the level of supervision and review.

Anticipated Reliance on Internal Control

During the preliminary planning phase, auditors estimate the reliance they may place on internal control. This permits them to plan the tentative nature, timing, and extent of substantive tests. Often auditors base their anticipated reliance on internal control on prior-year findings. If controls were found to be reliable and control risk was assessed at a low level in the prior year, the auditor would probably anticipate similar reliance on controls in the current year. Of course, the auditors subsequently will have to confirm their understanding of internal control and test it. The greater the anticipated reliance on internal control (lower control risk), the less substantive tests the auditor will plan to perform.

Preliminary Judgment about Materiality

Approaches to establishment of a materiality threshold and allocation of materiality to accounts in the form of tolerable misstatement are discussed in Chapter 7. One commonly used approach is to compute materiality as a percentage of some financial statement amount such as income before income taxes, revenues, net current assets, and so forth.

Preliminary planning is often done early in the year to be audited. How can an auditor determine an amount for the year, such as income before income taxes months before year end? The auditor may obtain copies of interim financial statements (e.g., for the first six months of the year) and annualize them to use as a basis for determining year-end amounts. (Factors such as seasonal variations and anticipated changes in operations during the subsequent six months should be considered.) In other situations, prior-year annual financial statements adjusted for known and anticipated changes could be used. As discussed in Chapter 7, the lower the materiality threshold (and tolerable misstatement), the more substantive tests that must be planned.

Potential Problem Areas

Auditors seldom plan an audit without having any idea of where potential errors may exist in the financial statements. Probably the best indication of where errors may exist is where they existed in the previous audit. If the client's personnel made errors in calculating deferred income taxes and earnings per share in the prior year due to lack of knowledge, they are likely to make similar errors in the current year. Auditors can identify these potential problem areas by a review of the prior-year audit working papers or, if the prior-year audit was performed by a predecessor auditor, a review of that auditor's working papers. The auditors then plan to spend additional audit time and effort in these areas. Potential problem areas may be created when the client's financial statements are affected by a new Financial Accounting Standards Board (FASB) accounting standard. Client personnel may be unaware of the new standard or may not understand its application. This could cause errors or omissions in the financial statements that the auditor should anticipate.

Another potential problem concerns *related parties*. Related parties include affiliated companies, owners, management, and any other party that does not fully pursue its own separate interests.

When auditors examine or obtain evidence from a third party, such as vendor invoices, confirmations, or sales agreements, they normally assume that the third party is independent of the client. If this assumption is invalid, the evidence will be less reliable. Moreover, the audit risk associated with related party transactions may be higher because of the possibility that the parties to the transactions are motivated by reasons other than those that may exist for most business transactions. Auditors have been victimized several times by clients who recorded large sales that later turned out to have been made to undisclosed related parties. Because the sales agreements were not with outside parties and sometimes contained contingencies that later led to reversal of the sale, they were improperly recorded as revenue and earnings. Related party transactions continue to create problems for auditors and are often difficult to detect.

Related parties should be identified early in the planning phase, so that the audit team can be alert for the existence of related party transactions during the subsequent phases of the audit. A list of previously identified related parties is usually maintained in the permanent audit file. Related parties may be identified by inquiries of management and predecessor auditors and by reviews of stockholder listings, SEC filings, and material investment transactions.

Auditors should also plan for difficult auditing situations. They may encounter situations that require special knowledge of a nonaccounting nature. In these instances, the auditor may plan to use *specialists* such as actuaries (to evaluate pension and other postretirement liabilities), appraisers (to value works of art or real estate), engineers (to estimate useful lives of plant and equipment), geologists (to estimate mineral reserves), and attorneys (to interpret legal agreements and regulations). When specialists are used, they preferably should not be related to the client. The auditor should make inquiries or perform other procedures to satisfy himself or herself concerning the specialist's professional qualifications and reputation. Identification of areas requiring the use of a specialist and consideration of the specialist's qualifications are part of the planning process.

Type of Report to Be Issued

The type of audit report to be issued may affect the extent of the auditor's work. If a client company has several subsidiary companies, substantially more work should be planned if the auditor is to report on the financial statements of each subsidiary company individually rather than on the consolidated financial statements. (Materiality would be lower for the individual subsidiary companies than for the consolidated total.) The client may also require additional special reports (described in Chapter 21) that would require the planning of more extensive work.

SOURCES OF PLANNING INFORMATION

Auditors have many sources from which to gain knowledge of a particular industry and general economic conditions.

General Sources

Auditors make inquiries of client management regarding the effects on the financial statements of production and marketing operations, industry conditions, new accounting pronouncements, unusual accounting transactions, and so forth. For example, if management states that the company was involved in a complex business combination during the year, the auditor would want to plan sufficient time to review the accounting for the transaction.

Periodicals and other publications are available for almost every industry, and government agencies publish a wide range of business statistics. Knowledge of general economic conditions can be obtained by reading such publications as the *Wall Street Journal* and *Business Week*.

Auditors may also consult published annual reports (e.g., SEC Form 10-Ks) of clients and others in a particular industry (available on National Automated Accounting Research System—NAARS—data file and on the internet). The AICPA publishes audit and accounting guides for specific industries that include discussions of industry operating characteristics and unusual industry accounting and auditing problems. Examples of industries for which such guides have been published are airlines, banks, brokers and dealers in securities, casinos, colleges and universities, credit unions, investment companies, and life insurance companies. Prior-year audit working papers, when available, should contain extensive information. Auditors typically tour a client's major plants and offices and make extensive inquiries of management.

Analytical Procedures

Analytical procedures are introduced in Chapter 6. The auditor is *required* to use analytical procedures in the planning and final review phases of all audits. The purposes of performing analytical procedures in the planning phase are to

1. Enhance the auditor's understanding of the client's business.
2. Direct the auditor's attention to balances and transactions that are unusual or unexpected.

Unusual or unexpected amounts suggest a higher risk of error, so the auditor will plan to perform extended audit procedures on these amounts. The auditor should obtain an understanding of the reasons for unusual variations before the audit is completed.

One form of analytical procedure is to compare current-year amounts with those of the prior year. (This assumes that there are no significant known changes from the prior year and that the prior year is therefore the expectation for the current year.) Consider the interim statements of income for the nine months ended September 30, 19X1 (the interim period of the year being audited) and 19X0 (an interim period of the prior year) shown below. All amounts are larger in the current period—a common occurrence for a growing company. But a closer analysis reveals that, although cost of sales has increased, the increase is not proportional to the increase in revenues. In 19X0 cost of sales was 31 percent of revenues, whereas in 19X1 cost of sales fell to 28 percent of revenues. This is the primary reason for the increase in net income. The auditors would ask themselves, "Why would cost of sales decline as a percentage of revenues?" There may be legitimate reasons for this decline, such as an increase in sales price or a decline in production cost; however, errors and fraud could also cause this result. These errors and fraud include fictitious revenues, omitted costs, and nonexistent or overpriced inventories. If the auditors are unable to document increased sales prices or decreased production costs, they may believe there may be a higher than normal risk of errors and fraud. The auditors would then plan additional audit procedures for revenues, costs, and inventories.

	Nine months ended September 30	
	19X1	19X0
Revenues	$18,228,000	$15,915,000
Operating costs and expenses		
Cost of sales	$ 5,121,000	$ 4,963,000
Operating and general costs	5,653,000	4,868,000
Depreciation	3,070,000	2,999,000
Taxes, other than income taxes	841,000	570,000
Interest expense	2,085,000	1,616,000
	$16,770,000	$15,016,000
Income before income taxes	$ 1,458,000	$ 899,000
Income tax expense	476,000	323,000
Net income	$ 982,000	$ 576,000

DEVELOPMENT OF AN AUDIT STRATEGY

The information described in the previous sections is usually gathered by the audit senior, audit manager, and audit partner. Based on identified risks, the size of the engagement, and personnel availability, an *audit team* is formed. The audit team should be assigned with the first general standard in mind:

> The audit is to be performed by a person or persons having adequate technical training and proficiency as an auditor.

The audit team generally consists of the following personnel:

1. One or more staff auditors, often with three years' experience or less, who perform audit procedures as directed by a senior auditor.
2. A senior or in-charge auditor with two to six years' experience who performs difficult audit procedures requiring more subjective judgment, and who supervises and reviews the daily work of the staff auditors. The senior auditor may have special training or experience in the client's industry.
3. A manager or supervisor who may have four to ten years' experience. The manager is responsible for arranging and requesting staff for each audit, reviewing the audit work performed by the staff and senior auditor, and billing and collecting the audit fee.
4. A partner with perhaps more than ten years' experience who has overall and final responsibility for the audit. The partner reviews the audit work of the staff, senior, and manager, resolves audit problems with the client, and approves the form of and signs the audit report.

There is normally some continuity of the audit team for a particular client from year to year, although resignations, terminations, and promotions may result in some changes. To obtain a fresh look at each client periodically, many accounting firms require a complete change in the audit team for a particular client every five or so years. Some critics of the accounting profession have maintained that this change is not sufficient and that accounting firms should be rotated periodically, but this idea has not been widely accepted.

An engagement team (composed not only of the audit team but also tax and management consulting personnel assigned to the client) meets to consider the preliminary planning information and develop an audit strategy. This strategy identifies the primary risk areas and considers such matters as whether there may be indications of

1. Management predisposition to distort financial statements.
2. Unreliable accounting estimates.
3. Constant crisis in operating or accounting areas.
4. Lack of control over computer processing.
5. Inadequate security of data or assets.

A determination then is made as to whether heavy reliance will be placed on (1) the internal control (referred to as the "lower control risk approach" in Chapter 9) or (2) substantive tests (referred to as the "primarily substantive approach" in Chapter 9) for various assertions, accounts, and groups of accounts. The audit manager summarizes the results of this meeting in an audit planning memorandum. This memorandum provides guidance to the audit senior in developing the audit program.

THE AUDIT PROGRAM

The most important control mechanism in an audit is the *audit program*. It should be prepared in writing and outline all of the audit procedures considered necessary for an auditor to express an opinion on the client's financial statements. Although audit programs should be specifically tailored to each audit engagement, computer-generated listings of audit procedures are sometimes utilized in audit program preparation.

An audit program that is properly prepared and used provides

1. Evidence of proper planning of the work and allows a review of the proposed scope of the audit. The program gives the partner, manager, and other members of the audit team an opportunity to review the proposed scope of the audit *before* the work is performed, when there is still time to modify the proposed audit procedures.
2. Guidance to less experienced staff members. The specific audit steps to be performed by each staff person are indicated in the program.
3. Evidence of work performed. As each audit step is performed, the staff person signs or initials in a space beside that step on the program to indicate that it has been completed.
4. A means of controlling the time spent on an audit. The audit program usually includes the estimated time required to perform each audit step and a space in which the actual time required can be recorded. Thus, a staff member knows approximately how much time a certain audit step should require and can ask the senior for assistance if appreciably more or less time appears to be needed.
5. Evidence of the consideration of control risk in designing the proposed audit procedures. Many programs include a brief summary of the important control features in each section of the audit and some evaluation of these controls. Thus, audit procedures can be restricted where controls are effective and expanded where they are ineffective.

The audit program is only a *tentative* program based on assumptions about the client's accounting procedures and controls. When the work begins, if the conditions are not as anticipated, the auditor should revise the audit program on the basis of conditions actually found.

▶ **EXAMPLE**

If an auditor designs the audit program to confirm only a few accounts receivable balances because control risk is believed to be low (on the basis of past experience), the program must be changed to confirm more accounts if the assessment of the level of control risk is increased.

The property and equipment and accumulated depreciation section of an audit program are illustrated in the appendix to this chapter. The program has four major sections: (1) an account description, which states briefly the nature of the items included in the account, (2) an evaluation of audit risk, which summarizes important controls and includes an evaluation of the component risks, (3) audit procedures, which outline the specific audit steps to be performed, who should perform them, and an estimate of the required time, and (4) a conclusion, which represents the opinion of the staff as to whether the audit objectives have been accomplished.

The illustration indicates that inherent and control risks relating to property additions are low, but inherent and control risks relating to property retirements are relatively high because no periodic review is made for unreported retirements, and individual pieces of equipment are not tagged or otherwise specifically identified as belonging to the company. The low risks relating to additions do not mean that additions need not be audited, but the lower risks do allow the auditor to restrict the extent of the procedures and increase detection risk (by exclusion of property additions of less than $4,000 in this case). In contrast, an extended search for unrecorded retirements is performed because of higher risks in this area.

Finally, the audit program in the appendix illustrates the division of the audit work between interim and final. Some procedures are performed at an interim date and are updated through the end of the year during the final audit work (tests of property additions and maintenance expense by examination of vendor invoices, etc.). Other procedures are performed only once (preparation of lead schedule) to avoid unnecessary duplication.

USE OF THE AUDIT RISK MODEL IN PLANNING

When preparing the audit program, auditors make use—implicitly or explicitly—of the audit risk model discussed in Chapter 7. Based on the factors discussed in previous sections, auditors make planning judgments about inherent risk and control risk. Audit risk should be set at a low level.

The other component of the audit risk model is the risk that, given that material errors exist in the financial statements, the auditor's substantive tests will fail to detect them (detection risk). The auditor controls this risk by varying the nature, timing, and extent of the tests of balances, transactions, and disclosures and analytical procedures. Thus, an inverse relationship exists between the strength of a client's controls and the effort an auditor expends in testing balances and disclosures in the financial statements. The relationships of these risks may be expressed in the form of the audit risk model.

$$AR = IR * CR * DR$$

where AR represents audit risk, IR inherent risk, CR control risk, and DR detection risk. The auditor considers the components of audit risk in planning the audit to reduce overall audit risk to an acceptably low level. These risks were discussed in detail in Chapter 7 and are summarized here because of their importance in the planning process.

The following examples illustrate how the audit risk model can be used to plan the extent of audit work to be performed.

Accounts Receivable

Accounts receivable consists of amounts due from the sale of a standard product to a few large companies under long-term contracts. Both quantity and price are established by contract, and customers remit weekly. Controls over shipping, billing, and collecting are strong and were tested with good results.

Because the existence assertion applicable to the account does not appear to be susceptible to error (low inherent risk) and controls appear to be strong (low control risk), the audit risk model appears as follows:

$$AR = IR * CR * DR$$

$$LOW = LOW * LOW * ?$$

This assessment indicates that the auditor can plan to take a high risk of not detecting an error in the existence of this account because the probability of one occurring and not being detected is low. The auditor would plan only limited substantive tests of the existence of the accounts receivable balance.

Inventory

Inventory consists of computer chips involving several stages of production. Standard costs are accumulated and transferred between stages. Exact specifications result in a high rate of rejection. Numerous differences are common between perpetual records and physical counts of inventory. Controls over the purchase and receipt of raw materials are weak.

Because the existence assertion of this account appears to be highly susceptible to error (high inherent risk) and controls are weak (high control risk), the audit risk model appears as follows:

$$AR = IR * CR * DR$$

$$LOW = HIGH * HIGH * ?$$

This assessment indicates that the auditor should plan to take a low risk of not detecting an error in the existence of this account balance because the probability of one occurring and not being detected is high. Therefore, the auditor would plan extensive substantive tests of the existence assertion of the inventory balance.

SCHEDULING THE AUDIT WORK

Efficient scheduling of audit work is the key to maximizing the effectiveness and monetary return of an accounting firm. This fact becomes clear when we consider the economics of a public accounting practice.

The Economics of Public Accounting

Because a majority of businesses prepare financial statements on a calendar-year basis, there is a greatly disproportional demand on auditors' time during the early months of the year. An accounting firm must employ enough personnel to meet the peak demands of its clients, which may occur in February. Consequently, in other months, such as May and June, the accounting firm will be paying a number of personnel who are not producing revenue. Other functions can be performed during these months, such as professional development and training, planning the next year's audits, and vacations. However, any audit time that can be moved out of the peak period and into another time of the year will increase the efficiency and monetary return of the accounting firm. Not all audit procedures must be performed after the end of the period being audited, and most accounting firms strive to perform as much work at an interim date as possible. This practice allows the accounting firm to reduce staff requirements and the clients to issue financial statements and annual reports at an earlier date. Auditors appreciate clients whose fiscal year ends other than on December 31.

Segments of an Audit

The audit work can be segmented in various ways, one of which is to split the work into the following phases:

Phase I—Planning
Phase II—Interim audit work
Phase III—Year-end audit work
Phase IV—Final audit work

Figure 8.6 illustrates how audit work could be scheduled for an entity with December 31 as the end of the fiscal year.

**FIGURE 8.6   Illustration of How Work Could Be Scheduled
for a Calendar-Year Audit**

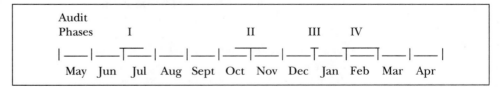

Phase I—Planning

Phase I is discussed earlier in this chapter. After considering the potential risks of material misstatements of the financial statements, the auditor prepares an audit program containing detailed audit procedures required to detect material misstatements in the financial statements. In Phase I the auditor should also consider more efficient audit methods and procedures and opportunities for shifting more work to the interim period, with primary emphasis on preparing or updating the audit program and reviewing prior-year audit working papers to find areas where the effectiveness of the audit work could be improved. The timing of this work is flexible, but the work should be completed before the beginning of the interim audit work.

The shifting of additional work to an interim period requires adequate internal control that permits effective substantive tests to be applied during the period from interim to year end. If the auditor's experience with the reliability of the accounting records and management's integrity has been good, some audit procedures normally performed after the end of the year may be moved to an interim date.

Phase II—Interim Audit Work

Phase II, performed perhaps one to four months before the end of the client's year, consists of the execution of audit procedures that need not be performed at year end or during the final audit work. Remember that the auditor's objective is to move as much work as possible into Phase II. There are no specific rules or guidelines as to exactly what work can be performed at this time. Each audit must be studied and the timing of the audit steps determined after careful consideration of the accounting procedures, controls, and other factors. Nevertheless, some audit procedures are *usually* performed in Phase II, others *may* be performed, and still others are *seldom* performed.

The assessment of control risk is usually performed in Phase II, because the extent and nature of subsequent audit procedures depend on the results of this assessment. One may wonder whether the auditor is required to perform the same assessment during Phase IV to cover the period from the interim audit work to year-end, inasmuch as the entire year is the subject of the audit. In practice, auditors do make inquiries and limited reviews of procedures and controls during Phase IV, but not in as much depth as in Phase II.

Other procedures usually carried out in Phase II include a review of minutes of the meetings of stockholders and board of directors (and any subcommittees thereof) and tests of additions to and reductions of accounts with balances that tend to carry forward rather than turn over rapidly. Examples are property and equipment, deferred charges, long-term debt, and stockholders' equity. Transactions in these accounts can be audited through an interim date and then audited from that date to year-end in Phase IV. This approach is more efficient than auditing transactions for the entire year in Phase IV.

Audit procedures that *may* be performed in Phase II depend on the auditor's evaluation of *incremental risk* (the increased risk that misstatements may not be detected at the balance sheet date because audit procedures were performed at an interim date). Incremental risk is affected by (1) whether the client's internal control will produce reliable records between the interim date and year-end, (2) whether there are rapidly changing business conditions that might predispose management to misstate the financial statements between the interim date and year-end, and (3) whether the year-end balances of accounts selected for interim testing are reasonably predictable. If the incremental risk of performing principal substantive tests at an interim date can be controlled because control risk is low, business conditions are not such as to predispose management to financial statement misstatement, and year-end balances are reasonably predictable, such procedures as confirmation of accounts receivable, observation of physical inventories, and confirmation of accounts payable may be performed in Phase II. If such procedures are performed in Phase II, the auditor must review transactions in the accounts from the interim date to year-end to be satisfied of the validity of the account balances at year-end.

Some audit procedures are seldom performed in Phase II, because they would duplicate work done in Phase IV. For example, tests of accrued liabilities, review of loan agreements for compliance with restrictions, an examination of the stockbook are normally done at year-end, and work done at and interim date would be an unnecessary duplication.

Phase III—Year-end Audit Work

Phase III involves audit procedures that are performed at the end of a client's year. Examples of such procedures include observation of physical inventories, count of cash funds, and inspection of marketable or investment securities. This work often must be done on the specific year-end date, because it may not be possible otherwise to determine that the asset was actually on hand at that date. Certain techniques, such as the use of seals on cash boxes and the limitation of access to bank safety deposit boxes, may allow some of these procedures to be moved from year-end to other dates.

Phase IV—Final Audit Work

Phase IV can begin as soon as the client has prepared and posted the final accounting entries and totaled, balanced, and closed the accounting records. This phase consists of the execution of all audit procedures not previously performed and preparation and issuance of the audit report. Auditors must resist tight time deadlines established by clients. Although sometimes pressured by a client to issue an audit report before all procedures have been completed, the auditor must insist on completing all aspects of the audit, no matter how minor, before issuing the audit report.

PLANNING THE FIRST-TIME AUDIT

A large majority of audits performed during a given year are repeat engagements; however, when an audit is performed for the first time for a client, additional audit procedures must be planned. If the client has never been audited, the auditor must first determine if the entity is auditable (i.e., that all necessary financial records are available). If the entity is deemed auditable, the auditor should plan to perform audit procedures on asset and liability account balances as of the beginning of the year. This is necessary because errors in beginning balances will cause errors in income statement accounts or ending balances of balance sheet accounts. For example, assume there is a material overstatement error in the beginning balance of accounts receivable. If the error is corrected during the year by a debit to sales and a credit to accounts receivable, sales for the current year will be understated by the amount of the error; if the error is not corrected, ending accounts receivable will be overstated by the amount of the error. The auditor is also interested in determining whether the accounting principles employed in the current year are consistent with those employed in the prior year. Application of audit procedures to prior-year balances helps to determine this fact.

If the client was audited in the prior year by a predecessor auditor, the successor auditor should make inquiries of the predecessor and review the predecessor's audit working papers (after obtaining the consent of the client and the predecessor auditor). These procedures are often sufficient to provide the successor with reasonable assurance that the beginning balances are not materially misstated.

INTERNATIONAL STANDARDS ON AUDITING

International standards on auditing presume the use of engagement letters, whereas U.S. auditing standards do not require the use of engagement letters.

APPENDIX: ILLUSTRATION OF THE PROPERTY AND EQUIPMENT AND ACCUMULATED DEPRECIATION SECTION OF AN AUDIT PROGRAM

X Co.
Property and Equipment
12-31-X8

Account Description

This group of accounts represents the land, building, and equipment used in the company's manufacturing process, as well as the salespeople's automobiles. Annual straight-line depreciation rates are 10 percent for buildings, 20 percent for equipment, and 33⅓ percent for automobiles.

Evaluation of Audit Risk

A detailed ledger is maintained showing the individual items of property and equipment, and it is balanced with the control account monthly. Capital expenditures in excess of $5,000 require the approval of the board of directors in the capital expenditures budget. Formal policies have been established to distinguish between capital and maintenance charges. Retirements of property are reported by the shop supervisors, but no periodic review is made for unreported retirements and individual pieces of equipment are not tagged or otherwise specifically identified as belonging to the company.

Overall, inherent and control risk relating to property additions and the assertions of rights, completeness, valuation, and presentation are assessed as low. Inherent and control risks relating to property retirements and existence are assessed as medium to high.

To maintain audit risk at a low level, detection risk will be set high (limited work) for property additions and medium to low (expanded work) for property retirements.

Audit Procedures

Time Required		Audit Step	Assigned to	Performed by/Date
Estimated	Actual			
Interim—				
4		1. Review and assess inherent and control risk relating to property and equipment assertions and accumulated depreciation assertions (see separate programs).	Staff 1	
3		2. Analyze property and equipment additions through the interim audit date listing all additions in excess of $4,000. For all additions in excess of $4,000, examine vendor invoice, canceled check, and receiving report and determine if classification as a capital item is proper. Also indicate on schedule if the addition is a new or replacement item.	Staff 2	
3		3. Analyze maintenance expense through the interim audit date listing all charges in excess of $4,000. For all maintenance charges in excess of $4,000, examine vendor invoice, canceled check, and receiving report and determine if classification as an expense item is proper.	Staff 2	
1		4. Trace all additions in excess of $5,000 to capital budget approved by the board of directors.	Staff 2	
3		5. Analyze retirements of property and equipment through the interim audit date. Trace the original cost of items retired, together with dates acquired and retired, to the detailed property ledger. Test calculation of accumulated depreciation to date of retirement and trace any salvage proceeds to cash receipts book. Investigate any significant retirements for which there is no salvage. Recompute gain or loss on the retirement and relate to other income or expense account.	Staff 1	
2		6. Review and supervision.	Senior	
Final—				
1		1. Review and assess inherent and control risk relating to property and equipment and accumulated depreciation for any material changes from interim review.	Staff 1	
1		2. Prepare or obtain client-prepared lead schedule of property and equipment and accumulated depreciation and trace beginning balances on lead schedule to prior-year audit working papers.	Staff 2	

Audit Procedures *Continued*

Time Required		Audit Step	Assigned to	Performed by/Date
Estimated	*Actual*			
1		3. Total the detailed property ledger and determine if it balances with the control account.	Staff 2	
2		4. Analyze property and equipment additions from interim to year-end, listing all additions in excess of $4,000. Cross-reference the total of this schedule to the lead schedule. For all additions from interim date to year-end in excess of $4,000, examine vendor invoice, canceled check, and receiving report and determine if classification as a capital item is proper. Also, indicate on schedule if the addition is a new or replacement item.	Staff 2	
1		5. Analyze maintenance expense from interim date to year-end, listing all charges in excess of $4,000. Cross-reference the total of this schedule to the operating expense lead schedule. For all maintenance charges from interim date to year-end in excess of $4,000, examine vendor invoice, canceled check, and receiving report and determine if classification as an expense item is proper.	Staff 2	
1		6. Trace all additions from interim date to year-end in excess of $5,000 to capital budget approved by the board of directors.	Staff 2	
1		7. Analyze retirements of property and equipment from interim date to year-end. Cross-reference the total of this schedule to the lead schedule. Trace the original cost of items retired after interim date, together with dates acquired and retired, to the detailed property ledger. Test calculation of accumulated depreciation to date of retirement and trace any salvage proceeds to cash receipts book. Investigate any significant retirements for which there is no salvage. Recompute gain or loss on the retirement and relate to other income or expense account.	Staff 1	
		8. Perform a search for unrecorded retirements including the following:		
1		(a) Determine whether a retirement was recorded for each addition identified as a replacement.	Staff 1	

Audit Procedures *Continued*

Time Required		Audit Step	Assigned to	Performed by/Date
Estimated	*Actual*			
1		(b) Investigate any significant reduction in property insurance coverage or property tax assessments to determine if it resulted from property retirements.	Staff 1	
1		(c) Review miscellaneous and other income accounts for salvage credits or scrap sales that may indicate the disposal of retired property and equipment.	Staff 1	
1		(d) Discuss property and equipment retirements with the shop supervisors and the plant manager.	Staff 1	
2		(e) Select 10 items of equipment from the detailed property and equipment ledger and locate them in the plant.	Staff 1	
1		(f) Write a memorandum outlining the work performed in the search for unrecorded retirements.	Staff 1	
		9. Test the current-year provision for depreciation:		
1		(a) Compare depreciation methods, estimated lives of assets, and estimated salvage values to prior year for consistency.	Staff 1	
2		(b) Make an overall test of depreciation expense by major asset category and investigate any significant variations.	Staff 1	
1		10. Review the balances of accumulated depreciation at year-end to determine the reasonableness of the undepreciated cost of the major assets in relation to their remaining depreciable lives. Consider such factors as obsolescence and technological changes, as well as physical characteristics.	Senior	
1		11. Consider whether the carrying amount of any significant property and equipment may be impaired. If carrying amounts are questionable, review client estimates of future cash flows expected from the use and disposal of the asset.	Senior	
2		12. Review and supervision.	Senior	
Conclusion—				

Chapter 8 ▶ GLOSSARY OF TERMS

Audit committee   A subcommittee of the board of directors, consisting of nonmanagement members, that deals with auditing (both internal and external) and financial reporting matters.

Audit program   A detailed written set of audit procedures that the auditor believes is necessary to accomplish the objectives of the audit.

Audit strategy   A general approach to planning an audit.

Audit team   The individuals assigned to a specific audit engagement.

Engagement letter   A letter from the CPA to the client confirming the scope of a professional engagement.

Incremental risk   The increased risk that misstatements may not be detected at the balance sheet date because audit procedures were performed at an interim date.

Interim audit work   Audit procedures performed before the audit date.

Internal control   Policies and procedures an entity establishes to assure reliability of its accounting records and to safeguard its assets.

Opinion shopping   An entity's search for support for a marginally acceptable accounting practice by soliciting opinions of different accounting firms as to the appropriateness of the accounting practice.

Professional skepticism   The mental attitude of a CPA when planning and performing an audit that assumes neither certain dishonesty nor unquestioned honesty on the part of management and employees of the audited entity.

Related parties   Parties related to the party being audited such as affiliated entities, subsidiaries, management, major stockholders, and any other party that does not fully pursue its own self-interests.

Specialist   A person or firm possessing special skill or knowledge in a particular field other than accounting or auditing, whose work is utilized by the auditor.

Chapter 8 ▶ REFERENCES

American Institute of Certified Public Accountants. *Professional Standards*
  AU Section 310—*Relationship Between the Auditor's Appointment and Planning*
  AU Section 311—*Planning and Supervision*
  AU Section 313—*Substantive Tests Prior to the Balance Sheet Date*
  AU Section 315—*Communications Between Predecessor and Successor Auditors*
  AU Section 322—*The Auditor's Consideration of the Internal Audit Function in an Audit of Financial Statements*
  AU Section 329—*Analytical Procedures*
  AU Section 334—*Related Parties*
  AU Section 336—*Using the Work of a Specialist*
  AU Section 625—*Reports on the Application of Accounting Principles*

Durbin, Timothy E., and Summo, Jeanne M. "When Auditors Use Specialists," *Journal of Accountancy* (August 1994), pp. 47–49.

Glezen, G. William, and Elser, Mark B. "The Auditor Change Process," *Journal of Accountancy* (June 1996), pp. 73–77.

Godwin, Larry. "Enhanced Engagement Letters," *Journal of Accountancy* (June 1993), pp. 53–58.

Hardy, John W., and Deppe, Larry A. "Client Acceptance: What to Look For and Why," *The CPA Journal* (May 1992), pp. 20–27.

Kunitake, Walter K., Luzi, Andrew D., and Glezen, G. William. "Analytical Review in Audit and Review Engagements," *The CPA Journal* (April 1985), pp. 18–26.

Marxen, Dale E. "A Behavioral Investigation of Time Budget Preparation in a Competitive Audit Environment," *Accounting Horizons* (June 1990), pp. 47–57.

Murray, Mark F. "When a Client Is a Liability," *Journal of Accountancy* (September 1992), pp. 54–58.

Serlin, Jerry E. "Shopping Around: A Closer Look at Opinion Shopping." *Journal of Accounting, Auditing & Finance* (Fall 1985).

Wolfe, Donald N., and Smith, Gerald. "Planning the Audit in a Distressed Industry," *The CPA Journal* (October 1988), pp. 46–50.

Chapter 8 ▶ REVIEW QUESTIONS

8-1 What is meant by opinion shopping?

8-2 Describe four potential duties of audit committees.

8-3 Who has the responsibility to initiate communications when a change of auditors occurs? What specific inquiries should be made?

8-4 List the matters normally included in an audit engagement letter.

8-5 Describe an auditor's attitude toward planning and performing an audit.

8-6 What matters should an auditor consider when planning an audit?

8-7 What are three global economic risks that an auditor should consider when planning an audit?

8-8 What are three U.S. economic risks that an auditor should consider when planning an audit?

8-9 What are two important industry risks that an auditor should consider when planning an audit?

8-10 What are three entity risks not controlled directly by management that an auditor should consider when planning an audit?

8-11 What are some potential problem areas that an auditor should consider when planning an audit?

8-12 When would an auditor consider the use of a specialist during the planning phase?

8-13 What are some general sources of planning information?

8-14 Why does an auditor perform analytical procedures in the planning phase of an audit?

8-15 Describe the composition of the audit team and the responsibilities of its members.

8-16 Why is an audit program considered tentative? What could cause it to be changed?

8-17 How does the auditor use the audit risk model to help plan the audit?

8-18 Why do auditors attempt to perform as much work as possible at an interim date?

8-19 Four audit segments or phases are identified in the chapter. When is each performed?

8-20 How does planning for a first-time audit differ from planning a continuing audit?

Chapter 8 ▶ OBJECTIVE QUESTIONS

(* = author prepared; ** = CPA examination; *** = CMA examination)

*8-21 If a CPA receives a request from an entity that is not a client to evaluate the use of an accounting principle, the CPA should

    a. Consult with the entity's auditor as required by the Code of Professional Conduct.

    b. Not consult with the entity's auditor because there is no requirement to do so.

    c. Consult with the entity's auditor to ascertain all available facts relevant to forming a professional judgment.

    d. Not consult with the entity's auditor because the evaluation should be made independently.

**8-22 As generally conceived, the "audit committee" of a publicly held company should be made up of

    a. Representatives of the major equity interests (bonds, preferred stock, common stock).

    b. The audit partner, the chief financial officer, the legal counsel, and at least one outsider.

    c. Members of the board of directors who are not officers or employees.

    d. Representatives from the client's management, investors, suppliers, and customers.

**8-23 Before accepting an audit engagement, a successor auditor should make specific inquiries of the predecessor auditor regarding the predecessor's

    a. Opinion of any subsequent events occurring since the predecessor's audit report was issued.

    b. Understanding as to the reasons for the change of auditors.

    c. Awareness of the consistency in the application of GAAP between periods.

    d. Evaluation of all matters of continuing accounting significance.

**8-24 A successor auditor most likely would make specific inquiries of the predecessor auditor regarding

    a. Specialized accounting principles of the client's industry.

    b. The competency of the client's internal audit staff.

    c. The uncertainty inherent in applying sampling procedures.

    d. Disagreements with management as to auditing procedures.

**8-25 Which of the following statements would *least* likely appear in an auditor's engagement letter?

    a. Fees for our services are based on our regular per diem rates, plus travel and other out-of-pocket expenses.

    b. During the course of our audit we may observe opportunities for economy in, or improved controls over, your operations.

c. Our engagement is subject to the risk that material errors, fraud, and defalcations, if they exist, will *not* be detected.

d. After performing our preliminary analytical procedures we will discuss with you the other procedures we consider necessary to complete the engagement.

**8-26 Because an audit in accordance with generally accepted auditing standards is influenced by the possibility of material misstatements, the auditor should plan the audit with an attitude of

a. Professional responsiveness.
b. Professional skepticism.
c. Conservative advocacy.
d. Objective judgment.

*8-27 A CPA is planning an audit of a client, a substantial portion of whose business consists of exports of microchips for sale in England. The CPA knows from reading the financial news that the U.S. dollar has risen relative to the British pound. Because of this knowledge the CPA will plan

a. More work on production costs.
b. Less work on shipping costs.
c. More work on inventory pricing.
d. Less work on foreign currency translation gains.

*8-28 A CPA is planning the audit of a hospital and is aware that the U.S. Congress recently passed a law limiting the amounts that can legally be charged for certain hospital services. Because of this knowledge, the CPA will plan more work on

a. Payroll.
b. Legal expense.
c. Sales and accounts receivable.
d. Purchases and accounts payable.

**8-29 To obtain an understanding of a continuing client's business in planning an audit, an auditor most likely would

a. Perform tests of details of transactions and balances.
b. Review prior-year working papers and the permanent file for the client.
c. Read specialized industry journals.
d. Reevaluate the client's internal control environment.

*8-30 Prior to beginning interim work on a recurring audit, an auditor makes a preliminary judgment about materiality. Which of the following would not be an appropriate base for this decision?

a. Current-year actual net income.

b. Annualized net income for the first nine months of the current year.
c. Prior-year audited net income.
d. Current-year budgeted net income.

**8-31 Which of the following events most likely indicates the existence of related parties?

a. Borrowing a large sum of money at a variable rate of interest.
b. Making a loan without scheduled terms for repayment.
c. Selling real estate at a price that differs significantly from its book value.
d. Discussing merger terms with a company that is a major competitor.

**8-32 An auditor obtains knowledge about a new client's business and its industry to

a. Make constructive suggestions concerning improvements to the client's internal control.
b. Develop an attitude of professional skepticism concerning management's financial statement assertions.
c. Evaluate whether the aggregation of known misstatements causes the financial statements taken as a whole to be materially misstated.
d. Understand the events and transactions that may have an effect on the client's financial statements.

**8-33 Which of the following situations would *most* likely require special audit planning by the auditor?

a. Some items of factory equipment do *not* bear identification numbers.
b. Depreciation methods used on the client's tax return differ from those used on the books.
c. Inventory is comprised of precious stones.
d. Assets costing less than $500 are expensed, even though the expected life exceeds one year.

**8-34 Which of the following procedures would an auditor most likely perform in planning a financial statement audit?

a. Inquiring of the client's legal counsel concerning pending litigation.
b. Comparing the financial statements to anticipated results.
c. Examining computer generated exception reports to verify the effectiveness of internal controls.
d. Searching for unauthorized transactions that may aid in detecting unrecorded liabilities.

8-35 The objective of performing analytical procedures in planning an audit is to identify the existence of
   a. Unusual transactions and events.
   b. Illegal acts that went undetected because of internal control weaknesses.
   c. Related party transactions.
   d. Recorded transactions that were *not* properly authorized.

8-36 In designing written audit programs, an auditor should establish specific audit objectives that relate primarily to the
   a. Timing of audit procedures.
   b. Cost-benefit of gathering evidence.
   c. Selected audit techniques.
   d. Financial statement assertions.

8-37 When planning an audit, the auditor needs to evaluate audit risk where the auditor may unknowingly fail to appropriately modify his or her opinion on financial statements that are materially misstated. Audit risk is composed of
   a. Tolerable error risk, sampling error risk, and inherent risk.
   b. Tolerable rate risk, sampling rate risk, and inherent risk.
   c. Allowance for sampling risk, allowance for nonsampling risk, and allowance for inherent risk.
   d. Risk of incorrect rejection, risk of incorrect acceptance, risk of overreliance, and risk of underreliance.
   e. Inherent risk, control risk, and detection risk.

8-38 Before applying substantive tests to the details of asset accounts at an interim date, an auditor should assess
   a. Control risk at below the maximum level.
   b. Inherent risk at the maximum level.

   c. The difficulty in controlling the incremental audit risk.
   d. Materiality for the accounts tested as insignificant.

8-39 Which of the following procedures would an auditor normally plan only for a first-time audit?
   a. Review litigation against the company that was settled in prior years.
   b. Review capital stock transactions from inception of the company.
   c. Review accounts receivable transactions from inception of the company.
   d. Review long-term debt repayments in prior years.

8-40 Match the term or terms that relate to each description. Each term may be used once, more than once, or not at all.

Description	Term
1. The confirmation of a CPA's responsibility for an audit.	a. A generally accepted auditing standard
2. In all matters relating to the engagement, the auditor or auditors must maintain an independence in mental attitude.	b. Inherent risk
3. The work is to be adequately planned, and assistants, if any, are to be properly supervised.	c. Engagement letter
4. The susceptibility of an account balance to misstatement.	d. Analytical procedures
5. A procedure to enhance the auditor's understanding of the client's business and direct the auditor's attention to balances and transactions that are unusual or unexpected.	e. A generally accepted accounting principle
6. The examination is to be performed by a person or persons with adequate technical training and proficiency as an auditor.	f. Control risk

Chapter 8 ► DISCUSSION/CASE QUESTIONS

(* = author prepared; ** = CPA examination)

8-41 The use of audit committees has become widespread. Independent auditors have become increasingly involved with audit committees and consequently have become familiar with their nature and function.

Required:

   a. Describe an audit committee.

   b. Identify the reasons audit committees have been formed and are currently in operation.

   c. List the functions of an audit committee.

*8-42 | Joe Melton, CPA, has been contacted by the president of Mudalum Company (a company developing a process to turn mud into aluminum) and asked to perform the company's audit for the current year. During a meeting with the president, Joe learned that the Securities and Exchange Commission had a suit pending against the company, charging it with an illegal distribution of securities. The president explained that it was an honest mistake by Mudalum because neither its former attorneys nor its former auditors informed him of the SEC registration requirements. For this reason, the president decided to change auditors and has threatened the former auditors with a lawsuit. Because of the threatened litigation, the former auditors refuse to discuss their audit of Mudalum Company with Joe.

If you were Joe, would you accept Mudalum Company as a client? Discuss your reasoning.

If you wished to make a further investigation of the situation, what would you investigate and what evidence would you gather?

May the former auditors properly refuse to discuss their audit of Mudalum Company with Joe?

*8-43 | Management of Consolidated Systems Company (CSC), a publicly held company, has asked three accounting firms, including yours, to bid on its annual audit. It has given permission to you and the predecessor firm, Andersen & Price, to communicate. In your discussion with Randel Mudge, the partner with Andersen & Price who supervised the CSC audit, you learn the following:

   a. Mudge has no reason to question the integrity of the CSC management.

   b. Mudge understands that the reason for the change in auditors was to obtain a lower audit fee. Andersen & Price charged $80,000 for the prior-year audit, of which $50,000 has not yet been paid by CSC.

   c. Mudge indicated that he had no disagreements with the management of CSC concerning accounting principles or auditing procedures. He did note that management had not informed the audit team of several canceled customer sales contracts for which revenue had been recorded. The auditors learned of the cancellations from their audit procedures, and management agreed to reduce revenue when questioned about the matter.

   d. Mudge stated that the management was very conscious of a perceived need to increase earnings per share each year. To help accomplish this, they would record the very minimum required costs where subjective estimates were involved, such as the allowance for doubtful accounts and the allowance for warranty costs. Where alternative accounting principles existed, CSC always selected the principle that resulted in the highest current net income.

   e. Mudge said that, because of significant losses in the last two years, he had seriously considered modifying the audit report last year to indicate substantial doubt as to CSC's ability to continue as a going concern. He discussed this matter with management, who were adamant that the company would continue as a going concern. Mudge agreed not to modify the report for last year, but he told management that a modified report might be necessary in the future.

Required:

   a. Describe how each of the above items—(a) through (e)—will affect your decision as to whether to accept CSC as an audit client.

   b. Assuming that all other information that you obtain about CSC is satisfactory, explain why you will or will not accept CSC as an audit client.

*8-44 The following audit engagement letter was drafted by D. Minus, a new staff assistant.

Ms. Patty Huff, Controller
Lurch Enterprises
1481 Big Mountain Road
Evening Shade, Arkansas   *no date at top*

Dear Ms. Huff:

This will confirm our arrangements with you to express an <u>unqualified</u> opinion on the financial statements of Lurch Enterprises for the year 19X4. We will do a <u>thorough</u> review of the balance sheet at December 31, 19X4, and the related statements of income and cash flow for the year then ending in accordance with <u>generally accepted</u> *GAAS* <u>auditing procedures</u>. This requires that we plan and perform the work to obtain a <u>high degree</u> of assurance about whether the financial statements are correct. An audit includes examining, on a test basis, evidence supporting the amounts and disclosures in the financial statements. An audit also includes assessing the accounting principles used and significant estimates made by management, as well as evaluating the overall financial statement presentation.

We intend to assess the company's existing internal control to see if it is adequate to prevent errors. Any errors not prevented by your internal control will be detected by our audit.

The charges for our services will be contingent upon how many hours we spend, which, in turn, is contingent upon the size of your company.

We appreciate this opportunity to provide you with the most outstanding auditing services available in this country.

Sincerely,
D. Minus
Staff Assistant

Required:
Identify the deficiencies in this audit engagement letter.

*8-45 Your knowledge of general economic conditions during the year ended December 31, 19X9, included the facts that inflation had been recorded at a high 12 percent rate, which caused a serious slowdown in business (real GNP declined 6 percent) and a steep drop in the stock market (approximately 25 percent). Unemployment was high, even though unions were demanding large wage increases. Because of high interest rates and the stock market decline, money supplies were tight, and long-term financing was practically unavailable.

Discuss the effects of these conditions on your audits of the following companies for the year ended December 31, 19X9:

a. A construction contractor specializing in small office buildings on fixed-price contracts.

b. An investment company with 50 percent of its portfolio in common stocks and 50 percent in long-term bonds.

c. A manufacturing company that has always been only marginally profitable and whose 4 percent bonds mature January 1, 19X0.

d. A small finance company specializing in consumer loans.

e. A manufacturer whose warranty costs have historically averaged 5 percent of sales.

*8-46 Your client, Kelting & Company, established a manufacturing facility in a Central American country several years ago because of the availability of cheap labor. Goods manufactured at this plant are shipped to and sold in the United States. This year the elected government was overthrown, and a military dictatorship is now in power. It is difficult to transfer funds out of the country, and business is suffering some disruption. Export licenses are subject to considerable delay. In addition, the U.S. Congress has imposed duties on goods the client manufactures at its Central American plant.

How are you likely to learn this information? How will this information affect your planning of the current-year audit?

*8-47   You are in the process of planning the audit of Computer Logic, a supplier of integrated circuits (chips) and associated software for complex peripheral control functions, including mass storage, graphics, and data communications. These devices play an integral role in the operation of personal computers, workstations, and related peripherals such as disk drives.

The mass storage devices consist primarily of 5¼-inch disk drives for personal computers. The graphics chips have not been successfully marketed yet because of intense foreign competition. The Federal Trade Commission is presently investigating whether foreign firms are illegally dumping graphic chips in this country. Management of Computer Logic is confident that U.S. government sanctions against the foreign companies in the form of tariffs will permit the sale of a large inventory of the graphic chips. Sales in the communications segment have not yet begun, but the company has spent significant funds to develop a pair of chips that will combine the capabilities of a fax machine, modem, and an answering machine into two integrated circuits, each of which is about the size of a postage stamp. The company has capitalized the cost of some prototypes as inventory, but the final product is not expected to reach the market for 18 months.

How would this information affect your planning of the current-year audit?

**8-48   Temple, CPA, is auditing the financial statements of Ford Lumber Yards, Inc., a privately held corporation with 300 employees and five stockholders, three of whom are active in management. Ford has been in business for many years but has never had its financial statements audited. Temple suspects that the substance of some of Ford's business transactions differs from their form because of the pervasiveness of related party relationships and transactions in the local business supplies industry.

Required:

Describe the audit procedures Temple should apply to identify related party relationships and transactions.

**8-49   Parker is the in-charge auditor with administrative responsibilities for the upcoming annual audit of FGH Company, a continuing audit client. Parker will supervise two staff assistants on the engagement and will visit the client before the fieldwork begins. Parker has started the planning process by preparing a list of procedures to be performed prior to the beginning of interim work. The list includes:

1. Review correspondence and permanent audit files.

2. Review prior-year's audit working papers, financial statements, and auditor's report.

3. Discuss with engagement team (firm personnel responsible for audit and nonaudit services to the client) matters that may affect the audit.

4. Discuss with management current business developments affecting the client.

Required:

Complete Parker's list of procedures to be performed prior to beginning the interim work.

*8-50   The first generally accepted auditing standard of fieldwork requires, in part, that "the work is to be adequately planned." An effective tool that aids the auditor in adequately planning the work is an audit program.

Required:

What is an audit program, and what purposes does it serve?

*8-51   You have been assigned to the audit of Hogeye Ranch Company. In assessing audit risk for various accounts, you have gathered the following information.

Accounts receivable   Accounts receivable consists of amounts due from the sale of cattle through four sales barns. All amounts are collected within one week. By state law, cattle cannot be sold without a certificate of inspection by a veterinarian, so all sales are easily accounted for by an examination of vet certificates. The number of cattle sold each month is reconciled with both vet certificates and sale barn receipts, and this control was tested with good results.

Cattle inventory   The herd numbers 500 cows and bulls. Cattle records are kept on notepads by the cowboys. Deaths and births are not always recorded promptly. Ear tag identifications are sometimes lost, so that specific animals may be difficult to identify. Also, a fence adjoining a neighbor's property is in poor condition, so that the client's and the neighbor's herds are sometimes mixed.

Property and equipment   Property consists mainly of land, a barn, and fencing. Equipment consists of a truck, a tractor, and minor other items. No control risk assessments tests have been performed on controls relating to property and equipment.

Required:

For the existence assertion of each account, assess each component of audit risk as high, medium, or low. Also indicate how your substantive tests for each account will be affected by your assessments.

*8-52   You have been assigned to the planning phase of the audit of ABC Company. One of the procedures that you have been assigned to perform is to compare a set of projected ratios and balances for 19X7 (the year under audit) with a set of ratios and balances computed from the unaudited book values for 19X7. The projected ratios and balances were computed by the audit team as summaries of expectations based on results from previous quarters of the current year, past audited results, and industry trends and are considered to be reliable. The ratios and balances are shown below.

		19X7 Projected	19X7 Unaudited	Percentage Change
Ratios				
	Current ratio = $\frac{\text{Current assets}}{\text{Current liabilities}}$	1.50	1.52	+1.3
	Quick ratio = $\frac{\text{Current assets less inventory}}{\text{Current liabilities}}$	1.00	0.98	<2.0>
	Gross margin %	28.7%	27.8%	<3.1>
	Income before taxes as % of sales	7.5%	10.0%	+33.3

		19X7 Projected	19X7 Unaudited	Percentage Change
	Inventory turnover = $\dfrac{\text{Cost of goods sold}}{\text{Ending inventory}}$	2.85	2.62	<8.1>
	Receivable turnover = $\dfrac{\text{Sales}}{\text{Ending receivables}}$	3.00	3.00	—
Balances	Inventory (FIFO), 12/31/X7	$1,500,000	$1,650,000	+10.0
	Current assets, 12/31/X7	4,496,000	4,646,000	+3.3
	Net income, 19X7 (Assume a marginal tax rate of 40%)	270,000	360,000	+33.3
	Sales, 19X7	6,000,000	6,000,000	—

Because some of the ratios and balances computed from the unaudited book values differ from what was anticipated, you inquired of management, who suggested that the cause of the discrepancy was a large year-end purchase of inventory at a favorable price.

Required:

a. Analyze the ratios and balances and explain why management's explanation is not sufficient to account for the discrepancies.

b. Assume that only one misstatement caused the discrepancies. State the most likely misstatement and describe how it affected each of the ratios and balances.

(*Source:* Adapted from "Pattern Recognition, Hypotheses Generation, and Auditor Performance in an Analytical Task" by Bedard and Biggs in *The Accounting Review.*)

*8-53   Late in the calendar year, Shallow and Shallow, a regional CPA firm, was approached by Undermyne Computers, Inc., a developer of innovative computer software, about changing auditors. Crest and Crest, another regional CPA firm, had been Undermyne's auditor since Undermyne listed its stock on the New York Stock Exchange several years ago.

Myron Shallow, the managing partner, held initial conversations with Stewart Marketo, who was president and majority stockholder of Undermyne Computers, Inc. The conversations were cordial until Shallow raised the question of why Crest and Crest was being replaced. Mr. Marketo was adamant in asserting that the sole basis for his "firing of Crest and Crest" was a disagreement on proper accounting procedures for several million dollars of software development costs of products whose marketability was showing signs of waning. Mr. Marketo insisted that these development costs continue to be amortized over the estimated original life of the software that was established when the products were conceived. Crest and Crest disagreed, maintaining that the amortization period should be shortened considerably, or perhaps the costs should be written off this year as a charge against earnings.

A week later, Mr. Shallow received a call from the managing partner of Crest and Crest who wished to discuss the audit of Undermyne Computers, Inc. Mr. Shallow indicated that his firm was still giving consideration to accepting the audit of Undermyne Computers, Inc., even though he had some reservations about the accounting treatment for Undermyne's software development costs. The managing partner of Crest and Crest described the many problems encountered during prior-year audits. He hinted strongly that continued amortization of certain computer-development costs would create serious problems for any further auditor of Undermyne Computers, Inc.

Mr. Shallow and the other partners of Shallow and Shallow considered the matter for several days and decided to accept the audit but to insist that the controversial computer development costs be examined carefully.

Required:

a. Create the sequence of events that should have occurred when Mr. Shallow was approached by Undermyne Computers, Inc. to consider the audit of that company.

b. All things considered, explain why Shallow and Shallow should or should not have accepted the audit.

During the next two weeks, Mr. Shallow had a number of conversations with Mr. Marketo about the scope of the audit. Although Mr. Marketo insisted that an engagement letter was "a waste of time and paper" because other services might be rendered by the CPA firm, Mr. Shallow believed that a nominal letter should be sent. The letter contained the following comments:

> This will confirm our arrangements with you to perform a variety of services for you during the coming calendar year, some of which will be determined at a later time.
>
> As part of the audit portion of our services, we will assess the company's existing internal control. However, there may be errors and fraud that we will not detect.
>
> The charges for our services will be determined after all services are performed.
>
> If these arrangements are in accordance with your understanding, please sign and return to us the enclosed copy of this letter. We appreciate this opportunity to be of service to you.

Required:

c. Describe the errors and omissions in this engagement letter.

During the planning stage of the audit, the following data were gathered on Undermyne Computers, Inc. and the industry in which it operates.

	From Prior-Year Financial Statements of Undermyne Computers, Inc.	From Computer Software Industry
Return on total assets	14%	15%
Gross profit margin	27%	27%
Net income margin	8%	10%
Inventory turnover	3	4
Day's sales in accounts receivable	26	20
Current ratio	0.90	1.00
Working capital to total assets	33%	32%

Required:

   d. Based on the above data, the other facts in the case, and your knowledge of the computer software market, describe the areas in which the auditors of Undermyne Computers, Inc. should concentrate their audit efforts. Do not list any specific audit procedures.

**8-54   Cook, CPA, has been engaged to audit the financial statements of General Department Stores, Inc., a continuing audit client, which is a chain of medium-sized retail stores. General's fiscal year will end on June 30, 19X3, and General's management has asked Cook to issue the auditor's report by August 1, 19X3. Cook will not have sufficient time to perform all the necessary fieldwork in July 19X3, but will have time to perform most of the fieldwork as of an interim date, April 30, 19X3.

    For the accounts to be tested at the interim date, Cook will also perform substantive tests covering the transactions of the final two months of the year. This will be necessary to extend Cook's conclusions to the balance sheet date.

Required:

   a. Describe the factors Cook should consider before applying principal substantive tests to General's balance sheet accounts at April 30, 19X3.

   b. For accounts tested at April 30, 19X3, describe how Cook should design the substantive tests covering the balances as of June 30, 19X3, and the transactions of the final two months of the year.

Internal Control—Obtaining an Understanding

"Tempt not a desperate man."

Shakespeare, *Romeo and Juliet*,
V, iii

LEARNING OBJECTIVES

After reading and studying the material in this chapter, the student should be able to

▶ Describe the five steps the auditor uses in assessing control risk.

▶ Write a short paragraph discussing the components of internal control.

▶ Describe the procedures for obtaining an understanding of internal control.

▶ Assess the ways of documenting the understanding of internal control.

▶ Write a brief narrative describing the logic of the flowcharts for the two audit strategies.

▶ Assess the reasons for using either of the two audit strategies.

▶ Analyze the illustrations of accounts receivable assertions and give reasons for the steps described in each illustration.

▶ Write a brief paragraph describing how the auditor can add value to the audit when obtaining an understanding of internal control.

In Chapter 7 we described the general framework of an audit as shown in Figure 9.1. In this chapter, we will discuss and illustrate the way control risk is assessed (block 2) using the following conceptual model.

1. Obtain an understanding of internal control for significant financial statement assertions. If appropriate, perform tests of controls on all or some of the internal control policies and procedures related to these significant assertions.

2. Assess control risk on these assertions.

FIGURE 9.1   General Flowchart of an Audit

Plan the audit	Understand and test internal control	Perform substantive tests	Issue audit report
Assess inherent risk	Assess control risk	Establish detection risk	Evaluate audit risk

3. Ascertain that the assessed level of control risk on these assertions corresponds with the planned level of substantive tests relating to these assertions.

4. Design the nature, timing, and extent of substantive tests relating to these assertions.

GENERAL DISCUSSION

The auditor should obtain and document a sufficient understanding of internal control to plan the audit. This includes the following steps:

1. An understanding should be obtained of each of the components of internal control that relates to assertions of significant accounts or classes of transactions. The five components of internal control (each of which is discussed later in the chapter) are (1) the control environment, (2) risk assessment, (3) control activities, (4) information and communication, and (5) monitoring. The auditor should become sufficiently familiar with the client's internal control to (1) identify types of potential misstatements, (2) consider factors that affect the risk of material misstatements, and (3) design substantive tests.

2. The auditor should assess control risk for assertions related to account balances and transaction classes. *Control risk* is

> the risk that a material misstatement that could occur in a financial statement assertion will not be prevented or detected on a timely basis by an entity's internal control policies or procedures.

In the auditor's *assessment of control risk,* he or she

> evaluates the effectiveness of an entity's internal control policies and procedures in preventing or detecting material misstatements in the financial statements.

▶ **EXAMPLE**

An auditor obtains an understanding of how orders from customers are processed. He or she may determine that inadequate controls for checking customers' credit could result in a significant misstatement of the allowance for uncollectible accounts and thus a material misstatement of the valuation assertion relating to the net amount of accounts receivable. If the auditor assesses the risk of a material misstatement to be at a high level, he or she may plan to perform a detailed examination of credit files to provide evidence as to the validity of this assertion. On the other hand, a low control risk assessment may allow the auditor to plan to rely more on discussions with client personnel about customers' credit histories.

The Role of Tests of Controls

Some *tests of controls* must be performed if the auditor plans to assess control risk below maximum or below 100 percent. Tests of controls are

> tests directed toward the design or operation of an internal control policy or procedure to assess its **effectiveness** in preventing or detecting material misstatements in a financial statement assertion.

> ▶ **EXAMPLE**
>
> Assume that an auditor is obtaining an understanding of internal control. He or she may learn that the duties of the client's credit department include reviews of the credit histories of customers to determine which accounts are doubtful of collection. Based on this review, the credit department prepares a monthly report that serves as a basis for adjusting the allowance for uncollectible accounts. The auditor wishes to learn how *effective* these credit department procedures actually are in preventing material misstatements in the allowance for uncollectible accounts (valuation of accounts receivable). Tests of controls (in-depth inquiries, observations, detailed examination of documentation, and reperformance of certain procedures) provide the auditor with the information necessary to evaluate the *effectiveness* of the procedures. Such information may allow the auditor to reduce the assessed level of control risk for the valuation assertion on net accounts receivable and alter substantive tests for this assertion.

DISCUSSION OF INTERNAL CONTROL

Internal control is defined by the Committee of Sponsoring Organizations of the Treadway Commission (COSO) as:

> A process—effected by an entity's board of directors, management, and other personnel—designed to provide reasonable assurance regarding the achievement of objectives in the following categories:
>
> (a) Reliability of financial reporting.
> (b) Compliance with applicable laws and regulations.
> (c) Effectiveness and efficiency of operations.

Internal control consists of five interrelated components. While they apply to all entities, the components are likely to be more formalized in large organizations than small ones. These components are:

Control Environment

This component basically reflects management's philosophy and attitude. It is sometimes referred to as the tone at the top. It defines the integrity, ethical values, and competence of individuals in the organization and is the foundation for all other components of internal control. An ineffective control environment can negate the benefits of the other parts of internal control.

▶ **EXAMPLE**

A company has a reliable system for recording credit sales and a proper segregation of duties between billing and accounts receivable clerks. But the company's top management has an attitude of "appearance of sales growth at all costs." They instruct both clerks to record fictitious sales near the end of the accounting period.

The control environment is influenced by such factors as the following.

A. Integrity and Ethical Values of the Client's Management

Management should issue appropriate policy statements and codes of conduct and should not adopt policies that encourage company personnel to falsify financial statement data.

▶ **EXAMPLE**

Management establishes a policy whereby supervisors have their bonuses reduced if the year-end physical inventories in their departments fall below a certain percentage of the departments' perpetual inventories. The supervisors arrange for small, temporary markups when pricing the physical inventories, so that quantity shortages are partially covered with pricing inconsistencies between the physical and perpetual inventories. The supervisors receive their full bonuses when they should not.

B. Commitment to Competence

For internal control to operate effectively, properly trained personnel must be performing appropriate tasks.

▶ **EXAMPLE**

The manager of the credit department has no experience in approving credit. The result could be a large volume of credit sales that cannot be collected.

C. Board of Directors or Audit Committee

An active board of directors and its audit committee can prevent concentration of control by management and can effectively interact with external and internal auditors.

▶ **EXAMPLE**

The board of directors requires management to adopt conservative accounting principles recommended by the external auditors.

D. Management Philosophy and Operating Style

Each manager has definite "ideas" about how the operations of an entity should be conducted. Some managers pay close attention to financial reporting, prepare and use budgets, and place emphasis on meeting operating goals; other managers do not. Some managements are dominated by a few individuals; other managements are more decentralized.

The auditor's assessment of management philosophy and operating style (as difficult as it may sometimes be) is a significant factor in the assessment of control risk. If current observation and prior experience convince the auditor that little importance is attached to proper financial reporting or if business risk is not adequately monitored, these may be early indications that control risk should be assessed at a high level.

E. Organizational Structure

The assignment of authority and responsibility within the company is also a criterion that the auditor will use in evaluating the control environment. Too much responsibility given to a few individuals may result in errors because of the excessive workload. Moreover, concentrated authority might create a climate in which fraud is more likely to occur. The delegation of responsibility and authority for specific tasks should be clearly defined.

Assume that the controller of a large company with many divisions has an inadequate staff to do the following:

1. Record and process all accounting transactions.
2. Maintain custody of all company securities.
3. Formulate investment policies and make all investments.

In such a case material errors are likely to occur. Such concentration of authority creates opportunities for fraud and diminishes the chances of such fraud being detected.

The auditor cannot observe the recording of every transaction. However, the more confidence the auditor has in the efficiency and effectiveness of the organizational structure, the more confident he or she will be that transactions have been properly recorded.

F. Assignment of Authority and Responsibility

Management's control over company operations is another matter that the auditor must consider. An effective method of establishing this control is the use of budgets and standards, including investigation and timely action on variances. A budgeting system that provides for investigating large deviations between actual and budgeted costs may reduce the risk of misstatement in the financial statements.

▶ **EXAMPLE**

If actual repair costs are substantially below the budgeted amounts, an investigation might disclose that significant amounts of repair costs were improperly recorded as additions to property and equipment.

The existence and effective use of internal auditors by the company might be one of the most important elements of the control environment. Internal auditors (unlike external auditors) are able to observe and influence, on a daily basis, the financial reporting process of the company. In fact, many audit procedures performed by external auditors are also performed more extensively by internal auditors.

G. Human Resource Policies and Practices

If sufficient numbers of competent individuals are involved in the financial reporting process, there is less probability that material misstatements will occur in the financial statements than if insufficient or incompetent individuals are involved. An entity should establish appropriate policies and procedures for hiring, training, promoting, and compensating employees.

Risk Assessment

All entities face risks, and this component relates to how effectively management identifies and controls those risks. Note that this is a risk assessment by management as opposed to the auditor's risk assessment.

Management must establish objectives for an entity before the risks of not accomplishing those objectives can be identified. Those objectives range from highly structured strategic plans for some organizations to informal goals for others. Setting objectives can help to identify critical success factors. These objectives and critical success factors relate to the (1) effectiveness and efficiency of an entity's operations, (2) preparation of reliable financial statements, and (3) adherence to laws and regulations. Risks threatening the meeting of these objectives can arise from

- Changes in the operating environment.
- New personnel.
- New or revamped information systems.
- Rapid growth.
- New technology.
- New products and activities.
- Corporate restructurings.
- Foreign operations.

   In addition to identifying risks, management should have plans for

- Estimating the likelihood and significance of the risks.
- Managing the risk, that is, determining what actions should be taken.

Control Activities

This component includes a range of activities such as approvals, authorizations, verifications, and reconciliations performed to address management-identified risks. These activities may be incorporated in

- Performance indicators (e.g., purchase price variances, number of days between sales order receipt and shipment of goods, returns of defective goods).
- Information processing (e.g., reconciliation of control totals, edit checks of data input).
- Physical controls (e.g., restricting access to inventory, maintaining investment securities in safe deposit boxes).
- Segregation of duties (e.g., separating the duties of authorizing a transaction, recording a transaction, having custody of the related asset, and reconciling the custody of the asset and its recorded amount).

Information and Communication

This component includes an accounting system that will identify, describe, measure, and record all valid financial transactions, but it is considerably broader. It includes other forms of communication such as policy manuals, memoranda, voice mail, electronic mail, and videotaped messages. It also includes a broad range of information including

- Brand profitability.
- Market share.
- Customer complaint trends.
- Accident statistics.
- Competitor product development activities.
- Legislative and regulatory initiatives.

    While some of this information does not relate directly to financial statements, auditors are beginning to focus on operating information as a way to add value to the audit.

Monitoring

Because internal control systems change over time, monitoring ensures that the systems continue to operate effectively. To a degree monitoring procedures are built into the normal operating activities of an entity. Controls are monitored internally by managers, internal auditors, and others. External monitors include customers, vendors, and regulators. Examples of monitoring activities include

- Identification of significant inaccuracies or exceptions to anticipated results.
- Communications from external parties.
- Independent reconciliations.
- Evaluations by internal and external parties.

► EXAMPLE

An entity receives numerous complaints from vendors that payments of invoices are for incorrect amounts. These complaints should alert management to potential weaknesses in internal control relating to purchases and accounts payable.

Limitations of Internal Control

There are certain inherent limitations in the effectiveness of an entity's internal control. These limitations arise from misunderstanding of instructions, mistakes in judgment, management override of controls, carelessness, and so forth. Therefore, internal control provides *reasonable* but not complete assurance that an entity's objectives will be achieved.

OBTAINING AN UNDERSTANDING OF INTERNAL CONTROL—GENERAL DISCUSSION

The Level of Understanding

For the relevant assertions of material accounts or classes of transactions, the auditor should obtain an *understanding of the internal control policies and procedures*. For each relevant assertion, the required level of understanding depends on

1. The complexity of the system that processes the transactions.
2. Experience gained from prior audits.
3. The auditor's assessment of inherent risk.
4. The auditor's understanding of the particular industry.
5. The auditor's judgment about materiality.

The auditor acquires an understanding of internal control to plan the audit. The understanding of internal control that relates to an assertion should be used to take the following actions:

1. Identify types of potential misstatements for that assertion.
2. Consider factors that affect the risk of material misstatement for that assertion and assess control risk.
3. Design substantive tests that correspond with the assessment of control risk.

▶ **EXAMPLE**

Assume that the assertion under examination is the existence of cash. What potential misstatements could occur? What factors affect the risk of material misstatement and what level of control risk should be assessed? What substantive tests should be designed? In obtaining an understanding of the policies and procedures that relate to the existence assertion, the auditor might consider (among other things) the possibility that recorded bank balances have been fabricated and do not actually exist. In obtaining an understanding of internal control relating to the existence assertion for cash, the auditor determines whether policies and procedures exist to provide reasonable assurance that cash transactions are properly accounted for, accurate and timely cash deposits are made, bank reconciliations are performed by independent parties, and so on. Therefore, control risk is assessed at a lower level, and substantive tests are restricted.

Procedures to Obtain an Understanding

Types of Procedures

To obtain an understanding of the relevant internal control policies and procedures, the auditor may (1) make *inquiries* of appropriate company personnel, (2) *inspect* documents and records, and (3) *observe* the company's activities and operations. The auditor can also make use of similar information obtained in prior-year audits.

▶ **EXAMPLE**

Assume that the auditor is obtaining an understanding of the policies and procedures related to the completeness assertion of accounts payable and purchase transactions. The auditor might wish to question purchasing agents as well as clerks who handle the purchases and accounts payable records. Inspection of purchases journals, accounts payable subsidiary ledgers, and supporting source documents would certainly be in order. The auditor also might observe the processing of purchases and accounts payable transactions. If the same policies and procedures had been evaluated as effective in prior-year audits, the auditor might restrict some of his or her procedures to determining whether changes in the policies and procedures have occurred.

What the Procedures Should Determine

Basically, the auditor is interested in obtaining two types of information about the internal control policies and procedures of each assertion under examination.

1. How relevant policies and procedures are *designed*.
2. Whether these policies and procedures have been *placed in operation*.

Design of certain policies and procedures may be critically important because their absence is an indication that the financial statements could contain material misstatements. One example is the lack of reconciliation between the accounts receivable control account and the accounts receivable subsidiary ledger. Another is the failure to segregate the duties of recording cash transactions and custody of cash.

It is equally important that these policies and procedures be placed in operation. It is one thing for the auditor to be told in response to an inquiry that one person records cash receipts and another person deposits them. It is another thing for the auditor to observe the separate performance of these functions.

An Example of Determining Design and Operation

Figure 9.2 contains examples of some procedures the auditor might use to obtain an understanding of internal control relating to a group of assertions for the accounts receivable balance and credit sales transactions.

FIGURE 9.2   Examples of Procedures to Obtain an Understanding of Internal Control

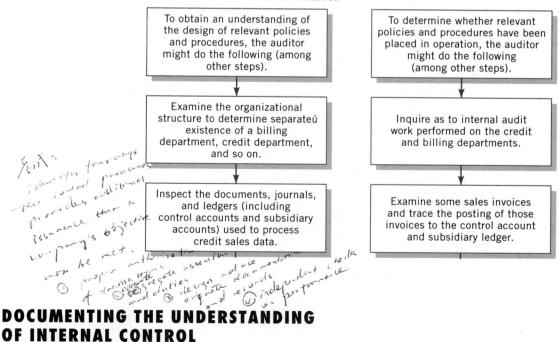

DOCUMENTING THE UNDERSTANDING OF INTERNAL CONTROL

The auditor is *required* to document his or her understanding of internal control. The extent and format of such documentation are a matter of judgment, however.

Generally, the more complex the company's internal control and the more procedures performed, the more extensive the documentation. Two traditionally popular forms of documentation are (1) flowcharts with accompanying narrative describing the document flows, and (2) questionnaires. In the remainder of this section, each of these forms is used to partially document the understanding of a system of cash receipts on account. This system relates to the existence and completeness assertions of the cash account.

Flowcharts

Flowcharts are graphic descriptions of the information flow in a system. The reader obtains a visual overview that may not be acquired from reading a narrative description of that same system. Thus, the auditor can often see control procedures in the system design more quickly and easily.

Flowcharts can be obtained from client personnel, if available, or the auditor can create them from observations, questions, and other available information. The advantages of obtaining client-prepared flowcharts are (1) time-saving and (2) possibly a more accurate overview of the system. The advantage of auditor-prepared flowcharts is the knowledge of the system obtained by the preparer. These flowcharts are often prepared and maintained in computer files.

Figure 9.3 shows the standard flowchart symbols normally used in flowcharts and the ones we will use in our illustrations.

FIGURE 9.3   Standard Flowchart Symbols

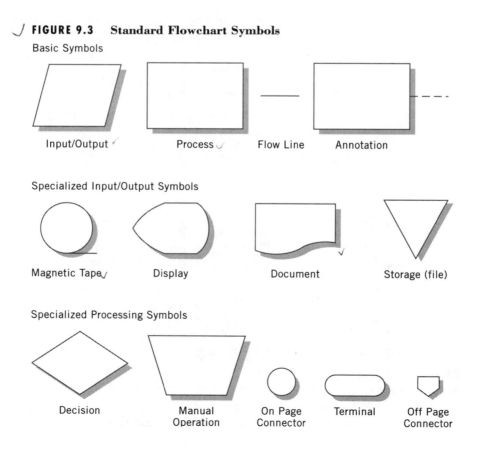

Basic Symbols

Input/Output   Process   Flow Line   Annotation

Specialized Input/Output Symbols

Magnetic Tape   Display   Document   Storage (file)

Specialized Processing Symbols

Decision   Manual Operation   On Page Connector   Terminal   Off Page Connector

Now look at Figure 9.4 on page 254 for an illustration of a flowchart of a system of cash receipts on account. Notice that the flowchart is sectioned according to the areas where the events and information flows occur. These sections, with accompanying narrative describing the document flows, are as follows.

1. The mail room where the checks and remittance advices are received from the customers.
   a. The checks are restrictively endorsed, and a two-part receipts listing is prepared. The checks are sent to the cashier.
   b. Copies of both the receipts listing and the remittance advices are sent to the accounts receivable department.
   c. A copy of the receipts listing is sent to the general ledger department.
2. The cashier department where the checks are received from the mail room.
   a. A deposit slip is prepared, and the checks are deposited at the bank.
   b. The bank returns the deposit slip to the cashier, and it is forwarded to the general ledger department.
3. The accounts receivable department where remittance advice and receipts listing are received from the mail room.
   a. The copy of the receipts listing and the remittance advice are reconciled, and the information is posted to the individual customer ledger accounts.
   b. The remittance advice and receipts listing are filed.
   c. Once a month, the total of the customer ledger accounts is reconciled with the accounts receivable control total maintained in the general ledger department.
4. The general ledger department where the receipts listing is received from the mail room.
   a. Total receipts are verified and posted to the cash account and accounts receivable control account.
   b. The total of the receipts listing is reconciled with the total of the deposit slip.
   c. The receipts listing and the deposit slip are filed.
   d. Once a month, the bank statement is reconciled with the cash balance in the general ledger.

Internal Control Questionnaires

In addition to examining a graphical design of the various systems of internal control, the auditor will ask and obtain answers to questions about these systems. Some of the answers might come from company employees and others from observations made while obtaining an understanding of internal control. Other answers could be provided by examination of policy manuals and flowcharts.

Such questions and answers are often documented in *internal control questionnaires,* an example of which is shown in Figure 9.5 on page 255. This questionnaire relates to the system of cash receipts on account illustrated in the flowchart in Figure 9.4. Check marks are placed in the Yes or No columns, and, where applicable, additional information is added, especially where there is a negative answer to the question. These questionnaires are often maintained on computer files.

Traditionally, internal control questionnaires have been important in obtaining

FIGURE 9.4   Flowchart for System of Cash Receipts on Account

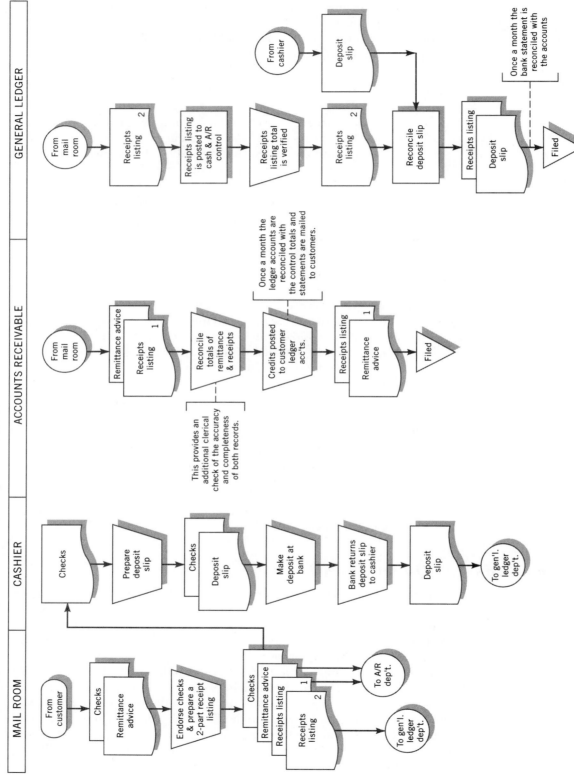

FIGURE 9.5   An Internal Control Questionnaire for Cash Receipts on Account

Question	Answer Yes	Answer No	Comments
1. Do different people handle the cash and have access to the records of cash receipts?		✓	The mail room has access to cash receipts and prepares receipts listing, but customer statements are mailed in accounts receivable.
2. Is immediate control established over mail receipts?	✓		
3. Are deposits made intact daily?	✓		
4. Do different individuals handle the detailed customer ledger accounts and control accounts?	✓		
5. Is the clerical accuracy of the cash receipts and remittance advices verified?	✓		
6. Is the bank-validated deposit slip returned to someone other than the cashier?		✓	The bank reconciliation is prepared in the general ledger department.
7. Is the total of the deposit slip reconciled with the remittance advice and receipt listing total before the deposit is made?		✓	No compensating strength found.

an understanding of internal control. Although other methods such as flowcharts have gained wide acceptance, the questionnaire approach is still popular among many CPA firms. The answers should be recorded only after proper investigation of flowcharts, narratives, results of conversations, and so on.

THE AUDIT STRATEGY

The auditor uses a variety of techniques to decide how much relative reliance to place on controls and substantive tests in gathering evidence. The auditor identifies controls and then makes a decision as to how those controls affect related substantive tests (e.g., after studying the controls over recording of accounts receivable, the auditor makes a preliminary decision that controls exist that may permit reductions in the number of confirmations sent to customers if tests of controls confirm that they are operating effectively.)

Studying and evaluating in depth each of the client's controls may not be an *efficient* way of determining the scope of related substantive tests. Some account balances and supporting assertions have weak or nonexistent controls and need not be studied and evaluated in depth. (Some clients, such as charitable organizations, have few controls because they cannot afford them.) In such cases the auditor anticipates, either from last year's audit or from a preliminary study, that most or all of the evidence must be gathered from substantive tests. Other account balances and supporting assertions may be believed by the auditor to have effective controls and may need to be studied and evaluated thoroughly to document the restriction of related substantive tests.

For a number of account balances and related assertions the auditor may use an *audit strategy* (relative emphasis placed on controls and substantive tests in gathering evidence) to make more efficient use of time during the audit.

▶ **EXAMPLE**

In auditing the existence of inventory and the occurrence of inventory transactions, it may be necessary to rely heavily on inventory controls because the volume of transactions makes it difficult to audit every transaction. Conversely, the existence of long-term debt may be audited efficiently by exclusive use of substantive tests because the volume of transactions is often small; controls need not be tested in this case.

Two alternative audit strategies may be developed for assertions related to significant account balances or classes of transactions.

1. A *primarily substantive approach.* The auditor gathers all or most of the evidence using substantive tests, and little or no reliance is placed on the controls. This approach usually results in an assessment of control risk at or near maximum. (This approach might be appropriate for the existence assertion for prepaid expenses because the balance may be easily tested by recalculation, a substantive test.)
2. A *lower control risk approach.* The auditor places moderate or considerable reliance on controls and, as a result, performs relatively few substantive tests. (The completeness assertion for accounts payable might be appropriate for this approach because the volume of transactions makes reliance on controls more efficient.)

The Primarily Substantive Approach—Flowchart

Figure 9.6 is a flowchart of the sequence of steps the auditor might take for some or all assertions for significant accounts if the primarily substantive approach is the audit strategy. In choosing this strategy, the auditor places heavy reliance on substantive tests and probably assesses control risk at maximum or near-maximum levels.

The Primarily Substantive Approach—Discussion

Reasons for Using the Primarily Substantive Approach

Basically, the auditor would use this approach for any of three reasons.

1. There are few (if any) internal control policies or procedures that are relevant. (A small owner-operated business is a possible example.) For such cases, only a minimum of audit effort is expended on controls, and almost all evidence supporting the assertion is gathered from substantive tests.

FIGURE 9.6　　**Flowchart of the Primarily Substantive Approach**

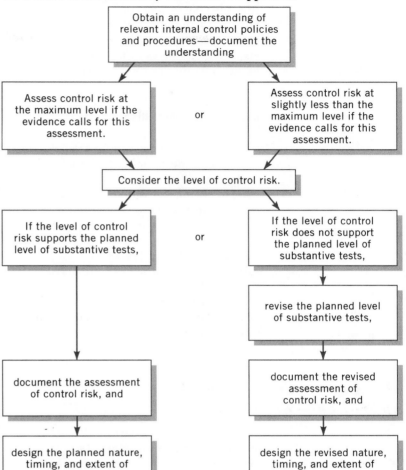

2. The internal control policies or procedures relating to assertions for significant accounts and classes of transactions are ineffective. For example, the controls over purchases and cash disbursements may be so inadequate that the auditor plans in advance to conduct extensive substantive tests for the completeness assertion of accounts payable (requesting a large percentage of the accounts payable vendors to independently verify the balances).

3. Heavy reliance on substantive tests is more efficient for a particular assertion. The cost and effort of spending considerable time testing controls for certain assertions are more than the saved cost and effort associated with the reduced level of substantive tests. In other words, "it isn't worth it." A case in point might be the existence assertion for property and equipment. If there are only a few transactions in the property and equipment account, the effort needed to test the controls regarding additions, retirements, and physical safeguarding may exceed the effort needed to gather the necessary evidence by examining documents supporting each addition and disposal.

Understanding Internal Control

If the primarily substantive approach is used, the auditor devotes less effort to obtaining an understanding of internal control than he or she would if the lower control risk approach is employed. Nevertheless, some basic knowledge must be acquired to design substantive tests, and the understanding of internal control must be documented in the workpapers.

Assessing Control Risk

When the primarily substantive approach is used for one or more assertions, the control risk probably will be assessed at or near the maximum level.

The assessment of control risk for the assertion must be documented regardless of its level. If the assessment is at maximum, the auditor needs only to document this fact. If the assessment is below maximum, however, the basis or reason for the assessment must be documented.

Designing Substantive Tests

After the auditor assesses control risk and decides on the planned level of substantive tests for the assertion, these tests are designed. Decisions are made on the nature (which tests), timing (when to perform them), and the extent (how much) of the related substantive tests for each appropriate assertion on which the auditor assessed control risk.

The Lower Control Risk Approach—Flowchart

Figure 9.7 is a flowchart of the sequence of steps the auditor might take if the auditor uses the lower control risk approach. In choosing this strategy, the auditor plans to obtain the necessary understanding of internal control and to perform enough tests of controls to support a lower assessed level of control risk.

The Lower Control Risk Approach—Discussion

Reasons for Using the Lower Control Risk Approach

A primary reason for using the lower control risk approach is increased audit efficiency. For certain assertions, internal control may consist of elaborate policies and procedures, which makes this approach more cost-beneficial.

One example of audit efficiency is a well-designed and efficiently operated perpetual inventory system that provides support for the existence assertion. The auditor plans to conduct the necessary tests of controls to assess control risk for this assertion at minimum. The time and effort saved from restricting substantive tests for this assertion will exceed the additional time and effort expended to lower the assessment of control risk from maximum to minimum.

The auditor also will consider the nature and location of the assets and related records that must be examined. Inventory may be maintained at dozens of locations throughout the country. Performing substantive tests at all sites may not be practi-

FIGURE 9.7   Flowchart of the Lower Control Risk Approach

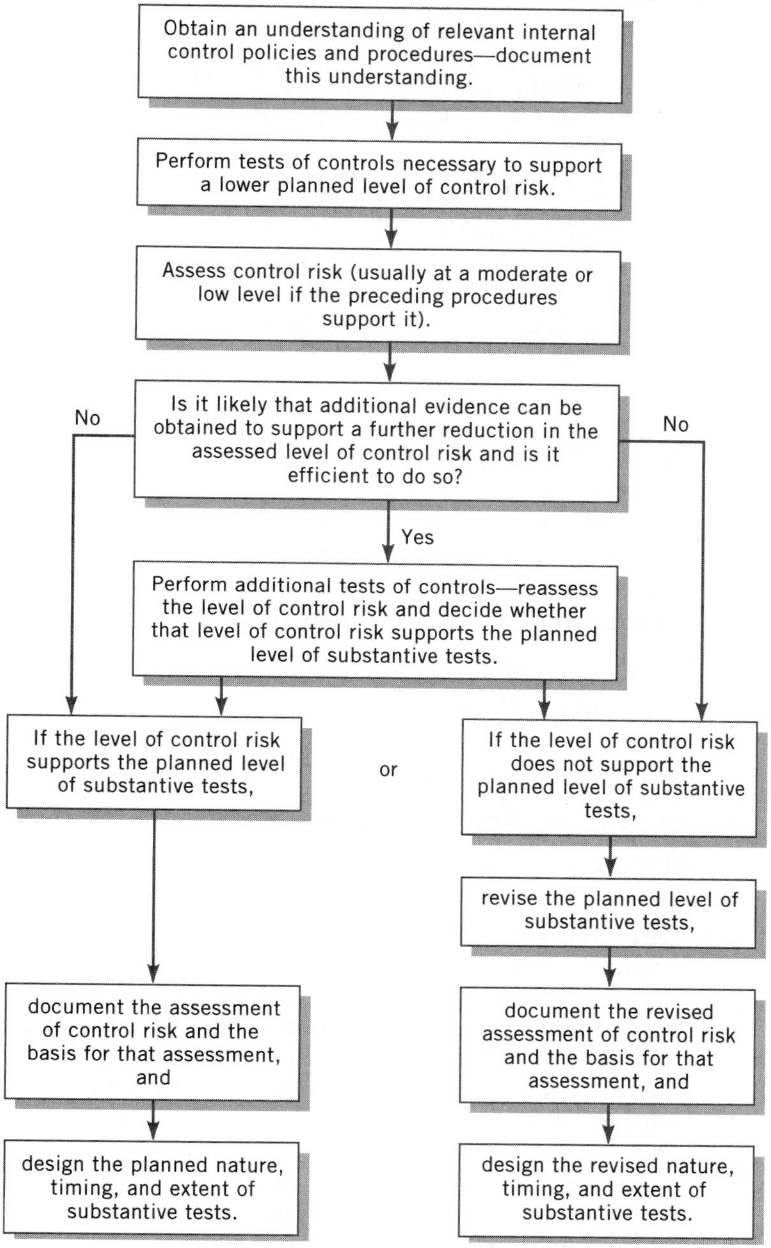

cal; therefore, extensive tests of controls may be the most appropriate audit approach.

COMPARISON OF THE TWO AUDIT STRATEGIES

A comparison of Figures 9.6 and 9.7 shows the basic differences in the two audit strategies (see Figure 9.8).

√ **FIGURE 9.8   Comparison of the Two Audit Strategies**

Primarily Substantive Approach	*Lower Control Risk Approach*
1. The auditor plans an assessment of control risk at a maximum or near-maximum level.	1. The auditor plans an assessment of control risk at a moderate or low level.
2. The auditor plans less extensive procedures to obtain an understanding of internal control.	2. The auditor plans more extensive procedures to obtain an understanding of internal control.
3. The auditor plans few, if any, tests of controls.	3. The auditor plans extensive tests of controls.
4. The auditor plans to conduct extensive substantive tests.	4. The auditor plans to restrict substantive tests.

AN ILLUSTRATION OF ACCOUNTS RECEIVABLE ASSERTIONS

Figure 9.9 on pages 261–262 provides additional insights into the concepts described and should be a valuable bridge to the material covered later in the chapter. We make the following assumptions.

1. A primarily substantive approach is used for the valuation assertion.
2. A lower control risk approach is used for the existence assertion.

VALUE-ADDED CONSIDERATIONS WHEN OBTAINING AN UNDERSTANDING OF INTERNAL CONTROL

An auditor can add value to the audit while obtaining an understanding of internal control. For example, while studying control activities related to the valuation assertion for accounts receivable the auditor should consider such questions as: Is management satisfied with the information generated about accounts receivable by the information system? How common are customer complaints? How is the issuance of credit memos controlled? Are credit terms similar to those of competitors? Has management considered substituting major credit cards for open accounts receivable? Are credit limits reviewed and adjusted periodically? Is interest charged on past-due accounts receivable? Questions such as these relate more closely to efficient operations than proper financial statement presentation, but auditors can add value to the audit by raising them with management.

APPENDIX: THE RELATIONSHIP AMONG TRANSACTION CYCLES, CONTROLS, AND ASSERTIONS

The auditor may wish to obtain an understanding of internal control by studying transaction cycles and the controls that relate to each of these cycles. In the following illustrations we show transaction cycles for purchases, accounts payable, and payroll; controls associated with parts of the cycles; and how these controls relate to account balance assertions when substantive tests are performed.

Description of Purchases Transaction System

1. When the stores department needs merchandise, two copies of a requisition are prepared. One copy is sent to the accounts payable department and the other to the purchasing department.
2. Upon receipt of the requisition, the purchasing department, after obtaining competitive bids, initiates a five-copy purchase order.
3. One copy of the purchase order is sent back to the stores department, where the quantities and descriptions are verified.

FIGURE 9.9   Illustration of Accounts Receivable Assertions

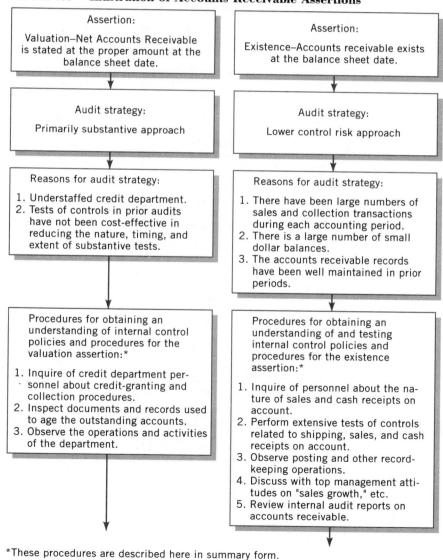

*These procedures are described here in summary form.

FIGURE 9.9   *(Continued)*

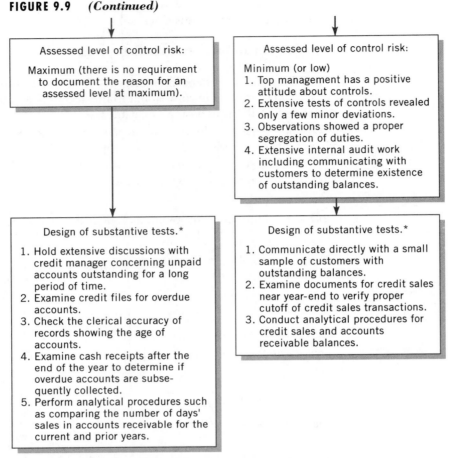

*These procedures are described here in summary form.

4. Copies of the purchase order are sent to the accounts payable and receiving departments to serve as file copies and as notification that merchandise has been ordered.

5. Two copies of the purchase order are sent to the vendor, who acknowledges receipt by sending one copy back to the purchasing department.

6. The vendor ships the merchandise to the receiving department, where an independent count of the merchandise is made and three copies of a receiving report are prepared.

7. The merchandise, after being counted and inspected, is sent to the stores department, along with two copies of the receiving report. The stores department compares the merchandise with the listings on the receiving report and sends one copy of the receiving report to the accounts payable department.

8. The third copy of the receiving report is sent from the receiving department to the purchasing department as notification that goods ordered were received.

9. Two copies of an invoice are sent from the vendor to the purchasing depart-

ment. The purchasing department retains the copy and sends the original to the accounts payable department.

10. The accounts payable department compares the details of the requisition, the purchase order, the invoice, and the receiving report. All four documents are filed together as documentation of the transaction.

Purchases

Description	Control	Assertion
One copy of the requisition is sent to accounts payable.	Establishes control over the pending purchase transaction.	Completeness
The purchasing agent obtains competitive bids.	Establishes control over prices.	Valuation
The purchasing department sends a copy of the purchase order to the receiving department.	Permits receiving department to determine that goods received have been ordered.	Existence
The receiving department makes an independent count of incoming merchandise.	Establishes control over incoming merchandise.	Completeness
The stores department compares merchandise with listings on the receiving report.	Continues control over incoming merchandise.	Completeness
The accounts payable department compares the details of the requisition, the purchase order, the invoice, and the receiving report.	Establishes control over the entire purchase transaction and ensures that what was requested, ordered, received, and billed are the same.	Existence

Description of Cash Disbursements Transaction System

1. To initiate a cash disbursement, a voucher is prepared in the accounts payable department. After the supporting documents (invoice, purchase order, requisition, and receiving report—see Description of Purchases Transaction System) and the account distribution are verified, the voucher is approved for payment.

2. The amount of the voucher is entered in the voucher register in the accounts payable department. Detail of the account distribution is sent to the general accounting department, where the amounts are posted to the applicable subsidiary ledger accounts. The voucher, together with the supporting documents, is sent to the cash disbursements department.

3. In the cash disbursements department, the supporting documents are examined and the voucher is approved for payment.

4. A check is prepared and signed after inspection of the approved voucher. The check is mailed to the payee by the signer. The amount of the check is entered in the check register. The supporting documents are canceled after the check is signed.

5. The check number and the amount of the paid voucher are sent to the accounts payable department and entered in the voucher register.

6. The general accounting department reconciles control totals from the subsidiary ledger accounts, the voucher register in the accounts payable department, and the check register in the cash disbursements department. Periodically, the total of unpaid items in the voucher register is compared with the vouchers payable control account maintained in the general accounting department.

7. The bank sends the bank statement and canceled checks directly to the internal audit department, where an independent bank reconciliation is performed.

Cash Disbursements

Description	Control	Assertion
The cash disbursement voucher is approved for payment.	Ensures that goods or services were received before payment is made.	Existence
The supporting documents are canceled when the check is signed.	Ensures that the voucher is not paid twice.	Existence
The total of unpaid items in the voucher register is compared with the vouchers payable general ledger control account.	Ensures agreement between the general ledger account and the voucher register.	Completeness
The bank statement is sent directly to the internal audit department, where an independent bank reconciliation is performed.	Ensures that unrecorded or inaccurately recorded cash disbursements are detected.	Existence

Description of Payroll Transaction System

1. The timekeeping department maintains two sets of time records. Employee clock cards, which originate in the timekeeping department, show the number of hours worked by each employee. Job time tickets, which come from the shops department, show the amount of time for each employee by job.

2. The timekeeping department reconciles the job time tickets with the employee clock cards. The job time tickets are then sent to the cost accounting department. The employee clock cards are sent to the payroll department.

3. The cost accounting department records the information from the job time tickets in a labor distribution journal. This journal is sent to the general accounting department, where an entry is made to a payroll clearing account.

4. The payroll department obtains employment and rate authorization records and deduction slips from the human resources department. These records and the employee clock cards are used to prepare the payroll register. A copy of the payroll register is forwarded to the accounts payable department.

5. The accounts payable department uses the payroll register to prepare a voucher that authorizes the writing of the payroll account reimbursement check. The voucher information is forwarded to the general accounting department for posting to the payroll clearing account. The voucher itself is forwarded to the cash disbursements department.

6. The cash disbursements department prepares the payroll account reimbursement check for the total amount of the payroll, as evidenced by the voucher received from the accounts payable department. The check is sent to the bank.

7. The bank deposits the payroll check in an imprest payroll account. This account is used to write individual checks to employees.

8. The payroll department writes the individual payroll checks from the imprest payroll account. On occasion, the individual checks are distributed to employees by the internal audit department. When this is done, identification is required of employees before payroll checks are released.

Payroll

Description	Control	Assertion
The timekeeping department reconciles the job time tickets with the employee clock cards.	Ensures that all employees' time is accounted for.	Completeness
The payroll department uses human resource department records and employee clock cards to prepare the payroll register.	Ensures that proper data are used to prepare the payroll register.	Existence
The cash disbursements department prepares one check for the total amount of the payroll.	Establishes control over the total amount of the payroll.	Valuation
Individual checks are sometimes distributed to employees by the internal audit department.	Ensures that payroll checks are not being paid to improper or nonexistent employees.	Existence

Chapter 9 ▶ GLOSSARY OF TERMS

Assessment of control risk Evaluation of the effectiveness of an entity's internal control policies and procedures in preventing or detecting material misstatements in the financial statements.

Audit strategy The relative emphasis the auditor places on controls and substantive tests in gathering evidence.

Control environment The collective effect of management operating and control techniques on establishing, enhancing, or mitigating the effectiveness of specific internal control policies or procedures.

Control activities The policies and procedures that help ensure management directives are carried out.

Control risk The risk that a material misstatement could occur in a financial statement assertion, which will not be prevented or detected on a timely basis by an entity's internal control.

Flowcharts Graphic descriptions of the information flow in a system.

Information and communication The accounting and other systems for identifying, capturing, and exchanging information.

Internal control A process—effected by an entity's board of directors, management, and other personnel—designed to provide reasonable assurance regarding the achievement of objectives in the following categories: (a) Reliability of financial reporting, (b) Compliance with applicable laws and regulations, and (c) Effectiveness and efficiency of operations.

Internal control questionnaire   A document that contains an auditor's questions about internal control. Answers are obtained from inquiry, observation, and inspection of records, flowcharts, and other documentation.

Lower control risk approach   An audit strategy in which the auditor is placing moderate or considerable reliance on controls and is conducting fewer substantive tests to gather evidence for assertions.

Monitoring   A process that assesses the quality of internal control over time.

Planned level of substantive tests   The nature, timing,

and extent of substantive tests for an assertion that should vary directly with the assessed level of control risk for that assertion.

Primarily substantive approach   An audit strategy in which the auditor is gathering all or most of the evidence with substantive tests; little or no reliance is placed on controls.

Risk assessment   Management's identification and control of risks facing the entity.

Tests of controls   Tests directed toward the design or operation of an internal control policy or procedure to assess its effectiveness in preventing or detecting material misstatements in a financial statement assertion.

Understanding of internal control policies and procedures   The knowledge of internal control that the auditor believes is necessary to plan the audit.

Chapter 9 ▶ REFERENCES

American Institute of Certified Public Accountants, Professional Standards
   AU Section 319—*Consideration of the Internal Control Structure in a Financial Statement Audit*
   AU Section 322—*The Auditor's Consideration of the Internal Audit Function in an Audit of Financial Statements*
American Institute of Certified Public Accountants, *Audit Guide for Statement on Auditing Standards No. 55, Consideration of Internal Control in a Financial Statement Audit.*
Committee of Sponsoring Organizations of the Treadway Commission (COSO). *Internal Control—Integrated Framework* (COSO, 1992).

Flagg, James C., Miller, Jeffrey R., and Smith, L. Murphy. "SAS 55 and the Small Business Engagement," *The CPA Journal* (January 1993), pp. 48–51.
Monk, Harold L., and Tatum, Kay W. "Applying SAS No. 55 in Audits of Small Businesses," *Journal of Accountancy* (November 1988), pp. 40–56.
Tanki, Frank J., and Steinberg, Richard M. "Internal Control— Integrated Framework: A Landmark Study," *The CPA Journal* (June 1993), pp. 16–20.
Temkin, Robert H., and Winters, Alan J. "SAS No. 55: The Auditor's New Responsibility for Internal Control," *Journal of Accountancy* (May 1988), pp. 86–98.

Chapter 9 ▶ REVIEW QUESTIONS

9-1   Name the five components of internal control.

9-2   Why is the control environment the foundation of internal control?

9-3   Describe the seven factors that influence the control environment.

9-4   Name eight examples of risk that management should identify and control.

9-5   Discuss four categories of control activities.

9-6   The information and communication component of internal control includes the accounting system. What other forms of communication are included?

9-7   What is the purpose of the monitoring component of internal control?

9-8   Describe the inherent limitations of internal control.

9-9   The understanding of internal control that relates to an assertion should be used to take three actions. Name these three actions.

9-10   Name the three procedures the auditor uses to obtain an understanding of relevant internal control policies and procedures.

9-11   What is the difference between a flowchart and an internal control questionnaire?

9-12   Why would studying and evaluating each of the client's controls not necessarily be the most efficient way of determining the scope of related substantive tests?

9-13   What is an audit strategy?

9-14   Describe two alternative audit strategies.

9-15 Give three reasons for using the primarily substantive approach.

9-16 Describe the steps in Figure 9.6.

9-17 Describe the steps in Figure 9.7.

9-18 Give a four-part comparison of the two audit strategies.

9-19 In Figure 9.9, why are there fewer substantive tests for the existence assertion than for the valuation assertion?

Chapter 9 ▶ OBJECTIVE QUESTIONS

(* = author prepared; ** = CPA examination)

 9-20 Which of the following is not a characteristic of the primarily substantive approach?
a. The auditor usually gathers all or most of the evidence with substantive tests.
b. Usually little or no reliance is placed on controls.
c. The assessment of control risk is usually at or near maximum level.
d. Extensive tests of controls are performed.

9-21 Which of the following is not a characteristic of the lower control risk approach?
a. Control risk is usually assessed at maximum level.
b. Substantive tests are usually restricted.
c. The auditor usually plans to place considerable reliance on the controls.
d. The auditor plans to perform extensive tests of controls.

9-22 Which of the following is not part of the control environment?
a. Management philosophy and operating style.
b. Organizational structure.
c. Information and communication systems.
d. Assignment of authority and responsibility.

9-23 If the auditor uses the primarily substantive approach instead of the lower control risk approach
a. A higher level of understanding of internal control is required.
b. The auditor plans to assess control risk at a lower level.
c. The auditor plans heavier reliance on substantive tests.
d. The auditor plans to restrict substantive tests.

9-24 The understanding of internal control that relates to a financial statement assertion should be used to do all of the following except
a. Determine inherent risk for that assertion.
b. Identify types of potential misstatements for that assertion.
c. Consider factors that affect the risk of material misstatement for that assertion and assess control risk.

d. Design substantive tests that correspond with the assessment of control risk.

 9-25 To obtain an understanding of the relevant policies and procedures of internal control, the auditor performs all of the following except
a. Make inquiries.
b. Inspect documents and records.
c. Make observations.
d. Design substantive tests.

9-26 After obtaining an understanding of an entity's internal control, an auditor may assess control risk at the maximum level for some assertions because the auditor
a. Believes the internal control policies and procedures are unlikely to be effective.
b. Determines that the pertinent internal control components are not well documented.
c. Performs tests of controls to restrict detection risk to an acceptable level.
d. Identifies internal control policies and procedures that are likely to prevent material misstatements.

9-27 An auditor may decide to assess control risk at the maximum level for certain assertions because the auditor believes
a. Sufficient evidential matter to support the assertions is likely to be available.
b. Evaluating the effectiveness of policies and procedures is inefficient.
c. More emphasis on tests of controls than substantive tests is warranted.
d. Considering the relationship of assertions to specific account balances is more efficient.

 9-28 An auditor's flowchart of a client's accounting system is a diagrammatic representation that depicts the auditor's
a. Assessment of control risk.
b. Identification of weaknesses in the system.
c. Assessment of the control environment's effectiveness.
d. Understanding of the system.

9-29 Management's attitude toward aggressive financial reporting and its emphasis on meeting projected profit goals most likely would significantly influence an entity's control environment when
  a. The audit committee is active in overseeing the entity's financial reporting policies.
  b. External policies established by parties outside the entity affect its accounting practices.
  c. Management is dominated by one individual who is also a shareholder.
  d. Internal auditors have direct access to the board of directors and entity management.

9-30 Which of the following questions would an auditor most likely include on an internal control questionnaire for notes payable?
  a. Are assets that collateralize notes payable critically needed for the entity's continued existence?
  b. Are two or more authorized signatures required on checks that repay notes payable?
  c. Are the proceeds from notes payable used for the purchase of noncurrent assets?
  d. Are direct borrowings on notes payable authorized by the board of directors?

9-31 Which of the following internal control procedures would an entity most likely use to assist in satisfying the completeness assertion related to long-term investments?
  a. Senior management verifies that securities in the bank safe deposit box are registered in the entity's name.
  b. The internal auditor compares the securities in the bank safe deposit box with recorded investments.
  c. The treasurer vouches the acquisition of securities by comparing brokers' advices with canceled checks.
  d. The controller compares the current market prices of recorded investments with the brokers' advices on file.

9-32 Equipment acquisitions that are misclassified as maintenance expense most likely would be detected by an internal control procedure that provides for
  a. Segregation of duties of employees in the accounts payable department.
  b. Independent verification of invoices for disbursements recorded as equipment acquisitions.
  c. Investigation of variances within a formal budgeting system.
  d. Authorization by the board of directors of significant equipment acquisitions.

9-33 Sound internal control procedures dictate that immediately upon receiving checks from customers by mail, a responsible employee should
  a. Add the checks to the daily cash summary.
  b. Verify that each check is supported by a prenumbered sales invoice.
  c. Prepare a duplicate listing of checks received.
  d. Record the checks in the cash receipts journal.

Chapter 9 ▶ DISCUSSION/CASE QUESTIONS

(* = author prepared; ** = CPA examination)

*9-34 During the course of acquiring an understanding of the internal control of her client, Consent Company, Ms. Search was pleased to discover that the recordkeeping in general and the accountability for assets were good. Also, transactions were approved by the proper individuals, and there was an adequate segregation of duties of sensitive responsibilities.

Ms. Search, however, was concerned about some aspects of the company's organizational structure and about the attitude of some of the company's top executives. For example:
  1. The company used a system of budgets and standards but paid little attention to deviations unless they were extremely large.
  2. The company had a credit manager who approved all credit sales above a certain amount. As far as Ms. Search could tell, the credit manager had no discernible criteria but simply approved or disapproved credit on an "intuitive" basis. Credit was rarely disapproved.
  3. The yearly financial statements were always compiled a few days after the end of the fiscal year. Many times, accruals were omitted and were subsequently recorded only at the insistence of the auditor.

4. The internal auditors did little except routine clerical work and reported to the controller.

5. The incentive pay of department heads was reduced if the departmental physical inventory count was less than 99 percent of the amount on the departmental perpetual inventory records.

Required:

a. Give reasons why Ms. Search might assess control risk at maximum and perform extensive substantive tests. Be specific as to which accounts (or account assertions) would require the most extensive substantive tests. (You need not name the substantive tests.)

b. Give reasons why Ms. Search might assess control risk below maximum.

*9-35 For each of the following situations, indicate whether the auditor would use a primarily substantive approach or a lower control risk approach for most or all of the assertions. Give reasons for your answers. (Consider only the information given here.)

1. The company is owned and managed by one person who employs two bookkeepers, a cashier, and one individual to manage the credit department.

2. The company has a sophisticated computer system that processes hundreds of transactions daily and has an elaborate set of computer controls. Few errors have been found during tests of controls in prior audits.

3. The company has a reasonably reliable information system and fairly good control activities. All members of top management believe that internal control is "a necessary evil" and pay little attention to problems reported by the auditor.

4. The company is a small service business that carries no inventory and a few accounts receivable. There is very little long-term debt, and short-term debt is almost always paid off the next month. Limited use is made of computers.

5. The company's internal control is poorly designed and the information system produces many errors. In prior audits, considerable time was devoted to tests of controls that resulted in a small restriction of substantive tests.

*9-36 For each of the procedures listed below, do the following.

a. Indicate what assertion(s) is being audited.

b. Indicate whether the procedure is (1) acquiring an understanding of internal control (which might include some tests of controls) or (2) a substantive test.

1. Ascertaining that the cash balance is on deposit in the bank at year-end.

2. Asking the credit department personnel about the policies for writing off uncollectible accounts. *evaluation*

3. Observing the procedures for entering and processing inventory purchase transactions.

4. Sending written requests to customers, asking them to reply directly to the auditors as to whether or not the accounts receivable balances on the company's books are the correct amounts.

5. Recalculating the amounts shown as accumulated depreciation on property and equipment. *allocation, substantive*

6. Inquiring about safeguards for the physical items of property and equipment. *existance, underst.*

7. Discussions with top management about credit-granting policies for sales made on account. *evaluation, understanding*

8. Examining documents near the end of the year to determine whether some purchases on credit were omitted in determining the accounts payable balance. *completness substantive*

**9-37 Examine the flowchart for sales, shipping, billing, and collecting on page 271 and do the following:

  a. Write a narrative description of the system.

  b. From a review of the flowchart and of the narrative written in (a), identify as many control activities as you can. Identify the financial statement assertion or assertions to which each control relates.

**9-38 Examine the flowchart for purchases on page 272 and do the following:

  a. Identify the sections of the flowchart and for each section write an accompanying narrative of the document flows (use pages 261–263 as a guide).

  b. Supply answers and comments to the internal control questionnaire for purchases controls shown below.

  c. From a review of the flowchart, the narrative description, and the questionnaire, identify as many control activities as you can. Identify the financial statement assertion or assertions to which each control relates.

An Internal Control Questionnaire for Purchases Controls

Question	Answer	Comments
1. Is there separation between authorizing, recording, and custody of merchandise purchases?		
2. Are steps taken to ensure the best prices for merchandise?		
3. Is immediate control established over merchandise received from vendors?		
4. Are receiving reports prepared after an independent count?		
5. Are procedures used to ensure that merchandise ordered is received?		
6. Are procedures used to ensure that merchandise invoiced by the vendor has been received?		

**9-39 Examine the flowchart for payroll shown on page 273 and do the following:

  a. Identify the sections of the flowchart and for each section write an accompanying narrative of the document flows (use pages 264–265 as a guide).

  b. Supply answers and comments to the internal control questionnaire for payroll controls on page 274.

  c. From a review of the flowchart, the narrative description, and the questionnaire, identify as many control activities as you can. Identify the financial statement assertion or assertions to which each control relates.

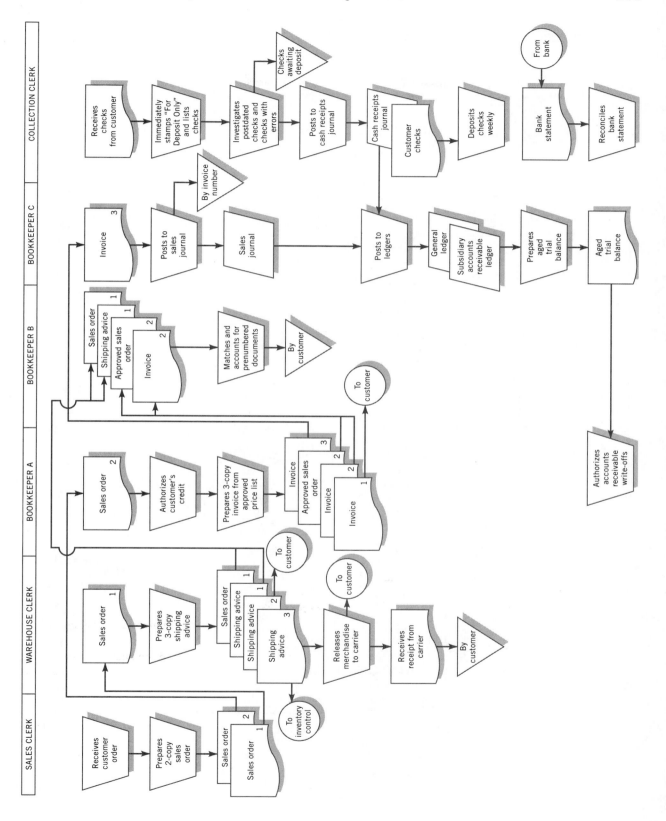

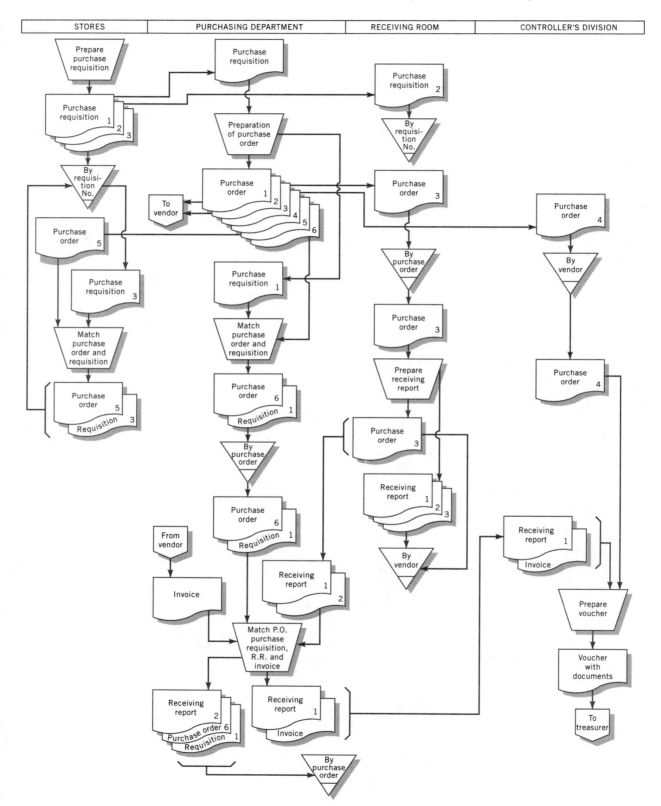

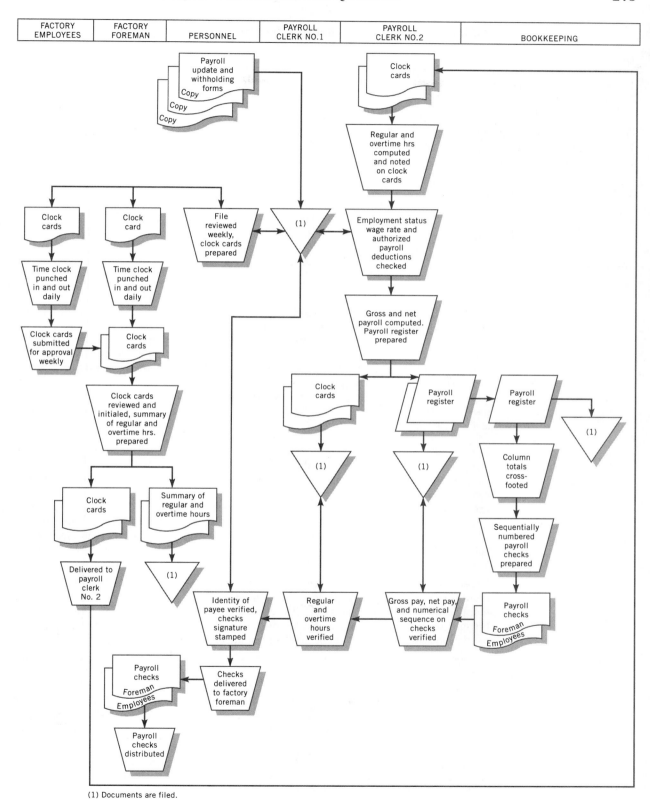

FACTORY EMPLOYEES	FACTORY FOREMAN	PERSONNEL	PAYROLL CLERK NO.1	PAYROLL CLERK NO.2	BOOKKEEPING

(1) Documents are filed.

An Internal Control Questionnaire for Payroll Controls

Question	Answer	Comments
1. Are the duties of recording the payroll and disbursing the payroll checks separate?		
2. Is an imprest payroll account used?		
3. Are steps taken to guard against paying checks to improper or fictitious employees?		
4. Are steps taken to ensure that the clock cards are accurate?		
5. Are employment records kept in a department separate from payroll preparation?		

**9-40   In 19X4 XY Company purchased more than $10 million of office equipment under its "special" ordering system, with individual orders ranging from $5,000 to $30,000. "Special" orders entail low-volume items that have been included in an authorized user's budget. Department heads include in their annual budget requests the types of equipment and their estimated cost. The budget, which limits the types and dollar amounts of office equipment a department head can requisition, is approved at the beginning of the year by the board of directors. Department heads prepare a purchase requisition form for equipment and forward the requisition to the purchasing department. XY's "special" ordering system functions as follows:

Purchasing: Upon receiving a purchase requisition, one of five buyers verifies that the person requesting the equipment is a department head. The buyer then selects the appropriate vendor by searching the various vendor catalogs on file. The buyer then phones the vendor, requesting a price quotation, and gives the vendor a verbal order. A prenumbered purchase order is then processed with the original sent to the vendor, a copy to the department head, a copy to receiving, a copy to accounts payable, and a copy filed in the open requisition file. When the buyer is orally informed by the receiving department that the item has been received, the buyer transfers the purchase order from the unfilled file to the filled file. Once a month the buyer reviews the unfilled file to follow up and expedite open orders.

Receiving: The receiving department receives a copy of the purchase order. When equipment is received, the receiving clerk stamps the purchase order with the date received, and, if applicable, in red pen prints any differences between quantity on the purchase order and quantity received. The receiving clerk forwards the stamped purchase order and equipment to the requisitioning department head and orally notifies the purchasing department.

Accounts payable: Upon receipt of a purchase order, the accounts payable clerk files the purchase order in the open purchase order file. When a vendor invoice is received, the invoice is matched with the applicable purchase order, and a payable is set up by debiting the equipment account of the department requesting the items. Unpaid invoices are filed by the due date, and, at the due date, a check is prepared. The invoice and purchase order are filed by purchase order number in a paid invoice file, and then the check is forwarded to the treasurer for signature.

Treasurer: Checks received daily from the accounts payable department are sorted into two groups: those over $10,000 and those $10,000 and less. Checks for $10,000 and less are machine-signed. The cashier maintains the key and signature plate to the check-signing machine and maintains a record of usage of the check-signing machine. All checks over $10,000 are signed by the treasurer or the controller.

Required:

a. Identify the sections of the narrative that describe aspects of the control environment for XY Company. What effect, if any, would these aspects of the control environment have on XY Company's accounting system and control activities relating to purchasing, receiving, accounts payable, and treasurer?

b. Identify the financial statement assertions for specific accounts covered by the narrative. For each assertion, identify potential misstatements that could occur in the financial statements.

c. Identify the control activities in the narrative that relate to each of the financial statement assertions in (b) above. Indicate in what way the control activities might prevent or detect these potential misstatements.

*9-41 Assume that an independent auditor is auditing the financial statements of a small not-for-profit institution. He finds that the information system is handled by one individual who writes checks, records and deposits the cash receipts, and records and posts all transaction entries. The independent auditor suggests that two additional people are needed to provide minimum control for the information system.

a. The directors of the institution agreed to hire two additional people. Suggest how the accounting duties can be divided between the three individuals so as to improve the controls.

b. The directors reject the suggestion of hiring another individual. What effect would this have on the audit?

*9-42 Listed hereafter are eight responsibilities that might be performed by individuals in an accounting department. Assume that five people are employed for the purpose of handling these eight responsibilities.

1. Responsible for the general ledger.
2. Responsible for the accounts receivable subsidiary ledger.
3. Responsible for deposit of cash receipts in the bank.
4. Responsible for the purchases journal.
5. Responsible for writing checks to creditors.
6. Responsible for the cash disbursements journal.
7. Responsible for the cash receipts journal.
8. Responsible for the payroll register.

Required:

a. Assuming that no employee will perform more than two jobs, list combinations of jobs for each of the five employees, considering the combinations that will provide the most effective control system. Support your listings with reasons.

b. List the *worst* combination of jobs that you can think of and support your reasoning.

*9-43 In an effective internal control system, the following functions are separated: (1) authorizing a transaction, (2) recording a transaction, (3) maintaining custody of assets that result from a transaction, and (4) comparing assets with the related amounts recorded in the accounting records. In each of the following situations, indicate which functions are combined and what misstatement or misstatements could occur.

a. The payroll supervisor disburses the payroll checks.

b. The general ledger clerk maintains the accounts receivable subsidiary ledger.

c. The cashier maintains the cash receipts journal.

d. The accounts payable supervisor writes and mails the checks.

e. The storeroom clerks count the physical inventory.

f. The cashier reconciles the bank statements.

**9-44   You have been engaged by the management of Alden, Inc. to review its internal control over the purchase, receipt, storage, and issue of raw materials. You have prepared the following comments to describe Alden's procedures.

Raw materials, which consist mainly of high-cost electronic components, are kept in a locked storeroom. Storeroom personnel include a supervisor and four clerks. All are well trained, competent, and adequately bonded. Raw materials are removed from the storeroom only on written or oral authorization of one of the production supervisors.

There are no perpetual inventory records; hence, the storeroom clerks do not keep records of goods received or issued. To compensate for the lack of perpetual records, a physical inventory count is taken monthly by the storeroom clerks, who are well supervised. Appropriate procedures are followed in making the inventory count.

After the physical count, the storeroom supervisor matches quantities counted against a predetermined reorder level. If the count for a given part is below the reorder level, the supervisor enters the part number on a materials-requisition list and sends this list to the accounts payable clerk. The accounts payable clerk prepares a purchase order for a predetermined reorder quantity for each part and mails the purchase order to the vendor from whom the part was last purchased.

When ordered materials arrive at Alden, they are received by the storeroom clerks. The clerks count the merchandise and reconcile counts to the shipper's bill of lading. All vendors' bills of lading are initialed, dated, and filed in the storeroom to serve as receiving reports.

Required:

a. Identify the inventory assertions covered by the narrative. For each assertion, identify potential misstatements that could occur in the financial statements.

b. Identify the control activities in the narrative that relate to each of the assertions in (a) above. Indicate whether or not the control activities might prevent or detect these potential misstatements. If they might, indicate how.

**9-45   The flowchart on page 277 depicts part of a client's revenue cycle. Some of the flowchart symbols are labeled to indicate control procedures and records. For each symbol numbered 61 through 73, select one response from the answer lists below. Each response in the lists may be selected once or *not* at all.

Answer Lists

Operations and Control Procedures

A. Enter shipping data

B. Verify agreement of sales order and shipping document

C. Write off accounts receivable

D. To warehouse and shipping department

E. Authorize account receivable write-off

F. Prepare aged trial balance

G. To sales department

H. Release goods for shipment

 I. To accounts receivable department

J. Enter price data

K. Determine that customer exists

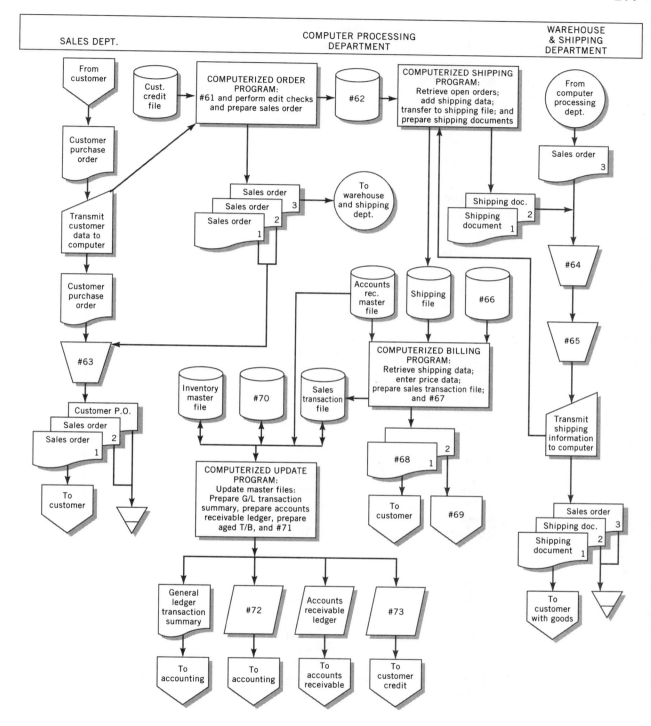

L.   Match customer purchase order with sales order

M.   Perform customer credit check

N.   Prepare sales journal

O.   Prepare sales invoice

Documents, Journals, Ledgers, and Files

P.   Shipping document

Q.   General ledger master file

R.   General journal

S.   Master price file

T.   Sales journal

U.   Sales invoice

V.   Cash receipts journal

W.   Uncollectible accounts file

X.   Shipping file

Y.   Aged trial balance

Z.   Open order file

**9-46   Butler, CPA, has been engaged to audit the financial statements of Young Computer Outlets, Inc., a new client. Young is a privately-owned chain of retail stores that sells a variety of computer software and video products. Young uses an in-house payroll department at its corporate headquarters to compute payroll data, and to prepare and distribute payroll checks to its 300 salaried employees.

Butler is preparing an internal control questionnaire to assist in obtaining an understanding of Young's internal control and in assessing control risk.

Required:

Prepare a "Payroll" segment of Butler's internal control questionnaire that would assist in obtaining an understanding of Young's internal control and in assessing control risk.

Do *not* prepare questions relating to cash payrolls, EDP applications, payments based on hourly rates, piecework, commissions, employee benefits (pensions, health care, vacations, etc.), or payroll tax accruals other than withholdings.

Use the format in the following example:

| *Question* | *Yes* | *No* |

Are paychecks prenumbered and accounted for?

**9-47   Field, CPA, is auditing the financial statements of Miller Mailorder, Inc. (MMI) for the year ended January 31, 19X5. Field has compiled a list of possible errors and fraud that may result in the misstatement of MMI's financial statements, and a corresponding list of control activities that, if properly designed and implemented, could assist MMI in preventing or detecting the errors and fraud.

Required:

For each possible error and fraud numbered 1 through 15, select one internal control procedure from the answer list on pages 279–280 that, if properly designed and implemented, most likely could assist MMI in preventing or detecting the errors and fraud. Each response in the list of control activities may be selected once, more than once, or not at all.

Possible Errors and Fraud

1. Invoices for goods sold are posted to incorrect customer accounts.
2. Goods ordered by customers are shipped, but are *not* billed to anyone.
3. Invoices are sent for shipped goods, but are *not* recorded in the sales journal.
4. Invoices are sent for shipped goods and are recorded in the sales journal, but are *not* posted to any customer account.
5. Credit sales are made to individuals with unsatisfactory credit ratings.
6. Goods are removed from inventory for unauthorized orders.
7. Goods shipped to customers do *not* agree with goods ordered by customers.
8. Invoices are sent to allies in a fraudulent scheme and sales are recorded for fictitious transactions.
9. Customers' checks are received for less than the customers' full account balances, but the customers' full account balances are credited.
10. Customers' checks are misappropriated before being forwarded to the cashier for deposit.
11. Customers' checks are credited to incorrect customer accounts.
12. Different customer accounts are each credited for the same cash receipt.
13. Customers' checks are properly credited to customer accounts and are properly deposited, but errors are made in recording receipts in the cash receipts journal.
14. Customers' checks are misappropriated after being forwarded to the cashier for deposit.
15. Invalid transactions granting credit for sales returns are recorded.

Control Activities

a. Shipping clerks compare goods received from the warehouse with the details on the shipping documents.
b. Approved sales orders are required for goods to be released from the warehouse.
c. Monthly statements are mailed to all customers with outstanding balances.
d. Shipping clerks compare goods received from the warehouse with approved sales orders.
e. Customer orders are compared with the inventory master file to determine whether items ordered are in stock.
f. Daily sales summaries are compared with control totals of invoices.
g. Shipping documents are compared with sales invoices when goods are shipped.
h. Sales invoices are compared with the master price file.
i. Customer orders are compared with an approved customer list.
j. Sales orders are prepared for each customer order.
k. Control amounts posted to the accounts receivable ledger are compared with control totals of invoices.
l. Sales invoices are compared with shipping documents and approved customer orders before invoices are mailed.
m. Prenumbered credit memos are used for granting credit for goods returned.
n. Goods returned for credit are approved by the supervisor of the sales department.
o. Remittance advices are separated from the checks in the mailroom and forwarded to the accounting department.
p. Total amounts posted to the accounts receivable ledger from remittance advices are compared with the validated bank deposit slip.
q. The cashier examines each check for proper endorsement.
r. Validated deposit slips are compared with the cashier's daily cash summaries.

s. An employee, other than the bookkeeper, periodically prepares a bank reconciliation.

t. Sales returns are approved by the same employee who issues receiving reports evidencing actual return of goods.

**9-48   An auditor's working papers include the narrative description below of the cash receipts and billing portions of internal control of Rural Building Supplies, Inc. Rural is a single-store retailer that sells a variety of tools, garden supplies, lumber, small appliances, and electrical fixtures to the public, although about half of Rural's sales are to construction contractors on account. Rural employs 12 salaried sales associates, a credit manager, three full-time clerical workers, and several part-time cash register clerks and assistant bookkeepers. The full-time clerical workers perform such tasks as cash receipts, billing, and accounting and are adequately bonded. They are referred to in the narrative as "accounts receivable supervisor," "cashier," and "bookkeeper."

Narrative

Retail customers pay for merchandise by cash or credit card at cash registers when merchandise is purchased. A contractor may purchase merchandise on account if approved by the credit manager based only on the manager's familiarity with the contractor's reputation. After credit is approved, the sales associate files a prenumbered charge form with the accounts receivable (A/R) supervisor to set up the receivable.

The A/R supervisor independently verifies the pricing and other details on the charge form by reference to a management-authorized price list, corrects any errors, prepares the invoice, and supervises a part-time employee who mails the invoice to the contractor. The A/R supervisor electronically posts the details of the invoice in the A/R subsidiary ledger; simultaneously, the transaction's details are transmitted to the bookkeeper. The A/R supervisor also prepares a monthly computer-generated A/R subsidiary ledger without a reconciliation with the A/R control account and a monthly report of overdue accounts.

The cash receipts functions are performed by the cashier who also supervises the cash register clerks. The cashier opens the mail, compares each check with the enclosed remittance advice, stamps each check "for deposit only," and lists checks for deposit. The cashier then gives the remittance advices to the bookkeeper for recording. The cashier deposits the checks daily separate from the daily deposit of cash register receipts. The cashier retains the verified deposit slips to assist in reconciling the monthly bank statements, but forwards to the bookkeeper a copy of the daily cash register summary. The cashier does not have access to the journals or ledgers.

The bookkeeper receives the details of transactions from the A/R supervisor and the cashier for journalizing and posting to the general ledger. After recording the remittance advices received from the cashier, the bookkeeper electronically transmits the remittance information to the A/R supervisor for subsidiary ledger updating. The bookkeeper sends monthly statements to contractors with unpaid balances upon receipt of the monthly report of overdue balances from the A/R supervisor. The bookkeeper authorizes the A/R supervisor to write off accounts as uncollectible when six months have passed since the initial overdue notice was sent. At this time, the credit manager is notified by the bookkeeper not to grant additional credit to that contractor.

Required:

Based only on the information in the narrative, describe the internal control weaknesses in Rural's internal control concerning the cash receipts and billing functions. Organize the weaknesses by employee job function: Credit manager, A/R supervisor, Cashier, and Bookkeeper. Do *not* describe how to correct the weaknesses.

**9-49   Taylor, CPA, has been engaged to audit the financial statements of University Books, Inc. University Books maintains a large revolving cash fund exclusively for the purpose of buying used books from students for cash. The cash fund is active all year because the nearby university offers a large variety of courses with various starting and completion dates throughout the year.

Receipts are prepared for each purchase, and reimbursement vouchers are submitted periodically.

Required:

Construct an internal control questionnaire to be used in the evaluation of internal control of University Books' buying segment's revolving cash fund. The internal control questionnaire should elicit a Yes or No response. Do *not* discuss the internal control procedures over the books that are purchased.

Internal Control— Testing, Assessing Control Risk, and Designing Substantive Tests

"Skepticism is the first step toward truth."

DIDEROT, *Pensées Philosophiques*

LEARNING OBJECTIVES

After reading and studying the material in this chapter, the student should be able to

▶ Describe the purpose of tests of controls and analyze situations that would and would not require tests of controls.

▶ Describe the four procedures for performing tests of controls.

▶ Give brief examples of the four factors the auditor considers when deciding what additional evidence is needed when tests of controls are performed during an interim period.

▶ Briefly describe eight factors the auditor should consider in using sampling techniques for tests of controls.

▶ Assess reasons for using, or not using, each of the sample selection methods for tests of controls.

▶ Analyze factors the auditor will use in setting (1) the risk of assessing control risk too low, (2) the planned tolerable rate, and (3) the expected deviation rate in the population.

▶ Analyze the decision rules for evaluating sample results for a test of controls.

▶ Describe the decision rules for assessing the level of control risk.

▶ Analyze the relationships among assertions, assessed levels of control risk, planned levels of related substantive tests, and revised levels of related substantive tests.

▶ Paraphrase the format of the report that communicates reportable conditions.

▶ Determine sample size, select the sample, and evaluate sample results for a test of controls using nonstatistical and statistical sampling.

In this chapter we discuss (1) tests of controls (including sampling), (2) assessment of control risk, and (3) design of related substantive tests. We will also show how and with whom to communicate internal control weaknesses (referred to as reportable conditions) noted during the audit.

THE PURPOSE OF TESTS OF CONTROLS

While the auditor is obtaining an understanding of internal control for a financial statement assertion, he or she may identify specific policies or procedures that are likely to prevent or detect material misstatements in the assertion. If appropriate, *tests of controls* are performed to provide reasonable assurance that these internal control policies and procedures are designed and operating *effectively*.

Tests of controls are *not necessary* if the auditor *plans* to use the primarily substantive approach and assess control risk at maximum. If the auditor *plans* to assess control risk below maximum, tests of controls *must* be performed.

The difference between obtaining an understanding and performing a test of controls is illustrated in Figure 10.1 where we assume that the financial statement assertion is the valuation of net accounts receivable.

FIGURE 10.1 **Comparison of Obtaining an Understanding and Performing Tests of Controls**

Procedures Used to Obtain an Understanding of Internal Control	*Tests of Controls Directed Toward Effectiveness of Design and Operation*
Read policy manual to determine that prices on invoices are compared with a master price list.	
Confirm by inquiry that comparisons are actually being made.	Select a sample of invoices and compare prices to master price list.

PROCEDURES FOR PERFORMING TESTS OF CONTROLS

Inquiry of Appropriate Company Personnel

To test controls for accounts receivable assertions the auditor interviews the individuals who handle (1) cash deposits, (2) records of cash deposits, (3) the accounts receivable subsidiary ledger, and (4) the general ledger. From the interview, the auditor determines whether internal control policies and procedures are operating effectively and as they are purported to operate (e.g., do different individuals handle the detailed customer ledger accounts and the control accounts?).

Inspection of Documents

The auditor also could examine records that are part of the design of the internal control policies and procedures.

> ▶ **EXAMPLE**
>
> The auditor examines such cash receipts documents as copies of remittance advices, receipts listings, deposit slips, and entries to the accounts receivable subsidiary ledger and the general ledger. By doing so, the auditor ascertains that the records *do exist,* that they have the proper format, and that the data are consistently recorded between records.

The auditor also could conduct a *walkthrough* by tracing one or more transactions from the receipt of cash to its deposit and to its recording in the subsidiary and general ledgers. The auditor is not conducting a scientific sample but is ascertaining whether the cash receipts transactions appear to be properly processed.

Observation of the Application of the Policy or Procedure

Sometimes the auditor might obtain evidence of operating effectiveness by watching the processing of the cash receipts transactions. To be most effective, this observation should probably be on a surprise basis. Also, an auditor must remember that an observation applies only to the point in time that it occurs, not the entire audit period.

Reperformance of the Policy or Procedure

The auditor can also test controls by examining client policies and procedures as if he or she were applying the policies or performing the procedures. Instead of performing the processes, however, the auditor ascertains that client personnel performed them properly to a degree satisfactory to him or her.

> ▶ **EXAMPLE**
>
> In evaluating the design of the cash disbursements system, the auditor observes that all vendor invoices are to be approved with a signature or initials of the controller before checks are prepared and issued to the vendor. The auditor could ascertain that this procedure is being effectively applied by examining a sample of purchase invoices to see whether they contain the proper signature or initials.

Another test of controls that involves reperformance is the tracing of dollar amounts from one record to another. These types of tests accomplish a dual purpose: (1) the auditor ascertains whether transaction processing procedures are carried out effectively in accordance with the design of the system, and (2) the auditor checks the validity of dollar amounts being processed.

In the case of a cash receipts on account system, the auditor might determine whether three controls are operating in this system. For each of these controls, a

FIGURE 10.2 Tests of Controls for Cash Receipts on Account

Control	Audit Test
Deposit of cash receipts on account	Trace information from the record of cash receipts to the record of deposits
Recording of cash receipts on account	Trace information from the record of deposits to the record of cash receipts
Postings of cash receipts on account	Trace postings from the cash receipts record to the customer ledger accounts

sample of information would be traced from one cash receipts record to another. Figure 10.2 is an example of three such tests.

TIMING OF TESTS OF CONTROLS

To increase audit efficiency, some tests of controls are performed during the interim period (e.g., from January to October 19X1 for financial statements covering the calendar year ending December 31, 19X1). When this is done, the auditor must decide what additional evidence, if any, needs to be obtained during the remaining period (e.g., from November 19X1 to December 31, 19X1), and should consider the following factors.

1. The significance of the financial statement assertion being tested.

▶ **EXAMPLE**

The existence of cash (many transactions) and inventory (often a large dollar total) and the valuation of net accounts receivable (highly subjective estimates) might require substantial additional evidence during the remaining period.

2. The specific internal control policies and procedures tested during the interim period.

▶ **EXAMPLE**

Because of the judgment involved, the testing of procedures relating to inventory obsolescence might require more additional evidence during the remaining period than, say, the testing of procedures for safeguarding securities.

3. The degree to which the policies and procedures were tested and the test results.

▶ **EXAMPLE**

If considerable time was spent testing the procedures for approving credit sales, less audit work may be necessary in the remaining period if the test results were positive.

4. The length of the remaining period.

▶ **EXAMPLE**

If the tests of controls are performed early in the audit period, more evidence may have to be obtained than if the tests are performed near the end of the audit period.

THE USE OF SAMPLING TO PERFORM TESTS OF CONTROLS[1]

Sampling cannot be used for tests of controls that involve inquiries, observations, and walkthroughs. Nor would sampling be applicable to a test that requires inspection of 100 percent of the documents.

Sampling is more likely to be used for tests of controls that involve reperformance of the application of the policy or procedure. The examples used here are the three tests of controls for cash receipts on account illustrated on page 285. For each test there is a population of cash receipts transactions from which the auditor selects a sample.

To properly implement sampling techniques for tests of controls, the auditor should give proper consideration to the following factors:

1. Identification—Tests of controls on which sampling can be used.
2. Definition—The definition of a deviation from an internal control procedure and conditions that indicate whether a deviation has or has not occurred.
3. Definition—How a population is defined.
4. Selection—Different methods available to select the sample.
5. Determination—Factors to consider in determining the sample size.
6. Performance—How to perform the sampling plan.
7. Evaluation—How to evaluate the sampling results.

We will cover these considerations in the seven following subsections.

Identification—Tests of Controls on Which Sampling Can Be Used

For sampling to be appropriate, the policies or procedures being tested should leave a trail of documentary evidence. Here are some examples of tests of controls that can be applied using sampling techniques.

---

[1] Refer to Appendices A and B at the end of this chapter for specific examples of how to perform nonstatistical and statistical tests of controls.

Some Tests of Controls for Inventory Purchases Procedures

Purpose of the Test	*Test*
1. To determine whether competitive bidding procedures are followed (valuation).	1. Compare invoice price with bids submitted by vendors.
2. To ascertain whether merchandise billed by the vendor was received by the company (existence).	2. Compare the vendor's invoice with the receiving report.

Some Tests of Controls for Cash Disbursement Procedures

Purpose of the Test	*Test*
1. To ascertain whether the entries were properly recorded (valuation and presentation).	1. Trace entries in the voucher register to the vouchers.
2. To determine whether goods recorded are owned and properly valued (rights and valuation).	2. Compare vouchers with supporting vendor invoices and canceled checks.
3. To ascertain that the probability of duplicate payment to creditors has been minimized (existence).	3. Examine supporting documents for indication of cancellation.

Some Tests of Controls for Payroll Procedures

Purpose of the Test	*Test*
1. To determine whether the time spent on jobs is approved (occurrence).	1. Inspect the job time tickets for proper approval by authorized official.
2. To determine whether the payroll checks agree with the payroll register (obligations and completeness).	2. Compare the payee and amount on the payroll check to the payroll register and examine signature and endorsement.
3. To determine whether proper rates and deductions are used in preparing the payroll (valuation).	3. Trace rates and deductions on the payroll to the authorizations and deduction slips kept in the Personnel Department.

Definition—The Definition of a Deviation from an Internal Control Procedure

To conduct an effective test of controls, the auditor must be able to identify a *deviation*, which is a departure from the prescribed internal control procedure. The deviation must relate to the specific internal control procedure being tested.

► EXAMPLE

A control activity calls for comparing the vendor's invoice with a copy of the receiving report to ascertain whether all purchased merchandise is received. A deviation exists when a receiving report does not contain the same items as the invoice.

Definition—Definition of the Population

For the test of controls to accomplish the audit objective, the *population* to which the test is applied must be appropriately defined.

▶ **EXAMPLE**

An auditor might compare items on the receiving report with items on the vendor invoice. If the audit objective is to determine that all merchandise billed from vendors was received (i.e., accounts payable exist), the population consists of all vendor invoices recorded during the year. If the audit objective is to determine that all merchandise received was billed by the vendors and recorded in accounts payable (i.e., accounts payable are complete), the population consists of all receiving reports prepared during the year.

Ideally, tests of controls should be applied to a sample of all applicable transactions in the audit period. For example, if the audit is for the calendar year 19X5, the sample should be drawn from items (receiving reports, time tickets, etc.) for the entire period of January through December.

Tests may be applied to transactions in periods of less than a year. To make more efficient use of time, auditors often obtain an understanding of internal control at an interim date. In such cases, it is not always necessary to conduct tests of controls covering the remainder of the year. If the interim date were late in the year (November for a December 31 year-end) and if the test results in the interim period were satisfactory, additional tests might not be necessary if the auditor is able to satisfy himself or herself that no changes in internal control have occurred. This satisfaction could be obtained by means of other auditing procedures such as inquiry.

Sample results in the interim period may lead the auditor to conclude that the operation of internal control procedures is unsatisfactory for the year. This conclusion would be based on the large number of deviations found in the interim period. In such a case, tests for the interim period are sufficient.

The auditor must be careful to define the unit that will be sampled within the population. For example, a *sampling unit* may be

1. A document, such as an invoice.
2. An entry, such as a posting to a subsidiary ledger.
3. A line within a document, such as lines within an invoice.

In deciding whether to sample a document or a line, the auditor considers the objective of the test.

▶ **EXAMPLE**

Assume that the purpose of comparing vendor invoices and receiving reports is to ascertain whether there is a receiving report to match each invoice. A deviation is a missing receiving report; therefore, the sampling unit is the invoice. If the purpose of this test is to ascertain whether all items on the invoice are matched by items on a receiving report, the sampling unit could be the line or the invoice.

The size of the population differs if the auditor defines lines rather than invoices as sampling units. For instance, 2,000 invoices processed during the year constitute a population of 2,000. If there is an average of 10 lines per invoice, the population of invoice lines is 20,000.

Selection—Methods of Selecting the Sample

Auditors are not required to use one particular method to select a sample. However, items should be selected in such a way that the sample is representative of the population. Otherwise, auditors cannot draw definitive conclusions about the effectiveness of internal control procedures. For a sample to be representative of the population, every item in the population must have an opportunity to be selected.

Two of the less rigorous sampling methods are (1) a block sample and (2) a haphazard sample. A *block sample* is the selection of a group of consecutive transactions, such as for a month of the year. Another type of block sample is the selection of transactions for groups of days, such as March 5, June 19, and so on. Block sampling is convenient but may not be representative of the population and so is generally not recommended.

Haphazard sampling is a method of selection that has no particular pattern or conscious bias toward selecting or omitting any particular items. For example, in examining a sample of checks for supporting documentation, no attempt is made to select or omit checks with an unusual volume of supporting documents. This method is convenient and could produce a sample that is representative of the population, but there is no scientific basis for judging sample results, and, without proper care the sample may contain bias.

Sampling Methodology—Random Numbers

Unrestricted random selection means that every element in the population has an equal chance of being selected. In a population of 200 lines, each one has a 1 in 200 chance of appearing in the sample. If the method is to be statistically defensible, a tested table of random numbers or computer-generated random numbers should be used. Such a table is illustrated in Table 10B.4 in Appendix B of this chapter.

What if an element in the population is selected more than once? If the test calls for *sampling with replacement* (replacing the item before continuing with the sample), the number should be reused. If *sampling without replacement* is used (not replacing the item before continuing with the sample), the number should be ignored. Audit samples are normally selected without replacement. The sample size is lower, and auditors have no need to examine a document or item more than once.

Sampling Methodology—Systematic Sampling

Unrestricted random sampling is not the only method available for selecting items to be examined. *Systematic sampling* can be used and every *n*th element selected. If such a technique is used, however, the auditor should ascertain that the population from which the sample is taken does not contain unusual items that appear at fixed intervals.

▶ **EXAMPLE**

During certain days of each week invoices are processed by a part-time employee who makes an unusually large number of mistakes. Approximately every tenth invoice contains a clerical deviation. If the auditors selected every tenth invoice as their sampling interval, the sampling results would not provide a good estimate of the deviations in the population.

Systematic sampling is easy to use and might provide results comparable to those gained from unrestricted random sampling. But the auditor should avoid using the method with populations that might contain nonrandom deviations. To introduce randomness into systematic sampling, a random starting point should be used—for example, by a blind stab into a random number table.

Determination—Determining the Sample Size

Whether statistical or nonstatistical sampling is used, auditors should consider a number of factors in deciding on the size of the sample:

1. The risk of assessing control risk too low.
2. The planned tolerable rate.
3. The expected deviation rate in the population.

Risk of Assessing Control Risk Too Low

The *risk of assessing control risk too low* is the risk that the sample results support the planned degree of reliance on the control when the true population deviation rate is large enough not to justify such reliance. Because the risk of assessing control risk too low relates to the effectiveness of the audit, it is kept at a relatively low level by auditors. If statistical sampling is used, the auditor will quantify the risk level. Risk levels of 1, 5, and 10 percent are examples. If nonstatistical sampling is used, the risk levels can be described as very low or low.

Whether statistical or nonstatistical sampling is used, there is an inverse relationship between the risk of assessing control risk too low and the sample size. Auditors determine the appropriate risk level by considering the reliance to be placed on a control. Reliance, as the term is used in planning a sample, does not refer to the strength of a control; reliance refers to the importance of a control in determining the extent to which substantive tests will be restricted. If a control on which auditors place heavy reliance is functioning properly, substantial restriction is placed on substantive tests of balances. On tests of controls of this type, auditors will set the risk of assessing control risk too low at a very low level. On the other hand, if a control on which auditors place little reliance is functioning properly, only a small restriction is placed on substantive tests of balances. On tests of controls of this type, auditors will set the risk of assessing control risk too low at a higher level.

It may be difficult to decide whether risk levels should be very low or low (or 1, 5, or 10 percent). For this reason, the same risk level is sometimes used for all tests of controls. This means that the sample size varies with the factors discussed in the next two subsections.

Planned Tolerable Rate

The *planned tolerable rate* is the maximum rate of deviations auditors will accept without altering the assessment of control risk and the planned substantive testing of an assertion. In setting the planned tolerable rate, the auditor considers how materially the financial statements would be affected if the control does not function properly. The auditor will set a relatively low planned tolerable rate on controls more likely to prevent or detect material errors in the financial statements; similarly, the auditor will set a relatively high planned tolerable rate on controls less likely to prevent or detect material errors in the financial statements.

▶ **EXAMPLE**

Compare two controls. One control is designed to prevent or detect errors in pricing sales invoices. (The test is comparing invoice prices to the master price list.) The other control is designed to prevent or detect the recording of a sale when the merchandise has not been shipped. (The test is comparing sales invoices to shipping documents.)

The pricing control might be less likely to prevent material errors in the financial statements than the sales recording control because repetitive errors in invoice pricing may produce lower dollar errors than repetitive errors in recording sales, and pricing errors may be detected before financial statements are prepared. Therefore, the auditor would set a relatively high planned tolerable rate on the pricing test and a relatively low planned tolerable rate on the sales recording test. The difference in rates is the auditor's assessment that errors in the pricing control are less likely to cause material errors in the financial statements.

If statistical sampling is used, planned tolerable rates must be quantified: 2 to 5 percent might be considered low; 6 to 9 percent could be considered moderate; 10 percent is probably considered high. There is an inverse relationship between the planned tolerable rate and the sample size.

Expected Population Deviation Rate

As the estimate of the population deviation rate approaches the planned tolerable rate, there is greater need for precise information from the sample because the allowance for sampling risk is smaller. Therefore, as the expected population deviation rate increases, the sample size should increase if all other factors remain constant.

The estimate of the population deviation rate is a matter of audit judgment. The sample deviation rate in the prior-period audit is one basis for making this judgment; a preliminary sample (e.g., 20 items) is another basis. There is a direct relationship between the estimate of the population deviation rate and the sample size.

Performance—Performing the Sampling Plan

Performance of the sampling plan is essentially an application of the appropriate audit procedure to the elements in the sample (comparison of invoices and receiving reports, examination of time tickets for proper approval, etc.). Here are some guidelines to use in performing the sampling plan.

1. Select extra sampling items to use as "replacements" in case a voided or unusable document is found.
2. Consider terminating the sampling process and drawing conclusions if too many errors are found early in the sampling process. For instance, assume that five checks with missing documentation are found in the first 50 checks examined. The control is not operating effectively even if no missing documentation is found for the remaining 50 checks to be examined. The test can be terminated, and the auditors can conclude that the control cannot be relied on.
3. Unlocated documentations should be considered a deviation.

Evaluation—Evaluating the Sample Results

The first step in evaluating sample results is to calculate the deviation rate in the sample. Five missing authorizations on 100 time tickets constitute a 5 percent deviation rate and is now the best estimate of the actual population deviation rate. From here, a set of decision rules can be followed if nonstatistical sampling is used. The techniques in Appendix B are applicable if statistical sampling is used.

1. If the *sample deviation rate (calculated estimate of the population deviation rate)* is higher than the planned tolerable rate, control risk is not at a sufficiently low level to restrict substantive tests of the financial statement assertions that relate to this control.

2. If the sample deviation rate is less than the planned tolerable rate, we should consider that these sample results could have occurred even if the actual population deviation rate is higher than the planned tolerable rate. Here are some additional guidelines.

   a. If the sample deviation rate is considerably lower than the planned tolerable rate (e.g., 1 percent compared to 8 percent), we can assume that control risk is at a sufficiently low level to restrict substantive tests of financial statement assertions that relate to this control.

   b. If the sample deviation rate is barely lower than the planned tolerable rate (e.g., 7 percent compared to 8 percent), we can generally conclude that control risk is not at a sufficiently low level to restrict substantive tests of financial statement assertions that relate to this control.

   c. If the sample deviation rate is higher than the estimate of the population deviation rate used to plan the sample size, the sample results should generally be interpreted to mean that control risk is not at a sufficiently low level to restrict substantive tests of financial statement assertions that relate to this control. Assume that in planning a sample the auditor estimated the deviation rate in the population to be 3 percent and found that the sample deviation rate is 4 percent (4 missing receiving reports for 100 invoices examined). Control risk is unacceptably high.

We can summarize by stating that if

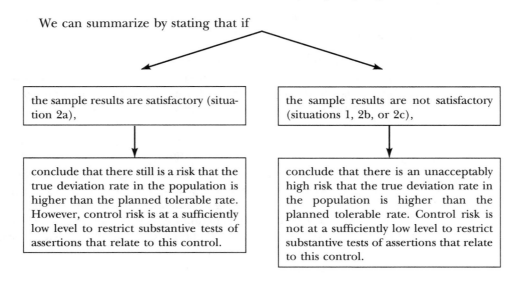

the sample results are satisfactory (situation 2a),	the sample results are not satisfactory (situations 1, 2b, or 2c),
conclude that there still is a risk that the true deviation rate in the population is higher than the planned tolerable rate. However, control risk is at a sufficiently low level to restrict substantive tests of assertions that relate to this control.	conclude that there is an unacceptably high risk that the true deviation rate in the population is higher than the planned tolerable rate. Control risk is not at a sufficiently low level to restrict substantive tests of assertions that relate to this control.

NONSTATISTICAL AND STATISTICAL SAMPLING

Auditors may use nonstatistical sampling techniques in which sample size and the evaluation of sample results are judgmentally determined. Much of the sampling used in auditing practice is nonstatistical because of its convenience and ease of application. If care is taken and appropriate factors are considered in sample selection and sample evaluation, the auditing results should be reliable and defensible. Appendix A in this chapter illustrates an application of nonstatistical sampling.

Auditors may also use statistical sampling techniques in which selection of the sample size and the evaluation of sample results are determined scientifically. Judgment is still used in all other phases of the sampling process, and the objective of the tests of controls is the same as when nonstatistical sampling is used. Appendix B to the chapter illustrates an application of statistical sampling.

THE ASSESSMENT OF CONTROL RISK

After performing tests of controls, the next step is the *assessment of control risk*. If the primarily substantive approach is used, the control risk assessment could be made after obtaining an understanding of internal control, in which case the assessment would be maximum.

If the lower control risk approach is used, the control risk assessment could be made after

1. Obtaining an understanding of internal control and performing tests of controls designed to lower the assessment of control risk below maximum (perhaps to moderate), or
2. Performing additional tests of controls designed to additionally lower the assessment of control risk (perhaps to low).

The Assessed Level of Control Risk

The conclusion the auditor reaches as a result of the assessment of control risk is called the *assessed level of control risk*. It can be expressed qualitatively or quantitatively. The following are examples.

Maximum	or	100%
Slightly below maximum	or	80%
Moderate	or	50%
Low	or	20%

The auditor assesses control risk at *maximum* if he or she uses the primarily substantive approach and does not perform any tests of controls. If the lower control risk approach is used, the auditor will consider an assessed level of control risk of something *less* than maximum. The decision depends on the results of the tests of controls.

1. If the tests show that the design and operation of the internal control policies and procedures for the assertion are effective, the assessed level of control risk will be less than maximum. How much less is a matter of audit judgment.

2. If the tests show that the design and operation of the policies and procedures are not effective, the auditor would assess control risk at *maximum*. Again, the final decision is a matter of audit judgment. Negative test results could be based on the auditor's qualitative considerations and/or the number of deviations discovered during sampling.

Documentation of the Assessed Level of Control Risk

If the auditor assesses control risk at maximum, a memorandum to that effect is sufficient; no documentation of the reason is necessary. However, an assessed level of control risk below maximum requires documentary support because the auditor is placing some reliance on internal control policies and procedures and is restricting related substantive tests. Figure 10.3 is a partial example of the documentation the auditor might provide. Notice that the following format is used:

1. The left column contains misstatements that could occur for some financial statement assertions relating to the inventory balance and purchases transactions.

2. The right column identifies internal control policies and procedures relevant to these assertions that are likely to prevent or detect material misstatements.

FIGURE 10.3   **Form for Assessing Control Risk by Considering Misstatements—Inventory Balance and Purchases Transactions**

Misstatements That Could Occur	Internal Control Policies and Procedures
1. The merchandise requested by the stores department could be different from that ordered and/or received.	1. The purchasing department compares receiving reports with the requisitions.
2. Merchandise could be taken by individuals in the receiving department and no receiving report prepared.	2. The accounts payable department matches the invoice with a copy of the receiving report. The stores department matches the receiving report with the merchandise.
3. The vendor may bill for merchandise not shipped.	3. The receiving department independently counts the merchandise but has no access to the invoice.

Other samples of documentation include flowcharts, with accompanying narratives, and questionnaires illustrated on pages 251–255. Also, to justify assessing control risk at less than maximum, the auditor should document results of tests of controls of the identified policies and procedures.

Assessing Control Risk by Assertion

The assessed control risk (together with the inherent risk) for *certain* assertions embodied within an account balance could be sufficiently low to *eliminate* the need for substantive tests for these assertions. For example, the auditor could conclude that the control environment may be relied on to eliminate substantive tests on the accounts receivable disclosure assertion. On the other hand, the auditor might conclude that certain control procedures relating to extension of credit are ineffective, necessitating a relatively high control risk assessment on the valuation assertion for accounts receivable. This assessment, in turn, will require a lower planned detection risk for the accounts receivable valuation assertion and will prevent the auditor from restricting tests of the allowance for doubtful accounts.

Is it possible for the assessment of control risk on each assertion for an account balance to be so low that it negates the necessity to perform any substantive tests on that account balance? As a practical matter this will not happen. Some substantive tests *should* be performed on every significant account balance or class of transactions, although in some cases substantive tests might be limited to analytical procedures.

EVALUATING THE LEVEL OF PLANNED SUBSTANTIVE TESTS

During the planning phase of the audit the auditor developed an audit program with a tentative level of substantive tests. Substantive tests performed in prior periods might serve as a basis for the planned level. After assessing control risk, the auditor must assure himself or herself that this assessment corresponds with the planned level of substantive tests.

When the level of substantive tests does not correspond with the assessment of control risk for an assertion, the substantive tests should be revised. The auditor is not correcting a mistake; he or she is reacting to additional information acquired when an understanding of internal control was obtained and tests of controls (if applicable) were performed.

The auditor may revise substantive tests in one or all of the following ways.

1. The *nature* of the related substantive tests may be changed from a more effective to a less effective test, or vice versa (evidence obtained from inside the company rather than outside the company, or vice versa).
2. The *timing* of the related substantive tests may be changed (tests performed at an interim date rather than at year end, or vice versa).
3. The *extent* of the related substantive tests may be changed (from a smaller to a larger sample, or vice versa).

Figure 10.4 demonstrates how to revise the planned level of substantive tests so that they correspond to the assessed level of control risk.

FIGURE 10.4   Revision of Planned Level of Substantive Tests

Assertion	Assessed Level of Control Risk	Level of Related Substantive Tests (based on planned levels)	Level of Related Substantive Tests (revised for assessed level of control risk)
Existence of accounts receivable	Maximum	Low level of confirmation requests to customers.	Change the *extent* by using a larger sample.
		Heavy emphasis on analytical procedures.	Change the *nature* by placing more emphasis on confirmations and less emphasis on analytical procedures.
		Considerable tests conducted at interim date.	Change the *timing* by performing the tests at year-end.
Valuation of net accounts receivable	Low	High level of examination of credit files.	Change the *extent* by examining only a few key credit files.
		Extensive examination of subsequent cash receipts.	Change the *nature* by eliminating these procedures and discussing very old accounts with the credit manager.

COMMUNICATING INTERNAL CONTROL RELATED MATTERS NOTED IN THE AUDIT

The major purpose of the auditor's study of internal control is to assess control risk for the purpose of determining the scope of related substantive tests. During the course of this study, however, the auditor will often find deficiencies in the internal control policies and procedures that are of interest to the company's audit committee. Such deficiencies are referred to as *reportable conditions,* which are defined as

> matters coming to the auditor's attention that, in his or her judgment, should be communicated to the audit committee because they represent significant deficiencies in the design or operation of internal control, which could adversely affect the organization's ability to record, process, summarize, and report financial data consistent with the assertions of management in the financial statements.

Examples of Reportable Conditions

Here are a few examples of reportable conditions:

1. Lack of segregation of duties. (The same person deposits cash and records cash receipts, or the same person counts inventory and maintains perpetual inventory records.)
2. Absence of approvals of transactions. (No one approves credit extensions to customers, or no one approves vendor invoices before payment.)
3. No procedures for assessing and applying accounting principles. (There is no policy for differentiating between capital and maintenance expenditures.)
4. Evidence of intentional override of internal control. (The president insists that a check be prepared without the necessary documentation and approvals.)
5. Failure to perform reconciliations. (Several months pass between reconciliation of the accounts receivable subsidiary ledger and the control account, and differences are not corrected.)
6. Falsification of accounting records. (Fictitious sales invoices are prepared and recorded.)

Communicating Reportable Conditions

Generally accepted auditing standards require the auditor to communicate reportable conditions to the audit committee or another appropriate body of the client's organization. The auditor should communicate orally most reportable conditions as soon as they are found. At the end of the audit a written report may be issued. The following illustrates the sections of such a report.

> In planning and performing our audit of the financial statements of the ABC Corporation for the year ended December 31, 19X1, we considered its internal control in order to determine our auditing procedures for the purpose of expressing our opinion on the financial statements and not to provide assurance on the internal control. However, we noted certain matters involving internal control and its operation that we consider to be reportable conditions under standards established by the American Institute of Certified Public Accountants. Reportable conditions involve matters coming to our attention relating to significant deficiencies in the design or operation of internal control that, in our judgment, could adversely affect the organization's ability to record, process, summarize, and report financial data consistent with the assertions of management in the financial statements.
>
> (Include paragraphs to describe the reportable conditions noted.)
>
> This report is intended solely for the information and use of the audit committee, management, and others within the organization.

Auditors may not issue a report stating that no reportable conditions were noted during an audit.

Material Weaknesses

A reportable condition may be so significant that the auditor considers it to be a *material weakness,* defined as a reportable condition in which the design and operation of one or more of the internal control components does not reduce to a relatively low level the risk that misstatements in amounts that would be material in relation to the financial statements being audited may occur and not be detected within a timely period by employees in the normal course of performing their assigned function.

Auditors may separately identify reportable conditions that they consider to be material weaknesses, but they are not required to do so.

ENGAGEMENTS TO REPORT ON INTERNAL CONTROL

Separate engagements to report on a client's internal control (as opposed to reports made in connection with an audit) are not common. However, the AICPA has provided guidelines for such reporting in *Statement on Standards for Attestation Engagements No. 2.* This standard provides that management must make an assertion (i.e., that internal control over financial reporting is adequate). The CPA then expresses an opinion on management's assertion. To express this opinion the CPA must plan the engagement, obtain an understanding of internal control, and test and evaluate the operating effectiveness of the internal control policies and procedures.

The accountant's report should include (1) a title that includes the word *independent,* (2) management's assertion about the effectiveness of internal control, (3) a description of the scope of the engagement, (4) the inherent limitations of internal control, and (5) an opinion on management's assertion as to the effectiveness of internal control.

A report on the effectiveness of internal control must disclose any reportable conditions and separately identify any material weaknesses found during the engagement. Restrictions on the scope of the accountant's engagement may require a modification of the report.

APPENDIX A

Example of a Test of Controls—Nonstatistical Sampling

To illustrate the concepts discussed in this chapter, we will use a test of controls to demonstrate how to (1) determine the sample size for the test, (2) apply a sampling technique to the test, and (3) evaluate the sampling results. In this appendix nonstatistical sampling techniques are used. Appendix B applies statistical sampling to the same test of controls.

Assume that we have already acquired an understanding of internal control for purchase transactions by using techniques illustrated in Chapter 9. We plan to assess control risk at less than maximum and restrict substantive tests of certain financial statement assertions for the purchases and accounts payable accounts that relate to purchases controls. We wish to ascertain, however, that these controls are operating effectively by conducting tests of controls. On the basis of these test results, we will decide whether the assessed level of control risk is sufficiently low to additionally restrict substantive tests of certain financial statement assertions for the purchases and accounts payable accounts.

Refer to page 287, which contains examples of tests of inventory purchases controls. Notice that the second test listed is a comparison of the vendor's invoice with the receiving report, the purpose being to ascertain whether merchandise billed by the vendor was received by the company (relates to the assertions that the accounts payable exist and the purchases occurred).

Assume that the population consists of the vendor invoice file for the year. A sample of invoices is to be compared with the related receiving reports. No deviation exists if we find the following:

1. A receiving report exists for each invoice and is attached or appropriately filed with the invoice.
2. The vendor's name, description of merchandise, and quantity received are the same on the invoice and the receiving report (or a satisfactory explanation is obtained if the information is different).

Otherwise a deviation exists for that invoice.

Determination of Sample Size   Our first step is to determine the number of invoices we will compare with a related receiving report. Assume that the client processed 20,000 invoices during the year.

The size of the sample in a test of controls is based on the following three factors:

1. Planned tolerable rate (the highest deviation rate that the auditor will tolerate)—Missing or improper receiving reports could indicate billed merchandise has not been received (i.e., purchases have not occurred and accounts payable do not exist). Planned tolerable rate is set at 8 percent. If the sample results indicate that the risk is sufficiently low that the deviation rate in the population of invoices is no more than 8 percent, the sample results are acceptable.
2. Risk of assessing control risk too low—When nonstatistical sampling is used, an amount is not assigned to the risk of assessing control risk too low. Because auditors use judgment to determine an appropriate sample size, they could set this risk nonquantitatively at high, moderate, or low. For this example, this risk is set at a moderate level to provide moderate reliance that the deviation rate in the sample is a reliable predictor of the deviation rate in the population.
3. Expected population deviation rate—For our purposes, we will assume a 2 percent rate.

The relationships between sample size and these three factors are shown in the following table.

	Factor		Sample Size	
	Higher	*Lower*	*Larger*	*Smaller*
Planned tolerable rate	X			X
		X	X	
Risk of assessing control risk too low		X	X	
	X			X
Estimate of the population deviation rate	X		X	
		X		X

For purposes of this illustration, we subjectively decide on a sample size of 100 based on a planned tolerable rate of 8 percent, an expected deviation rate of 2 percent, and a moderate risk of assessing control risk too low.

Method of Sample Selection   We will assume the use of systematic sampling with a random start in which every two-hundredth invoice is selected to ascertain whether it is accompanied by a matching and properly completed receiving report.

Evaluation of Sample Results   In the following illustration, we will assume several sampling results and will explain why each of these results would be acceptable or unacceptable using the three decision rules discussed on page 292. An acceptable sampling result means that control risk is at a sufficiently low level to restrict substantive tests of assertions that relate to this purchases control. An unacceptable sampling result means that control risk is not at a sufficiently low level to restrict substantive tests of assertions that relate to this purchases control.

Evaluation of Sampling Results and the Assessment of Control Risk

Planned Tolerable Rate—8 percent

Risk of Assessing Control Risk Too Low—moderate

Estimate of Deviation Rate in the Population—2 percent

	Sample Size	*Number of Deviations*	*Sample Deviation Rate (number of deviations divided by the sample size)*
Test Result 1	100	10	10%
Test Result 2	100	0	0%
Test Result 3	100	6	6%

The first test result shown above is unacceptable because the sample deviation rate is 10 percent and the planned tolerable rate is 8 percent. There is an unacceptably high risk that the true deviation rate in the population of 20,000 invoices is higher than 8 percent.

The second test result is acceptable because the sample deviation rate is zero and is considerably lower than the planned tolerable rate of 8 percent. There is an acceptably low risk that the true deviation rate in the population is higher than 8 percent.

What about the third test result? The sample deviation rate is slightly lower than the planned tolerable rate of 8 percent but is higher than the 2 percent estimate of the population deviation rate. Auditor judgment is always the ultimate criterion, but this test result would probably be considered unacceptable. The sample deviation rate is too close to the planned tolerable rate and is higher than our estimate of the population deviation rate.

Other Considerations in Evaluating the Sample Results

The auditor should look beyond the sample deviation rate and examine the types of deviations found. For example, six missing receiving reports might be more serious than six receiving reports that include all but a few minor items shown on the related invoice. Qualitative factors would be a part of the auditor's judgment as to whether control risk is at a sufficiently low level to restrict substantive tests of assertions affected by this control.

APPENDIX B

Example of a Test of Controls—Statistical Sampling—Estimation Sampling for Attributes

In Appendix A we discussed the use of nonstatistical sampling to perform a test of controls. In this section, we will demonstrate the same type of test using statistical sampling.

The objective of the test of controls is the same regardless of the sampling method selected. Also, systematic or random sampling techniques are just as applicable to nonstatistical as to statistical sampling. The factors that are different, however, are the ways in which (1) the size of the sample is determined and (2) the sampling results are evaluated. We will cover each of these factors in the following subsections.

Determination of Sample Size   Because we are looking for an *attribute* (a properly completed receiving report for each invoice), we will make use of statistical sampling tables that assume the use of the technique called *estimation sampling for attributes*. For given risk levels (risk of assessing control risk too low), we can determine the optimum sample size for given planned tolerable rates and estimates of the expected deviation rate in the population.

An examination of Tables 10B.1 and 10B.2 shows that a wide variety of sample sizes can be selected by (1) referring to the appropriate risk level table (Table 10B.1 for 5 percent and Table 10B.2 for 10 percent), (2) selecting the planned tolerable rate, and (3) using the estimate of the deviation rate in the population.

Each table shows larger sample sizes as the planned tolerable rates become smaller with the same estimate of the population deviation rate. This is a quantitative expression of the inverse relationship between the planned tolerable rate and the sample size. If the auditor wants a "tighter tolerance" or "more precise estimate," he or she must take a larger sample.

TABLE 10B.1
Determination of Sample Size—One-Sided Risk of Assessing Control Risk Too Low (5 percent)

Sample size	\begin{tabular}{c} *Tolerable rates for various deviation rates* \end{tabular}																				
	0.5	.5	1.0	2.0	3.0	4.0	5.0	6.0	7.0	8.0	9.0	10.0	12.0	14.0	16.0	18.0	20.0	25.0	30.0	40.0	50.0
50	5.8			9.1		12.1		14.8		17.4		19.9	22.3	25.1	27.0	29.6	31.6		42.4	52.6	62.4
100	3.0		4.7	6.2	7.6	8.9	10.2	11.5	13.0	14.0	15.4	16.4	18.7	21.2	23.3	25.6	27.7	33.1	38.4	48.7	56.8
150	2.0		5.1		7.7		10.2		12.6		15.0	17.3	19.6	21.7	24.0	26.1		36.7	47.0	56.6
200	1.5	2.4	3.1	4.5	5.8	7.1	8.3	9.5	10.8	11.9	13.1	14.2	16.4	18.7	20.9	23.1	25.2	30.5	35.7	45.7	55.6
250	1.2		4.2		6.7		9.1		11.4		13.7	15.9	18.1	20.3	22.4	24.6		34.8	44.8	54.7
300	1.0		2.6	3.9	5.2	6.4	7.6	8.8	10.0	11.1	12.2	13.3	15.5	17.7	19.8	22.0	24.1	29.1	34.1	44.1	54.1
350	.9		3.7		6.2		8.5		10.8		13.0	15.2	17.4	19.5	21.7	23.6		33.6	43.6	53.6
400	.7	1.6	2.3	3.6	4.8	6.0	7.2	8.3	9.5	10.6	11.7	12.8	15.0	17.2	19.2	21.2	23.2	28.2	33.2	43.2	53.2
450	.7		3.5		5.9		8.2		10.4		12.6	14.8	16.8	18.9	20.9	22.9		32.9	42.9	52.9
500	.6		2.1	3.4	4.6	5.8	6.9	8.0	9.2	10.3	11.4	12.5	14.6	16.7	18.6	20.7	22.6	27.6	32.6	42.6	52.6
550	.5		3.3		5.7		7.9		10.1		12.3	14.4	16.4	18.4	20.4	22.4		32.4	42.4	52.4
600	.5	1.3	2.0	3.2	4.4	5.6	6.7	7.8	9.0	10.0	11.2	12.2	14.2	16.2	18.2	20.2	22.2	27.2	32.2	42.2	52.2
650	.5		3.2		5.5		7.7		10.0		12.1	14.1	16.1	18.1	20.1	22.1		32.1	42.1	52.1
700	.4		1.9	3.1	4.3	5.4	6.6	7.7	8.8	9.9	10.8	11.9	13.9	15.9	17.9	19.9	21.9	26.9	31.9	41.9	51.9
750	.4		3.1		5.4		7.6		9.8		11.8	13.8	15.8	17.8	19.8	21.8		31.8	41.8	51.8
800	.4	1.1	1.8	3.0	4.2	5.3	6.4	7.5	8.7	9.7	10.7	11.7	13.7	15.7	17.7	19.7	21.7	26.7	31.7	41.7	51.7
850	.4		3.0		5.3		7.5		9.6		11.6	13.6	15.6	17.6	19.6	21.6		31.6	41.6	51.6
900	.3		1.7	3.0	4.1	5.2	6.3	7.5	8.5	9.5	10.5	11.5	13.5	15.5	17.5	19.5	21.5	26.5	31.5	41.5	51.5
950	.3		2.9		5.2		7.4		9.4		11.4	13.4	15.5	17.4	19.5	21.4		31.5	41.5	51.5
1000	.3	1.0	1.7	2.9	4.0	5.2	6.3	7.4	8.4	9.4	10.4	11.4	13.4	15.4	17.4	19.4	21.4	26.4	31.4	41.4	51.4
1500	.2		1.5	2.7	3.8	4.9	5.9	6.9	7.9	8.9	9.9	10.9	12.9	14.9	16.9	18.9	20.9	25.9	30.9	40.9	50.9
2000	.1	.8	1.4	2.6	3.7	4.7	5.7	6.7	7.7	8.7	9.7	10.7	12.7	14.7	16.7	18.7	20.7	25.7	30.7	40.7	50.7
2500	.1		1.4	2.6	3.6	4.6	5.6	6.6	7.6	8.6	9.6	10.6	12.6	14.6	16.6	18.6	20.6	25.6	30.6	40.6	50.6
3000	.1	.8	1.4	2.5	3.5	4.5	5.5	6.5	7.5	8.5	9.5	10.5	12.5	14.5	16.5	18.5	20.5	25.5	30.5	40.5	50.5
4000	.1	.7	1.3	2.4	3.4	4.4	5.4	6.4	7.4	8.4	9.4	10.4	12.4	14.4	16.4	18.4	20.4	25.4	30.4	40.4	50.4
5000	.1	.7	1.3	2.3	3.3	4.3	5.3	6.3	7.3	8.3	9.3	10.3	12.3	14.3	16.3	18.3	20.3	25.3	30.3	40.3	50.3

Note: The numbers in the first column represent sample sizes (50, 100, etc.). The numbers in the first row represent deviation rates (0.0, .5, 1.0, etc.). The rest of the numbers represent tolerable rates.

If the auditor uses a tolerable rate that is not shown in the table, two alternatives are available.

1. The auditor can find the next lowest listed planned tolerable rate below the one he or she wishes to use. The sample size for that listed planned tolerable rate is the one used for the test. Look at Table 10B.2 and note the planned tolerable rates of 7.6 and 5.2 associated with the expected population deviation rate of 2.0. If the auditor's planned tolerable rate is 6.0, a sample size of 100 can be selected because 5.2 is the next lowest listed planned tolerable rate below 6.0.

2. The auditor can interpolate. Using the same example as above, he or she would make the following calculation where *n* equals sample size.

TABLE 10B.2
Determination of Sample Size—One-Sided Risk of Assessing Control Risk Too Low (10 percent)

Sample size	\multicolumn{21}{c}{*Tolerable rates for various deviation rates*}

Sample size	0.5	.5	1.0	2.0	3.0	4.0	5.0	6.0	7.0	8.0	9.0	10.0	12.0	14.0	16.0	18.0	20.0	25.0	30.0	40.0	50.0
50	4.5			7.6		10.3		12.9		15.4		17.8	20.1	22.7	24.7	27.2	29.1		39.8	50.0	59.9
100	2.3		3.3	5.2	6.6	7.8	9.1	10.3	11.7	12.7	14.0	15.0	17.3	19.6	21.7	24.0	26.1	31.4	36.6	46.9	56.8
150	1.5			4.4		6.9		9.3		11.6		13.9	16.1	18.4	20.5	22.7	24.8		35.2	45.5	55.4
200	1.1	1.9	2.6	4.0	5.2	6.4	7.6	8.8	10.0	11.0	12.2	13.3	15.5	17.7	19.8	22.0	24.0	29.3	34.5	44.4	54.4
250	.9			3.7		6.1		8.4		10.7		12.9	15.1	17.2	19.3	21.5	23.6		33.7	43.7	53.7
300	.8		2.2	3.5	4.7	5.9	7.0	8.2	9.3	10.4	11.5	12.6	14.7	16.9	19.0	21.1	23.2	28.2	33.2	43.2	53.2
350	.7			3.3		5.7		8.0		10.2		12.3	14.5	16.7	18.8	20.9	22.8		32.8	42.8	52.8
400	.6	1.3	2.0	3.2	4.4	5.6	6.7	7.8	8.9	10.0	11.1	12.2	14.3	16.5	18.5	20.5	22.5	27.5	32.5	42.5	52.5
450	.5			3.1		5.5		7.7		9.9		12.0	14.2	16.3	18.3	20.3	22.3		32.3	42.3	52.2
500	.5		1.8	3.1	4.2	5.4	6.5	7.6	8.7	9.8	10.9	11.9	14.1	16.1	18.1	20.1	22.1	27.1	32.1	42.1	52.0
550	.4			3.0		5.3		7.5		9.7		11.8	13.9	15.9	17.9	19.9	21.9		31.9	41.9	51.9
600	.4	1.1	1.7	2.9	4.1	5.2	6.3	7.4	8.5	9.6	10.7	11.7	13.7	15.7	17.7	19.7	21.7	26.7	31.7	41.7	51.7
650	.4			2.9		5.2		7.4		9.5		11.6	13.6	15.6	17.6	19.6	21.6		31.6	41.6	51.6
700	.3		1.7	2.9	4.0	5.1	6.2	7.3	8.4	9.5	10.5	11.5	13.5	15.5	17.5	19.5	21.5	26.5	31.5	41.5	51.5
750	.3			2.8		5.1		7.3		9.4		11.4	13.4	15.4	17.4	19.4	21.4		31.4	41.4	51.4
800	.3	1.0	1.6	2.8	3.9	5.0	6.1	7.2	8.3	9.3	10.3	11.3	13.3	15.3	17.3	19.3	21.3	26.3	31.3	41.3	51.3
850	.3			2.8		5.0		7.2		9.2		11.2	13.2	15.3	17.3	19.3	21.3		31.3	41.3	51.3
900	.3		1.6	2.7	3.9	5.0	6.0	7.1	8.2	9.2	10.2	11.2	13.2	15.2	17.2	19.2	21.2	26.2	31.2	41.2	51.2
950	.2			2.7		4.9		7.1		9.1		11.1	13.1	15.1	17.1	19.1	21.1		31.1	41.1	51.1
1000	.2	.9	1.5	2.7	3.8	4.9	6.0	7.1	8.1	9.1	10.1	11.1	13.1	15.1	17.1	19.1	21.1	26.1	31.1	41.1	51.1
1500	.2		1.4	2.5	3.6	4.7	5.7	6.7	7.7	8.7	9.7	10.7	12.7	14.7	16.7	18.7	20.7	25.7	30.7	40.7	50.7
2000	.1	.8	1.3	2.5	3.5	4.5	5.5	6.5	7.5	8.5	9.5	10.5	12.5	14.5	16.5	18.5	20.5	25.5	30.5	40.6	50.6
2500	.1		1.3	2.4	3.4	4.4	5.4	6.4	7.4	8.4	9.4	10.4	12.4	14.4	16.4	18.4	20.4	25.4	30.4	40.4	50.4
3000	.1	.7	1.3	2.4	3.4	4.4	5.4	6.4	7.4	8.4	9.4	10.4	12.4	14.4	16.4	18.4	20.4	25.4	30.4	40.4	50.4
4000	.1	.7	1.2	2.3	3.3	4.3	5.3	6.3	7.3	8.3	9.3	10.3	12.3	14.3	16.3	18.3	20.3	25.3	30.3	40.3	50.3
5000	.0	.7	1.2	2.3	3.2	4.2	5.2	6.2	7.2	8.2	9.2	10.2	12.2	14.2	16.2	18.2	20.2	25.2	30.2	40.2	50.2

Copyright © (1974) by the American Institute of Certified Public Accountants, Inc., reprinted with permission. (Adapted for changes in terms.)

Note: The numbers in the first column represent sample sizes (50, 100, etc.). The numbers in the first row represent deviation rates (0.0, .5, 1.0, etc.). The rest of the numbers represent tolerable rates.

$$n = 50 + \frac{7.6 - 6.0}{7.6 - 5.2} \times 50$$

$$n = 84$$

Method of Sample Selection   Either systematic or unrestricted random number sampling can be used for tests of controls. Although unrestricted random number sampling may be theoretically preferable, systematic sampling is acceptable as long as there is a random start and the auditor believes that no deviation patterns exist in the population (e.g., every tenth invoice has a missing or improperly completed receiving report).

Evaluation of Sample Results   Statistical sampling tables are available to provide auditors with a quantitative evaluation of the sample results. Table 10B.3 is an

TABLE 10B.3
Evaluation of Sample Results

	Number of deviations	Risk level 10%	Risk level 5%	Risk level 1%		Number of deviations	Risk level 10%	Risk level 5%	Risk level 1%
Sample	0	8.80	11.29	16.82	Sample	0	1.83	2.37	3.62
Size	1	14.69	17.61	23.75	Size	1	3.08	3.74	5.19
25	2	19.91	23.10	29.59	125	2	4.20	4.95	6.55
	3	24.80	28.17	34.88		3	5.27	6.09	7.81
	4	29.47	32.96	39.79					
						4	6.29	7.17	9.00
Sample	0	4.50	5.82	8.80		5	7.29	8.23	10.15
Size	1	7.56	9.14	12.55		6	8.27	9.25	11.26
50	2	10.30	12.06	15.77		7	9.24	10.26	12.34
	3	12.88	14.78	18.72					
						8	10.19	11.25	13.40
	4	15.35	17.38	21.50		9	11.13	12.23	14.14
	5	17.76	19.88	24.15					
	6	20.11	22.32	26.71		10	12.06	13.19	15.47
	8	24.69	27.02	31.61		11	12.98	14.15	16.48
Sample	0	3.02	3.92	5.96		12	13.89	15.09	17.47
Size	1	5.09	6.17	8.53		13	14.80	16.03	18.45
75	2	6.94	8.16	10.74		19	20.14	21.50	24.16
	3	8.69	10.01	12.78					
					Sample	0	1.52	1.98	3.02
	4	10.38	11.79	14.70	Size	1	2.57	3.12	4.34
	5	12.02	13.51	16.55	150	2	3.51	4.14	5.49
	6	13.62	15.18	18.34		3	4.40	5.09	6.54
	7	15.20	16.82	20.08					
						4	5.26	6.00	7.54
	8	16.75	18.42	21.77		5	6.10	6.88	8.50
	12	22.78	24.63	28.25		6	6.92	7.74	9.44
						7	7.72	8.59	10.35
Sample	0	2.28	2.95	4.50					
Size	1	3.83	4.66	6.45		8	8.52	9.42	11.24
100	2	5.23	6.16	8.14		9	9.31	10.24	12.12
	3	6.56	7.56	9.70		10	10.09	11.05	12.98
						11	10.86	11.85	13.83
	4	7.83	8.92	11.17					
	5	9.08	10.23	12.58		12	11.62	12.64	14.67
	6	10.29	11.50	13.95		13	12.39	13.43	15.50
	7	11.49	12.75	15.29		14	13.14	14.21	16.32
						15	13.89	14.98	17.13
	8	12.67	13.97	16.59					
	9	13.83	15.18	17.87		16	14.64	15.75	17.94
	10	14.99	16.37	19.13		23	19.79	21.02	23.42
	11	16.13	17.55	20.37					
	15	20.61	22.15	25.18					

TABLE 10B.3 *Continued*

	Number of deviations	Risk level				Number of deviations	Risk level		
		10%	*5%*	*1%*			*10%*	*5%*	*1%*
Sample	0	1.31	1.70	2.60	Sample	0	1.14	1.49	2.28
Size	1	2.20	2.68	3.73	Size	1	1.93	2.35	3.27
175	2	3.01	3.55	4.72	200	2	2.64	3.11	4.14
	3	3.78	4.37	5.63		3	3.31	3.83	4.93
	4	4.52	5.15	6.49		4	3.96	4.52	5.69
	5	5.24	5.91	7.32		5	4.59	5.18	6.42
	6	5.94	6.65	8.12		6	5.21	5.83	7.13
	7	6.63	7.38	8.91		7	5.82	6.47	7.82
	8	7.32	8.10	9.68		8	6.42	7.10	8.50
	9	8.00	8.80	10.43		9	7.01	7.72	9.16
	10	8.67	9.50	11.18		10	7.60	8.33	9.82
	11	9.33	10.19	11.91		11	8.18	8.94	10.46
	12	9.99	10.87	12.64		12	8.76	9.54	11.10
	13	10.65	11.55	13.36		13	9.34	10.14	11.73
	14	11.30	12.22	14.07		14	9.91	10.73	12.36
	15	11.95	12.89	14.77		15	10.48	11.31	12.98
	16	12.59	13.55	15.47		16	11.04	11.90	13.59
	17	13.23	14.21	16.16		17	11.61	12.48	14.20
	18	13.87	14.87	16.85		18	12.17	13.05	14.81
	27	19.51	20.64	22.84		19	12.73	13.63	15.41
						20	13.38	14.20	16.01
						21	13.84	14.77	16.60
						30	18.75	19.79	21.82

adaptation of a statistical sampling table published by the American Institute of Certified Public Accountants.

We must quantify the risk of assessing control risk too low. We will assume a 5 percent risk of assessing control risk too low for our example. As noted in Table 10B.3, the numbers below the risk level percentages represent the achieved tolerable rates at given risk levels if a certain number of deviations is found when a certain sample size is used. The *planned tolerable rate* (8 percent in our example) is the planned highest deviation rate in the population that the auditor can accept and still conclude that the control is operating as prescribed. The *achieved tolerable rate* is based on the sample results and is the highest probable deviation rate in the population at a designated risk of assessing control risk too low.

Look at Table 10B.3. With a sample size of 100, a risk of assessing control risk too low of 5 percent, and one deviation, the achieved tolerable rate is 4.66 percent. If the auditor takes a sample of 100 and finds one improperly completed receiving report, there is a 5 percent risk that the true deviation rate in the population exceeds 4.66 percent.

TABLE 10B.4
Table of Random Numbers

							Column							
Line	*(1)*	*(2)*	*(3)*	*(4)*	*(5)*	*(6)*	*(7)*	*(8)*	*(9)*	*(10)*	*(11)*	*(12)*	*(13)*	*(14)*
1	10480	15011	01536	02011	81647	91646	69179	14194	62590	36207	20969	99570	91291	90700
2	22368	46573	25595	85393	30995	89198	27982	53402	93965	34095	52666	19174	39615	99505
3	24130	48360	22527	97265	76393	64809	15179	24830	49340	32081	30680	19655	63348	58629
4	42167	93093	06243	61680	07856	16376	39440	53537	71341	57004	00849	74917	97758	16379
5	37570	39975	81837	16656	06121	91872	60468	81305	49684	60672	14110	06927	01263	54613
6	77921	06907	11008	42751	27756	53498	18602	70659	90655	15053	21916	81825	44394	42880
7	99562	72905	56420	69994	98872	31016	71194	18738	44013	48840	63213	21069	10634	12952
8	96301	91977	05463	07972	18876	20922	94595	56869	69014	60045	18425	84903	42508	32307
9	89579	14342	63661	10281	17453	18103	57740	84378	25331	12566	58678	44947	05585	56941
10	85475	36857	53342	53988	53060	59533	38867	62300	08158	17983	16439	11458	18593	64952
11	28918	69578	88231	33276	70997	79936	56865	05859	90106	31595	01547	85590	91610	78188
12	63553	40961	48235	03427	49626	69445	18663	72695	52180	20847	12234	90511	33703	90322
13	09429	93969	52636	92737	88974	33488	36320	17617	30015	08272	84115	27156	30613	74952
14	10365	62219	87529	85689	48237	52267	67689	93394	01511	26358	85104	20285	29975	89868
15	07119	97336	71048	08178	77233	13916	47564	81056	97735	85977	29372	74461	28551	90707
16	51085	12765	51821	51259	77452	16308	60756	92144	49442	53900	70960	63990	75601	40719
17	02368	21382	52404	60268	89368	19885	55322	44819	01188	63255	64835	44919	05944	55157
18	01011	54092	33362	94904	31273	04146	18594	29852	71585	85030	51132	01915	92747	64951
19	52162	53916	46369	58586	23216	14513	83149	98736	23495	64350	94738	17752	35156	35739
20	07056	97628	33787	09998	42698	06691	76988	13602	51851	46104	88916	19509	25625	58104
21	48663	91245	85828	14346	09172	30168	90229	04734	59193	22178	30421	61666	99904	32812
22	54164	58492	22421	74103	47070	25306	76468	26384	58151	06646	21524	15227	06909	44592
23	32639	32363	05597	24200	13363	38005	94342	28728	35806	06912	17012	64161	18296	22851
24	29334	27001	87637	87308	58731	00256	45834	15398	46557	41135	10367	07684	36188	18510
25	02488	33062	28834	07351	19731	92420	60952	61280	50001	67658	32586	86679	50720	94953
26	81525	72295	04839	96423	24878	82651	66566	14778	76797	14780	13300	87074	79666	95725
27	29676	20591	68086	26432	46901	20849	89768	81536	86645	12659	92259	57102	80428	25280
28	00742	57392	39064	66432	84673	44027	32832	61362	98947	96067	64760	64584	96096	98253
29	05366	04213	25669	26422	44407	44048	37937	63904	45766	66134	75470	66520	34693	90449
30	91921	26418	64117	94305	26766	25940	39972	22209	71500	64568	91402	42416	07844	69618
31	00582	04711	87917	77341	42206	35126	74087	99547	81817	42607	43808	76655	62028	76630
32	00725	69884	62797	56170	86324	88072	76222	36086	84637	93161	76038	65855	77919	88006
33	69011	65795	95876	55293	18988	27354	26575	08625	40801	59920	29841	80150	12777	48501
34	25976	57948	29888	80604	67917	48708	18912	82271	65424	69774	33611	54262	85963	03547
35	09763	83473	73577	12908	30883	18317	28290	35797	05998	41688	34952	37888	38917	80050
36	91567	42595	29758	30134	04024	86385	29880	99730	55536	84855	29080	09250	79656	73211
37	17955	56349	90999	49127	20044	59931	06115	20542	18059	02008	73708	83517	36103	42791
38	46503	18584	18845	49618	02304	51038	20655	58727	28168	15475	56942	53389	20562	87338
39	92157	89634	94824	78171	84610	82834	09922	25417	44137	48413	25555	21246	35509	20468
40	14577	62765	35605	81263	39667	47358	56873	56307	61607	49518	89656	20103	77490	18062
41	98427	07523	33362	64270	01638	92477	66969	98420	04880	45585	46565	04102	46880	45709
42	34914	63976	88720	82765	34476	17032	87589	40836	32427	70002	70663	88863	77775	69348
43	70060	28277	39475	46473	23219	53416	94970	25832	69975	94884	19661	72828	00102	66794
44	53976	54914	06990	67245	68350	82948	11398	42878	80287	88267	47363	46634	06541	97809
45	76072	29515	40980	07391	58745	25774	22987	80059	39911	96189	41151	14222	60697	59583
46	90725	52210	83974	29992	65831	38857	50490	83765	55657	14361	31720	57375	56228	41546
47	64364	67412	33339	31926	14883	24413	59744	92351	97473	90297	38931	04110	23726	51900
48	08962	00358	31662	25388	61642	34072	81249	35648	56891	69352	48373	45578	78547	81788
49	95012	68379	93526	70765	10592	04542	74663	54328	02349	17247	28865	14777	62730	92277
50	15664	10493	20492	38391	91132	21999	59516	81652	27195	48223	46751	22923	32261	85653

Source: Interstate Commerce Commission, *Table of 105,000 Random Decimal Digits* Washington, D.C.: Bureau of Transport, Economics and Statistics, 1949).

Therefore, in using Table 10B.3 to evaluate the sampling results quantitatively, we use these decision guides.

1. If the achieved tolerable rate is equal to or lower than the planned tolerable rate, the sample results are acceptable and control risk is sufficiently low to restrict the substantive tests of assertions that relate to the purchases control.
2. If the achieved tolerable rate is higher than the planned tolerable rate, the sample results are not acceptable and control risk is not sufficiently low to restrict the substantive tests of assertions that relate to the purchases control.

Table 10B.3 illustrates what our sampling results will be for various deviation rates. With a sample size of 100, we must find three deviations or less for our sampling results to be acceptable.

A Table of Random Numbers is provided in Table 10B.4.

Chapter 10 ▶ GLOSSARY OF TERMS

Achieved tolerable rate The tolerable rate that is based on the sample results.

Assessed level of control risk The conclusion reached by the auditor as a result of assessing control risk.

Assessment of control risk The process of evaluating the effectiveness of an entity's internal control policies and procedures in preventing or detecting material misstatements in assertions regarding accounts in the financial statements.

Attribute A condition in the population that does or does not exist (such as a matching receiving report for an invoice or dual signatures on a payroll check).

Block sample The selection of a group of consecutive transactions.

Deviation A departure from a prescribed internal control policy or procedure.

Estimation sampling for attributes Sampling to ascertain whether an attribute does or does not exist for the purpose of estimating the rate of attribute deviations in the population.

Haphazard sampling A method of sample selection that has no particular pattern or conscious bias toward selecting or omitting any particular item.

Planned tolerable rate The maximum rate of deviations an auditor will accept without altering the assessment of control risk.

Population The complete group of items with similar characteristics of interest from which the sample is drawn.

Reportable conditions Matters coming to the auditor's attention that, in his or her judgment, should be communicated to the audit committee because they represent significant deficiencies in the design or operation of internal control, which could adversely affect the organization's ability to record, process, summarize, and report financial data consistent with the assertions of management in the financial statements.

Risk of assessing control risk too low The risk that the sample results support the planned degree of reliance on the control when the true deviation rate in the population is so large as not to justify such reliance.

Sampling unit or element The characteristic being sampled, such as a document, an entry, or a document line.

Sampling with replacement A sampling selection method where, as each sampling unit is selected, it is replaced in the population so that it is subject to being selected again.

Sampling without replacement A sample selection method where a selected sampling unit is not replaced in the population and therefore is not subject to being selected again.

Systematic sampling A sample selection method where sampling units are selected at fixed intervals in a population (e.g., selecting every fifth item in a population after a random start).

Test of controls Tests that provide auditors with reasonable assurance of the effective design and operation of internal control policies and procedures.

Unrestricted random selection Selection of a sample in such a way that every sampling unit in the population has an equal chance of being selected.

Chapter 10 ► REFERENCES

American Institute of Certified Public Accountants. Professional
Standards
    AT Section 400—*Reporting on an Entity's Internal Control Over Financial Reporting.*
    AU Section 319—*Consideration of the Internal Control in a Financial Statement Audit.*
    AU Section 325—*Communication of Internal Control Related Matters Noted in an Audit.*
    AU Section 350—*Audit Sampling.*
Meservy, Rayman D., Bailey, Andrew D., Jr., and Johnson, Paul

E. "Internal Control Evaluation: A Computational Model of the Review Process," *Auditing: A Journal of Practice and Theory* (Fall 1986), pp. 44–74.
Srinidhi, B. N., and Vasarhelyi, M. A. "Auditor Judgment Concerning Establishment of Substantive Tests Based on Internal Control Reliability," *Auditing: A Journal of Practice and Theory* (Spring 1986), pp. 64–76.
Willingham, John J., and Wright, William F. "Financial Statement Errors and Internal Control Judgments," *Auditing: A Journal of Practice and Theory* (Fall 1985), pp. 57–70.

Chapter 10 ► REVIEW QUESTIONS

10-1   What is the purpose of tests of controls?

10-2   Describe the four procedures that can be used in conducting tests of controls.

10-3   Why are some tests of controls performed during the interim period?

10-4   What four factors should the auditor consider in deciding what evidence, if any, needs to be obtained during the period from the interim date to the balance sheet date?

10-5   Sampling is more likely to be used for certain types of tests of controls. What types are these?

10-6   For what types of procedures would sampling be appropriate?

10-7   For purposes of tests of controls, what is a deviation?

10-8   Give three examples of a sampling unit.

10-9   What is the difference between block sampling and haphazard sampling?

10-10   What is the difference between unrestricted random selection and systematic sampling?

10-11   Name the factors the auditor should consider in deciding on the size of a sample for a test of controls.

10-12   In performing the sampling plan, how should the auditor classify unlocated documents?

10-13   List the decision rules the auditor can use in evaluating sample results.

10-14   When nonstatistical sampling is used, two decisions are made judgmentally. These two are determined scientifically when statistical sampling is used. What are these two decisions?

10-15   In what situation is the assessed level of control risk most likely to be maximum?

10-16   What assessed level of control risk requires documentary support?

10-17   Describe the three ways in which substantive tests may be revised.

10-18   What is a reportable condition?

10-19   To whom should reportable conditions be communicated?

10-20   What is a material weakness?

Chapter 10 ► OBJECTIVE QUESTIONS

(* = author prepared; ** = CPA examination)

*10-21   Which of the following statements is true?
    a. Tests of controls are necessary if the auditor plans to use the primarily substantive approach.
    b. Tests of controls are necessary if the auditor plans to assess the level of control risk at maximum.

    c. The auditor can simultaneously obtain an understanding of internal control and perform tests of controls.
    d. After performing tests of controls, the auditor will always assess control risk at maximum.

*10-22   In considering the evidence needed to assess control risk during the period from interim to year-end, all of the following should be considered except the

a. Significance of the assertion being tested.

b. Specific internal control policies and procedures tested during the interim period.

c. Degree to which the policies and procedures were tested and the test results.

d. Control risk on other assertions.

*10-23 The assessment of control risk can be made at any of the following times except

a. Immediately after obtaining an understanding of internal control.

b. After some tests of controls are performed concurrently with obtaining an understanding.

c. After the performance of additional tests of controls designed to additionally lower the assessment of control risk.

d. After performing all necessary substantive tests.

*10-24 Which of the following statements is true?

a. If control risk is assessed at maximum, the nature of related substantive tests should be changed from more to less effective.

b. If control risk is assessed at maximum, the nature of related substantive tests should be changed from less to more effective.

c. If control risk is assessed at maximum, the timing of related substantive tests should be changed from year-end to an interim date.

d. If control risk is assessed at maximum, the extent of related substantive tests should be changed from a larger to a smaller sample.

*10-25 Which of the following would not be a method used to conduct tests of controls?

a. Inquiry.   c. Confirmation.
b. Walkthrough.   d. Observation.

*10-26 What is the reason for ensuring that every copy of a vendor's invoice has a receiving report?

a. To ascertain that merchandise billed by the vendor was received by the company.

b. To ascertain that merchandise received by the company was billed by the vendor.

c. To ascertain that the invoice was correctly prepared.

d. To ascertain that a check was prepared for every invoice.

*10-27 Which of the following procedures is most likely to ensure that employee job time tickets are accurate?

a. Approve the payroll voucher in the accounts payable department.

b. Keep employment information in the human resources department.

c. Make sure that the number of hours per week on each employee's job time ticket is 40.

d. Check the employee clock cards against the job time tickets.

**10-28 Which of the following audit techniques most likely would provide an auditor with the most assurance about effectiveness of the operation of an internal control procedure?

a. Inquiry of client personnel.

b. Recomputation of account balance amounts.

c. Observation of client personnel.

d. Confirmation with outside parties.

**10-29 The likelihood of assessing control risk too low is the risk that the sample selected to test controls

a. Does not support the tolerable misstatement for some or all of management's assertions.

b. Does support the auditor's planned assessed level of control risk when the true operating effectiveness of the control does not justify such an assessment.

c. Contains misstatements that could be material to the financial statements when aggregated with misstatements in other account balances.

d. Contains proportionately more deviations from prescribed internal control policies or procedures than exist in the population.

**10-30 The likelihood of assessing control risk too low relates to the

a. Effectiveness of the audit.

b. Efficiency of the audit.

c. Preliminary estimates of materiality levels.

d. Allowable risk of tolerable misstatement.

*10-31 Which of the following is *not* an auditing procedure that is commonly used in performing tests of controls?

a. Inquiry.   c. Comparison.
b. Observation.   d. Inspection.

**10-32 The proper use of prenumbered termination notice forms by the payroll department should provide assurance that all

a. Uncashed payroll checks were issued to employees who have *not* been terminated.

b. Personnel files are kept up to date.

c. Employees who have *not* been terminated receive their payroll checks.

d. Terminated employees are removed from the payroll.

10-33 As a result of tests of controls, an auditor assessed control risk too low and decreased substantive testing. This assessment occurred because the true deviation rate in the population was
   a. Less than the risk of assessing control risk too low, based on the auditor's sample.
   b. Less than the deviation rate in the auditor's sample.
   c. More than the risk of assessing control risk too low, based on the auditor's sample.
   d. More than the deviation rate in the auditor's sample.

10-34 After obtaining an understanding of internal control and assessing control risk, an auditor decided to perform tests of controls. The auditor most likely decided that
   a. It would be efficient to perform tests of controls that would result in a reduction in planned substantive tests.
   b. Additional evidence to support a further reduction in control risk is *not* available.
   c. An increase in the assessed level of control risk is justified for certain financial statement assertions.
   d. There were many internal control weaknesses that could allow errors to enter the accounting system.

10-35 Which of the following statements is correct concerning reportable conditions in an audit?
   a. An auditor is required to search for reportable conditions during an audit.
   b. All reportable conditions are also considered to be material weaknesses.
   c. An auditor may communicate reportable conditions during an audit or after the audit's completion.
   d. An auditor may report that *no* reportable conditions were noted during an audit.

10-36 Which of the following statements is correct concerning statistical sampling in tests of controls?
   a. As the population size increases, the sample size should increase proportionately.
   b. Deviations from specific internal control procedures at a given rate ordinarily result in misstatements at a lower rate.
   c. There is an inverse relationship between the expected population deviation rate and the sample size.
   d. In determining tolerable rate, an auditor considers detection risk and the sample size.

10-37 The likelihood of assessing control risk too high is the risk that the sample selected to test controls
   a. Does *not* support the auditor's planned assessed level of control risk when the true operating effectiveness of the control justifies such an assessment.
   b. Contains misstatements that could be material to the financial statements when aggregated with misstatements in other account balances or transactions classes.
   c. Contains proportionately fewer monetary errors or deviations from prescribed internal control policies or procedures than exist in the balance or class as a whole.
   d. Does *not* support the tolerable misstatement for some or all of management's assertions.

Chapter 10 ▶ DISCUSSION/CASE QUESTIONS

(* = author prepared; ** = CPA examination; *** = other sources)

10-38 A partially completed charge sales systems flowchart is on page 312. The flowchart depicts the charge sales activities of the Bottom Manufacturing Corporation.

A customer's purchase order is received, and a six-part sales order is prepared from it. The six copies are initially distributed as follows:

   Copy No. 1—Billing copy, to billing department.
   Copy No. 2—Shipping copy, to shipping department.
   Copy No. 3—Credit copy, to credit department.
   Copy No. 4—Stock request copy, to credit department.
   Copy No. 5—Customer copy, to customer.
   Copy No. 6—Sales order copy, file in sales order department.

When each copy of the sales order reaches the applicable department or destination, it calls for specific internal control procedures and related documents. Some of the procedures and related documents are specified on the flowchart. Others are indicated only by the letters *a* to *r*.

Required:

a. List the procedures or the internal documents that are labeled letters *a* to *r* in the flow-chart of Bottom Manufacturing Corporation's charge sales system.

b. From the flowchart and the answers to (a), identify the financial statement assertions and the control procedures that relate to each assertion.

c. Identify the potential misstatements that could occur for each assertion. Indicate whether the control procedures in (b) would or would not prevent or detect these misstatements.

d. List the tests of controls you could perform on each control applicable to each assertion.

e. Assess control risk on each assertion. In each case, indicate whether this assessment would correspond with a high, medium, or low level of related substantive tests. (Do not list any substantive tests.)

**10-39 The flowchart on page 313 depicts the activities relating to the shipping, billing, and collection processes used by Smallco Lumber, Inc.

Required:

a. Identify the financial statement assertions and the internal control procedures that relate to each assertion.

b. List the tests of controls you could perform on each internal control procedure.

**10-40 The Art Appreciation Society operates a museum for the benefit and enjoyment of the community. During hours when the museum is open to the public, two clerks who are positioned at the entrance collect a $5 admission fee from each nonmember patron. Members of the Art Appreciation Society are permitted to enter free of charge on presentation of their membership cards.

At the end of each day, one of the clerks delivers the proceeds to the treasurer. The treasurer counts the cash in the presence of the clerk and places it in a safe. Each Friday afternoon the treasurer and one of the clerks deliver all cash held in the safe to the bank and receive an authenticated deposit slip, which provides the basis for the weekly entry in the cash receipts journal.

The board of directors of the Art Appreciation Society has identified a need to improve its internal control relating to cash admission fees. The board has determined that the cost of installing turnstiles, sales booths, or otherwise altering the physical layout of the museum will greatly exceed any benefits that may be derived. However, the board has agreed that the sale of admission tickets must be an integral part of its improvement efforts.

Smith, CPA, has been asked by the board of directors of the Art Appreciation Society to audit the financial statements of the society. During the audit Smith is expected to review internal control relating to cash admission fees and provide suggestions for improvement.

Required:

a. Indicate weaknesses in the existing internal control relating to cash admission fees that Smith should identify, and recommend one improvement for each of the weaknesses identified.

b. Give reasons why you might assess control risk at maximum.

c. Give reasons why you might assess control risk below maximum.

**10-41 Dunbar Camera Manufacturing, Inc., is a manufacturer of high-priced precision motion picture cameras in which the specifications of component parts are vital to the manufacturing process. Dunbar buys valuable camera lenses and large quantities of sheetmetal and screws.

BOTTOM MANUFACTURING CORPORATION
Flowchart of Credit Sales Activities

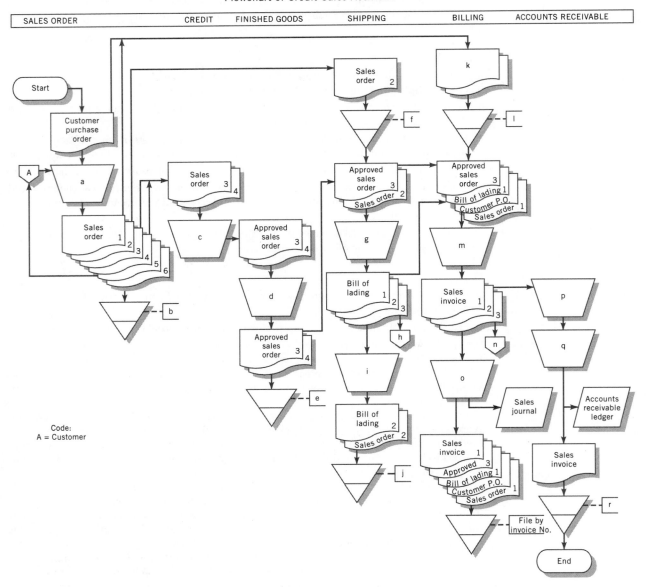

Screws and lenses are ordered by Dunbar and are billed by the vendors on a unit basis. Sheetmetal is ordered and billed by the vendors on the basis of weight. The receiving clerk is responsible for documenting the quality and quantity of merchandise received.

Your understanding of internal control indicates that the following procedures are being followed:

Receiving Report: Properly approved purchase orders, which are prenumbered, are filed numerically. The copy sent to the receiving clerk is an exact duplicate of the copy sent to the vendor. Receipts of merchandise are recorded on the duplicate copy by the receiving clerk.

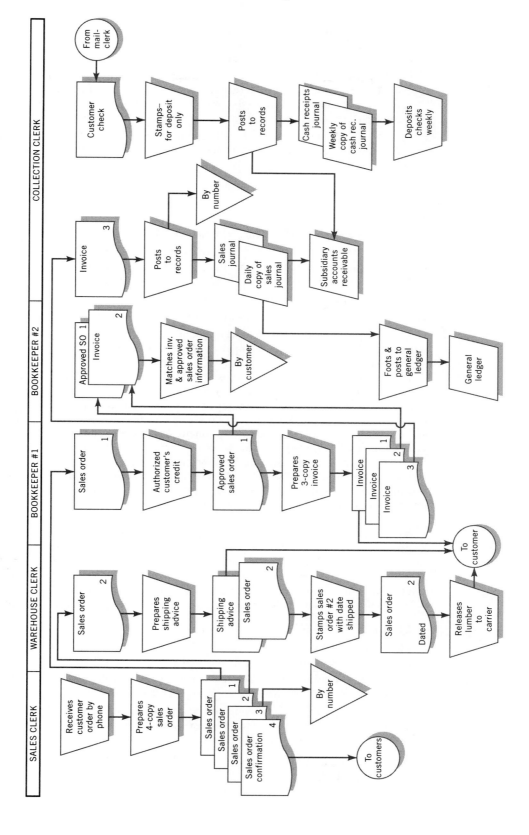

Sheetmetal: The company receives sheetmetal by railroad. The railroad independently weighs the sheetmetal and reports the weight and date of receipt on a bill of lading that accompanies all deliveries. The receiving clerk checks the weight on the bill of lading against the purchase order.

Screws: The receiving clerk opens cartons containing screws, then inspects and weighs the contents. The weight is converted to number of units by means of conversion charts. The receiving clerk then checks the computed quantity against the purchase order.

Camera Lenses: Each camera lens is delivered in a separate corrugated carton. Cartons are counted as they are received by the receiving clerk and the number of cartons is checked against purchase orders.

Required:

a. Explain why the internal control procedures as they apply individually to receiving reports and the receipt of sheetmetal, screws, and camera lenses are adequate or inadequate.

b. What financial statement misstatements may arise because of the inadequacies in Dunbar's internal control procedures, and how may they occur?

c. What tests of controls could be performed?

d. At what level (quantitative or qualitative) would you assess control risk? Why?

***10-42** You were engaged to audit the financial statements of Blank City Newspapers, Inc., for the year ended December 31. The company publishes a newspaper with a daily circulation of approximately 65,000.

During your examination of accounts receivable, certain unusual transactions were noted and discussed with company executives. When questioned about the transactions, the cashier admitted to a defalcation and gave company executives 298 remittance advices consisting of either the top half of the newspaper's monthly statement, the voucher portion of the customers' checks, or the cashier's memo of payment. The cashier said these remittance advices (amounting to $74,437.38) were the record of payments made by customers for which the checks had been deposited in the bank but no credit had been given in the customers' accounts. She had diverted some previous checks received by mail to an unauthorized bank account that she established in the company's name using a forged corporate resolution. Funds could be withdrawn upon her signature.

The company was shocked because the cashier was an old and faithful employee who was never sick and so interested in her work that she never took a vacation.

To conceal the irregularity, the cashier was lapping accounts receivable by withholding cash receipts from some customers and posting later cash receipts to these earlier customers' accounts. As the total misappropriated grew to a sizable amount, the process became so involved that most customers were receiving credit up to two weeks late.

A review of the company's internal control for cash receipts disclosed the following:

The cashier reported directly to the controller.

Mail was opened by another employee of the company. This employee did not prepare a record of the money and checks received before he distributed them.

All mail and over-the-counter receipts (cash sales and payments on account) were given to the cashier. Receipts included approximately $100 to $200 daily in currency.

The cashier prepared a daily report showing customer and amount of payment. She gave this report, together with remittance advices, to the accounts receivable department for posting to the customers' accounts receivable ledger cards.

The cashier prepared the bank deposit and took the deposit to the bank. She obtained an authenticated deposit slip from the bank.

The cashier gave the authenticated deposit slip to the controller, who compared the total shown thereon with the total shown on the daily cash receipts report. These totals were always in agreement.

Required:

a. Write a letter to the audit committee listing the reportable conditions noted in the company's accounting procedures for cash receipts and recommendations for improvement.

b. List the tests of controls that might have disclosed the fraud by the cashier.

c. What should you do when you discover unusual items that might indicate a fraud by one of the company's employees?

Source: Adapted and used with permission of Ernst & Young.

*10-43   During the audit of Clements Manufacturing Company, Bill Gahagan, CPA, noticed that scrap steel from the manufacturing process was piled in an unfenced vacant lot next to the plant. No records were kept of the amount of scrap generated in the manufacturing process or the amount on hand at any time. Scrap sales were recorded when made by the maintenance foreman.

Gahagan included these weaknesses in his report of reportable conditions to management, together with his recommendations for strengthening controls by fencing the area and weighing and recording the daily scrap production; however, the management of Clements took no action on the recommendations included in the report.

Six months later, it was discovered that the maintenance supervisor reported only a small portion of the actual scrap that was sold and had kept most of the proceeds from the scrap sales for himself. The president of Clements then called Gahagan and asked him why he had not caught the maintenance supervisor in his audit and suggested that he might hold Gahagan liable for the loss.

Discuss how Gahagan should handle this situation and how he would reply to the president. What liability do you think Gahagan would have in this situation? Would your answer be different if the letter was sent to the audit committee?

*10-44   During the course of an audit, Mr. Robin, CPA, observed that one of the clerks in the small toy department consistently was taking money from the customers in areas other than at the cash register. At the time, he gave little thought to this practice, because most items were priced in "whole dollars" and the customer did not need any change. He did mention this to the controller, who had the same reaction. The audit was completed, and the report was issued.

The following year it was discovered that the clerk had been keeping the money from these "whole dollar purchases" rather than putting it in the cash register.

Required:

a. Could the auditor be held liable for failure to detect this fraud? Should his comment to the controller make any difference?

b. Assume that the auditor decided to include his observation in a letter of reportable conditions, along with his recommendation on how to eliminate this weakness and provide reasonable assurance that currency receipts are placed in the cash register drawer. Draft such a letter.

*10-45   During an audit of a loan company, the auditor discovered that the recipient of a loan with a principal balance of $2,100 had received only $2,000 when the loan was written. The auditor read the loan agreement and noted that it called for a $2,000 check and $100 in currency to be given to the customer who borrowed the money.

The auditor read other loan agreements and found similar wording in each of them. When the controller was asked about this practice, she replied that this "service" was given to the customers so that they could have immediate access to currency. She thought that the $100 inconsistency was an error and could be corrected easily. The auditor decided to drop the matter.

Early the following year, a class-action lawsuit was brought against the loan company by several customers who discovered that they had received less than the principal amount of the loans. It was discovered that the controller had kept the currency. The company's board of directors notified the auditor that they would take legal action against him because of his failure to inform them of what he had learned about this matter.

Required:

a. Could the auditor be held liable for either ordinary negligence or gross negligence in this case?

b. Assume that the auditor chose to include this loan agreement practice in a letter of reportable conditions to the audit committee. Draft such a letter. Include a recommendation of the controls that can be implemented to prevent such an occurrence.

*10-46 During the course of an audit, Ms. Command, the senior, decided to use nonstatistical sampling (per *SAS No. 39* guidelines) on a test of controls. The sampling plan included the following.

1. The planned tolerable rate was set at 6 percent because only a moderate effect on the financial statements would occur if the control being tested did not function properly.

2. The risk of assessing control risk too low was set at a low level because of the need for high assurance that the control was functioning as prescribed.

3. The estimated deviation rate in the population was set at 2 percent, based on the deviation rate found in the prior year.

Although nonstatistical sampling was used, Ms. Command computed a sample size based on numerical guidelines in the auditing literature. The performance of the test of controls was assigned to Mr. Critical, an assistant.

Mr. Critical selected and audited the sample and calculated a sample deviation rate of 2.5 percent. However, he was puzzled as to how to evaluate the sample results. He remembered reading the guidelines in the auditing literature. If the sample deviation rate is far enough below the planned tolerable rate, there is an acceptably low risk that the true deviation rate in the population exceeds the planned tolerable rate; 2.5 percent seemed to be sufficiently low to accept the sampling results.

The auditing literature, however, also suggests that the sampling results would not generally be accepted if the sample deviation rate exceeded the estimate of the deviation rate in the population (2.5 percent compared to 2 percent). Mr. Critical took the question to Ms. Command, who stated that the sampling results should be accepted and related substantive tests restricted.

Mr. Critical questioned whether the sampling results should be accepted if the sample deviation rate is 2.5 percent. It seemed that the "careful" course of action was to expand the substantive tests. To accept the results seemed "out of line" with guidelines in the auditing literature. Ms. Overhear, another assistant, injected an opinion. She thought that the sample should be expanded. Her reasoning was that the sample deviation rate "should be 2 percent or under," based on knowledge of the population characteristics and prior-year audits.

Required:

Evaluate the strengths and weaknesses of each person's argument.

*10-47 An auditor is applying statistical sampling for attributes to the testing of extensions on sales invoices. There are 250 invoices with an average of four sales on each invoice. The auditor uses 1,000 as the population total and classifies each extension mistake as a deviation. The auditor decides to use a 10 percent risk of assessing control risk too low, a planned tolerable rate of 5.2 percent, and an estimated deviation rate of 2 percent.

Assume the following deviation condition exists in the population. (The invoices are numbered 1–250; the lines are numbered 1–1000.)

Invoice no.	Line no.	Amount of deviation	Error results in overstatement (O) or understatement (U) of sales
10	39	$ 100	U
21	81	350	O
51	202	900	O
53	220	700	O
61	240	950	O
70	291	300	U
102	410	41	U
103	413	850	O
150	600	1000	O
170	674	150	O
192	798	500	O
203	840	350	O
210	855	520	U
215	890	925	O
224	906	820	O
225	908	1000	O
231	930	10	O
250	971	900	O

Required:

a. Calculate the sample size.

b. Take the sample using random selection. Identify the numbers in the random number set with the lines 1–1000. For example, random number 102 is line 102, and so on. If you select a line number listed in the preceding deviation chart, assume that a deviation is located.

c. Quantitatively evaluate your sample results. If you incorrectly rejected the sample results, why did this happen?

d. Would the dollar amount of the deviations you found change the evaluation of your results? Why or why not?

**10-48 Jiblum, CPA, is planning to use sampling in a test of controls relating to sales. Jiblum has begun to develop an outline of the main steps in the sampling plan as follows:

1. State the objective or objectives of the audit test (e.g., to test the effectiveness of an internal control procedure for the sales occurrence assertion).

2. Define the population. (Define the period covered by the test; define the completeness of the population.)

3. Define the sampling unit (e.g., client copies of sales invoices).

Required:

What are the remaining steps in the preceding outline that Jiblum should include in the test of sales invoices? Do not present a detailed analysis of tasks that must be performed to carry out the objectives of each step. Parenthetical examples need not be provided.

*10-49 While obtaining an understanding of internal control for a client's system of cash disbursements, an auditor decided to test the controls by taking a sample of vendor invoices and examining them to determine whether they were properly approved for payment. Therefore, a deviation would be an invoice with no evidence of approval prior to payment.

The population of invoices is shown below and on pages 319–320. A check mark in the deviation column beside an invoice number means that no approval was indicated for that invoice, and, if the auditor includes that invoice in his or her sample, a deviation will be detected. (There are deviations in 22 of the invoices, but the auditor would not know this.)

Assume that the auditor decides on a risk of assessing control risk too low of 10 percent, a planned tolerable rate of 8 percent, and an estimate of the deviation rate in the population of 2 percent. The sample size is 50.

Required:

a. Assume that nonstatistical sampling is used and that a systematic sampling technique is employed. Using a one-digit number from the table of random numbers in Appendix B as a starting point (number 4 means invoice no. 02362), list the 50 invoice numbers that would be examined. Indicate how many deviations were found, the sample deviation rate, and whether you consider the sampling results to be acceptable or unacceptable. Given the deviation rate in the population, did the sampling results lead you to the correct conclusion?

b. Assume that statistical sampling is used and that random number sampling is employed. Using the table of random numbers, list the 50 invoice numbers that would be examined. Indicate how many deviations were found, the sample deviation rate, the achieved tolerable rate, and whether you consider the sampling results to be acceptable or unacceptable. Given the deviation rate in the population, did the sampling results lead you to the correct conclusion? (Use the tables in Appendix B.)

The Population of Invoices

Invoice no.	Deviation (no approval)	Sample selection	Invoice no.	Deviation (no approval)	Sample selection
2359			84		
60			85		
61			86		
62			87		
63			88		
64			89		
65			90		
66			91		
67			92	✓	
68	✓		93		
69			94		
70			95		
71			96		
72			97		
73			98		
74			99		
75			2400		
76			01		
77			02		
78			03		
79			04		
80	✓		05		
81			06	✓	
82			07		
83			08		

The Population of Invoices *Continued*

Invoice no.	Deviation (no approval)	Sample selection	Invoice no.	Deviation (no approval)	Sample selection
09			59		
10			60		
11	✓		61		
12			62		
13			63		
14			64	✓	
15			65		
16			66		
17			67		
18			68		
19			69		
20	✓		70		
21			71		
22			72		
23			73		
24			74		
25			75		
26	✓		76	✓	
27			77		
28			78		
29			79		
30			80		
31			81		
32			82		
33			83		
34	✓		84		
35			85		
36			86		
37			87		
38			88	✓	
39			89		
40			90		
41			91		
42			92		
43			93		
44			94		
45			95		
46			96	✓	
47			97		
48			98		
49	✓		99		
50			2500		
51			01		
52			02		
53			03		
54			04		
55			05		
56			06		
57			07	✓	
58			08		

The Population of Invoices *Continued*

Invoice no.	Deviation (no approval)	Sample selection	Invoice no.	Deviation (no approval)	Sample selection
09			59		
10			60		
11			61	✓	
12			62		
13			63		
14			64		
15			65		
16			66		
17			67		
18	✓		68		
19			69	✓	
20			70		
21			71		
22			72		
23			73		
24			74		
25			75		
26			76		
27			77		
28			78		
29			79		
30			80		
31			81	✓	
32			82		
33			83		
34	✓		84		
35			85		
36			86		
37			87		
38			88		
39			89		
40			90		
41			91		
42			92		
43			93	✓	
44			94		
45			95		
46			96		
47			97		
48			98		
49	✓		99		
50			2600	✓	
51			01		
52			02		
53			03		
54			04		
55			05		
56			06		
57			07		
58			08		

Obtaining an Understanding of Internal Control in a Computer Environment

"The machine does not isolate man from the great problems of nature but plunges him more deeply into them."

ANTOINE DE SAINT-EXUPÉRY, *Wind, Sand and Stars*

LEARNING OBJECTIVES

After reading and studying the material in this chapter, the student should be able to

► Write a brief paragraph on six ways the auditor's approach to obtaining an understanding of internal control is different when computers are used.

► Describe the factors the auditor considers when obtaining an understanding of the control environment that affects computer processing.

► Analyze a flowchart for a computer system using batch processing.

► Analyze a flowchart for a computerized online system.

► Analyze a data flow diagram showing the use of a microcomputer.

► Briefly describe the four general controls in a computerized system.

► Briefly describe the three application controls in a computerized system.

► Briefly describe the special control problems that may exist in independent minicomputer and microcomputer systems.

► Describe the controls in independent minicomputer or microcomputer systems.

► Analyze the factors that determine the extent of understanding that auditors need about computer control procedures.

Computers have been so thoroughly integrated into the business world that sometimes it is difficult to categorize internal control as either manual or computerized. In many audit engagements, procedures designed to acquire an understanding of internal control and conduct tests of controls require examination both of records and documents produced manually and by the computer. In prior years, it was considered unwise to ignore computer processing; today, it is often impossible. For this reason, we consider the material in this chapter to be an extended coverage of discussions and illustrations contained in Chapter 9. Similarly, Chapter 12 has the same relationship to Chapter 10.

INTERNAL CONTROL

Different Approach in a Computer System

The auditor's approach to obtaining an understanding of internal control is sometimes different when computers are used to process much of the data and generate much of the output. For example:

1. The traditional audit trails that are familiar in manual systems may exist in computer systems only for a short time and only in computer-readable form. An *audit trail* is a chain of evidence provided through coding, cross-references, and documentation connecting account balances and other summary results with original transactions and calculations. Here is an example of an audit trail in a manual system.

   In a computer system, the cash receipts data are transformed into machine-readable form when or soon after the transaction occurs. In certain types of computer systems, the data may be transcribed from a remittance advice (a form of source document) to a computer file. The data appear as output in the form of computer files representing a sales journal and a cash receipts journal. The general ledger data are stored in computer memory. In other computer systems, the data are transformed into machine-readable form and processed into a general ledger entry as the cash receipts transactions occur.

2. Computer programming instructions process similar transactions in the same way. Random error associated with manual processing does not exist. However, incorrect programming instructions result in incorrect processing of transactions. In auditing computer systems, auditors usually pay more attention to the accuracy and validity of the programming process than to casual errors normally created in a manual system.

3. Procedures performed by separate individuals in a manual system are often performed by one person in a computer system. The segregation of duties control that auditors rely on in manual systems does not exist in its traditional form in a computer system. Other segregation of duties (such as within the computer department) must be substituted for the traditional ones.

4. Data stored in machine-readable rather than visible form can be inappropriately accessed or altered. Because the data are processed with a relatively small amount of human involvement, the potential for observing errors or fraud is less than in a manual system.

5. A computer system can produce a wide variety of information used by management to more effectively supervise the operations of the entity. A wider variety of information is also available to the auditor, analytical information being a prime example.

6. In a manual system, transactions are usually authorized before they are executed and recorded. Checks to vendors and writeoffs of accounts receivable are examples. In a computer system, some transactions are automatically executed and recorded without explicit management authorization. In accepting the design of the computer system, management implicitly grants its authorization to these transactions. For instance, accounts receivable may be automatically written off if the customer's credit status reaches a certain point.

Control Environment

In obtaining an understanding of the control environment that affects computer processing, the auditor considers the following factors.

1. What is management's attitude toward the investments, risks, and benefits of computerized data processing?

▶ **EXAMPLE**

If management uses outdated hardware or software in a rapidly expanding high-technology industry, it might expect more than can be reasonably produced, creating an environment conducive to processing errors.

2. The centralization or decentralization of computerized processing is also important to an auditor's understanding of internal control. In some companies almost all authority is delegated to the computer center manager, and little supervision of these operations is exercised. In these situations, the traditional segregation of duties may not exist and should be considered in assessing control risk.

3. In a computer environment, it is important for the auditor to note management's attitude and actions on such matters as
   a. Approving changes in systems and control policies and procedures.
   b. Safeguarding programs and files.
   c. Restricting access to computer files and records.

Sometimes, the computer center manager is in charge of policies and procedures relating to these matters, with senior management's role confined to reviewing computer output and controlling overall operations. Such an arrangement can be efficient if the computer center manager is competent, but the potential for material undetected errors or fraud should be considered by the auditor.

4. What are management's policies and procedures for hiring, training, evaluating, promoting, and compensating employees with computer-related responsibilities?

► **EXAMPLE**

If management's policies result in excessive employee turnover, the auditor must consider the risk of computer processing errors. Also, the lack of job rotation or periodic vacations in such sensitive areas as programming and data reconciliation might increase the risk of fraud.

Methods of Processing Transactions

The techniques used to obtain an understanding of a computerized accounting system depend partly on the entity's method of processing such transactions. Basically, there are two methods, batch processing and online processing.

Batch Processing

Source documents are created when the transactions occur. Data from these source documents are periodically entered into a computer file. Periodic computer processing is performed that produces various types of output such as updated computer files and printed reports. Thus, *batch processing* is sometimes called a method of periodic preparation and periodic processing.

When auditors are obtaining an understanding of a batch processing accounting system, it is sometimes helpful to study a *systems flowchart,* which describes the sequence of major processing operations and the data flow to and from the files used in processing; it provides an overview of the system. Figure 11.1 is an example of a systems flowchart for a computer system.

Illustration of a Systems Flowchart Using Batch Processing

Figure 11.1 is an example of a systems flowchart for the processing of credit sales, noncash credits, and cash receipts on account. It shows the processing operations

FIGURE 11.1   **An Example of a Systems Flowchart for a Computer System Using Batch Processing**

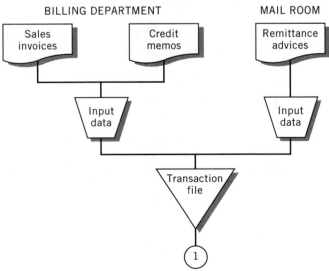

FIGURE 11.1 *(Continued)*

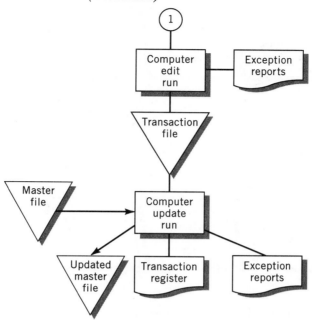

and flow of data from source document to computer-generated output. Here is a description of the flowchart.

1. Data from sales invoices, credit memos, and remittance advices (all in manual form) are entered at a terminal in the respective departments and recorded in a transaction file.
2. A *computer edit program* performs tests of the data in the transaction file for accuracy, validity, reasonableness, and completeness. Exception reports are printed.
3. A computer update program takes data from the edited transaction file and the master file and generates an updated master file, a printed transaction register, and printed exception reports.

Value of Flowcharts

Auditing standards do not require the use of flowcharts. Nonetheless, a systems flowchart can be a useful tool for understanding the overall processing flow of a computerized credit sales, purchases, or payroll system. Auditors should probably use systems flowcharts unless alternative documentation is available to aid them in obtaining an understanding of a computer system.

Online Processing

Data from source documents need not be transferred to a machine-readable device in a separate operation before computer processing takes place. In fact, it is not necessary that a source document be created when *online processing* is used (although one may be created). When the transaction occurs, it can be entered at a terminal and used for immediate file updating. A file inquiry can be made at any time.

FIGURE 11.2   Computerized Online System

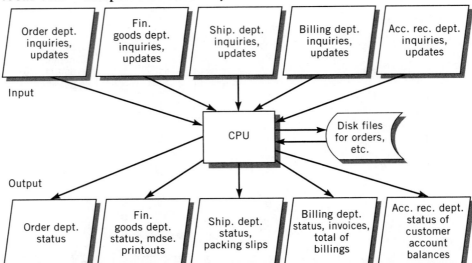

Illustration of Online Processing

Figure 11.2 contains an overview of a sales and accounts receivable system using online processing. Each of the five departments uses a microcomputer to enter transactions and update their central files as well as files in their own department.

▶ **EXAMPLE**

The order department could enter customer orders at a microcomputer as they are received. These orders are immediately edited by a mainframe central processing unit and stored in a pending order file both on the central and department magnetic disks. The same microcomputer could also be used to print a status report of pending orders whenever needed.

▶ **EXAMPLE**

The billing department could produce sales invoices as shipping information is entered from the shipping department. The information on the sales invoices is immediately used to update the customers' accounts. The balance in each customer's account can be accessed through terminal inquiry in the accounts receivable department.

Use of the Microcomputer in a Small Accounting System

Some accounting systems use *microcomputers* in a partially computerized system. The data flow diagram in Figure 11.3 illustrates the use of a microcomputer in a credit sales system. Note the limited but important use made of the microcomputer that performs a variety of functions on a standalone basis. The microcomputer is independent of a *mainframe central processing unit* (although several may be connected in an area network). In a small company, one microcomputer can be used for such applications as inventory, payroll, and sales (as shown in Figure 11.3).

FIGURE 11.3   Use of Microcomputer in a Partial Computer System

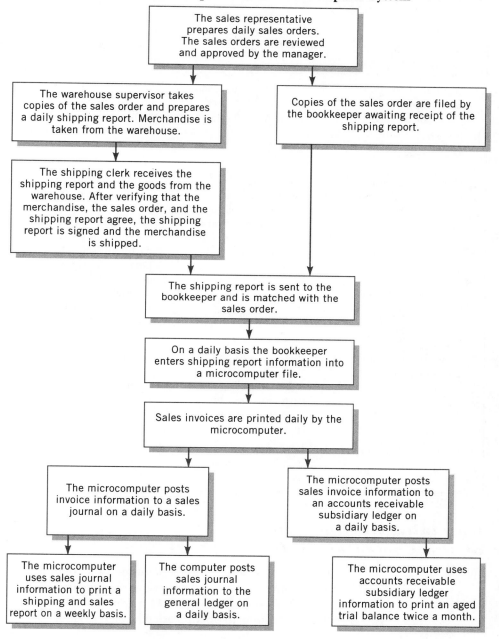

FIGURE 11.4   **Questions and Answers about Computer Systems**

Questions about the Computer System	Answers for the Batch Processing System with a Mainframe (Figure 11.1)	Answers for the Online System with a Mainframe (Figure 11.2)	Answers for the Batch Processing System with a Microcomputer (Figure 11.3)
1. What are the significant actions and classes of transactions processed by the computer?	1. Credit sales, noncash credits, and cash receipts on account.	1. Sales orders, removal of finished goods, shipments, billings, posting to customers' accounts.	1. Sales invoices, sales journal, shipping and sales report, general ledger, accounts receivable subsidiary ledger, aged trial balance.
2. How are the transactions initiated? What are the source documents?	2. Sales invoices and credit memos are prepared in the billing department. Remittance advices are prepared in the mail room.	2. Sales orders are prepared in the order department, merchandise transfer report in the finished goods department, shipping reports in the shipping department, accounts receivable subsidiary ledger in the accounts receivable department.	2. Microcomputer creates sales invoices from shipping reports; creates sales journal from sales invoices; creates shipping and sales reports and general ledger from sales journal; creates subsidiary ledger and aged trial balance from sales invoices.
3. How are the data entered into the computer?	3. Sales invoices and credit memos from terminals in billing department, cash receipts from terminals in mail room.	3. From microcomputers in each of the five departments.	3. By the bookkeeper on a microcomputer.
4. What computer master files are used?	4. Customer accounts are stored in computer files.	4. Disk files for customer accounts.	4. General ledger and accounts receivable subsidiary ledger.

Obtaining an Understanding of the Computer System

The auditor obtains an understanding of a computer system by asking questions, making observations, and reviewing documentation.

The first column of Figure 11.4 contains some questions for which the auditor will need answers to obtain basic knowledge about the computer system. The other columns have the answers based on the information contained in the flowcharts of the batch processing and online systems (Figures 11.1 and 11.2) and the data flow diagram of the small company system that uses a microcomputer (Figure 11.3).

COMPUTER CONTROL PROCEDURES

Sometimes auditors find it convenient to divide computer control procedures into two groups—*general* and *application*.

General controls are defined as follows:

1. The plan of organization and operation of computer activity.
2. The procedures for documenting, reviewing, testing, and approving systems or programs and changes thereto.
3. Controls built into the equipment by the manufacturer (commonly referred to as "hardware" controls).
4. Controls over access to equipment and data files.
5. Other data and procedural controls that affect overall computer operations.

Application controls are more specific. Their function is to provide reasonable assurance that the recording, processing, and reporting of specific data processing applications (e.g., credit sales and cash receipts) are properly performed.

For discussion, these controls are divided into the following categories.

General Controls
1. Organization and operation controls.
2. Systems development and documentation controls.
3. Access controls.
4. Data and procedural controls.

Application Controls
1. Input controls.
2. Processing controls.
3. Output controls.

In the remainder of this section we will discuss these controls.

Organization and Operation Controls

Organization and operation controls consist of the general plan designed to effect a smooth operation, accomplish the assigned tasks, and minimize the opportunity for errors or fraud in the system.

▶ **EXAMPLE**

Controls such as proper job segregation, periodic rotation of duties, and effective operational supervision are conceptually the same as those in a manual system. Others, such as proper scheduling of computer operations and proper control over program changes, are unique to computer systems.

Different Job Responsibilities

One obvious difference in the organization and operation controls of a computer system is the functions performed by personnel who operate the system.

► **EXAMPLE**

Systems analyst (This function may not be present if packaged software is used.)

a. Reviews potential applications of data processing and works with users in defining information and control requirements.

b. Designs and reviews the documentation for computerized systems.

c. Designs the various computerized and manual controls.

d. Monitors the program maintenance function and maintains systems documentation.

► **EXAMPLE**

Programmer (This function may not be present if packaged software is used.)

a. Codes (not designs systems for) various computerized applications.

b. Codes the computer procedures for programmed controls.

c. Maintains the computer programs by coding, testing, and debugging modifications.

► **EXAMPLE**

Computer operator

a. Operates equipment and in general maintains custody of the computer hardware.

b. Provides physical security over data and program files.

► **EXAMPLE**

Control group (This function is often performed in the various user departments such as shipping, payroll, and accounts payable.)

a. Monitors manual input from the user areas. This position includes the origination and comparison of control totals.

b. Monitors computer output and reconciles this output with the input, including control totals.

c. Corrects errors detected by editing procedures.

► **EXAMPLE**

Input data operator (This function is often performed in the various user departments such as shipping, payroll, and accounts payable.)

a. Converts transactions to machine-readable form.

b. Verifies the machine-readable data produced from manual input.

No one of the listed groups should have direct and complete access to the recordkeeping system. The systems analysts and programmers should have no control over the day-to-day computer operations. The computer operator's knowledge of detailed programs and records should not be comprehensive. Input and output controls should be maintained by the control group or user department.

Unique Computer Control Problems

In computerized installations access to assets can exist *without* the individuals maintaining *physical* contact with the assets.

► **EXAMPLE**

Computer personnel have access to assets if the computer activity includes the preparation or processing of documents that lead to the use or disposition of the assets. Computer personnel have direct access to cash if the computer activity includes the preparation and signing of disbursement checks.

▶ EXAMPLE

Sometimes access by computer personnel to assets may not be readily apparent because the access is indirect. Computers may generate payment orders authorizing issuance of checks, shipping orders authorizing release of inventory, or authorization of other transactions.

Several steps are advisable to improve internal control when computer personnel have this type of indirect access to assets.

1. Access to computer programs should be limited so that only authorized changes can be made. Normally, the computer programmers should not be allowed to make changes without proper approval (a program change control).
2. The programmers should not operate the computers.
3. All programs should be documented with flowcharts, listings of the programs, and input, output, and file descriptions. Periodic runs should be made by independent personnel to ensure that the actual programs are processing as described in the listings and flowcharts.
4. Errors or exceptions that are detected by the computer should be communicated to the appropriate person who has the responsibility to correct them. Operator errors are normally detected by the system aborting, a message printed by the computer, or the reconciliation of controls by the control group. Routine errors or exceptions resulting from conditions tested by the computer programs should be reported to the control group for disposition. Errors resulting from hardware or vendor software failures should be reported to management.
5. Records should be kept of all processing actions involving the computer to lower the probability of unauthorized operation and to provide a documented log for management.
6. Job rotation among computer operators is desirable. If one operator were running a deliberately altered program, collusion might be necessary to continue the fraud.

Segregation between Computer Department and Users

There should be a segregation of certain functions between the computer department and users of computer-processed data. Specifically, those who perform computer functions should not

1. Authorize transactions.
2. Correct errors in transactions.
3. Initiate the preparation of data.
4. Have custody or control of assets.
5. Be able to change the controls.
6. Originate changes in master files (such as files for accounts receivable customers).

In smaller companies, the computer function may be part of a user department. In addition, the increasing use of microcomputers has made it more difficult to separate the use of data and computer processing of data.

Segregation of Functions within the Computer Department

The following policies should be followed within the computer department:

1. Separate people should write the programs and operate the equipment.
2. Duties should be rotated among computer operators.
3. Vacations should be required for all employees.

Systems Development and Documentation Controls

Documentation controls consist of procedures designed to ensure the integrity of computer storage devices and systems documentation.

► **EXAMPLE**

The grandfather–father–son principle can be used so that if a critical file becomes unreadable, a backup will be available. The transaction file of a processing run is called the "father," the output master file is called the "son," and the master file produced by the previous updating is called the "grandfather." The grandfather and father files are stored at a remote location.

► **EXAMPLE**

Access to computer documentation should be controlled, with records maintained of each usage and each modification.

► **EXAMPLE**

Nonresident files should be stored in a secure, fireproof storage area under the strict control of a person charged with these responsibilities; backup copies of critical files should be stored at off-site locations.

► **EXAMPLE**

Computer programs should be duplicated with a securely stored backup file, and strict control over changes should be followed.

In addition, computer documentation should consist of at least the following items.

1. Program listing. A listing of a program that shows steps written by the programmer in the specific computer language.
2. Error listing. A list of all types of errors a program has been designed to detect, the probable causes of such errors, and the most likely necessary corrective actions. The programmer prepares this listing when he or she writes the program.
3. Log. A listing of the detail of all computer runs. The logs include (a) errors

detected and printed by the computer; (b) everything pertinent to a computer run, such as identification of the run, setup actions taken, input–output files used, and actions taken by the operator each time the computer halted; (c) an accounting of all computer time, including productive time, idle time, rerun time, and so forth; and (d) a listing of all files used, showing date, time, and application.

4. Record layout. A listing of all fields of information in a record and how they are arranged in the record.
5. Flowcharts (discussed and illustrated in a previous section).

Access Controls

Access controls are designed to help prevent or detect errors or fraud caused by (1) improper use or manipulation of data files, (2) unauthorized or incorrect use of a computer program, or (3) improper use of computer resources or a combination of these. These controls are similar to the systems development and documentation controls. Access controls, however, emphasize ways to prevent or detect improper or incorrect use of computer resources.

► **EXAMPLE**

Access to program documentation should be limited to those persons who require it in the performance of their duties. Unlimited access to program documentation could result in unauthorized changes to computer programs and data files. Placing specific people in charge of the documentation and maintaining logs of program and data use are some ways to prevent improper or incorrect program changes.

► **EXAMPLE**

Access to data files and programs should be limited to those individuals authorized with passwords or personal identification codes to process or maintain particular files. Computer program documentation should be restricted to people authorized to make modifications to programs.

► **EXAMPLE**

Access to computer hardware should be limited to computer operators. Physical security devices can be used to partially implement this control. In addition, reviews of utilization reports and console logs can be made on a regular basis.

Data and Procedural Controls

Data and procedural controls provide a framework for controlling daily operations and establishing safeguards against processing errors. They are designed to ensure prompt and accurate processing of data.

► **EXAMPLE**

There should be a written manual of systems and procedures for all computer operations. This manual should provide for management's general or specific authorizations to process transactions. For example, if management authorizes writeoffs of customer accounts that are outstanding for more than 120 days, this policy should be included in the systems and procedures manual so that computer personnel will follow this authorization in processing transactions.

▶ **EXAMPLE**

Internal auditors or some other independent group within the organization should review and evaluate proposed systems at critical stages of development.

▶ **EXAMPLE**

Internal auditors or some other independent group within the organization should review and test computer processing activities (such as computer programs).

Commentary on General Controls

General controls must be in place for application controls to be effective. It would be of little benefit to an entity to have computer programs that edit input data for accuracy, validity, and completeness if these same computer programs could be improperly altered. Similarly, it would be of limited benefit to an entity to have verification of input data if verification was performed by the same personnel who processed the transactions.

Input, Processing, and Output Controls

Application controls have been defined as follows.

Input controls are designed to provide reasonable assurance that data received for processing by computers have been properly authorized, converted into machine-sensible form and identified, and that data (including data transmitted over communication lines) have not been lost, suppressed, added, duplicated, or otherwise improperly changed.

Processing controls are designed to provide reasonable assurance that computer processing has been performed as intended for the particular application.

Output controls are designed to assure the accuracy of the processing result (such as account listings or displays, reports, magnetic files, invoices, or disbursement checks) and to assure that only authorized personnel receive the output.

Input and Output Control Terms

1. *Batch control.* This technique helps ensure that data flowing through the system are complete and accurate. At an early point in the system, independent totals of documents are accumulated by a unit of the company, such as a control or user group, and are later matched against totals derived from the processing of the same documents by the computer department. The three most common types of batch totals are the following:
   a. Control total—usually a meaningful dollar total such as total charge sales.
   b. Hash total—a total that need not have any significance other than as a batch total. The total of customer account numbers is an example.
   c. Record count—a count of the number of documents or transactions processed.

FIGURE 11.5   Three Types of Batch Totals

If the Following Receipts Were Processed on a Given Day	Customer Number	Customer Name	Amount
	053	Leven Bros.	$ 590.00
	007	Alpha	3,525.00
	056	Wolsey	480.00
	081	Eastgate	347.00
	036	Keller-Goodman	480.00
	012	Gamma	5,210.00
	043	Bart Bros.	288.00
	008	Griffin	750.00
	057	Cardwell	1,020.00
	063	Mann's	2,820.00
The control total would be			$15,510.00
The hash total would be	416 (the sum of customer numbers)		
The record count would be		10 (the number of documents)	

The three types of batch totals are illustrated in Figure 11.5.

2. *Check digit.* This digit is an extra digit of an identification number that is algebraically computed from the other digits and serves to detect data transmission or conversion errors.

Processing Control Terms

Processing controls are program steps to ascertain that predetermined conditions will be tested and certain errors in the input records will be detected when computer processing occurs. The major categories are as follows:

1. *Completeness test.* A test to ascertain that all information fields are complete.
2. *Validation test.* A test to ascertain that all information fields contain appropriate data. A dollar amount field should not contain alphabetic characters, for example.
3. *Sequence test.* A test to ascertain that data being processed are in the correct sequence.
4. *Limit or reasonableness test.* A matching of certain data in the input records being processed against a predetermined limit in the computer program. The purpose is to detect data above or below this limit. For example, if the number of hours worked falls outside certain upper or lower limits, a payroll transaction will be listed for investigation.

Individual Input Controls

Only transactions that have management's general or specific authorization should be accepted for computer processing. If a transaction is supported by a document, some evidence of approval is needed. Time cards and purchase invoices are examples. If a transaction is entered without a supporting document, a terminal user identification or some other means of authorization should be used.

Conversion of data into machine-readable form should be controlled. The use of control totals, hash totals, and record counts will help to detect errors made when data from source documents are transferred to computer files. When data are entered directly into a computer file through a scanner or a terminal, a computer edit program will help to detect errors.

Movement of data between one processing step and another, or between files, should be controlled. When data are moved, they can be lost, added, or altered. Control totals, hash totals, and record counts are helpful here.

Discussion of Processing Controls

Processing controls are sometimes called program controls. They consist of computer application programs that read the input data, test it for certain types of errors, and print messages if such errors are found in the data. These computer programs also test for certain error conditions in files as updating runs are made.

In general, processing controls are designed to prevent or detect the following types of errors:

1. Incomplete or duplicate processing of input transactions.
2. Processing and updating of the wrong files.
3. Processing of illogical, incomplete, or unreasonable input.
4. Loss or distortion of data during processing.

Individual Processing Controls

Control totals should be produced at an early point in the application by originators of source documents or by a control group. They should not be forwarded to the computer department. The computer then produces a set of control totals; a group independent of the computer department (the *control group,* for example) reconciles the two sets of totals.

Limit and reasonableness checks should be incorporated into the computer programs that edit the input data for errors. In this application, the computer program tests the input data for illogical conditions that should not exist. Some examples are 120 hours on a weekly time card, inventory quantity reduced to a negative value, an unusually large check issued to a small-volume vendor, or acceptance of a credit sale for a closed account.

Discussion of Output Controls

Output controls are designed to ensure that (1) the processing results are accurate and (2) only authorized personnel receive the output. A control group may be given the responsibility for implementing this control. They see that input data with errors are returned to the original source, properly corrected, and resubmitted. A control group reconciles control totals generated by the computer with the same totals originated at an earlier point in the system. Finally, the control group sees that output reports are given to the appropriate personnel.

Individual Output Controls

Some examples of individual output controls include the following:

1. Output control totals should be reconciled with input control totals.

2. Output should be scanned and tested by comparison to original source documents.
3. Output should be distributed only to authorized users.

APPROPRIATE CONTROLS FOR AN ONLINE SYSTEM

For an online system, access to the terminal should be controlled through use of periodically changed passwords. Unsuccessful attempts to access the system should be monitored.

In addition, this type of system should

1. Permit only terminal operators to enter or recall data. No terminal operator should have access to files or programs.
2. Contain appropriate edit steps in the computer programs so that unauthorized or improper transactions are rejected. Control totals of transactions should also be part of the computer programs. These control totals should be compared with similar totals generated when files are updated.

All processed transactions and master file changes should be recorded on another set of files accessible only to authorized personnel. For example, a record of every transaction and every master file change would be recorded in a file. Such a file could be used to review transactions and recreate master files.

CONTROL CONSIDERATIONS IN MINICOMPUTER AND MICROCOMPUTER SYSTEMS

The controls that auditors should evaluate in a minicomputer system depend on the type of system in use. Some minicomputer systems operate from a central computer with data stored in a central location as illustrated in Figure 11.2. Each minicomputer in the system updates the central database, as well as maintains files in its own areas. In this regard, a minicomputer system has some of the same characteristics as online systems with terminals at various locations, a significant difference being the processing and data storage capability of a minicomputer.

Other minicomputer systems have their own independent equipment and files and are similar to microcomputers. The files are updated when processing takes place; a central database is not updated. Audit trails must be created (if at all) on printed output rather than through magnetic media. To provide an adequate audit trail for logging transactions, it might be necessary to add a disk storage device to the system. If the minicomputer system is connected to a central computer, the auditor's control considerations are not significantly different from those already discussed. If the minicomputer system has independent equipment and files, each minicomputer location may have its own set of controls.

Microcomputers have some of the same characteristics as independent minicomputers; the equipment and files are independent of a central processor (although they may be connected in a network).

Given these characteristics, independent minicomputers and microcomputers have special control problems that may not exist in mainframe installations.

▶ **EXAMPLE**

Lack of segregation of duties among programming, operations, and control of data within the computer department.

▶ **EXAMPLE**

Inadequate processing controls in programs furnished by vendors, especially controls applicable to online processing.

▶ **EXAMPLE**

Access to data files and programs by a number of individuals.

▶ **EXAMPLE**

Files stored on removable disks.

▶ **EXAMPLE**

Lack of control over program changes, because the same person who makes program changes often controls data files and enters transactions.

Specifically, the control problems in an independent minicomputer or a microcomputer system can be divided into the following categories.

1. *General controls*
   a. *Segregation between computer functions and users.* This segregation of functions often does not exist because users also perform computer functions. Some segregation of functions between users may be feasible—for example, having one person enter and process data and another person maintain a control log.
   b. *Segregation within computer functions.* If the users perform computer functions, the segregation of functions suggested in (a) may be applicable. If computer processing and use of the computer are separated (unlikely in many systems), programming and computer operations should be segregated. If packaged software is used, this segregation of duties may occur automatically. If the company develops programs, the same person often performs programming and computer operations.
2. *Application controls*
   a. *Control of conversion of data into machine-readable form.* If some form of batch processing is used, this control can take the form of batch totals. A powerful computer edit program is also desirable.
   b. *Limit or reasonableness checks.* This control can often be accomplished by selecting appropriate application software packages.
   c. *Control over distribution of output to authorized users.* In small minicomputer or microcomputer systems, the familiarity of personnel makes it likely that output will be distributed correctly.

Given these problems, there are limited, but nevertheless vital, controls that an auditor should look for in reviewing independent minicomputer or microcomputer systems.

1. Adequate training of personnel who use the computers. The duties of these personnel should be documented.
2. Labeling of diskettes and separate secure storage.
3. Making of backup files.
4. Protection of critical software.
5. Frequent printouts of data processed on the computer.
6. If there is segregation between computer functions and users, the users should do the following:
   a. Authorize transactions.
   b. Use batching or other appropriate procedures to determine that all input is processed.
   c. Have control over changes to master files and resubmission of transactions rejected by computer edit programs.
   d. Balance master files from one processing cycle to another.

If there is no segregation between computer functions and users (which is often the case), the auditor may have to rely on extensive substantive tests.

OBTAINING AN UNDERSTANDING OF COMPUTER CONTROL PROCEDURES

The extent of understanding that auditors need about computer control procedures depends on a number of factors.

1. The complexity of the computerized operations.
   a. For the online operation illustrated in Figure 11.2, the auditor may need to obtain considerable knowledge. Each of the five departments has a separate microcomputer that processes transactions as they occur. All input occurs at the terminals, and files are updated as transactions are processed.
   b. For the batch processing operation illustrated in Figure 11.1 some knowledge of the computer operations would be necessary because computers are editing, updating, and processing the transactions. But the required knowledge might be less than in (a) because some parts of the system do not utilize computer processing. The source documents (sales invoices, credit memos, and remittance advices) are created independently, thus producing backup documentary evidence. Also, a batch processing system often has a better audit trail than an online processing system.
   c. For the microcomputer operation illustrated in Figure 11.3, less knowledge of computer operations is required than in (a). Part of the document processing is done manually, and the computer processing is limited by the software package.

2. The audit strategy. Again, using the operations illustrated in Figures 11.1 through 11.3, we can assume that different audit strategies might be employed for each of them.

    a. For the online operation illustrated in Figure 11.2, the auditor might use a *lower control risk approach* because of the extensive use made of computer processing. It might be more effective and efficient to perform tests of controls of the system than to conduct extensive substantive tests of related sales and accounts receivable assertions.

    b. For the batch processing operation illustrated in Figure 11.1 the auditor might also use a *lower control risk approach,* although tests of controls might be less extensive than those conducted on an online system. Also, the source documents and printed computer output provide a partial audit trail that may be used for substantive testing.

    c. For the microcomputer operation illustrated in Figure 11.3, the auditor might use a *primarily substantive approach.* The lack of segregation of duties in computer processing might cause the auditor to assess a high level of

FIGURE 11.6   **Controls in Different Types of Computerized Systems**

Questions Related to Control	Answer and Reason(s) for Answer		
	Batch Operation (Figure 11.1)	Online Operation (Figure 11.2)	Microcomputer Operation (Figure 11.3)
1. Is there proper job segregation?	Yes—a programmer codes programs, a machine operator runs the programs, and users enter data.	Yes—although the users perform some computer functions, one person enters data, and another person keeps a control log.	No—the bookkeeper prepares source documents, enters data, and receives output.
2. Is there adequate computer documentation?	Yes—there are program listings, logs of computer runs, etc.	Yes—there are program listings, logs of computer runs, etc.	No—commercial software is used.
3. Is there controlled access to computers, files, and programs?	Yes—only the computer operator has access to computer and files, and only the programmer can make changes to programs.	Yes—passwords and identification codes restrict access to data files and programs.	No—all office personnel have access to files, programs, and computer.
4. Are batch totals used?	Yes—control totals and record counts are used.	Yes—users make record counts of documents processed.	No—the bookkeeper informally reviews totals.
5. Is an edit program used?	Yes—data are edited before file updating or computer output.	Yes—comprehensive edit program checks data during online processing.	Yes—but the edit program is very limited.
6. Are control totals reconciled with input?	Yes—control group performs this function.	Yes—performed automatically by program; internal auditors review periodically.	No.

control risk and rely primarily on substantive tests for the related sales and accounts receivable assertions.

OBTAINING AN UNDERSTANDING OF COMPUTER CONTROL PROCEDURES—AN ILLUSTRATION

We will now assume that the auditor is obtaining an understanding of computerized control procedures for the operations illustrated in Figures 11.1 through 11.3. Taking the general and three application controls discussed earlier in the chapter, we will use Figure 11.6 to identify some of the computer controls (or lack of controls) the auditor might find for each of these operations.

SUMMARY

Using the material in Chapter 9 as a conceptual foundation, we discussed the controls that may exist in an entity with computerized operations. We also illustrated how the auditor would obtain an understanding of internal control of such an entity. In Chapter 12, we will continue our coverage of the computer environment by discussing and illustrating tests of controls and the assessment of control risk.

Chapter 11 ▶ GLOSSARY OF TERMS

Access controls   Controls designed to help prevent or detect errors or fraud caused by (1) improper use or manipulation of data files, (2) unauthorized or incorrect use of a computer file, or (3) improper use of computer resources.

Application controls   Controls that provide reasonable assurance that the recording, processing, and reporting of data are properly performed.

Audit trail   A chain of evidence provided through codes, cross-references, and documentation connecting account balances and other summary results with original transactions and calculations.

Batch control   A technique to help ensure that data flowing through the system are complete and accurate.

Batch processing   Processing of similar data at intervals or in batches.

Computer edit program   A computer program that subjects data to tests for accuracy, validity, reasonableness, and completeness.

Control group   An independent group of employees that performs tests of the accuracy of data flow to and from the computer and sees that output is distributed properly.

Data and procedural controls   Controls that provide a framework for controlling daily operations and establishing safeguards against processing errors.

Flowcharts   Diagrams of sequence, data flow, and processing logic in information processing.

General controls   The plan of organization and operation of the computer activity; the procedures for documenting, reviewing, testing, and approving systems or programs and changes thereto; controls built into the equipment by the manufacturer; controls over access to equipment and data files; and other data and procedural controls that affect the overall computer operations.

Input controls   Controls designed to provide reasonable assurance that data received for processing by computer have been properly authorized, converted into machine-sensible form, and identified and that data have not been lost, suppressed, added, duplicated, or otherwise improperly changed.

Microcomputers   Personal computers that perform a variety of functions; the equipment and files can be independent of a mainframe central processing unit.

Minicomputers   Physically small but powerful computer systems that often are used for single applications in larger systems.

Online processing   Processing of data as transactions occur; processing usually takes place when data are entered at a terminal.

Organization and operation controls   The general plan designed to effect a smooth operation, accomplish the assigned tasks, and minimize the opportunity for errors or fraud in the system.

Output controls   Controls designed to ensure the accuracy of the processing result and limit output to authorized personnel.

Processing controls   Controls designed to provide rea-

sonable assurance that data have been properly processed in a particular application.

Systems flowchart   A diagram that describes the sequence of major processing operations and the data flow to and from the files used in processing.

Chapter 11 ▶ REFERENCES

American Institute of Certified Public Accountants. *Professional Standards*
AU Section 319—*Consideration of Internal Control in a Financial Statement Audit*
Forgione, Dana, and Blankley, Allan. "Microcomputer Secu-

rity and Control," *Journal of Accountancy* (June 1990), pp. 83–90.
Steinberg, Richard M., and Johnson, Raymond N. "Implementing SAS No. 55 in a Computer Environment," *Journal of Accountancy* (August 1991), pp. 60–68.

Chapter 11 ▶ REVIEW QUESTIONS

11-1   Briefly describe six reasons why the auditor's approach to obtaining an understanding of internal control is different when a computer is used rather than manual processing.

11-2   In obtaining an understanding of the control environment that affects computer processing, the auditor will often consider several matters. Briefly describe these matters.

11-3   What is batch processing?

11-4   What function is performed by an edit program?

11-5   What is online processing?

11-6   What is the difference between a minicomputer and a microcomputer?

11-7   What three methods or audit techniques are used to obtain an understanding of the computerized elements of an accounting system?

11-8   Define each of the general controls.

11-9   Define each of the application controls.

11-10   Describe the three most common types of batch totals.

11-11   Describe five potential control problems in an independent minicomputer or microcomputer system.

11-12   Describe six controls that an auditor should look for in an independent minicomputer or microcomputer system.

11-13   Name two factors that determine the extent of knowledge that auditors need to obtain about computer control procedures.

11-14   Why might an auditor use a primarily substantive approach for the operation illustrated in Figure 11.3?

Chapter 11 ▶ OBJECTIVE QUESTIONS

(* = author prepared; ** = CPA examination)

*11-15   Which of the following is a systems flowchart?
  a. A description of the sequence of operations and logic in a computer program.
  b. A description of the sequence of major processing operations and the data flow to and from the files used in processing.

  c. A performance of tests of the data on the transactions record.
  d. A computer update program.

*11-16   Which of the following is not an application control?
  a. Input controls.

b. Processing controls.

c. Output controls.

d. Organization and operation controls.

*11-17 Which of the following procedures would not improve internal control in a computer system?

a. One computer operator running all programs.

b. Limited access to computer programs.

c. Programmers not operating the computers.

d. Programs documented with flowcharts.

*11-18 Which of the following is not a batch control?

a. Control total.

b. Hash total.

c. Record count.

d. Parity check.

**11-19 Which of the following *best* describes a fundamental control weakness often associated with computer systems?

a. Computer processing equipment is more subject to systems error than manual processing is subject to human error.

b. Computer processing equipment processes and records similar transactions in a similar manner.

c. Computer processing procedures for detection of invalid and unusual transactions are less effective than manual control procedures.

d. Functions that would normally be separated in a manual system are combined in the computer system.

**11-20 Matthews Corporation has changed from a system of recording time worked on clock cards to a computerized payroll system in which employees record time in and out with magnetic cards. The computer system automatically updates all payroll records. Because of this change

a. A generalized computer audit program must be used.

b. The potential for payroll-related fraud is diminished.

c. Part of the audit trail is altered.

d. Transactions must be processed in batches.

**11-21 Internal control procedures are ineffective when computer department personnel

a. Participate in computer software acquisition decisions.

b. Design documentation for computerized systems.

c. Originate changes in master files.

d. Provide physical security for program files.

**11-22 Which of the following is an example of application controls in computer processing systems?

a. Hardware controls.

b. Input controls.

c. Documentation procedures.

d. Controls over access to equipment and data files.

**11-23 Which of the following would most likely be a weakness in internal control of a client that utilizes microcomputers rather than a larger computer system?

a. Employee collusion possibilities are increased because microcomputers from one vendor can process the programs of a system from a different vendor.

b. The microcomputer operators may be able to remove hardware and software components and modify them at home.

c. Programming errors result in all similar transactions being processed incorrectly when those transactions are processed under the same conditions.

d. Certain transactions may be automatically initiated by the microcomputers, and management's authorization of these transactions may be implicit in its acceptance of the system design.

**11-24 Program controls in a computer processing system are used as substitutes for human controls in a manual system. Which of the following is an example of a program control?

a. Dual read.

b. Echo check.

c. Limit and reasonableness tests.

d. Key verification.

**11-25 Some computer processing internal control procedures relate to all computer activities (general controls), and some relate to specific tasks (application controls). General controls include

a. Controls designed to ascertain that all data submitted to the computer system for processing have been properly authorized.

b. Controls for documenting and approving programs and changes to programs.

c. Controls that relate to the correction and resubmission of data that were initially incorrect.

d. Controls designed to ensure the accuracy of the processing results.

**11-26 Which of the following employees normally would be assigned the operating responsibility for designing a computer processing installation, including flowcharts of data processing routines?

a. Computer programmer.
b. Systems analyst.
c. Data processing manager.
d. Internal auditor.

**11-27 When an online computer system is in use, internal control can be strengthened by
a. Providing for the separation of duties between data input and error listing operations.
b. Attaching plastic file protection rings to reels of magnetic tape before new data can be entered on the file.
c. Making a validity check of an identification number before a user can obtain access to the computer files.
d. Preparing batch totals to provide assurance that file updates are made for the entire input.

**11-28 When erroneous data are detected by computer program controls, such data may be excluded from processing and printed on an error report. The error report should probably be reviewed and followed up by the
a. Supervisor of computer operations.
b. Systems analyst.
c. Computer programmer.
d. Control group.

**11-29 Which of the following would increase control risk in a computer processing system?
a. The custodian of computer records maintains custody of computer program instructions and detailed listings.
b. The control group is solely responsible for the distribution of all computer output.
c. Computer operators have access to operator instructions and detailed program listings.
d. Computer programmers write and debug programs that perform routines designed by the systems analyst.

**11-30 The computer system most likely to be used by a large savings bank for customers' accounts would be
a. A batch processing system.
b. An online system.
c. A generalized utility system.
d. A direct-access database system.

**11-31 Which of the following would an auditor most likely use in obtaining an understanding of internal control?

a. Systems flowcharts.
b. Record counts.
c. Program listings.
d. Record layouts.

**11-32 Which of the following is not a characteristic of a batch processing computer system?
a. The collection of like transactions that are sorted and processed sequentially against a master file.
b. Keying of transactions, followed by machine processing.
c. The posting of a transaction, as it occurs, to several files, without intermediate printouts.
d. The production of numerous printouts.

**11-33 If a control total were to be computed on each of the following data items, which would best be identified as a hash total for a payroll computer application?
a. Department numbers.
b. Net pay.
c. Hours worked.
d. Total debits and total credits.

**11-34 When computer programs or files can be accessed from terminals, users should be required to enter a (an)
a. Parity check.
b. Personal identification code.
c. Self-diagnosis test.
d. Echo check.

**11-35 Misstatements in a batch computer system caused by incorrect programs or data may *not* be detected immediately because
a. Errors in some transactions may cause rejection of other transactions in the batch.
b. The identification of errors in input data typically is *not* part of the program.
c. There are time delays in processing transactions in a batch system.
d. The processing of transactions in a batch system is *not* uniform.

**11-36 Which of the following controls is a processing control designed to ensure the reliability and accuracy of data processing?

	Limit test	*Validity check test*
a.	Yes	Yes
b.	No	No
c.	No	Yes
d.	Yes	No

Chapter 11 ▶ DISCUSSION/CASE QUESTIONS

(* = author prepared; ** = CPA examination)

*11-37   For a number of years, the Keep Company had used a computer batch processing system for its credit sales transactions. As clerks made credit sales, a copy of the sales invoice was given to the customer and another copy was placed in the register drawer. At the end of each day, these sales invoice copies were batched by a control group. The data on the invoices were keyed into a transactions file. As the keying took place, an edit program checked data for certain error conditions and calculated batch totals. The control group compared the computer-generated batch totals with their own and made sure that rejected data were re-keyed. The file updating was performed in a manner similar to that shown in the systems flowchart in this chapter. The system seemed to work well and there were few complaints from customers.

However, Ms. Change, a new employee who worked in the computer department, suggested that an online system be installed. She contended that the batch processing system was too slow and inefficient. Under her suggested system, a terminal would be located in each department that sold merchandise. As a credit sale was made, the clerk would key the transaction at the terminal and the data would update the customer's account, which would be maintained on magnetic disk files. A sales invoice would be prepared and a copy given to the customer; but nothing would be done with the store's copy, except to place it in a file.

Mr. Keep, the owner, decided to follow Ms. Change's suggestion. The change was made, and for a short time everything seemed to work well.

Several months later, numerous customers began to complain of erroneous account balances. Some customers said that all items they purchased had not been charged to them. Other customers claimed that incorrect charges had been made to their accounts.

In an attempt to correct the problems, the controller tried to reconstruct all sales transactions made since the new system was installed. He discovered that all sales invoice copies had been thrown away and no separate computer record of the sales transactions had been made.

When the independent auditor (who had not been told of the change) obtained an understanding of internal control, she assessed control risk at maximum. An unusually large number of substantive tests were performed, including 100 percent confirmation of all accounts receivable balances. The auditor also wrote a long letter to the owner describing several reportable conditions and suggesting numerous controls for the new system.

Required:

a. Describe how this situation could have occurred (what improper functions were performed or what proper functions were not performed).

b. What controls were probably suggested by the auditor? Give reasons for each suggested control.

**11-38   Talbert Corporation hired an independent computer programmer to develop a simplified payroll application for its newly purchased computer. The programmer developed an online, data-based microcomputer system that minimized the level of knowledge required by the operator. It was based on typing answers to input cues that appeared on the terminal's screen, examples of which follow:

a. Access routine

1. Operator access number to payroll file?

2. Are there new employees?

b. New employees routine

1. Employee name?
2. Employee number?
3. Social security number?
4. Rate per hour?
5. Single or married?
6. Number of dependents?
7. Account distribution?

c. Current payroll routine

1. Employee number?
2. Regular hours worked?
3. Overtime hours worked?
4. Total employees this payroll period?

The independent auditor is attempting to verify that certain input validation (edit) checks exist to ensure that errors resulting from omissions, invalid entries, or other inaccuracies will be detected during the typing of answers to the input cues.

Required:

Identify the various types of input validation (edit) checks the independent auditor would expect to find in the computer system. Describe the assurances provided by each identified validation check.

*11-39   Examine Figure 11.3 and describe as many control problems as you think exist. (Use the diagram and any other logical assumptions from the diagram.) Classify the controls according to the following:

a. Organization controls.
b. Documentation controls.
c. Access controls.
d. Input controls.
e. Processing controls.
f. Output controls.

*11-40   Examine the systems flowchart shown on page 347 and write a detailed narrative of the procedures shown in the flowchart.

*11-41   Examine the program flowchart on pages 348–349 and write a narrative description of the computer processing shown. Include in your narrative a general description of the error messages. In the flowchart a transaction code one is a credit sale, a transaction code two is a cash receipt, and a transaction code three is a noncash credit.

*11-42   Ineffective internal control may allow errors or fraud to occur. For each of the following situations, indicate the error or fraud that could occur.

a. The computer operator, who has some knowledge of programming, is allowed unlimited access to programs.
b. The control totals are forwarded to the computer operator.
c. Computer files are not properly named.
d. The computer program has no programming controls.
e. No log is kept of computer operations.

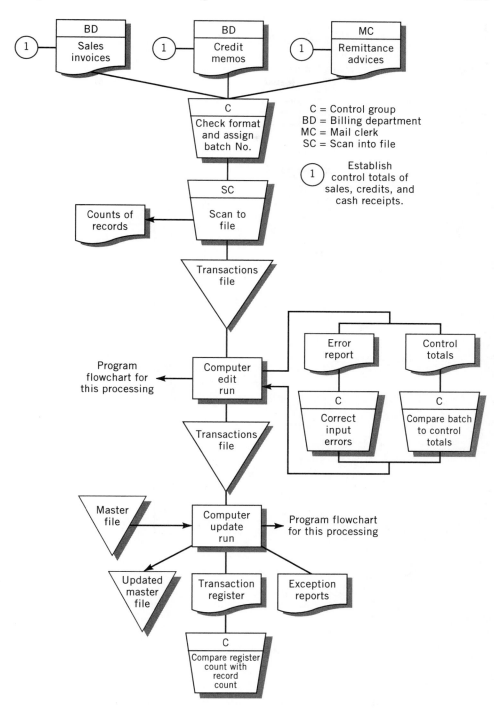

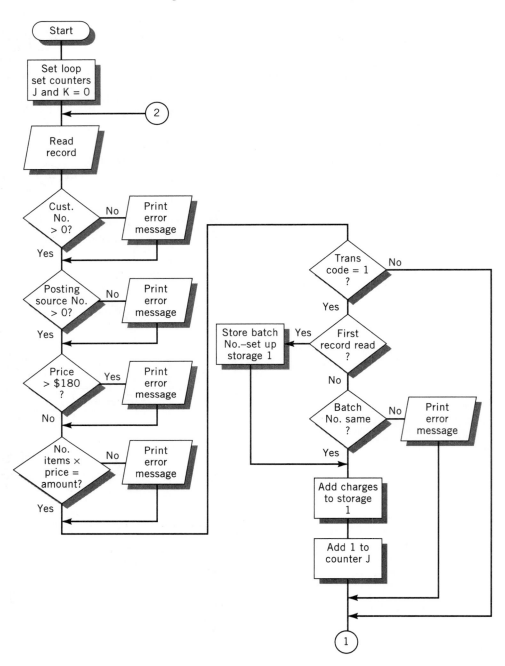

*11-43   Mr. A. O. Steady, a programmer for One Corporation, had been employed in his job for a number of years. He was the only programmer. There was a separate computer operator and input data operator.

The computer system provides for data from purchase invoices to be entered at a terminal. The data are processed through the computer, and checks for vendors are printed by the computer. Each check is compared with the purchase invoice by another individual before mailing.

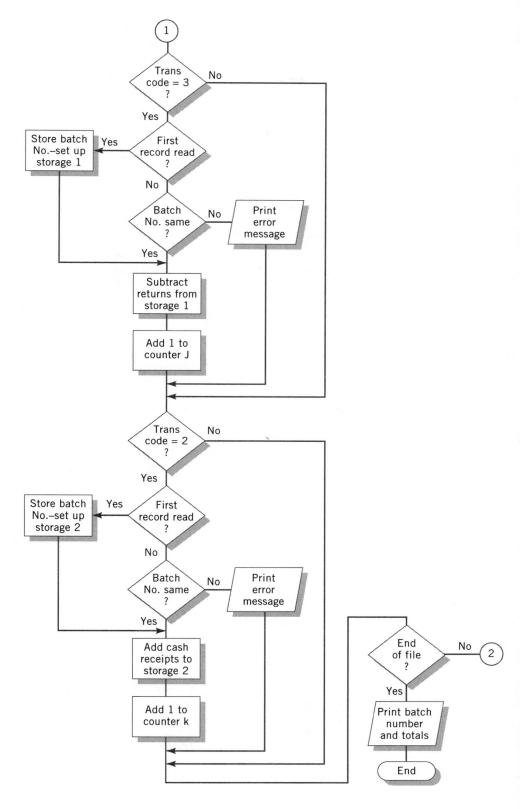

One day it was discovered that Mr. Steady had been receiving kickbacks from a company that had received money from One Corporation without sending them any merchandise. The president of the company was puzzled about how Mr. Steady could have perpetrated this fraud. There seemed to be a proper segregation of duties, and the programmer never handled the checks that were printed by the computer.

Required:

a. Explain how this fraud may have occurred and remained undetected.

b. Discuss some controls, including noncomputer types, that might have prevented or uncovered the fraud.

**11-44   George Beemster, CPA, is auditing the financial statements of the Louisville Sales Corporation, which recently installed a new computer. The following comments have been extracted from Mr. Beemster's notes on computer operations and the processing and control of shipping notices and customers invoices:

> To minimize inconvenience, Louisville converted without change its existing data processing system. The computer vendor supervised the conversion and has provided training to all computer department employees (except input data operators) in systems design, operations, and programming.
>
> Each computer run is assigned to a specific employee, who is responsible for making program changes, running the program, and answering questions. This procedure has the advantage of eliminating the need for records of computer operations, because each employee is responsible for his or her own computer runs.
>
> At least one computer department employee remains in the computer room during office hours, and only computer department employees have keys to the computer room.
>
> System documentation consists of those materials furnished by the computer vendor—a set of record formats and program listings. These and the tape library are kept on a desk in the computer department.
>
> The data processing manager considered the desirability of programmed controls but decided to retain the manual controls from the existing system.
>
> Company products are shipped directly from public warehouses, which forward shipping notices to general accounting. There a billing clerk enters the price of the item and accounts for the numerical sequence of shipping notices from each warehouse. The billing clerk also prepares daily control totals of the units shipped and the unit prices.
>
> Shipping notices and control totals are forwarded to the computer department for data entry and processing. Extensions are made on the computer. Output consists of invoices (in six copies) and a daily sales register. The daily sales register shows the aggregate totals of units shipped and unit prices, which the computer operator compares to the control totals.

Required:

Indicate the weaknesses that you see in the system and your recommendations for correcting these weaknesses.

**11-45   You are reviewing audit work papers containing a narrative description of the Tenney Corporation's factory payroll system. A portion of that narrative is as follows:

> Factory employees punch time cards each day when entering or leaving the shop. At the end of each week, the timekeeping department collects the time cards and prepares duplicate batch control slips by department showing total hours and number of employees. The time cards and original batch control slips are sent to the payroll accounting section. The second copies of the batch control slips are filed by date.
>
> In the payroll accounting section, payroll transaction data from the information on the time cards are keyed through a terminal to a transactions tape, and a batch total for each batch is keyed from the batch control slip. The time cards and batch

TENNEY CORPORATION
FLOWCHART OF FACTORY PAYROLL SYSTEM

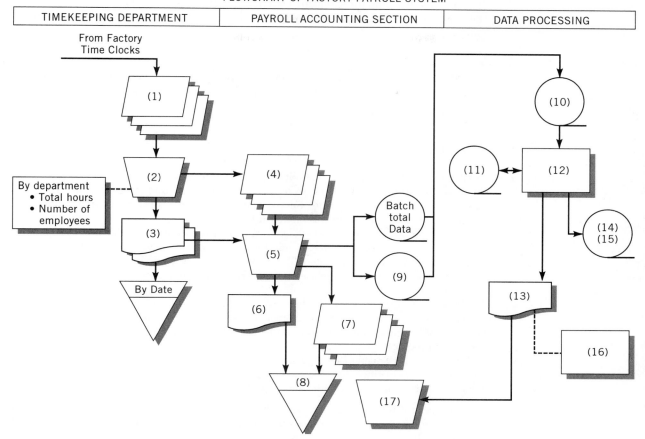

| TIMEKEEPING DEPARTMENT | PAYROLL ACCOUNTING SECTION | DATA PROCESSING |

control slips are then filed by batch for possible reference. The payroll transaction data and batch total data are transmitted to data processing. Each batch is edited by a computer program that compares each employee number against a master employee file and the total hours and number of employees against the batch total data. A detailed printout by batch and employee number indicates batches that do not balance and invalid employee numbers. This printout is returned to payroll accounting to resolve all differences.

In searching for documentation, you found a flowchart of the payroll system that included all appropriate symbols but was only partially labeled. The portion of this flowchart just described appears above.

Required:

a. Number your answers 1 through 17. Next to the corresponding number of your answer, supply the appropriate labeling (document name, process description, or file order) applicable to each number symbol on the flowchart.

b. Flowcharts are one of the aids an auditor may use to obtain an understanding of a client's internal control. List advantages of using flowcharts in this context.

**11-46 When auditing a computer accounting system, the independent auditor should understand how the use of computers affects the various characteristics of internal control. The independent auditor should be aware of those control procedures that are commonly referred to as "general" controls and those that are commonly referred to as "application" controls. General controls relate to all computer activities, and application controls relate to specific accounting tasks.

Required:

a. What are the general controls that should exist in computer-based accounting systems?

b. What are the purposes of each of the following categories of application controls?

    (1) Input controls.

    (2) Processing controls.

    (3) Output controls.

*11-47 Smaller Company is a manufacturer of plastic golf balls. Since the company was organized, it has used central processing for all of its computerized accounting operations. Early this year management decided to use microcomputers to process inventory transactions and maintain inventory records in the branch offices.

Several operators (who had previous word processing experience with microcomputers) were hired in each branch office. A number of programmers and computer operators in central processing were terminated. The newly hired microcomputer operators were given a two-week training course in the use of the appropriate software to process inventory transactions.

The microcomputers were located wherever they "would fit" in the respective branch offices. Diskettes were used for file storage and were stored in the same file drawers as the printouts of inventory transactions and records. All employees had access to the files. Only one set of diskettes was maintained.

The auditor for Smaller Company had not been consulted about the change to microcomputers for processing inventory transactions at the branch offices. Therefore, when he arrived late in the year to update his understanding of internal control, he discovered the following:

1. No one at the branch offices knew the correct amount of inventory for each type of plastic golf ball. The inventory amounts on printouts did not match the inventory control account in the general ledger maintained in the central accounting offices.

2. Diskettes were not labeled, and no one seemed to know the contents of each diskette.

3. Discounts were being lost because no one in the branch offices had the necessary invoice information to know when merchandise orders had been filled by vendors.

Because of these and other microcomputer inventory problems at the branches, the auditor was considering assessing a maximum control risk to inventory controls and performing extensive substantive tests on inventory assertions of existence and completeness.

Required:

a. Give probable reasons why the auditor found the previously described conditions.

b. What controls should now be put in or strengthened?

c. What potential problems are inherent in the use of microcomputers for accounting applications of this type?

Testing Controls and Gathering Evidence in a Computer Environment

"The real problem is not whether machines think, but whether men do."

B. F. SKINNER, *Contingencies of Reinforcement*

LEARNING OBJECTIVES

After reading and studying the material in this chapter, the student should be able to

▶ Analyze the difference between the following in a computer environment: (1) procedures for obtaining an understanding of controls and (2) related tests of controls.

▶ Describe the test data process.

▶ Design examples of (1) test data, (2) predetermined auditor's output, and (3) output for the computer edit program.

▶ Describe an integrated test facility, online audit monitoring, and parallel simulation.

▶ Assess computer controls by writing potential misstatements that could occur in a computerized system and controls that should prevent or detect these misstatements.

▶ Describe the detailed functions performed by computer-assisted audit programs.

▶ Write a brief paragraph describing computer-assisted audit programs.

▶ Provide examples of (1) output produced by a computer-assisted audit program and (2) audit procedures performed with this output.

▶ Provide examples of (1) spreadsheet working papers and (2) uses made of these working papers.

▶ Analyze the uses made of microcomputer systems in audit engagements.

▶ Write a brief critique of computer-assisted audit programs.

▶ Briefly describe expert systems.

Some methods used to conduct tests of controls do not require use of the computer and are common to all internal control processes. Observation of operations and examination of records and documents are examples. Other methods require use of the computer and are unique to internal control processes that are partially or completely computerized. We will illustrate the former set of methods in the following section and the latter set in the section entitled "Tests of Controls That Require Use of the Computer."

TESTS OF CONTROLS THAT DO NOT REQUIRE USE OF THE COMPUTER

Illustration of Tests of Controls

Figure 12.1 contains a list of (1) procedures the auditor might use for obtaining an understanding of controls and (2) related tests of controls the auditor might use to measure the effectiveness of design and operation of such controls in a computer environment. These procedures and tests do not relate to any particular system and are arranged according to the categories of general and application controls.

Discussion of Tests of Controls

Segregation of Duties Between the Computer Department and Computer Users

This control is one of the most important because it could determine whether control risk is assessed at or below maximum. (Refer to the batch processing system illustrated in Figure 11.1.) Because a mainframe is used for all computer processing, the auditor should be able to observe the operations of computer personnel in one area or department and determine that users are not involved in this operation. Segregation between computer personnel and users may be a major strength of this type of system.

Conversely, the auditor would have to separately observe each of the five departments shown in Figure 11.2. Such observation might show that the users perform computer operations, although other controls could exist that partially mitigate this weakness.

In the case of the microcomputer system shown in Figure 11.3, there is no comparable segregation of duties because the bookkeeper performs all key duties in the computer department. No observation is necessary, and the auditor would consider the implications of this lack of control in his or her assessment of control risk.

Segregation of Duties Within the Computer Department

Observation of operations and examination of documents in the computer department of the batch processing system illustrated in Figure 11.1 might show that (1) there are separate programmers and computer operators and (2) the duties of computer operators are rotated. The auditor could *observe* that control (1) is in place and could *examine* the computer usage logs to determine that control (2) is being effectively implemented. In Figure 11.3 there is no similar control to test because there is no separate computer department.

FIGURE 12.1 **Procedures for Obtaining an Understanding of Controls and Related Tests of Controls in a Computer Environment**

Procedures for Obtaining an Understanding	*Tests of Controls*
Organization and Operation Controls	
Review organization charts and job descriptions for evidence of proper segregation of duties between the computer department and computer users.	Observe the actual operation.
Inquire as to whether there is a policy prohibiting the computer department from correcting errors.	Observe the reconciliation of control totals with computer processing results.
Review appropriate documentation and make inquiries for evidence of proper segregation of duties within the computer department.	(a) Observe the operation. (b) Examine usage records for evidence of proper authorization for use of data files. (c) Examine logs to determine that computer operators' duties are rotated.
Review the organizational structure and relationships of the control group.	Examine, on a test basis, reconciliation of control totals by the control group.
Discuss with internal auditors their procedures for reviewing and testing computer processing activities.	Examine internal auditors' reports and workpapers.
Systems Development and Documentation Controls	
Review plans for controlling the conversion from one computer record to another to prevent unauthorized changes on master and transaction files.	(a) Observe conversion procedures. (b) Trace detailed records from old files to new ones.
Interview appropriate personnel to determine whether computer program changes have been authorized, tested, and documented.	Trace selected computer program changes to the appropriate supporting records and approvals.
Review documentation standards to determine whether they appear to provide for adequate documentation.	Examine selected documentation to assess conformance with the documentation standards.
Review the methods for determining that access to data files and programs are limited to authorized individuals.	Examine access records and attempt to access restricted files.
Input Controls	
Review procedures for determining that only properly authorized and approved input is accepted for computer processing.	(a) Examine, on a test basis, evidence of transaction authorization. (b) Investigate exceptions in the authorization process.
Review the procedures for controlling the conversion of input to machine-readable form.	(a) Observe verification procedures. (b) Compare edited transactions to original input.
Review the procedures used to determine that data movement from one processing step to another does not result in lost, added, or altered data.	Observe the procedures for moving data from one processing step to another and compare data between steps.

FIGURE 12.1   *(Continued)*

Procedures for Obtaining an Understanding	Tests of Controls
Processing Controls	
Review the controls used to prevent processing the wrong file or to detect errors in file manipulation.	Examine the console log for error messages and determine how errors are resolved.
Review the control totals used to verify data at appropriate points in the processing.	Observe the procedures for reconciling control totals.
Output Controls	
Review the procedures for reconciling output with control totals.	Observe the reconciliations.
Review the procedures for scanning output and comparing it to original source documents.	(a) Observe the verification procedures. (b) On a test basis, compare output with source documentation.
Inquire about the procedures for determining that output is distributed only to authorized users.	(a) Observe the distribution of the output. (b) Test the distribution of the output and determine that recipients are authorized personnel.

Documentation Standards for Adequate Documentation

In the case of all the systems illustrated in Chapter 11 (Figures 11.1 through 11.3), the auditor could examine selected documentation and evaluate it for completeness. For the small system illustrated in Figure 11.3, system documentation may be limited.

Limited Access to Data Files and Programs

If logs and records exist, the auditor would make inquiries and observe procedures to determine whether access is limited to authorized persons. For the batch system in Figure 11.1, the auditor might find that programmers are the only persons who have access to and can make changes to programs. The auditor might find extensive access to the microcomputer files in Figure 11.3. The online system in Figure 11.2 might allow employees to access only specific files relating to their duties.

Control to Prevent Lost, Added, or Altered Data

Observation of the movement of data would be different in Figures 11.1, 11.2, and 11.3. In each case, the auditor should observe the data input operations at the terminals.

Verification of Data During Processing

Some of the testing of processing controls might be performed with the computer, as discussed in the next section. But if control totals are used, the auditor could observe the procedures for reconciling control totals generated by the computer to those generated when the data are entered at terminals.

Procedures for Comparing Computer Output with Source Documents

In larger systems, this procedure might not be performed because of the volume of transactions and more efficient controls. If it were done (perhaps in the small system in Figure 11.3), the auditor could reperform the procedures on a test basis. In the past, some auditors relied heavily on this test because they were not able to use computer-assisted tests or it was impractical to do so.

TESTS OF CONTROLS THAT REQUIRE USE OF THE COMPUTER

Auditors may wish to test the computer programs themselves. Such methods are sometimes referred to as *through the computer approaches*. Some of the techniques, such as test data, test the functioning of computer programs on a "static" basis; that is, the program is not being processed by the client at the time it is tested. Other techniques, such as parallel simulation or integrated test facility, test the functioning of the computer programs as they are being processed by the client.

Auditing standards do not require that computer programs be tested, but if the auditor intends to assess control risk at less than maximum, one or more of these techniques may prove useful.

Test Data

One technique of testing through the computer, which involves the use of *test data*, was designed for batch systems. The method operates as follows.

1. Client documentation is reviewed, and controls are identified.
2. Simulated transactions, including records with errors, are created to test the identified controls.
3. These transactions are entered on the auditor's worksheet, along with the predetermined computer results.
4. The simulated transactions are processed with the client's computer program, and the computer results are compared with the predetermined results. If the two sets match, the controls are assumed to be functioning as called for in the program documentation.

The test data procedure is depicted in Figure 12.2, and shows the auditors' test data being entered from magnetic tape. If they wish, auditors could create the transactions in the source documents, which would be tantamount to testing the client's data entry technique.

What assurance do auditors have that they are using the correct program? If a different program is being used to perpetuate a fraud, the client might furnish the auditors with a program that correctly processes the test data, while he or she uses the other program to process the real data. This substitution is possible, but precautionary steps can be taken to lower the probability of such an occurrence.

For instance, the test data could be run on a surprise basis. However, a more practical approach might be for auditors to copy the client's program in advance of the test data run. Then, at the client's convenience, the test data could be processed, and the program used in this processing could be compared with the copy of the program obtained earlier.

FIGURE 12.2   Diagram of Test Data

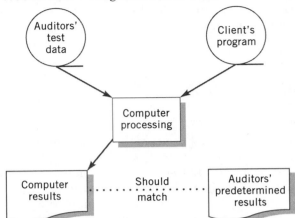

An Example of Test Data

Here is a specific illustration of the test data procedure. The systems flowchart in Figure 11.1 shows that there are two computer programs. The first program is an edit program designed to (1) print an error message for certain inaccurate or invalid data from the invoices, credit memos, and remittance advices and (2) print control totals for comparison with similar totals produced in the billing department and the mail room. The second program is an updating program that merges current transactions into the master file records. Although the auditor should test both computer programs, we will discuss only the edit program.

Some edit tests are incorporated in the edit program in Figure 11.1.

1. Completeness tests of the customer and posting source numbers. If the computer reads a record that has a blank or zeroes in either of these fields, an error message is printed.

2. A limit test of the price. The price of the most expensive item sold by the client is $180. If the computer reads a record that has a price in excess of this amount, an error message is printed.

3. A validity test of the amount. If the computer reads a record that contains an extension error on the total amount of the sale, an error message is printed.

Next, there are three sets of batch numbers. If the batch number is incorrect for any or all of the transaction codes, an error message or messages are produced. Finally, record counts and control totals are accumulated for all records that contain the daily batch numbers.

Figure 12.3 contains partially completed illustrations of (1) test data designed by auditors, (2) auditors' predetermined results, and (3) the actual computer output. Auditors enter one input record without errors to test the program output under conditions in which there are no inaccuracies. In addition, auditors enter one record for every type of error condition tested in the edit program. Because seven errors are possible, eight records are illustrated.

FIGURE 12.3   **Examples of Test Data**

Examples of Test Data Designed by Auditors

Type of Error	Transaction Code	Batch No.	Customer No.	Source No.	Name	Date	Description	No. of Items	Price	Amount
No errors	1	501	07	2102	Alpha	X91003	DX1 sofa	12	180.00	2,160.00
Invalid customer no.	2	2499		2349	Leven	X91003				590.00
Invalid source no.	3	501	10		Kellon	X91003	TX1 sofa	1	112.00	112.00
Excess price	1	501	07	2102	Alpha	X91003	G57 chair	11	245.00	2,695.00
Extension error	1	501	07	2102	Alpha	X91003	G57 chair	11	145.00	1,455.00
Billing batch no. in error	1	502	10	2103	Kellon	X91003	DX1 sofa	1	180.00	180.00
Billing batch no. in error										
Mail room batch no. in error										

Examples of Predetermined Output Designed by Auditors

The first record's processing should not show any errors.

The second record's processing should produce an error message: Invalid customer number.

The third record's processing should produce an error message: Invalid source number.

The fourth record's processing should produce an error message: Price in excess of limit.

The fifth record's processing should produce an error message: Extension error.

The sixth record's processing should produce an error message: Incorrect billing batch number.

The seventh record's processing should produce an error message: Incorrect billing batch number.

The eighth record's processing should produce an error message: Incorrect mail room batch number.

The batch totals produced by the computer should be

(1) Billing dept. record count _____   Control total _____

(2) Mail room record count _____   Control total _____

Form of Output for Computer Edit Program for Customer Charges and Credits

Transaction Code	Batch No.	Customer No.	Document No.	Date	No. of Items	Price	Amount
2	2499	0	2349	X91003			590.00
Invalid customer no.							
3	501	10	0	X91003	1	112.00	112.00
Invalid document no.							
1	501	7	2101	X91003	11	245.00	2,695.00
Price over limit							
1	501	7	2102	X91003	11	145.00	1,455.00
Incorrect extension							
Incorrect billing batch no.							
Incorrect billing batch no.							
Incorrect mail room batch no.							
billing batch no.		Mail room batch no.			No. records		Total

Critique of the Test Data Approach

A major benefit of using test data is the greater assurance that is gained about the reliability of the client's computer programs. The auditors have reasonable assurance that the programs tested function as prescribed, even though they may not be completely certain that they are testing the right programs.

However, the use of test data does have certain limitations.

1. A successful test data run does not necessarily indicate effective internal control because other types of errors or fraud could occur outside the computer processing area. A prime example is the failure of a mail clerk to report all cash receipts.

2. Test data determine whether the program that has been *furnished* the auditor is functioning as it should. The auditor cannot be *certain* that this is the same program used in daily operations, although proper precautions can greatly increase that assurance.

3. The test data approach is limited to a test of the functions in the *client's* program, and that program may be inadequate to edit the client's transactions.

4. The test data approach was designed for a batch processing system. The approach may not be suitable for online systems where there is no intermediate processing between the input devices and the central processing unit, and where more continuous processing takes place.

5. Developing test data can be time consuming, and the test data must be tailor-made for every application.

Regardless of these drawbacks, the use of test data can provide auditors with insights into the computer system that are not gained by ignoring the computer.

Integrated Test Facility

A variation of test data is the *integrated test facility*. Instead of running simulated data on a static basis with the client's computer program, the auditor runs simulated data while actual client data are being processed with the client's computer program. Like test data, computer results are compared with the auditor's predetermined results. To avoid contamination of actual client data, the simulated transactions are coded to a dummy subsidiary or branch, so that they can be extracted from the system when the processing is completed.

One advantage of using an integrated test facility is that it permits the auditor to test the processing of data under actual operating conditions. Another advantage is that the client's computer does not have to be dedicated entirely to testing simulated transactions. Figure 12.4 is a diagram of an integrated test facility. Note the similarity to the test data method illustrated in the previous section.

Online Audit Monitor

In Chapter 11, we described an online entry system as one in which transactions are captured and processed as they occur. If such a system is properly designed, it will include edit programs that test the accuracy, validity, and completeness of all transactions entering the system. In such a system, batch entry is not used; therefore, testing techniques such as test data may not be feasible.

FIGURE 12.4   **Diagram of Integrated Test Facility**

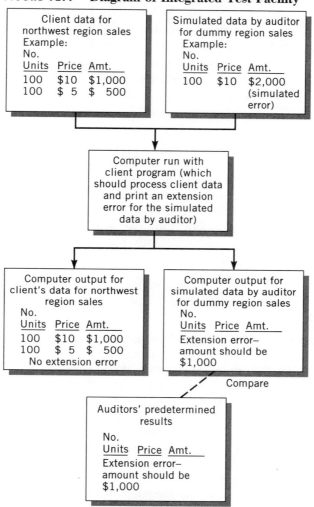

A testing technique that has been devised to test transactions as they are entered into the system on an online basis is called an *online audit monitor.* Basically, this monitor is a set of auditor's criteria that is added to the computer edit programs used by the client to edit transactions. The criteria might call for certain transactions entering the system to be "flagged" and printed (or written to a file) for review by the auditor. For example, the auditor may designate that charge sales be flagged if those sales were made to a customer who had an outstanding balance more than 90 days overdue. The auditor can follow up to see if these sales are a violation of the credit limit policy (a test of controls of credit policy procedures).

Online audit monitoring generally follows this sequence.

1. As a transaction is entered into the system, the standard edit program checks are applied to the data (checking the proper number of numeric characters, for example).

2. When the standard edit checks are completed, the auditor's specified criteria are applied to the transaction. In our example, charge sales would be edited to ascertain if they were made to customers who have balances 90 days overdue.

3. Any transaction that meets the auditor's criteria is flagged and written to a file or is displayed on an online terminal located in the auditor's office.

4. The transaction is marked with a special character or code that identifies it as a transaction subject to auditor's review.

5. The transaction is released for normal processing.

Online audit monitoring has a number of advantages. First, it can be used with a system that processes transactions as they occur. Second, it can be used without interfering with the client's normal processing routine. In fact, auditors can enter criteria from their own terminal if proper arrangements are made with the client.

If the auditor selects too many transactions, it can impact the client's normal processing. The possibility also exists that users might alter transactions that they know will be subjected to the auditor's edit process. For this reason, the auditor's edit criteria should be kept confidential or revealed only to selected client personnel.

Parallel Simulation

In the computer testing techniques illustrated in the three previous sections, the auditor tests the client's program with simulated data or tagged client transactions. In the *parallel simulation* method, actual client data are processed both with the client's program and a program written by the auditor. The computer results of processing data with both programs are compared.

One advantage of parallel simulation is that tests can be made for error conditions that may not be detected by the client's program. When test data are used, the auditor must confine his or her testing to controls contained in the client's program. An obvious disadvantage of parallel simulation is the cost of writing a unique computer program for each audit.

To illustrate, assume that the client's program *does not* contain a test for extension errors, but the auditor's program *does* contain such a test. Figure 12.5 shows the different computer results produced by parallel processing of actual client data.

ASSESSMENT OF CONTROL RISK

The guidelines for assessing control risk are the same regardless of whether the system is computerized.

1. The auditor will assess control risk at maximum if the primarily substantive approach is used and no tests of controls are performed.

2. If tests of controls are performed, the auditor will use this decision criterion.

   a. If the tests show that the internal control policies and procedures for the assertion have an effective design and operation, the assessed level of control risk will be less than maximum.

FIGURE 12.5   **Diagram of Parallel Simulation**

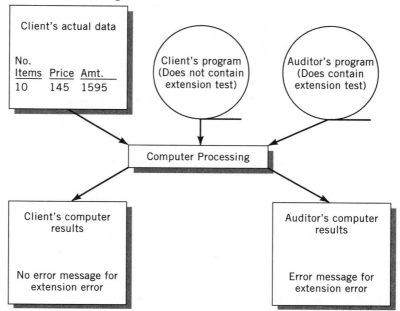

b. If the tests show that the policies and procedures are not designed or operating effectively, the auditor will assess control risk at maximum.

In Figure 12.6, assume that the auditor is assessing control risk for assertions embodied in the three operations shown in Figures 11.1 through 11.3. In Figure 12.6 we use a form for assessing control risk by considering misstatements (similar to Figure 10.2).

DEFINITION OF COMPUTER-ASSISTED AUDIT PROGRAMS

A *computer-assisted audit program* (sometimes referred to as a generalized computer audit program) involves the use of *auditor-developed* computer programs to perform certain data processing functions, such as (1) reading computer files, (2) selecting information, (3) performing calculations, and (4) printing reports in a format specified by the auditor. Such programs are useful because auditors can learn to use them quickly, they allow direct access to the data, and documentation is often a byproduct of their use.

DETAILED FUNCTIONS OF COMPUTER-ASSISTED AUDIT PROGRAMS

A computer-assisted audit program can perform many detailed functions. Here is a comprehensive, but not exhaustive, list of program capabilities. Many of the audit procedures are discussed in Chapters 15 through 18.

FIGURE 12.6   **Assessment of Computer Controls**

Misstatements That Could Occur	*Internal Control Policies and Procedures*		
	Batch Processing System	*Online System*	*Microcomputer System*
1. Unauthorized changes could be made to the programs by the computer operator.	Programmer and computer operator are separate.	Users enter data, but other functions are separate.	Commercial software package is used by bookkeeper.
2. Unauthorized programs could be run.	There are program listings and logs.	There are program listings and logs.	There are no program listings or logs.
3. Unauthorized changes could be made to master files.	Only users have access to master files.	Only users have access to master files.	Bookkeeper has access to all files.
4. Computer programs could contain errors that cause data to be improperly processed.	An independent group tests all programs on a periodic basis.	Internal auditors test all programs.	Commercial software is used.
5. Input data could be lost or altered during processing.	Batch totals are used.	Record counts are made.	No batch totals are used.
6. Data could contain blank fields, illogical conditions, out-of-limit amounts, etc.	Data are subjected to computer edit program before file updating.	Computer edit program checks data.	Limited edit program is used.
7. Computer output may not be consistent with data input from terminals.	Control totals are reconciled with input.	Control totals are reconciled with input.	No control totals are generated.
Overall control risk assessment	Less than maximum	Less than maximum	Maximum

1. Scanning computer records for exceptional or unusual characteristics and preparing a file of these characteristics for the auditors' investigation. Some examples are as follows:
   a. Accounts receivable balances over a certain amount, over the credit limit, or containing a credit balance.
   b. Unusually large inventory balances.
   c. Unusual payroll situations such as terminated employees or excessive overtime.
2. Making or checking computations and listing for the auditors' review computations that are incorrect. Some examples are as follows:
   a. Payroll calculations.
   b. Interest calculations.
   c. Depreciation calculations.
   d. Calculations of various prepaid items.

3. Comparing data on different records or files and listing unusual or irregular results, such as the following:

    a. Comparing accounts receivable master file balances between two dates with credit sales, cash collections, and noncash credits between the same dates.

    b. Comparing number of employees on the master payroll files with number of employees on personnel records.

4. Selecting and obtaining various types of samples. Included among these might be the following:

    a. Accounts receivable and accounts payable confirmations.
    b. Property and equipment additions.
    c. Inventory items.
    d. Charges to an expense account.

5. Preparing various analyses and listings that facilitate the audit of certain accounts. Some of these are the following:

    a. Accounts receivable aging schedules.
    b. Analysis of inventory by date of purchase.
    c. Statistics relating to various accounts, such as accounts receivable and inventory turnover.
    d. Trial balances and lead schedules.

All these listed capabilities of computer-assisted audit programs have one common trait. The auditor employs a developed series of computer programs to produce various lists, analyses, and so on from data maintained in the client's computerized files. Access to this information is considered essential, or certainly desirable, to perform the audit. If a computer-assisted audit program was not available, printouts of data would probably be obtained from the client's computer files. Manual analyses would then be made from such data.

DESCRIPTION OF COMPUTER-ASSISTED AUDIT PROGRAMS

Figure 12.7 shows the *general* method that is employed, although individual systems differ from one CPA firm to the next. The *auditors' specifications* are the descriptions of the audit objectives and the types of files to be used in computer processing. The computer-assisted audit program is written for the individuals performing the audit. It is not necessary for the auditors to understand the minute features of the programming techniques, but they need to be knowledgeable of the audit objectives and the characteristics of the client's system from which the information is taken.

An added feature sometimes used is a special software processor that converts the auditors' specification data into a problem-oriented or high-level language program. This program, in turn, processes the client's files, producing the desired information to be used in the examination of the appropriate amount. Such a technique reduces the auditors' need for firsthand knowledge of the programming lan-

FIGURE 12.7   **Diagram of Computer-Assisted Audit Program**

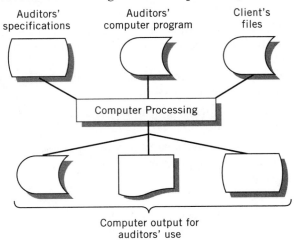

Computer output for
auditors' use

guage. It does, however, sharpen the necessity of understanding the audit objectives and the manner in which the data are stored in the client's computer files.

AUDIT OBJECTIVES AND COMPUTER CAPABILITIES

A computer-assisted audit program does not produce all the necessary evidence in the audit of a company's financial statements. Although computations, comparisons, and other clerical functions may be performed with this computerized process, it remains for the auditors to use much of the output in conducting the *same*

FIGURE 12.8   **Uses of Computer-Assisted Audit Program**

Output Produced by the Computer-Assisted Audit Program	Audit Procedures Performed with This Output
1. Listing of accounts receivable balances that exceed the credit limit.	1. Discussions with client personnel on causes and effect on allowance for doubtful accounts.
2. Listing of accounts receivable credit balances.	2. Inquiries concerning the question of reclassifying such balances as current liabilities.
3. Listing of unusually large inventory balances.	3. Investigation of possible obsolescence and errors in computation; observation of client's inventory count.
4. Accounts receivable and accounts payable confirmations.	4. Summarization of confirmation results and followup on customer's or vendor's exceptions.
5. Listing of property and equipment additions.	5. Examination and analyses of vendor invoices supporting such additions.

procedures that they would have if the information had been acquired through manual methods.

To illustrate this point, Figure 12.8 on page 366 again lists some of the output obtained from processing the client's files by a computer-assisted audit program. To the right of each listing are descriptions of appropriate audit steps to be taken *with* the information produced by computer processing.

Computer-assisted audit programs produce necessary information for the conduct of an audit, but in many instances additional work must be performed. Such programs provide the most aid during the phases of the audit that call for calculations, listings, clerical comparisons, and so on. On the other hand, although computer printouts furnish information that can be used to make inquiries and conduct observations, this computer output is no substitute for these audit procedures themselves.

THE USE OF MICROCOMPUTERS TO GATHER AND DOCUMENT AUDIT EVIDENCE

Since being introduced into commercial use, auditors have developed numerous applications for the use of microcomputers to gather and document audit evidence. The use of spreadsheets has been particularly prevalent because many audit working papers are in this form.

Some descriptions of spreadsheet working papers now being used by many CPA firms are shown in Figure 12.9 and illustrated in Chapters 15–18 of this text. Discussions in Chapters 15–18 provide explanations of how these working papers are used to document the evidence gathered on the various financial statement accounts.

FIGURE 12.9   Descriptions of Spreadsheet Working Papers

Spreadsheet Working Paper	Use Made of Working Paper	Text Reference
Customer trade receivables aged listing	To document customers to whom accounts receivable confirmations are sent and to aid in ascertaining the reasonableness of the allowance for doubtful accounts	Chapter 15
Accounts payable confirmation control	To document the vendors to whom accounts payable confirmations are sent and to describe the audit procedures performed on these accounts	Chapter 16
Equipment additions	To document the individual additions to equipment selected for testing and to describe the audit procedures performed on these additions	Chapter 17
Analysis of legal expense	To document the detail of the expenditures for legal expense and to describe the auditing procedures performed on these expenditures	Chapter 18

MICROCOMPUTER SYSTEMS
IN AUDIT ENGAGEMENTS

Laptop computer systems can be carried to an audit engagement and set up quickly for on-site work. This tool may eventually automate most aspects of the audit.

Mircrocomputer-based audit tools developed by CPA firms assist auditors in gathering, analyzing, and distributing information for a variety of uses but primarily for auditing. Computer systems capitalize on the development of the microcomputer, which permits a variety of computer applications to be performed on equipment that can be transported easily and set up on a desktop. Computer systems enable auditors to complete more quickly and efficiently many time-consuming functions that have traditionally been performed manually. They improve the quality of audits by allowing auditors to use more time to solve complex auditing problems.

These standalone microcomputer systems do not require but are likely to have a connection with client computer systems. The auditor uses these systems to accumulate, analyze, and evaluate data.

The following descriptions show some of the uses of these computer systems.

1. *Trial balance and financial statement processing.* These systems permit the preparation of trial balances, including posting audit adjustments and reclassifications, and the drafting of financial reports to be accomplished more efficiently and reliably.

2. *Audit programming.* These systems assist in designing for each client an efficient and complete audit program that takes into consideration all relevant factors. Through its integration of a variety of audit information, these systems are able to consolidate and analyze data developed from such diverse sources as the trial balance, various client files, workpapers, and public databases.

3. *Detailed workpaper preparation.* Auditors have traditionally spent considerable time preparing detailed analyses. These systems assist in this preparation by providing automated mechanisms to handle detailed clerical functions. With an automated spreadsheet, auditors can improve the reliability of such workpapers and reduce preparation time.

4. *Audit confirmations.* Confirmation preparation and control represent a time-consuming audit task that will be assisted by computerization. Statistics regarding confirmations that have been mailed and received, or are still outstanding, can be analyzed quickly.

5. *Statistical sampling.* Statistical sampling capabilities that were previously available only from a timesharing network or had to be produced manually can be applied by auditors using these systems to provide timely and accurate information needed to prepare audit samples and analyze results.

6. *Database retrieval.* Data related to the client's industry, including financial or product news and other relevant information, can be obtained quickly and efficiently by using these systems to draw directly on public databases. This capability will assist auditors in pricing client investment portfolios, comparing client and industry data, and preparing background information for client reports.

7. *Engagement management.* Audit administration also benefits from these systems.

Through access to operating office scheduling and time-gathering databases, audit managers have the tools available for better execution of their engagement responsibilities.

8. *Word processing.* Word processing can be used by auditors for preparing audit and client memoranda, correspondence, and reports more efficiently.

CRITIQUE OF COMPUTER-ASSISTED AUDIT PROGRAMS

The Auditors' Computer Proficiency

The most efficient use of these software packages occurs when the auditors comprehend the computer system in use. To possess this understanding, auditors should have a workable computer "vocabulary" and should be familiar with the way data are processed on machine-readable records and stored in computerized files.

Auditors also need an understanding of flowcharting and should be able to read various types of documentation, such as record layouts. They should be able to visualize their objectives, the file systems used by the client, and the output required from application of the computer-assisted audit program to these files.

Fraud Detection

Computer-assisted audit programs are generally not designed to detect fraud. However, the use of auditors' software provides some advantages over manual auditing should certain types of fraud exist in the client's organization. If computers are being employed to perpetrate fraud, an "around-the-computer" approach is less likely to provide evidence of these occurrences.

One of the most publicized frauds in recent years was the *Equity Funding* case. This case was not technically a computer fraud but a fraud aided and partially concealed through the *use* of computers. In this case, the company maintained a set of fictitious insurance policies on computer files (accessible for manual scrutiny only through printouts).

Through the use of some clever programming techniques, Equity Funding restricted the policy information shown on the printouts, so that all such policies had the appearance of legitimacy. Client computer printouts of data stored in the files did not provide sufficient evidence to detect the fraud.

Whenever data are stored on magnetized "invisible" devices, the application of a CPA firm's own program is expected to produce more reliable results than other approaches. An important question is whether the cost of developing and applying such methods is worth the benefit to be derived.

At the present time, many CPA firms use computer-assisted audit programs. Supervisory responsibility for program operation is placed on specially trained individuals who acquire the necessary computer knowledge either through in-house seminars or prior academic background. However, the option of using such programs is evolving into a necessity as more companies develop computerized systems. Understanding of computer-assisted audit programs is becoming more commonplace.

EXPERT SYSTEMS

As computer power is enhanced and auditors are faced with making decisions in more complex environments, some accounting firms have begun to develop expert systems to assist their personnel in the audit process. An expert system is a complex system of computer programs that models the decision process of a human expert. The psychological methods used to gain an understanding of the human expert's decision processes and the conversion of these decision processes into mathematical equations and computer programs are far beyond the scope of this text. However, auditing students should be aware that such systems are under development and, in some cases, in limited use. Some of the initial expert systems are used to assess control risk, evaluate loan collectivity, and evaluate whether a company can continue as a going concern. Additional expert systems may be developed to support other auditor judgments.

Chapter 12 ▶ GLOSSARY OF TERMS

Auditors' specifications   Descriptions of the audit objectives and the types of files to be used in computer processing.

Computer-assisted audit program   A computer program or set of computer programs designed by the auditor to gather evidence.

Integrated test facility   A variation of test data whereby simulated data and actual client data are run simultaneously with the client's program and computer results are compared with auditors' predetermined results.

Online audit monitor   A set of auditors' criteria that is added to the computer edit programs used by the client to test transactions entered into the system through a terminal.

Parallel simulation   A method whereby actual client data are processed with both client's and auditors' programs and the computer results are compared.

Test data   Simulated transactions created by the auditor and processed by the client's computer program(s). The computer output is compared with the auditors' predesigned output.

Through the computer approaches   Methods for testing computer programs.

Chapter 12 ▶ REFERENCES

Jacobson, Scott D., and Wolfe, Christopher. "Auditing with Your Microcomputer," *Journal of Accountancy* (February 1990), pp. 70–80.

Lovata, Linda M. "The Utilization of Generalized Audit Software," *Auditing: A Journal of Practice and Theory* (Fall 1988), pp. 72–86.

Chapter 12 ▶ REVIEW QUESTIONS

12-1   What is the purpose of tests of controls?

12-2   What is meant by "through the computer approaches" to performing tests of controls?

12-3   Contrast the purpose of and the methods of performing the four following tests of controls in a computer system.
   a. Test data.
   b. Integrated test facility.

c. Online audit monitor.

d. Parallel simulation.

12-4 What are some of the limitations of using test data?

12-5 Describe the advantages and disadvantages of using online audit monitoring.

12-6 Describe the use of parallel simulation to test the client's computer program.

12-7 Describe the guidelines for assessing control risk.

12-8 What are computer-assisted audit programs?

12-9 Give five examples of functions that can be performed by a computer-assisted audit program.

12-10 Name four types of spreadsheet working papers that can be produced with microcomputers.

12-11 What items should auditors consider when deciding whether to use computer-assisted audit programs?

Chapter 12 ▶ OBJECTIVE QUESTIONS

(* = author prepared; ** = CPA examination)

*12-12 Which of the following tests of controls require use of the computer?

a. Observe the reconciliation of control totals with computer processing results.

b. Design and process test data.

c. Examine usage records for evidence of proper authorization for use of data files.

d. Examine internal auditors' reports and workpapers.

*12-13 Which of the following tests of controls do not require use of the computer?

a. Compare computer output with source documentation.

b. Test data.

c. Integrated test facility.

d. Parallel simulation.

*12-14 Which of the following is a description of the integrated test facility?

a. Simulated data and actual client data are processed with the client's computer program.

b. Simulated data are processed on a static basis with the client's computer program.

c. Auditors' criteria are added to the computer edit programs used by the client.

d. Actual client data are processed with both the client's computer program and the auditors' computer program.

*12-15 Which of the following is not performed by computer-assisted audit programs?

a. Scanning or examining computer records.

b. Checking computations.

c. Comparing data on different records.

d. Assessing the sufficiency of the client's adjustment for inventory obsolescence.

**12-16 Which of the following statements most likely represents a disadvantage for an entity that keeps microcomputer-prepared data files rather than manually prepared files?

a. Attention is focused on the accuracy of the programming process rather than errors in individual transactions.

b. It is usually easier for unauthorized persons to access and alter the files.

c. Random error associated with processing similar transactions in different ways is usually greater.

d. It is usually more difficult to compare recorded accountability with physical count of assets.

**12-17 An auditor most likely would introduce test data into a computerized payroll system to test internal controls related to the

a. Existence of unclaimed payroll checks held by supervisors.

b. Early cashing of payroll checks by employees.

c. Discovery of invalid employee I.D. numbers.

d. Proper approval of overtime by supervisors.

**12-18 Assume that an auditor estimates that 10,000 checks were issued during the accounting period. If a computer application control that performs a limit check for each check request is to be subjected to the auditor's test data approach, the sample should include

a. Approximately 1,000 test items.

b. A number of test items determined by the auditor to be sufficient under the circumstances.

c. One transaction.

d. A number of test items determined by the auditor's reference to the appropriate sampling tables.

Question 12-19 is based on the following flowchart.

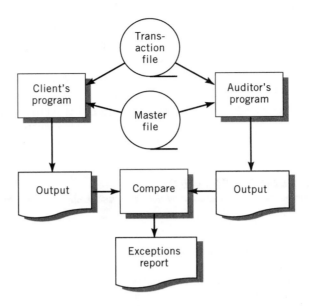

**12-19 The above flowchart depicts
  a. Program code checking.
  b. Parallel simulation.
  c. Test data.
  d. Controlled reprocessing.

**12-20 Auditing by testing the input and output of a computer system instead of the computer program itself will
  a. Detect all program errors, regardless of the nature of the output.
  b. Not detect program errors that do not show up in the output sampled.
  c. Provide the auditor with the same type of evidence.
  d. Not provide the auditor with confidence in the results of the auditing procedures.

**12-21 Which of the following is *not* among the errors that an auditor might include in test data when auditing a client's computer system?
  a. Numeric characters in alphanumeric fields.
  b. Differences in description of units of measure.
  c. Authorization code.
  d. Illogical entries in fields whose logic is tested by programmed consistency checks.

**12-22 When an auditor tests a computerized accounting system, which of the following is true of the test data approach?
  a. Test data must consist of all possible valid and invalid conditions.
  b. The program tested is different from the program used throughout the year by the client.

  c. Several transactions of each type must be tested.
  d. Test data are processed by the client's computer programs under the auditor's control.

**12-23 A primary advantage of using computer-assisted audit programs to audit the financial statements of a client that uses a computer system is that the auditor may
  a. Consider increasing the use of substantive tests of controls in place of analytical procedures.
  b. Substantiate the accuracy of data through self-checking digits and hash totals.
  c. Reduce the level of required tests of controls to a relatively small amount.
  d. Access information stored on computer files while having a limited understanding of the client's hardware and software features.

**12-24 An auditor would least likely use computer software to
  a. Access client data files.
  b. Prepare spreadsheets.
  c. Access control risk.
  d. Perform parallel simulations.

**12-25 An auditor using audit software probably would be least interested in which of the following fields in a computerized perpetual inventory file?
  a. Economic order quantity.
  b. Warehouse location.
  c. Date of last purchase.
  d. Quantity sold.

Chapter 12 ► DISCUSSION/CASE QUESTIONS

(* = author prepared; ** = CPA examination)

**12-26 Johnson, CPA, was engaged to audit the financial statements of Horizon Incorporated, which has its own computer installation. While obtaining an understanding of internal control, Johnson found that Horizon lacked proper segregation of the programming and operating functions. As a result, Johnson assessed control risk at maximum.

Required:

a. Give reasons why Johnson made this assessment.

b. What are compensating general controls that Johnson might find to lower his assessment of control risk? Do not discuss hardware and application controls.

c. If no compensating general controls were found by the auditor, what effect would this have on substantive tests?

*12-27 Refer to Question 11-44 in Chapter 11. For each weakness noted in the question, indicate a general control or an application control that would overcome that weakness and how that control could be tested. Be specific in discussing the type of control (for example, an access control relating to access to computer programs or a processing control that edits the data, etc.). Give reasons why the controls that you describe relate to the weaknesses.

*12-28 During an audit of a company that uses computers, Mr. Sure, the auditor, decided to process test data with some of the client's computer programs. The computer output matched his predesigned output. Later, however, Mr. Sure discovered that some of these computer programs were producing improper output. Indicate reasons why this could have happened.

**12-29 The following five topics are part of the relevant body of knowledge for CPAs who have fieldwork or immediate supervisory responsibility in audits involving a computer:

1. Computer equipment and its capabilities.

2. Organization and management of the computer function.

3. Characteristics of computer-based systems.

4. Fundamentals of computer programming.

5. Tests of computer programs.

CPAs who are responsible for computer audits should possess certain general knowledge on each of these five topics. For example, on the subject of computer equipment and its capabilities, the auditor should have a general understanding of computer equipment and should be familiar with the uses and capabilities of the central processor and microcomputers.

Required:

For each of the topics two through five, describe the general knowledge that should be possessed by CPAs responsible for computer audits.

*12-30 Two auditors for the CPA firm of Alford & Alford were engaged in a discussion about the best way to test the computer controls of their client, Mod-Comp., Inc. Jane Tester contended that the traditional test data method would be best because the client's computer system still used batch processing in some of its applications. Jim Progemer stated that they should develop their own computer program so that they would have more flexibility in testing the client's computer controls.

Required:

[If you wish to test only the general knowledge in the chapter, cover only requirement (a); requirement (b) is more specific.]

a. Discuss the advantages and disadvantages of the two techniques advocated by each of the auditors. (*Note:* Try to develop some answers in addition to those you obtain from reading the appropriate sections of the chapter.)

b. Show how each of these techniques would operate by developing your own data, such as the following:

   (1) Develop five items of test data, the predetermined output, and the form of the computer output for the test data approach.

   (2) Develop five items of client's actual data and develop a description of the auditors' computer program that would test these data. Show the form of the computer results and the client's output and indicate why they do or do not match.

*12-31 Refer to Chapter 11 and review Figures 11.1 through 11.3. Then review Figure 12.6 in this chapter.

a. The auditor decided to use the following audit strategies.

   (1) A lower control risk approach for the batch processing system in Figure 11.1.

   (2) A lower control risk approach for the online system in Figure 11.2.

   (3) A primarily substantive approach for the microcomputer system in Figure 11.3.

   Give reasons why the auditor probably used each of these audit strategies.

b. The auditor assessed control risk at a lower level for the batch processing system in (1) than for the online system in (2). Give reasons why.

*12-32 The auditors of Update Company were considering the use of a computer-assisted audit program to gather and document evidence from their client's computerized files. Most of the transactions, including accounts receivable and inventory, were processed by Update Company's computer system.

One of the auditors, Ms. Current, suggested that as much information as possible be taken from Update Company's computerized system by the use of a computer-assisted audit program. She made a list of each financial statement account on which information could be taken from computerized files with the use of a computer-assisted audit program. She also made a list of the information for each account that could be taken from the computer files in this manner. The other auditor, Mr. Leave, agreed that much information could be obtained from Update Company's computer files in an efficient way by using the computer-assisted audit program. He contended, however, that the information itself was not an audit procedure and that audit procedures would have to be performed on each item of information taken from the computer files. He wondered whether it would be more efficient simply to obtain printouts of the computer files and select the information they needed from these printouts to conduct the necessary audit procedures.

Required:

a. List the accounts and the information for each account that Ms. Current probably had in mind. (*Hint:* Consider each account on which computer files are probably maintained and list the information the auditor would probably need.)

b. List the audit procedures that Mr. Leave probably has in mind that will be conducted with the use of the information taken (at Ms. Current's suggestion) from Update Company's computer files.

c. What potential problems could the auditor have if no computer-assisted audit program is used?

**12-33 A CPA's client, Boos & Baumkirchner, Inc., is a medium-sized manufacturer of products for the leisure-time activities market (camping equipment, scuba gear, bows and arrows, etc.). A computer system maintains inventory records of finished goods and parts. The inventory master file is maintained on a disk. Each record of the file contains the following information:

Item or part number
Description
Size
Unit of measure code
Quantity on hand
Cost per unit
Total value of inventory on hand at cost
Date of last sale or usage
Quantity used or sold this year
Economic order quantity
Code number of major vendor
Code number of secondary vendor

In preparation for year-end inventory, the client has two identical sets of preprinted inventory count cards prepared. One set is for the client's inventory counts, and the other is for the CPA's use to make audit test counts. The following information has been recorded on records that can be scanned:

- Item or part number
- Description
- Size
- Unit of measure code

In taking the year-end inventory, the client's personnel will write the actual counted quantity on the face of each record. When all counts are complete, the counted quantity will be processed against the disk file, and quantity-on-hand amounts will be adjusted to reflect the actual count. A computer listing will be prepared to show any missing inventory count records and all quantity adjustments of more than $100. These items will be investigated by client personnel, and all required adjustments will be made. When adjustments have been completed, the final year-end balances will be computed and posted to the general ledger.

The CPA has available a computer-assisted audit program that will run on the client's computer and can process disk files.

Required:

a. In general and without regard to the preceding facts, discuss the nature of computer-assisted audit programs and list the various types and uses of such programs.

b. List and describe at least five ways a computer-assisted audit program can be used to assist in all aspects of the audit of the inventory of Boos & Baumkirchner, Inc. (For example, the program can be used to read the disk inventory master file and list items and parts with a high unit cost or total value. Such items can be included in the test counts to increase the dollar coverage of the audit verification.)

*12-34 The following is a list of tasks performed by auditors in gathering evidence to support their opinion. For each task, indicate whether a computer-assisted audit program could be used. Indicate the reasons for your answer.

a. Selecting accounts receivable confirmations.

b. Comparing subsidiary amounts to general ledger control amounts.

c. Investigating accounts receivable confirmation responses.

   d. Inquiries on the collectibility of customer accounts.

   e. Extracting important items from the minutes of meetings of the board of directors.

   f. Preparing a list of property and equipment additions in excess of a certain dollar amount.

   g. Comparing capital stock issuances with legal authorizations.

   h. Determining the adequacy of insurance coverage.

   i. Testing the accounts receivable aging schedule to supporting documents.

*12-35   In many cases, the auditor uses the output of a computer-assisted audit program for the same purpose as if the output were obtained through manual means. For each of the following examples of computer-assisted audit program output, indicate the use that the auditor would make of the output in conducting the audit. For example, a computer-generated list of unusually large inventory balances might be used to test for possible inventory obsolescence.

   a. Bank reconciliations for all the company's cash accounts.

   b. An aged accounts receivable schedule.

   c. A list of unusually large inventory balances (list a procedure other than testing for possible inventory obsolescence).

   d. A list of property and equipment additions and retirements.

   e. A list of vendors from whom large dollar purchases were made during the year.

   f. A list of employees who have received overtime pay in excess of a certain amount.

   g. A set of comparative financial statements for the two previous years.

**12-36   An auditor accesses a magnetic disk file that contains the dollar amounts of all client inventory items by style number. The information on the disk is in no particular sequence. By use of a computer-assisted audit program, how can the auditor best ascertain that no consigned merchandise is included in the file?

*12-37   An auditor's client has a magnetic disk that contains the detail of its customers' insurance policies by policy number. Unknown to the auditor is the fact that many of the policies are for nonexistent customers. To prevent these nonexistent policies from being printed and tested by the auditors, a special code was placed in the account number of fictitious policies. When the computer read this code, the policy data associated with it were not printed.

   Required:

   Indicate how the auditor could have used a computer-assisted audit program to detect this coverup.

**12-38   In the past, the records to be evaluated in an audit have been printed reports, listings, documents, and written papers, all of which are visible output. However, in fully computerized systems that employ daily updating of transaction files, output and files are frequently in machine-readable forms. Thus, they often present the auditor with an opportunity to use the computer in performing an audit.

   Required:

   Discuss how the computer can be used to aid the auditor in examining accounts receivable in such a fully computerized system.

**12-39   After determining that computer controls are valid, Hastings is reviewing the sales system of Rosco Corporation to determine how a computer-assisted audit program may be used to assist in performing tests of Rosco's sales records.

   Rosco sells crude oil from one central location. All orders are received by mail and indicate the preassigned customer identification number, desired quantity, proposed delivery date, method of payment, and shipping terms. Since price fluctuates daily, orders do not indicate a price. Price sheets are printed daily, and details are stored in a disk file. The details of orders are also maintained on a disk file.

Each morning the shipping clerk receives a computer printout that indicates details of customers' orders to be shipped that day. After the orders have been shipped, the shipping details are entered into the computer, which simultaneously updates the sales journal, perpetual inventory records, accounts receivable, and sales accounts.

The details of all transactions, as well as daily updates, are maintained on disks that are available for Hastings' use in the performance of the audit.

Required:

a. How may Hastings use a computer-assisted audit program to perform substantive tests of Rosco's sales records in their machine-readable form? *Do not discuss accounts receivable and inventory.*

b. After having performed these tests with the assistance of the computer, what other auditing procedures should Hastings perform to complete the audit of Rosco's sales records?

**12-40 Microcomputer software has been developed to improve the efficiency and effectiveness of the audit. Electronic spreadsheets and other software packages are available to aid in the performance of audit procedures otherwise performed manually.

Required:

Describe the potential benefits to an auditor of using microcomputer software in an audit as compared to performing an audit without the use of a computer.

Evidence of Financial Statement Assertions

"The most savage controversies are about those matters as to which there is no good evidence either way."

BERTRAND RUSSELL, *An Outline of Intellectual Rubbish in Unpopular Essays*

LEARNING OBJECTIVES

After reading and studying the material in this chapter, the student should be able to

► Describe guidelines for assessing the (1) competency of audit evidence and (2) sufficiency of audit evidence.

► Describe each of the means of gathering audit evidence.

► Analyze the different characteristics of audit evidence and the reliance that can be placed on each type.

► Analyze how auditors (1) use management assertions to establish audit objectives and (2) reason from audit objectives to audit procedures.

► Compare audit evidence obtained by inquiry and by confirmation.

► Assess special problems associated with auditing accounting estimates.

► Describe guidelines that may affect the use of analytical procedures used as substantive tests.

► Describe the business approach to gathering evidence.

► Describe how ratio analysis can be a tool in detecting financial statement misstatements.

► Describe the characteristics of regression analysis and how it can be used to determine where special audit effort is needed.

► Illustrate how audit work can be performed on pairs of accounts.

► Describe how auditors detect transactions with related parties.

► Describe how auditors make an evaluation of the client's ability to continue as a going concern.

► Describe how the review process provides the means for controlling the quality of the performance of the audit procedures.

► Assess how auditors use known, projected, and likely misstatements to evaluate audit findings.

► Describe the ways audit findings are communicated to the client.

In this chapter we explore the general characteristics of evidence-gathering techniques for financial statement assertions. Comprehensive coverage of selected audit procedures is included in subsequent chapters. These chapters relate to the third symbol in Figure 13.1, which illustrates that the purpose of evidence gathering for financial statement assertions is to establish detection risk.

FIGURE 13.1   General Flowchart of an Audit

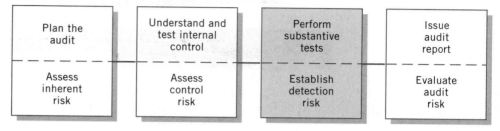

The Philosophy of Evidence Gathering

THE PHILOSOPHY OF EVIDENCE GATHERING

The Third Standard of Fieldwork

AU Section 326 (*SAS No. 31*) describes the third standard of fieldwork as follows:

> Sufficient competent evidential matter is to be obtained through inspection, observation, inquiries, and confirmations to afford a reasonable basis for an opinion regarding the financial statements under audit.

The term *evidence gathering* may be used to refer to the acquisition of evidence regarding assertions embodied in year-end financial statement balances and disclosures, however, in a broader context the term represents most of the acts performed by auditors to form an opinion as to the fairness of financial statements. In the latter sense evidence gathering includes the assessment of inherent and control risks.

The auditor's report presented in Chapter 1 stated that an audit is designed to provide *reasonable assurance* that the financial statements are not materially misstated. Thus, the auditor will not attempt to obtain evidence that would provide absolute or complete assurance, even if that were possible. Rather, the auditor evaluates the competency and sufficiency (as those terms are described in the next section) of evidence to decide whether it meets the reasonable assurance standard.

Guidelines for Evidence Gathering

Auditors evaluate the competency and sufficiency of audit evidence. Competency refers to the validity and relevance of the evidence, whereas sufficiency refers to the amount of evidence to be obtained. Some *general* guidelines are furnished in AU Section 326 (*SAS No. 31*), but otherwise auditors apply judgment in selecting specific audit procedures and deciding the amount and types of evidence to be gathered.

The Competency of Audit Evidence

Certain types of audit evidence may be more competent, that is, more valid and relevant, than others. The following guidance assists auditors in evaluating the competency of various types of audit evidence.

Evidence from Independent Sources

AU Section 326 (*SAS No. 31*) states that

> When evidential matter can be obtained from independent sources outside an entity, it provides greater assurance of reliability for the purposes of an independent audit than that secured solely within the entity.

Two landmark fraud cases (*Ultramares* and *McKesson & Robbins*) might have been detected in the audits if evidence of accounts receivable and inventory had been obtained from independent outside sources. There is general agreement with the theoretical guideline that "outside" evidence should be obtained, if possible. The auditors' practical problem, however, is determining whether specific outside evidence can be gathered. Discussion of certain accounts shows which ones might be susceptible to outside corroboration.

The key is whether the information in question is known by some outside party. For example, the amounts of cash and marketable securities probably can be substantiated independently if they are held by outside entities. In contrast, deferred income taxes and goodwill are created as the result of internal calculations, and outside confirmation of authenticity cannot be obtained by auditors.

Accounts receivable and accounts payable usually qualify for independent outside verification because they represent individual balances owed by customers and to creditors. Sales and cost of products sold typically do not qualify for the same basic reason that deferred income tax and goodwill do not—these two income statement accounts cannot be authenticated by outside entities in the aggregate.

As a general rule auditors will attempt to confirm with an independent outside source (1) tangible assets held by outside organizations, (2) debts owed to or by the client, and (3) other information that there is reason to believe an outside source can verify.

Evidence and Control Risk

When accounting data and financial statements are developed under conditions of low control risk there is more assurance about their reliability than when they are developed under conditions of high control risk.

> The more effective the internal control, the more assurance it provides about the reliability of the accounting data and financial statements.

The question of how much or what type of audit scope adjustment to make for the quality of internal control is a matter of judgment for which there are few definite criteria. Some auditors might confine tests of certain accounts to analytical procedures if internal control is exceptionally strong. Other auditors might take a different viewpoint and make a smaller change in the amount of testing.

The inventory account can be used to illustrate the relationship between control risk and substantive testing. What change can auditors make in the nature, timing, or extent of substantive tests of the existence of inventory if control risk is assessed at a low level? One answer is that the client's inventory count may be observed at times other than year-end *if* an accurate perpetual inventory system is in use.

If the auditors observed the client's inventory count at an interim date and a review of the inventory system and tests of the perpetual inventory records gave them reasonable assurance that these records were reliable, the year-end balance probably would be acceptable. Some review would be made of the intervening transactions in the client's perpetual inventory records from interim date through year-end. But because the reliability of the inventory records has already been established, this would not be a detailed review.

If control risk relating to the existence of inventories is assessed at maximum, an extensive year-end inventory observation by the auditor might not produce audit evidence as competent as the preceding interim observation.

Evidence from Direct Personal Knowledge

The third guideline for judging the competency of audit evidence is as follows:

> The independent auditor's direct personal knowledge, obtained through physical examination, observation, computation, and inspection, is more persuasive than information obtained indirectly.

Inventories again provide an example of the relative competency of evidence. Assume that this account consists of physical quantities held for the client by a public warehouse. A letter from the warehouse attesting to the existence of the inventories furnishes auditors with evidence that the inventories do exist. However, physical observation of the inventories gives auditors *more persuasive* evidence of existence.

Even physical observation of the inventories may not furnish auditors with completely reliable evidence. For example, the inventory may consist of grain stored in a storage silo, and an auditor may be unable to distinguish his or her client's grain from that owned by others. Therefore, the term *persuasive* is used rather than *convincing*.

One can easily ascertain some accounts that are suitable for evidence gathering through direct personal knowledge.

1. Marketable securities can be examined.
2. The client's count of physical inventories can be observed.
3. Taxes on income can be computed and compared with the client's computation.

Direct personal knowledge by the auditor may not produce competent evidence if specialized knowledge is required. As discussed in Chapter 8, the auditor may consider the use of a specialist to value works of art, estimate mineral reserves, make actuarial determinations, and so forth.

The Sufficiency of Audit Evidence

The Persuasiveness of Evidence

AU Section 326 also contains criteria for judging the sufficiency of audit evidence; that is, how much and what type should be gathered. One guideline relates to persuasiveness:

The amount and kinds of evidential matter required to support an informed opinion are matters for the auditor to determine in the exercise of his professional judgment after a careful study of the circumstances in the particular case. In the great majority of cases, the auditor finds it necessary to rely on evidence that is persuasive rather than convincing.

A good illustration of the difficulty of gathering convincing evidence is the process of evaluating the allowance for doubtful accounts. The account is an estimate of the amount necessary to reduce the accounts receivable balance to its realizable amount. The estimate is based on the client's judgment as to which accounts or what percentage of the accounts receivable balance will be uncollectible.

There is no way to confirm the collectibility of the account balance with an independent source, and it cannot be verified by inspection. Auditors usually determine what method the client used to calculate the allowance (perhaps from an aging schedule). Next, the auditors test the accuracy of the client's calculations. Finally, the auditors render a *judgment* as to whether the client's assumptions are reasonable. In all likelihood, some of the best evidence that auditors can acquire is a summary of the collection history and some opinions (often from the client) on the collectibility of slow-paying accounts. This evidence may be persuasive but far from completely convincing.

The Cost of Obtaining Evidence

Another guideline on the sufficiency of evidence is contained in AU Section 326.

An auditor typically works within economic limits; his opinion, to be economically useful, must be formed within a reasonable length of time and at reasonable cost. . . . As a guiding rule, there should be a rational relationship between the cost of obtaining evidence and the usefulness of the information obtained.

This guideline suggests that auditors should consider the relationship between (1) the value of additional assurance that can be obtained by gathering further evidence and (2) the cost of gathering such evidence. Assume that an audit client has 1,000 individual customer accounts that comprise total accounts receivable. The auditor has decided to gather evidence regarding the existence of accounts receivable by confirmation procedures and considers the following sample sizes and related levels of assurance. (These levels of assurance may be considered implicitly and may not be quantified.)

Number of confirmations	Level of assurance	Increase in Confirmations	Increase in Assurance
100	80%	100	80%
200	90	100	10
300	95	100	5
400	97	100	2
500	98	100	1
.	.	.	.
1000	99+	100	—

Each additional 100 confirmations, at approximately the same cost, provides less and less *additional* assurance. An auditor uses professional judgment to determine the point at which additional confirmations cost more than the value of the additional assurance obtained. It is not unlikely that different auditors may select different cutoff points because professional judgments may vary.

Although an auditor considers the cost of obtaining evidence in relation to its usefulness, the difficulty and expense involved in testing a particular item do not constitute valid reasons for omitting a test that, in the auditor's judgment, is required to comply with generally accepted auditing standards. For example, if a significant portion of inventory is stored at a remote location, the extra time and expense required to observe that inventory would not justify omitting the procedure if the auditor believed that observation was necessary.

To be useful, an auditor's opinion must be formed within a reasonable period of time. For example, if auditors could wait one year after the balance sheet date to issue their reports, they could make more precise estimates of the allowance for doubtful accounts because they could determine which accounts receivable balances were subsequently collected and which were subsequently written off. However, financial statements that are a year old would be of little use to stockholders and creditors. Therefore, to permit issuance of their reports on a timely basis, auditors consider less precise and more subjective evidence to be sufficient.

The Evaluation of Evidence

A criterion for evaluating audit evidence is contained in AU Section 326.

> In developing his opinion, the auditor should give consideration to relevant evidential matter regardless of whether it appears to corroborate or to contradict the assertions in the financial statements.

Auditors may be tempted to search for evidence that confirms their beliefs about the accounting records. For example, if an auditor believes that the error rate in a population is 5 percent, he or she is likely to be satisfied with the result of a sample that indicates an error rate of 5 percent or less. On the other hand, if the result of a sample indicates a 6 percent error rate, the auditor may be tempted to increase the sample by the number of items which, if they contain no errors, will reduce the sample error rate to 5 percent. This practice seems contrary to the preceding criterion. The auditor should not attempt to convert contradictory evidence to corroborative evidence or vice versa. If the preceding sample size was originally too small, it should have been increased regardless of the sample outcome, not because of it. Auditors should maintain an attitude of *professional skepticism* toward the evidence they obtain and client assertions in the financial statements.

EVIDENCE GATHERING

The collective purpose of all audit procedures is to gather sufficient competent evidence to form an opinion regarding the financial statements taken as a whole. In a narrower sense, however, the individual audit procedures depend on (1) the nature of the account or assertion under examination, (2) the objectives of auditing that account or assertion, (3) the risks associated with that account or assertion, and (4) the documents or records used to compile the account balance or assertion.

For example, certain accounts, such as sales and expenses, represent totals of transactions for a certain period, usually a year. Other accounts, such as property and equipment, represent accumulated balances from several years. Still other accounts represent balances with a rapid turnover, such as cash and accounts receivable. Other aspects of an account that influence audit procedures are volume of transactions (usually small for capital stock and long-term debt and large for cash and accounts payable), and verifiability (such as physical observation of inventories and calculation of deferred charges).

Audit procedures also depend on individual assertions within an account balance. For example, audit procedures for the existence assertion relating to accounts receivable will be different from audit procedures for the valuation assertion relating to the same account.

A discussion of evidence gathering, then, must include consideration of the following factors:

1. The means of gathering audit evidence.
2. The characteristics of such evidence.
3. The objectives of auditing a particular account (including their relationship to assertions regarding that account).
4. The audit procedures required to satisfy the objectives.

The first two factors are generally applicable to the audit of any account, whereas the last two are unique to each account.

The Means of Gathering Audit Evidence

Generally, evidence-gathering techniques can be categorized as follows. (Not all these methods may be applicable to each account.)

1. *Observation.* Auditors observe or watch the performance of some function. This means of gathering evidence is often used to obtain assurance that physical items, such as inventories, exist by observing client personnel counting them. The auditor should recognize, however, that the counting procedures might not be performed in the same manner when the auditor is not present. This may be particularly important when the auditor cannot observe all client count teams over the entire inventory counting period.

2. *Confirmation.* Auditors obtain acknowledgments in writing directly from third parties of transactions, balances, and other information. Because confirmations produce evidence from sources outside an entity, they are generally considered to result in competent evidence.[1]

3. *Calculation.* Auditors recompute certain account balances. Amounts such as

---

[1] However, the auditor should not consider confirmations to produce infallible evidence because in studies where erroneous confirmations have been intentionally mailed to customers, a surprisingly low number (47 percent) of customers reported the discrepancies to the auditor. See "An Empirical Study of Accounts Receivable Confirmations as Audit Evidence," by Paul Caster in *Auditing: A Journal of Practice and Theory* (Fall 1990), pp. 75–91.

depreciation expense and amortization of goodwill are created by client calculations and can only be tested by the auditor's calculation. Because calculation involves the direct personal knowledge of the auditor, it generally produces competent evidence.

4. *Analysis.* Auditors combine and decompose amounts in meaningful ways to allow application of audit judgment. For example, an auditor analyzes an aged trial balance for accounts receivable to assist in forming a judgment as to the adequacy of the allowance for doubtful accounts.

5. *Inquiry.* Auditors question client personnel about company policies, transactions, and balances, and they listen and evaluate their responses. Inquiries may be the least competent means of gathering evidence because they are directed to the individuals who are the subject of the audit and who may have reasons to provide biased answers. For this reason, inquiry alone will seldom provide sufficient competent evidence for an important assertion of a material account balance.

6. *Inspection.* Auditors inspect documents relating to transactions and balances. Examples are the inspection of vendor invoices and canceled checks to obtain assurance regarding the rights and valuation assertions of property and equipment. This means of gathering evidence is generally competent if the documents inspected are valid and relevant.

7. *Comparison.* Auditors relate two or more transactions or balances. A common example is the performance of analytical procedures where a current-year balance is compared with the prior-year and budgeted balances. This means of gathering evidence involves evaluating the reasonableness of the assumption that an account balance is not materially misstated, but it does not directly determine an account's validity.

For the audit of certain accounts, all seven techniques might be used. The inventory account serves as an example.

1. Normally, the client counts inventory quantities at year-end. The evidence of these quantities can be obtained by *observation* of the client's count.

2. Some of the year-end inventory may be on consignment or in public warehouses. Evidence of the existence of this merchandise can be acquired by *confirmation* from the party holding the inventory.

3. Evidence that inventory listings have been properly extended and totaled is acquired by *calculation*.

4. For inventory to be stated fairly at the balance sheet date, the client should make a proper year-end cutoff (a determination that only goods on hand at the end of the year are included in inventory and that all liabilities for goods on hand are recorded properly). To determine that a proper inventory cutoff is made, the auditors use *analysis*.

5. During the process of observing the client's inventory count, auditors sometimes have questions about the manner in which various quantities are determined and the possible obsolescence of certain items. The auditors may attempt to obtain answers to these questions by *inquiry* of client personnel.

6. The testing of inventory transactions represented by vendor invoices, material

issue tickets, shipping records, and so on is a necessary part of determining the reliability of the records that support the inventory account. These documents can be tested by *inspection*.

7. Inventory should be priced at the lower of cost or market. Auditors can gather evidence that this procedure is used by making *comparisons* of inventory cost to vendor invoices and price lists.

The auditor uses the seven techniques to design the specific audit procedures to be applied in each area of the audit.

The Characteristics of Audit Evidence

The auditor should appreciate the different characteristics of audit evidence and the reliance that can be placed on each type. Audit evidence can be characterized as one of the following types:

1. Direct personal knowledge of the auditor.
2. Evidence from third parties received directly by the auditor.
3. Evidence generated by third parties, but received and held by the client.
4. Evidence generated by the client.

The first and second types of evidence are generally considered to be the most persuasive, as noted earlier in the chapter. The first type consists of observations and calculations made by the auditor. The second type consists of direct communications with customers, creditors, and others who have information concerning the client.

The third type of evidence includes purchase orders from customers, purchase invoices from vendors, bank statements, titles to properties, insurance policies, and so forth. The fact that independent parties prepare the documents and send them to the client adds reliability to this type of evidence. Client custody of these documents takes away some of their reliability.

Comment   Cases have occurred where auditors have been misled by altered copies of documents. Copying machines were used to change original documents and to create false documents. To alleviate this risk, auditors should be sensitive to the possibility that a document is false and should insist on inspecting only original documents.

The fourth type consists of the client's underlying accounting data as well as corroborating documents. This type of evidence is illustrated in Figure 13.2.

An auditor normally prefers evidence of the first or second type if available, but in many situations it is impossible or impracticable to obtain (as in the audit of payroll expense, unamortized debt discount, etc.). In using evidence of the fourth type, the auditor must be particularly alert and consider, among other things, the source from which the evidence originated within the client company. For example, more reliance may be placed on a sales invoice supported by a shipping ticket from the shipping department than on a journal entry prepared within the accounting department. Similarly, an auditor may place more reliance on an explanation for a variation in annual sales received from a plant manager than on a similar explana-

FIGURE 13.2   Examples of Client-Generated Evidential Matter

Underlying Accounting Data	Corroborating Evidence
General ledger	Copies of sales invoices
Subsidiary ledgers	Copies of purchase orders
General journal	Canceled checks
Sales journal	Purchase requisitions
Purchases journal	Receiving reports
Voucher register	Check requests
Cost allocation worksheets	Minutes of meetings of board of directors and stockholders
Bank reconciliations	

tion received from the chief accountant. The reason for this bias is that the chief accountant generally will give an explanation to support the amounts shown in the accounting records, whereas the plant manager, who may be unaware of what is shown in the accounting records, is more likely to base the explanation on actual operating factors. The auditor attempts to obtain the most independent evidence that is available. As mentioned earlier, however, the auditor's decisions concerning what evidence to gather are complicated by time constraints and cost-benefit considerations.

In the audit of accounts receivable, the auditors could use the second type of evidence to satisfy the objective of ascertaining the existence of the balances that constitute this account. Evidence of proper valuation, however, would require some use of the third and fourth evidence categories.

AUDIT OBJECTIVES

Before beginning an audit, the auditor must define carefully the audit objectives for each account. Auditors should not begin their work by mailing confirmations to customers, examining invoices and canceled checks, and performing numerous other tasks without first considering what they are attempting to accomplish for each account and then determining the best, most efficient way to proceed. Only by knowing what the objectives are can an auditor know whether they have been accomplished. For example, an auditor may decide that one objective in auditing cash is to determine that it is not restricted and is subject to immediate withdrawal; but if this objective is not specified, the auditor may omit the audit steps necessary to accomplish it. Similarly, by establishing objectives, the auditor may avoid excess work that does not contribute to their accomplishments.

An auditor determines the objectives of auditing each account by relating them to the assertions, either explicit or implicit, that management makes regarding that account. The general assertions that are made regarding an account are described in Chapter 6 and restated here.

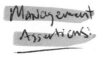 Management Assertions:

1. Existence or occurrence.
2. Rights and obligations.
3. Completeness.

4. Valuation or allocation.

5. Presentation and disclosure.

Audit procedures are designed to provide evidence regarding each audit objective or assertion for each account. The process is shown in Figure 13.3.

FIGURE 13.3 **The Process of Reasoning from Management Assertions to Audit Evidence**

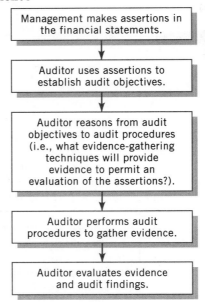

Management makes assertions in the financial statements.

↓

Auditor uses assertions to establish audit objectives.

↓

Auditor reasons from audit objectives to audit procedures (i.e., what evidence-gathering techniques will provide evidence to permit an evaluation of the assertions?).

↓

Auditor performs audit procedures to gather evidence.

↓

Auditor evaluates evidence and audit findings.

AUDIT PROCEDURES

Although an all-inclusive list of audit procedures cannot be prepared, the following procedures are representative of those often followed in the audit of inventories. The procedures are keyed to the objectives (assertions) to which they relate.

1. Obtain an understanding of internal control, and test and evaluate the inherent and control risks relating to inventories. (Normally, this would include controls in the purchasing and payroll areas.)

2. At year end, *observe* the client's inventory counting and recording procedures to determine whether they are adequate to result in an accurate inventory. Make and record test counts of inventory and *compare* them with those made by the client. Recount any items for which differences are found (existence and completeness).

3. *Confirm* the existence and ownership of inventory held on consignment or in public warehouses (existence and rights).

4. Test the propriety of the cutoff of inventory shipments and receipts by (a) recording the numbers and descriptions of the last five shipping and

receiving reports during the year-end inventory observation, and at a later date, (b) *inspecting* the first five shipping and receiving documents after the end of the year. *Analyze* the sales and purchase invoices that correspond with those shipping and receiving documents and determine whether (a) items recorded as sales in the current period were excluded from inventory, (b) items recorded as sales in the subsequent period were included in inventory, (c) items recorded as purchases in the current period were included in inventory, and (d) items recorded as purchases in the subsequent period were excluded from inventory (existence, completeness, and rights).

5. During the inventory observation, look for and *inquire* about any excess, slow-moving, obsolete, or unsalable inventory. Indications of such items would be a covering of dust or rust, or prior-year inventory tags (valuation and presentation).

6. *Compare* and account for all prenumbered inventory tags before and after the physical inventory (existence and completeness).

7. Obtain a copy of the final inventory listing and test *clerical accuracy. Compare* inventory prices with purchase invoices. *Test the calculation* of the inventory amount on the basis of the method used (i.e., FIFO, LIFO, average) and *compare* with market—the lower of replacement cost or net realizable value (valuation and rights).

8. Review *confirmations* received from banks and other creditors and minutes of the board of directors for indications of pledges or assignments of inventories (rights and disclosures).

9. Apply analytical procedures to the inventory balance in relation to sales, production, shipments, and purchases and *compare* with prior year and budget (existence, completeness, and valuation).

These procedures are necessarily more general than those in an actual audit, but they demonstrate how audit procedures are designed to accomplish the audit objectives. Normally, several procedures are required to achieve an objective fully, and, in many cases, one procedure will contribute to the fulfillment of more than one objective. A summary of the above procedures as they relate to individual inventory assertions is shown in Figure 13.4. Notice that each technique affects more than one assertion and that several techniques may be applied to each assertion.

FIGURE 13.4   Summary of Evidence-Gathering Procedures Applied to Inventory

Procedures	Assertions				
	Existence	Rights	Completeness	Valuation	Presentation
Observation	x		x		
Confirmation	x	x			x
Inspection	x	x	x	x	
Analysis	x	x	x		
Inquiry				x	x
Comparison	x	x	x	x	
Calculation				x	

Obtaining Audit Evidence by Inquiry

Inquiry is one means of obtaining evidence. It deserves special consideration because it is used so extensively. Auditors are constantly communicating with client personnel during an audit. Inquiries range from "Where are the invoices filed?" to "How are cash disbursements processed?" to "What caused the change in the accounts receivable balance from the prior year?"

Auditors generally should use open-ended questions and avoid conveying an expected answer. For example, the question "Did operating costs increase this year because of the opening of the new branch office in Kansas City?" is likely to result in an affirmative answer. A better phrased open-ended and unbiased question is, "What caused the variation in operating costs this year?" Another example of open/closed and biased/unbiased questions is shown in Figure 13.5.

FIGURE 13.5   Examples of Open/Closed and Biased/Unbiased Interview Questions

	Classification of interview questions	
	Unbiased	*Biased*
Open	"How was the allowance for uncollectibles estimated?"	"Why do you believe the allowance for uncollectibles is adequate?"
Closed	"Has the allowance for uncollectibles been estimated using the same methods as last year?"	"The allowance for uncollectibles is fairly stated in all material respects, wouldn't you say?"

Source: "Effective Interviewing Skills for Auditors," by Thomas R. Craig in *Journal of Accountancy* (July 1991), pp. 121–126.

Inquiry involves more than merely asking questions. The auditor must also listen to and evaluate answers to the questions. Answers should not be accepted without a careful evaluation. Sometimes client personnel fail to understand a question or lack the technical background to properly answer it. Auditors must be alert to these situations and seek other sources of information.

To a great extent, individual auditors will create either favorable or unfavorable impressions of themselves and their firms in their communications with client personnel. Thus, communication skills are critical to success in public accounting.

Confirmations

Confirmations are another important source of audit evidence. For our purposes, confirmation refers to obtaining written correspondence directly from a third party (i.e., someone other than the client or client personnel) to evaluate financial statement assertions. Such third parties include banks (bank balance and loan balance and terms), customers (accounts and notes receivable balances), warehouses (inventory quantities), vendors (accounts payable balances), lenders (note payable balances), trust companies (number of shares outstanding), and attorneys (litigation, claims, and assessments).

In all the above cases, the confirmation takes the form of a written request (developed by the auditor) from the client to the third party. The third party is asked to provide information directly to the auditor. Note that the request is *not* from the auditor to the third party. Third parties have no basis to release client information to the auditor without authorization from the client.

Clients often word-process the confirmations for the auditor on client letterhead. (Auditors use a preprinted form for bank confirmations.) The auditor reads the letters for accuracy and inserts them, together with a postage-paid return envelope addressed to the auditor, into an envelope showing the auditor's address as the return address. The auditor wants all responses, both deliverable and undeliverable, sent to his or her office. The envelopes are then deposited in a postal depository. (They should *not* be given to the client's mail room.)

Special problems can arise when confirmations are received by facsimile or FAX. They are (1) the source of the FAX can be false (transmitting FAX machines can be reprogrammed with a false FAX number and name) and (2) the FAX is vulnerable to deterioration. If the auditor has any reason to be suspicious of a FAX confirmation, he or she can call the sender of the FAX for confirmation of the transmission. The deterioration problem can be solved by reproducing the FAX on a copying machine.

The procedures to be performed in the event no response is received or the response from the third party differs from the client's information are discussed together with specific types of confirmations in subsequent chapters.

AUDITING ACCOUNTING ESTIMATES

Accounting estimates present special challenges to auditors because they are based on subjective as well as objective factors. The subjective factors increase the opportunity for intentional and unintentional bias in the estimates. The subjective factors also make controls more difficult to establish over accounting estimates. Auditors should identify all accounting estimates early in the audit.

The need for accounting estimates may be identified from knowledge of the client's business and a review of pertinent documentation. For example, an auditor may know from prior experience or a review of sales contracts that a client provides a warranty on its product. This would identify a need to estimate an allowance for warranty costs. Examples of accounting estimates often encountered by the auditor are shown in Figure 13.6.

To determine a reasonable amount or range of amounts for an accounting esti-

FIGURE 13.6   Accounting Estimates that Auditors Often Encounter

Allowance for doubtful accounts
Allowance for warranty costs
Allowance for inventory obsolescence
Valuations of securities not traded
Percentage of completion construction contracts
Residual values of leases
Useful lives and salvage value of leases

mate, the auditor must first understand how the client developed the estimate. The auditor may then evaluate the estimate by the following means:

1. Test the process used by management to develop the estimate. Using warranty cost as an example, the auditor would
   a. Identify controls relating to the estimate (e.g., the client may use a standard journal entry each month to record the warranty accrual; this reduces the possibility of inadvertently omitting the warranty accrual entry).
   b. Evaluate the sources of data used to determine the accrual (e.g., determine that adequate statistical data regarding prior period warranty costs are used in making the estimate).
   c. Determine if assumptions are reasonable and consistent (e.g., an increase in the number of units sold should normally cause an increase in the warranty accrual).
   d. Test the calculations management used to translate the assumptions into the accounting estimate (e.g., multiply the period's sales by the warranty accrual rate).
2. Develop an independent expectation. For example, historical data in the auditor's permanent audit file may indicate that on average one-tenth of one percent of all sales are returned for repair or replacement within a 30-day warranty period. The auditor is not aware of any change in the client's operations that would affect this historical average. The auditor may make an independent estimate of the allowance for warranty costs at the balance sheet date of one-tenth of one percent of sales for the last month of the year. Client personnel may calculate their estimate by a different method. The auditor would compare his or her independently derived estimate with the client's estimate. As will be discussed later in this chapter, differences between the auditor's estimate and the client's estimate would generally be considered a likely misstatement.
3. Review subsequent events or transactions. Auditors may evaluate the accrual for warranty costs at the balance sheet date by comparing it with actual warranty repairs made in the first month of the following year, which apply to sales made prior to the balance sheet date.

Some estimates, such as a potential loss from litigation, are very difficult to estimate because there are no relevant historical data or transactions in the subsequent period. In these cases, disclosure may be all that is required by generally accepted accounting principles.

ANALYTICAL PROCEDURES AS SUBSTANTIVE TESTS

In Chapter 8 we discussed the use of analytical procedures in the planning process to help identify accounts or transactions with a high risk of material misstatement. Analytical procedures may also be used as substantive tests. Here are some guidelines that may affect the use of analytical procedures in those circumstances.

Nature of Assertion

Analytical procedures may be more effective than other substantive tests when gathering evidence about certain assertions. Consider the audit of the completeness assertion for property tax expense. Inspection of paid tax receipts will not disclose unpaid property taxes; however, an analytical procedure of comparing property tax expense with the prior period or with the amount budgeted may indicate inadequate property tax expense and disclose the misstatement.

Plausibility and Predictability of the Relationship

Relationships involving income statement accounts are generally more predictable than relationships involving only balance sheet accounts. Many income statement accounts such as administrative salaries, office rent, and depreciation expense have relatively large fixed components. Unless there are changes in operations or errors in recording, these accounts should be comparable from one period to the next. Conversely, balance sheet accounts such as cash are often affected by random events such as the timing of payments to vendors, collections from customers, and borrowings from banks.

Availability and Reliability of Data

Data may be more readily available in certain entities than in others. For example, revenues in a manufacturing company may be subjected to analytical procedures using prior period amounts, budgeted amounts, and shipping department statistics. On the other hand, if a museum relies primarily on donations for revenue, shipping department statistics will not exist and prior-period and budgeted amounts may not be meaningful.

The auditor should have some assurance concerning the reliability of the data used to develop the expectations. For example, a common analytical procedure is to compare an account balance in the current year to the prior year. This assumes that the prior year is the expectation for the current year. If the prior year has been audited, the auditor would have more assurance from the application of the analytical procedure than if the prior year had not been audited.

Precision of the Expectation

The more assurance an auditor expects from applying an analytical procedure, the more precise the expectation should be. Generally, expectations developed at detailed levels are less likely to be obscured by offsetting factors than expectations developed at general levels. Consider the analysis of revenues on page 394.

The month of March contains a $100,000 overstatement of revenue while the remaining months are legitimate random differences. A comparison of monthly amounts should identify the misstatement while a comparison of only annual amounts is unlikely to identify it. An auditor would have more assurance of detecting the material misstatement in the monthly data than in the annual data. Other examples of detail data that may yield more precise expectations include data developed by location or line of business.

Month	Expected revenues*	Recorded revenues	Difference
Jan.	$ 110,000	$ 100,000	$(10,000)
Feb.	114,000	105,000	(9,000)
Mar.	103,000	203,000	100,000
Apr.	113,000	100,000	(13,000)
May	111,000	98,000	(13,000)
Jun.	111,000	101,000	(10,000)
Jul.	107,000	108,000	1,000
Aug.	108,000	100,000	(8,000)
Sept.	109,000	100,000	(9,000)
Oct.	112,000	113,000	1,000
Nov.	115,000	99,000	(16,000)
Dec.	120,000	106,000	(14,000)
	$1,333,000	$1,333,000	—

* Could be prior-year or budgeted amounts.

Analytical procedures are powerful tools for detecting material misstatements that result in deviations of unaudited book amounts from expectations. However, the agreement of expectations and book amounts provides no assurance that a misstatement is not present. Thus, tests of balances and transactions are often necessary when audit risk is high or the balances or transactions are material.

A BUSINESS APPROACH TO GATHERING EVIDENCE

Auditors should maintain an overall perspective of the financial statements they are auditing. They may easily become involved in the details and forget to ask, "Does this answer or presentation make good sense in light of present industry and economic conditions?" To be able to answer that question adequately, auditors must understand the client's business operations and have some knowledge of industry and economic conditions. This means that auditors must be more than number checkers; they must develop business judgment and knowledge equal to or greater than those of their clients.

This knowledge will help auditors performing substantive tests to determine the appropriateness of accounting principles and the adequacy of disclosure. In addition, the auditors will be in a better position to evaluate the reasonableness of estimates and representations made by management.

Auditors acquire an understanding of the client's business operations during the planning process by discussions with operating personnel as well as with financial personnel. While performing substantive tests, they should not isolate themselves in the accounting department, but should seek explanations for variations in the client's operations from engineers, operation managers, marketing managers, and others. After all, it is the client's business operations that are reflected in the financial statements. Who could be more qualified to discuss and explain them than the people directly involved? Such discussions not only provide audit evidence, but also broaden auditors' understanding of the operation of business in general and the client's business in particular. This understanding allows them to use such techniques as operating and financial ratio analyses as effective audit tools to evaluate account balances. Analytical procedures are applications of the business approach.

The use of operating, industry, and general economic knowledge can enhance the quality of an audit. Some examples of how this could be useful follow.

1. You are reviewing the audit trial balance of a sugar refiner, and you are surprised by a large increase in sales during the current year. Because of your knowledge of the industry, you know the approximate average price per pound of sugar during the year; dividing this price into total sales gives you approximately 10 million pounds sold during the year. You recall that the production capacity of your client's plant is only 6 million pounds per year. Although there may be a reason for this difference (reduction of inventory, purchase of refined sugar from others for resale, etc.), you perform other substantive tests in the sales area.

2. In your audit of a manufacturing company, you note that the gross profit ratio has increased from 20 to 30 percent, but you know that because of overcapacity in the industry, several sales price reductions were made during the year which alone would result in a decline in the gross profit ratio. When the client is unable to explain the increase satisfactorily, you revise your audit program to increase substantive tests of inventory (for possible overstatement), accounts payable (for possible unrecorded purchases), and sales (for possible overstatements).

3. While reviewing the audit trial balance, you note that interest income on short-term investments has increased from that of the prior year. You mentally calculate that the average rate of interest received during the year, based on an average of the beginning and ending amounts invested, was 12 percent; however, from your knowledge of general economic conditions, you know that short-term interest rates did not exceed 8 percent during the entire year. You extend your substantive tests to recompute interest income for the year because you believe it is overstated and find that the client did make an error by accruing interest receivable for the last quarter of the year twice.

Ratio Analysis

One specific application of a business approach to auditing is the use of analytical procedures to calculate and evaluate certain financial statement ratios. These data should not be computed and appraised mechanically without regard for the business and industry environment in which the client operates. If such computations are used properly, however, and are integrated with pertinent information obtained from other sources, they can be valuable tools in detecting financial statement misstatements.

As an illustration, assume the calculation of the following ratios for the client's current and prior years' financial statements. (The current year's statements are unaudited.)

Ratio	*19X8*	*19X9*
Gross profit	32.1	27.3
Accounts receivable turnover	5.5	4.2
Inventory turnover	6.3	6.2

What audit significance can be attached to these ratios? Taken in the abstract, they probably mean little. But coupled with business information obtained from other sources, they could show the auditor where to concentrate audit effort. Here are some examples.

1. For an auditor to evaluate properly the decline in the gross profit ratio, several factors must be considered, such as (a) variations in sales volume, (b) relationships of fixed and variable costs, (c) variations in sales price, (d) variations in production costs, (e) variations in production volume, and (f) method of inventory computation. The decline in the gross profit ratio could properly result from such factors as lower sales volume, higher production costs, and lower sales prices. The auditor is concerned that it did not result from understated inventory, overstated purchases, or understated sales.

2. Accounts receivable turnover decreased from 19X8 to 19X9. In 19X9 credit sales increased, credit terms remained the same, and a new system of more rapid billing was introduced. Under these conditions, the auditor concludes that accounts receivable turnover *should* have increased in 19X9 unless slow-paying customers caused collections to falter. The auditor should expand the scope of the work in auditing the allowance for doubtful accounts.

3. The inventory turnover remained stable in 19X9. But considering the introduction of a new line of high-turnover merchandise, an increase was expected. During the inventory observation, it was noted that there were unusually large stocks of certain lines of merchandise on hand. The auditor should devote special attention to audit procedures designed to detect obsolete inventory.

A number of financial ratios commonly used as analytical procedures is shown in Figure 13.7. Effective use of ratio analysis may identify financial statement errors and result in a better quality audit.

Regression Analysis

Another specific application of the business approach to auditing is the use of regression analysis to predict the dollar amount of an account. If this predicted amount is materially different from the actual amount recorded on the client's records, special audit effort is devoted to that account. *Regression analysis* measures the rate at which a dependent variable changes in relation to one or more independent variables.

The independent variable can be expressed as number of units, number of hours, number of dollars, and so forth. The dependent variable can also be expressed as one of several measures. Some examples of independent and dependent variables are (1) machine hours and repair expenses, (2) direct labor hours and labor costs, and (3) sales and delivery expenses. We will use the third example for illustration.

A first-order regression function[2] may be expressed as

[2] For information regarding the use of regression analysis in auditing, see Kenneth W. Stringer and Trevor R. Stewart, *Statistical Techniques for Analytical Review in Auditing* (New York: Wiley, 1986).

FIGURE 13.7   Financial Ratios Commonly Used as Analytical Procedures

Ratio	*Calculation of ratio*
Income statement accounts	
Return on sales	$\dfrac{\text{Net income}}{\text{Sales}}$
Gross profit ratio	$\dfrac{\text{Gross profit}}{\text{Sales}}$
Effective income tax rate	$\dfrac{\text{Provision for income taxes}}{\text{Income before income taxes}}$
Ratio of selling expense (and other variable costs) to sales	$\dfrac{\text{Selling expense}}{\text{Sales}}$
Balance sheet account	
Current ratio	$\dfrac{\text{Current assets}}{\text{Current liabilities}}$
Quick ratio	$\dfrac{\text{Cash + marketable securities + net accounts receivable}}{\text{Current liabilities}}$
Debt to equity ratio	$\dfrac{\text{Total liabilities}}{\text{Total equity}}$
Income statement and balance sheet accounts	
Accounts receivable turnover	$\dfrac{\text{Sales}}{\text{Average accounts receivable}}$
Days' sales in accounts receivable	$\dfrac{\text{Accounts receivable}}{\text{Sales}/365}$
Inventory turnover	$\dfrac{\text{Cost of goods sold}}{\text{Average inventory}}$
Interest expense to notes payable	$\dfrac{\text{Interest expense}}{\text{Average notes payable}}$
Depreciation expense to property	$\dfrac{\text{Depreciation expense}}{\text{Average gross property}}$
Investment income to investments	$\dfrac{\text{Dividend and interest income}}{\text{Average investments}}$
Amortization expense to deferred charges	$\dfrac{\text{Amortization expense}}{\text{Average deferred charges}}$
Return on assets	$\dfrac{\text{Net income}}{\text{Total assets}}$

$$E(Y) = B_0 + B_1 X$$

where

$E(Y)$ is the expected value of Y (the account to be predicted).

X is the account believed to have a relationship with Y.

B_0 is often thought of as the fixed element of the account to be predicted, but it may have no particular meaning as a separate term in the regression function.

B_1 is the rate of change of Y for each unit change in X.

The auditor may have independently audited sales and may believe there should be a close relationship between the client's dollar sales for the year and delivery expense because most sales are delivered by company truck. Sales can be used to predict the amount of delivery expense by using simple linear regression analysis.

To predict the delivery expense rate of variability in relation to dollar sales, the auditor collects the actual dollar amounts of both accounts for the previous 10 years. (In practice, three years of monthly data are often used.) It is assumed that the dollar relationships that exist between these accounts for the 10-year period are typical of the relationship that should exist in the current year.

Sales and delivery expense for the 10-year period follow.

Year	Sales (in thousands of dollars)	Delivery expense (in thousands of dollars)
19W9	$10,019	$ 78
19X0	11,904	94
19X1	13,638	110
19X2	15,622	127
19X3	19,431	151
19X4	22,774	175
19X5	26,058	183
19X6	31,354	210
19X7	35,900	255
19X8	41,895	317

Using the ordinary least squares statistical technique, the auditor calculates the estimated fixed portion of delivery expense at $10,000 and the estimated variable portion at $0.007 per sales dollar. The auditor could plot the data on a chart and draw the calculated variable expense line. Such a graph is shown on page 399.

An examination of the graph shows that the correlation between sales and delivery expense appears to be very high (the coefficient of determination is 0.98). Unless the auditor has other evidence to contradict the appearance of high correlation, he or she may assume that $10,000 plus $0.007 per sales dollar is a good predictor of delivery expense.

The next step is to calculate the predicted amount of delivery expense for the current year and compare it with the actual figure on the client's 19X9 income statement. If, in the auditor's judgment, the difference is not too large, the delivery expense account may be accepted as not materially in error.[3]

Assume that 19X9 sales are $45,000,000 and 19X9 delivery expense is $300,000. The predicted delivery expense is $325,000 [$10,000 + (0.007 × $45,000,000)]. The auditor must make a judgment on the materiality of this difference. If $25,000 is not considered to be material, the account balance is accepted. If the auditor considers the $25,000 to be material, he or she might examine a significant portion

---

[3] The auditor may calculate confidence intervals at a certain risk level to aid in identifying material variations.

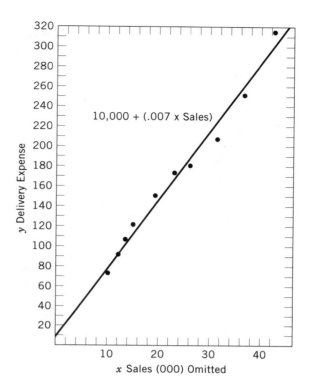

10,000 + (.007 x Sales)

y Delivery Expense

x Sales (000) Omitted

of the evidence supporting the delivery expense account. Such an examination could reveal misclassifications of expenditures between delivery expense and other accounts.

The auditor may have made the same decision by a cursory examination of delivery expense and sales for the prior 10 years. Regression analysis refines the process. The methodology is easy to apply, and with microcomputers the calculations can be made quickly.[4] However, the auditor should be aware that a number of statistical assumptions are involved in the use of regression analysis and that violation of these assumptions may bias the results. These assumptions are found in most basic statistics books.

Relationships among Accounts

Auditors must be aware of the natural flow of funds through a set of financial statements. This flow of funds and the resulting relationships are such that evidence gathered to support the propriety of one account often contributes to the accomplishment of the audit objectives for another account. For example, audit procedures performed and evidence gathered in the audit of inventory, cash, and accounts payable contribute to the audit of cost of goods sold. Similarly, the auditor who has satisfactorily tested the client's procedures for recording sales and cash transactions has a certain amount of evidence in support of accounts receivable

[4] See Terry L. Brock, "Multiple Regression on Lotus 1-2-3," *Journal of Accountancy* (July 1986), pp. 106–110.

TABLE 13.1
Accounts on Which Audit Work Is Often Performed Simultaneously

Balance sheet accounts	Income statement accounts
Accounts receivable	Sales and bad debt expense
Inventories	Cost of goods sold
Investment securities	Other income (dividends and interest)
Property and equipment	Maintenance and depreciation expense
Prepaid insurance	Insurance expense
Notes payable	Interest expense
Accrued income taxes	Income tax expense

before performing any audit procedures listed in that section. Table 13.1 illustrates pairs of accounts on which audit work is often performed simultaneously.

Many of the balance sheet accounts listed in Table 13.1 can be confirmed by outside parties (accounts receivable and notes payable) or observed by the auditor (inventories and investment securities). Many of the income statement accounts represent a large number of individual items flowing through the accounts during the year (sales and cost of goods sold). The double-entry accounting system allows accounts to be audited from two directions.

Consider sales. This account can be, and to some extent is, audited by examining evidence to support the amounts recorded in the account, such as sales invoices and shipping documents. This is only a portion of the evidence gathered for the audit of sales, however. The following equation

$$\begin{array}{l}\text{Accounts} \\ \text{receivable} \\ \text{at beginning} \\ \text{of a period}\end{array} + \begin{array}{l}\text{Credit} \\ \text{sales} \\ \text{for a} \\ \text{period}\end{array} - \begin{array}{l}\text{Cash} \\ \text{collections} \\ \text{of accounts} \\ \text{receivable}\end{array} = \begin{array}{l}\text{Accounts} \\ \text{receivable} \\ \text{at end of} \\ \text{a period}\end{array}$$

can be written as

$$\begin{array}{l}\text{Credit} \\ \text{sales} \\ \text{for a} \\ \text{period}\end{array} = \begin{array}{l}\text{Accounts} \\ \text{receivable} \\ \text{at end of} \\ \text{a period}\end{array} + \begin{array}{l}\text{Cash} \\ \text{collections} \\ \text{of accounts} \\ \text{receivable}\end{array} - \begin{array}{l}\text{Accounts} \\ \text{receivable} \\ \text{at beginning} \\ \text{of a period}\end{array}$$

Many companies record all sales through accounts receivable, so credit sales are often equivalent to total sales. In these cases, by auditing the accounts receivable balance at the end of a period (assuming that the balance at the beginning of the period was audited in the prior year), and by testing cash receipts, the auditor adds evidence to the audit of sales without gathering any evidence in direct support of the amounts recorded in the sales account.

EVIDENCE OF RELATED PARTY TRANSACTIONS

In Chapter 8 we discussed how auditors attempt to identify related parties during the planning process. If related parties are identified, the auditor attempts to detect transactions with such parties by:

Review of minutes.

Review of accounting records for large or unusual transactions.

Review of confirmations and loan agreements for the existence of guarantees.

Review of "conflict-of-interest" statements obtained by the company.

Auditors should pay particular attention to nonmonetary exchanges that provide gains to one or more parties and to year-end transactions that aid the client in reaching its earnings forecasts or meeting its debt covenant requirements.

If related party transactions are detected, the auditor must first gain an understanding of the business purposes of the transactions. The auditor cannot complete the audit until he or she understands the business sense of material related party transactions. The auditor should also be aware that the substance of a related party transaction may be significantly different from its form and that financial statements should recognize the substance of transactions rather than their legal form. If valid business purposes exist, the auditor should examine or obtain appropriate evidence of the transactions and determine that they have been approved by the board of directors.

▶ EXAMPLE

The following illustration of a related party transaction is condensed from a case reported by the SEC. Company A, a real estate broker, purportedly sold properties to Company B, an unaffiliated company, for $5,400,000 and recognized profit of $550,000 from the transaction. However, a provision of the agreement guaranteed Company B that it would suffer no loss from operation of the properties and that it could sell the properties back to Company A. Later, Company B did request that Company A take back the properties. At this point, Company A formed two companies, undisclosed related parties, to purchase the properties from Company B. Company A knew that no profit could be recognized if it took the properties back, but by transferring the properties to undisclosed related parties it concealed the fact that no income should have been recognized because the risk of loss from the properties remained with it. The SEC concluded that the auditors failed to review adequately the agreements related to this transaction or to pursue the implications of the disposition of the properties by Company B.

If related party transactions are material, the auditor should determine whether the financial statements disclose the nature of the relationships and a description of the transactions, including dollar volume and year-end balances.

EVIDENCE FOR THE CONSIDERATION OF AN ENTITY'S ABILITY TO CONTINUE AS A GOING CONCERN

In addition to the requirement that an auditor evaluate evidence regarding amounts shown in the client's financial statements, professional standards require an overall evaluation of the client's ability to *continue as a going concern* for a period of one year from the balance sheet date. This evaluation relates to the viability of the entity, not just whether its assets are recoverable and its liabilities are properly classified. This is an important extension, because auditors are charged with the responsibility under professional standards of interpreting financial statements in addition to expressing an opinion as to whether or not they conform with generally accepted accounting principles.

Auditors are not required to design audit procedures solely to detect going concern problems. Rather, auditors evaluate the effect of transactions and events identified during the audit and the results of audit procedures performed to accomplish other audit objectives. Although different auditors may place different degrees of importance on the following events and factors, they are illustrative of the matters considered.

The first indication of a problem is often an operating loss by the client in the current year. The auditor then considers whether (1) operating losses have occurred in prior years, (2) cash flows from operations have been positive or negative in the current and prior years, and (3) key financial ratios such as the current ratio, quick ratio, and debt-to-equity ratio exhibit adverse trends. Other indicators are defaults under loan agreements, denial of normal trade credit from suppliers, and the necessity to restructure debt or seek new sources of financing. In addition, factors that may not have an immediate effect on solvency might include work stoppages; legal proceedings; loss of important franchises, patents, customers, or suppliers; and uninsured catastrophes.

Some auditors have used bankruptcy prediction models as an aid in this assessment. One popular model was developed by Edward Altman, using the multiple discriminate analysis statistical technique.[5] This model uses the following financial ratios to compute an index that can be used to predict bankruptcy.

Working capital/total assets
Retained earnings/total assets
Earnings before interest and taxes/total assets
Market value of equity/book value of total liabilities
Sales/total assets

The predictive accuracy of this model one year prior to bankruptcy has been relatively high.

If conditions or events such as those identified previously create *substantial doubt* as to the ability of the entity to continue as a going concern, the auditor should consider whether management has plans for and the ability to implement alternative means of maintaining adequate cash flows. Examples include plans and the ability to (1) dispose of assets, (2) renew or extend existing loans, (3) reduce or dispose of operations producing negative cash flows, and (4) obtain new equity capital and reduce dividend payments. The auditor should attempt to examine evidence to support management's ability to carry out these plans. Examples of such evidence would be appraisals or bids for assets held for disposition and correspondence from banks indicating an agreement to renew or extend loans.

If the necessary evidence to support management's plans cannot be obtained or if substantial doubt remains about the client's ability to continue as a going concern, the auditor should evaluate whether the matter is adequately disclosed in the financial statements and consider whether his or her audit report requires modification.

[5] Edward I. Altman, *Corporate Financial Distress* (New York: Wiley, 1983).

The appropriate audit report modification in these circumstances is discussed in Chapter 20.

REVIEW AND EVALUATION OF EVIDENCE

The auditor must remain keenly alert while performing audit procedures, no matter how routine a step appears to be. One brief period of carelessness can have a devastating effect on the quality of the audit. Although the senior, manager, and partner will review the audit working papers prepared by the staff, none of these people will see the invoice, canceled check, or other document that was examined. Therefore, a basic responsibility for the audit rests with the staff.

The staff is assisted in meeting this responsibility by senior supervision. The senior should explain the purpose and means of accomplishing the audit steps assigned to the staff. Although the staff may be encouraged to develop their own solutions to problems encountered on the audit, the senior should review the soundness of these solutions with them and assist them when they encounter significant difficulties.

Each firm should establish a formal set of procedures to be followed if differences of opinion concerning accounting or auditing issues arise among firm personnel involved in an audit. These procedures should enable the staff to document the reason for disagreement and, if necessary, to be disassociated from the resolution of the issue.

The Review Process

The review process provides the means for controlling the quality of the performance of the audit procedures. The audit working papers should be reviewed at each level of responsibility from the senior through the partner. In other words, the senior reviews the working papers prepared by the staff, the manager reviews the working papers prepared by the staff and the senior, and the partner reviews all of the working papers, including any prepared by the manager. As the reviews are conducted at each level, the reviewer makes notes or points about the audit work. These notes may be answered or cleared either personally or by someone at a lower level. An example of review notes prepared by Joe Jones (J.J.) and cleared by Mary Smith (M.S.) are shown in Figure 13.8. Satisfactory disposition must be made of all such notes before the audit can be considered complete. After disposition such notes are usually destroyed.

In reviewing the audit work, the supervisors must be satisfied that the working papers contain evidence that the scope of the work was adequate and that the work was actually performed using appropriate care and skill. For example, each level of supervision must be satisfied that an adequate *number* of confirmations of accounts receivable was obtained and that *care and skill* were employed in obtaining, recording, reconciling, and evaluating the confirmations received. The supervisors must also concentrate on the meaning of the *audit findings* and their implications with respect to the financial statements and the auditor's report. For example, if the auditor does not receive an adequate response to accounts receivable confirmation requests or finds material unreconcilable differences between the client and cus-

FIGURE 13.8   Illustration of Review Notes for the Audit of Cash

Working Paper Index	Review Note	By	Disposition	By
A-2	1. Sign and date the schedule.	JJ	1. Done	MS
A-2	2. Trace bank balance to year-end bank statement.	JJ	2. Done and now indicated on A-2.	MS
A-2	3. Trace book balance to general ledger.	JJ	3. Now done.	MS
A-2	4. Indicate if dates, payees, signatures, and endorsements on canceled checks were examined.	JJ	4. Done. See $\vee$ on A-2.	MS

tomer records, consideration must be given to proposing an adjustment to the financial statements or modifying the auditor's report.

Audit findings may be recorded in the working papers in (1) memoranda regarding specific audit and reporting problems encountered and their disposition, (2) audit staff conclusions on various working papers, and (3) support for adjusting and reclassifying entries. Should any audit finding made by the audit team indicate that an error or fraud may have occurred, the finding should be investigated until the facts that are reasonably obtainable have been assembled or until it becomes clear that the matter is immaterial. Such findings should immediately be reported to the audit partner, who must review the available evidence, consider its implications, consult with other designated partners, if necessary, and discuss the matter and the extent of further investigation with an appropriate level of management.

A required part of the overall review process is the performance of analytical procedures. The purpose of analytical procedures at this point is to assess the conclusions reached during the audit and to evaluate the overall financial statement presentation. The procedures generally involve reading the financial statements and notes to determine that satisfactory explanations have been obtained for all unusual amounts and relationships.

Known, Projected, and Likely Misstatements

Auditors frequently find misstatements during their audits, although many of them are immaterial.[6] The evaluation of these misstatements is a critical aspect of an audit.

In evaluating audit findings, the auditor considers known and projected *misstatements. Known misstatements* are those specifically identified in the audit process. *Projected misstatements* arise when sampling is used and consist of the projection of

---

[6] Icerman and Hillison reported that only 12.3 percent of 147 audits performed by seven large accounting firms resulted in no detected errors in five accounts (accounts receivable, inventory, accounts payable, revenue, and cost of sales) studied ["Disposition of Audit-Detected Errors: Some Evidence on Evaluation Materiality," *Auditing: A Journal of Practice and Theory* (Spring 1991), pp. 22–34].

known misstatements identified in a sample to the population from which the sample was selected. *Likely misstatements* consist of the auditor's best estimate of the total misstatements in an account balance. Likely misstatements include (1) known misstatements, (2) misstatements projected to a total account balance from auditing only a sample of the individual items included in the account, (3) unreasonable estimates affecting an account balance, and (4) prior-period misstatements that affect the current period. An example of the computation of likely misstatements for accounts receivable (net of allowance for doubtful accounts) is shown in the table below.

| | Effect on | |
Misstatement	Accounts receivable	Net income[a]
Known misstatement—invalid accounts receivable detected by sending confirmations to all accounts in excess of $50,000	$40,000	$26,000
Known misstatement—invalid accounts receivable detected by sending confirmations to a sample of 20 percent of all accounts below $50,000	2,000	1,300
Projected misstatement—projection of confirmation sample results to remaining 80 percent of all accounts below $50,000	8,000	5,200
Unreasonable estimate—difference between estimated allowance for doubtful accounts per books ($200,000) and nearest reasonable estimate by auditor ($230,000)	30,000	19,500
Uncorrected prior-year misstatement—difference between estimated allowance for doubtful accounts per books at end of prior year ($150,000) and nearest reasonable estimate by auditor at end of prior year ($170,000) that was accepted by auditor as immaterial	—	(13,000)
Likely misstatement	$80,000	$39,000

[a] The effect on net income is reduced by 35 percent to allow for the estimated income tax effect.

In evaluating the materiality of likely misstatement, the auditor should consider the risk of even further misstatement due to sampling risk and the imprecise nature of certain audit procedures. For example, if likely misstatement is $39,000 and the auditor has established $40,000 as a material misstatement, he or she may conclude that there is an unacceptably high risk that undetected misstatements could cause the financial statements to be materially misstated. In this case, the auditor may perform additional audit procedures, ask the client to correct some or all of the identified misstatements, or consider modification of the audit report.

All likely misstatements that are determined to be immaterial should be reported to the client's management to determine whether they want to correct them. Clients often wish to correct minor misstatements so they can begin a new year with a more accurate set of accounting records. The auditor will prepare a schedule summarizing all uncorrected misstatements to be reasonably assured that, in the aggregate, they do not have a material effect on the financial statements. This schedule is often called a summary of immaterial entries or a summary of entries passed. Figure 13.9 is an example of such a schedule. The net amount of the entries not made is compared with the amounts to be shown in the financial statements to determine whether it is material in the aggregate.

If an auditor determines that a proposed adjustment is due to fraud (as opposed to an error), then he or she must consider the implications for other aspects of the audit as well as the monetary effect. If the proposed adjustment involving a fraud is immaterial, the auditor should (1) refer the matter to a level of management at least one level above those involved[7] and (2) determine that those involved do not have duties that could permit further fraud, which would materially misstate the financial statements. If the proposed adjustment involving a fraud is material, the auditor should (1) consider the implications for all aspects of the audit, (2) determine that the audit committee is adequately informed, and (3) suggest that the client consult with legal counsel.[8]

COMMUNICATING AUDIT FINDINGS

Audit findings are communicated through the auditor's report and less formally by communications with the client's audit committee.

Issuing the Audit Report

At the end of the audit, the auditors must carefully read the financial statements to determine whether they are in conformity with generally accepted accounting principles and whether they contain all information necessary for a clear understanding of the company's operations and its financial position. Auditors often recommend additional footnote disclosure or clarification of footnote wording as a result of a careful reading of the financial statements. Only after the financial statements are in final form can the auditor decide on the type of audit report to be issued (discussed in Chapters 19 and 20).

Once the financial statements and audit report are in final form, most accounting firms subject them to some type of quality control review. Quality control reviews often include (1) proofreading and clerical check, (2) tracing amounts and disclosures in the financial statements to the audit working papers to be sure that they are the same in both documents and have been subjected to audit, and (3) reading of the audit report and financial statements by another audit partner who was not associated with the engagement. (Some accounting firms carry this step further by requiring a complete review of the audit working papers by the second audit partner.)

The first procedure listed involves a comparison of the final typed or printed copy of the audit report and financial statements with the draft copy to detect the

---

[7] If an immaterial fraud involves senior management, the audit committee should be informed.

[8] In some circumstances, the auditor may also have a responsibility to report fraud to outside parties such as the SEC, successor auditors, and funding agencies of entities receiving government assistance.

FIGURE 13.9   X Company Summary of Entries Passed 12-31-X8

X Co.
Summary of Entries Passed
12-31-X8

R. Smith
2-1-x9

PBC

Index	Description	Increase/(Decrease) in					
		Current Assets	Current Liabilities	Long-term Assets	Long-term Liabilities	Stockholders Equity	Net Income
10/B	Sales	(350)					(350)
	Accounts receivable						
	To record credit memo issued in Jan, X9 applicable to Dec, X8 sales						
9/20	Accumulated depreciation			200			200
	Depreciation expense						
	To correct error in calculation of depr.						
p/20	Accrued liabilities		(230)				230
	Property tax expense						
	To correct overaccrual of property taxes						
	Total	(975)	0	200	0	0	(125)
	Income tax effect	0	(60)	0	0	0	60
	Net	(975)	(710)	200	0	0	(65)
	Per Audit Trial Balance	473,990	314,084	512,901	250,000	422,807	71,229

In my opinion, the entries passed are immaterial in relation to the financial statements.   R. Senior   M. Manager   P. Partner

omission of words or sentences and misspellings, and a check of the clerical accuracy of all totals. The second procedure is performed to determine that there is support in the audit working papers for all amounts and disclosures in the financial statements. This step is usually done by a senior or manager who has had no prior association with the engagement. The final procedure is sometimes thought of as a test to determine whether an individual knowledgeable about accounting but unfamiliar with the particular financial statements being read finds the financial statements to be presented in a clear and understandable manner.

The auditor's report is signed and released to the client only after all the foregoing procedures have been performed and all the questions or comments raised as a result have been cleared.

Communicating with the Audit Committee

In addition to the formal audit report, the auditor should determine that the audit committee[9] is informed of the following matters:

1. The initial selection of significant accounting policies, methods used to account for significant unusual transactions, and the effect of continuing accounting policies in controversial areas.
2. The processes used by management in formulating accounting estimates and the bases for the auditor's conclusions about the reasonableness of those estimates.
3. The implications of errors (both corrected and uncorrected), fraud, and illegal acts (unless clearly inconsequential) discovered during the audit.
4. The auditor's responsibility for information other than the audited financial statements in documents such as corporate annual reports.[10]
5. The level of responsibility an auditor assumes under generally accepted auditing standards, that is, reasonable but not absolute assurance.
6. Any disagreements between the auditor and management, whether or not satisfactorily resolved.
7. Any major issues discussed by management and the auditor before the auditor was hired and issues on which other accountants were consulted.
8. Any serious difficulties the auditor encountered that were detrimental to the effective completion of the audit.
9. Significant deficiencies in internal control (discussed in Chapter 10).

Audit committees may find the foregoing information useful in fulfilling their responsibilities for accounting and auditing matters.

OMITTED AUDIT PROCEDURES

Occasionally, usually as the result of a peer review, an auditor may become aware after an audit report has been delivered that a necessary audit procedure was not performed during the audit, although there is no indication that the financial state-

---

[9] If a client does not have an audit committee, the communications should be to other financial oversight groups, such as finance or budget committees, if they exist.

[10] The auditor's responsibility for this other information is discussed in Chapter 19.

ments are misstated. If the auditor believes that the omission of the procedure impairs his or her ability to support the previously expressed opinion and that shareholders, creditors, or others are continuing to rely on the opinion, the omitted procedure should be performed. The auditor also would be well advised to seek legal counsel.

Chapter 13 ▶ GLOSSARY OF TERMS

Accounting estimate An approximation of a financial statement element, item, or account.

Audit procedures Specific acts to be performed when gathering evidence.

Business approach to auditing Application of business and economic knowledge to evaluate the reasonableness of account and transaction balances.

Competence of evidential matter The validity and relevance of audit evidence.

Going concern An entity's ability to continue to meet its obligations as they become due without substantial disposition of assets outside the ordinary course of business, restructuring of debt, externally forced revisions of operations, or similar actions.

Known misstatements Misstatements detected by the auditor in the audit process.

Likely misstatements The sum of known and projected misstatements, unreasonable estimates, and uncorrected prior year errors.

Projected misstatements The projection of known misstatements from a sample to the population.

Ratio analysis The evaluation of financial ratios to identify potential misstatements in the financial statements.

Regression analysis A statistical measurement of the rate of change of a dependent variable in relation to one or more independent variables.

Sufficiency of evidential matter The amount or extent of audit evidence.

Chapter 13 ▶ REFERENCES

American Institute of Certified Public Accountants. *Professional Standards*
   AU Section 312—*Audit Risk and Materiality in Conducting an Audit*
   AU Section 326—*Evidential Matter*
   AU Section 329—*Analytical Procedures*
   AU Section 334—*Related Parties*
   AU Section 341—*The Auditor's Consideration of an Entity's Ability to Continue as a Going Concern*
   AU Section 342—*Auditing Accounting Estimates*
   AU Section 380—*Communication with Audit Committees*
   AU Section 390—*Consideration of Omitted Procedures After the Report Date*
Bamber, E. Michael, Bamber, Linda S., and Bylinski, Joseph H. "A Descriptive Study of Audit Managers' Working Paper Review," *Auditing: A Journal of Practice and Theory* (Spring 1988), pp. 137–149.
Canfield, Gary A. "A Guide for Effectively Questioning Clients," *Journal of Accountancy* (September 1985), pp. 162–168.
Coglitore, Frank, and Berryman, R. Glen. "Analytical Procedures: A Defensive Necessity," *Auditing: A Journal of Practice and Theory* (Spring 1988), pp. 150–163.
Craig, Thomas R. "Effective Interviewing Skills for Auditors," *Journal of Accountancy* (July 1991), pp. 121–126.
Craig, Thomas R. "Combining Prior and Current Misstatements When Evaluating Audit Findings," *Journal of Accountancy* (July 1990), pp. 103–109.
Ellingsen, John E., Pany, K., and Fagan, P. "SAS No. 59: How to Evaluate Going Concern," *Journal of Accountancy* (January 1989), pp. 24–31.
Holstrum, Gary L., and Mock, Theodore J. "Audit Judgment and Evidence Evaluation," *Auditing: A Journal of Practice and Theory* (Fall 1985), pp. 101–108.
Kunitake, Walter K., and Glezen, G. William. "The Use of Analytical Review Procedures and Their Effectiveness in Signaling Financial Statement Errors," *The Ohio CPA Journal* (Summer 1987), pp. 45–49.
Pearson, David B., and Sauter, Douglas P. "Assessing the Risks of FAX Confirmations," *Journal of Accountancy* (March 1990), pp. 75–79.

Chapter 13 ► REVIEW QUESTIONS

13-1 How does the auditor evaluate the competency of audit evidence obtained from outside sources?

13-2 Describe the relationship between reliability of accounting data and internal control.

13-3 Differentiate between the competency of audit evidence gained through personal knowledge of the auditor and evidence obtained indirectly.

13-4 What is the difference between convincing and persuasive audit evidence?

13-5 How does the cost of obtaining evidence affect its sufficiency?

13-6 How does an auditor make an objective evaluation of audit evidence?

13-7 List and describe seven techniques for gathering audit evidence. State how each could be applied to the audit of inventory.

13-8 List the characteristics of audit evidence and give an example of each.

13-9 By what three means may an auditor evaluate the reasonableness of the amount of an accounting estimate?

13-10 Describe four guidelines that affect the use of analytical procedures as substantive tests.

13-11 What is the "business approach" to substantive testing?

13-12 How does an auditor gain knowledge of his or her client's business operations?

13-13 How is ratio analysis used in an audit?

13-14 How does the auditor use regression analysis?

13-15 List six pairs of accounts on which audit work is often performed simultaneously.

13-16 What records does an auditor review to detect related party transactions?

13-17 Describe five transactions or events that may create substantial doubt as to the ability of an entity to continue as a going concern.

13-18 Explain the review process for audit working papers.

13-19 Differentiate among known, projected, and likely misstatements.

13-20 Describe nine matters about which the auditor should determine that the audit committee is informed.

Chapter 13 ► OBJECTIVE QUESTIONS

(* = author prepared; ** = CPA examination; *** = CMA examination)

**13-21 Which of the following statements is generally correct about the competence of evidential matter?

  a. Competence of evidential matter refers to the amount of corroborative evidence obtained.

  b. The more effective the internal control, the more assurance it provides about the reliability of the accounting data and financial statements.

  c. Information obtained indirectly from independent outside sources is more persuasive than the auditor's direct personal knowledge obtained through observation and inspection.

  d. Competence of evidential matter refers to the audit evidence obtained from outside the entity.

**13-22 Although the validity of evidential matter is dependent on the circumstances under which it is obtained, there are three general presumptions that have some usefulness. The situations given below indicate the relative reliability a CPA has placed on two types of evidence obtained in different situations. Which of these is an exception to one of the general presumptions?

  a. The CPA places more reliance on the balance in the scrap sales account at Plant A, where the CPA has made limited tests of transactions because of effective controls, than at Plant B, where the CPA has made extensive tests of transactions because of ineffective controls.

  b. The CPA places more reliance on the CPA's computation of interest payable on outstanding bonds than on the amount confirmed by the trustee.

  c. The CPA places more reliance on the report of an expert on an inventory of precious gems than on the CPA's physical observation of the gems.

   d. The CPA places more reliance on a schedule of insurance coverage obtained from the company's insurance agent than on one prepared by the internal audit staff.

**13-23 In testing the existence assertion for an asset, an auditor ordinarily works from the

   a. Financial statements to the potentially unrecorded items.

   b. Potentially unrecorded items to the financial statements.

   c. Accounting records to the supporting evidence.

   d. Supporting evidence to the accounting records.

*13-24 An auditor audits an accounting estimate by any of the following means except

   a. Testing the process used by management to develop the estimate.

   b. Obtaining a confirmation from an independent source.

   c. Developing an independent expectation.

   d. Reviewing subsequent events or transactions.

*13-25 When analytical procedures are used as substantive tests, some account relationships are more predictable than others. For which of the following accounts is the prior-year balance likely to be the best predictor of the current year balance?

   a. Accounts payable.   **c.** Cash.

   b. Revenues.   **d.** Inventory.

**13-26 For audits of financial statements made in accordance with generally accepted auditing standards, the use of analytical procedures is required to some extent

As a substantive test	In the final review stage
a. Yes	Yes
b. Yes	No
c. No	Yes
d. No	No

**13-27 Which of the following *best* describes the most important stage of an auditor's statistical analysis of significant ratios and trends?

   a. Computation of significant ratios and trends.

   b. Reconciliation of statistical data to the client's accounting ratios.

   c. Interpretation of significant variations and unusual relationships.

   d. Comparison of statistical data to prior-year

statistics and to similar data published by government and private sources.

***13-28 Which one of the following items is not a measure of a company's liquidity?

   a. Accounts receivable turnover.

   b. Acid test ratio.

   c. Debt-to-equity ratio.

   d. Operating cycle.

   e. Days' sales in inventory.

*13-29 An auditor may use regression analysis to predict an account balance. In the regression equation $E(Y) = B_0 + B_1X$, B_1 represents the

   a. Account being audited.

   b. Fixed cost in the account being audited.

   c. Expected amount.

   d. Relationship between the account being audited and another account.

*13-30 Audit work is often performed simultaneously on all the following pairs of accounts except

   a. Cash and common stock.

   b. Inventories and cost of goods sold.

   c. Property and depreciation expense.

   d. Accrued income taxes and income tax expense.

**13-31 An auditor searching for related party transactions should obtain an understanding of each subsidiary's relationship to the total entity because

   a. This may permit the audit of intercompany account balances to be performed as of concurrent dates.

   b. Intercompany transactions may have been consummated on terms equivalent to arm's-length transactions.

   c. This may reveal whether particular transactions would have taken place if the parties had *not* been related.

   d. The business structure may be deliberately designed to obscure related party transactions.

*13-32 If related party transactions are detected, the auditor cannot complete the audit until he or she

   a. Sends confirmations to all parties.

   b. Determines what the comparable arm's-length transaction would have been.

   c. Understands the business purpose of the transaction.

   d. Notifies the SEC.

*13-33 An auditor has a responsibility to evaluate the going concern status of an audit client for a(an)

a. Period of one year from the balance sheet date.

b. Period of one year from the date of the auditor's report.

c. Period of two years from the balance sheet date.

d. Indefinite period.

*13-34 All the following may indicate substantial doubt as to an entity's ability to continue as a going concern except

a. Work stoppages.

b. Legal proceedings.

c. Purchase of catastrophe insurance.

d. Operating losses.

*13-35 If an auditor has substantial doubt as to an entity's ability to continue as a going concern, he or she should

a. Discontinue the audit.

b. Consider management's plans for generating additional cash flow.

c. Perform additional audit work on long-term assets.

d. Contact legal counsel.

**13-36 Analytical procedures used in the overall review stage of an audit generally include

a. Gathering evidence concerning account balances that have *not* changed from the prior year.

b. Retesting control procedures that appeared to be ineffective during the assessment of control risk.

c. Considering unusual or unexpected account balances that were *not* previously identified.

d. Performing tests of transactions to corroborate management's financial statement assertions.

**13-37 In the course of an audit, the auditor will normally prepare a schedule of unadjusted differences for which the auditor did not propose adjustment when they were uncovered. What is the primary purpose served by this schedule?

a. To point out to the responsible client officials the errors made by various company personnel.

b. To identify the potential financial statement effects of misstatements that were considered immaterial when discovered.

c. To summarize the adjustments that must be made before the company can prepare and submit its federal tax return.

d. To summarize the misstatements made by the company so that corrections can be made after the audited financial statements are released.

*13-38 In the audit of accounts receivable an auditor sends confirmations to all customers with balances of $50,000 or more and to a sample of 25 percent of the customers with balances of less than $50,000. Overstatement errors of $12,000 were found in the accounts of $50,000 or more, and understatement errors of $3,000 were found in the sample. Likely misstatement for accounts receivable is

a. $0. **c.** $15,000.

b. $9,000. **d.** $24,000.

**13-39 An auditor would *least* likely initiate a discussion with a client's audit committee concerning

a. The methods used to account for significant unusual transactions.

b. The maximum dollar amount of misstatements that could exist without causing the financial statements to be materially misstated.

c. Indications of fraud and illegal acts committed by a corporate officer that were discovered by the auditor.

d. Disagreements with management as to accounting principles that were resolved during the current year's audit.

**13-40 An auditor is considering whether the omission of a substantive procedure considered necessary at the time of an audit may impair the auditor's present ability to support the previously expressed opinion. The auditor need *not* apply the omitted procedure if the

a. Financial statements and auditor's report were *not* distributed beyond management and the board of directors.

b. Auditor's previously expressed opinion was qualified because of a departure from GAAP.

c. Results of other procedures that were applied tend to compensate for the procedure omitted.

d. Omission is due to unreasonable delays by client personnel in providing data on a timely basis.

*13-41 For each description, match the term or terms that relates to the description. Each term may be used once, more than once, or not at all.

Description	Term

1. Sufficient competent evidential matter is to be obtained through inspection, observation, inquiries, and confirmations to afford a reasonable basis for an opinion regarding the financial statements under audit.

2. Auditors obtain acknowledgments in writing directly from third parties of transactions, balances, and other information.

3. Auditors combine and decompose amounts in meaningful ways to allow application of audit judgment.

4. Auditors relate two or more transactions or balances.

5. Assertion that may be made regarding an account.

6. Measures the rate at which a dependent variable changes in relation to an independent variable.

Term

a. Confirmations
b. Analysis
c. Regression analysis
d. Third standard of fieldwork
e. Audit procedure
f. Existence or occurrence

Chapter 13 ▶ DISCUSSION/CASE QUESTIONS

(* = author prepared; ** = CPA examination; *** = CMA examination)

*13-42   In each of the following cases, rank the various items of evidence on a scale from most persuasive to least persuasive. Furnish support for your rankings.

    a. Evidence to support the cash account.

      (1) Bank reconciliation prepared by the client.

      (2) A written confirmation of the bank balance, sent directly by the bank to the auditor.

      (3) Written certification by the client that the bank balance is correct.

      (4) The year's canceled checks and validated deposit slips held by the client.

    b. Evidence to support accounts receivable (not including the allowance for doubtful accounts).

      (1) Sales invoices held by the client.

      (2) Written certification by the client that the balance is correct.

      (3) Written confirmation of the balances, sent by the customers directly to the auditor.

      (4) An accounts receivable aging schedule prepared by the client.

      (5) Shipping documents held by the client, showing the dollar amount of merchandise sent to customers.

      (6) Deposit slips held by the client, showing the cash received from customers during the month after year-end.

    c. Evidence to support inventory quantities.

      (1) Purchase invoices held by the client.

      (2) Canceled checks issued to vendors.

      (3) Observations of the client's physical count.

      (4) A written certification from the client that the amount shown as inventory is correct.

      (5) Written confirmation of inventory quantities sent by a public warehouse directly to the auditor.

*13-43   One of the audit clients of Brown and Brown, CPAs, is We-Fit Manufacturing Company, makers of shirts, sweaters, and other clothing items. The finished goods inventory consists of merchandise placed in hundreds of sealed boxes on the warehouse floor. The client's inventory count consists of a count of boxes that are supposed to contain a standard number of shirts or sweaters. The only way the auditors can be certain about the contents of the boxes is to break them open and count the pieces of clothing. They do not wish to use this method of verification except on a few selected boxes.

Required:

a. What criterion would you use in deciding how many boxes to open, if any, during the inventory observation?

b. What are the possible legal implications associated with a massive number of empty boxes?

c. Would you seek extra audit evidence on the validity of inventory simply as a result of the client's count procedure? If so, what types?

*13-44   One of the clients of Cain, CPA, is a local financial institution. As part of the standard audit procedures, Cain sent notes receivable confirmations to 50 of the 2,000 customers.

Although a return envelope was sent with the confirmations, most of the customers chose to bring the letter to the office. Cain was interrupted constantly to explain orally the nature of the confirmation letter. Customers were told that their signatures were to be placed on the letter without any additional comment only if they agreed that they owed the amount printed on the letter. Otherwise, the customers were asked to indicate the amount they believed they owed.

Few of the customers seemed to understand the oral instructions given by Cain, and most merely signed the letter and left it. Cain was perplexed by these responses, but did not know whether to send additional letters, look for alternative types of evidence, or simply accept these signatures without additional audit procedures.

Required:

a. Which of the three courses of action would you recommend? If you reject all three courses of action, what would you recommend?

b. Comment in general on the validity and limitations of audit evidence gained from confirmation letters sent to the public.

*13-45   Classify the following items of audit evidence from most reliable (1) to least reliable (17). Discuss the reasons for your classifications.

a. Canceled payroll check.

b. Copy of client sales invoice.

c. Request for a travel advance.

d. Client-prepared receiving report for merchandise.

e. Client-prepared depreciation worksheet.

f. Journal entry to correct an account classification.

g. Board of director minutes signed by the corporate secretary.

h. Vendor invoice for merchandise purchased.

i. Client-prepared purchase order for merchandise.

j. Copy of client articles of incorporation.

k. Bank statement.

l. Cutoff bank statement received directly by the auditor.

m. Positive accounts receivable confirmation.

n. Client-prepared inventory count sheet.

o. Oral client representations.

p. Written client representations.

q. Representation letter from client's attorney.

*13-46 Mary Smith, a new staff auditor, has been assigned to interview Mad Dog Clancy, controller, about variations between expected and book amounts noted in performing analytical procedures as substantive tests. The interview went as follows:

MARY: Good morning, Mr. Clancy.

MAD DOG: What's good about it?

MARY: Well, not much, I suppose. I would like to talk with you about some potential errors in your financial statements.

MAD DOG: Errors! What do you mean "errors"? What errors are you talking about?

MARY: I'm referring to the fact that your revenue increased 15 percent this year, but the quantity shipped was not significantly different from last year and unit prices didn't change. How do you explain that?

MAD DOG: The answer is so simple that even a high school student should see it. While *total* quantities and *individual* prices didn't change, the mix of high- and low-priced items did change. We sold more of our more expensive products. Didn't you learn anything at that university you attended?

MARY: Well, that does seem like a logical explanation. I'll check it out. But I also would like to know why your freight expense is lower this year than last year.

MAD DOG: Mary, can't you put two plus two together and get four? You were in here yesterday asking about the increase in our equipment account, and I told you that we purchased our own trucks for delivery so we could save money from paying contract truckers. When is your firm going to start hiring people with some business sense?

MARY: Oh yes, I remember that now. I just didn't put the two together. Let me ask you about the decline in your inventory turnover. Was that caused by a deliberate inventory increase in anticipation of a large sales campaign this spring?

MAD DOG: Yeah, that's as good an answer as any. Now look, I have my own work to do, and I don't have any more time to talk with you.

MARY: That's all the help I need right now. I'll just check out your answers to be sure you are telling the truth. If I have any other problems I'll get back to you.

MAD DOG: I can hardly wait.

Required:

a. Evaluate Mary's interview techniques. What was wrong with each of Mary's statements or questions?

b. Except for her greeting, reword in an appropriate way each of Mary's statements or questions.

c. How do you discuss auditing matters with a disagreeable client?

**13-47 You are the auditor of Star Manufacturing Company. A trial balance taken from the books of Star at year-end follows.

Account	Dr. (Cr.)
Cash in bank	$ 87,000
Trade accounts receivable	345,000
Notes receivable	125,000
Inventories	317,000
Land	66,000
Buildings, net	350,000
Furniture, fixtures, and equipment, net	325,000
Trade accounts payable	(235,000)
Mortgages payable	(400,000)
Capital stock	(300,000)

Account	Dr. (Cr.)
Retained earnings	(510,000)
Sales	(3,130,000)
Cost of sales	2,300,000
General and administrative expenses	622,000
Legal and professional fees	3,000
Interest expense	35,000

There are no inventories consigned either in or out. All notes receivable are due from outsiders and held by Star.

Required:

a. Which accounts should be confirmed with outside sources?

b. Describe by whom they should be confirmed and the information that should be confirmed.

c. Organize your answer in the following format.

Account Name	By Whom Confirmed	Information to Be Confirmed

13-48 The purpose of all auditing procedures is to gather sufficient competent evidence to form an opinion regarding the financial statements taken as a whole.

Required:

a. In addition to the example below, identify and describe five techniques of gathering audit evidence to evaluate a client's inventory balance.

Technique	Description
Observation	An auditor watches the performance of some function, such as a client's annual inventory count.

b. Identify the five general assertions regarding a client's inventory balance and describe one *different* substantive auditing procedure for each assertion. Use the format illustrated below.

Assertion	Substantive Auditing Procedure

13-49 Bill Kelting, audit senior from New York City, was assigned to be in charge of the Hogeye Ranch Company audit. Before this engagement the only cows Bill had seen were in pictures. However, Bill knew how to perform an audit. A large sample of sales was traced to sales barn receipts, and expenses were traced to vendor invoices. Cattle were accounted for as purchased, sold, or on hand. All amounts in the financial statements were tied down to Bill's satisfaction. While reviewing the audit working papers on the last day of the audit, the manager inquired as to what happened to the calves. Bill replied that there were no calf transactions because no calves had been purchased during the year. The manager reminded Bill that calves could be acquired on a ranch without being purchased. Bill spent three days past the expected end of the job reviewing birthing records and accounting for the calves. The calves had been exchanged in one transaction for "next spring delivery" of heifers, but the transaction had not been recorded. Substantial changes were required in the financial statements and tax returns, and a large time overrun occurred.

How might this problem have been avoided?

**13-50   Analytical procedures are an important part of the audit process and consist of evaluations of financial information made by the study of plausible relationships among both financial and nonfinancial data. Analytical procedures are used to assist in planning other auditing procedures, as substantive tests in obtaining evidential matter, and as an overall review of the financial information.

Required:

a. Describe the factors that influence an auditor's decision to select analytical procedures as substantive tests, including the factors that affect their effectiveness and efficiency.

b. Describe an auditor's objectives in applying analytical procedures in the overall review stage of an audit and which analytical procedures generally would be included in the overall review stage.

*13-51   Trend and Jones, CPAs, were planning their initial audit of Kargo Corporation, whose stock traded on the New York Stock Exchange. Although the partners had consulted with the predecessor auditor and had reviewed prior-year working papers, they still had a number of questions about the areas that should be given special attention in the audit. To provide them with more insight, Ms. Trend and Mr. Jones decided to take the published financial statements of Kargo Corporation for the last two years and the statements for the first quarter of this year and develop some ratios. They calculated the following amounts.

	19X6	19X7	1st Quarter 19X8
Current ratio	2.1 to 1	2.0 to 1	1.8 to 1
Accounts receivable turnover	8.3	8.4	8.6[a]
Inventory turnover	7.4	9.2	10.8[a]
Times interest earned	1.7	1.6	1.4
Earnings per share	10.50	11.62	3.45
Debt/equity ratio	.95	1.20	1.24
Dividends per share	2.50	3.00	.90

[a]Annualized.

In addition to these ratios, the following information is available.

1. Kargo's credit terms are 30 days net.

2. The Kargo Corporation has a loan restriction that requires it to maintain at least a 2 to 1 current ratio.

3. The "normal" inventory turnover for the industry in which Kargo Corporation operates is 10.

Required:

   a. Indicate the areas in which the auditors should concentrate special effort. Consider only the areas revealed by the ratio analysis. Do not name specific audit procedures.

   b. Discuss actions that the management of Kargo might be inclined to take to cover up any possible adverse effects of these listed ratios. What could the auditors do to provide reasonable assurance that they found these actions?

*13-52   Joyce Cover, CPA, was engaged to audit the financial statements of Extensive, Inc., a first-time audit client, for the year ended December 31, 19X6. The assessment of control risk was conducted during the late fall of 19X6 and, with the exception of accounts receivable and sales, control risk was assessed at a low level. Extensive, Inc. compiled the following financial statement data as of December 31, 19X6 and for the year 19X6.

Sales		$800,000
Cost of goods sold		500,000
Gross margin		$300,000
Operating expenses:		
Salaries	$ 60,000	
Depreciation	40,000	
Uncollectible accounts	20,000	
Commissions	8,000	
Supplies	12,000	
Travel	15,000	
Miscellaneous	15,000	170,000
Net income before tax		$130,000
Income tax expense		60,000
Net income		70,000

Assets

Current assets:		
Cash	$ 2,000	
Marketable securities	5,000	
Accounts receivable (net of allowance		
for doubtful accounts of $22,000)	78,000	
Inventory	50,000	$135,000
Long-term assets:		
Equipment	$200,000	
Less: Accumulated depreciation	80,000	120,000
Other assets		17,000
Total assets		$272,000

Liabilities and Equities

Current liabilities:		
Accounts payable	$ 15,000	
Accrued expenses	2,500	$ 17,500
Long-term liabilities:		
Notes payable		110,000
Total liabilities		$127,500
Capital stock	$100,000	
Retained earnings	44,500	144,500
Total liabilities and equities		$272,000

Required:

a. On which of the above accounts would evidence be obtained through

   (1) Inspection?
   (2) Observation?
   (3) Inquiry?
   (4) Confirmation?

(The same account may be listed more than once. Give reasons for your listings.)

b. On which of the above accounts could evidence be obtained from independent outside sources? Name the independent outside sources for each listed account.

c. On which accounts would the evidence gathered be affected by the high level of control risk? Give reasons for your answers.

d. On which accounts is the evidence gathered likely to be most persuasive? Least persuasive? Give reasons for your answers.

e. On which accounts is the cost of obtaining evidence likely to be the highest? The lowest? Give reasons for your answers.

f. On which accounts is the evaluation of evidence likely to be the most subjective? The least subjective? Give reasons for your answers.

*13-53 You are completing your audit of Carleson Motorcycle Manufacturing Company and evaluating the going concern status of the company. Competition from foreign motorcycle makers has been severe. The company incurred losses this year and last year. Management is projecting a loss for next year but a sizable profit in the following year because of the introduction of a new model and anticipated cost reductions. At the audit date, current assets exceed current liabilities although there has been a decline in cash and an increase in inventory. The company is near its long-term borrowing limit.

The company has been slow in paying its suppliers because of the cash shortage, but all suppliers continue to extend normal trade credit. The company's union agreement expires next year, and union leaders have indicated that they expect to obtain large wage increases for their members. Management believes that a new union agreement containing a small wage increase can be reached without a strike.

The company's management is stable and experienced. It has overcome other serious business problems in the past and believes that its current problems can be resolved without substantial disposition of assets outside the ordinary course of business, restructuring of debt, externally forced revisions of its operations, or similar actions.

Required:

Consider the preceding information and decide whether you have substantial doubt as to the ability of the company to continue as a going concern for a reasonable period of time. Support your decision with reasons in a memorandum to the audit manager.

*13-54 You have completed your audit of Ethridge Construction Company for the year ended November 30, 19X5, and have scheduled a meeting with the company's audit committee for the next day. The company builds small apartment buildings in a three-state area and has been only marginally profitable during the last five years. Ethridge uses the percentage-of-completion method to recognize revenue, and although you were generally satisfied with the overall fairness of the financial statements after your audit last year, you believe the company tends to be optimistic in estimating the stage of completion of its work-in-process.

You did not receive the assistance you anticipated from the company's internal auditor because she was working on a special project for the controller. This resulted in your performing more work, which resulted in a higher-than-anticipated audit fee. The client protested the higher audit fee but has agreed to pay it.

One of Ethridge's competitors issued its annual report a week before Ethridge. The president has asked that you complete next year's audit two weeks earlier than this year so that Ethridge can issue its annual report first. You worked an excessive amount of overtime just to meet this year's deadline.

Prepare an outline of all the points you would like to discuss with the audit committee.

*13-55 Presented below are two sets of financial ratios. The ratios in the first column were computed from EAZ Manufacturing's *prior-year audited* statements. In the second column are ratios computed from the *current-year unaudited* statements. The difference between the two years' ratios could be the result of *normal year-to-year variation* and/or an *error* in the unaudited statements which has a material effect on net income or, if only the balance sheet is affected, is material in relation to total assets or total liabilities. You have no other reason to expect major changes from the prior year's financial relationships. Assume that any financial statement error is caused by a *single* mistake or multiple occurrences of the *same mistake*. (There is only one cause.)

For example: The change in the ratios might have resulted from *next period's credit sales recorded in the current period.*

Financial Ratios

Ratio	Prior year audited	Current year Unaudited
Gross margin		
$\dfrac{\text{Gross profit}}{\text{Net sales}}$	26.1%	26.3%
Current ratio		
$\dfrac{\text{Current assets}}{\text{Current liabilities}}$	2.43	2.72
Quick ratio		
$\dfrac{\text{Quick assets}}{\text{Current liabilities}}$	1.04	1.25

Source: Adapted from Robert Libby and David M. Frederick, "Experience and the Ability to Explain Audit Findings," *Journal of Accounting Research* (Autumn 1990), pp. 348–367.

Required:

List all the possible errors that you can think of that may have caused the changes in the ratios.

*13-56   For each audit procedure, indicate (1) the assertion to which it relates, (2) the means of gathering audit evidence, and (3) the characteristic of the audit evidence gathered. The first audit procedure is shown as an example.

Audit Procedure	Assertion	Means of Gathering Evidence	Characteristic of Audit Evidence
1. Send letters to customers with accounts receivable balances. (Example)	Existence	Confirmation	Evidence from third parties received directly by the auditor
2. Examine schedule showing the age of each customer's accounts receivable balance.			
3. Compare sales for current and prior accounting periods.			
4. Inspect credit files of customers with past due accounts receivable balances.			
5. Ask management about any accounts receivable pledged during the period.			
6. Inspect due dates of accounts receivable balances to determine their current/noncurrent status.			

Sampling for Substantive Tests of Account Balances—Nonstatistical and Statistical

''How prone to doubt, how cautious are the wise!''

HOMER, *Odyssey*

LEARNING OBJECTIVES

After reading and studying the material in this chapter, the student should be able to

▶ Compare the risks of incorrect rejection and incorrect acceptance.

▶ Define the population on which sampling will be performed.

▶ Compare the three sampling techniques for a substantive test.

▶ Determine the sample size for a substantive test by considering the (1) variation in the population, (2) risk levels, (3) tolerable misstatement, (4) expected dollar misstatement, and (5) population size.

▶ Compare the three methods of selecting a sample.

▶ Perform quantitative and qualitative evaluations of sample results.

▶ Compare the following three statistical methods of estimating the dollar amount of a population: (1) mean estimation; (2) ratio estimation; and (3) difference estimation.

▶ Apply mean estimation as a classical statistical sampling technique.

▶ Describe the characteristics of probability proportional to size sampling.

▶ Select and evaluate a probability proportional to size sample.

In Chapter 10, we discussed tests of controls that require the use of sampling techniques, both nonstatistical and statistical. In this chapter we discuss the use of sampling techniques, both nonstatistical and statistical, for substantive tests of account balances.

We begin with discussions and illustrations of the general concepts of sampling for substantive tests, followed by the application of these concepts to (1) nonstatistical, (2) classical statistical, and (3) probability proportional to size sampling techniques.

SAMPLING FOR SUBSTANTIVE TESTS

A number of substantive tests lend themselves to the use of sampling methods. Confirmation of accounts receivable, comparison of physical inventory counts and perpetual inventory records, and inspection of invoices for additions to property are examples discussed in Chapters 15 through 18. When the auditor decides that sampling is appropriate for a given substantive test, the objective is to test the reasonableness of the amount on the client's records. The audit procedure is a form of hypothesis test.

Assume that the auditor is testing the clerical accuracy of the client's perpetual inventory records. The hypothesis is that the evidence supports the recorded inventory amount; the dollar difference between the recorded amount and the correct amount is not so large that when it is added to errors in all other accounts it will make the financial statements materially misstated. The sample results will lead the auditor either to accept or reject the hypothesis.

Thus, the acceptance or nonacceptance of the hypothesis carries with it two sampling risks.

1. The *risk of incorrect rejection* is the risk that the auditor will incorrectly reject the hypothesis that the evidence supports the account balance. The sampling results would lead the auditor to believe incorrectly that the account balance contains more dollar misstatement than can be tolerated.

2. The *risk of incorrect acceptance* is the risk that the auditor will incorrectly accept the hypothesis that the evidence supports the account balance. The sampling results would lead the auditor to believe incorrectly that the account does not contain more dollar misstatement than can be tolerated.

When sampling is used as a hypothesis test, the sampling objectives are twofold:

1. To determine by *estimation sampling* techniques the estimated account balance the auditor considers to be correct.

2. To determine whether the difference between the estimated amount and the recorded amount allows the auditor to accept the evidence as supporting the account balance at a given risk level.

In most audit sampling applications, the characteristic of interest is the *projected misstatement,* which is the difference between the estimated and recorded amounts. In testing the accuracy of inventory records, for example, assume that the recorded amount on the client's records is $100,000. As a result of the sample, the auditor estimates the inventory to be $90,000. The auditor must consider all available evidence and make a judgment as to whether this projected misstatement of $10,000 is so large as to cause rejection of the hypothesis that the evidence supports the account balance at a given risk level. The discussion in the remainder of this chapter illustrates the sampling tools and other guidelines used to aid the auditor in making these types of judgments.

DEFINING THE POPULATION

The objective of the substantive test affects how the auditor defines the population on which the test will be performed. Basically, this is a fairly simple task; *the population* may consist of all items in the account balance. If the records show 1,000 accounts receivable customer balances, the population may be defined as 1,000 units.

In defining the population, however, the auditor should consider the following situations.

1. If the objective of the test is to detect unrecorded items (completeness), the population is *not* the items recorded on the client's books. Accounts payable is a case in point. For purposes of confirmation requests, the population is not the recorded amounts, but the list of vendors that did business with the client during the audit period (the source of potential accounts payable).
2. The physical representation of the population may not include all items in the population. If this is true, then a sample of items from the physical representation may not be representative. In testing the proper classification of additions to property and equipment, the auditor may be shown a file drawer of invoices supporting this class of transactions. The auditor should determine that this file drawer of invoices is, indeed, the complete population of additions to property and equipment (i.e., no invoices are missing from the file drawer).

It may be desirable to test 100 percent of some part of an account balance. Many accounting populations consist of a few large amounts, a moderate number of reasonably large amounts, and a large number of small amounts. A few large accounts receivable may need to be confirmed on a 100 percent basis. A few large inventory balances may need to be compared to the physical count on a 100 percent basis. Sampling techniques discussed in this chapter are not applicable to these balances.

Sampling units are individual elements in the population and, for sampling purposes, could consist of the following:

1. An account balance.
2. A transaction within an account.
3. A document evidencing a transaction.

In defining the sampling unit, the auditor must consider the objective of the sample and the likelihood of obtaining usable results. Sometimes consideration should be given to confirming individual customer invoices rather than the total accounts receivable balances. If the auditor believes that there will be a large number of differences between the recorded amounts and confirmation replies and that these differences will be difficult to resolve, consideration might be given to defining individual invoices as the population.

SAMPLING TECHNIQUES

Basically, there are three sampling techniques for a substantive test.

1. The auditor can use *nonstatistical sampling techniques,* which rely solely on the use of judgment in determining the sample size and evaluating the sample results. Although tables are available to aid the auditor in deciding on the size of the sample, it is not necessary to use these tables. Nonstatistical sampling is convenient and does not require knowledge of statistical methods. If the auditor has a thorough understanding of the objective of the test and a good knowledge of the population characteristics, a nonstatistical sample may produce reliable results.

2. *Classical statistical sampling techniques* may be used. The auditor needs some understanding of normal distribution theory (or available help from other auditors) to effectively use these methods. The auditor couples judgmental factors with statistical equations and tables to determine the sample size and quantitatively evaluate the sample results. Classical statistical sampling may be useful when the population contains many differences between the recorded and audited amounts.

3. A statistical sampling technique that has gained popularity is *probability proportional to size sampling.* Although some knowledge of statistical theory is desirable, the formulas are relatively easy to use and tables are available to aid in determining the sample size and quantitatively evaluating the sample results. This technique is particularly useful when the population contains a small number of large dollar overstatements. However, if the population contains a large number of small overstatements and understatements, classical statistical sampling or nonstatistical sampling may be more useful.

DETERMINING THE SAMPLE SIZE

Whether nonstatistical or statistical sampling methods are used in the substantive test, the auditor must make a number of judgments to determine an optimum sample size. The following factors must be considered:

1. The variation in the population.
2. Risk levels the auditor is willing to accept.
3. The tolerable misstatement the auditor is willing to accept.
4. The dollar misstatement the auditor expects to exist in the population.
5. The size of the population.

In the following subsections, we discuss each of these judgmental factors.

Variation in the Population

Many accounting populations have a high variability (or dispersion). Statistically, this variability is measured by the *standard deviation.* Nonstatistically, it is measured judgmentally by a review of the dispersion or range of the values of the sampling units. For example, an inventory population may have the following characteristics:

20 items each with dollar amounts over $40,000

100 items each with dollar amounts between $10,000 and $39,999

1,000 items each with dollar amounts under $10,000

Such a wide variation necessitates a relatively large sample for the sample to be representative of the population. If all other factors remain the same, wider variations in the population call for larger sample sizes, and vice versa. Generally, the sample size can be smaller and more efficient if a population with high variability is stratified into meaningful groups. Then, a sample or a 100 percent test is taken from each group (or stratum).

An obvious basis for dividing this population is the recorded dollar amount. The auditor could do the following:

1. Audit all 20 items over $40,000.
2. Select a relatively large sample of items with dollar amounts between $10,000 and $39,999.
3. Select a relatively small sample of items with dollar amounts under $10,000.

Recorded dollar amount is not the only basis for dividing the population into groups or strata. Another basis is the likelihood of misstatement. Prior experience may show that a certain group of inventory items consistently contains differences between the perpetual records and the physical counts. In this case, the auditor may wish to test these error-prone items on a 100 percent basis.

The variation in the population may be estimated by conducting a pilot sample or by measuring the variation of the recorded amounts. Note that the auditor is trying to estimate the variation in the correct (but unknown) amounts, which may or may not be the recorded amounts. A pilot sample (20 to 30 items) is selected and audit procedures are performed on those items. Such a sample enables the auditor to gain a better understanding of the difference in variation between recorded and audited (correct) amounts. Such a test may show that the physical counts of these items vary more widely than the amounts on the perpetual records. This may demonstrate to the auditor a need for a large sample size.

If the auditor has no reason to believe that there are significant differences between recorded and audited amounts, an estimate of the variability of the recorded amounts might be sufficient. If statistical sampling is used, this variability is measured by computing the standard deviation of the recorded amounts. If nonstatistical sampling is used, the estimated variability can be measured by the standard deviation of recorded amounts or by the use of judgment.

In the latter part of this chapter, we demonstrate how stratification can be used in nonstatistical sampling and classical statistical sampling. Stratification is not necessary when probability proportional to size sampling is used because stratification is inherent in this sampling technique.

Considerations in Setting the Risk of Incorrect Acceptance

Audit risk is the risk that material errors will occur in the financial statements and not be detected by internal control or the auditor. Audit risk is also described as the risk that there is a misstatement in an account balance greater than is tolerable and that the auditor fails to detect this error. Audit risk, which is to be set at a low level, is composed of three factors that have been discussed in earlier chapters, particularly Chapter 7.

1. *Inherent risk.* The risk that misstatements that are more than tolerable will occur in the accounting process.
2. *Control risk.* The risk that misstatements that are more than tolerable will not be prevented or detected by internal control.
3. *Detection risk.* The risk that misstatements that are more than tolerable will not be detected by substantive tests.

Professional standards do not specify the degree of reliance that should be placed on each factor. That decision is made in the context of a specific audit situation. The descriptive relationships among these factors, sample size, and planned sampling risk of incorrect acceptance for substantive tests are shown in the following table.

Factor	Planned sampling risk of incorrect acceptance	Sample size of substantive test of details
1. Susceptibility of account balance or assertion to misstatement		
a. Greater	Lower	Larger
b. Lesser	Higher	Smaller
2. Assessed level of control risk related to account balance or assertion		
a. Greater	Lower	Larger
b. Lesser	Higher	Smaller
3. Risk that analytical procedures and other substantive tests of details will not detect misstatements in account balance or assertion		
a. Greater	Lower	Larger
b. Lesser	Higher	Smaller

If the auditor wishes to quantify the risk of incorrect acceptance as a planning tool for a substantive test of details, the following form of the audit risk model may be used (*TD* is the risk of incorrect acceptance in the following audit risk models).

$$AR = IR \times CR \times APR \times TD$$

$$TD = \frac{AR}{IR \times CR \times APR}$$

where

AR = audit risk

IR = inherent risk

CR = control risk

APR = the risk that analytical procedures and other related substantive tests of details will not detect misstatements greater than are tolerable

TD = the allowable risk of incorrect acceptance on a substantive test of details

Assume that an auditor accepted an audit risk of 5 percent that an account balance or assertion contained misstatements that when added to misstatements in other accounts or assertions would cause the financial statements to be materially misstated. Assume, also, that IR, CR, and APR were set at 100 percent each (i.e., there is a 100 percent probability that a misstatement will occur, a 100 percent probability that internal control will not detect it, and a 100 percent probability that analytical procedures and other substantive tests of details will not detect it). The TD risk is computed as follows:

$$TD = 0.05/(1.00 \times 1.00 \times 1.00)$$

$$TD = 0.05 \text{ or } 5 \text{ percent}$$

The auditor is placing no reliance on the lack of susceptibility of the account balance to error, internal control, analytical procedures, or other substantive tests. The risk of incorrect acceptance is low, and the sample size is large. An example is a small organization without adequate accounting expertise, without segregation of duties, and where there are no reliable amounts with which to perform analytical procedures. In this case, the auditor would lower the sampling risk and perform extensive substantive tests.

Assume that the auditor sets audit risk (AR) at 5 percent. The planned substantive test using sampling is a test of the clerical accuracy of items on the physical inventory listings. There are several thousand items on the list, so a sample will be taken.

Assume that the inherent processes and internal control procedures that relate to inventory summarization are reliable in some respects. However, some weaknesses exist in compiling inventory listings because inexperienced personnel are used. On this basis, the auditor assigns IR a risk factor of 0.80 and CR a risk factor of 0.60.

Most of the analytical procedures are designed to test for proper valuation and disclosure of inventories. However, the auditor does conduct another test of details by tracing test counts made during the physical inventory observation to the inventory listings. The auditor also accounts for physical inventory count sheets. On this basis, the auditor assigns APR a risk factor of 0.50.

The risk that the auditor may incorrectly accept the inventory listings as being accurately compiled is calculated as follows:

$$TD = AR/(IR \times CR \times APR)$$

$$TD = 0.05/(0.80 \times 0.60 \times 0.50)$$

$$TD = 0.20 \text{ or } 20 \text{ percent}$$

If the auditor did not wish to quantify the risk associated with the planned substantive test of details, the following nonquantitative set of decision rules could be used, assuming that audit risk is kept at a low level.

1. If an account or assertion is inherently susceptible to misstatement and there is no reliance on internal control and other substantive tests, set the risk of incorrect acceptance at a very low level.

2. If an account or assertion is inherently susceptible to some misstatement and there is moderate reliance on internal control and other substantive tests, set the risk of incorrect acceptance at a moderate level.

3. If an account or assertion is not inherently susceptible to misstatement and there is high reliance on internal control and other substantive tests, set the risk of incorrect acceptance at a high level.

4. If an account or assertion is inherently susceptible to some misstatement and there is moderate reliance on internal control and low reliance on other substantive tests, or vice versa, set the risk of incorrect acceptance somewhere between moderate and low.

If the risk of incorrect acceptance is set too low, the auditor performs excessive work and the audit is inefficient. If it is set too high, the auditor does not perform enough work and the audit may be ineffective (sometimes resulting in a lawsuit against the auditor).

Considerations in Setting the Risk of Incorrect Rejection

The consequences of incorrectly rejecting an account balance are additional audit cost or an incorrect audit adjustment. Therefore, these two consequences should be prime factors in deciding on the appropriate risk level. The auditor should consider the type of audit procedure used and the viable alternatives should the audit procedure result in a rejection of the account balance. For example, the auditor may examine the client's shipping records if the evaluation of the confirmation requests results in a conclusion that the client's accounts receivable balance might be materially misstated. If the examination of shipping records is not a costly audit procedure, the risk of incorrect rejection is set at a relatively high level.

Similarly, if observation of the client's physical inventory results in a conclusion that the client's inventory balance might be materially misstated, the auditor may reexamine the control procedures in the purchases/inventory cycle. If this reexamination is a costly process, the risk of incorrect rejection may be set at a relatively low level and the sample size of the physical observation tests may be set at a relatively high level.

Tolerable Misstatement the Auditor Is Willing to Accept

Recall from Chapter 10 that in conducting tests of controls the auditor is required to estimate the highest population deviation rate that can be tolerated without altering planned reliance on the internal control procedure being tested. This deviation rate is called the tolerable rate.

In conducting substantive tests, the auditor is required to estimate the misstatement that can exist in an account balance which, when added to the misstatements in all other accounts, will not cause the financial statements to be materially misstated. This estimate is called *tolerable misstatement* and is a planning concept related to the auditor's estimate of materiality. The establishment of tolerable misstatement is discussed in Chapter 7.

Although the dollar amount of a potential misstatement is only one measure of materiality, let us use it for illustrative purposes. Assume that recorded net income before income taxes is $500,000. The auditor has determined that the financial statements are materially misstated if there is a misstatement in net income before income taxes of more than $40,000. Assume, too, that the auditor is conducting a substantive test of the clerical accuracy of the perpetual inventory records. To determine sample size, an estimate of tolerable misstatement must be made for this account balance. The auditor might follow this line of reasoning.

1. Misstatements in other account balances could create a misstatement in net income before income taxes as high as $30,000. The tolerable misstatement for inventory should be set in such a way that materiality for the entire financial statements does not exceed $40,000.

2. Based on these prior estimates and the auditor's estimate of materiality, the tolerable misstatement for inventory might be set at $10,000.

The auditor must carefully consider the dollar amount of tolerable misstatement for a given substantive test of an account balance. A higher tolerable misstatement causes the sample size to decrease, and a lower tolerable misstatement causes the sample size to increase. A smaller sample size lowers the probability of detecting a given misstatement; a sample size that is too large results in an inefficient use of time.

The Expected Misstatement in the Population

Recall, again, from Chapter 10 that as the expected amount of deviation in the population approaches the tolerable rate, there is a smaller *allowance for sampling risk*. In conducting substantive tests, the same logic is applied to the auditor's estimate of the expected dollar misstatement in the population. The difference between expected misstatement (estimated deviation rate in attribute sampling) and tolerable misstatement (tolerable rate in attribute sampling) represents the allowance for sampling risk. So as expected misstatement increases, the allowance for sampling risk decreases and the sample size of the substantive test increases.

An estimate of the dollar amount of misstatement in the population can be made in a number of ways. (Note some similarity to the ways of estimating the deviation rate in attribute sampling.)

1. Information from the prior year's audit may be used.

2. The auditor may consider the type of account being examined. For example, the customer billing process may be less effective than the methods of calculating perpetual inventory amounts. Therefore, on the basis of this information, the auditor may estimate a higher dollar misstatement in accounts receivable than in inventory.

3. The auditor may use similar tests to estimate the dollar misstatement. In examining the documentation supporting additions to property, the auditor may estimate the dollar misstatement in this class of transactions to be the same

as the dollar misstatement found when documentation supporting additions to another account was examined.

If auditors have no reason to expect misstatements, this amount may be set at zero.

Size of the Population

Generally, the larger the population, the larger the required sample size for substantive tests. This principle differs from attribute sampling discussed in Chapter 10, where population size has no effect except for very small populations. Usually, population size is easily determined by a count of the elements in the population (e.g., number of customer accounts that comprise total accounts receivable).

METHOD OF SAMPLE SELECTION

In substantive testing, as in tests of controls, the sample should be selected in such a way that it is expected to be representative of the population. For example, several methods are discussed in Chapter 10; in this section we will briefly review these methods.

1. The sample can be selected judgmentally in such a way that no obvious or apparent bias exists (haphazard sampling).
2. Systematic sampling can be used. This sampling method is convenient and under certain conditions can produce sampling results as reliable as random number sampling.
3. Random number sampling can be used. Each time a sample item is selected, every item in the population has an equal chance of selection.

PERFORMING THE SAMPLING PLAN

After selecting the sample, the applicable audit procedure should be applied to each sample item. In this respect, there is no difference between nonstatistical, classical statistical, and probability proportional to size sampling. The audit procedure is the same regardless of which sampling technique is used.

What if a sample item is missing, such as an invoice? In this case, the auditor must exercise judgment and take one of two courses of action.

1. If the auditor believes the evaluation of misstatement in the account balance would not be altered if the missing item were misstated, alternative procedures may be omitted.
2. If the auditor believes the evaluation of misstatement in the account balance might be altered if the missing item were misstated, alternative procedures should be used.

The decision to use alternative procedures depends on the auditor's assessment of the importance of the missing item. A missing page from an inventory listing that represents 20 percent of the total account balance would be assessed differently than a missing purchase invoice that supports a small addition to property. The auditor should also consider whether his or her previous assessment of control risk should be reevaluated because of the missing items.

EVALUATING SAMPLE RESULTS

Quantitative Evaluation

After the sample is selected and the audit procedure performed, the last step is to evaluate the sample results. If statistical sampling is used, part of the evaluation will be made with the aid of tables and computations. With nonstatistical sampling, only professional judgment is used to make the quantitative and qualitative evaluations.

First, the audited values should be compared with the recorded values and misstatements compiled. The auditor should be certain that differences between the audited and recorded values are misstatements. For example, any difference between an accounts receivable confirmation reply and the amount on the books should be reviewed for possible reconciling items. If the difference can be resolved (a payment in transit by a customer), it is not considered a misstatement.

Next, the misstatement found in the sample should be projected to the population. The techniques for projecting misstatements and computing likely misstatements are explained and illustrated on pages 404–406 of Chapter 13. Note that the projected misstatement is more than the sum of the misstatements found in the sample. The projection is actually an estimate of what the misstatement in the population would be if every item were examined.

To illustrate, assume that no category of items is examined on a 100 percent basis. A sample of 100 items is taken from a population of 2,500 items; four percent of the population items (10 percent of the dollar amount of the population) is sampled. The total misstatement detected in the sample is $1,000.

There are two ways to calculate a projected misstatement in the population.

1. Divide the total misstatement in the sample by the percentage of dollars in the population that was sampled. In this illustration, the projected misstatement is $10,000 ($1,000 misstatement divided by 10 percent dollar percentage of the population in the sample).

2. Calculate an average misstatement per sampled item and multiply it by the number of items in the population. In this illustration, the projected misstatement is $25,000 ($1,000 misstatement divided by 100 items in the sample = $10, the average misstatement per sampled item, times 2,500, the number of items in the population).

This difference between the two projected misstatements results because 10 percent of the dollar amount but only 4 percent of the number of items in the population are sampled. Which method should be used? The decision depends on whether the misstatements in the sample relate better to the dollar amount of the items sampled or are fairly constant among all items. If the former is true, the projected misstatement should be $10,000; if the latter is true, the projected misstatement should be $25,000.

To elaborate further, assume that an audit procedure such as confirmation is applied to individual accounts receivable. A $110 misstatement is found in a recorded amount of $1,000, a $45 misstatement is found in a recorded amount of $500, and so on. It appears that misstatements relate to recorded dollar amounts and that $10,000 is a more reliable projected misstatement. However, assume that the amounts of the misstatements range from $8 to $12 per account. In this case, the amounts of the misstatements appear to be fairly constant, and $25,000 appears to be a more reliable projected misstatement.

Assume that both four percent of the items and four percent of the dollar amount of the population were sampled. The projected misstatement is the same using either method. Under method one, the projected misstatement is $25,000 ($1,000/0.04). Under method two, the projected misstatement is $25,000 ($1,000/100 = $10 × 2,500 = $25,000).

When the auditor is satisfied that differences between recorded and audited amounts in the sample are misstatements, the client should be asked to adjust the recorded amounts. After calculating the projected misstatement, any adjustments agreed on and recorded by the client can be subtracted from this projected misstatement. The remaining part of the projected misstatement is used to determine the likely misstatement, illustrated in Chapter 13.

Even if the likely misstatement is not considered to be individually material, the auditor should not dismiss it as immaterial. All likely misstatements in all audit tests should be combined and a decision made as to whether the financial statements taken as a whole are materially misstated. Misstatements in individual accounts may be singularly immaterial, but collectively all the misstatements may be material. See page 407 of Chapter 13 for an example of an audit working paper that combines such immaterial misstatements.

Qualitative Evaluation

In addition to projecting misstatements found in a sample and quantitatively evaluating sample results, the auditor should make qualitative evaluations. Consideration should be given to the cause and nature of misstatements and the relationship of the misstatements to other phases of the audit.

For example, the likely misstatements may be small, but they occurred in a clustered group of items. All the misstatements found in the sample may be of a certain type, giving the auditor reason to believe that there may be a pattern in the population.

If many significant unexpected misstatements are found, the auditor may reevaluate the assessment of control risk related to the account balance. This reevaluation may, in turn, result in an expanded sample or an extension of other related tests of the same account balance.

AN ILLUSTRATION OF A SUBSTANTIVE TEST USING NONSTATISTICAL SAMPLING

The Sampling Plan

For our illustration of nonstatistical sampling, we will use Table 14.1, which contains the following information for 100 accounts receivable amounts:

TABLE 14.1
Information for Nonstatistical and Classical Statistical Sampling Illustrations

Account number	Client book amount	Audit confirmation amount	Difference	Account number	Client book amount	Audit confirmation amount	Difference
1	$10,200	$10,200	$ —	41	$ 9,880	$ 9,880	$ —
2	6,960	15,340	8,380	42	3,060	3,060	—
3	2,080	2,180	100	43	—	—	—
4	18,470	19,070	600	44	55,510	55,510	—
5	—	—	—	45	26,520	20,160	(6,360)
6	12,400	12,400	—	46	1,950	1,950	—
7	53,910	54,180	270	47	9,500	9,500	—
8	11,900	11,900	—	48	3,060	3,060	—
9	24,540	25,540	—	49	—	—	—
10	2,180	2,180	—	50	26,050	26,050	—
11	50,000	40,270	(9,730)	51	31,960	28,360	(3,600)
12	46,060	53,600	7,540	52	8,500	8,500	—
13	21,060	21,060	—	53	—	—	—
14	4,020	4,020	—	54	37,220	37,220	—
15	13,350	13,350	—	55	145,220	145,220	—
16	32,400	32,400	—	56	—	—	—
17	25,070	25,070	—	57	—	—	—
18	28,240	27,940	(300)	58	5,820	5,820	—
19	6,500	6,500	—	59	149,410	149,770	360
20	—	—	—	60	17,800	8,900	(8,900)
21	1,440	1,440	—	61	30,080	30,080	—
22	6,690	6,690	—	62	33,290	33,290	—
23	5,430	5,430	—	63	31,750	29,750	(2,000)
24	7,300	7,300	—	64	10,800	10,800	—
25	7,700	3,850	(3,850)	65	4,250	4,250	—
26	1,450	1,450	—	66	5,690	5,690	—
27	70,490	71,930	1,440	67	20,640	20,640	—
28	6,400	6,400	—	68	—	—	—
29	8,900	8,900	—	69	18,600	18,600	—
30	—	—	—	70	6,600	7,600	1,000
31	2,380	2,380	—	71	2,000	2,000	—
32	7,420	7,240	(180)	72	24,550	24,550	—
33	4,800	—	(4,800)	73	39,500	40,500	1,000
34	2,400	2,400	—	74	—	—	—
35	4,800	4,800	—	75	9,060	9,060	—
36	—	7,740	7,740	76	1,000	1,000	—
37	8,450	8,450	—	77	10,410	10,410	—
38	3,450	3,450	—	78	11,900	11,900	—
39	10,300	10,300	—	79	5,760	5,760	—
40	20,350	20,350	—	80	—	—	—

TABLE 14.1 *Continued*

Account number	Client book amount	Audit confirmation amount	Difference	Account number	Client book amount	Audit confirmation amount	Difference
81	$ 100	$ 100	$ —	91	$ 52,180	$ 52,180	$ —
82	48,600	48,600	—	92	1,190	1,190	—
83	8,850	8,850	—	93	7,200	7,200	—
84	1,040	1,040	—	94	—	—	—
85	—	—	—	95	9,750	9,750	—
86	29,400	29,400	—	96	11,600	11,600	—
87	5,760	5,760	—	97	5,400	5,400	—
88	10,200	10,200	—	98	1,450	1,450	—
89	—	—	—	99	7,100	7,100	—
90	8,730	8,730	—	100	3,600	3,600	—
				Totals	$1,559,980	$1,548,690	$(11,290)

1. Account numbers.
2. Client book or recorded amounts.
3. The audited amounts or the amounts that would be correctly confirmed by the customers if confirmation letters were sent to them.
4. The differences or misstatements in the account balances. For purposes of this illustration, assume that no differences can be resolved by the auditor and all of them are classified as misstatements.

The audit test consists of positive confirmation requests sent to a sample of the 100 accounts. This small population is used only for teaching purposes and does not represent the typical size of an accounts receivable population on which sampling techniques would be used.

The objective of the test is to ascertain whether the accounts exist and are owned by the client. Other substantive tests of accounts receivable are also performed, but we will concentrate on this one.

A 100 percent test is conducted on the 16 accounts with recorded balances of $30,000 or more. Positive confirmation requests are sent to all 16 of these customers. In doing so, the auditor will send confirmations to $907,580 of the $1,559,980 recorded balance, and the variability of the other accounts will be lowered considerably.

No letters will be sent to the 15 accounts with zero balances. The auditor is concerned with existence (possible overstatement of accounts receivable rather than understatement). The zero balance accounts cannot be overstated (except for a credit balance), and professional judgment leads the auditor to believe that any possible understatement of the recorded amounts would not be significant. The completeness assertion is the subject of other audit procedures.

Confirmation letters are sent to a sample of the remaining 69 accounts. Judgmental sampling techniques are used to select the sample and evaluate the sampling results. A projected misstatement of the population of 69 accounts is calculated and combined with other misstatements found in the 16 accounts tested on a 100 percent basis. This total likely misstatement in accounts receivable is aggregated with likely misstatements in all other accounts to form a basis for the auditor to determine whether the financial statements are materially misstated.

After considering possible misstatements in the other account balances and a materiality level for the financial statements taken as a whole, the auditor sets $30,000 as the tolerable misstatement for accounts receivable. Based on prior years' audits and professional judgment, the auditor estimates zero expected dollar misstatement in the population.

In the auditor's professional judgment, there is a moderate risk that misstatements greater than the tolerable amount will occur and that internal control procedures and other substantive tests will not detect them. Therefore, the auditor decides to set a moderate risk of incorrect acceptance.

If the sampling decision results in rejection of the hypothesis that the evidence supports the account balance, alternative procedures to determine whether this is an incorrect rejection will be costly and time-consuming. Therefore, the auditor decides on a low risk of incorrect rejection to increase the sample size and more effectively guard against this possibility.

After considering all these factors, the auditor uses professional judgment to decide on a sample size of 23 of the 69 accounts. Systematic sampling is used with a random start.

Selection of the Sample

Examination of Table 14.1 shows that the following 16 accounts have a recorded balance of $30,000 or more. Confirmation requests are sent to 100 percent of these accounts. Here are the results.

Account number	Recorded amount	Audit amount	Difference
7	$ 53,910	$ 54,180	$ 270
11	50,000	40,270	(9,730)
12	46,060	53,600	7,540
16	32,400	32,400	—
27	70,490	71,930	1,440
44	55,510	55,510	—
51	31,960	28,360	(3,600)
54	37,220	37,220	—
55	145,220	145,220	—
59	149,410	149,770	360
61	30,080	30,080	—
62	33,290	33,290	—
63	31,750	29,750	(2,000)
73	39,500	40,500	1,000
82	48,600	48,600	—
91	52,180	52,180	—
	$907,580	$902,860	$(4,720)

The known and projected misstatement for these 16 accounts is $4,720, the net difference between the recorded and audited amounts.

Confirmation requests are sent to 23 of the remaining 69 accounts with balances in excess of zero. A letter is sent to every third customer beginning with customer number two. In selecting every third account, the amounts of $30,000 or more are omitted because they are included in the 16 accounts audited on a 100 percent basis. Following are the sample results.

Account number	Recorded amount	Audit amount	Difference
2	$ 6,960	$ 15,340	$ 8,380
6	12,400	12,400	—
10	2,180	2,180	—
15	13,350	13,350	—
19	6,500	6,500	—
23	5,430	5,430	—
26	1,450	1,450	—
31	2,380	2,380	—
34	2,400	2,400	—
38	3,450	3,450	—
41	9,880	9,880	—
46	1,950	1,950	—
50	26,050	26,050	—
60	17,800	8,900	(8,900)
66	5,690	5,690	—
70	6,600	7,600	1,000
75	9,060	9,060	—
78	11,900	11,900	—
83	8,850	8,850	—
87	5,760	5,760	—
92	1,190	1,190	—
96	11,600	11,600	—
99	7,100	7,100	—
	$179,930	$180,410	$ 480

The confirmation results are summarized in the table below.

Group	Total recorded amount on books	Recorded amount of group	Audit amount of group	Difference
100% tested	$907,580	$907,580	$902,860	$(4,720)
Sample of 23	652,400	179,930	180,410	480
Known and projected misstatement { 100% tested				$(4,720)
Sample of 23 ($179,930/$652,400 = .276)(480/.276) =				1,740
Likely misstatement				$(2,980)

The likely misstatement of $2,980 is well below the tolerable misstatement of $30,000. Therefore, the risk that the actual misstatement in the population exceeds $30,000 is low. The hypothesis that the evidence supports the account balance is not rejected. However, the $2,980 is combined with likely misstatements found in other account balances so that the total can be considered in the aggregate.

Qualitative Evaluation of Sample Results

Although the likely misstatement is relatively small, the auditor should consider several qualitative factors. Following are two examples:

1. Out of 39 accounts examined, misstatements were found in 11. One reason for the relatively low likely misstatement is the offset effect of the overstatements and understatements. The auditor might wish to investigate this large percentage of misstatements.
2. If none of the misstatements was corrected on the books by the client, this might indicate an unwillingness to concede that misstatements exist in the population. This attitude could be a source of auditor–client conflict in other phases of the audit.

CLASSICAL STATISTICAL SAMPLING METHODS

Statistical sampling provides a scientific basis for evaluating sampling risk, whereas nonstatistical sampling does not. Classical statistical methods may be efficient for sampling populations that contain a number of differences between recorded and audited amounts. The illustration we are using (Table 14.1, used to demonstrate nonstatistical sampling) contains several overstatements and understatements.

Generally, auditors use one of three statistical methods to estimate the dollar amount of a population:

1. Mean estimation.
2. Ratio estimation.
3. Difference estimation.

Mean Estimation

In *mean estimation* a sample mean of the audited values is calculated by dividing the total audited value of the sample items by the number of items in the sample. The sample mean is multiplied by the number of items in the population to obtain an estimate of the total dollar amount in the population.

The optimum sample size for estimating the dollar amount of a population can be found by using the following four items.

1. An estimate of the standard deviation of the population. Estimates may be obtained from prior-year audits. Also, if significant misstatements are not anticipated, the standard deviation of the recorded amounts in the population may be used as an estimate.

2. The auditor's planned levels of sampling risks. Risk of incorrect rejection is based on the difficulty and cost of additional investigation. Risk of incorrect acceptance is derived from the audit risk model.
3. The auditor's planned *allowance for sampling risk,* which is the difference between the expected misstatement (see pages 430–431) and the tolerable misstatement.
4. The number of items in the population.

The effect of each of these four items on sample size is demonstrated in the following table:

	Factor		Sample Size	
	Higher	Lower	Larger	Smaller
1. Estimated standard deviation of the population	X		X	
		X		X
2. Planned levels of sampling risks	X			X
		X	X	
3. Planned allowance for sampling risk	X			X
		X	X	
4. Number of elements in the population	X		X	
		X		X

After selecting and auditing the sample, the following steps are used to obtain the sample results.

1. Compute the mean of the sample and multiply it by the number of items in the population. The result is an estimate of the total dollar amount of the population.
2. Compute the achieved allowance for sampling risk around the population estimate, expressed as, for example, ±$10,000. This computation is illustrated later.
3. Add the achieved allowance to and subtract the achieved allowance from the estimate of the dollar amount of the population. The result is the achieved allowance interval at a specified risk level.
4. Determine if the book value falls within the interval.

Generally, mean estimation as well as ratio and difference estimation provide more efficiency if the population is stratified into subgroups.

Ratio Estimation

Ratio estimation is appropriate when auditors want to estimate a population value based on the ratio of recorded amounts and audited amounts. In unstratified populations, the standard deviation of ratios is usually smaller than the standard deviation of account balances, thus resulting in smaller sample sizes. Although the method is suitable for such procedures as tests of extension of inventory amounts and confirmation of accounts receivable, it is not compatible with procedures in which no book value exists for individual items.

For an example of *ratio estimation,* assume that an account balance totals $100,000. The auditors sample $20,000 of this amount, and their calculated audit amount is $21,000 or 105 percent of the sampled book figure. They then estimate the population total as $105,000 (105 percent of $100,000).

Ratio estimation can be used most effectively when the calculated audit amounts are approximately proportional to the book amounts. For example, the following situation is appropriate for ratio estimation because the ratios of audited to book amounts are fairly consistent.

Book amounts	Audited amounts	Difference	Ratio
$ 80,000	$ 79,000	$(1,000)	0.99
100,000	102,500	2,500	1.03
120,000	117,000	(3,000)	0.98
90,000	93,000	3,000	1.03
$390,000	$391,500	$ 1,500	

The following situation would *not* be as suitable for ratio estimation because the relationship between book and audited amounts is not proportional, and the audit to book ratios are not consistent.

Book amounts	Audited amounts	Difference	Ratio
$ 80,000	$ 80,500	$ 500	1.01
100,000	86,000	(14,000)	0.86
120,000	118,000	(2,000)	0.98
90,000	107,000	17,000	1.19
$390,000	$391,500	$ 1,500	

If a small number of audit/book differences exist in the population, the use of ratio estimation may not be appropriate. A relatively large sample would be necessary to ensure that the differences between book and audited values found are representative of the population. Such a large sample would erase much of the benefit of ratio estimation. However, stratification of the population may be useful in this situation.

Difference Estimation

The objective of *difference estimation* is to estimate a population value based on the difference between the client's book amount and the audited amount (same as ratio estimation), but the method is *slightly* different because the auditor uses dollar rather than ratio differences. Difference estimation is also incompatible with procedures in which no book value exists for individual items.

Assume that a book amount is $100,000 for a population of 1,000 accounts. A sample of $20,000 of this book amount revealed an audited amount of $21,000. The sample size is 100. The total difference in the sample is $1,000 or an average difference of $10 ($1,000 difference divided by the sample size of 100) per item. To estimate the population difference, the auditors multiply the average difference of $10 by the population total of 1,000. The estimated population difference is $10,000, and the estimate of the population total is $110,000.

Difference estimation may be used if the dollar amount (not ratios) of audit/book differences is fairly consistent. Otherwise, the method's advantages and disadvantages are essentially the same as for ratio estimation.

APPLICATION OF MEAN ESTIMATION

Steps in Applying Mean Estimation

Mean estimation, as well as other classical statistical sampling techniques, can be applied more efficiently by following a sequence of logical steps. These steps are outlined in the following list and discussed more fully in the remainder of the section.[1]

1. Determine the distribution of the account balances to assess the need for stratification.
2. Stratify the accounts if high variability is a problem.
3. Determine the appropriate sample size by
   a. Determining the risks of incorrect acceptance and incorrect rejection.
   b. Determining the tolerable misstatement and the planned allowance for sampling risk.
   c. Estimating the population standard deviation.
   d. Estimating expected misstatement.
   e. Determining the number of items in the population.
4. Select the sample and perform the necessary audit procedures.
5. Quantitatively evaluate the sample results by estimating the population value, calculating an achieved allowance for sampling risk, and accepting or rejecting the hypothesis that the evidence supports the recorded amount.
6. Perform a qualitative evaluation of the sample results.

Estimation of an Accounts Receivable Balance

Distribution of the Account Balances

Assume that the auditors wish to estimate the balance of accounts receivable and test the hypothesis that the evidence supports the recorded balance. One of the

---

[1] Auditors would not usually select the mean estimation method for auditing accounts with recorded balances. However, it illustrates estimation sampling concepts and avoids some of the complications of ratio and difference estimation techniques. If mean estimation is understood, other techniques will not be difficult to comprehend.

TABLE 14.2
Distribution of the Accounts

Range of account balances	Number of accounts	Total dollar amount of accounts
$ 0– 9,999	61	$ 237,050
10,000– 19,999	13	167,930
20,000– 29,999	10	247,420
30,000– 39,999	7	236,200
40,000– 49,999	2	94,660
50,000– 59,999	4	211,600
60,000– 69,999	0	0
70,000– 79,999	1	70,490
80,000– 89,999	0	0
90,000– 99,999	0	0
100,000–109,999	0	0
110,000–119,999	0	0
120,000–129,999	0	0
130,000–139,999	0	0
140,000–149,999	2	294,630
	100	$1,559,980

first steps taken by the auditors is to review the numerical distribution of the accounts. Such a distribution is shown in Table 14.2.[2]

The distribution of the 100 accounts is skewed heavily and has a relatively high standard deviation. Following is some information about the population of the book values of accounts receivable:

1. The mean is $15,600.
2. The total is $1,559,980.
3. The standard deviation is $24,177.

A statistically derived sample for this accounts receivable distribution would be inefficient because the size of such a sample probably would be very large.

Stratification—A Solution to High Variability

How can statistical sampling methods be applied to a distribution of accounts receivable balances with such a large variability? Stratify the accounts into two or more subgroups and then treat each subgroup as a separate population. Review of the distribution of accounts shows the strata into which each dollar group can be placed.

One first notices two very large account balances totaling $294,630 (out of a population total of $1,559,980). Clearly, these two accounts should be audited separately with positive confirmation requests. By doing so, we reduce the variability in

[2] This distribution is taken from Table 14.1. This table was used to illustrate nonstatistical sampling. It is also used to illustrate classical statistical sampling so that the results may be compared.

the remaining population of 98 and cover approximately 20 percent of the total dollar balance in accounts receivable.

A further examination of the account balance distribution shows that an additional 14 accounts are listed in the dollar categories starting at $30,000 and ending at $79,999. Positive confirmation requests on a 100 percent basis might also be appropriate for these balances.

Among the 61 accounts listed in the $0–999 classification are 15 with zero balances. Extracting these accounts will lower the variability of the remaining distribution.

After separation of the accounts according to the criteria explained in the foregoing paragraphs, the following groups emerge.

Type of account	Number of accounts	Type of evidence
Balances ≥$30,000	16	Positive confirmation on a 100 percent basis
Balances between $1 and $29,999	69	Positive confirmation on a sample of accounts—statistical sampling techniques applied

The new population to which variable sampling methods can be applied has a different and more suitable set of statistical measures.

1. The mean is $9,455.
2. The total is $652,400.
3. The standard deviation is $7,538.

Audit Risks

Using the audit risk model equation, $TD = AR/[IR \times CR \times APR]$, discussed earlier in the chapter, the auditor has a 20 percent risk of incorrect acceptance calculated by assigning the values 0.05 to AR, 1.0 to IR, 0.50 to CR, and 0.50 to APR, as follows:

$$0.20 = 0.05/[1.0 \times 0.50 \times 0.50]$$

Using judgment, the auditor sets the risk of incorrect rejection at 5 percent.

Allowance for Sampling Risk

Using judgment, the auditor sets the tolerable misstatement at $210,000. (Recall that tolerable misstatement is the amount of overall financial statement materiality that is allocated to individual accounts.) The planned allowance for sampling risk is a percentage of tolerable misstatement based on the risks of incorrect acceptance

TABLE 14.3
Ratio of Planned Allowance for Sampling Risk to Tolerable Misstatement[a]

Risk of incorrect acceptance	Risk of incorrect rejection			
	.20	.10	.05	.01
.01	.355	.413	.457	.525
.025	.395	.456	.500	.568
.05	.437	.500	.543	.609
.075	.471	.532	.576	.641
.10	.500	.561	.605	.668
.15	.511	.612	.653	.712
.20	.603	.661	.700	.753
.25	.653	.708	.742	.791
.30	.707	.756	.787	.829
.35	.766	.808	.834	.868
.40	.831	.863	.883	.908
.45	.907	.926	.937	.952
.50	1.000	1.000	1.000	1.000

[a] This table is derived from *Statistical Auditing* by Donald Roberts (New York: AICPA, 1978). Copyright © (1978) American Institute of Certified Public Accountants, Inc., reprinted with permission.

and incorrect rejection and is calculated by reference to Table 14.3. This table gives the ratio of planned allowance for sampling risk to tolerable misstatement for several combinations of risks of incorrect acceptance and incorrect rejection. The table factor of 0.700, based on risks of incorrect acceptance of 0.20 and incorrect rejection of 0.05, is multiplied by $210,000 to calculate an allowance for sampling risk of $147,000. This amount is usually expressed as ±$147,000. Based on this sampling plan, if the recorded amount is within ±$147,000 of the estimated population value, the auditor can state, at a 20 percent risk of incorrect acceptance, that the evidence supports the recorded amount.

Estimation of the Population Standard Deviation

The auditors also need a reasonably good estimate of the population standard deviation to determine an optimum sample size. In this case, the auditors estimate the standard deviation of the 69 recorded amounts to be $7,900.

Use of the Variables to Determine Sample Size

The planned risks of 20 and 5 percent, the planned allowance for sampling risk of $147,000, a $7,900 estimate of the population standard deviation, and the population size of 69 can be used to derive a sample size. If sampling is conducted with replacement, the equation is

$$\text{Sample size} = \left(\frac{\left(\begin{array}{c}\text{Estimate of the}\\ \text{population}\\ \text{standard deviation}\end{array}\right)\left(\begin{array}{c}\text{Reliability}\\ \text{coefficient}\end{array}\right)\left(\begin{array}{c}\text{Population}\\ \text{size}\end{array}\right)}{\text{Planned allowance for sampling risk}} \right)^2$$

TABLE 14.4
Reliability Factors

Reliability	One-tailed factor	Two-tailed factor
80	0.84	1.28
85	1.04	1.44
90	1.28	1.64
95	1.64	1.96
99	2.33	2.58

The reliability coefficient refers to a standard deviation multiple associated with a certain reliability (the complement of risk) for the risk of incorrect rejection. See Table 14.4, which provides a list of reliability factors. A 5 percent risk of incorrect rejection is a 95 percent reliability. The two-sided factors from the table are used for the risk of incorrect rejection.

The statistical notation is

$$n = \left(\frac{s \times U_R \times N}{A} \right)^2$$

$$n = \left(\frac{7,900 \times 1.96 \times 69}{147,000} \right)^2$$

$$n = 53$$

As applied to confirmation requests, sampling with replacement does not mean that two letters are mailed to the same customer if the same number is selected in the random sample. It simply means that a larger sample must be selected to overcome the possible obstacle of choosing the same number more than once when only one is used.

A more practical approach is to sample without replacement and thus derive n separate customer numbers. If this method is adopted, the following correction factor is applied to the sample of 53.

$$n' \text{ (without replacement)} = \frac{n \text{ (with replacement)}}{1 + \dfrac{n \text{ (with replacement)}}{N}}$$

$$n' = \frac{53}{1 + \dfrac{53}{69}}$$

$$n' = 30 \text{ (without replacement)}$$

Selecting the Sample and Performing the Audit Procedures

There are two common techniques for deriving a set of random numbers. One method is to draw samples from a random number table. Another is to list the numbers from a computer-generated random number program. Assume that the latter method is used. Because accounts receivable customer numbers are available,

TABLE 14.5
Customers Selected to Receive Confirmation Requests

Random number	Customer number	Book balance	No error indicated	Amount of customer reply (error in records)	Amount used in population estimate
1	1	$10,200	x		$ 10,200
2	2	6,960		$15,340	15,340
10	14	4,020	x		4,020
11	15	13,350	x		13,350
14	19	6,500	x		6,500
15	21	1,440	x		1,440
17	23	5,430	x		5,430
22	29	8,900	x		8,900
34	45	26,520		20,160	20,160
37	48	3,060	x		3,060
38	50	26,050	x		26,050
43	65	4,250	x		4,250
44	66	5,690	x		5,690
45	67	20,640	x		20,640
46	69	18,600	x		18,600
49	72	24,550	x		24,550
50	75	9,060	x		9,060
51	76	1,000	x		1,000
52	77	10,410	x		10,410
53	78	11,900	x		11,900
54	79	5,760	x		5,760
57	84	1,040	x		1,040
58	86	29,400	x		29,400
59	87	5,760	x		5,760
61	90	8,730	x		8,730
62	92	1,190	x		1,190
65	96	11,600	x		11,600
66	97	5,400	x		5,400
67	98	1,450	x		1,450
69	100	3,600	x		3,600
					$294,480

they can be identified easily with the numbers produced by the computerized random number generator.

Once the 30 customer numbers are selected, confirmation requests are sent to those customers and the auditors wait for replies. If a letter is returned by a customer and contains an indication of a disagreement with the book balance, the auditors seek to find the reason for this difference. A satisfactory resolution of this discrepancy is tantamount to a reply from the customer with no difference. If the client's amount is wrong, the customer amount should be used to estimate the population total.

Assume that the sample is selected, the confirmation letters are mailed, and the customer replies are received. Table 14.5 lists the 30 customers receiving confirmation requests. Assume that unresolved discrepancies are misstatements in the records; therefore, to estimate the population total, the amount confirmed by the customer is used as the correct amount.

Estimate of the Population Total and the Achieved Allowance for Sampling Risk

The next step for the auditor is to use the confirmation results to make an estimate of the total accounts receivable. A range (the achieved allowance for sampling risk) is developed around this estimate, and the auditor may then accept, at a 20 percent risk of incorrect acceptance, if the book value falls within the range, or reject, at a five percent risk of incorrect rejection, if the book value falls outside the range.

These sets of calculations are performed by taking the $294,480 total of the confirmation results (see Table 14.5) and developing the sample mean (the mean value of an item in the sample, referred to as $\bar{x}$).

$$\text{Sum of sample values} \div n = \bar{x}$$

$$\$294,480 \div 30 = \$9,820$$

Then an estimate of the population (accounts receivable) value is made.

$$\bar{x} \times N = \text{Estimate of population value}$$

$$\$9,820 \times 69 = \$677,580$$

Note that $677,580 is only one of *many* population estimates that could have been derived by the auditors. How many could be selected if, from a population of 69, a random sample of 30 is selected without replacement? The answer is

$$\frac{69 \text{ (Factorial)}}{30 \text{ (Factorial)} \ (69 - 30) \text{ (Factorial)}}$$

(31,627,280,000,000,000,000). The reason statisticians consider 30 to be a large sample is that there are so many population estimates (and sample means) that the sample distribution is expected to be fairly close to normal, even if the population from which the sample is taken is skewed.

The achieved allowance for sampling risk (A') is developed by use of the following equation.

$$A' \text{ (achieved allowance for sampling risk)} = \frac{S_{\bar{x}}}{\sqrt{n}} \times U_R \times N$$

where $S_{\bar{x}}$ is the standard deviation of the sample items (note that except for the substitution of $S_{\bar{x}}$ for S this is the sample size equation rearranged).

$$A' = \frac{7,830}{\sqrt{30}} \times 1.96 \times 69 = 193,390 \text{ (achieved allowance for sampling risk with replacement)}[3]$$

---

[3] The $7,830 standard deviation of the sample is different from the $7,900 standard deviation of the recorded amounts.

This allowance is multiplied by a finite correction factor because sampling is done without replacement.

$$193,390 \times \sqrt{\frac{N - n}{N - 1}}$$

$$193,390 \times \sqrt{\frac{69 - 30}{69 - 1}} = 146,580 \text{ (achieved allowance for sampling risk without replacement).}$$

The auditors then have the following range: \$531,000 (\$677,580, the population estimate, minus \$146,580) to \$824,160 (\$677,580, the population estimate, plus \$146,580).

The achieved allowance for sampling risk will be larger than the planned allowance if the sample standard deviation is larger than the estimated population standard deviation used to compute the sample size. If this occurs, a new and larger sample size could be computed by using the standard deviation of the first sample.

However, in this example, the achieved allowance of \$146,580 is less than the planned allowance of \$147,000. The reason is that the sample standard deviation of \$7,830 is smaller than the estimated population standard deviation of \$7,900.

The following graph describes the normal distribution into which the population estimates of the sample of 30 are assumed to fall. The population estimate of the sample is \$677,580. The achieved allowance for sampling risk range is \$531,000 to \$824,160.

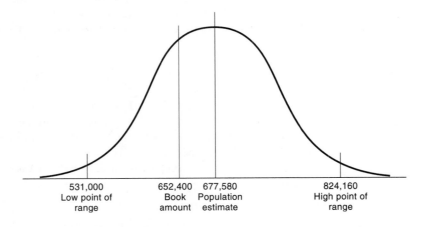

531,000	652,400	677,580	824,160
Low point of range	Book amount	Population estimate	High point of range

The Decision to Reject or Not Reject the Hypothesis
That the Evidence Supports the Recorded Balance

For the \$652,400 recorded amount, the following decision criteria would be used.

1. If the client's recorded balance falls within the achieved allowance range (as it does in the preceding graph) and if the achieved allowance is smaller than the planned allowance, the auditor will accept the hypothesis that the evi-

dence supports the recorded balance. This acceptance is at a risk of incorrect acceptance equal to or less than 20 percent. One way of describing the risk is as follows. There is one chance in five or less that the recorded balance is in error by more than the $210,000 tolerable misstatement and that an incorrect acceptance is made.

2. If the likely misstatement of $25,180 ($677,580, population estimate, minus $652,400, the recorded balance) plus the achieved allowance for sampling risk of incorrect acceptance is equal to or less than the tolerable misstatement, the hypothesis that the evidence supports the recorded balance will still be accepted. The likely misstatement of $25,180 plus the achieved allowance for risk of incorrect acceptance of $63,420 (tolerable misstatement of $210,000 less $146,580) equals $88,600, which is less than the tolerable misstatement of $210,000. Therefore, the hypothesis is accepted with a risk of incorrect acceptance of 20 percent or less.

3. If the likely misstatement plus the allowance for sampling risk of incorrect acceptance is more than the tolerable misstatement, the hypothesis that the evidence supports the recorded balance will be rejected. A risk of incorrect rejection of 2.5 percent or less accompanies the decision to reject the hypothesis.

To evaluate the entire accounts receivable balance of $1,559,980, the auditor must combine the errors found in the 16 accounts tested 100 percent with the projected misstatement calculated in the sample. This total likely misstatement is aggregated with misstatements in all other accounts and compared with materiality for the overall financial statements.

PROBABILITY PROPORTIONAL TO SIZE SAMPLING

Sometimes the auditor may decide to use statistical sampling on populations of account balances or classes of transactions that normally contain a few overstatements, some of which may be large. Accounts receivable is an example. In auditing this type of population, the major criterion is to ascertain, at a desired risk level, whether the dollar overstatement does or does not exceed a certain amount.

Unless the population is stratified, the classical statistical sampling procedures discussed in this chapter may not be appropriate. Mean estimation sometimes proves to be inefficient because of large sample sizes. Allowance for sampling risk intervals cannot be calculated for ratio and difference estimation unless a sufficient number (at least 30) of differences between book and audited amounts are found in the sample. For a population with few errors, a small sample may produce no differences. Even if differences are found, they may be the smaller ones and the population estimate may be poor.

Probability proportional to size sampling, sometimes called dollar-unit sampling, overcomes these potential problems with these types of populations. In fact, even if the dollar amount of the misstatements is not large and the misstatements are few, probability proportional to size sampling (PPS) has some advantages over mean, ratio, and difference estimation. The sampling method is more likely to result in the selection of a few large dollar overstatements, should such a condition exist in the population.

Characteristics of PPS

PPS uses each dollar in the population as a separate sampling unit, as contrasted with mean, ratio, and difference estimation, which use such items as account balances as the sampling unit. Each dollar has an equal chance of selection. However, if any dollar of an account balance is selected, the entire balance is audited (e.g., a confirmation letter sent, physical and perpetual inventory compared, etc.). This procedure results in large recorded account balances in the population having a greater chance of being selected and audited. The greater the overstatement in an account, the greater the probability that the account will be selected and the overstatement detected (unless a nonsampling error occurs).

PPS is performed on the assumption that no recorded account balance is overstated by more than its recorded amount. For instance, an assumption is made that a recorded customer accounts receivable balance of $10,000 could not actually be as low as −$5,000 (or a $5,000 credit balance).

To determine an appropriate sample size for PPS sampling, the following items are needed.

1. Tolerable misstatement.
2. Risk of incorrect acceptance.
3. Number of misstatements anticipated in the sample.
4. Recorded book value of the population.

An Illustration of PPS—Assuming No Misstatements Are Found

The mechanics of selecting and evaluating a PPS sample can be shown by reference to Table 14.1, used to illustrate nonstatistical and classical statistical sampling. The 100 accounts are listed in Table 14.6. Note that some audit amounts are changed to create a population that consists for the most part of a few large dollar overstatements. The audit procedure is a positive confirmation request. The objective of the audit procedure is to determine whether the amounts exist and are owned by the client. The following data are assumed:

1. Tolerable misstatement (TM)—$100,000.
2. Risk of incorrect acceptance (derived from the audit risk model)—15 percent.
3. Number of misstatements anticipated—0.
4. Recorded book value (BV)—$1,559,980.

The sample size is computed by using the equation

$$n = \frac{\text{Reliability factor for misstatements anticipated and risk of incorrect acceptance}}{TM/BV}$$

TABLE 14.6
Information for Probability Proportional to Size Sampling Illustration

Account number	Client recorded amount	Audit confirmation amount	Difference	Account number	Client recorded amount	Audit confirmation amount	Difference
1	$10,200	$10,200	$ —	41	$ 9,880	$ 9,880	$ —
2	6,960	6,960	—	42	3,060	3,060	—
3	2,080	2,080	—	43	—	—	—
4	18,470	18,470	—	44	55,510	55,510	—
5	—	—	—	45	26,520	20,160	(6,360)
6	12,400	12,400	—	46	1,950	1,950	—
7	53,910	54,180	270	47	9,500	9,500	—
8	11,900	11,900	—	48	3,060	3,060	—
9	25,540	25,540	—	49	—	—	—
10	2,180	2,180	—	50	26,050	26,050	—
11	50,000	40,270	(9,730)	51	31,960	28,360	(3,600)
12	46,060	46,060	—	52	8,500	8,500	—
13	21,060	21,060	—	53	—	—	—
14	4,020	4,020	—	54	37,220	37,220	—
15	13,350	13,350	—	55	145,220	145,220	—
16	32,400	32,400	—	56	—	—	—
17	25,070	25,070	—	57	—	—	—
18	28,240	28,240	—	58	5,820	5,820	—
19	6,500	6,500	—	59	149,410	149,410	—
20	—	—	—	60	17,800	8,900	(8,900)
21	1,440	1,440	—	61	30,080	30,080	—
22	6,690	6,690	—	62	33,290	33,290	—
23	5,430	5,430	—	63	31,750	31,750	—
24	7,300	7,300	—	64	10,800	10,800	—
25	7,700	3,850	(3,850)	65	4,250	4,250	—
26	1,450	1,450	—	66	5,690	5,690	—
27	70,490	70,490	—	67	20,640	20,640	—
28	6,400	6,400	—	68	—	—	—
29	8,900	8,900	—	69	18,600	18,600	—
30	—	—	—	70	6,600	7,600	1,000
31	2,380	2,380	—	71	2,000	2,000	—
32	7,420	7,420	—	72	24,550	24,550	—
33	4,800	—	(4,800)	73	39,500	39,500	—
34	2,400	2,400	—	74	—	—	—
35	4,800	4,800	—	75	9,060	9,060	—
36	—	—	—	76	1,000	1,000	—
37	8,450	8,450	—	77	10,410	10,410	—
38	3,450	3,450	—	78	11,900	11,900	—
39	10,300	10,300	—	79	5,760	5,760	—
40	20,350	20,350	—	80	—	—	—

TABLE 14.6 *Continued*

Account number	Client recorded amount	Audit confirmation amount	Difference	Account number	Client recorded amount	Audit confirmation amount	Difference
81	100	100	—	92	1,190	1,190	—
82	48,600	48,600	—	93	7,200	7,200	—
83	8,850	8,850	—	94	—	—	—
84	1,040	1,040	—	95	9,750	9,750	—
85	—	—	—	96	11,600	11,600	—
86	29,400	29,400	—	97	5,400	5,400	—
87	5,760	5,760	—	98	1,450	1,450	—
88	10,200	10,200	—	99	7,100	7,100	—
89	—	—	—	100	3,600	3,600	—
90	8,730	8,730	—	Totals	$1,559,980	$1,524,010	$(35,970)
91	52,180	52,180	—				

The numerator is a table factor based on an anticipation of a certain number of misstatements and a risk of incorrect acceptance (see Table 14.7). In this case, zero misstatements and a 15 percent risk of incorrect acceptance provide a table factor of 1.90.

The denominator is the tolerable misstatement (*TM*) divided by the recorded book value (*BV*). In this case $100,000 ÷ $1,559,980. Therefore

$$n = \frac{1.90}{100,000/1,559,980} = 30 \text{ (rounded)}$$

The sampling method is systematic, and the sampling interval is computed as follows on page 453:

TABLE 14.7
Probability Proportional to Size Sampling Tables:
Reliability Factors for Overstatement

Number of overstatements	Risk of incorrect acceptance								
	1%	5%	10%	15%	20%	25%	30%	37%	50%
0	4.61	3.00	2.31	1.90	1.61	1.39	1.21	1.00	.70
1	6.64	4.75	3.89	3.38	3.00	2.70	2.44	2.14	1.68
2	8.41	6.30	5.33	4.72	4.28	3.93	3.62	3.25	2.68
3	10.05	7.76	6.69	6.02	5.52	5.11	4.77	4.34	3.68
4	11.61	9.16	8.00	7.27	6.73	6.28	5.90	5.43	4.68
5	13.11	10.52	9.28	8.50	7.91	7.43	7.01	6.49	5.68
6	14.57	11.85	10.54	9.71	9.08	8.56	8.12	7.56	6.67
7	16.00	13.15	11.78	10.90	10.24	9.69	9.21	8.63	7.67
8	17.41	14.44	13.00	12.08	11.38	10.81	10.31	9.68	8.67

Source: Audit and Accounting Guide—Audit Sampling (AICPA, 1983). Copyright © (1983) American Institute of Certified Public Accountants, Inc., reprinted with permission.

$$BV \div n = \text{Sampling interval}$$

$$\$1,559,980 \div 30 = \$52,000 \text{ (rounded)}$$

The sample is selected by assuming that there are 1,559,980 sampling units and that every 52,000th unit is selected. The chart below shows some of the selection process from the 100 accounts in Table 14.6. Assume a random start at the 10,000th dollar with the 62,000th dollar being the second dollar selected.

Recorded amount	Cumulative recorded amount	Sampling interval	Recorded amount of account selected
$10,200	$ 10,200	$10,000	$10,200
6,960	17,160		
2,080	19,240		
18,470	37,710		
12,400	50,110		
53,910	104,020	62,000	53,910

The next account selected would be the account that falls into the $114,000 cumulative book amount ($62,000 + $52,000). As can be seen, the largest account balances have the largest chance of selection.

Assume that no misstatements are detected in the sample. The auditor could then state with a 15 percent risk that the maximum dollar overstatement in the population does not exceed $100,000 (tolerable misstatement, which is the allowance for sampling risk).

A More Detailed Illustration of PPS

In the previous illustration, the sample results were assumed to be satisfactory because the upper limit on net overstatement (or maximum dollar overstatement in the population) was not in excess of the tolerable misstatement. There was a 15 percent risk that the true overstatement in the population was in excess of the tolerable misstatement and that the auditor incorrectly accepted the estimate of misstatement in the account. The results occurred because no misstatements were anticipated in determination of the sample size and no misstatements were found when the sample was audited.

In the illustration in Table 14.8, we also assume a 15 percent risk of incorrect acceptance, a tolerable misstatement of $100,000, no anticipated errors, a sample size of 30, and a sampling interval of $52,000. However, all 100 account balances (except zero balances) are used to select the sample. In so doing, we will demonstrate how a PPS systematic sample is drawn from an unstratified population, how the projected misstatement is calculated, and how the sample results are evaluated.

Note that the PPS method does not require the division of the population into strata, which is generally required when classical statistical sampling is used on populations with high variability. Note also that all accounts with balances of $52,000 or more are selected when a sampling interval of $52,000 is used. When a dollar in the sampling interval is selected, the entire account balance containing the dollar

TABLE 14.8
Illustration of PPS Using All Population Items[a]

Recorded amount	Cumulative recorded amount	Sampling interval	Recorded amount of account selected	Audit amount
$ 10,200	$ 10,200	$ 10,000	$ 10,200	$ 10,200
6,960	17,160			
2,080	19,240			
18,470	37,710			
12,400	50,110			
53,910	104,020	62,000	53,910	54,180
11,900	115,920	114,000	11,900	11,900
25,540	141,460			
2,180	143,640			
50,000	193,640	166,000	50,000	40,270
46,060	239,700	218,000	46,060	46,060
21,060	260,760			
4,020	264,780			
13,350	278,130	270,000	13,350	13,350
32,400	310,530			
25,070	335,600	322,000	25,070	25,070
28,240	363,840			
6,500	370,340			
1,440	371,780			
6,690	378,470	374,000	6,690	6,690
5,430	383,900			
7,300	391,200			
7,700	398,900			
1,450	400,350			
70,490	470,840	426,000	70,490	70,490
6,400	477,240			
8,900	486,140	478,000	8,900	8,900
2,380	488,520			
7,420	495,940			
4,800	500,740			
2,400	503,140			
4,800	507,940			
8,450	516,390			
3,450	519,840			
10,300	530,140	530,000	10,300	10,300
20,350	550,490			
9,880	560,370			
3,060	563,430			
55,510	618,940	582,000	55,510	55,510
26,520	645,460	634,000	26,520	20,160
1,950	647,410			
9,500	656,910			
3,060	659,970			
26,050	686,020	686,000	26,050	26,050
31,960	717,980			
8,500	726,480			

TABLE 14.8 *Continued*

Recorded amount	Cumulative recorded amount	Sampling interval	Recorded amount of account selected	Audit amount
37,220	763,700	738,000	37,220	37,220
145,220	908,920	790,000	145,220	145,220
145,220[b]	908,920[b]	842,000	145,220	145,220
145,220[b]	908,920[b]	894,000	145,220	145,220
5,820	914,740			
149,410	1,064,150	946,000	149,410	149,410
149,410[b]	1,064,150[b]	998,000	149,410	149,410
149,410[b]	1,064,150[b]	1,050,000	149,410	149,410
17,800	1,081,950			
30,080	1,112,030	1,102,000	30,080	30,080
33,290	1,145,320			
31,750	1,177,070	1,154,000	31,750	31,750
10,800	1,187,870			
4,250	1,192,120			
5,690	1,197,810			
20,640	1,218,450	1,206,000	20,640	20,640
18,600	1,237,050			
6,600	1,243,650			
2,000	1,245,650			
24,550	1,270,200	1,258,000	24,550	24,550
39,500	1,309,700			
9,060	1,318,760	1,310,000	9,060	9,060
1,000	1,319,760			
10,410	1,330,170			
11,900	1,342,070			
5,760	1,347,830			
100	1,347,930			
48,600	1,396,530	1,362,000	48,600	48,600
8,850	1,405,380			
1,040	1,406,420			
29,400	1,435,820	1,414,000	29,400	29,400
5,760	1,441,580			
10,200	1,451,780			
8,730	1,460,510			
52,180	1,512,690	1,466,000	52,180	52,180
1,190	1,513,880			
7,200	1,521,080	1,518,000	7,200	7,200
9,750	1,530,830			
11,600	1,542,430			
5,400	1,547,830			
1,450	1,549,280			
7,100	1,556,380			
3,600	1,559,980			

[a] Zero balances are not included because the purpose of the test is to detect overstatements.

[b] These accounts are selected three times because of their dollar size. The PPS sampling method takes this into account, and the method should not be altered because this occurs. The accounts would be audited only once.

is audited. This automatic selection of large balances is popular with many auditors because these accounts are more likely to contain large overstatements.

Following is a summary of the misstatements found in the sample:

Recorded amount	Audited amount	Misstatement
$53,910	$54,180	$ 270
50,000	40,270	(9,730)
26,520	20,160	(6,360)
Net overstatement found in the sample		$(15,820)

Because the sampling interval started at $10,000, 30 accounts were selected. Only 26 different accounts were used, however. Two accounts, $145,220 and $149,410, are so large that the sampling interval caused each of them to be selected three times. The sample size without replacement is 26, and this is the number of confirmation requests sent to customers.

One way to think about PPS sampling is that the auditor is auditing the individual intervals. If the account selected from an interval is equal to or greater than the size of the interval, the auditor has audited 100 percent of the dollars in that interval. If the account selected from an interval is smaller than the interval, the auditor has *sampled from* the dollars in that interval (and must project findings from the sample to the entire interval).

If misstatements occur in recorded amounts that are equal to or greater than the sampling interval of $52,000, the amounts of the misstatements are classified as projected misstatements. Thus, the $270 understatement in $53,910 is classified as a projected misstatement of $270. Misstatements in recorded amounts less than the sampling interval of $52,000 must be projected to the entire sampling interval of $52,000. We do this by determining the percent that the recorded amount is in error (the error divided by the recorded amount). We call this a "tainting" factor. The tainting factor is then multiplied by the interval. For example, if an audited amount was 20 percent less than its recorded amount, it is "tainted" by 20 percent; if the actual misstatement is $9,730 ($50,000 − $40,270) the projected misstatement is $10,400, or $52,000 times 0.20.

The following table is a compilation of the likely misstatement (sum of the projected misstatements) in the population based on the three misstatements found in the sample.

Recorded amount	Audited amount	Tainting[a]	Sampling interval	Projected misstatement[b]
$53,910	$54,180	—	$ —	$ 270
50,000	40,270	20%	52,000	(10,400)
26,520	20,160	24	52,000	(12,480)
Total likely overstatement				$(22,610)

[a] The recorded amount minus the audit amount divided by the recorded amount, or the misstatement divided by the recorded amount.

[b] The sampling interval times the tainting percentage.

As in nonstatistical sampling, this likely misstatement is aggregated with misstatements in all other accounts and compared with materiality for the overall financial statements.

In PPS sampling, an allowance for sampling risk can be calculated and added to the likely misstatement to derive an upper limit on net overstatement. This upper limit can then be compared to the tolerable misstatement.

In PPS sampling, the allowance for sampling risk has two parts:

1. An allowance based on the projected misstatements of accounts smaller than the sampling interval. Each projected misstatement is multiplied by an increment in the table of reliability factors (see Table 14.7). Notice that the projected misstatements are listed in descending dollar order.
2. A "basic" allowance. This allowance is tolerable misstatement or the sampling interval times the factor for the specified risk of incorrect acceptance and no misstatements. This factor is taken from the same table of reliability factors used to calculate the sample size (Table 14.7).

Following are calculations of the *upper limit on the net overstatement* (projected misstatement plus allowance for sampling risk).

Projected misstatement of accounts smaller than the sampling interval		Reliability factor increment (from Table 14.7)		Projected misstatement plus allowance for sampling risk
$12,480	×	1.48[a]	=	$18,470
10,400	×	1.34[b]	=	13,940
$22,880				$32,410

[a] Table 14.7. The factor for a 15 percent risk of incorrect acceptance for one misstatement (3.38) minus the factor for a 15 percent risk of incorrect acceptance for no misstatements (1.90).

[b] The table factor for 15 percent risk and two misstatements (4.72) minus the table factor for 15 percent risk and one misstatement (3.38).

The allowance for sampling risk based on increments of projected misstatement of accounts smaller than the $52,000 sampling interval is:

$$\$32,410 - \$22,880 = \$9,530$$

The basic allowance for sampling risk is tolerable misstatement or the sampling interval times the factor for 15 percent risk and no misstatements taken from Table 14.7:

$$\$52,000 \times 1.90 = \$100,000 \text{ (rounded)}$$

Total allowance for sampling risk	$109,530
Total likely overstatement (from page 456)	22,610
Upper limit on net overstatement	$132,140

The sample results are not acceptable because the tolerable misstatement is $100,000. No misstatements were anticipated in the sample but three misstatements, with a net overstatement of $15,820, were found. The actual overstatement in the population is $35,970; therefore, the account balance is incorrectly rejected.

To avoid the possibility of an incorrect rejection for this reason, a larger sample could be taken. One or more misstatements could be anticipated when the sample size is determined, thus lowering the upper limit on net overstatement.

ANTICIPATING MISSTATEMENTS IN PPS SAMPLING

Although an auditor would not normally use PPS sampling if many misstatements are expected, he or she may wish to anticipate one or a few misstatements to reduce the risk of incorrect rejection. One approach is as follows:

1. Estimate the amount of misstatement in the sample.
2. Multiply the estimated misstatement in the sample by an expansion factor (see Table 14.9) to determine the effect of the expected misstatement.
3. Subtract the expected misstatement from tolerable misstatement.
4. Calculate sample size and sampling interval using the method described on pages 450–453 for zero misstatements.

The previously described zero-misstatement sample size calculation would be modified as follows:

1. Assume the auditor estimates that $20,000 of misstatements will be found in the sample.
2. Multiply the estimated misstatement of $20,000 times the expansion factor (Table 14.9) for a risk of incorrect acceptance of 15 percent (1.4) giving $28,000.
3. Subtract the expected misstatement ($28,000) from tolerable misstatement ($100,000) giving $72,000.

TABLE 14.9
Expansion Factors for Expected Misstatement

	Risk of incorrect acceptance							
	1%	*5%*	*10%*	*15%*	*20%*	*25%*	*30%*	*50%*
Factor	1.9	1.6	1.5	1.4	1.3	1.25	1.2	1.0

4. Calculate sample size as follows:

$$n = \frac{1.90}{72,000/1,559,980} = 41$$

Thus, the anticipation of $20,000 of misstatement in the sample increases sample size from 30 to 41.

SUMMARY

If the auditor decides to use sampling to conduct a substantive test of details, either nonstatistical or statistical methods may be used. The major advantages of nonstatistical sampling are its convenience and the fact that no special knowledge of statistical theory is required. Its major disadvantage is that no scientific evaluation of sampling risk can be made. However, a nonstatistical sampling plan that is well designed and executed can produce reliable results.

If the auditor decides to use statistical sampling, two methods are generally available. Classical statistical sampling requires some knowledge of normal distribution theory or the availability of other people who understand such theory and can review the plan. This sampling method is useful for populations that contain a large number of small dollar understatements or overstatements. With large variation in the population, stratification is usually necessary if mean estimation is used. There is less need for stratification if either ratio estimation or difference estimation is employed, but a minimum number of differences is required for their use.

The other statistical sampling method is probability proportional to size sampling. The availability of tables makes the determination of the sample size and the evaluation of sample results generally easier than classical statistical sampling. Also, PPS is more effective for finding large dollar overstatements in the population. For this reason, PPS is often preferred when the population is believed to contain few, if any, large dollar overstatements. It is not necessary to stratify the population when PPS is used.

Thus, there is no one "best" sampling method. The auditor selects the most efficient method based on the anticipated characteristics of the population to be audited.

There are concepts common to all of the sampling techniques. The sequence of steps discussed in the first part of this chapter is a logical way to sample for substantive tests.

Chapter 14 ▶ GLOSSARY OF TERMS

Allowance for sampling risk The acceptable difference between the expected misstatement (often zero) and the tolerable misstatement.

Classical statistical sampling techniques Sampling techniques that use normal distribution theory to quantify sampling risk, determine sample size, and evaluate sample results.

Difference estimation A technique of estimating the dollar amount of a population by calculating the average difference between the audited and recorded amounts in the sample and projecting this difference to the population. This technique is a type of classical statistical sampling.

Estimation sampling A sampling approach that involves the use of sample results to estimate the dollar amount of the population from which the sample is taken.

Mean estimation   A technique of estimating the dollar amount of a population by calculating the mean of the sample and projecting this mean to the population. This technique is a type of classical statistical sampling.

Nonstatistical sampling techniques   Sampling techniques that do not quantify sampling risk in determining sample size and evaluating sample results.

Population   All the units in an account balance or class of transactions.

Probability proportional to size sampling   A sampling technique that uses a combined attributes and variable approach to quantify risk and estimate the amount of error in a population.

Projected misstatement   The difference between the estimated and recorded amount of a population; projected from misstatements found in the sample.

Ratio estimation   A technique of estimating the dollar amount of a population by calculating the ratio between the audited and recorded amounts in the sample and using this ratio to make the estimate. This technique is a type of classical statistical sampling.

Risk of incorrect acceptance   The risk that the auditor will incorrectly accept the hypothesis that the evidence supports the account balance.

Risk of incorrect rejection   The risk that the auditor will incorrectly reject the hypothesis that the evidence supports the account balance.

Sampling unit   Individual elements in a population that contain the characteristic of interest.

Standard deviation   Statistical measure of variability in a population; used in classical statistical sampling to determine sample size.

Stratification   Dividing the population into subgroups or strata and treating each subgroup as a separate population.

Tolerable misstatement   The planned dollar misstatement that can exist in an account balance which, when added to misstatements in all other accounts, will not exceed materiality for the overall financial statements.

Upper limit on net overstatement   A term used in probability proportional to size sampling to indicate the projected misstatement plus the allowance for sampling risk.

Chapter 14 ▶ REFERENCES

Akresh, Abraham D., and Tatum, Kay W. "Audit Sampling—Dealing with the Problems," *Journal of Accountancy* (December 1988), pp. 58–64.

American Institute of Certified Public Accountants, *Professional Standards*
AU Section 312 [*SAS No. 47*]—Audit Risk and Materiality in Conducting an Audit.
AU Section 350 [*SAS No. 39*]—Audit Sampling.

Robertson, Jack C., and Rouse, Robert. "Substantive Audit Sampling—The Challenge of Achieving Efficiency Along With Effectiveness," *Accounting Horizons* (March 1994), pp. 35–44.

Windsor, Sean. "The Use of Audit Sampling Techniques to Test Inventory," *Journal of Accountancy* (January 1991), pp. 107–111.

Chapter 14 ▶ REVIEW QUESTIONS

14-1   Describe the two types of sampling risks for substantive tests.

14-2   When sampling is used to test the hypothesis that the evidence supports the account balance, what are the two parts of the sampling objective?

14-3   In most audit sampling situations, what is the characteristic of primary interest?

14-4   What situations should the auditor consider when defining the population for a substantive test?

14-5   In what three ways could the sampling unit be defined for a substantive test?

14-6   What three sampling techniques can the auditor use for a substantive test?

14-7   What five items must the auditor consider to determine the sample size when using statistical or nonstatistical sampling methods for a substantive test?

14-8   What is stratification, and how does it affect sample size for substantive tests?

14-9   What are the consequences of incorrectly rejecting a hypothesis that the evidence supports an account balance?

14-10   What is the relationship between tolerable misstatement and sample size?

14-11   Why does the sample size of a substantive test increase as the expected misstatement in the population increases?

14-12   Discuss three ways that a sample can be selected in substantive testing.

14-13 Describe two ways to calculate a projected misstatement in the population when nonstatistical sampling is used.

14-14 What three methods can be used to estimate the dollar amount of a population when classical statistical sampling is used?

14-15 In classical statistical sampling, what four items are used to obtain the optimum sample size for estimating the dollar amount of a population?

14-16 Why do ratio and difference estimation methods usually produce smaller sample sizes than the mean estimation method?

14-17 In classical statistical sampling, what six steps should be followed in applying mean estimation?

14-18 In classical statistical sampling, how does the auditor determine whether to accept or reject the hypothesis that the evidence supports the account balance?

14-19 What are the characteristics of a population to which an auditor would apply probability proportional to size sampling?

14-20 What four items are needed to determine the sample size when probability proportional to size sampling is used?

Chapter 14 ▶ OBJECTIVE QUESTIONS

(* = author prepared; ** = CPA examination)

*14-21 Sampling results could lead the auditor to believe erroneously that the account does not contain more dollar error than can be tolerated. Which of the following corresponds to the preceding statement?
   a. The risk of incorrect acceptance.
   b. The risk of incorrect rejection.
   c. Estimation sampling.
   d. Projected misstatement.

*14-22 To determine an optimum sample size when sampling methods are used in a substantive test, all of the following factors must be considered except the
   a. Variation in the population.
   b. Risk levels the auditor is willing to accept.
   c. Deviation occurrence rate the auditor expects to exist in the sample.
   d. Tolerable misstatement.

**14-23 Which of the following sample planning factors would influence the sample size for a substantive test of details for a specific account?

	Expected amount of misstatements	Measure of tolerable misstatement
a.	No	No
b.	Yes	Yes
c.	No	Yes
d.	Yes	No

*14-24 The relationship between the sampling risk of incorrect acceptance and the sample size of substantive tests is
   a. Inverse.

   b. Positive.
   c. Indeterminate.
   d. None of the above.

**14-25 Which of the following sampling methods would be used to estimate a numerical measurement of a population, such as a dollar value?
   a. Discovery sampling.
   b. Sampling for variables.
   c. Sampling for attributes.
   d. Numerical sampling.

**14-26 In assessing sampling risk, the risk of incorrect rejection of an account balance relates to the
   a. Efficiency of the audit.
   b. Effectiveness of the audit.
   c. Selection of the audit.
   d. Audit quality controls.

**14-27 Which of the following statements is correct concerning the auditor's use of statistical sampling?
   a. An assumption of PPS sampling is that the underlying accounting population is normally distributed.
   b. An auditor needs to estimate the dollar amount of the standard deviation of the population to use classical variable sampling.
   c. A classical variable sample needs to be designed with special considerations to include negative balances in the sample.
   d. The selection of zero balances usually does not require special sample design considerations when using PPS sampling.

**14-28 In statistical sampling methods used in substantive testing, an auditor most likely would stratify a population into meaningful groups if

a. Probability proportional to size sampling is used.

b. The population has highly variable recorded amounts.

c. The auditor's estimated tolerable misstatement is extremely small.

d. The standard deviation of recorded amounts is relatively small.

**14-29 An advantage of statistical sampling over nonstatistical sampling is that statistical sampling helps an auditor to

a. Minimize the failure to detect errors and fraud.

b. Eliminate the risk of nonsampling errors.

c. Reduce the level of audit risk and materiality to a relatively low amount.

d. Measure the sufficiency of the evidential matter obtained.

**14-30 If the achieved allowance for sampling risk of a statistical sample is greater than the planned allowance for sampling risk, this is an indication that the

a. Standard deviation was larger than expected.

b. Standard deviation was less than expected.

c. Population was larger than expected.

d. Population was smaller than expected.

**14-31 An auditor is performing substantive tests of pricing and extensions of perpetual inventory balances consisting of a large number of items. Past experience indicates numerous pricing and extension errors. Which of the following statistical sampling approaches is most appropriate?

a. Unstratified mean estimation.

b. Ratio estimation.

c. PPS.

d. Stop or go.

**14-32 Using statistical sampling to assist in auditing the year-end accounts payable balance, an auditor has accumulated the following data:

	Number of accounts	Book balance	Balance determined by the auditor
Population	4,100	$5,000,000	?
Sample	200	$ 250,000	$300,000

Using the ratio estimation technique, the auditor's estimate of year-end accounts payable balance would be

a. $6,150,000.

b. $6,000,000.

c. $5,125,000.

d. $5,050,000.

**14-33 Use of the ratio estimation sampling technique to estimate dollar amounts is *inappropriate* when

a. the total book value is known and corresponds to the sum of all the individual book values.

b. There are some observed differences between audited values and book values.

c. The audited values are nearly proportional to the book values.

d. A book value for each sample item is unknown.

**14-34 In classical statistical sampling, which of the following must be known to estimate the appropriate sample size?

a. The total amount of the population.

b. The planned standard deviation.

c. The planned risk levels.

d. The estimated rate of error in the population.

**14-35 The major reason that the difference and ratio estimation methods would be expected to produce audit efficiency compared to mean estimation is that the

a. Number of members of the populations of differences or ratios is smaller than the number of members of the population of book values.

b. Variability of populations of differences or ratios is less than that of the populations of book values or audited values.

c. Risk of incorrect acceptance may be ignored.

d. Calculations required in using difference or ratio estimation are less arduous and fewer than those required when using mean estimation.

*14-36 Probability proportional to size sampling (PPS) is normally used when it is thought that the population contains a

a. Few understatements.

b. Large number of understatements.

c. Few overstatements.

d. Large number of overstatements.

**14-37 Vale has decided to use PPS sampling in the audit of a client's accounts receivable balances. Vale plans to use the following PPS sampling table:

Reliability Factors of Overstatement

Number of overstatements	Risk of incorrect acceptance				
	1%	5%	10%	15%	20%
0	4.61	3.00	2.31	1.90	1.61
1	6.64	4.75	3.89	3.38	3.00
2	8.41	6.30	5.33	4.72	4.28

Additional information

Tolerable misstatement	$ 24,000
Risk of incorrect acceptance	5%
Number of misstatements anticipated	0
Recorded amount of accounts receivable	$240,000
Number of accounts	360

What sample size should Vale use?
a. 120
b. 108
c. 60
d. 30

**14-38 In a PPS sample with a sampling interval of $10,000, an auditor discovered that a selected account receivable with a recorded amount of $5,000 had an audit amount of $3,000. The projected misstatement of this sample is

a. $3,000.
b. $4,000.
c. $6,000.
d. $8,000.

**14-39 In a PPS sample with a sampling interval of $5,000, an auditor discovered that a selected account receivable with a recorded amount of $9,000 had an audit amount of $8,000. If this were the only error discovered by the auditor, the projected error of this sample would be
a. $1,000.
b. $2,000.
c. $4,000.
d. $5,000.

**14-40 Which of the following statements is correct concerning PPS sampling?
a. The sampling distribution should approximate the normal distribution.
b. Overstated units have a lower probability of sample selection than units that are understated.
c. The auditor controls the risk of incorrect acceptance by specifying that risk level for the sampling plan.
d. The sampling interval is calculated by dividing the number of physical units in the population by the sample size.

Chapter 14 ▶ DISCUSSION/CASE QUESTIONS AND PROBLEMS

(* = author prepared; ** = CPA examination)

*14-41 In each of the following cases involving nonstatistical sampling, indicate what conclusions the auditor might draw and why.
a. The likely misstatement is more than the tolerable misstatement.
b. The likely misstatement is considerably lower than the tolerable misstatement.
c. The likely misstatement is lower than, but close to, the tolerable misstatement.
d. The likely misstatement is more than the preliminary estimate of the population misstatement.

*14-42 Assume that an account has the following characteristics:

Number of items in the account—300

Recorded amount—$600,000

Sample size—100

Required:
a. If the sample mean is $1,800 and mean estimation is used, the estimate of the account total is $_____.

b. If ratio estimation is used and (1) the recorded amount of the sample is $200,000 and (2) the audit amount of the sample is $210,000, the estimate of the account total is $_____.

c. If difference estimation is used and (1) the recorded amount of the sample is $200,000 and (2) the audit amount of the sample is $195,000, the estimate of the account total is $_____.

*14-43 The following data for a substantive test using sampling are available:

Population recorded amount—$200,000

Tolerable misstatement—$10,000

Number of items in the population—200

Risk of incorrect acceptance—20 percent

Estimated misstatement in the population—0

Required:

a. Assume the use of nonstatistical sampling and a sample size of 50. Assume that the recorded amount of the sample is $40,000 and the audited amount of the sample is $35,000. Calculate the projected misstatement using the two methods illustrated in the chapter. Using both methods, indicate why the sampling results are acceptable or unacceptable.

b. Assume the use of PPS sampling with zero anticipated misstatements.

    (1) Calculate the sample size using the equations and tables illustrated in the chapter.

    (2) Disregarding Problem (1), assume a sample size of 40. What is the sampling interval? If a misstatement is found in an account with a recorded balance of $50,000, would "tainting" have to be used to calculate a projected misstatement? Why or why not? Calculate the projected misstatement if a $400 overstatement is found in an account with a recorded balance of $4,000.

*14-44 Take the population in the table on pages 465–466 and perform the following (use sampling without replacement and a standard deviation of the recorded amounts of 20).

a. Determine the sample size for a classical statistical sample using mean estimation. Assume a tolerable misstatement of $2,000, a risk of incorrect rejection of 20 percent, and a risk of incorrect acceptance of 10 percent.

b. Take the sample using either systematic or unrestricted random sampling. Assume that the recorded and audited amounts are the same except for the following.

Account number	Recorded amount	Audited amount
1	$218	$118
20	211	0
27	224	37
68	202	0
69	207	407
126	173	373
143	198	98

c. Calculate a projected misstatement. Calculate an achieved allowance for sampling risk.

d. Indicate whether the sampling results are acceptable or unacceptable. Explain your reason.

Number	Amount	Number	Amount	Number	Amount
1	218	54	169	107	232
2	209	55	234	108	234
3	200	56	190	109	235
4	196	57	191	110	210
5	170	58	180	111	190
6	178	59	181	112	185
7	180	60	182	113	220
8	199	61	209	114	215
9	201	62	208	115	210
10	230	63	214	116	205
11	228	64	188	117	200
12	212	65	193	118	195
13	197	66	196	119	190
14	190	67	194	120	185
15	202	68	202	121	185
16	196	69	207	122	180
17	233	70	206	123	175
18	181	71	184	124	170
19	196	72	182	125	172
20	211	73	178	126	173
21	210	74	175	127	174
22	208	75	209	128	175
23	186	76	213	129	176
24	190	77	215	130	177
25	191	78	231	131	178
26	183	79	232	132	179
27	224	80	175	133	180
28	226	81	176	134	118
29	215	82	178	135	180
30	208	83	180	136	191
31	200	84	182	137	192
32	193	85	185	138	193
33	183	86	188	139	194
34	203	87	189	140	195
35	181	88	191	141	196
36	228	89	193	142	197
37	230	90	195	143	198
38	232	91	197	144	199
39	188	92	199	145	200
40	199	93	202	146	201
41	187	94	204	147	202
42	212	95	206	148	203
43	230	96	208	149	204
44	201	97	210	150	205
45	214	98	212	151	206
46	215	99	215	152	207
47	189	100	218	153	208
48	178	101	220	154	209
49	234	102	221	155	210
50	204	103	224	156	211
51	205	104	226	157	212
52	220	105	228	158	213
53	198	106	230	159	214

Number	Amount	Number	Amount	Number	Amount
160	215	175	197	190	196
161	216	176	196	191	206
162	158	177	102	192	216
163	171	178	198	193	226
164	240	179	195	194	236
165	235	180	206	195	196
166	234	181	206	196	186
167	190	182	205	197	185
168	182	183	205	198	184
169	203	184	174	199	183
170	171	185	174	200	186
171	220	186	180	Total	$39,816
172	198	187	179		
173	233	188	188	Mean	$199.08
174	202	189	178		

*14-45   During the planning of the audit of Strong Company, the partner in charge of the audit was discussing sampling plans with a manager and a senior. The discussion centered on the potential use of sampling in testing the clerical accuracy of the perpetual inventory records.

The senior maintained that a classical statistical sampling technique was the appropriate method. Experience has shown that the dollar amounts of misstatements in the inventory records are small, although the number of misstatements is often large.

The manager disagreed with the suggestion. He contended that increasing numbers of auditors are using PPS, which does not require stratification. If a few large dollar misstatements existed in the population and none was found in the sample, the results could be misleading.

The senior believed that the potential problem presented by the manager was overrated. Experience shows that perpetual inventory records contain small dollar misstatements.

At this point, the audit partner became a bit impatient. She suggested that the group confer with a newly promoted senior who had recently taken an up-to-date auditing course and had attended a professional development course in statistical sampling.

Required:

Assume that you are the newly promoted senior and have been asked to suggest a sampling plan for the inventory testing.

a. Summarize the merits and flaws in each argument.

b. Suggest the conditions under which either classical statistical sampling or PPS sampling might be appropriate.

**14-46   You desire to estimate the amount of the inventory of your client. Draper, Inc. You satisfied yourself earlier as to the inventory quantities. During the audit of the pricing and extension of the inventory, the following data were gathered using appropriate unrestricted random sampling with replacement procedures.

- Total items in the inventory (N)   12,700
- Total items in the sample (n)   400
- Total audited value of items in the sample $38,400

Required:

    a. According to the sample results, what is the estimate of the total value of the inventory using mean estimation? Show computations.

    b. Independent of your answer to problem (a), assume that the book value of Draper's inventory is $1,700,000, and on the basis of the sample results, the estimated total value of the inventory is $1,690,000. The tolerable misstatement is $15,000, and the achieved allowance for sampling risk is $8,000. Discuss the audit and statistical considerations the auditor must evaluate before deciding whether to accept the hypothesis that the evidence supports the book value.

*14-47   In the following situations solve the problems and answer the questions.

    a. Nonstatistical sampling is used. The number of items in the population is 1,000, and the recorded amount on the books is $100,000. The sample size is 250, and the recorded amount of the sample is $40,000. The audit amount of the sample is $35,000 based on five misstatements.

       (1) Calculate the projected misstatement using two methods. Show the calculations for both methods.

       (2) Explain why there was a difference in the projected misstatements. Under what conditions should each projected misstatement be used?

    b. PPS sampling is used. The sampling interval is $6,000. One misstatement is found. The recorded amount of the account in which the misstatement was found is $5,000, and the audited amount is $3,500.

       (1) Calculate the projected misstatement. Show calculations.

       (2) Explain the commonality between the method of calculating the projected misstatement here and one of the methods of calculating the projected misstatement in (a) above.

**14-48   Smith, CPA, has decided to assess control risk applicable to the existence of accounts receivable at a low level. Smith plans to use sampling to obtain substantive evidence concerning the existence of the client's accounts receivable balances. Smith has identified the first few steps in an outline of the sampling plan as follows:

    a. Determine the audit objectives of the test.

    b. Define the population.

    c. Define the sampling unit.

    d. Consider the completeness of the population.

    e. Identify individually significant items.

Required:

Identify the remaining steps that Smith should include in the outline of the sampling plan. Illustrations and examples need not be provided.

**14-49   Edwards has decided to use probability proportional to size (PPS) sampling in the audit of a client's accounts receivable balance. Few, if any, account balance overstatements are expected. Edwards plans to use the following PPS sampling table:

Reliability Factors for Overstatement

Number of overstatements	Risk of incorrect acceptance				
	1%	*5%*	*10%*	*15%*	*20%*
0	4.61	3.00	2.31	1.90	1.61
1	6.64	4.75	3.89	3.38	3.00
2	8.41	6.30	5.33	4.72	4.28
3	10.05	7.76	6.69	6.02	5.52

Required:

a. Identify the advantages of using PPS sampling over classical statistical sampling.
(*Note:* Requirements (b) and (c) are *not* related.)

b. Calculate the sampling interval and the sample size Edwards should use given the following information:

Tolerable misstatement	$15,000
Risk of incorrect acceptance	5%
Number of misstatements anticipated	0
Recorded amount of accounts receivable	$300,000

(*Note:* Requirements (b) and (c) are *not* related.)

c. Calculate the total projected misstatement if the following three misstatements were discovered in a PPS sample:

	Recorded amount	*Audit amount*	*Sampling interval*
1st error	$ 400	$ 230	$1,000
2nd error	500	0	1,000
3rd error	3,000	2,500	1,000

*14-50 Take the illustration of PPS sampling starting on page 450 of the chapter material and do the following:

a. Assume a tolerable misstatement of $150,000 instead of $100,000, leaving all other variables on page 450 the same. Calculate the sample size and the sampling interval.

b. Repeat (a), assuming a tolerable misstatement of $120,000.

**14-51 Mead, CPA, was engaged to audit Jiffy Co.'s financial statements for the year ended August 31, 19X8. Mead is applying sampling procedures.

During the prior year's audits Mead used classical variables sampling in performing tests of controls on Jiffy's accounts receivable. For the current year Mead decided to use probability proportional to size (PPS) sampling in confirming accounts receivable because PPS sampling uses each account in the population as a separate sampling unit. Mead expected to discover many overstatements, but presumed that the PPS sample still would be smaller than the corresponding size for classical variables sampling.

Mead reasoned that the PPS sample would automatically result in a stratified sample because each account would have an equal chance of being selected for confirmation. Additionally, the selection of negative (credit) balances would be facilitated without special considerations.

Mead computed the sample size using the risk of incorrect acceptance, the total recorded book amount of the receivables, and the number of misstated accounts allowed. Mead divided the total recorded book amount of the receivables by the sample size to determine the sampling interval. Mead then calculated the standard deviation of the dollar amounts of the accounts selected for evaluation of the receivables.

Mead's calculated sample size was 60 and the sampling interval was determined to be $10,000. However, only 58 different accounts were selected because two accounts were so large that the sampling interval caused each of them to be selected twice. Mead proceeded to send confirmation requests to 55 of the 58 customers. Three selected accounts each had insignificant recorded balances under $20. Mead ignored these three small accounts and substituted the three largest accounts that had not been selected in the sample. Each of these accounts had balances in excess of $7,000, so Mead sent confirmation requests to those customers.

The confirmation process revealed two differences. One account with an audited amount of $3,000 had been recorded at $4,000. Mead projected this to be a $1,000 misstatement. Another account with an audited amount of $2,000 had been recorded at $1,900. Mead did not count the $100 difference because the purpose of the test was to detect overstatements.

In evaluating the sample results, Mead determined that the accounts receivable balance was not overstated because the projected misstatement was less than the allowance for sampling risk.

Required:

Describe each incorrect assumption, statement, and inappropriate application of sampling in Mead's procedures.

Auditing the Working Capital Assertions— Part I

''A billion here and a billion there and pretty soon you're talking big money.''

Senator Everett Dirksen, *attributed*

LEARNING OBJECTIVES

After reading and studying the material in this chapter, the student should be able to

▶ Paraphrase the objectives in the audit of cash.

▶ Compare examples of (1) internal control policies and procedures and (2) substantive tests for each of the five assertions relating to cash.

▶ Describe the contents of working papers for (1) cash in bank schedules, (2) bank confirmations, and (3) interbank transfer schedules.

▶ Describe how value can be added to the audit of cash.

▶ Paraphrase the objectives in the audit of receivables.

▶ Compare examples of (1) internal control policies and procedures and (2) substantive tests for each of the five assertions relating to receivables.

▶ Describe the contents of working papers for (1) accounts receivable aged listing schedules and (2) accounts receivable confirmations.

▶ Describe how value can be added to the audit of receivables.

▶ Paraphrase the objectives in the audit of prepayments.

▶ Compare examples of (1) internal control policies and procedures and (2) substantive tests for each of the five assertions relating to prepayments.

▶ Describe the contents of a working paper for prepayments.

Although assets may be understated as well as overstated, auditors normally find few cases of unrecorded or understated assets. Management's desire for increased earnings tends to result in more auditor-proposed adjustments to reduce earnings and assets than to increase them (though there may be exceptions motivated by income tax factors). Thus, auditors place primary emphasis on verifying recorded amounts (existence, rights, and valuation) when they audit assets. (The emphasis is on completeness in the audit of liabilities.)

Because working capital accounts turn over rapidly, the balance at the end of a period contains few if any elements that were included in the balance at the beginning of the period. Thus, audit emphasis is placed on the ending account balance rather than on changes in the account during the period being audited.

CASH

Although the cash balance is seldom one of the larger amounts on the balance sheet, the volume and dollar amount of transactions flowing through the cash account are usually greater than for any other account, because most business transactions ultimately are settled in cash. In addition, being the most liquid of all assets, cash is susceptible to defalcation (high inherent risk). For these reasons, the audit procedures applied to cash are often more extensive than the dollar size of the account might seem to warrant.

Most business transactions are carried out by check, although businesses commonly maintain small petty cash funds for minor disbursements. Unless the balance or volume of transactions in a petty cash fund is large, the auditor seldom makes a count of the fund. Cash may be counted, however, if it is material or if unusual circumstances exist.

Unless otherwise disclosed in the financial statements, the cash balance included in current assets is considered to be unrestricted and available for immediate withdrawal. Restrictions on cash can take many forms, from an informal agreement with a bank to maintain an average balance above a certain amount to support borrowing and other credit arrangements (referred to as a compensating balance) to formally restricted escrow or other accounts from which immediate withdrawal cannot be made. Compensating balance arrangements should be disclosed in a note to the financial statements, whereas formally restricted accounts may be classified as noncurrent assets.

A general concept of internal control—the separation of responsibilities for recording transactions affecting an asset from custody of the asset—has special applicability to cash. The implementation is sometimes referred to as a separation of the accounting and treasury functions. In large companies, these functions frequently are separated into different departments, with a controller supervising the recording function (e.g., recording transactions in journals and ledgers) and a treasurer supervising the custody function (e.g., preparing disbursement checks and receiving and depositing cash).

Even if such a complete separation of functions is not possible, certain specific duties can be separated among the available personnel to achieve the most effective internal control possible under the circumstances. For example, an employee who receives and deposits cash and checks should not prepare sales invoices, post detail accounts receivable records, reconcile the detail of accounts receivable to the control account, prepare or mail customer statements, approve writeoffs of customer accounts, or receive or reconcile the bank statements. Similarly, an authorized check-signer should not receive or reconcile the bank statement, open the mail, approve vouchers for payment, and so on.

Audit Objectives

The objectives (assertions) in the audit of cash are as follows:

1. To determine whether the amount shown as cash in the financial statements constitutes all (completeness) cash on hand, in banks, or in transit (existence) that is owned (rights) by the company.
2. To determine whether any restricted cash is properly classified and disclosed (presentation).

Note that cash is generally asserted to be valued at face amount so that no specific audit objective is shown for this assertion. There could be exceptions to this general assertion, as in the case of translation of foreign currencies.

Audit Procedures and Working Papers

The first procedure to accomplish these objectives should be to assess control risk for the assertions relating to cash. The following are some examples of internal control policies and procedures that the auditor would consider in determining the scope of substantive tests of cash: (1) receipt and reconciliation of monthly bank statements by parties with no other cash duties may allow the auditor to reduce the number of bank reconciliations tested, limit the extent of audit procedures applied, and perform the bank reconciliation work at an interim date; (2) the com-

FIGURE 15.1   Cash Lead Schedule

X Co.
Cash Lead Schedule
12–31–X8

A

J. Jones
1-18-x9

	Index	As Adjusted 12–31–X7	Per Books 12–31–X8	Adjustments Dr.	Cr.	As Adjusted
Bank A	A-1	51,315 ✓	46,782 ∧			46,782
Bank B	A-2	12,065 ✓	8,309 ∧			8,309
Bank C	A-3	10,000 ✓	10,000 ∧			10,000
Petty Cash		50 ✓	50 ∧			50
		73,430	65,141			65,141
		TB-1	TB-1			TB-1

✓ Traced to prior year working papers.
∧ Traced to general ledger.

parison of checks to supporting documentation, such as a vendor's invoice, by the check-signer may reduce the number of such comparisons made by the auditor; or (3) lack of segregation of check-preparation and check-signing functions may increase the number of checks and supporting documentation examined by the auditor. Other examples of internal control policies and procedures and substantive tests related to specific assertions for the cash account are shown below.

Assertions	Examples of internal control policies and procedures	Examples of substantive tests
1. Existence	1. Bank reconciliation by an independent party.	1. Confirmation of bank balance and reconciliation to book balance.
2. Rights	2. Control environment (require board of director approval for pledging of certificates of deposit).	2. Inquiry and review of board of director minutes and loan documents for evidence of pledging.
3. Completeness	3. Separation of duties for custody of cash and recording of cash transactions; control environment (require board of director approval to open and close bank accounts).	3. Send accounts receivable confirmations (to detect lapping); send bank confirmations to all banks with which the client did business during the year whether the account is open or has been closed.
4. Valuation	4. Not applicable unless foreign currencies are involved.	4. Not applicable unless foreign currencies are involved.
5. Presentation	5. Control environment (require board of director approval of compensating balance and escrow deposits).	5. Inquiry and review of board of director minutes for evidence of compensating balances and escrow deposits.

The next procedure could be to prepare a lead schedule analyzing the amount shown in the audit trial balance by bank account (Figure 15.1). The amounts on the lead schedule should be compared with the general ledger and prior-year working papers. The company's procedures provide that only a limited number of minor items may be purchased with petty cash. The auditor's review of procedures indicates that this policy is being followed, and therefore no additional work will be performed on the petty cash balance.

Analytical Procedures
The auditor will review changes in cash balances during the audit period for reasonableness and compare ending balances with cash budget balances; explanations should be obtained for significant or unusual variations.

Bank Reconciliations and Cutoff Statements
The auditor can then prepare or obtain a copy of the client's bank reconciliation for each account. The bank reconciliation provides the auditor with an important means of accomplishing an important objective regarding cash—to determine that

FIGURE 15.2   Cash in Bank A

A-1

X Co.
Cash in Bank A
12–31–X8

J. Jones
1-18-x9

List of
Outstanding Checks

		Check No.	Amount
Balance per bank	59,650 ₵✓Ⓜ	3014	3 ⊘
Deposits in transit–		3175	416 ⊗
Dates deposited		3180	2,650 ⊘
		3181	718 ⊘
Per Books Per Bank		3183	4,377 ⊘
12-30-X8 ʌ 1-2-X9 Ⓜ A/1 606 Ⓜ		3184	8,288 ⊘
12-31-X8 ʌ 1-2-X9 Ⓜ 5,879 Ⓜ 4,485		3185	1,935 ⊗
		3186	966 ⊗
Outstanding checks	(19,353) ⊘		19,353
Other reconciling			⊘
items	0		
Balance per books	46,782 ʌ		

A

₵ Confirmed by bank - See A-1/1
✓ Traced to December bank statement.
Ⓜ Traced to cutoff statement received directly from bank.
ʌ Traced to cash book.
⊘ Examined canceled check and compared with cash book as to date, number, payee, and amount. Also examined endorsement and compared signature with authorized signers.
⊗ Compared with cash book as to check number and amount.

Note 1- The first bank endorsements of all checks clearing with the cutoff bank statement were examined; none preceded the audit date.

Note 2- Numbers of all checks issued during the month of December, 19X8 were accounted for as clearing with the December bank statement or as being on the outstanding check list.

the cash is represented by deposits in banks or in transit (existence). If the amount shown as the balance in the bank is confirmed directly with the bank, and if the reconciling items (deposits in transit and outstanding checks) are audited satisfactorily, substantial persuasive evidence will have been accumulated in support of the existence of the cash balance shown in the accounting records. These procedures might appear in the audit program as follows.

1. Foot the bank reconciliation and any supporting details (performed by microcomputer when the schedule was prepared).
2. Confirm the balance per bank directly with the bank by means of a standard bank confirmation (indicated by ₵ in Figure 15.2; also see Figure 15.3).
3. Obtain a cutoff bank statement directly from the bank for the period from 1-1-X9 to 1-15-X9. A cutoff bank statement is a bank statement covering a portion of the month following the audit date that is used to test the validity of cash balances and reconciling items.
4. Trace the balance per bank in the reconciliation to the year-end bank state-

FIGURE 15.3 Bank A Confirmation

STANDARD FORM TO CONFIRM ACCOUNT
BALANCE INFORMATION WITH FINANCIAL INSTITUTIONS

Bank A
Fayetteville, Arkansas

X Company
CUSTOMER NAME

We have provided to our accountants the following information as of the close of business on December 31, 19X8, regarding our deposit and/or loan balances. Please confirm the accuracy of the information, noting any exceptions to the information provided. If the balances have been left blank, please complete this form by furnishing the balance in the appropriate space below.* Although we do not request nor expect you to conduct a comprehensive, detailed search of your records, if during the process of completing this confirmation additional information about other deposit and loan accounts we may have with you comes to your attention, please include such information below. Please use the enclosed envelope to return the form directly to our accountants.

1. At the close of business on the date listed above, our records indicated the following deposit balance(s):

ACCOUNT NAME	ACCOUNT NO.	INTEREST RATE	BALANCE*	
Regular	10 0000	0	59,650	A-1

2. We were directly liable to the financial institution with respect to loans at the close of business on the date listed above as follows:

ACCOUNT NO./ DESCRIPTION	BALANCE*	DATE DUE	INTEREST RATE	DATE THROUGH WHICH INTEREST IS PAID	DESCRIPTION OF COLLATERAL
Note	300,000	12-01-Y4	8%	12-01-X8	Land and Buildings
Note	60,000	10-30-X9	8%	12-31-X8	Accounts Receivable

Bruce Lee   _1-4-X9_
(Customer's Authorized Signature)   (Date)

The information presented above by the customer is in agreement with our records. Although we have not conducted a comprehensive, detailed search of our records, no other deposit or loan accounts have come to our attention except as noted below.

R. Senneff   _1-16-X9_
(Financial Institution Authorized Signature)   (Date)

Internal Auditor
(Title)

EXCEPTIONS AND/OR COMMENTS

Please return this form directly to our accountants:

* Ordinarily, balances are intentionally left blank if they are not available at the time the form is prepared.
Revised 1990

ment and the beginning balance of the cutoff bank statement (indicated by $\checkmark$ and Ⓦ in Figure 15.2)

5. Trace the balance per books to the cash book (indicated by Ⱳ in Figure 15.2).

6. Trace the dates and amounts of deposits in transit to the cutoff bank statement obtained directly from the bank (indicated by Ⓦ in Figure 15.2).

7. For canceled checks received in the cutoff bank statement and dated on or before the audit date, perform the following steps (indicated by Ⓥ in Figure 15.2).

   a. Trace to the outstanding check list supporting the bank reconciliation to determine whether they are shown properly.
   b. Compare the signature with the list of authorized check-signers in the permanent audit file.
   c. Examine the endorsement to see that the check is endorsed by the payee and that there are no unusual second endorsements.
   d. Review payees for any that appear unusual such as checks payable to cash.
   e. Compare with cash book as to date, number, payee, and amount.

8. For checks received in the cutoff bank statement and dated after the audit date, examine the first bank endorsement to see that it does not precede the audit date (indicated by Note 1 in Figure 15.2).

9. For checks on the outstanding check list that did not clear with the cutoff bank statement, compare check number and amount with cash book and investigate any that have been outstanding for an unusually long time (indicated by Ⓧ in Figure 15.2).

10. Account for all check numbers issued during the month as having cleared with the year-end bank statement or as being on the outstanding check list (indicated by Note 2 in Figure 15.2).

Effective internal control includes a separation of duties for authorization of cash disbursements, signing and mailing checks, and preparation of the bank reconciliation. If such separation exists, audit procedures 7 through 10 might be applied on a test basis. Auditors sometimes use a minimum dollar amount as a basis for selecting the items to be tested in this type of situation to be sure of testing all significant items. Other types of sample selection previously discussed could also be used.

The auditor normally sends confirmation requests to every bank with which the client has an account or has done recent business. This helps to detect unrecorded bank accounts (completeness) and direct liabilities. Note that Item 2 on the form is a request for information on outstanding loans that the client has with the bank as of the balance sheet date. Thus, this form can serve as a working paper for both cash and liabilities. The auditor may also wish to confirm with the bank other transactions and agreements between the client and the bank, but these requests should be conveyed in a separate letter rather than as part of the standard bank confirmation. Examples of such transactions and agreements include certificates of deposit, collateral and pledged assets, compensating balance requirements, contingent liabilities, letters of credit, lines of credit, loan agreements, securities held in safekeeping, and repurchase/reverse repurchase transactions.

The auditor may also ask banks with accounts that were closed during the year and show a zero book balance whether they have been notified formally of the closing of the accounts (often they are not) and whether there have been any transactions after the date of the last book entry. Unless the necessary formal steps are taken by the client to close such accounts, they could be used for unauthorized deposits and subsequent misappropriation of funds.

If an auditor has reason to suspect lapping (a fraud involving the substitution of cash items to cover misappropriated funds and the delayed posting of collections to the detailed accounts receivable records), authenticated deposit slips may be requested from the bank. Authenticated deposit slips are copies of deposit slips that are mailed to the bank for comparison with copies in its files. The bank indicates on the deposit slip that this has been done (authenticates the deposit slip) and mails it directly to the auditor. The effectiveness of this procedure is limited, however, if details of the deposit are not included on the deposit slip or if the bank does not make an item-by-item comparison of the deposit slip. (Banks sometimes decline to do so.) Lapping is illustrated on page 487.

Interbank Transfers

The foregoing procedures would provide evidence of the existence of individual cash account balances, but the auditor must also consider the effect of transactions between accounts, often referred to as *interbank transfers*. (Intrabank, interdivision, and intercompany transfers should also be tested.) Companies often have several bank accounts (some for special purposes such as payroll), and transfers among them are common. The objective of testing interbank transfers is to determine that for each transfer near the end of the year, the amount added (deposited) to one account was subtracted (withdrawn) from another account during the same year (existence and completeness). For example, if a transfer is added to one account on December 31 and subtracted from another on January 2, the cash balance as of December 31 would be overstated by the amount of the transfer (another account such as vouchers payable would also be overstated). The following illustration shows how cash is overstated.

Illustration of Kiting

	Bank A	Bank B
Transfer between bank accounts		
Transaction	Withdrawal	Deposit
Date recorded on books	January 2, 19X9	December 31, 19X8
Amount	$10,000 $\longrightarrow$	$10,000

Result—Cash is overstated by $10,000 at December 31, 19X8.

This practice, sometimes called *kiting,* has been used by companies to conceal weak cash positions and to increase their current ratios. (If current liabilities exceed current assets, an equal increase in each will improve the current ratio.) Auditors test interbank transfers for kiting with an interbank transfer schedule such as that shown in Figure 15.4. The time period covered by this schedule depends on the normal time for a check to clear the banks involved. One or two weeks is not unusual.

FIGURE 15.4   **Interbank Transfer Schedule**

X Co.
Interbank Transfer Schedule
For the Period 12-22-X8 to 1-10-X9
12-31-X8

$\frac{A}{1}$

J. Jones
1-19-x9

		Deposits		Withdrawals		Dates of		
Check Number	Description	Per Books	Per Bank	Per Books	Per Bank	Bank A	Bank B	Bank C
3183	Transfer from A to B	12-30-X8 ✓	12-30-X8 ⌐	12-30-X8 ✓	12-31-X8 ⌐	(10,000)	10,000	
0613	Transfer from B to A	12-31-X8 ⌐	1-2-X9 ⌐	12-31-X8 ✓	1-3-X9 ⌐	5,879	(5,879)	
						A-1	A-2	

✓ Traced to cash book.
⌐ Traced to bank statement.

The first transfer in Figure 15.4 was recorded on the books and cleared both banks in the same year and therefore is not a reconciling item. The second transfer was recorded on the books in one year and cleared both banks in the subsequent year. Therefore, it should appear in Bank A's reconciliation as a deposit in transit (as in Figure 15.2) and in Bank B's reconciliation as an outstanding check.

Kiting may also be used to temporarily conceal a cash shortage. If a bookkeeper misappropriates funds from a bank account or petty cash fund by unauthorized withdrawals, the shortage may be covered at the audit date by writing, but not recording, a check on another company bank account, preferably in a distant city to increase the time required for clearance. That check is deposited to cover the shortage. The concealment is temporary because the unrecorded check will clear the bank after the audit date and create another shortage. Auditors trace canceled checks dated prior to the audit date and returned with the cutoff bank statement to the list of outstanding checks supporting the bank reconciliation to detect this type of kiting. This step is indicated by $\checkmark$ in Figure 15.2.

Retail stores that sell to the general public and accept cash have special risks. Normally, cash registers are used to control and safeguard cash receipts; however, clerks can under-ring or fail to ring up some sales. Although much more difficult, employees may be able to manipulate cash register records to conceal removal of cash from the cash register. Manager supervision and control of cash register readings help curb this type of theft.

Classification and Disclosure

Most of the procedures discussed previously in this section relate to the objective of determining the existence, completeness, and rights regarding the cash balance. To determine that restricted cash is properly presented (classified and disclosed), the auditor must gather additional evidence. This evidence may take the form of answers to inquiries of management and a special confirmation letter to each bank requesting specific confirmation of compensating balances and other agreements between the bank and the client. Another source for detecting restrictions on cash is the audit of liabilities, particularly the review of the provisions of lease and loan agreements and related documents. Board of director minutes may also disclose restrictions of cash.

Managements of companies occasionally attempt to "window dress" their cash balance by borrowing funds immediately prior to year-end and repaying the loans immediately after year-end so that a large cash balance will appear in the financial statements. This practice is not improper as long as it is adequately disclosed.

Value-Added Audit Considerations for Cash

While performing audit procedures applicable to cash the auditor should consider such matters as: Does the entity have a cash management plan to optimize earnings on excess cash balances? Are payments of vendor invoices delayed until the discount or due date? Are preestablished wire transfers used to maintain minimum balances at decentralized locations? The auditor should discuss these business questions with client management to add value to the audit.

▶ **EXAMPLE**

While auditing cash, the auditor observes that the cash balance exceeds normal operating needs. The auditor suggests that the client study its cash needs for the next 12 months. As a result, the client adopts a policy of investing excess cash in short-term securities and adds several thousand dollars a month to net income.

Summary of Important Substantive Tests for Cash

- Perform analytical procedures.
- Obtain or prepare copies of bank reconciliations, and

    foot the reconciliations,
    confirm the bank balance,
    trace the bank balance to year-end and cutoff bank statements,
    trace balance per books to cash book,
    trace deposits in transit to cutoff bank statements,
    compare outstanding check list with canceled checks included with the cutoff bank statement and examine checks for date, number, payee, amount, signature, and endorsement,
    examine canceled checks included with the cutoff bank statement dated after the audit date for date of first bank endorsement,
    investigate any long outstanding checks, and
    account for all check numbers issued during the month ending on the audit date.

- Schedule and review interbank transfers.
- Inquire of management and review special bank confirmations, lease and loan agreements, and minutes for restrictions on cash that may require reclassification or disclosure.

RECEIVABLES

Accounts receivable included in current assets are considered to be collectible within one year or during a company's natural operating cycle. Other receivables are classified as long-term assets. Notes or accounts receivable due from officers, employees, affiliated enterprises, and other related parties should be shown separately and not included under a general heading, such as notes receivable or accounts receivable.

Receivables are sometimes pledged as collateral for a loan, and sometimes discounted or sold (with or without recourse). Disclosure is required of the direct or contingent liabilities that may arise from such transactions.

Receivables should not be stated at an amount in excess of net realizable value. An allowance account is used to reduce the receivable balance to the amount expected to be realized. The allowance for doubtful accounts should be sufficient to cover not only losses from accounts known to be uncollectible, but also an estimate of current receivables that subsequently will become uncollectible.

The internal control relating to accounts receivable is discussed in Chapter 9. The basic concept of segregation of duties requires that such responsibilities as maintaining detailed receivable ledgers, receiving cash, maintaining the receivable control account, preparing sales documents, writing off bad debts, and approving credit be separated to the extent possible.

Audit Objectives

The objectives (assertions) in the audit of receivables are as follows:

1. To determine whether the amount shown as receivables in the financial statements represents all (completeness) bona fide amounts due from others (existence) and owned by the client (rights).
2. To determine whether receivables are stated at net realizable value (valuation).
3. To determine whether receivables are classified properly (presentation).
4. To determine whether all liens on and pledges of receivables are disclosed properly (disclosures).

Audit Procedures and Working Papers

The auditor should begin work in this section by obtaining an understanding of the client's internal control relating to sales, shipping, billing, and accounts receivable and by assessing control risk for assertions relating to accounts receivable. An example of some of these controls is shown in Chapter 9. The assessment of these controls should affect directly the work performed in this section and particularly the scope of one of the most important procedures in this section—the direct confirmation of account balances.

FIGURE 15.5   Receivables Lead Schedule

X Co.
Receivables Lead Schedule
12–31–X8

J. Jones
1-20-x9

B

	Index	As Adjusted 12–31–X7	Per Books 12–31–X8	Adjustments Dr.	Cr.	As Adjusted 12–31–X8
Customer trade receivables	B-1	129,576 ✓	143,400 ᴎ			143,400
Officer and employees	B-2	600 ✓	550 ᴎ			550
Other	B-3	1,013 ✓	1,817 ᴎ			1,817
Allowance for doubtful accounts	B-4	(10,000) ✓	(5,000) ᴎ	(1) (6,000)		(11,000)
		121,189	140,767	(6,000)		134,767
		TB-1	TB-1			TB-1

✓ Traced to prior year working papers.
ᴎ Traced to general ledger.

Effective internal control, such as shown in the cash receipts system in Chapter 9, might allow the auditors to reduce the number of confirmations sent. Other examples of controls that would affect the nature, timing, and extent of substantive tests of assertions regarding accounts receivable are (1) lack of a policy to reconcile detailed accounts receivable records to the general ledger control account, or an out-of-balance condition, should cause the auditor to significantly increase the number of confirmations requested, (2) periodic confirmation by internal auditors may allow the external auditor to reduce the number of confirmations requested, and (3) the existence of a separate credit and collections department with effective procedures for collecting customer accounts may allow the auditor to reduce the extent of his or her analysis and tests of the aging schedule and to perform them at an interim date. Other examples of internal control policies and procedures and substantive tests related to specific assertions for receivables are shown in the following table.

Assertions	Examples of internal control policies and procedures	Examples of substantive tests
1. Existence	1. Require evidence of shipment before sales invoice is prepared and recorded.	1. Confirmation of account balance with customer.
2. Rights	2. Control environment (require board of director approval for pledging of accounts receivable).	2. Inquiry and review of board of director minutes and loan agreements for evidence of pledging.
3. Completeness	3. Require that prenumbered shipping documents be accounted for and reconciled with invoices.	3. Analytical procedures (particularly the comparison of units shipped per sales records with units shipped per shipping records).
4. Valuation	4. Require the preparation of a monthly report by the credit department evaluating the collectibility of all past due accounts.	4. Inquiry of credit manager and review of aged accounts receivable trial balance and credit files.
5. Presentation	5. Control environment (require board of director approval of related party transactions).	5. Inquiry and review of board of director minutes for evidence of related party transactions.

The auditor must prepare a lead schedule for receivables to determine types and amounts of major subaccounts. Figure 15.5 (page 481) shows that X Company's receivables consist primarily of customer accounts receivable. The officer and employee and other accounts should be reviewed to determine there were no significant transactions through them during the year. If there were none, no additional work would normally be performed on these accounts, because they are clearly immaterial.

Analytical Procedures

Numerous opportunities exist to employ analytical procedures to accounts receivable. Some of the more common comparisons are

1. Current-year balance to current-year budget and prior-year actual.
2. Units shipped per sales records with units shipped per shipping records.
3. Number of days' sales in accounts receivable for current and prior year.
4. Accounts receivable turnover ratio for current and prior year.
5. Ratio of bad debt expense to sales for current and prior year.
6. Ratio of allowance for doubtful accounts to accounts receivable for current and prior year.
7. Ratio of past due accounts receivable to total accounts receivable for current and prior year.

Unusual and unexplained variations may raise questions as to the propriety of the accounts receivable balance and the adequacy of the allowance for doubtful accounts (existence and valuation).

The Aging Schedule

The auditor ordinarily would obtain a listing of the individual customer trade receivables to have sufficiently detailed information to which he or she can apply audit procedures. A detailed listing of customer trade receivables is combined with an aging schedule in Figure 15.6. Note the following audit procedures that have been performed on this schedule.

1. The listing was totaled by the microcomputer and determined to be in agreement with the general ledger (by cross-referencing to the lead schedule where the balance had been traced to the general ledger).
2. The aging of the accounts was tested (valuation).
3. Customer account balances were confirmed on a test basis (existence of and rights to the receivable).
4. Alternative procedures (the examination of invoice, shipping documents, and remittance advice evidencing subsequent payment by the customer) were applied to customer balances selected for confirmation but for which no reply was received (existence of the receivable).
5. The adequacy of the allowance for doubtful accounts was tested by (a) review of credit files and discussions of the collectibility of all accounts over $2,000 with the credit manager, (b) review of subsequent collection of account balances, and (c) comparison with the prior year of the percentage of accounts receivable in each of the aging categories (valuation at net realizable value and proper classification).

Confirmations

Confirmation of accounts receivable is a generally accepted auditing procedure. An auditor should employ this procedure during an audit unless:

- Accounts receivable are immaterial.
- The use of confirmations would be ineffective.
- The level of audit risk is at an acceptably low level because of low assessed inherent and control risks and evidence obtained from other substantive tests.

FIGURE 15.6   Customer Trade Receivables Aged Listing

B-1

J. Jones
1-20-x9

X Co.
Customer Trade Receivables
Aged Listing
12-31-X8

Account No.	Customer Name	Balance 12-31-X8	Current	30-60 Days	60-90 Days	Over 90 Days	Subsequent Collections	Comments
1103	Cunningham Inc.	5,630 C	5,630 (v)				0	
1110	Litton & Co.	1,935	1,860		75		1,860	
1112	La Fleur & Sons, Ltd.	278				278	0	Bankrupt
1120	March Co.	3,811 √n	2,701	1,110			3,811	
	Total	B 143,400	110,745	18,759	8,286	5,610	64,423	
	Percent of total	100%	77%	13%	6%	4%		
	Prior year percentages	100%	83%	11%	5%	1%		

C Confirmed by customer - See B-1.
√ Second request mailed.
n Non-reply. Examined invoice, shipping documents, and remittance advice for subsequent collection.
(v) Tested the aging of the accounts.

Client computes allowance for doubtful accounts as 100% of accounts over 90 days old. I reviewed credit files and discussed all accounts over $2000 with the credit manager and noted approximately $6000 of accounts in the 30-60 and 60-90 day columns that are doubtful. Recommend the following adjustment:

Bad debt expense   6000
    Allowance for doubtful accounts   6000

J. Jones
1-20-X9

FIGURE 15.7 Accounts Receivable Confirmation

X CO.
122 WEST AVE.
FAYETTEVILLE, ARKANSAS

January 19, 19X9

Mr. Harold Cunningham
Cunningham, Inc.
423 Best Road
Fayetteville, Arkansas 72701

Dear Mr. Cunningham:

Our auditors, Partner & Co., are now engaged in an audit of our financial statements. In connection therewith, they desire to confirm the balance due us on your account as of December 31, 19X8, which was shown on our records (and the enclosed statement) as $5,630.00.

B-1

Please state in the space below whether or not this is in agreement with your records at that date. If not, please furnish any information you may have which will assist the auditors in reconciling the difference. After signing and dating your reply, please mail it directly to Partner & Co., 100 Main Street, Fayetteville, Arkansas 72701. A stamped, addressed envelope is enclosed for your convenience.

It is very important that Partner & Co. receive your prompt reply. We sincerely appreciate your assistance and will return the courtesy extended to us whenever X Co. receives your corresponding audit request.

Very truly yours,

Bruce Lee
Bruce Lee
Controller

B-1

The above balance of $ *5,630.00* due X Co. agrees with our records at December 31, 19X8 with the following exceptions (if any):

none

Date __*1-20-X9*__ Signed __*Harold Cunningham*__

Figure 15.7 is an example of a *positive* confirmation request in which the customer is asked to return the confirmation directly to the auditor, indicating thereon agreement or disagreement with the amount shown on the client's records. Often the confirmation request is accompanied by a statement showing the detail of the accounts receivable balance, which allows the customer to determine agreement or disagreement more accurately. Positive confirmations are preferable when individual account balances are relatively large, or when inherent and control risks are believed to be high and there is reason to believe that there may be a substantial number of misstatements in the accounts.

A negative confirmation request contains much of the same wording as a positive request, except that the customers are asked to return the confirmation directly to the auditor *only* if they disagree with the amount shown on the confirmation. Therefore, the auditor cannot be completely sure that customers do not return negative confirmations because they (1) agree with the clients' balances, or (2) neglect to give them proper consideration. Negative confirmations may be used when there are a large number of relatively small account balances, inherent and control risks are believed to be low, and the individuals receiving the confirmation requests are likely to give them adequate consideration.

If a positive confirmation request is sent and no reply is received within a reasonable period of time, a second request is sent. If a reply is not received after the second request, the auditors will apply *alternative procedures* (inspection of internal records such as copies of sales invoices, shipping documents, and evidence of payment). Once an account has been selected for verification, some type of evidence ordinarily should be obtained.

Some entities such as government agencies frequently do not answer confirmation requests, thus requiring the adoption of alternative procedures. However, the belief that no reply will be forthcoming is not a valid reason for omitting the request for confirmation, nor is it appropriate in such circumstances to use a negative form of confirmation.

The auditor should investigate all exceptions to both positive and negative confirmation requests. Often the difference between the client's records and the customer's reply can be explained by a cash receipt in transit or a late charge by the client. Sometimes the client has made an error, in which case an adjusting entry would be proposed if the difference is material. Not only exceptions but also gratuitous comments should be investigated. For example, if the comment "Paid in full on January 8, 19X9" were added by a customer to a confirmation as of December 31, 19X8, the auditor should examine the cash receipts book for a payment on or near January 8, 19X9.

Auditors often summarize the results of their confirmation procedures to facilitate the review of this work. An example of the form such a summary may take is as follows.

	Number	Amount
Accounts confirmed without exception	41	$681,321
Accounts confirmed with exception but exception cleared	5	66,094
Accounts confirmed with exception and adjusting entry proposed	2	14,756
Accounts for which no reply was received—alternative procedures performed	6	54,312
Total accounts selected for confirmation	54	$816,483

Auditors often send confirmations to 100 percent of the accounts that exceed tolerable misstatement and to a sample of all others. In determining the size of the sample, the auditor would consider factors discussed in Chapter 14 such as the amount of tolerable misstatement, the risk of incorrectly accepting a materially incorrect amount, and so forth.

The auditor should understand that a confirmation is evidence of the existence of a receivable but is *not* evidence of its collectibility. A customer may agree completely that a balance is due but may be without funds to make payment. Similarly, the collection of a receivable after the audit date is evidence of its collectibility but may not be evidence of its existence at the audit date. (The receivable and related sale may actually have occurred after the audit date.)

Confirmation of accounts receivable may disclose a fraud referred to as *lapping*. If a client employee has access to both cash receipts and accounts receivable records, cash receipts from one customer may be diverted to personal use and a subsequent cash receipt from a second customer posted to the account of the first customer. This leaves an incorrect balance in the account of the second customer that must be covered by the cash receipt from a third customer, and so on. Naturally, this type of fraud is not permanently concealed and must be continually manipulated. However, some significant losses have occurred because of lapping.

Lapping may be temporarily concealed by changing the client's copy of the deposit slip to show what was improperly posted to customer accounts rather than what was actually received. In addition, monthly statements to customers may be prepared to show a balance different from the incorrect balance shown in the ledger. Here is a brief example of how the accounts could be manipulated.

| | | Customers | | | | | |
| | | A | | B | | C | |
	Theft	Book Balance	Correct Balance	Book Balance	Correct Balance	Book Balance	Correct Balance
Balance		$400	$400	$600	$600	$200	$200
Receipt from A	400		(400)				
Balance	400	400	—	600	600	200	200
Receipt from B	200	(400)			(600)		
Balance	600	—	—	600	—	200	200
Receipt from C				(200)			(200)
Balance	600	—	—	400	—	200	—

Lapping may come to light when it breaks down due to its complexity. Note that because the shortage is continually being shifted among accounts, the bookkeeper cannot afford to take a vacation or otherwise allow others to post the receipts. This is one reason why lapping is sometmes discovered when a "loyal, hard-working" employee becomes seriously ill or is otherwise prevented from performing his or her job. In addition to the confirmation of the balance of a customer's account that is being manipulated (customers B and C in the preceding example), the tracing of individual amounts shown on deposit slips authenticated or obtained directly from the bank (see page 477) to the cash book may disclose this irregularity. Lapping is deterred by a separation of the cashier and accounts receivable functions and by requiring all employees to take regular vacations.

Red flags in the accounts receivable area include:

- An increase in the amount of writeoffs.
- A general slowdown in cash collections.
- An increase in slow-paying accounts.
- An increase in customer complaints about their accounts.
- An increase in interest and late charges made to customer accounts and their subsequent writeoff.

Valuation of Receivables

Because the determination of the adequacy of the allowance for doubtful accounts can be very subjective, it is crucial that the auditor exercise good business judgment in this area. An auditor cannot automatically accept amounts computed by standard client procedures (such as a percentage of sales, a percentage of accounts past due, etc.), even if such procedures produced proper results in the past. Conditions change, and procedures that produced reliable results at one time may not do so later. Among the factors an auditor would consider in evaluating the adequacy of the allowance for doubtful accounts are:

1. *An assessment of the effectiveness of the client's credit and collection policies and the procedures for estimating the allowance for doubtful accounts.* A client with a credit department that checks customers' credit carefully before approving sales and that follows up aggressively on past due accounts is less likely to have extensive uncollectible accounts. Moreover, preparation of the estimate of the allowance for doubtful accounts by qualified individuals using reliable data, reasonable assumptions, and appropriate methods reduces the risk of misstatement.

2. *Ratios and statistical analyses.* Auditors evaluate and compare over time such measures as number of days' sales in accounts receivable, bad debts written off as a percentage of sales, bad debt expense as a percentage of sales, and percentage of sales in each aging category. (This is most useful if the volume of accounts is high and the dollar value of individual accounts is low.)

3. *Review of credit files and payment histories of individual customers.* Auditors review individual customer credit files that include Dun and Bradstreet reports, customer financial statements, and correspondence with customers regarding terms and payments. Auditors also review customer payment histories to determine patterns or trends in a customer's payment habits. These are effective procedures but may be impractical if more than a few large accounts are involved.

4. *Review of subsequent collections.* Auditors can use the benefit of hindsight to determine which accounts were collected subsequent to the balance sheet date. If an auditor determines that an account is collected in the period subse-

quent to the balance sheet date, the auditor has evidence that it was collectible at the balance sheet date. Of course, many collectible accounts may not be collected in the normal course of business before the audit is completed; these accounts must be subjected to other procedures.

5. *Consideration of general economic and industry conditions.* Auditors apply the business approach when evaluating the allowance for doubtful accounts. For example, an auditor would intuitively expect the allowance for doubtful accounts of a consumer loan company to be higher during a period of recession and high unemployment because many customers would be out of work and unable to repay their loans.

In evaluating the risk that the allowance for doubtful accounts is misstated, the auditor may disaggregate the overall risk into the following categories:[1]

- *Credit risk.* This is the risk that the customer lacks the ability and/or the willingness to pay the amount owed; it is the focal point of much of the auditor's work.
- *Collateral risk.* Some receivables, particularly notes, may be secured by collateral. The risk here is that the legal status of the collateral may be imperfect or the value of the collateral may be less than the balance due. Auditors use the services of specialists if collateral is an important consideration in determining the collectibility of an account.
- *Concentration risk.* If most of an entity's customers are in the same industry or geographic area, which is not uncommon, an economic recession in that industry or area will increase the risk of an inadequate allowance for doubtful accounts.
- *Management risk.* Management policies that are established for the granting of credit, whether liberal or strict, are factors that auditors must consider.
- *Operations risk.* Failure of client personnel to adequately monitor potentially uncollectible accounts and to take effective action on a timely basis is an operations risk.
- *Fraud or insider risk.* Sales made to accomplices of employees or to related parties without proper authorization may expose the entity to loss if the party has no intent to make full repayment.

Auditors will test the accounts written off for proper authorization. Unless write-offs are properly authorized, an employee could intercept a customer's remittance and then conceal the theft by writing off the customer's account.

Auditors also review sales returns and allowances that are recorded after the balance sheet date. If sales that were recorded prior to the balance sheet date are returned after that date, an allowance should be recorded at the balance sheet date to properly match the sale and return in the same period. Auditors have been sued because they failed to detect a large overstatement of net income when large sales made near the end of a year were subsequently returned by customers the next year.

---

[1] See "Auditing the Allowance for Credit Losses," by Michael D. Foley in *Journal of Accountancy* (September 1989), pp. 140–144.

Matters Requiring Disclosure

To search for receivables from related parties that require disclosure, auditors use inquiry and inspection of documents as described in Chapters 8 and 13.

To identify liens or pledges of receivables that require disclosure, the auditor would (1) inquire of management as to any financial arrangements made to assign, discount, or pledge receivables, (2) inspect loan agreements for the existence of and minutes for the approval of such financial arrangements, and (3) request confirmation of the existence of such arrangements from financial institutions with which the client transacts business. The business approach is useful here. For example, an auditor should know that a client company that is short of cash and already has pledged its property and equipment is much more likely to have pledged its receivables than a client with an adequate cash flow.

Other Receivables

In addition to accounts receivable, clients may have notes receivable and interest receivable. Notes receivable are audited with procedures similar to those discussed previously, with the following differences. Confirmation letters should include a request for confirmation of the interest rate, due date, and collateral of the notes receivable as well as the outstanding balance. In addition, the auditor should inspect the original notes, which should be kept in a secure place such as a bank safe deposit box. (Procedures for inspecting securities are discussed in Chapter 17.) Interest receivable is audited by recalculation and is discussed in Chapter 17.

Value-Added Audit Considerations for Accounts Receivable

While performing audit procedures applicable to accounts receivable the auditor should consider such matters as: How is customer satisfaction measured (e.g., by survey, tabulation of number of complaints, etc.)? Are customer needs changing? How long does it take to process a customer's order, and how does this compare with best practices in the industry? Can invoices be sent more frequently (e.g., weekly rather than monthly)? Can credit policies be safely relaxed? Are bad debts referred to a collection agency? Does management monitor accounts receivable statistics common to the industry? Is interest charged on overdue accounts receivable? Although satisfactory answers to these questions do not add to the reliability of the financial statements, they help management focus on business problems related to accounts receivable and thereby add value to the audit.

▶ EXAMPLE

While auditing accounts receivable an auditor learns that it takes approximately three days to process a customer's order. From consulting industry statistics the auditor determines that, on average, companies in this industry take less than a day to process a customer's order. An investigation reveals that orders are being held in the order department until inventory control confirms that adequate goods are available for shipment. Immediate transmission of the order to the shipping department, with adequate backorder procedures for out-of-stock items, reduces order-processing time to less than one day. Shipments are made sooner, cash flow improves, and customers are happier. The auditor has added value to the audit.

Summary of Important Substantive Tests for Accounts Receivable

- Perform analytical procedures.
- Obtain and test the clerical accuracy of an accounts receivable trial balance.
- Send confirmations (positive or negative) to selected customers; send second requests to customers who fail to respond to first requests for positive confirmations.
- Perform alternative procedures for customers who fail to respond to second requests for positive confirmations.
- Obtain and test the accuracy of an aged trial balance, and evaluate the adequacy of the allowance for doubtful accounts by inquiry of credit manager, comparison with prior year of percentages and amounts in each aging category, examination of credit files and payment histories for large delinquent accounts, and review of subsequent collection of account balances.
- Inquire of management and review agreements and minutes for related parties and liens or pledges of accounts receivable that require disclosure.

PREPAYMENTS

Prepayments represent costs incurred that are applicable to future periods. Prepayments are short term in nature and are usually associated with services to be received within the next year, such as prepaid insurance, rent, and taxes.

Audit Objectives

The objectives (assertions) in the audit of prepayments are as follows:

1. To determine whether the amounts shown as prepayments in the financial statements constitute all such prepayments (completeness), are computed in accordance with generally accepted accounting principles (valuation), and are applicable to future periods (existence and rights).
2. To determine whether the amounts can reasonably be expected to be realized (valuation).
3. To determine whether the amounts are classified properly in the financial statements and whether disclosure is adequate (presentation).

Audit Procedures and Working Papers

The internal control policies and procedures to be considered by the auditor in the audit of prepayments include those applicable to cash disbursements, the client's policies regarding the kinds of costs that are subject to deferral, and the systematic procedure for amortizing such costs to expense. Tests of the procedures for proper deferral and amortization, described in this section, are dual-purpose tests. The evaluation of the effectiveness of these procedures is a significant factor in determining the scope of the auditor's work in this area. For example, a consistently followed policy of deferring the cost of only certain appropriate items might enable the auditor to substantially limit his or her examination of invoices supporting additions to the prepayments account. In addition, the test of prepayment amortizations by internal auditors should allow the external auditor to restrict substantive tests in this area. Other examples of internal control policies and procedures and substantive tests related to specific assertions for prepayments are shown below.

Assertions	Examples of internal control policies and procedures	Examples of substantive tests
1. Existence	1. Documented accounting policies for differentiating between amounts to be expensed (e.g., current period rent) and amounts to be deferred (e.g., future period rent).	1. Inspect vendor invoices charged to prepayments to determine the period to which the cost relates and evaluate propriety of accounting treatment.
2. Rights	2. Control environment (require board of director approval of pledging of such items as insurance policies).	2. Inquiry and review of board of director minutes and loan agreements for evidence of pledging.
3. Completeness	3. Same as for existence.	3. Inspect vendor invoices charged to expense to determine the period to which the cost relates and evaluate the propriety of the accounting treatment.
4. Valuation	4. Use of standard monthly journal entries to record monthly amortization of prepayments.	4. Recalculate amortization of prepayments.
5. Presentation	5. Documented accounting policies for identifying prepayments applicable to a period in excess of one year from the balance sheet date.	5. Inspect vendor invoices charged to prepayments to determine the period to which the cost relates.

After the auditor's assessment of control risk for assertions relating to prepayments, the next step normally would be the preparation of a lead schedule. In the X Company example, however, there is only one prepayment account. Therefore, in this case, the auditor would reference directly from the detail audit schedule for prepaid insurance (Figure 15.8) to the audit trial balance. This schedule (unlike working papers in the cash, accounts receivable, and inventory sections) shows the transactions for the year that affect prepaid insurance and insurance expense. (The procedures result in evidence about an expense account as well as an asset account.)

Analytical Procedures
The auditor should compare current-year prepayment balances by major category (insurance, rent, etc.) with the prior year. Because prepayment balances often apply to a specific period at the end of each year (e.g., an insurance policy covers the period July 1 to June 30 so that there are always six months of unexpired premium each December 31), variations in balances may relate primarily to variations in cost.

FIGURE 15.8 Prepayments

X Co.
Prepayments
Analysis of Prepaid Insurance and Expense
12-31-X8

J. Jones
1-22-X9

Description	Prepaid Balance 12-31-X7	Current Premium	Amortization to Expense	Prepaid Balance 12-31-X8
Policy No. REC 12233 for fire and extended coverage on building and contents in the amount of $600,000 for the year from 6-30-X7 to 6-30-X8	5,742	0	(5,742)	0
Increase in above policy to $625,000 and extensions to 6-30-X9	0	12,624 ✓	(6,312) X	6,312
Policy No. WC 22244 for workman's compensation coverage of $100,000 from 1-1-X8 to 12-31-X8 ✓	0	3,291 ✓	(3,291)	0
Policy No. CC 3719 – Blanket fidelity bond coverage in the amount of $200,000 from 1-1-X8 to 12-31-X8 ✓	0	1873 ✓	(1,873)	0
	11,343	37,898	36,986	12,255
	TB-1			TB-1

20
40

29,704
7,282
36,986

I discussed the Company's insurance coverage with Mr. Lee, Controller. He is satisfied that insurance coverage is adequate to cover the replacement cost of the assets and anticipated liability claims. I noted no significant omissions or inadequacies of insurance coverage.

J. Jones
1-22-X9

✓ Examined insurance policy noting provisions of the policy and annual premium.
↖ Examined insurance company invoice and canceled check.
X Checked calculation of amortization.

This allows the auditor to make effective tests of balances of prepayments by using analytical procedures. Any new categories of prepayments in the current year should be investigated to determine whether their deferral (existence) is appropriate.

Tests of Balance and Amortization

Under generally accepted accounting principles, prepayments generally are stated at cost. The auditor has tested this aspect in Figure 15.8 by examination of invoices from insurance companies and the related canceled checks (see ⋁). Additional evidence of the annual premium cost is obtained from examination of the insurance policy (see ✓). The auditor must be aware that the premium on certain types of policies, such as workman's compensation, are sometimes based on the injury experience of the insured and are subject to retroactive adjustment. In this case, a review of the client's injury experience and consultation with the client's insurance agent may be necessary to arrive at an estimate of the final premium. The applicability of the prepaid portion of the cost to future periods is tested by calculating the current-year amortization on the basis of the percentage of the total policy period included in the current year (see ⋌). An examination of the policy periods shown in the description column indicates that all will expire within one year and that the classification of the prepaid balance as a current asset is proper. The objective of determining that the amounts can reasonably be expected to be realized is usually self-evident with prepaid insurance, because the balance generally is refunded on cancellation of the policy. This is not the case for all prepaid items, however. Consider prepaid rent on a plant that is shut down permanently. Although the cost in this case may apply to some future period, prepayments must generate some future benefit or value at least equal to their cost to be classified properly as assets. If such items do not produce revenues to absorb their costs, they will not be realized.

Review of Insurance Coverage

On Figure 15.8 is a notation of a review of the company's insurance coverage with the controller and the auditor's observation of no significant omissions or inadequacies in the coverage. Disclosure of significantly inadequate insurance coverage may be necessary for a fair presentation of financial statements. The auditor is not an insurance expert with the qualifications to reach an informed opinion about insurance coverage, although he or she should be familiar with typical business insurance coverage. For example, most businesses maintain fidelity bond coverage to insure against loss from embezzlement and theft, and auditors consider this coverage in their evaluation of the control environment. The auditor should recommend that the client consult with an insurance representative about any obvious deficiencies in coverage.

Important audit information sometimes can be obtained from a review of insurance coverage. A reduction in insurance coverage of property and equipment, for example, may lead the auditor to an unrecorded property retirement, and the existence of a loss-payable clause in a policy could result in the detection of an unrecorded liability.

The audit procedures for other types of prepayments are similar to those for prepaid insurance and are not illustrated in detail. A common problem in auditing prepayments is the auditor's tendency to perform excessive work on relatively immaterial balances. This problem is due in part to the usually uncomplicated and easily verifiable nature of the accounts. An auditor must resist the temptation to dwell on immaterial and uncomplicated accounts and concentrate on the more difficult audit areas.

Summary of Important Substantive Tests for Prepayments

- Perform analytical procedures.
- Examine invoices and other documents for additions to prepayments.
- Test calculation of amortization for the period and ending balances.
- Review insurance coverage.

Chapter 15 ▶ GLOSSARY OF TERMS

Alternative procedures Procedures employed when the audit procedure producing the most competent evidence cannot be completed; for example, internal documents such as sales invoices, shipping documents, and evidence of collection may be examined if a customer fails to reply to positive accounts receivable confirmation requests.

Cutoff bank statement A bank statement, usually for a portion of a month following the audit date, sent directly from the bank to the auditor for use in testing the validity of cash balances and reconciling items.

Kiting The practice of (1) recording an interbank transfer as a deposit in one period and as a disbursement in the subsequent period to improperly inflate the cash balance or (2) covering a cash shortage with an unrecorded check on an out-of-town bank.

Lapping A fraud involving the substitution of cash items to cover misappropriated funds and the delayed posting of collections to the detailed accounts receivable records.

Chapter 15 ▶ REFERENCES

American Institute of Certified Public Accountants. *Professional Standards.* AU Section 330—The Confirmation Process.

Bailey, Charles D., and Ballard, Gene. "Improving Response Rates to Accounts Receivable Confirmations: An Experiment Using Four Techniques," *Auditing: A Journal of Practice & Theory* (Spring 1986), pp. 77–85.

Caster, Paul. "The Role of Confirmations as Audit Evidence," *Journal of Accountancy* (February 1992), pp. 73–76.

Compton, John C., and Van Son, W. Peter. "Check Truncation: The Auditor's Dilemma," *Journal of Accountancy* (January 1983), pp. 36–38.

Foley, Michael D. "Auditing the Allowance for Credit Losses," *Journal of Accountancy* (September 1989), pp. 140–144.

Johnson, Johnny R., Leitch, Robert A., and Neter, John. "Characteristics of Errors in Accounts Receivable and Inventory Audits," *The Accounting Review* (April 1981), pp. 270–293.

Sauter, Douglas P. "Bank Confirmation Form Receives a Facelift," *Journal of Accountancy* (March 1991), pp. 82–89.

Chapter 15 ▶ REVIEW QUESTIONS

15-1 Why are assets more likely to be overstated than understated, and what effect does this have on the auditor's emphasis in the audit of assets?

15-2 Give an example and explain the importance of restrictions on cash.

15-3 State the objectives in the audit of cash.

15-4 What analytical procedures may an auditor apply to cash?

15-5 The auditor gathers evidence regarding the amounts shown in a bank reconciliation. Indicate the evidence he or she would gather or examine in support of

  a. The bank balance.   **c.** Deposits in transit.
  b. The book balance.   **d.** Outstanding checks.

15-6 The standard bank confirmation provides the auditor with evidence relating to accounts other than cash. State how this is done.

15-7 What is the objective of testing interbank transfers?

15-8 Explain what is meant by "kiting."

15-9 What are some inquiries an auditor can make when examining the cash account to add value to the audit?

15-10 State the objectives in the audit of receivables.

15-11 How can analytical procedures be applied to accounts receivable?

15-12 What are "alternative procedures" and when are they performed?

15-13 List the factors an auditor would consider in evaluating the adequacy of the allowance for doubtful accounts.

15-14 Discuss the audit procedures an auditor would employ to detect liens on or pledges of receivables.

15-15 What are some inquiries an auditor can make when examining accounts receivable to add value to the audit?

15-16 State the objectives in the audit of prepayments.

15-17 Explain how internal control relating to prepayments could affect the scope of the auditor's work in that section.

15-18 What analytical procedures may an auditor apply to prepayments?

15-19 What evidence would an auditor examine in support of additions to prepaid insurance?

15-20 Why does an auditor review a client's insurance coverage?

Chapter 15 ▶ OBJECTIVE QUESTIONS

(* = author prepared; ** = CPA examination)

**15-21 To gather evidence regarding the balance per bank in a bank reconciliation, an auditor would examine all of the following *except* the
   a. Cutoff bank statement.
   b. General ledger.
   c. Year-end bank statement.
   d. Bank confirmation.

**15-22 An auditor ordinarily sends a standard confirmation request to all banks with which the client has done business during the year under audit, regardless of the year-end balance. A purpose of this procedure is to
   a. Provide the data necessary to prepare a proof of cash.
   b. Request a cutoff bank statement and related checks be sent to the auditor.
   c. Detect kiting activities that may otherwise not be discovered.
   d. Gather evidence regarding the completeness assertion.

**15-23 The cashier of Rock Company covered a shortage in the cash working fund with cash obtained on December 31 from a local bank by cashing, but not recording, a check drawn on the company's out-of-town bank. How would the auditor discover this manipulation?
   a. Confirming all December 31 bank balances.
   b. Counting the cash working fund at the close of business on December 31.
   c. Investigating items returned with the bank cutoff statements.

   d. Preparing independent bank reconciliations as of December 31.

*15-24 An auditor gathers evidence regarding the validity of deposits in transit by examining the
   a. Bank confirmation.
   b. Cutoff bank statement.
   c. Year-end bank statement.
   d. Bank reconciliation.

*15-25 Which of the following audit procedures is most likely to detect a cash balance that is restricted as to withdrawal?
   a. Review the cutoff bank statement.
   b. Prepare an interbank transfer schedule.
   c. Make inquiries of management.
   d. Compare cash balance with cash budget.

**15-26 An auditor should trace bank transfers for the last part of the audit period and the first part of the subsequent period to detect whether
   a. The cash receipts journal was held open for a few days after the year-end.
   b. Cash balances were overstated because of kiting.
   c. The last checks recorded before the year-end were actually mailed by the year-end.
   d. Any unusual payments to or receipts from related parties occurred.

**15-27 An auditor will request a cutoff bank statement primarily to
   a. Verify the cash balance on the client's bank reconciliation.

b. Detect lapping.

c. Verify reconciling items on the client's bank reconciliation.

d. Detect kiting.

15-28 On the last day of the fiscal year, the cash disbursements clerk drew a company check on Bank A and deposited the check in the company account in Bank B to cover a previous theft of cash. The disbursement has not been recorded. The auditor will best detect this form of kiting by

a. Comparing the detail of cash receipts as shown by the cash receipts records with the detail on the authenticated duplicate deposit tickets for three days prior to and subsequent to year-end.

b. Preparing from the cash disbursements books a summary of bank transfers for one week prior to and subsequent to year-end.

c. Examining the composition of deposits in both Bank A and Bank B subsequent to year-end.

d. Examining paid checks returned with the cutoff bank statement.

15-29 Cash receipts from sales on account have been misappropriated. Which of the following acts would conceal this defalcation and be *least* likely to be detected by an auditor?

a. Understating the sales journal.

b. Overstating the accounts receivable control account.

c. Overstating the accounts receivable subsidiary ledger.

d. Understating the cash receipts journal.

15-30 Which of the following statements is correct concerning the use of negative confirmation requests?

a. Unreturned negative confirmation requests rarely provide significant explicit evidence.

b. Negative confirmation requests are effective when detection risk is low.

c. Unreturned negative confirmation requests indicate that alternative procedures are necessary.

d. Negative confirmation requests are effective when understatements of account balances are suspected.

15-31 Which of the following internal control procedures most likely would deter lapping of collections from customers?

a. Independent internal verification of dates of entry in the cash receipts journal with dates of daily cash summaries.

b. Authorization of writeoffs of uncollectible accounts by a supervisor independent of credit approval.

c. Segregation of duties between receiving cash and posting the accounts receivable ledger.

d. Supervisory comparison of the daily cash summary with the sum of the cash receipts journal entries.

15-32 Which of the following statements regarding the audit of negotiable notes receivable is *not* correct?

a. Confirmation from the debtor is an acceptable alternative to inspection.

b. Physical inspection of a note by the auditor does not provide conclusive evidence of existence.

c. Materiality of the amount involved is a factor considered when selecting the accounts to be confirmed.

d. Notes receivable discounted with recourse need to be confirmed.

15-33 To conceal defalcations involving receivables, the auditor would expect an experienced bookkeeper to charge which of the following accounts?

a. Sales returns.

b. Miscellaneous income.

c. Petty cash.

d. Miscellaneous expense.

15-34 Returns of positive confirmation requests for accounts receivable were very poor. As an alternative procedure, the auditor decided to check subsequent collections. The auditor has satisfied himself that the client satisfactorily listed the customer name next to each check listed on the deposit slip. Hence, he decided that for each customer for which a confirmation was not received, he would add all the amounts shown for that customer on each validated deposit slip for the two months following the balance sheet date. The major fallacy in the auditor's procedure is that

a. By looking only at the deposit slip, the auditor would not know if the payment was for the receivable at the balance sheet date or a subsequent transaction.

b. Checking of subsequent collections is not an acceptable alternative auditing procedure for confirmation of accounts receivable.

c. The deposit slip would not be received directly by the auditor, as a confirmation would be.

d. A customer may not have made a payment during the two-month period.

**15-35 An auditor's purpose in reviewing credit ratings of customers with delinquent accounts receivable most likely is to obtain evidence concerning management's assertions about
a. Valuation or allocation.
b. Presentation and disclosure.
c. Existence or occurrence.
d. Rights and obligations.

*15-36 An auditor's risk of misstatement of accounts receivable is least likely to increase if there is
a. An increase in customer complaints about their accounts.
b. A general slowdown in cash collections.
c. An increase in the allowance for doubtful accounts.
d. An increase in slow-paying accounts.

*15-37 Which of the following ratios is least applicable to the audit of the valuation assertion of accounts receivable?
a. Ratio of bad debt expense to sales.
b. Current ratio.
c. Accounts receivable turnover ratio.
d. Ratio of allowance for doubtful accounts to accounts receivable.

*15-38 Which of the following questions would an auditor ask while auditing accounts receivable to add value to an audit?
a. Are accounts receivable pledged?
b. Are customers satisfied with your billing procedures?
c. Are any accounts receivable due from related parties?
d. Is there a separation of duties between the recording of cash receipts and the handling of cash?

**15-39 When auditing prepaid insurance, an auditor discovers that the original insurance policy on plant equipment is not available for inspection.

The policy's absence most likely indicates the possibility of a(an)
a. Insurance premium due but *not* recorded.
b. Deficiency in the coinsurance provision.
c. Lien on the plant equipment.
d. Understatement of insurance expense.

**15-40 When auditing the prepaid insurance account, which of the following procedures would generally *not* be performed by the auditor?
a. Recompute the portion of the premium that expired during the year.
b. Prepare excerpts of insurance policies for audit working papers.
c. Confirm premium rates with an independent insurance broker.
d. Examine support for premium payments.

**15-41 Items a through f represent the items that an auditor ordinarily would find on a client-prepared bank reconciliation. The accompanying List of Auditing Procedures represents substantive auditing procedures. For each item, select one or more procedures, as indicated, that the auditor most likely would perform to gather evidence in support of that item. The procedures on the List may be selected once, more than once, or not at all.

Assume:

• The auditor received a cutoff bank statement dated 10/7/X4 directly from the bank on 10/11/X4.
• The 9/30/X4 deposit in transit, outstanding checks #1281, #1285, #1289, and #1292, and the correction of the error regarding check #1282 appeared on the cutoff bank statement.
• The auditor assessed control risk concerning the financial statement assertions related to cash at the maximum.

General Company
Bank Reconciliation
1st National Bank of U.S. Bank Account
September 30, 19X4

a. Select 2 Procedures—<u>Balance per bank</u>			$28,375
b. Select 5 Procedures—<u>Deposits in transit</u>			
9/29/X4		$4,500	
9/30/X4		1,525	6,025
			34,400
c. Select 5 Procedures—<u>Outstanding checks</u>			
# 988 8/31/X4		2,200	
#1281 9/26/X4		675	
#1285 9/27/X4		850	
#1289 9/29/X4		2,500	
#1292 9/30/X4		7,225	(13,450)
			20,950
d. Select 1 Procedure—<u>Customer note collected by bank</u>			(3,000)
e. Select 2 Procedures—<u>Error: Check #1282, written on 9/26/X4 for $270 was erroneously charged by bank as $720; bank was notified on 10/2/X4</u>			450
f. Select 1 Procedure—<u>Balance per books</u>			$18,400

LIST OF AUDITING PROCEDURES

a. Trace to cash receipts journal.

b. Trace to cash disbursements journal.

c. Compare to 9/30/X4 general ledger.

d. Confirm directly with bank.

e. Inspect bank credit memo.

f. Inspect bank debit memo.

g. Ascertain reason for unusual delay.

h. Inspect supporting documents for reconciling item *not* appearing on cutoff statement.

i. Trace items on the bank reconciliation to cutoff statement.

j. Trace items on the cutoff statement to bank reconciliation.

Chapter 15 ▶ DISCUSSION/CASE QUESTIONS AND PROBLEMS

(* = author prepared; ** = CPA examination; *** = CMA examination)

*15-42   In your audit of Ryan Company for the year ended December 31, 19X8, you note that the bank reconciliation for the Third National Bank Account contains a large unlocated difference, as shown below.

Balance per bank statement	$142,267
Deposit in transit	3,864
Outstanding checks	(40,793)
Unlocated difference	10,846
Balance per general ledger	$116,184

From the bank statements (including the cutoff statement you received directly from the bank) and cash records, you determine the following:

1. A deposit in the amount of $3,678 of Rain Company was credited against the company's account in error in December.
2. A check in payment of an advertising invoice cleared the bank in December in the amount of $10,318 that was recorded in the cash book at $2,318.
3. Unrecorded bank service charges for December amounted to $125.
4. Proceeds of a bank loan on December 1, 19X8, discounted for three months at 8 percent, had not been recorded by the company in the amount of $9,800.
5. No entry had been made to record the return for NSF of a customer's check of $8,798.
6. A deposit for the collection of accounts receivable was recorded as $21,079, whereas the actual deposit in the bank was $13,678.
7. A check for a salesperson's expenses recorded in the cash disbursement books and shown on the outstanding check list as $612 cleared with the cutoff bank statement and was noted to be in the amount of $216.
8. The company is required by an informal agreement with the bank to maintain a compensating balance of $100,000.

Required:

a. State the objectives for the audit of cash.
b. State the procedures you would consider using to accomplish the objectives. (The final determination would depend on your evaluation of internal control, although it appears to be ineffective from some of the items noted above.)
c. Prepare the adjusting entry and footnote disclosures necessary for a fair presentation of cash.

*15-43　The following interbank transfer schedule has been prepared in connection with the audit of Panther Creek Properties, Inc.

Deposit date		Withdrawal date		Amount of deposit/ (withdrawal)		
Per books	Per bank	Per books	Per bank	First bank	Second bank	Third bank
12/30	1/2	12/31	1/3		8,000	(8,000)
12/31	12/31	12/30	1/2	(3,500)		3,500
12/29	1/2	12/31	12/31	5,000	(5,000)	
12/31	1/2	1/2	1/3	9,000		(9,000)

Complete the following summary as of December 31, assuming no deposits in transit or outstanding checks other than any that would result from the above transfers.

	First bank	Second bank	Third bank
Total deposits in transit	_____	_____	_____
Total outstanding checks	_____	_____	_____
Total over/(under) statement of cash	_____	_____	_____

**15-44　During the year Wimberly Corporation began to encounter cash flow difficulties, and a cursory review by management revealed receivable collection problems. Wimberly's management engaged Starr, CPA, to perform a special investigation. Starr studied the billing and collection cycle and noted the following:

The accounting department employs one bookkeeper who receives and opens all incoming mail. This bookkeeper is also responsible for depositing receipts, filing remittance advices on a daily basis, recording receipts in the cash receipts journal, and posting receipts in the individual customer accounts and the general ledger accounts. There are no cash sales. The bookkeeper prepares and controls the mailing of monthly statements to customers.

The concentration of functions and the receivable collection problems caused Starr to suspect that a systematic defalcation of customers' payments through a delayed posting of remittances (lapping of accounts receivable) is occurring. Starr was surprised to find that no customers complained about receiving erroneous monthly statements.

Required:

Identify the procedures that Starr should perform to determine whether lapping exists. *Do not discuss deficiencies in internal control.*

15-45   Your firm has been engaged to audit the financial statements of RST Inc. for the year ending December 31. RST Inc. is a medium-sized manufacturing company that has approximately 400 trade accounts receivable and does not prepare monthly statements. The manager assigned to the audit has decided to circularize the trade accounts receivable as of September 30 (three months before year-end). The senior on the job asks you to be at the company on October 1 to mail requests for confirmation. He tells you to ask the company's personnel to prepare 25 positive confirmation requests and 100 negative confirmation requests. These sample sizes are based on a sampling plan developed by the senior. He further asks you to obtain an aged trial balance as of September 30, to trace the balances of the accounts to the trial balance from the subsidiary ledgers, to test the aging, to foot the trial balance, and to compare the total of the trial balance with the accounts receivable control account in the general ledger. The senior also informs you that detailed tests of sales and cash receipts will be made.

Required:

a. Enumerate the types of accounts you would want to include in your selection of accounts to be circularized by the positive method.

b. Enumerate the types of accounts you would want to include in your selection of accounts to be circularized by the negative method.

c. Outline a plan for maintaining adequate control over confirmation requests.

d. Outline the additional audit steps that should be undertaken at December 31 in support of the amounts shown as accounts receivable; the company is preparing for your use an aged trial balance of accounts receivable as of that date.

(*Used with permission of Ernst & Young*)

*15-46   Susan Start, a new staff assistant of a CPA firm, was assigned to the audit team auditing the financial statements of Rel-Hep Finance Company. The senior in charge of the audit assigned Susan to the audit of the allowance for doubtful accounts.

During the course of this work, Ms. Start noticed that the allowance for doubtful accounts was only one percent of the accounts receivable balance, despite the fact that many large accounts were very old. She passed this information on to the senior who, in turn, asked the client about the low allowance percentages.

The client indicated that there was no problem, because the company's policy was to refinance slow-paying customers. For example, if Customer A had not made any recent monthly payments on a $5,000 one-year note, the company would refinance the note over a two- or three-year period, thus lowering the monthly payments. Generally, additional credit was not refused a customer, regardless of the status of payments on an existing account. The client maintained that this policy made possible a low allowance because few accounts had to be written off.

Required:

a. If you were suspicious of the small size of the allowance account, what evidence would you gather to verify or alleviate your suspicions?

b. With accounts constantly being refinanced, what evidence can be gathered to provide reasonable assurance that these accounts are collectible?

**15-47   The CPA firm of Wright & Company is in the process of auditing William Corporation's 19X4 financial statements. The following open matter must be resolved before the audit can be completed.

No audit work has been performed on nonresponses to customer accounts receivable confirmation requests. Both positive and negative confirmations were used. A second request was sent to debtors who did not respond to the initial positive request.

Required:

What alternative audit procedures should Wright consider performing on the nonresponses to customer accounts receivable confirmation requests?

***15-48   Chem Inc., a public company, manufactures pesticides and other chemical products and has its main manufacturing facilities in the United States. Chem does business primarily with other U.S. companies; however, the company is contemplating expanding its operations overseas.

Johnson & Smith, CPAs, are Chem Inc.'s auditors and have assigned Jean Davis to be in charge of the current audit engagement. It is Davis's responsibility to plan and conduct the audit. Davis reviewed past and current financial statements and prepared the following worksheet.

Chem Inc.
Operating Results
for the Years Ended May 31
($000 omitted)

	19X6	19X7	19X8	19X9 (Preliminary)
Sales	$12,000	$12,500	$8,500	$7,600
Cost of goods sold	6,000	6,500	6,000	6,500
Gross profit	6,000	6,000	2,500	1,100
Expenses	2,400	2,400	1,200	800
Operating income	$3,600	$3,600	$1,300	$300

While examining the company's preliminary 19X9 statement of financial position, Davis noted that the accounts receivable balance had increased substantially. The balance of $6,250,000 represents 25 percent of total assets and 45 percent of current assets. A review of accounts receivable and the revenue cycle indicated that internal control was adequate. However, Davis is concerned about this increase in accounts receivable and the increasing slowness in customer payments.

Based on an assessment of control risk and analytical procedures, Davis chose to use positive confirmations for all accounts receivable balances over $5,000 and a random sampling of the smaller account balances. Because of the significance of accounts receivable to the financial statements taken as a whole, Davis decided to confirm at least 90 percent of the amounts due. First and second confirmation requests were mailed. Any discrepancies received were resolved, and the following statistics are available for the confirmed accounts receivable.

Amount requested	
(90 percent × $6,250,000)	$5,625,000
Amount confirmed	3,551,000
Confirmations requested	
but not received	$2,074,000

An examination of the unconfirmed accounts receivable balances at May 31, 19X9, revealed the following amounts by major customer.

Bug-b-Gone	$ 450,000
Wasp Company	800,000
Roach Inc.	750,000
	2,000,000
Other	74,000
Total	$2,074,000

Management provided Davis with the following data for the allowance for doubtful accounts at May 31, 19X9.

Accounts receivable	$6,250,000
Less: Allowance for doubtful accounts	50,000
Accounts receivable (net)	$6,200,000

Management indicated that all known uncollectible accounts had been written off in accordance with company policy, and the provision for uncollectible accounts was adequate.

Burt Johnson, the partner in charge of the audit engagement, is planning to visit Davis and review the progress of the audit. Davis continues to be concerned with the audit work done to date on accounts receivable and the results that have been presented above, and intends to discuss this matter with Johnson.

Required:

a. List five audit objectives (assertions) for auditing accounts receivable.

b. With respect to accounts receivable, identify four additional audit steps Jean Davis needs to perform so that she may be able to recommend an unqualified opinion for the Chem Inc. financial statements dated May 31, 19X9.

c. Explain the operational significance of the unconfirmed accounts receivable balances at May 31, 19X9.

15-49 You have been assigned to the audit of a medium-sized manufacturer of machine parts whose fiscal year ends October 31. You and the senior arrive on Monday, November 13, to start the fieldwork for completing the audit. The senior gives you a copy of the accounts receivable aging schedule prepared by the company, the audit program, the control risk evaluation, and a file containing all working papers in connection with confirmation of receivables mailed on November 2. The file contains the following information:

Computer listing of accounts receivable at October 31.

A working paper showing the name, address, and balance of 12 customers to whom positive requests for confirmation were mailed.

Four customers' statements marked across the face "Do not mail."

Five positive requests that have been returned by customers confirming the balances as being correct.

Eight negative confirmations that have been returned with notations made thereon by customers.

Two positive requests and one negative request returned by the post office marked "unknown" or with a similar designation.

The senior introduces you to the credit manager, the accounts receivable bookkeeper, and the billing clerk. She then instructs you to proceed with the tests of the aging schedule and completion of the audit work on accounts receivable, as outlined in the audit program, and advises that she will return the next day to answer any questions you have with respect to the accounts receivable.

The senior informs you that the computer listing of accounts receivable was prepared by the accounts receivable bookkeeper for your use in sending out the confirmations. Your representative checked the customers' statements against the listing and the accounts receivable detail ledger, but did not check the total of the listing. However, you note that the total at the bottom of the listing does agree with the total shown on the aging schedule prepared by the company. You are told that either positive or negative requests were sent to all of the 50 accounts.

The aging schedule is shown on page 505. You are to assume that internal control is effective. You should study the aging schedule and answer the questions that follow. The normal credit terms are net 30.

Required:

a. What auditing procedures should the audit program call for with respect to the aging schedule?

b. Which items on the aging schedule would you select for additional auditing procedures, why would you select them, and what procedures would you use?

c. What would you do with the computer listing prepared at the time the confirmations were mailed?

d. What would you do with the statements marked "Do not mail"?

e. Which items would you select for discussion with the senior?

f. What would you do with the five positive requests that were returned indicating no exceptions?

g. In examining these positive requests, what would you look for?

h. What would you do with the requests returned by the post office marked "Unknown" or with a similar designation?

i. What would you do with the negative requests returned with notations made by customers?

j. What is your evaluation of the extent of substantive tests of accounts receivable?

(Used with permission of Ernst & Young)

Aged Trial Balance—Accounts Receivable October 31

	Balance Dr.	Balance Cr.	Oct.	Sept.	Aug.	May–June–July	Prior
Allied Products Co.	$ 12,618.32				$12,618.32		
American Manufacturing Co.		$ 612.00					
B & D Machinery, Inc.	57,538.79		$ 35,123.76	$10,078.12	6,312.45	$ 6,024.46	
Best Equipment, Inc.	1,098.45		198.45				$ 900.00
Cooper, Frank M. (employee)	5,000.00					5,000.00	
Chalmers Motors, Inc.	7,445.83			1,263.17	2,376.28	3,806.38	
Davidson Engineering Company	3,573.35					3,573.35	
Drake Press Division	78,396.21		78,396.21				
Erie Machine Works, Inc.	6,215.63						6,215.63
Evans and Co. (deposit)	10,000.00		10,000.00				
Franklin Motors, Inc.	17,624.91		11,784.16	5,840.75			
Franklin Motors, Inc. (note)	25,000.00				25,000.00		
Globe Machinery, Inc.	30,248.65		25,932.40				4,316.25
Globe Machinery, Inc. (consignment)	103,487.98		50,116.73	28,745.27	12,678.93	8,319.00	3,628.05
Goldman Sachs	14,750.00		14,750.00				
Watkins Company	4,728.16		4,728.16				
Whitman, Inc.	16,512.54		16,512.54				
Young Machinery Co.	8,378.05		6,873.00	1,505.05			
	$495,444.00	$5,612.00	$328,577.92	$53,932.36	$66,768.91	$31,104.88	$15,059.93

*15-50 Taylor Wholesalers distributes golf equipment to about 100 retail sporting goods stores. At June 30, 19X7, the end of the company's fiscal year, the distribution of the accounts receivable balances was as follows:

10 accounts over $50,000	$ 780,000
60 accounts under $50,000	1,100,000
30 accounts with zero balances	—
	$1,880,000

No accounts receivable are past due. Internal control affecting accounts receivable is considered to be effective. You have been furnished with the following audit program for substantive tests of accounts receivable.

1. Foot the detailed accounts receivable ledger and compare the total with the balance in the accounts receivable control account.

2. Using customer numbers, randomly select 50 accounts for positive confirmation. Send second requests and perform alternative procedures where necessary.

3. Obtain a detailed aged trial balance and test the schedule to the detailed accounts receivable ledger. Select every third account and discuss its collectibility with the credit manager.

4. Examine all subsequent collections of accounts receivable during the month of July 19X7.

What changes to the program, if any, would you suggest?

**15-51   Mary Jones, CPA, is engaged to audit the financial statements of Cook Wholesaling for the year ended December 31, 19X8. Jones obtained and documented an understanding of internal control relating to accounts receivable and assessed control risk for the assertions relating to accounts receivable at the maximum level. Jones requested and obtained from Cook an aged accounts receivable schedule listing the total amount owed by each customer as of December 31, 19X8, and sent positive confirmation requests to a sample of the customers.

Required:

What additional substantive audit procedures should Jones consider applying in auditing the accounts receivable?

**15-52   During an audit of the financial statements of Gole Inc., Robbins, CPA, requested and received a client-prepared property casualty insurance schedule, which included appropriate premium information.

Required:

a. Identify the type of information, in addition to the appropriate premium information, that would ordinarily be expected to be included in a property casualty insurance schedule.
b. What are the basic audit procedures that Robbins should perform in examining the client-prepared property casualty insurance schedule?

*15-53   Listed below are misstatements that could occur in cash, accounts receivable, and prepayments. Indicate the substantive test that should provide reasonable assurance of detecting each misstatement.

a. There is no disclosure of the pledging of accounts receivable.
b. The mail clerk diverts an incoming check from a customer. The check is endorsed with the client's name and is deposited to the mail clerk's account.
c. A clerk has made unrecorded withdrawals from a client's inactive bank account. Knowing that the auditor will send a bank confirmation as of the end of the year, he writes but does not record a check to cash on the client's out-of-town bank on the last day of the year and deposits it to the inactive bank account.
d. A client records sales to a customer, but the goods are not shipped.
e. The client uses the wrong time period to calculate prepaid insurance.
f. The client ships goods to a customer and records a sale; however, the client has an understanding with the customer that the goods can be returned after the end of the year.
g. The client has not disclosed a compensating balance arrangement with a bank.
h. The client has understated the allowance for doubtful accounts.

Auditing the Working Capital Assertions— Part II

"Imagination is more important than knowledge."

ALBERT EINSTEIN, *On Science*

LEARNING OBJECTIVES

After reading and studying the material in this chapter, the student should be able to

▶ Paraphrase the objectives in the audit of inventories.

▶ Compare examples of (1) internal control policies and procedures and (2) substantive tests for each of the five assertions relating to inventories.

▶ Describe the contents of working papers for (1) finished goods inventory listings, (2) finished goods inventory test counts, (3) inventory observation memoranda, (4) finished goods sales cutoff schedules, and (5) raw materials price tests.

▶ Describe how value can be added to the audit of inventories.

▶ Paraphrase the objectives in the audit of current liabilities.

▶ Compare examples of (1) internal control policies and procedures and (2) substantive tests for each of the five assertions relating to current liabilities.

▶ Describe the contents of working papers for (1) accounts payable confirmation control schedules and (2) accounts payable confirmations.

▶ Describe how value can be added to the audit of accounts payable.

▶ Compare examples of (1) internal control policies and procedures and (2) substantive tests for each of the five assertions relating to accrued liabilities.

▶ Describe the contents of a working paper for accrued property taxes.

This chapter continues the discussion of the audit objectives, procedures, and selected working paper examples of the working capital accounts.

INVENTORIES

Inventories is one of the most significant accounts for many manufacturing and retail companies. Because of its effect on both working capital and gross profit, the determination of inventory amounts can involve some of the most complex calculations in a company's accounting process. Also, the susceptibility of inventories to misappropriation and misstatement (high inherent risk) often requires extensive audit procedures if the amounts are material.

The Hermetite Audit

The SEC issued Accounting and Auditing Enforcement Release (AAER) No. 2 which describes deficiencies in the audit performed by an accounting firm of Hermetite Corporation. Because the deficiencies affected the inventory and accounts payable accounts, sections of the release are described in this chapter. The SEC found that the Hermetite audit was conducted "with a marked disregard for generally accepted accounting principles and generally accepted auditing standards."

The valuation of inventories has been the subject of several accounting pronouncements. Basically, these statements provide that inventories should be stated at cost, that cost may be determined under any one of several assumptions as to the flow of cost factors (first-in first-out, last-in first-out, average, etc.), and that inventories should not be valued in excess of market (generally, the lower of replacement cost or net realizable value).

Although the principles used to value inventory appear to be straightforward, the auditor will encounter many situations that do not fit precisely within the principles. Consider the following examples. A plant, because of lack of sales orders, operates below capacity. Is the increased fixed cost per unit a properly inventoriable cost, or is it an excess capacity cost that should be charged to expense as incurred? A client markets a new product that fails to gain customer acceptance and is selling very slowly. What is the net realizable value of the 100,000 units on hand when only 100 are sold each week at a retail price of $50 per unit? The client sells a chemical, the price of which fluctuates widely in the open market. Shortly after the end of the year, the price drops sharply. Should the client reduce the value of inventory to reflect the lower market price, or ignore the price drop on the basis that such fluctuations are normal and expected?

An auditor normally reviews and tests the client's cost accounting system in the tests of inventory pricing. To do so, the auditor must be knowledgeable of the most generally used cost accounting systems, including process cost, job order cost, and standard cost systems. The auditor must also understand the physical flow of material and labor through the client's facilities to fully understand the operation of the cost system. Thus, it is necessary to look beyond the numbers.

Internal control related to purchasing, receiving, and accounts payable affect inventories. The responsibilities for ordering, receiving, storing, shipping, and accounting for the goods should be separated to the extent possible. In addition, the client should adopt procedures to ensure an accurate physical inventory (including specific written instructions, prenumbered inventory cards or listings, double counts of inventory items, etc.) and pricing. Because internal control affecting inventories involves several types of transactions, the auditor must consider the result of several tests of controls. Tests of purchasing (purchasing and receiving), cash disbursements (accounts payable), payroll (labor costs), and sales (shipping) affect inventories. Dual-purpose tests in the inventory area include physical inventory test counts and inventory pricing tests, both of which are illustrated later in this section. The auditor's assessment of these controls determines the extent of subsequent audit procedures. As an example, the authorization of purchases, the recording of purchases, and the custody of the assets resulting from purchases should be separated. If such segregation of duties exists, the auditors might be willing to reduce the audit procedures that test inventory quantities.

Audit Objectives

The objectives (assertions) in the audit of inventories are as follows.

1. To determine whether the amount shown as inventories in the financial statements is represented by all (completeness) physical items on hand, in transit, or on consignment (existence).
2. To determine whether the inventory is calculated properly at the lower of cost or market in accordance with generally accepted accounting principles consistently applied (valuation).
3. To determine whether the inventory belongs to the company and whether any liens on the inventory are disclosed properly (rights and disclosure).
4. To determine whether any excess, slow-moving, or special-purpose items are properly valued and classified (valuation and presentation).

Audit Procedures and Working Papers

The first step is to assess control risk relating to inventory assertions. As a result of this assessment, the auditor establishes the scope of work for each assertion. For example, if perpetual records are kept and inventory is maintained in secure storage areas under the control of a storekeeper with no incompatible duties, the auditor will perform a more limited inventory observation and make fewer test counts than if all employees had unrestricted access to inventory. In addition, an auditor will perform more limited inventory pricing tests where a current, effective, and integrated cost accounting system is in operation than where such a cost system does not exist. Finally, the auditor will perform more extensive inventory cutoff procedures where there is no separate receiving department and prenumbered receiving reports are not used than where such controls do exist. Other examples of internal control policies and procedures and substantive tests related to specific assertions for the inventory accounts are shown on page 510.

Assertions	Examples of internal control policies and procedures	Examples of substantive tests
1. Existence	1. Maintenance of an effective perpetual inventory system with periodic test counts by internal auditors.	1. Observation of physical inventory counts and reconciliation of test counts with perpetual inventory records.
2. Rights	2. Control environment (require board of director approval for pledging of inventory).	2. Inquiry and review of board of director minutes and loan agreements for evidence of pledging.
3. Completeness	3. Require that prenumbered receiving reports be accounted for and matched with vendor invoices.	3. Test receiving cutoff procedures.
4. Valuation	4. Maintenance of an integrated cost accounting system with periodic investigation of variances.	4. Inspect vendor invoices, payroll records, and overhead application worksheets.
5. Presentation	5. Control environment (adequately trained personnel who are familiar with GAAP disclosure requirements applicable to inventory, e.g., bases of valuation).	5. Compare disclosures in financial statements with requirements of GAAP.

An illustration of the inventory lead schedule is shown in Figure 16.1, and the amount of finished goods is analyzed further by item in the summary of finished goods inventory shown in Figure 16.2. This illustration provides an example of how auditors satisfy themselves as to a total amount by systematically analyzing and auditing the components of that amount. By totaling the amount column, the auditor determines that the amount shown as finished goods is correct, *provided that* the individual amounts are correct. The individual amounts are determined by (a) the number of units, (b) the unit cost, and (c) the multiplication of the two. Thus, if the auditor is satisfied as to these three factors, he or she is satisfied as to the total finished goods inventory. Conversely, if any step is omitted (such as totaling the amount column), a link between the amount shown on the audit trial balance (and ultimately the financial statements) and the detail audit work (such as physical observation of the inventory) is broken. In this case, the auditor has no assurance that the individual amounts audited are represented in the financial statements. If they are not, any audit procedures performed on them are meaningless. Therefore, it is important that the auditor maintain the audit link between the amounts audited and the amounts shown in the financial statements.

Analytical Procedures
The auditor may place considerable reliance on analytical procedures in the inventory area. Some important comparisons (by department or product line) that are often made include

FIGURE 16.1 **Inventory Lead Schedule**

	Index	As Adjusted 12–31–X7	Per Books 12–31–X8	Dr.	Cr.	As Adjusted 12–31–X8
						C
		X Co. Inventory Lead Schedule 12–31–X8		*J. Jones 1–20–x9*		
Raw Materials	C–1	76,425 ✓	51,014 ⋏			
Work in process	C–2	29,760 ✓	36,253 ⋏			
Finished goods	C–3	151,903 ✓	137,692 ⋏			
Supplies	C–4	18,414 ✓	18,071 ⋏			
		276,502	243,030 ①			
		TB–1	*TB–1*			

① *The plant manager stated that the decline in inventory was due to a decline in sales orders during the last quarter of 19X8. This was confirmed by examination of the sales backlog report as of 12–31–X8.*
✓ *Traced to prior year working papers.*
⋏ *Traced to general ledger.*

1. Gross profit ratios in current and prior year.
2. Inventory turnover in current and prior year.
3. Inventory and cost of sales in current year with current-year budget and prior-year actual.
4. Standard and unit costs of major items of inventory in current and prior years.

Significant and unusual variations should alert the auditor to possible errors or inconsistencies in counting (existence), pricing, including obsolescence (valuation), or summarizing (completeness) inventories.

The Inventory Observation

The primary procedure for auditing the existence of inventory is the inventory observation. AU Section 331.01 (*SAS No. 1*) states, "Observation of inventories is a generally accepted auditing procedure. The independent auditor who issues an opinion when he has not employed them must bear in mind that he has the burden of justifying the opinion expressed."

The client has the responsibility for *taking* an accurate physical inventory. Auditors *observe* this inventory-taking to satisfy themselves that the client-prescribed counting procedures are being conscientiously followed by client personnel, thereby providing reasonable assurance of an accurate final count. This distinction is important, because if auditors take, rather than observe, the inventory, they as-

FIGURE 16.2   Finished Goods Inventory Listing

X Co.
Finished Goods Inventory Listing
12–31–X8

C-3

J. Jones
1-21-x9

Part Number	Description	Number of Units	Unit Cost	Amount
3001	Widget, small	1,042 ✓	31.50 ∧ ✗	32,823
3002	Widget, medium	613	35.00 ✗	21,455
3003	Widget, large	368	39.50	14,536
3101	Gidget, small	2,527 ✓	14.00 ✗	35,378

137,692
=====
C

✓ *Test counted during inventory observation - See C-3/1.*
∧ *Standard cost buildups tested on C-3/2.*
✗ *Cost to market comparison made on C-3/5.*

Note - All extensions and footings were computer tested.

sume responsibility for a significant step involved in preparing the financial statements. Their independence regarding those statements would be jeopardized.

Before the start of the physical inventory, auditors should review the client's written inventory instructions, looking for procedures that promote a complete and accurate inventory count by the client. To the extent they find such controls as double counts of high-value items, identification procedures to prevent double counting, or procedures for accurate recording and collecting of count totals, the auditors adjust the scope of their observation procedures.

During the actual inventory, auditors' emphasis should be on observing the counting procedures of the client's inventory teams to determine whether they understand the inventory instructions and are careful and diligent in carrying them out. Auditors also should *test-count* some of the items (the number depends on their evaluation of the client's procedures) as an additional test of the effectiveness of the procedures. Auditors normally record some of their counts (Figure 16.3) for subsequent comparison with the final inventory listing. The purpose of this step is to detect any changes of the counts after they have been completed, as well as to provide a record of specific items counted by the auditors.

FIGURE 16.3   Finished Goods Inventory Test Counts

X Co.					*C-3* / 1		
Finished Goods Inventory *Test Counts* *12-31-X8*				Prepared By Approved By	Initials *J. Jones*	Date *1 - 1 -X9*	
Inventory Sheet Number	*Part Number*	*Description*	*Client Count*			*Audit Count*	
1051	*3001*	*Small widget*	*1042* ✓			*1042*	
5053	*3101*	*Small gidget*	*2527* ✓			*2527*	
✓ *Agrees with inventory listing on C-3*							

Although the recorded test counts provide evidence that counts of actual items are not changed later, they do not prevent the subsequent inclusion of additional count sheets or tags containing fictitious items. To guard against this deception, auditors should account for the numbers of all inventory sheets or tags as either used or unused. Also, they should record the number of the last line used on several inventory sheets. Later when the inventory is compiled, the auditors should determine that it includes only items from inventory sheets they recorded as actually being used and that no items were added to the sheets for which they recorded the last line used.

Inventory Observations

Some interesting inventory observation situations in which an audit staff assistant might find himself or herself include:

- Determining the number of tons of coal in a coal pile.
- Spending eight hours observing the counts of frozen TV dinners in a walk-in freezer where the temperature is minus 10 degrees centigrade.
- Climbing and gauging 500,000 gallon tanks at a refinery.
- Observing the count of millions of dollars of gems in a jewelry store.
- Observing the number of cattle during a roundup.
- Estimating the percentage of completion of a jumbo jet passenger plane.
- Determining the number of board feet of lumber in a lumber yard.

The next time you walk into a grocery store or department store ask yourself how you could be reasonably sure that a physical count of inventory was accurate. Physical inventory observations are sometimes an awesome task.

Auditors must also be concerned during the inventory observation with the exis-

tence of obsolete, excess, or slow-moving items (valuation). Often the plant personnel involved in taking the physical inventory, such as production and shop supervisors, storekeepers, and others, are very knowledgeable in this area, and some
well-directed inquiries may yield pertinent information. The possibility of obsolescence may also be detected by the alert and inquisitive auditor who notes items
with unusual amounts of dust or rust or prior-year inventory tags.

Because many of the audit procedures performed at an inventory observation
cannot be quantified in working papers in a reasonable manner (such as observations of count teams and inquiries regarding obsolescence), it is common to summarize the work performed in a memorandum such as that shown in Figure 16.4.
The memorandum describes the steps taken to give the auditor reasonable assurance that a correct count was made. The last paragraph of the memorandum is
the auditor's opinion concerning the client's inventory count. The writer of the
memorandum noted a possible problem of slow-moving and obsolete items. The
note at the bottom of the memorandum indicates that a problem did exist and
subsequently was solved by recognition of the obsolescence factor in valuing the
inventory. All problems raised during an audit, both major and minor, must be
resolved. Unresolved problems in an auditor's working papers may be damaging
evidence in any subsequent litigation.

The Hermetite Audit-Inventory Observation

Hermetite determined its inventory quantities for purposes of its financial statements by
means of physical inventory counts. The auditing firm made no review of Hermetite's
inventory-taking plans or procedures. Its own procedures consisted solely of test-counting
a minimal number of items included in Hermetite's inventory. Although the results of the
limited test counts of raw materials showed material error rates in Hermetite's inventory
records of 23 percent in one year, 17 percent in a second year, and 12 percent in a
third year, no additional testing or other audit procedures were performed by the firm.
Moreover, the firm did not observe or inquire about the actual inventory counting methods
used by Hermetite.

(Extracted from SEC AAER No. 2)

As noted in Chapter 8, auditors may observe the client's physical inventory at
an interim date if incremental risk can be adequately controlled. Well-maintained
perpetual inventory records normally permit such control.

Inventories Held by Others

If significant amounts of inventories are held by public warehouses or other custodians, the auditor may decide between direct observation and confirmation. The general presumption is that personal knowledge of the auditor is more competent evidence than knowledge of third parties. There are exceptions, however, such as bulk
commodity storage. An auditor would probably receive little assurance that his or
her client's inventory of 5,000 bushels of corn existed by observing a grain storage
facility containing 100,000 bushels, some or none of which may represent the client's inventory. In this case confirmation with the facility may produce more competent evidence. If confirmation procedures are used to obtain evidence as to the
existence of inventories, additional procedures should be performed such as investigating the client's internal control applicable to the warehouse activity, reviewing

FIGURE 16.4 **Inventory Observation Memorandum**

X CO.

INVENTORY OBSERVATION MEMORANDUM

Prepared by: Dan Sharp

Date: 1-1-X9

Kim McDaniel and I arrived at the Manufacturing Plant at 7:00 a.m. on 1-1-X9 to begin our inventory observation. First, we obtained a copy of the inventory instructions and discussed them with the Controller. We took a plant tour and discussed with the Controller the sequence in which he wished to have the inventory observed and cleared since the Company wanted to begin production as soon as possible in every area and wanted to do so in the production cycle sequence.

Kim McDaniel and I began observing the count team procedures and making test counts in the designated areas. Upon completion of one area, we would clear it and production would begin. The client was to work only within that area, i.e., there was no movement from that area into other areas of the plant. Then we would go to the next area that was ready.

Kim called me to the raw materials area where she had been observing procedures and making test counts while I was clearing the area. She indicated that several dozen feet of pipe were not on the inventory at all and other items were recorded at obviously wrong amounts. According to the monthly inventory summaries, it would have been impossible to use the quantities that would have been necessary to get this amount reduced to what the inventory showed at this time. I discussed this with the Controller who assigned a new count team to the area with instructions to recount all items. Subsequent test counts by Kim indicated that the recounts were accurate. In all other cases, the inventory teams appeared to understand their instructions and to be working conscientiously.

We went back to the main plant and continued the inventory in all areas and cleared them as soon as possible. Kim and I split up these areas and made selected test counts on Xerox copies of the client's count sheets which we maintained for controls and as a record of our test counts. We inquired of the individuals in charge of the inventory in each area as to obsolete, excess, or slow-moving goods, and they knew of none except for a small pile of scrap which was excluded from the inventory. We saw no items during our observation that appeared obsolete, excess, or slow-moving.

We accumulated the last five receiving documents before inventory and the first five after the inventory that had been received on 1-1-19X9. We also had the shipping cut-off accumulated. This amounts to five shipping documents before inventory and one shipping document for a shipment on 1-1-19X9.

Per the inventory instructions, the client personnel were to place an X beside each item on their count sheets if it had not been used at all in the last 6 months. This was done and there are several throughout the count sheets. These will have to be followed up at final to see that they are properly valued in the final inventory listing.

FIGURE 16.4   *Continued*

Inventory Observation Memorandum
Page 2
Date: 1-1-X9

See ① below.

In my opinion, the procedures followed by the client provide reasonable assurance of a correct and accurate count of all goods on hand at 12-31-19X8, and all slow moving material was properly identified as such for later follow-up.

Dan Sharp
1-1-X9

① All items indicated by an X were reduced in value by 25% in the final inventory listing to recognize their slow-moving and possibly obsolete nature. Our review indicates that the 25% is reasonable.

J. Jones
1-21-X9

---

a report on internal control of the warehouse prepared by other CPAs, or observing physical counts at the warehouse. The point is to obtain evidence of the existence of the warehouse and inventory independent of and as a supplement to the confirmation. Auditors have been victimized by obtaining what appeared to be proper confirmations of what turned out to be nonexistent inventories in nonexistent warehouses.

Inventory Cutoff Tests

During the inventory observation, auditors also obtain and test the information necessary to evaluate the client's *inventory cutoff;* that is, they determine that the physical item and its related cost were treated in a consistent manner (completeness). In the finished goods example, the cutoff must be tested to determine whether items included in inventory are excluded from sales, and vice versa. To test the sales cutoff, auditors prepare a schedule such as the one shown in Figure 16.5. The shipping number, description, quantity, and date shipped are obtained from the shipping department records during the inventory observation. The year in which the shipping number is included in sales is determined at a later date after all accounting transactions have been recorded. The schedule indicates that the sales cutoff was proper and that items shipped prior to the audit date were excluded from inventory and included in sales. Evidence regarding the sales cutoff is also gathered with the confirmation procedures in the accounts receivable section. If an item is recorded as a sale (and accounts receivable) before the end of the year but is not shipped until after the end of the year, the customer should take exception to a confirmation request that includes the unshipped item in the balance. This is one of many examples of the relation of audit procedures between working paper sections.

Auditors perform a similar test of the cutoff of raw materials received. The objective here is to determine whether items that are received near the end of the year and included in inventory also are recorded as purchases and accounts payable.

FIGURE 16.5 Finished Goods Sales Cutoff

	X Co.				$\frac{C-3}{3}$	
	Finished Goods Sales Cutoff					Initials · Date
				Prepared By	*J. Jones*	
	12-31-X8			Approved By	*1 - 1 -X9*	

Shipping Number	*Per Examination of Shipping Records* Description	Quantity	Date Shipped	*Year Shipping Number Included In Sales*	
A-366	Medium gidget	37	12-30-X8	19X8 ✓	
A-367	Large widget	6	12-30-X8	19X8 ✓	
A-368	Large widget	118	12-30-X8	19X8 ✓	
A-369	Small widget	44	12-31-X8	19X8 ✓	
A-370	Small gidget	25	12-31-X8	19X8 ✓	
A-371	Unused			19X9 ✓	
✓	Per sales journal				

Auditors record the last several receiving report numbers used prior to the taking of the inventory. All items recorded on these documents should be recorded as purchases during the period being audited. All items included on subsequent receiving reports should be recorded as purchases during the following year.

An Inventory Cutoff Problem

A shipment of raw materials was received on December 31, 19X3 (the last day of the year) and was counted during the client's physical inventory. Items included in this physical inventory listing are priced, and the total of the priced listing is recorded as the ending inventory. The receiving report is not sent to the accounting department until several days later (in January 19X4), and the vendor's invoice is not received until January 19X4. Personnel in the accounting department record the purchase in January 19X4.

To see the result of this error, examine the following statement of cost of goods sold as of December 31, 19X3.

Beginning inventory	$XX	
Add purchases	XX ←	Understated—excludes the goods purchased
	$XX	
Less ending inventory	(XX) ←	Includes the goods purchased
Cost of goods sold	$XX ←	Understated

Cost of goods sold is understated (and net income is overstated) because items are included in ending inventory that are not recorded as being purchased as of December 31.

In some large companies, the physical inventory may extend over several days. This creates difficulties in determining whether materials received during this period were included or excluded from inventory (and therefore should be included or excluded from purchases). Auditors must plan their cutoff tests carefully in these situations.

Although the point at which title passes legally determines when a purchase or sale should be recorded, this is often ignored for routine immaterial transactions. To simplify the recording process, the date of receipt or shipment of the goods rather than the freight terms (FOB shipping or destination point) is normally the date the purchase or sale is recorded. Of course, the date of legal title transfer may be used for material or unusual transactions. However, the auditor would seldom spend time examining invoices for freight terms when auditing the shipping and receiving cutoffs.

Tests of Inventory Pricing

The inventory pricing method and the type of cost system used by the client determine the audit procedures employed in testing inventory pricing. Because pricing methods and cost systems vary widely, so do the related audit procedures. The calculation of LIFO inventory requires not only the pricing of individual items, but also overall calculations of inventory layers based on price index numbers. Compliance with federal income tax regulations is an important aspect of the audit of LIFO inventory calculations. Finished goods prices based on the FIFO or average cost method can be determined by the use of job-order, process, or standard costs. The audit of a job-order cost system involves a review of the categories of cost flowing through the control accounts (material, labor, and overhead) and tests of these costs in the jobs in progress at year-end. The auditor of a process cost system concentrates on the flow and accumulation of costs by cost center for the major products. In a standard cost system, the audit emphasis is on testing the standard cost buildups for major inventory items and reviewing variances for an approximation of actual costs.

Cost, however, is only one aspect of inventory pricing. The auditor also must determine that cost does not exceed market. As previously noted, the lower of current replacement cost or net realizable value is the proper accounting principle for inventory pricing. The replacement cost test is often made on an overall basis by reviewing the unit cost of production after the end of the year as well as reviewing the unit cost of major raw material items. A decline in either of these costs may indicate that replacement cost is lower than inventory cost and that a detailed analysis by product should be made. Net realizable value normally is defined as net selling price less estimated cost to sell. Cost to sell is often estimated as a percentage of the net selling price and computed by dividing total selling expense by sales.

The Hermetite Audit—Inventory Valuation

Hermetite priced its work-in-process and finished goods inventories at selling price instead of cost, and submitted those inventory computations to the auditing firm. The auditing firm then determined the amounts to be reported in the financial statements for work-in-process and finished goods by using a trial and error method to determine an estimate of the actual cost of the inventories. The method involved the use of estimated gross profit percentages that the auditing firm did not test. This method produced materially incorrect results because it failed to consider changes in the company's product mix.

(Extracted from SEC AAER No. 2)

An example of a raw materials price test is shown in Figure 16.6, where the prices used to calculate the inventory are compared with the purchase prices of the items. (This is a simplified example that assumes a FIFO method; many inventory pricing tests are more complicated.) Note that the auditor lists and examines the number of most recent vendor invoices necessary to cover the quantity of each inventory item tested.

Tests of Summarization

The auditor must ascertain whether the inventory has been properly summarized (existence, completeness, and valuation). Tests of the client's inventory summary schedules include (1) tracing physical quantities to the client's count records and the auditor's recorded test counts, (2) tracing prices to the client's cost accounting records and the auditor's price test working papers, (3) reviewing the unit of measure for reasonableness in relation to quantity and price (e.g., if paint is counted and recorded in units of gallons but is priced in units of barrels, a substantial inventory error could result), (4) testing the calculations of quantity times price, and (5) adding the dollar amounts of individual inventory items to arrive at the total inventory amount. If the client's inventory is maintained in computer files and the auditor uses a computer-assisted audit program, most of these procedures would be applied to all inventory items; otherwise, the procedures would probably be applied on a test basis.

The Hermetite Audit—Inventory Summarization

The auditing firm failed to perform sufficient tests or other audit procedures with regard to Hermetite's inventory compilation and summarization process. In one year Hermetite made summarization errors totaling $164,976 which the firm failed to detect because of its failure to audit the inventory summary. Those errors caused Hermetite's pretax income to be overstated by 15 percent.

(Extracted from SEC AAER No. 2)

Review for Obsolete, Excess, or Slow-Moving Inventory

The auditor's review for obsolete, excess, or slow-moving inventory must extend beyond the inquiries and observations during the inventory observation to include inquiry of top management and a review of perpetual or other inventory usage records. Although top management may not be as familiar with the usage of individual items as a shop supervisor, they will be more knowledgeable of major policy decisions that could result in large-scale obsolescence, such as plans to discontinue a product line or to make significant changes in a product. Perpetual or other inventory usage records of major items are examined to determine whether the quantity on hand will be used in a reasonable time on the basis of past usage. The business approach can be useful also if the auditor is aware of industry trends in product changes, supplies of raw materials, and manufacturing processes.

Review for Liens or Pledges of Inventory

The inventory audit procedures designed to detect liens and pledges of inventories are similar to those for accounts receivable, including the review of minutes and debt instruments, confirmation with financial institutions with which the client does

FIGURE 16.6 Raw Materials Price Test

X Co.
Raw Materials Price Test
12-31-X8

J. Jones
1-27-x9

$\frac{C-1}{2}$

		Per Inventory Records			Per Vendor Invoice				Inventory Price Over (Under) Invoice Price
Part Number	Description	Quantity	Unit Price	Unit Cost	Quantity	Date	Vendor		
1404	4" steel pipe	936	2.33√	2.33⌃	1,000⌃	11-4-X8⌃	U S Steel⌃		0
1406	Red paint	206	10.14√	10.14⌃	300⌃	12-1-X8⌃	Grayson Co.⌃		0
1407	Gaskets	10,500	.10√	.10⌃	5,000⌃	12-3-X8⌃	Hutson Gasket⌃		
				.10⌃	6,000⌃	12-15-X8⌃	Hutson Gasket⌃		0

√ *Agrees with price used in inventory listing - See C-1.*
⌃ *Agrees with vendor invoice.*

business, and inquiry of management. One unique aspect of inventory subject to lien is that it sometimes is fenced or otherwise segregated from other inventory; financial institutions occasionally place signs in the area stating that the inventory is pledged. Such restrictions on the inventory should be noted during the inventory observation.

Inventory Fraud

Inventory fraud is an important cause of audit failures. A *Wall Street Journal* article[1] described some of the problems that can arise when auditing inventory.

- "... some (auditors) who showed up at plants were fresh out of college ... the faces kept changing and there was little continuity ... (it was a) standing joke that the next outside auditor would be fresh out of high school ... (the partner) never showed up at plants during inventory counts."
- "auditors are often fooled (because they take) a very small sample of the goods ... and (compare) the count with management's tallies."
- "... (companies) count inventory that they pretend they have ordered but that will never arrive."
- "... auditors permitted company officials to follow the auditors and record where they were making test counts. Then the managers simply falsified counts for inventory that wasn't being tested."
- "shipments between plants were recorded as stocks located at both plants ... documentation supposedly showing they were being transferred to the second plant appeared to be largely fictitious."
- "... the auditor spotted a barrel whose contents management had valued at thousands of dollars. Actually, the barrel was filled with floor sweepings. The auditor forced the company to subtract the false amount from inventory, but it never occurred to the auditor that this was an egregious example of intentional and pervasive fraud."
- "... (auditors) observed the taking of inventory at no more than five stores and advised (the client) in advance of the specific stores. (The client) refrained from making fraudulent adjustments at the five stores where it knew that inventories would be observed ... instead, it made its fraudulent adjustments to the inventory records of the vast majority of other stores that it knew in advance (the auditors) would not review."
- "... the auditor test-counted two types of computer chips, finding 500 of one and 300 of the second at the acquired company. The next day, the company's controller called the auditor and told him that an hour after he left, 1,500 more chips of the first variety and 1,000 of the second arrived in a shipment ... the auditor never checked back to see if the new chips were real."

Value-Added Audit Considerations for Inventories

While performing audit procedures applicable to inventory the auditor should consider such matters as: Has the entity developed any new products in the last two years? How does management obtain feedback from customers about its products?

---

[1] "Inventory Chicanery Tempts More Firms, Fools More Auditors," *Wall Street Journal*, December 14, 1992, p. 1.

How does management monitor products of competitors? Are inventory components subjected to make-versus-buy analysis? Are activity-based costing and just-in-time inventory methods used? How are employee and customer theft discouraged? Are income tax effects considered in pricing inventory? How often do out-of-stock conditions occur? Is management aware of and do they monitor common inventory ratios for the industry? Is obsolete inventory promptly identified and disposed of? Questions such as these need management attention and can add value to the audit.

▶ **EXAMPLE**

While auditing inventory of a manufacturer of lamps, the auditor inquired as to how management decided whether to make or buy the various lamp components. The client had always manufactured all components, but as a result of the auditor's inquiry decided to obtain bids from outside suppliers for various components such as switches, cords, and shades. The client found that certain components could be purchased for less than the cost to manufacture them, resulting in substantial cost savings to the client.

Summary of Important Substantive Tests for Inventory

- Perform analytical procedures.
- Observe client counts of inventory quantities and perform test counts.
- Account for and control inventory tags or listings.
- Test inventory shipping and receiving cutoffs.
- Test inventory pricing to determine that the lower of cost or market concept is used.
- Test summarization of inventory.
- Review for obsolete, excess, or slow-moving inventory through inquiry, observation, and review of perpetual inventory records.
- Search for liens or pledges of inventory by review of minutes, debt instruments, and confirmations.

CURRENT LIABILITIES

In auditing assets, an auditor places primary emphasis on verifying the amounts recorded as assets (existence). In auditing liabilities, however, the auditor should place primary emphasis not on what is recorded, but on what is *not* recorded but should be (completeness). The auditor seldom finds amounts recorded as liabilities that are not liabilities, but unrecorded liabilities are not unusual.

Current liabilities include both amounts currently due (such as accounts payable) and amounts that have been incurred but are not yet due (such as accrued interest payable). Normally, the amounts not due are expected to be due within one year.

Although accounts payable and accrued liabilities normally are unsecured, in some circumstances assets can be held by others or pledged to secure their payment. Also, officers, stockholders, or other companies may guarantee payment. Short-term notes payable and the current portion of long-term debt often are collateralized. All of these conditions should be disclosed in the financial statements. Any other factors regarding current liabilities that are important in evaluating the financial statements should be disclosed, such as amounts due related parties or significant amounts of past-due accounts payable.

The accounting records in support of current liabilities usually are much less extensive than those supporting current assets. Many companies merely list and record by journal entry in one year all unpaid invoices applicable to that year that are received by some specified cutoff date (say the 20th of the following month) in the next year. Accrued liabilities usually are recorded by journal entry and supported by worksheet computations.

Internal control for accounts payable assertions is related closely to controls over purchasing, receiving, cash disbursements, and inventory, whereas control over accruals normally is exercised by controlling the related expense account.

Audit Objectives

The objectives (assertions) in the audit of current liabilities are as follows:

1. To determine whether all (completeness) current liabilities existing or incurred (existence and obligations) as of the audit date are reflected properly in the financial statements (valuation).
2. To determine whether current liabilities consist of amounts due within one year or the natural operating cycle of the business (presentation).
3. To determine whether disclosures concerning current liabilities are adequate (presentation).

Audit Procedures and Working Papers

The audit procedures and working papers applicable to accounts payable and accrued liabilities are considered in this section; the current portion of long-term debt and notes payable are considered in the long-term liability section.

Analytical Procedures

For accounts payable and accrued liabilities the auditor may compare

1. Current-year balances with current-year budget and prior-year actual.
2. Ratio of accounts payable to purchases for current and prior years.
3. Balances due to related parties for current and prior years.

It is not sufficient to establish that there is no change between periods; the auditor must also consider whether there should be a change that does not appear. If the auditor knows property tax rates increased in the current year, for example, substantially equal accrued property tax balances between years should be investigated.

Accounts Payable

As part of the first step of evaluating control risk for accounts payable assertions, the auditor must consider, on the basis of the procedures and controls used, the potential for material unrecorded liabilities. The potential for unrecorded liabilities is evaluated in part on the results of tests of controls for the purchasing and cash disbursements functions and in part on dual-purpose tests of procedures for recording liabilities and the resulting account balances. The magnitude of this potential determines the scope of subsequent procedures.

A comparison of the vendor's invoice and the company's receiving report in the accounts payable department should lower the probability that received merchandise is not accounted for and that some accounts payable invoices might be unrecorded. On this basis, the auditor might reduce the tests that search for unrecorded liabilities. Other examples are (1) client reconciliation of monthly statements received from vendors to recorded accounts payable and (2) monthly reconciliation of detail accounts payable with the general ledger control account. Examples of internal control policies and procedures and substantive tests related to specific assertions for accounts payable are shown below.

Assertions	Examples of internal control policies and procedures	Examples of substantive tests
1. Existence	1. Require that accounts payable cannot be processed unless a copy of the receiving report or other evidence of receipt of goods or services is matched with vendor invoice.	1. Compare recorded accounts payable with vendor invoice and accompanying evidence of receipt of goods or services.
2. Obligations	2. Same as for existence.	2. Same as for existence.
3. Completeness	3. Establish policy to review and investigate prenumbered purchase orders and receiving reports that are unmatched with vendor invoices at month end.	3. Send positive confirmation requests to vendors with whom the client has significant purchase transactions.
4. Valuation	4. Not applicable (accounts payable are generally recorded at face value).	4. Not applicable.
5. Presentation	5. Control environment (require board of director approval of transactions with related parties).	5. Inquiry and review of minutes of board of directors for indication of related party transactions.

Effective control procedures should reduce the likelihood of unrecorded accounts payable and allow the auditor to reduce the number of accounts payable confirmations sent. The completeness assertion for accounts payable generally is tested by confirmation of balances with vendors and a review of disbursements after the audit date.

Confirmation   Confirmation of accounts payable is not designated specifically as a generally accepted auditing procedure in *SAS No. 1,* as is the confirmation of accounts receivable; nevertheless, it is a procedure that many auditors use. One must keep in mind the difference in approaches to auditing assets and liabilities to understand the method of selecting the accounts to which confirmation requests will be sent. Recall that in the audit of liabilities the auditor is more concerned with what is not recorded but should be (completeness) than with what is recorded (existence). Therefore, confirmation requests generally are sent to a client's principal vendors and suppliers, regardless of their account balance at the audit date. Principal vendors can be determined from a vendor file (a file showing payments made to individual vendors). The auditor's objective is usually to obtain confirmations from the accounts *most likely* to have large accounts payable balances, not necessarily from the accounts that have large *recorded* balances. For this reason, the auditor often sends confirmation requests to accounts with zero balances. The auditor is not attempting to obtain a high dollar coverage of recorded account balances but is searching for unrecorded liabilities. Consider the following example.

Vendor	Purchases from vendor during the year	Payable balance at end of year
A Company	$ 35,000	$ 11,000
B Company	1,150,000	110,000
C Company	1,200,000	—
D Company	246,000	30,000

In this case, the auditor is likely to select B and C for confirmation, even though both A and D have larger year-end balances than C. A sample of other accounts also may be sent confirmation letters.

Accounts selected for confirmation are listed on a confirmation control schedule such as Figure 16.7. This schedule serves the dual purpose of recording the amount confirmed by the vendor and reconciling it to the amount shown in the client's detailed accounts payable listing. All differences between the client's accounting records and the confirmation from the vendor should be not only reconciled but also audited. In Figure 16.7, the payment in transit from the client to the vendor has been traced to the outstanding checklist in the bank reconciliation (indicated by $\checkmark$; also see Figure 15.2). The auditor must understand the relationships of the various sections of the audit well enough to realize instinctively that if a vendor had not received a payment from the client that was made before or on the audit date, the check could not have cleared the bank by the audit date and, therefore, must be listed as outstanding. In Figure 16.7, the unrecorded liability was traced to the vendor's invoice for a December purchase that was recorded by the client in January (indicated by Ⓥ). Because the amount is immaterial, it has been posted to the summary of entries passed for consideration in the aggregate.

An illustration of an accounts payable confirmation is shown in Figure 16.8 on page 527. It is similar to an accounts receivable confirmation in that it requests an outside party to provide information about the client directly to the auditor; however, an important difference is that whereas the accounts receivable confirmation contains the customer's balance according to the client's records, the accounts payable confirmation contains a request for the vendor to state the balance due from the client and attach a statement of the items making up the balance. The difference is due to the different emphasis in auditing assets and liabilities. With the accounts receivable confirmation, the auditor is attempting to verify the recorded balance; with the accounts payable confirmation, he or she is attempting to learn of all amounts due to a vendor, whether or not recorded.

FIGURE 16.7   Accounts Payable Confirmation Control Schedule

N-1

X Co.
Accounts Payable Confirmation Control
12-31-X8

J. Jones
1-26-x9

Vendor	Balance Per Books	Payment in Transit Check No.	Payment in Transit Amount	Explanation of Difference Mdse. in Transit	Unrecorded Liability	Other	Balance Per Vendor
Standard Supply Co.	3,810 ⋋	3183	4,377 √				8,187 ⋋
Webster Pipe Co.	0 ⋋				415 (ᴠ)		415 ⋋
Hewlett Paint Corp.	11,081 ⋋						11,081 ⋋

√ Traced to outstanding check list - See A-1.
⋋ Agrees with accounts payable listing - See N.
⋋ Confirmed by vendor. See N-1.
(ᴠ) Examined December invoice recorded in January. Posted to summary of adjustments passed.

The 10 vendors with the largest dollar volume during the year per review of vendor files were selected for confirmation.

FIGURE 16.8   Accounts Payable Confirmation

X CO.
122 WEST AVE.
CENTER CITY, ARKANSAS 70000

$\frac{N\text{-}1}{1}$

January 2, 19X9

Standard Supply Co.
222 Elm Street
Center City, Arkansas 70000

Gentlemen:

Our auditors, Partner & Co., are now engaged in an audit of our financial statements. In connection therewith, please advise them in the space provided below whether or not there is a balance due you by this company as of December 31, 19X8. If there is a balance due, please attach a statement of the items making up such balance.

After signing and dating your reply, please mail it directly to Partner & Co., 999 Verify Street, Center City, AR 70000. A stamped, addressed envelope is enclosed for your convenience.

Very truly yours,

Bruce Lee

Bruce Lee
Controller

Partner & Co.:

N-1

Our records indicate that a balance of $\$\underline{\quad 8187^{00}\quad}$ was due from X Co. at December 31, 19X8, as itemized in the attached statement.

Date __*1-11-X9*__   Signed: __*Von Graham, Treas.*__

The Hermetite Audit—Accounts Payable

Hermetite had no formal accounts payable system, and invoices were not recorded until they were paid. Because the auditing firm was aware of the lack of a system to record accounts payable, it sent confirmation requests to all the vendors with which Hermetite did business. The confirmations received by the auditing firm revealed material differences between client and vendor records. The accounts payable confirmed by the vendors exceeded the balances according to Hermetite's listing by 68 percent in one year, 53 percent in a second year, and 126 percent in a third year. The firm's working papers contained no indication that the differences were reconciled or accounted for by the audit team.

(Extracted from SEC AAER No. 2)

Although confirmation of accounts payable is widely used, in cases where accounts payable are not significant (as in many service industries) or control risk for the completeness assertion of accounts payable is assessed at a low level, auditors may substitute vendor statements received by the client for confirmations. Vendor statements, which list all unpaid vendor invoices, provide the same information as a confirmation, but the evidence provided by vendor statements is not considered to be as competent because the statements are not received directly from the vendor by the auditor. For this reason, their use is restricted to situations where inherent and control risks for the completeness assertion are assessed at low levels.

Review of Subsequent Disbursements   The second procedure used in the audit of accounts payable is the review of disbursements subsequent to the audit date. In making this review, which normally covers the period from the audit date to the date of completion of work in the client's office, the auditor inspects unpaid invoices and the invoices or other support for disbursements to determine the period to which they are applicable. (Often a minimum amount is established to avoid examining minor items.) If a disbursement is found that is applicable to the period before the audit date, the auditor reviews the accounts payable (and accrued liabilities) listing to determine whether the amount owed is recorded properly as a liability at the audit date. If it is not, it represents an unrecorded liability.

The advantage of this procedure is that it provides much broader account coverage than would be practicable with confirmations; the disadvantage is that any invoice representing an unrecorded liability not paid or received by the client prior to the end of the auditor's work in the client's office would not be detected. Such amounts may be detected by confirmation. Thus, a combination of accounts payable confirmation and a review of subsequent disbursements, together with work performed in other sections such as cash, inventories, and cost of sales, normally provides the audit evidence necessary to satisfy the auditor regarding the completeness of accounts payable.

Other audit procedures   Most of the audit work in accounts payable is directed toward the completeness assertion, but the other assertions should also be considered. Although there is only a small risk that accounts payable have been recorded that don't exist, the auditor should select several balances from the accounts payable trial balance and examine the underlying support (e.g., vendor invoices and receiving report) to test the existence and obligation assertions. The auditor should also consider the results of audit procedures applied to identify amounts due to related parties and other unusual accounts payable that may require special disclosure to test the presentation assertion.

Value-Added Audit Considerations for Accounts Payable   While performing audit procedures applicable to accounts payable the auditor should consider such matters as: Has management identified which critical suppliers could effectively put the entity out of business? How long does it take to process a payment transaction, and how does this time compare with best practices in the industry? Are competitive bids requested on major purchases? Are all purchase discounts taken? The auditor adds value to the audit by discussing business problems such as these with management.

▶ **EXAMPLE**

While auditing accounts payable an auditor computed the client's average cost to pay a vendor's invoice and compared this with an average cost to pay vendors' invoices from a best practices database (this database may have been developed by the accounting firm, an industry association, the AICPA, or other sources). The auditor found that the client's average cost was $18 while the average of best practices was $12. A review of the client's payment procedures revealed that the client required redundant approvals and documents that could be eliminated for substantial cost savings.

Summary of Important Substantive Tests for Accounts Payable

- Perform analytical procedures.
- Send confirmations to selected vendors; send second requests to vendors who fail to respond to first requests.
- Review disbursements subsequent to the audit date and unpaid invoices to determine whether any represent unrecorded liabilities.
- Trace a sample of balances on the accounts payable trial balance to supporting documents.
- Determine that all necessary disclosures concerning accounts payable have been identified.

Accrued Liabilities

Some accrued liabilities can be tested by reference to the subsequent payment of the liability (accrued payroll and payroll taxes), whereas others must be estimated or calculated on the basis of transactions in other accounts (accrued interest on the basis of interest-bearing debt outstanding and accrued royalties on the basis of sales). Figure 16.9 on page 531 illustrates an audit lead schedule for accrued liabilities.

The following are examples of internal control policies and procedures that an auditor would consider in establishing the scope of substantive tests of accrued liabilities: (1) client use of standard monthly journal entries to record recurring accruals such as property taxes, interest, and so forth should reduce the likelihood of omitting the accruals and allow the auditor to make overall tests of reasonableness rather than detail calculations, and (2) client preparation and use of a tax calendar to serve as a reminder of tax return due dates should reduce the likelihood of overlooking the payment of various taxes, which in turn should permit the auditor to spend less time examining tax payments. Other examples of internal control policies and procedures and substantive tests related to specific assertions for accrued liabilities (using accrued interest payable as an illustration) are shown on page 530.

Assertions	Examples of internal control policies and procedures	Examples of substantive tests
1. Existence	1. Establish policy that accrued interest payable is computed for individual notes payable outstanding at the end of each month.	1. Recalculate accrued interest payable on notes payable.
2. Obligation	2. Same as existence.	2. Same as existence.
3. Completeness	3. Same as existence.	3. Analytical procedures (compare ratios of accrued interest payable to notes payable for current and prior year).
4. Valuation	4. Not applicable (accrued interest payable is shown at calculated amount).	4. Not applicable.
5. Presentation	5. Control environment (require board of director approval of transactions with related parties).	5. Inquiry and review of board of director minutes for evidence of related parties to whom accrued interest may be payable.

In Figure 16.9 accrued payroll has been recomputed on an overall basis by reference to the total payroll paid in the subsequent period. The auditor has determined the total payroll for the two-week period ended January 3, 19X9, by examination of the payroll register (indicated by χ). This amount was multiplied by the fraction representing the payroll period in 19X8 (11 of the 14 days). The computed amount does not agree exactly with the amount recorded on the books because it was computed on an overall basis, whereas the book amount was computed by payroll group or individual employee. Variations such as this are to be expected when overall tests are used, and they do not imply that the client's records are incorrect.

Accrued interest is cross-referenced to *R,* which is the schedule reference for long-term debt. The audit of accrued interest is discussed in that section.

Accrued property taxes are cross-referenced to a detail audit schedule, *P-1,* which is shown in Figure 16.10 on page 532. This schedule summarizes the transactions in accrued property taxes for the year. The provision for property tax expense for the current year has been related to the expense section of the working papers and reviewed for reasonableness. This provision is an example of a situation in which an estimate must be made by the client and reviewed by the auditor, because it is assumed that the actual tax for the year will not be known until the tax bills are received at some date after the financial statements are issued. In practice, the period covered by the tax and the date the tax bills are rendered vary by taxing authority within each state. The auditor should be familiar with the practices of the taxing authorities within whose states his or her clients operate. In the example, the auditor was aware that there had been no tax rate increases and, from the audit of property, knew that there had been no significant variations in property balances. Thus, the auditor found that property tax expense in an amount approximately equal to the amount paid for the prior year was reasonable (indicated by ①). Note that merely comparing the provision for the current year with the amount paid for the prior year, without considering the factors that could make them different, is

FIGURE 16.9   **Accrued Liability Lead Schedule**

X Co.
Accrued Liability Lead Schedule
12–31–X8

P

J. Jones
1–20–x9

Account	Index	As Adjusted 12–31–X7	Per Books 12–31–X8	Adjustments Dr.	Adjustments Cr.	As Adjusted
Accrued payroll	①	13,079 ✓	10,390 ⋏			10,390
Accrued interest	R	2,333 ✓	2,000 ⋏			2,000
Accrued property taxes	P-1	22,199 ✓	22,529 ⋏			22,529
Accrued income taxes	P-2	43,012 ✓	46,859 ⋏	5,000		41,859
		80,623	81,778	5,000		76,778
		TB-2	TB-2			TB-2

① *Overall test of accrued payroll —*
Payroll for the two week period ended 1–3–X9   *13,177* ✗
Portion applicable to 19X8   *x* ¹¹/₁₄
   10,353
Per books   *10,390*
Difference is reasonable   *37*

⋏ *Traced to general ledger.*
✓ *Traced to prior year working papers.*
✗ *Traced to payroll register.*

not effective auditing. The auditor also has examined *receipted* tax bills and canceled checks to substantiate the tax payments (indicated by ✓).

Because of the significance of income tax expense and the related accrued tax liability, the auditor should have a basic understanding of federal income tax laws and regulations, as well as those of the states and any foreign countries in which his or her clients operate. In addition, the auditor must comprehend the differences between pretax accounting income and taxable income, timing differences and permanent differences, income taxes and deferred taxes, and the myriad of other concepts in FASB pronouncements covering accounting for income taxes. With this knowledge, the auditor is prepared to begin an audit of income taxes. The procedure consists generally of an analysis of the accrual account for the year and the testing of payments during the year by reference to canceled checks and prior-year tax returns. The auditor should also check the calculation of income tax expense for the current year and the amount of any deferred taxes arising from timing differences, in all cases considering the propriety of the amounts used in the calculations. In addition, the auditor should inquire as to the status of all unsettled prior-year returns and any revenue-agent examinations in progress. In many accounting firms, auditors prepare the income tax returns for the clients they audit, unless the client prepares his or her own return. In some cases, particularly in the larger accounting firms, a separate tax department prepares all tax returns.

FIGURE 16.10   Accrued Property Taxes

```
                                                              P-1
                            X Co.
                    Accrued Property Taxes              J. Jones
                         12-31-X8                       1-20-x9


    Balance 12-31-X7                                     22,199  P
    Accrual for property tax expense               ①  22,500  20
    Payments during the year—
                Check No.   Taxing Authority    Amount
                  2119      State of Arkansas    12,376  ✓
                  2280      City of Hypothetical  9,794  ✓    22,170

    Balance 12-31-X8                                     22,529  P


    ① Provision for the year is reasonable as it approximates
      the amount actually paid in the prior year and
      there have been no tax rate increases or significant
      property additions.

    ✓ Examined receipted tax bill and canceled check.
```

In auditing accrued liabilities, the auditor must not become so involved with testing calculations and reviewing the reasonableness of estimates that he or she forgets where the emphasis should be placed in the audit of liabilities. The auditor must consider what accrued liabilities should be recorded that are not recorded (completeness). Because accrued liabilities generally are accrued expenses, a good starting point in a search for unrecorded accrued liabilities is the client's expense accounts. It is often necessary to accrue such expenses as payroll, payroll taxes, vacation pay, sick pay, commissions, insurance, income, property and excise taxes, pensions, bonuses, interest, profit-sharing, and royalties. The auditor should consider the necessity of these as well as other accruals in each audit.

Summary of Important Substantive Tests for Accrued Liabilities

- Perform analytical procedures.
- Examine subsequent payments of accrued liabilities made before the fieldwork is completed and compare payment with accrued balance.
- Test computations of accrued balances by reference to such factors as interest rates, commission rates, royalty rates, tax rates, and historical data for accruals such as warranty costs, insurance, and so on.
- Determine that all necessary accrued liabilities have been recorded.

Chapter 16 ▶ GLOSSARY OF TERMS

Inventory cutoff   A determination that items received before the inventory date are included in inventory, accounts payable, and purchases and that items shipped before the inventory date are excluded from inventory and included in sales and accounts receivable.

Tests counts   Verification, by the auditor's inspection, of the number of physical objects comprising an item of inventory on hand at the inventory date.

Chapter 16 ▶ REFERENCES

American Institute of Certified Public Accountants. *Professional Standards*
AU Section 331—*Inventories*
AU Section 901—*Public Warehouses—Internal Control Policies and Procedures and Auditing Procedures for Goods Held*

Peavey, Dennis E., and Nurnberg, Hugo. "FASB 109: Auditing Considerations of Deferred Tax Assets," *Journal of Accountancy* (May 1993), pp. 77–81.

Chapter 16 ▶ REVIEW QUESTIONS

16-1 State the objectives in the audit of inventories.

16-2 Give three examples of internal control policies and procedures that may affect the scope of substantive tests of inventories.

16-3 What analytical procedures may an auditor apply to inventories?

16-4 Discuss the auditor's responsibility for an accurate physical inventory.

16-5 How does the auditor guard against inclusion in the final inventory listing of count sheets or tags containing fictitious inventory items?

16-6 Why does an auditor record some inventory test counts?

16-7 What is the purpose of inventory cutoff tests?

16-8 What procedures can the auditor perform during the inventory observation to test for obsolete, excess, or slow-moving items?

16-9 State the general approaches to auditing job-order, process, and standard cost systems.

16-10 Describe the audit tests made of the client's inventory summary schedules.

16-11 Describe the audit procedures designed to detect liens and pledges of inventory.

16-12 What are some inquiries an auditor can make when examining inventories to add value to the audit?

16-13 How do the auditor's approach and emphasis in auditing assets differ from those in auditing liabilities?

16-14 State the objectives in the audit of current liabilities.

16-15 Describe how analytical procedures may be applied to accounts payable and accrued liabilities.

16-16 The auditor normally uses two approaches to the audit of accounts payable. What are they and why are both used?

16-17 How does the auditor select the accounts to which accounts payable confirmations will be sent? Why is this method of selection used?

16-18 What are the similarities and differences in the form of accounts receivable and payable confirmation letters?

16-19 How and for what period is the review of subsequent disbursements made?

16-20 What are some inquiries an auditor can make when examining accounts payable to add value to the audit?

16-21 Name two approaches to auditing accrued liabilities.

16-22 What is a good starting point in an auditor's search for unrecorded accrued liabilities?

Chapter 16 ▶ OBJECTIVE QUESTIONS

(* = author prepared; ** = CPA examination)

**16-23 Which of the following internal control procedures would most likely be used to maintain accurate perpetual inventory records?
  a. Independent storeroom count of goods received.
  b. Periodic independent comparison of records with goods on hand.
  c. Periodic independent reconciliation of control and subsidiary records.
  d. Independent matching of purchase orders, receiving reports, and vendors' invoices.

**16-24 An auditor most likely would make inquiries of production and sales personnel concerning possible obsolete or slow-moving inventory to support management's financial statement assertion of
  a. Valuation or allocation.
  b. Rights and obligations.
  c. Existence or occurrence.
  d. Presentation and disclosure.

**16-25 Periodic or cycle counts of selected inventory items are made at various times during the year rather than a single inventory count at year end. Which of the following is necessary if the auditor plans to observe inventories at interim dates?
  a. Complete recounts by independent teams are performed.
  b. Perpetual inventory records are maintained.
  c. Unit cost records are integrated with production accounting records.
  d. Inventory balances are rarely at low levels.

*16-26 Which of the following matters would auditors discuss with management to add value to the audit?
  a. Methods of measuring customer satisfaction with the client's products.
  b. Inventory instructions for client count teams.
  c. Financial statement presentation of inventory.
  d. Means of maintaining an accurate perpetual inventory system.

**16-27 To gain assurance that all inventory items in a client's inventory listing schedule are valid, an auditor most likely would trace
  a. Inventory tags noted during the auditor's ob-
servation to items listed in the inventory listing schedule.
  b. Inventory tags noted during the auditor's observation to items listed in receiving reports and vendors' invoices.
  c. Items listed in the inventory listing schedule to inventory tags and the auditor's recorded count sheets.
  d. Items listed in receiving reports and vendors' invoices to the inventory listing schedule.

**16-28 While observing a client's annual physical inventory, an auditor recorded test counts for several items and noticed that certain test counts were higher than the recorded quantities in the client's perpetual records. This situation could be the result of the client's failure to record
  a. Purchase discounts.
  b. Purchase returns.
  c. Sales.
  d. Sales returns.

**16-29 A client maintains perpetual inventory records in both quantities and dollars. If the assessed level of control risk is high, an auditor would probably
  a. Insist that the client perform physical counts of inventory items several times during the year.
  b. Apply gross profit tests to ascertain the reasonableness of the physical counts.
  c. Increase the extent of tests of controls of the inventory cycle.
  d. Request the client to schedule the physical inventory count at the end of the year.

**16-30 A CPA is engaged in the annual audit of a client for the year ended December 31, 19X9. The client took a complete physical inventory under the CPA's observation on December 15 and adjusted its inventory control account and detail perpetual inventory records to agree with the physical inventory. The client considers a sale to be made in the period that goods are shipped. Listed in the following table are four items taken from the CPA's sales cutoff worksheet. Which item does *not* require an adjusting entry on the client's books?

	Shipped	Recorded as a sale	Credited to inventory control
a.	12/31	1/2	12/31
b.	1/2	12/31	12/31
c.	12/14	12/16	12/16
d.	12/10	12/19	12/12

**16-31 In an audit of inventories, an auditor would *least* likely verify that

   a. All inventory owned by the client is on hand at the time of the count.

   b. The client has used proper inventory pricing.

   c. The financial statement presentation of inventories is appropriate.

   d. Damaged goods and obsolete items have been properly accounted for.

**16-32 Which of the following auditing procedures most likely would provide assurance about a manufacturing entity's inventory valuation?

   a. Testing the entity's computation of standard overhead rates.

   b. Obtaining confirmation of inventories pledged under loan agreements.

   c. Reviewing shipping and receiving cutoff procedures for inventories.

   d. Tracing test counts to the entity's inventory listing.

**16-33 Which of the following audit procedures probably would provide the most reliable evidence concerning the entity's assertion of rights and obligations related to inventories?

   a. Trace test counts noted during the entity's physical count to the entity's summarization of quantities.

   b. Inspect agreements to determine whether any inventory is pledged as collateral or subject to any liens.

   c. Select the last few shipping advices used before the physical count and determine whether the shipments were recorded as sales.

   d. Inspect the open purchase order file for significant commitments that should be considered for disclosure.

**16-34 Cutoff tests designed to detect purchases made before the end of the year that have been recorded in the subsequent year most likely would provide assurance about management's assertion of

   a. Valuation or allocation.

   b. Existence or occurrence.

   c. Completeness.

   d. Presentation and disclosure.

**16-35 Which of the following audit procedures is best for identifying unrecorded trade accounts payable?

   a. Reviewing cash disbursements recorded subsequent to the balance sheet date to determine whether the related payables apply to the prior period.

   b. Investigating payables recorded just prior to and just subsequent to the balance sheet date to determine whether they are supported by receiving reports.

   c. Examining unusual relationships between monthly accounts payable balances and recorded cash payments.

   d. Reconciling vendors' statements to the file of receiving reports to identify items received just prior to the balance sheet date.

**16-36 To determine whether accounts payable are complete, an auditor performs a test to verify that all merchandise received is recorded. The population of documents for this test consists of all

   a. Vendors' invoices.

   b. Purchase orders.

   c. Receiving reports.

   d. Canceled checks.

*16-37 An auditor is performing a review of subsequent disbursements to search for unrecorded liabilities. All goods received are FOB destination. Which of the following disbursements represents an unrecorded liability as of December 31, 19X2?

	Date of receipt of goods	Date of invoice	Date recorded in books
a.	12-31-X2	1-3-X3	1-3-X3
b.	1-3-X3	12-31-X2	Unrecorded
c.	1-4-X3	12-31-X2	1-4-X3
d.	12-31-X2	1-5-X3	12-31-X2

**16-38 Only one of the following four statements, which compare confirmation of accounts payable with suppliers and confirmation of accounts receivable with customers, is true. The true statement is that

   a. Confirmation of accounts payable with suppliers is a more widely accepted auditing procedure than is confirmation of accounts receivable with customers.

b. It is less likely that the confirmation request sent to the supplier will show the amount owed him or her than that the request sent to the customer will show the amount due from him or her.

c. Statistical sampling techniques are more widely accepted in the confirmation of accounts payable than in the confirmation of accounts receivable.

d. Compared to the confirmation of accounts payable, the confirmation of accounts receivable will tend to emphasize accounts with zero balances at the balance sheet date.

**16-39 Which of the following procedures relating to the audit of accounts payable could the auditor delegate entirely to the client's employees?

a. Foot the accounts payable ledger.

b. Reconcile unpaid invoices to vendors' statements.

c. Prepare an audit lead schedule of accounts payable.

d. Mail confirmations for selected account balances.

**16-40 Which of the following *best* explains why accounts payable confirmation procedures are *not* always used?

a. Accounts payable are generally insignificant and can be audited by utilizing analytical procedures.

b. Monthly statements from vendors are generally available for audit inspection on the client's premises.

c. The auditor may feel certain that the creditors will press for payment.

d. Creditors seldom respond to confirmation requests so results are of questionable use.

**16-41 The audit procedures applied to accrued liabilities differ from those applied to accounts payable because

a. Accrued liabilities balances are less material than accounts payable balances.

b. Evidence supporting accrued liabilities is nonexistent, whereas evidence supporting accounts payable is readily available.

c. Accrued liabilities usually pertain to services of a continuing nature, whereas accounts payable are the result of completed transactions.

d. Accrued liabilities at year-end will become accounts payable during the following year.

*16-42 Match each assertion to the related audit objective. Each assertion may be used once, more than once, or not at all.

Audit objective	Assertion
1. To determine whether the amount shown as inventories in the financial statements is represented by all physical items on hand, in transit, or on consignment.	a. Existence or occurrence
2. To determine whether the inventory belongs to the company and whether any liens on the inventory are disclosed properly.	b. Rights and obligations
3. To determine whether current liabilities consist of amounts due within one year or the natural operating cycle of the business.	c. Completeness
4. To determine whether disclosures concerning current liabilities are adequate.	d. Valuation or allocation
	e. Presentation or disclosure

Chapter 16 ▶ DISCUSSION/CASE QUESTIONS AND PROBLEMS

(* = author prepared; ** = CPA examination)

*16-43 Audit procedures should be designed to accomplish specific audit objectives. Review the following inventory audit procedures and indicate which audit objectives are being accomplished and how.

a. Observe the taking of the client's physical inventory.

b. Account for the sequence of inventory tags and trace each tag to the physical inventory listing.

c. Compare the unit prices on the client's final inventory listing with vendor invoices.

  d. Inquire of management as to obsolete goods.

  e. Test the receiving cutoff to determine that all goods on hand are included in the final inventory listing.

  f. Confirm inventory held by a public warehouse.

**16-44 Your audit client, Household Appliances, Inc., operates a retail store in the center of town. Because of lack of storage space, Household keeps inventory that is not on display in a public warehouse outside of town. The warehouse supervisor receives inventory from suppliers and, on request from your client by a shipping advice or telephone call, delivers merchandise to customers or to the retail outlet.

  The accounts are maintained at the retail store by a bookkeeper. Each month the warehouse supervisor sends to the bookkeeper a quantity report indicating opening balance, receipts, deliveries, and ending balance. The bookkeeper compares book quantities on hand at month-end with the warehouse supervisor's report and adjusts his books to agree with the report. No physical counts of the merchandise at the warehouse were made by your client during the year.

  You are now preparing for your audit of the current year's financial statements in this recurring engagement. Last year you rendered an unqualified opinion.

  Required:

  a. Prepare an audit program for the observation of the physical inventory of Household Appliances, Inc. (1) at the retail outlet and (2) at the warehouse.

  b. As part of your audit, would you verify inventory quantities at the warehouse by means of (1) a warehouse confirmation (Why?) or (2) test counts of inventory at the warehouse? (Why?)

  c. Since the bookkeeper adjusts the books to quantities shown on the warehouse supervisor's report each month, what significance would you attach to the year-end adjustments if they were substantial? Discuss.

**16-45 Brown, CPA, is auditing the financial statements of Big Z Wholesaling, Inc., a continuing audit client, for the year ended January 31, 19X2. On January 5, 19X2, Brown observed the tagging and counting of Big Z's physical inventory and made appropriate test counts. These test counts have been recorded on a computer file. As in prior years, Big Z gave Brown two computer files. One file represents the perpetual inventory (FIFO) records for the year ended January 31, 19X2. The other file represents the January 5 physical inventory count.

  Assume:

  • Brown issued an unqualified opinion on the prior year's financial statements.

  • All inventory is purchased for resale and located in a single warehouse.

  • Brown has appropriate computerized audit software.

  • The perpetual inventory file contains the following information in item number sequence:

    Beginning balances at February 1, 19X1: Item number, item description, total quantity, and prices.

    For each item purchased during the year: Date received, receiving report number, vendor, item number, item description, quantity, and total dollar amount.

    For each item sold during the year: Date shipped, invoice number, item number, item description, quantity shipped, and dollar amount of the cost removed from inventory.

    For each item adjusted for physical inventory count differences: Date, item number, item description, quantity, and dollar amount.

  • The physical inventory file contains the following information in item number sequence: Tag number, item number, item description, and count quantity.

Required:

Describe the substantive auditing procedures Brown may consider performing with computerized audit software using Big Z's two computer files and Brown's computer file of test counts. The substantive auditing procedures described may indicate the reports to be printed out for Brown's followup by subsequent application of manual procedures. Do *not* describe subsequent manual auditing procedures.

Group the procedures by those using (a) the perpetual inventory file and (b) the physical inventory and test count files.

16-46   To audit a company's sales and purchases cutoffs at the close of the fiscal year ended December 31, 19X1, you have compiled the data listed on the following schedule. All sales and purchases of significant amount from December 26, 19X1, to January 4, 19X2, inclusive, are included. Refer to page 539.

The company realized a gross profit of 30 percent on each sale, and all sales and purchases were recorded as of the invoice dates. Items marked "B" were FOB destination; all other items were FOB shipping point.

The physical inventory taken by the company included only those items actually on hand as of the close of business December 31, 19X1. All items on hand were included except a special machine (see "A" on the cutoff schedule). This special machine was made to order by the company's supplier for one of the company's customers and was in the shipping room ready for shipment. It was excluded from the physical inventory.

The company maintains a perpetual inventory system. The inventory account and the subsidiary records have been adjusted to the physical inventory.

Complete the schedule on page 539 by showing for each item the required adjustment, if any.

(Used with permission of Ernst & Young)

*16-47   Assume that a CPA's client proposes to have an independent firm that specializes in inventory taking count the merchandise rather than use their own employees. Under these conditions, would it be acceptable for the CPA to forgo the inventory observation? Support your answer.

**16-48   Late in December 19X9, your CPA firm accepted an audit engagement at Fine Jewelers, Inc., a corporation that deals largely in diamonds. The corporation has retail jewelry stores in several Eastern cities and a diamond wholesale store in New York City. The wholesale store also sets the diamonds in rings and in other quality jewelry.

The retail stores place orders for diamond jewelry with the wholesale store in New York City. A buyer employed by the wholesale store purchases diamonds in the New York diamond market, and the wholesale store then fills the orders from the retail stores and from independent customers and maintains a substantial inventory of diamonds. The corporation values its inventory by the specific identification cost method.

Required:

Assume that at the inventory date you are satisfied that Fine Jewelers, Inc., has no items left by customers for repair or sale on consignment and that no inventory owned by the corporation is in the possession of outsiders.

a. Discuss the problems the auditor should anticipate in planning for the observation of the physical inventory on this engagement because of the

  (1)   Different locations of inventories.

  (2)   Nature of the inventory.

b. (1)   Explain how your audit program for this inventory would be different from that used for most other inventories.

  (2)   Prepare an audit program for the verification of the corporation's diamond and diamond jewelry inventories, identifying any steps that would apply only to the retail stores or the wholesale store.

Inventory Cutoff Test
Acs Company
12-31-X1

		Initials	Date
Prepared			

Description		Selling Price	Invoice Date	Shipping Date	Receiving Date	Accounts Receivable Dr./<Cr.>	Sales Dr./<Cr.>	Inventory Dr./<Cr.>	Cost of Sales Dr./<Cr.>	Accounts Payable Dr./<Cr.>
Sales:	a	6000—	12-28-X1	12-27-X1						
	b	8000—	12-28-X1	12-29-X1						
	c	5000—	A12-29-X1	1-3-X2						
	d	6000—	12-31-X1	1-3-X2						
	e	7000—	12-31-X1	1-2-X2						
	f	9000—	B12-31-X1	12-31-X1						
	g	4000—	1-3-X2	1-4-X2						
	h	5000—	1-3-X2	12-31-X1						
	i	6000—	1-4-X2	1-5-X2						
Purchases:	a	5000—	12-27-X1	12-27-X1	12-31-X1					
	b	7000—	B12-28-X1	12-31-X1	1-3-X2					
	c	8000—	12-31-X1	12-31-X1	1-3-X2					
	d	7000—	12-31-X1	12-31-X1	1-4-X2					
	e	6000—	1-3-X2	12-31-X1	12-31-X1					
	f	9000—	1-3-X2	12-31-X1	1-3-X2					
	g	7000—	B 1-4-X2	12-31-X1	1-3-X2					
	h	4000—	1-4-X2	1-5-X2	1-6-X2					

c. Assume that a shipment of diamond rings was in transit by corporation messenger from the wholesale store to a retail store on the inventory date. What additional audit steps would you take to satisfy yourself as to the gems that were in transit from the wholesale store on the inventory date?

*16-49 You have been assigned to the audit of Hogeye Manufacturing Company as of December 31, 19X8. Hogeye maintains its raw material inventory on a FIFO basis. The balance at December 31, 19X8 was $216,385. In performing the raw material inventory price test, you prepared an audit working paper that included the following items to which you wish to give further attention.

Item	Per books		Per vendor invoices		
	Price	Quantity	Price	Quantity	Date received
Springs	$1.15	1,037	$1.11	5,000	11-3-X8
Clips	.52	3,816	0.52	4,000	1-6-X9
			0.40	4,000	10-14-X8
Bars	2.50	11,509	2.50	5,000	11-18-X8
			2.05	7,000	10-31-X8
Paint	5.05	619	5.05	750	1-13-X7
Tin	3.13	7,616	3.15	10,000	8-20-X8

Other raw material items included in your sample and price tested with no exception total $53,118.

Required:

a. Determine the amount of pricing misstatement in the sample.

b. Project the sample results to the population.

c. Discuss any of the preceding items you would investigate further and describe what revisions you would suggest to the format of the preceding audit schedule.

**16-50   Kane, CPA, is auditing Star Wholesaling Company's financial statements and is about to perform substantive audit procedures on Star's trade accounts payable. After obtaining an understanding of Star's internal control for accounts payable, Kane assessed control risk at near the maximum. Kane requested and received from Star a schedule of the trade accounts payable prepared using the trade accounts payable subsidiary ledger (voucher register).

Required:

Describe the substantive audit procedures Kane should apply to Star's trade accounts payable. Do *not* include procedures that would be applied only in the audit of related party payables, amounts withheld from employees, and accrued expenses such as pensions and interest.

16-51   The following are situations or questions pertaining to the audit of accounts payable:

a. With regard to statements requested from vendors, the auditor's memo states, "We requested statements from all vendors with balances over $2,000 as shown by the trial balance." Do you feel this procedure is satisfactory? Give reasons for your answer.

b. Why should an auditor be particularly careful to investigate past-due accounts payable?

c. Discuss some of the sources from which the auditor can prepare a list of vendors from whom statements should be requested.

d. All vendors' statements on hand and received by the auditor have been reconciled by the company at the auditor's request. How much testing of the reconcilements should be done?

e. In connection with the year-end audit of trade accounts payable, the following are noted; describe briefly what each could indicate and what audit procedures you would follow in the circumstances:

(1)   Several long-standing credit balances.

(2)   A number of debit balances included in accounts payable.

(3)   A substantial dollar amount of purchase commitments in a situation of declining market prices.

(Used with permission of Ernst & Young)

*16-52   Listed below are several misstatements that could occur in the inventory, accounts payable, and accrued liabilities accounts. For each misstatement, design a substantive audit procedure that would provide reasonable assurance of detecting it.

a. When client employees counted the physical inventory, they included a number of items that were consigned to, but did not belong to, the client.

b. Several accounts payable to vendors that the client has never purchased from before are omitted from the accounts payable listing.

c. A bonus earned by the president of the company has not been recorded.

d. One-third of the inventory of precious gems is actually worthless glass.

e. There is no disclosure in the financial statements that a large accounts payable is due to a related party.

   f. Accrued payroll is overstated.

   g. During the year being audited, a competitor of the client markets a product that renders a client product obsolete. A substantial stock of this product is on hand at year-end.

   h. The client paid the same accounts payable balance twice.

   i. The client failed to record warranty expenses incurred after year-end applicable to sales made before year-end.

   j. Client personnel informed the auditors that underground petroleum tanks contained an inventory of high-octane gasoline when they actually contained water.

   k. The client failed to record sales commissions applicable to sales during the last month of the year.

   l. The client uses a job-order cost system. During the year costs were charged to the wrong jobs with the result that some jobs showed profits and others showed losses. The jobs with profits were closed, and those with losses remained in inventory.

   m. Inventory in one corner of the warehouse is overlooked and not counted during the client's physical inventory count.

   n. During the afternoon of the last day of the year, the client shipped and recorded as a sale items that had been counted and included as part of the physical inventory that morning.

   o. Because of the installation of new high-tech equipment at the end of the year, production cost of the company's product was reduced significantly.

*16-53   Billy Joe Atlas, an experienced senior with a CPA firm, was sent to the hospital with intense chest pains after watching his favorite college football team lose a bowl game on December 31. He was scheduled to be in charge of the January 1 inventory observation of Heave Industries, a maker of specialty wool sweaters. Vincent Whimp, a newly promoted senior with considerably less experience, had to be called in at the last minute to head the inventory observation team, which consisted of himself and two staff persons who had never observed an inventory. On January 2, Vincent prepared an inventory observation memorandum, part of which contained these comments.

   Bill Turncoat, Janice Swemish, and I arrived at the manufacturing plant at Heave Industries at 9:00 A.M. after taking a wrong turn at the freeway intersection. When we arrived, Mr. Dandurth, the controller, told us that the count teams had already been working for an hour and that several dozen boxes of sweaters had been counted, packed up, and sent to the docks for shipping the next day. I insisted that he instruct the count teams to unpack the boxes so we could see the contents. After a harsh exchange of words, Mr. Dandurth agreed to break open three boxes and recount the contents. There was some discrepancy between the recounts and the original counts of the reopened boxes. However, we took the recounts as the actual figures and did not look at any more boxes of sweaters sent to the dock.

   At 11:00 A.M. Janice told me that she wanted to do something other than watch inventory teams count the sweaters and that members of the team were laughing at her. I asked her why she was not making any test counts, and she indicated that no one had told her to do so. I was extremely annoyed but handed her a sheet of paper and instructed her to begin making some counts.

   At 2:00 P.M. I checked with Bill, who seemed very nervous. I asked him if there was any problem, and he said that many of the sweaters being counted were torn or had grease marks on them. I asked Mr. Dandurth whether these sweaters were being excluded from the inventory. He said that they were not because retailers were willing to pay full price for such sweaters since they could hide the blemishes and sell them at full price. This explanation seemed reasonable.

   We asked Mr. Dandurth whether prenumbered receiving reports and shipping documents were being used. He said that a prenumbered system was in use for both types of documents but that no cutoff was necessary because nothing was received or shipped for a week before and a week after January 1. We accepted his explanation.

After the inventory observation was completed, we apologized for arriving late and packed up our working papers. In my opinion the inventory count on January 1 was accurate.

Required:

a. Describe the mistakes that were made by the inventory observation team.

b. Draft the inventory observation memorandum that probably would have been written if Billy Joe's favorite football team had won its bowl game.

On January 15, Billy Joe was scheduled to be released from the hospital. But he read in the morning paper that a discovery of an ineligible player on his favorite football team had resulted in forfeiture of all conference games for the previous fall season. He had a relapse and had to be confined again to intensive care. As a result, Vincent became the temporary senior on the audit of Heave Industries.

Vincent obtained a trial balance of accounts payable as of the previous December 31. He asked one of his assistants to prepare accounts payable confirmation requests for the largest amounts on the schedule. The assistant had misplaced the prior-year working papers, so she prepared a confirmation "from scratch," part of which is shown below. She then gave them to Mr. Dandurth for signing and mailing.

Our auditors, Stretch and Co., are now engaged in an examination of our financial statements. In connection therewith, please indicate in the space provided whether the amount shown on this confirmation form is the correct amount owed to you. If the amount is not correct, please indicate the correct amount we owe you.

Required:

c. Describe the mistakes made by Vincent in the confirmation of accounts payable.

d. Draft the above portion of the accounts payable confirmation form that probably would have been written if no player had been declared ineligible on Billy Joe's favorite football team.

Auditing the Capital Asset and Financing Base Assertions

"Skepticism is the first step toward truth."

DIDEROT, *Pensées Philosophiques*

LEARNING OBJECTIVES

After reading and studying the material in this chapter, the student should be able to

▶ Paraphrase the objectives in the audit of property and equipment and related accumulated depreciation.

▶ Compare examples of (1) internal control policies and procedures and (2) substantive tests for each of the five assertions relating to property and equipment and related accumulated depreciation.

▶ Describe the contents of working papers for (1) equipment additions vouching schedules and (2) property retirements schedules.

▶ Describe how value can be added to the audit of property and equipment and related accumulated depreciation.

▶ Paraphrase the objectives in the audit of long-term investments and intangibles.

▶ Compare examples of (1) internal control policies and procedures and (2) substantive tests for each of the five assertions relating to long-term investments and intangibles.

▶ Describe the contents of a working paper for a security count of long-term investments.

▶ Paraphrase the objectives in the audit of long-term liabilities.

▶ Compare examples of (1) internal control policies and procedures and (2) substantive tests for each of the five assertions relating to long-term liabilities.

▶ Describe how value can be added to the audit of long-term liabilities.

▶ Paraphrase the objectives in the audit of equity accounts.

▶ Compare examples of (1) internal control policies and procedures and (2) substantive tests for each of the five assertions relating to equity accounts.

▶ Describe the contents of working papers for (1) tests of dividend payments and (2) stockbook examination schedules.

The approaches to capital asset and financing base accounts are similar in that the beginning balance is established first (normally from the prior-year audit), and then the current-year transactions are audited. The audit of these accounts differs from the audit of working capital accounts, in which the auditor anticipates an almost complete turnover of the amounts included in the balance at the end of the year compared with those at the beginning of the year. Items such as property and equipment, long-term debt, and equity tend to have long lives, and once they have been established as properly recorded amounts, the auditor's concern is with the accounting for the ultimate realization or disposition of these items. Thus, if the auditor is satisfied with the beginning balance and current transactions, he or she generally is satisfied with the ending balance.

PROPERTY AND EQUIPMENT AND ACCUMULATED DEPRECIATION

The property and equipment accounts represent the cost of a company's productive facilities, which may be depreciable (costs of buildings and machinery), depletable (costs of natural resources such as oil and gas), amortizable (cost of leasehold improvements), or fixed (such as land). Leased property and equipment also are included in the balance sheet if they are capitalizable under generally accepted accounting principles. In certain limited situations, such as in a quasi-reorganization or in personal financial statements, property and equipment are stated on a basis other than cost. Generally accepted accounting principles generally provide, however, that property and equipment shall not be written up by an enterprise to reflect appraisal, market, or current values that are above cost to the enterprise. FASB Statement No. 121 requires that long-lived assets be reviewed for impairment when events or changes in circumstances indicate that the carrying amount of assets may not be recoverable.

Because of the low volume of activity and the long-term nature of the assets, a company's detailed accounting records for property and equipment often are not as elaborate or as carefully maintained as those for other accounts such as cash, accounts receivable, or inventories. Property and equipment records normally should include a detail property ledger and, if construction activity is significant, a construction work order system. These records are important to the company's determination and the auditor's examination of the cost of retired or abandoned assets. Formal policies regarding approval of capital expenditures, distinction between capital and maintenance expenditures, and the reporting and recording of asset retirements are significant aspects of internal control in the property section.

Audit Objectives

The objectives (assertions) in the audit of property and equipment and related accumulated depreciation are as follows.

1. To determine whether the amount shown as property and equipment in the financial statements represents all (completeness) physical facilities (existence) owned by the company (rights) and associated with the productive

process (presentation), and all retired or abandoned property is removed properly from the accounts.

2. To determine whether property and equipment are stated at cost that is properly capitalizable and whether depreciation expense is adequate and is computed in accordance with generally accepted accounting principles (valuation and allocation).

3. To determine whether the accumulated depreciation is reasonable in relation to the expected useful life of the property (allocation).

4. To determine whether the disclosures concerning property and equipment are adequate and in accordance with generally accepted accounting principles (disclosure).

Audit Procedures and Working Papers

The procedures depend on the auditor's assessment of control risk for assertions applicable to the property section, as well as related areas such as purchasing and cash disbursements. For example, if supporting documents are examined by an independent party at the time accounts payable vouchers are prepared, the auditors might adjust the substantive tests of property purchases. Tests of procedures for distinguishing between capital and expense transactions and computing depreciation are dual-purpose tests; they will be explained later in this section.

Examples of the effect of internal control on the scope of substantive tests of property and equipment are as follows: (1) a formal budgeting system with investigation of variances is likely to detect payments that are misclassified between maintenance and property and allow the auditor to reduce the scope of his or her work on property additions and repairs and maintenance, (2) failure of the client to tag and periodically account for property and equipment is likely to cause the auditor to increase the scope of his or her search for unrecorded retirements, or (3) review and approval of the monthly depreciation entry by a supervisor who did not participate in its preparation is likely to allow the auditor to reduce the scope of his or her tests of depreciation expense. Other examples of internal control policies and procedures and substantive tests related to specific assertions for the property and equipment account are shown below.

Assertions	Examples of internal control policies and procedures	Examples of substantive tests
1. Existence	1. Require approved vendor invoice with related receiving report before recording additions to property and equipment.	1. Inspect approved vendor invoice with related receiving report for additions to property and equipment.
2. Rights	2. Control environment (require board of director approval to mortgage property and equipment).	2. Inquiry and review of board of director minutes and loan agreements for indication of mortgages of property and equipment.

Assertions	*Examples of internal control policies and procedures*	*Examples of substantive tests*
3. Completeness	3. Establish formal accounting policy to distinguish between property additions and repairs and maintenance.	3. Analyze the repairs and maintenance account and review charges to the account for improperly classified property and equipment additions.
4. Valuation	4. Establish formal accounting policy to capitalize acquisition and other appropriate costs (freight, installation, etc.).	4. Examine vendor invoices to determine if appropriate costs were capitalized.
5. Presentation	5. Control environment (adequately trained personnel who are familiar with GAAP requirements applicable to property and equipment, e.g., disclosure of depreciation methods and lives).	5. Determine that depreciation methods and lives are disclosed in notes to financial statements.

The lead schedule for property and equipment and accumulated depreciation summarizes the activity in the subaccounts for the year and relates the accumulated depreciation to the applicable asset account (Figure 17.1). The auditor will add the amounts of the individual property and equipment items in the detailed property ledger and determine that the sums agree with the amounts shown for each property and equipment subaccount on the lead schedule.

Analytical Procedures
The auditor should compare

1. The property and equipment account balances for the current year with the current-year budget and prior-year actual balances.
2. Property and equipment additions to the capital budget.
3. Depreciation expense for the current year with the prior year.
4. Ratios of accumulated and current-year depreciation expense to property and equipment balances of the current and prior years.

Significant unexpected variations, or lack thereof, should be investigated for misclassified additions (presentation), unrecorded retirements (existence), or erroneous depreciation calculations (allocation).

Audit of Property Additions
The audit procedures for property additions are designed to determine whether the additions represent physical facilities owned by the company (existence and rights), are stated at cost (valuation), and are properly capitalized (presentation). The auditor analyzes additions in greater detail than shown on the lead schedule. An example of such an analysis, often referred to as a *vouching schedule,* is shown

FIGURE 17.1 Property and Equipment and Accumulated Depreciation Lead Schedule

X Co.
Property and Equipment and Accumulated Depreciation Lead Schedule
Dec. 31, 19X8

A
J. Jones
1-24-x9

Depr. Rate	Description	Property and Equipment				Allowance for Depreciation			
		Balance 12-31-X7	Additions	Retirements	Balance 12-31-X8	Balance 12-31-X7	Additions	Retirements	Balance 12-31-X8
—	Land	55,041	0	0	55,041	0	0	0	0
5%	Buildings	287,869	19,013	10,854	296,028	21,751	13,037	10,379	24,409
10%	Equipment	226,526	24,757	9,678	241,605	61,702	21,065	8,374	74,393
33%	Automobiles	12,314	0	0	12,314	5,813	4,101	0	9,914
		581,750	43,770	20,532	604,988	89,266	38,203	18,753	108,716

G-1 G-2 TB-1 Q-3 TB-1 TB-1 20 Q-3 TB-1

FIGURE 17.2 Equipment Additions Vouching Schedule

X Co.
Equipment Additions
12-31-X8

F-2
J. Jones
1-11-x9

Scope: All over $2,000

Voucher No.	Vendor	Amount	Description
(1) 2-376	Electric Supply Co.	2,835✓	Electric motor for drill press
(2) 5-814	Maple Machine Co.	6,719✓	Plant sprayer and dryer ∧
	Total examined	19,460	
	Below minimum	5,297 (∧)	
	Total additions	24,757 F	

✓ Examined vendor invoice, receiving report, and canceled check and noted that the expenditure was a proper capital charge.
∧ Examined asset during inventory observation.
(∧) Reviewed ledger to determine that no items above the minimum were omitted.
(1) Replacement-noted retirement on F-3.
(2) New addition-no retirement required per discussion with plant engineer.

in Figure 17.2. In this example, the auditor has chosen to examine all additions to equipment in excess of $2,000, although sampling plans could also be used. The audit procedure indicated by ✓ includes (1) examination of vendor invoice and canceled check, indicating that the item was owned by the company and recorded at cost, (2) examination of receiving report, indicating that a physical item was received, and (3) review of the capitalization decision based on the description of the item. Major additions should be traced to board of director approval in the minutes. Additional evidence of the physical existence of the item may be gained from inspecting it during the inventory observation. The auditor also has noted by (1) and (2) whether each addition was a new or replacement item. This information is useful in auditing property retirements.

As a test for property units that may have been charged to expense (completeness), an analysis similar to that described above is made of the maintenance and repair expense accounts, and the work indicated by ✓ is performed. Because the review of the capitalization/expense decision is a significant aspect of this work, it often is performed simultaneously with the work on property additions.

Audit of Property Retirements

In the audit of property retirements, the auditor wants to determine whether recorded retirements are shown properly and, more important, whether there are significant *unrecorded property retirements*. Often, inherent and control risks relating to property retirements are high. Figure 17.3 illustrates some audit procedures that are likely to be applied to property retirements.

The recorded retirements are tested by tracing the original cost of the item, together with the dates acquired and retired, to the detail property ledger (indicated by √). Accumulated depreciation, if not recorded separately for each item, must be recomputed on the basis of the depreciation rate applicable to such assets and the periods they were held (indicated by ⋀). Salvage proceeds can be traced to the cash receipts book or deposit slip (indicated by Ж). With this information, the resulting net gain or loss from property retirements can be recomputed and related to an income or expense account (see the reference to the *40* schedule in Figure 17.3). The auditor uses the federal income tax status of the transactions in auditing the income tax liability and expense accounts.

A plant tour provides the auditor with knowledge of the production process that will be important in other sections of the audit, as well as in the search for unrecorded retirements. It sometimes is coordinated with the physical inventory observation. To be an effective procedure in the search for unrecorded retirements, the plant tour must be planned properly. To stroll through a plant inspecting certain items of equipment provides no evidence about unrecorded retirements (although it may be useful in verifying the physical existence of additions). During the search for unrecorded retirements, the auditor is interested in the pieces of equipment that are *not* in the plant but are still recorded in the accounting records. To make the test effective, the auditor must select certain items of equipment from the accounting records and then locate and identify them during the plant tour. Any items that cannot be located would represent unrecorded retirements and should be removed from the accounting records. Because of the nature of the audit work performed in the search for unrecorded property retirements, the auditor normally documents it in a memorandum.

The effectiveness of the auditor's search for unrecorded property retirements depends on his or her business knowledge and vigilance. In the work on property additions, the auditor noted whether major additions represented new or replacement items (see ① and ② in Figure 17.2). Because a replacement implies that an old asset was retired when the new asset was placed in service, the auditor can use this information to determine whether the retirement was recorded in the accounting records.

Other procedures used in the search for unrecorded retirements include a review of the miscellaneous or other income account for salvage credits and scrap sales and inquiry of operating and management personnel. Proceeds from the sale of scrap or used equipment may indicate unrecorded retirements and should be investigated if material. In this connection, the auditor should consider the internal control policies and procedures over the accumulation and sale of scrap. Lack of controls in this area (which is not unusual) can result not only in unrecorded property retirements, but also in misappropriation of proceeds from the sale of scrap and salvaged items.

Unrecorded Retirements of Property and Equipment

When reviewing transactions in the other income account, an auditor may note the following entry to record the sale of scrap:

Cash	XX	
Other income—scrap sales		XX

FIGURE 17.3   Property Retirements Schedule

X Co.
Property Retirements
12-31-X8

G-3

J. Jones
1-24-x9

Eqt. No.	Description	Date Acquired	Date Retired	Cost	Accumulated Depreciation	Salvage Proceeds	Gain (Loss)	Federal Tax Status
M482	Electric motor	3-30-X3 ✓	11-14-X8 ✓	1,976 ✓	1,083 ∿	25 X	(868) ∿	L.T. ∿
G312	Grinding machine	1-20-X5 ✓	9-3-X8 ✓	2,501 ✓	938 ∿	1,750 X	187 ∿	L.T. ∿
				20,532	18,753	1,893	114	
				φ	φ		40	

✓ Traced to detail property ledger.
X Traced to cash receipt book.
∿ Recalculated.

If the scrap was a piece of obsolete equipment, the auditor should be aware that perhaps the entry is incomplete and should have been:

Cash	XX	
Accumulated depreciation	XX	
Loss on sale of assets	XX	
Property and equipment		XX

The improper recording of the transaction changed it from a loss to income. The auditor should investigate the transaction by inquiry and inspection of relevant documents.

Audit of Depreciation

Auditors can become so involved in the detailed calculations of depreciation expense that they lose overall perspective of the account. They should remember that depreciation expense results from the allocation of the cost of assets over an *estimated* time period by an *arbitrary* method and that it may be unrealistic to expect to calculate and verify this allocation to the nearest dollar. Usually, groups of assets with similar lives and the same depreciation method, such as buildings and equipment, can be tested on an overall basis. For example, if equipment is depreciable on a straight-line basis over ten years with a 5 percent salvage value, the auditor could average the beginning and ending balances of the asset account, reduce it by 5 percent, and multiply the remaining balance by 10 percent. This figure is seldom exactly equal to the client's depreciation expense because of the uneven rate of additions and retirements during the year, fully depreciated assets, and other factors, but it gives the auditor an idea of the reasonableness of the calculation. If the overall calculation is materially different from the client's amount, detailed tests of individual items may be necessary. Auditors must also be satisfied that all depreciation calculations are made on a basis consistent with the calculations of the prior year.

Auditing Depreciation Expense

When auditing depreciation expense, it is helpful to consider what could be misstated and what audit procedure is likely to detect the misstatement. Consider the following calculation:

Cost	$10,000	◄—The cost of the asset may be incorrect. (1)
Rate (10 year-straight-line method)	× 0.10	◄—The life of the asset may be inappropriate (2) and the method may not be generally accepted. (3)
Depreciation expense	$ 1,000	◄—The mathematical calculation may be incorrect. (4)

Audit procedures

1. Trace the cost to the detailed property ledger or auditor working paper.
2. Evaluate the reasonableness of the estimated life based on age, technological changes, and lives of similar assets.

> 3. Auditors need only determine if the method is generally accepted. They do not have to evaluate whether one generally accepted depreciation method is more appropriate than another generally accepted depreciation method unless there is a change in method.
> 4. Recompute the amount.
>
> The auditors should also consider whether anything has been omitted from the computation—such as salvage value.

In addition to testing depreciation expense for the year, the auditor must evaluate the adequacy of the balance of accumulated depreciation. The auditor is not an appraiser, but depreciation is not a valuation process. It is a process of allocation, and the auditor can use his or her business judgment to determine the reasonableness of the allocation of the remaining cost of an asset over its remaining useful life. In considering the reasonableness of the remaining useful life of an asset, the auditor must take into account not only its physical condition, but technological innovations and other factors as well. For example, a remaining estimated life of 15 years for a TV camera owned by a TV station would be unreasonable if the camera was incompatible with newly acquired equipment. Also, an estimated life of 30 years for a natural gas pipeline might be unreasonable if the natural gas reserves amounted to only a 10-year supply. Such examples show the importance of the business approach in the audit.

Property Disclosures

The auditor should determine that adequate disclosure is made of the functional nature of property and equipment. Disclosures of depreciation amounts and methods of calculation are required by generally accepted accounting principles. In addition, disclosure should be made of any mortgages or liens. Many, though not all, mortgages arise in the initial acquisition of an item of property. In the audit of property additions, the auditor must be alert for mortgages associated with any noncash acquisitions of property. Mortgages and liens may also be detected by inspection of notes, bonds, and loan agreements, confirmation with financial institutions, review of minutes, and inquiry of management, all of which have been discussed in other sections.

Value-Added Audit Considerations for Property and Equipment

While performing procedures applicable to property and equipment the auditor should consider such matters as: Has management considered alternative methods of acquiring property and equipment? Are idle assets promptly converted into cash? How does the entity maintain security for its property and equipment? When will new property and equipment be needed, and how will it be financed? Helping management focus on questions such as these adds value to the audit.

▶ **EXAMPLE**

An auditor noted that a not-for-profit (tax-exempt) hospital client purchased all of its equipment. The auditor suggested that the equipment be purchased by a financing institution that could utilize the income tax deductions generated by the purchase of the equipment.

The financing institution could lease the equipment to the hospital at a reduced rate because of the benefits it obtained from the tax deductions. This plan added value to the audit by saving substantial sums for the hospital over the life of the equipment.

Summary of Important Substantive Tests for Property and Equipment

- Perform analytical procedures.
- Analyze property and equipment additions and examine supporting vendor invoices, canceled checks, receiving reports, and capitalization decisions.
- Analyze repair and maintenance expense and examine supporting vendor invoices, canceled checks, receiving reports, and expense decisions.
- Test recorded property and equipment retirements by tracing cost and accumulated depreciation to the detail property ledger.
- Search for unrecorded property and equipment retirements by inquiry of management and operating personnel, tour of plant to identify selected items, and investigation of major additions that represent replacements, reduction of insurance coverage or property tax base, and salvage credits and scrap sales.
- Test depreciation expenses by reference to the asset base, expected useful life, and depreciation method.
- Evaluate the adequacy of the accumulated depreciation.
- Review property additions, loan agreements, minutes, and confirmations and inquire of management regarding liens, mortgages, and other disclosures.

LONG-TERM INVESTMENTS AND INTANGIBLES

Long-term investments can take many forms. They may be debt or equity, marketable or nonmarketable, affiliated or nonaffiliated, and so on. Auditors depend on their knowledge of generally accepted accounting principles to determine the appropriate valuations and disclosures in each case. Long-term investments may not be significant for a manufacturing company but are likely to constitute the most significant asset of an investment company.

The physical evidence of long-term investments usually takes the form of stock or bond certificates (other forms include joint venture agreements, real estate deeds, and mineral leases), with evidence of ownership indicated either on the certificate (registered form) or by possession (bearer form). Certificates may be held by the company that owns them or by a bank or other financial institution as custodian for the company. If held by the company, the certificates should be stored in a bank safe deposit box. The level of control risk is reduced if dual access (the requirement that two individuals be present for access) is required for entry to the box.

Long-term investments may be valued on the basis of cost, underlying equity, or market value. General disclosures relating to long-term investments include the type of investment and basis of valuation; additional disclosures apply in many cases.

Intangibles include goodwill, franchises, patents, and organizational costs. The existence and ownership of goodwill subsequent to the transaction in which it is established are subjective and difficult to evaluate. However, other intangibles are represented by legal documents, such as franchise agreements, patents, or corporate articles of incorporation. Acquisition cost, less amortization, is generally the valuation basis for intangibles. Costs of developing, maintaining, or restoring intangible assets that are not specifically identifiable, have indeterminate lives, or are inherent in a continuing business and related to an enterprise as a whole—such as goodwill—should be deducted from income when incurred. Amortization is usually computed on the straight-line method over the periods estimated to be benefited but not to exceed 40 years.

Audit Objectives

The objective (assertions) in the audit of long-term investments and intangibles are as follows.

1. To determine whether all (completeness) long-term investments are represented by certificates of ownership owned by and held by or for the company, and that intangibles are represented by contractual rights, privileges, or earning power (goodwill) owned by the company (existence and rights).
2. To determine whether long-term investments are properly stated on the basis of accounting principles applicable in the circumstances, and whether intangibles are stated at cost less amortization (valuation and presentation).
3. To determine whether disclosures concerning long-term investments and intangibles are adequate and in accordance with generally accepted accounting principles (presentation).

Audit Procedures and Working Papers

The auditor must consider internal control policies and procedures for the physical security or evidence of ownership of long-term investments, cash disbursements for long-term investments and intangibles, and amortization policies for intangibles.

The following are some of the possible effects of internal control on the scope of substantive tests: (1) maintaining investment securities in a bank safe deposit box, as opposed to an office safe, is likely to allow the auditor to perform the security count at a time other than year-end, (2) board of director authorization and approval of acquisition of investments, patents, and so forth may allow the auditor to reduce the scope of work on additions to these accounts, and (3) standard monthly journal entries to amortize the balances of intangibles should reduce the chance of omitting amortization and allow the auditor to reduce the extent of tests of amortization. Other examples of internal control policies and procedures and substantive tests related to specific assertions for the investment account are shown below.

Assertions	Examples of internal control policies and procedures	Examples of substantive tests
1. Existence	1. Require signatures of two officers for access to bank safe deposit box.	1. Examine securities maintained in bank safe deposit box.

Assertions	Examples of internal control policies and procedures	Examples of substantive tests
2. Rights	2. Control environment (require board of director approval for pledging of investments).	2. Examine securities to determine if they are registered in the client's name with no indication of pledging.
3. Completeness	3. Control environment (have internal auditors compare contents of safe deposit box with related investments on a periodic basis).	3. Analytical procedures (match dividend and interest income with related investments).
4. Valuation	4. Control environment (adequately trained personnel with expertise to determine proper valuation of investments under GAAP).	4. Review method of valuation for compliance with GAAP and test computation by reference to brokers' advices, market quotations, or audited financial statements of investees.
5. Presentation	5. Control environment (adequately trained personnel with expertise to determine proper classification under GAAP).	5. Review classification of investments as long or short term and confirm management intentions in a representation letter.

Analytical Procedures

The auditor may make the following comparisons in performing analytical procedures for these accounts:

1. Current-year balance with current-year budget and prior-year actual.
2. Ratio of investment income (dividends and interest) to balance in investment accounts for the current and prior year.
3. Amortization costs for the current and prior year.
4. Ratio of amortization costs to unamortized balances for the current and prior year.

Such comparisons may identify improperly recorded purchases and sales of investments and intangible assets and erroneous recording of investment income or amortization of intangible assets.

Security Count

One means of determining that long-term investments exist and are owned by the company is physical inspection of the certificates, often referred to as a *security count*.

Security counts must be made as of the audit date, unless provisions can be made to verify that there has been no access to the certificates between the audit date and the date they are inspected. This verification can often be provided by examination of banks' records of access to safe deposit boxes (usually confirmed to the auditor by the bank in writing) or the use of seals by the auditor. This precaution

FIGURE 17.4   Long-Term Investments—Security Count Schedule

X Co.
Long-Term Investments
Security Count Listing
12–31–X8

H-2

J. Jones
1-2-x9

Box 43 at First National Bank

Certificate No.	Description	No. of shares or Face Value
OC1141 ✓	Beta Company ✓ common stock, ✓ no par ✓ value, dated 9-26-X5 ✓	100 ✓
X5303 ✓	Buff Co. subordinated convertible ✓ debentures, 6%, ✓ dated 9-28-X8, ✓ due 9-29-Y3 ✓	$10,000 ✓

✓ *Inspected certificate in the name of X Co. with no endorsements.*
The above listed securities were counted in my presence and returned to me intact on 1-2-X9 at 11:00 a.m.
Jerry Armstrong, Vice Pres.
William Snow, Treasurer
Note: I examined the bank entry records and noted the last entry to Box 43 was on 11-4-X8. See confirmation letter from bank on H-3.   *J. Jones*

is necessary to prevent the removal and sale or pledge of the investments as of the audit date to cover a shortage, and their subsequent replacement without the auditor's knowledge.

A security count of any size requires careful planning because, once the count is under way, it is very difficult to modify the procedures to any great extent. Among the more essential matters that should be considered are (1) obtaining a list of the locations of all securities, and the type and volume of securities at each place, (2) providing for the simultaneous control or count of all securities and cash, (3) arranging for the continuous presence of representatives of the client during the count, and (4) preparing lists of securities to be counted.

The working paper schedule evidencing the security count should include such details as company name, certificate number, number of shares, par value, face value, interest rate, due date, and issue date. An example of such a working paper is shown in Figure 17.4. Note that there is evidence on the working paper that the auditor inspected each certificate, that the inspection was performed in the presence of company officers, and that the certificates were returned intact to the company officers. The security count schedule is later compared with the description of the investments in the accounting records.

Although the auditor cannot be expected to recognize or uncover expertly forged securities, tests of apparent authenticity should be made during the count by noting the signatures of the trustee, registrar, transfer agent, and corporate officers, the presence of a corporate seal, and so forth.

Confirmation

Certificates evidencing long-term investments may be held for the company by financial institutions or others. If certificates are held by a reputable bank or other financial institution, the auditor will normally use a confirmation letter to confirm their existence with the holder. If, however, the certificates are held by an institution that is unknown to the auditor, he or she should not accept a confirmation without some inquiry into the nature of the institution. In addition, in the case of bonds, debentures, loans, and other debt obligations, the amount due should be confirmed directly with the debtor.

Valuation

Once the auditor has established the proper valuation basis for an investment under generally accepted accounting principles, he or she should perform audit procedures to determine whether that basis is being used. If **cost** is the valuation basis, the auditor should examine documentation (broker's advice, canceled check, etc.) for the acquisition of the investment. If **underlying equity** is the valuation basis, *audited* financial statements of the investee constitute sufficient evidential matter as to the equity in the underlying net assets, but unaudited financial statements do not. Therefore, if an investment accounted for by the equity method is material, the scope of an auditor's examination may be limited if the financial statements of the investee company are not audited. Finally, if **market** is the valuation basis, market quotations from such sources as the *Wall Street Journal* or *Barron's* may be used if the prices are based on a reasonably broad and active market and there are no restrictions on the transfer of the investment.

Because intangible assets are generally valued on the basis of cost less amortization, the auditor should evaluate the propriety of their deferral, examine documentation of their acquisition cost (franchise and merger agreements, invoices, canceled checks, etc.), and test the accuracy of the amortization. He or she also should evaluate the amortization period to determine whether any current events or circumstances warrant revision. Disposition or discontinuance of all or a portion of a business acquired in a business combination accounted for as a purchase would require the writeoff of the related goodwill.

Purchases and Sales of Investments

Some evidence regarding existence, rights, and valuation of investments is obtained by examining relevant documents. For the purchase of a publicly traded security, the auditor examines a *broker's advice* (a statement from a broker that shows the securities purchased, the date, the price, the commission, the total cost, and other germane information). When a security is sold, the auditor also examines a broker's advice, but it will show the sales price, which is not necessarily the cost, underlying equity, or other amount to be removed from the investment account. The difference between the amount at which the investment was recorded and the proceeds from the sale as shown on the broker's advice represents a gain or loss. This amount will be recalculated by the auditor.

Investment-Related Income

It is often convenient and efficient to audit dividend and interest income at the time investments are audited, and the audit procedures are usually recorded on the same audit working papers. Dividends can be tested by multiplying the number of shares (from the security count schedule if there were no changes during the year) by the dividend rate (per *Standard & Poor's Dividend Record,* audited financial statements of the investee, etc.). Interest income can be recomputed on the basis of face amount, interest rate, and period held (from the security count schedule or confirmation). Auditors account for all investment securities for which dividend or interest income was received as a test of the completeness assertion for investments.

**Summary of Important Substantive Tests
For Long-Term Investments and Intangibles**

- Perform analytical procedures.
- Perform security count or obtain confirmation to establish existence and rights of ownership.
- Test valuation by reference to broker's advice, canceled check, audited financial statements of investee, market values from financial publications, and franchise and merger agreements.
- Test purchases and sales of investments by reference to brokers' advices and other documents.
- Test investment-related income by reference to published dividend and interest sources.
- Test amortization of intangibles for accuracy and consistency.
- Review agreements and minutes for necessary disclosures.

LONG-TERM LIABILITIES

Long-term liabilities include loans, bonds, and notes payable that generally are due after one year from the balance sheet date, although certain amounts due within one year may be classified as long-term if both the intention and ability to refinance on a long-term basis are demonstrated.

Long-term liabilities, such as loans, bonds, and notes, have several characteristics that require particular attention from the auditor. First, they are often collateralized or secured by certain of the company's assets. The result is restriction of the free transferability of such assets.

Second, the debt instrument may be subject to the provisions of a separate but related *debt agreement* that may also place restraints on the company's operations. Provisions commonly found in debt agreements include requirements that the company maintain specified working capital and debt to equity ratios, as well as restrictions on payment of dividends, purchase of treasury stock, and merger or sale of the company or a significant portion of its assets. Violation of any of these provisions constitutes an event of default, which allows the debtholder to require immediate payment. If a provision is violated inadvertently and the debtholder has no reason to believe the loan is in danger, he or she will usually, on request from the company, waive the right to immediate payment. If a waiver is obtained, the financial statements should disclose that a violation occurred and was waived by the debtholder. If a waiver is refused, the debt should be classified as a current liability because payment can be demanded at any time by the debtholder. Obviously, such an event could have a catastrophic effect on a company.

Control features specifically applicable to long-term debt include the requirements that all borrowings be approved by the board of directors and that a checklist of requirements and restrictions in debt agreements be maintained to prevent inadvertent noncompliance.

Audit Objectives

The objectives (assertions) in the audit of long-term liabilities are as follows.

1. To determine whether all (completeness) long-term liabilities existing or incurred (existence and obligations) as of the audit date are reflected properly in the financial statements (valuation).
2. To determine whether long-term liabilities consist of amounts due after one year from the audit date (or operating cycle), or short-term obligations for which the intention and ability to refinance on a long-term basis have been demonstrated (presentation).
3. To determine whether disclosures regarding long-term liabilities are adequate (disclosure).

Audit Procedures and Working Papers

The first step is to assess control risk applicable to long-term debt assertions. Specific examples of the effect of internal control on substantive tests for long-term liabilities are as follows: (1) the requirement that the board of directors authorize all borrowings reduces the probabilities of unrecorded borrowings and may allow the auditor to limit the search for unrecorded borrowings by confirmation and other means, (2) the utilization of a bond trustee would allow the auditor to limit confirmation work to one confirmation with the trustee, and (3) a calendar of principal and interest payments helps to prevent overlooking a payment and lets the auditor reduce the time spent in determining that all required principal and interest payments have been made. Other examples of internal control policies and procedures and substantive tests related to specific assertions for long-term liability accounts are shown below.

Assertions	Examples of internal control policies and procedures	Examples of substantive tests
1. Existence	1. Control environment (adequately trained personnel—entities seldom record long-term debt that does not exist).	1. Confirmation of balance due to creditor.
2. Obligations	2. Control environment (adequately trained personnel—entities seldom record long-term debt that is not owed).	2. Confirmation of obligation with creditor.
3. Completeness	3. Control environment (require board of director approval of all borrowings).	3. Send confirmations to all financial institutions with which business was transacted during the period.

Assertions	Examples of internal control policies and procedures	Examples of substantive tests
4. Valuation	4. Control environment (adequately trained personnel with expertise to account for debt premium and discount).	4. Recalculate the computation of debt premium and discount.
5. Presentation	5. Control environment (adequately trained personnel with expertise to compute current portion of long-term debt).	5. Recalculate current portion of long-term debt.

The auditor prepares an audit lead schedule similar to the one in Figure 17.5 for long-term debt.

Analytical Procedures

In performing analytical procedures on long-term liabilities, the auditor may compare

1. Balances of the current and prior year.
2. Recorded borrowings and repayments to cash flow budgets.
3. Computed average interest rate (calculated by dividing interest expense by the average of the beginning and ending debt balances) with the stated interest rate.

The auditor should investigate significant variations to determine whether borrowings and repayments are properly recorded and interest expense is properly calculated.

Tests of Borrowings, Repayments, and Accrued Interest

Because long-term debt transactions often are few but relatively important, the auditor often examines all transactions in the account for the year, although samples may be used if the volume of transactions is large and the size of individual transactions is small. The auditor traces the proceeds from any borrowings to the cash receipts records, deposit slips, and bank statement, and audits payments by examining canceled checks (indicated by $\checkmark$ in Figure 17.5) and canceled notes, if paid in full. The authorization of all significant borrowings and any repayments not made in accordance with the terms of the debt instrument should be traced to minutes of meetings of the board of directors.

Interest payable is tested on the same schedule as long-term debt so that it can be related visually to the long-term debt balance. The simple example with only one note presents no problem, but if 30 or 40 notes were outstanding, this format would allow the auditor to determine quickly whether interest had been computed for each note and that there were recorded notes (completeness) for all interest expense. The fact that interest has been computed for each note, however, does not guarantee that it is computed correctly. The auditor tested interest expense at ① in Figure 17.5 by multiplying the outstanding balance by the interest rate and the fraction of the year it was outstanding. The accrued balance at the end of the year was tested in a similar manner at ② with the further step of relating

FIGURE 17.5 Long-term Debt Lead Schedule

X Co.
Long-Term Debt Lead Schedule
12-31-X8

J. Jones
1-18-X9

R

Debt

Description	Balance 12-31-X7	Additions	Retirements	Balance 12-31-X8	Balance 12-31-X7
¢ 8% note payable to a bank, due $50,000 per year to 12-1-Y4, secured by land and building ¢	350,000 ✗	0	50,000 √	300,000 ¢ √	2,333 ✗
	TB-2			TB-2	ρ

Interest Payable

	Provision	Payments	Balance 12-31-X8
	27,665 ①	27,998 ✗	2,000 ②
	40	ρ	ρ

Test of accrued interest

Note balance	300,000
Interest rate	0.08
	24,000
Accrual period ¢ 12-1 to 12-31 or one month	1/12
	2,000 ②

Test of interest expense

350,000 × .08 × 11/12	=	25,665	
300,000 × .08 × 1/12	=	2,000	
		27,665 ①	

¢ Confirmed by bank—See A-1.
✗ Traced to prior year working papers.
√ Examined canceled check.
√ Traced to general ledger.
✗ Examined canceled checks for the February and November payments.

the date to which interest was paid (the beginning of the accrual period) to the bank confirmation filed in the cash section (Figure 15.3). In addition, canceled checks were examined for two months' interest payments (indicated by χ in Figure 17.5), and the provision for interest expense was cross-referenced to the related expense account.

Confirmation

If the debtholder is a bank, the standard bank confirmation form (Figure 15.3) should be used; otherwise, a separate letter requesting similar information must be prepared. Note that in Figure 17.5 the pertinent data have been indicated as confirmed by the bank and cross-referenced to the bank confirmation (see $\mathbb{C}$). Confirmations normally are sent to all financial institutions with which the client has had dealings during the year, regardless of whether or not there is a balance at the end of the year. Although auditors anticipate that they will not receive replies to all of their requests for confirmation of accounts receivable and accounts payable, they usually require confirmation from all significant debtholders before releasing their report on the financial statements. Thus, personal followup by the auditor and the client may be needed in addition to second requests.

Review of Debt Agreements

The auditor's review of debt agreements must be performed carefully and thoroughly. If the meaning or intent of a provision in an agreement is unclear, the auditor should ask the client to request an interpretation from the debtholder. All violations of a debt agreement, no matter how minor, should be referred to the client so that waivers can be requested.

Examples of Provisions of Debt Agreements

The following are examples of provisions often found in debt agreements that are of particular interest to auditors.

Provision	*Audit evidence*
1. The client must maintain a current ratio of at least 2 to 1.	1. Compute current ratio, considering total likely misstatements, to determine if it equals or exceeds 2 to 1.
2. The client cannot pay cash dividends in any year in excess of $1 million.	2. Compare total cash dividends paid during the year with $1 million.
3. The client must maintain a debt to equity ratio of not more than 0.75 to 1.0.	3. Compute the debt to equity ratio, considering total likely misstatements, to determine if it exceeds 0.75 to 1.0.

The review of debt agreements often is documented with the use of a checklist of the debt agreement provisions in the permanent audit file. This checklist must be reviewed each year and an indication made by each provision as to whether or not it was complied with. Because this procedure requires a knowledge of all aspects of the audit, it generally is performed by the audit senior and is reviewed closely by the audit manager and partner.

Classification and Disclosure

Although the stated maturity date of a note often determines its classification as either a long- or short-term liability, other factors, such as the intent and ability to refinance or an unwaived violation of a debt agreement, may change that classification. The information about long-term liabilities that is to be disclosed in the financial statements should be requested in the confirmation from the debtholder.

Value-Added Audit Considerations for Long-Term Debt

While performing audit procedures applicable to long-term debt the auditor can add value to the audit by being sure that management considers such matters as: Does the entity have the ability to repay its debt? Is short-term debt being used for long-term purposes? Is the debt-to-equity ratio reasonable considering the entity's risk? Is additional debt financing available if needed? Does the entity maintain relationships with more than one financial institution?

▶ EXAMPLE

An auditor became concerned upon noting that a client was using short-term debt to finance long-term projects. If the short-term debt could not be refinanced, the company could be forced into a financial reorganization even though it was profitable. The auditor encouraged management to consider the establishment of a long-term line of credit at a bank or the sale of additional equity to prevent a potential financial crisis.

Summary of Important Substantive Tests for Long-Term Liabilities

- Perform analytical procedures.
- Trace new borrowings to authorizations in minutes and cash receipts records, deposit slips, and bank statements.
- Trace repayments to canceled checks and canceled notes.
- Recompute interest expense for the period and accrued interest at end of period.
- Obtain confirmation of amount and terms of long-term debt.
- Review the provisions of debt agreements to determine compliance.
- Evaluate the propriety of classification and disclosure of long-term liabilities.

EQUITY ACCOUNTS

Equity accounts include common and preferred stock, additional paid-in capital, retained earnings, valuation accounts for marketable securities and foreign currency translation, and treasury stock. (Partnership and proprietorship capital also would be included, but are not discussed in this text.) Transactions in these accounts are relatively infrequent but can be important.

The articles of incorporation of a company state the classes of stock it is authorized to issue, as well as the rights and preferences of each class, the number of shares of each class that is authorized, the par value, if any, of such stock, and any restrictions that may attach to it. The articles of incorporation of some companies provide for the restriction of dividends on common stock in the event that all preferred dividends are not paid; those of other companies, particularly companies that are closely held, require stock to be offered to the company at a certain price (such as book value) before it can be sold to another party. Thus, the articles of incorporation are the source of many financial statement disclosures.

The corporate secretary is normally responsible for the records relating to the number of shares of issued and outstanding stock. The procedures used by a company to account for and control the number of shares of stock issued and outstanding are determined largely by the number of its stockholders. If the number of stockholders is small, a company usually maintains a stock certificate book or stockbook. This book is similar to a checkbook in that it consists of a detachable stock certificate attached to a permanently bound stub on which can be entered the number of shares, date the certificate was issued, and name of the stockholder. When stock is sold or transferred, the stock certificate of the original stockholder is surrendered to the company so that it can be marked "canceled" and reattached to the stub from which it was issued. A new certificate is issued to the new stockholder. The number of shares issued at any time is determined by adding the numbers of shares shown on all stock certificate stubs that do not have canceled certificates attached to them. This procedure is adequate if the number of stockholders and stock transfers is small but obviously would be impractical if hundreds or thousands of shares were transferred daily.

Public companies whose stock is traded actively on stock exchanges usually employ banks or other financial institutions to act as transfer agents and registrars. As transfer agents, these institutions receive and issue certificates and maintain lists of stockholders for use in mailing stockholder reports, paying dividends, and so forth. As registrars, they maintain records of the number of shares issued and canceled to check on the transactions of the transfer agent and to guard against mistakes that could result in an overissue of stock.

Treasury stock should be recorded at cost, and it is generally shown as a deduction from other equity items in the balance sheet. Treasury stock certificates should be stored in a safe deposit box and safeguarded in the same manner as investment securities.

The retained earnings account should contain few transactions other than net income or loss and dividend contributions. *FASB Statement No. 16* requires, with certain exceptions, that all items of profit and loss recognized during a period be included in earnings for that period. Only two items may be treated as prior-period adjustments—corrections of errors in the financial statements of a prior period and tax adjustments resulting from realization of income tax benefits of preacquisition operating loss carry-forwards of purchased subsidiaries.

Many companies have stock option plans for officers and key employees. If these plans are used, records must be maintained of the number of options authorized, granted, exercised, and expired, as well as option prices and periods covered.

Audit Objectives

The objectives (assertions) in the audit of the equity accounts are as follows.

1. To determine whether the equity accounts and all (completeness) of the transactions therein as shown in the financial statements (existence) are presented in accordance with generally accepted accounting principles (valuation).

2. To determine whether adequate disclosure is made of all restrictions, rights, options, and other matters important to an understanding of the financial statements (presentation).

Audit Procedures and Working Papers

In examining equity accounts, an auditor must keep in mind that the audit is being made of the company and *not* of its stockholders. Transfers of shares between stockholders and the number of shares owned by individual stockholders are theoretically of no concern to the auditor, because they have no effect on the financial statements being audited. The auditor is concerned only with the total authorized, issued, and outstanding stock and not with its ownership, although knowledge of ownership may aid the auditor in identifying related parties. For this reason, auditors normally do not confirm stock ownership with individual stockholders.

The auditor should understand the internal control applicable to the equity accounts and may conduct tests of controls over cash receipts and cash disbursements. However, because of the limited number of transactions and their importance, the auditor often examines all transactions in the accounts. The cost of performing tests of controls applicable to assertions for this account may exceed the benefits from reduction of substantive tests. However, certain controls may affect the extent of substantive tests. Some examples are: (1) the use of independent transfer agents and registrars allows the auditor to gather evidence of the number of shares issued and outstanding with a confirmation rather than through an examination of the stockbook and (2) the use of an imprest bank account may allow the auditor to reduce the scope of examination of individual dividend payments. Other examples of internal control policies and procedures and substantive tests related to capital stock are shown below.

Assertions	Examples of internal control policies and procedures	Examples of substantive tests
1. Existence	1. Maintain stockbook showing number of shares issued, canceled, and outstanding.	1. Examination of stockbook.
2. Obligations	2. Not applicable.	2. Not applicable.
3. Completeness	3. Maintain stockbook showing number of shares issued, canceled, and outstanding.	3. Examination of stockbook.

Assertions	Examples of internal control policies and procedures	Examples of substantive tests
4. Valuation	4. Control environment (adequately trained financial personnel who can record capital stock transactions in accordance with GAAP).	4. Calculate par value or other basis of stock issued and retired.
5. Presentation	5. Control environment (adequately trained financial personnel who can determine disclosures necessary for compliance with GAAP; e.g., dividend restrictions).	5. Review financial statements for appropriate disclosures under GAAP.

All equity accounts should be analyzed (often on a schedule maintained in the permanent audit file), and transactions during the year should be audited by examination of supporting documents and authorizations. For example, if additional stock is sold during the year, the proceeds should be traced to the cash receipts book and bank statement and the authorization of the sale should be traced to minutes of stockholder or directors' meetings. Particular attention should be paid to the valuation attributed to stock issued for noncash consideration, the treatment of gains or losses from sale or retirement of treasury stock, the propriety of entries to retained earnings other than net income or loss and dividends, and the accounting treatment of stock dividends and splits.

Analytical Procedures
For the equity section of the balance sheet the auditor will compare

1. The current balance with the budgeted and prior-year amounts.
2. Dividend payments with cash flow budgets.

All significant differences should be investigated.

Tests of Dividends
Total dividends declared during a year can be tested on an overall basis by multiplying the number of shares outstanding at the dividend record date by the dividend rate per share. This procedure provides evidence that the proper amount was calculated, but the auditor should also obtain evidence that it was paid to the stockholders.

Some companies engage a bank or trust company as a dividend-paying agent. In these cases, the company pays the total dividend to its dividend-paying agent, which makes the dividend distributions to the individual stockholders. The auditor examines the canceled check for the total dividend and the notice of receipt from the agent.

If a company pays its own dividends, the auditor should test the propriety of the payments to the individual stockholders. An example of such a test, which may be

FIGURE 17.6 Test of Dividend Payments

X Co.					*I-1*
Test of Dividend Payments					*J. Jones*
12–31–X8					*1-10-x9*

Shareholder	Shares of Record	Dividend Rate	Amount	Check Number
C. H. Dahl ✓	10,500 ✓	.50 ∧	5,250 ⚹	318 X
F. W. Tucei ✓	100 ✓	.50 ∧	50 ⚹	319 X
L. W. Lane ✓	638 ✓	.50 ∧	319 ⚹	320 X
J. W. Miley ✓	24 ✓	.50 ∧	12 ⚹	321 X

	100,000		50,000	
	I-4		*TB-2*	

✓ *Per stock record as of dividend date.*
∧ *Per 12-15-X8 minutes of B/D.*
⚹ *Calculation checked by computer.*
X *Examined properly endorsed canceled check.*

done on a sample basis, is shown in Figure 17.6. The auditor obtained the stockholder's name and number of shares owned of record as of the dividend record date from the stockbook (indicated by ✓). He or she also totaled the number of shares owned by all stockholders and related it to the total shares outstanding as shown in the account analysis in the permanent audit file. (*I-4* is an illustration of a method of indexing the permanent audit file.) The auditor then compared the dividend rate with that shown in the minutes of the specific meeting at which the dividend was declared and recomputed the calculation of the individual dividend payments. Finally, he or she examined the canceled check in payment of the dividend, noting particularly that it was endorsed properly by the stockholder.

Examination of Stockbook and Treasury Stock

If a company maintains its own stock records, the auditor should examine the stockbook to determine whether the proper number of shares is shown as being issued in the financial statements. Because many of the same stockbook stubs and canceled certificates are examined each year, the auditor commonly maintains a permanent audit file schedule that can be used to document the examination for several years. An illustration of such a schedule is shown in Figure 17.7. The auditor must account for all certificate numbers by examining the stockbook stubs for outstanding shares (indicated by ∧), canceled certificates for retired shares (indicated by ✓), and unissued certificates for the balance. The total of the shares outstanding has been

FIGURE 17.7   **Stockbook Examination Schedule**

Certificate Number	Stockholder	Date Issued	Number of Shares	Date Retired	No. of New Certificate (if transfer)	Shares 19X7	Outstanding 19X8	Per Examination 19X9
								J-4
21	C. R. Dahl	3-3-X6	10,000			10,000	10,000 ⋏	
22	R. W. Roth	3-3-X6	24	1-6-X8	25	24	0 ✓	
23	F. W. Tucei	6-10-X7	100			100	100 ⋏	
24	L. W. Lane	11-30-X7	638			638	638 ⋏	
25	J. W. Miley	1-6-X8	24				24 ⋏	
						100,000 ✗		
						* $1	100,000 ✗	
						100,000	* $1	
							100,000	

✗ *Par value per articles of incorporation.*
⋏ *Examined stock book stub with Federal tax stamp.*
✓ *Examined canceled stock certificate attached to stub.*

Unused stock certificates remaining in Stockbook per examination   .25-100   26-100

R. Parker   J. Jones
1-3-X8   1-7-X9

multiplied by the par value to produce the dollar amount of capital stock shown in the financial statements.

If the client possesses treasury stock, it should be inspected. The schedule evidencing this inspection should include the certificate number, date, and number of shares. All treasury stock certificates should be in the name of the company. The inspection should be made in a manner similar to that of a security count, described earlier in this chapter.

Confirmation

If the client employs a transfer agent and registrar, there will be no stock certificate book to examine. Instead, the number of shares issued and outstanding should be confirmed in writing directly from the transfer agent and registrar to the auditor.

Review of Articles of Incorporation

The auditor reviews the articles of incorporation (updated for any amendments during the year noted while reading the minutes) for descriptions, par values, numbers of shares authorized, and other pertinent information concerning both common and preferred stock.

Matters Requiring Disclosure

The general disclosures required of all companies under generally accepted accounting principles, such as capital changes, stock options, liquidation value of preferred stock, and limitations on stock transfers, can usually be related to corporate documents such as the articles of incorporation or minutes of meetings of stockholders or directors. Normally, they present no special problems.

Disclosures of restrictions such as limitations or prohibitions on payment of cash dividends and purchase of treasury stock are more difficult to detect. Most restrictions of this nature are due to provisions in debt and lease agreements and should be found by use of the procedures discussed in the long-term debt section, such as review of debt (and lease) agreements and minutes, and confirmations with debtholders. Other restrictions may arise from the laws of the state in which a company is incorporated. For example, several states have laws prohibiting the payment of dividends to the extent of the cost of treasury stock, thereby necessitating the disclosure of a restriction of retained earnings if treasury stock is held. To discover these disclosures the auditor must be familiar with the corporate codes of the states in which clients operate.

Value-Added Audit Considerations for the Equity Accounts

While performing audit procedures applicable to the equity accounts the auditor should consider such matters as: Is the company organized in the most appropriate business form (e.g., proprietorship, partnership, or corporation)? Is the company's equity properly structured, and are there plans to obtain additional equity as needed? Have stock options been properly used as a compensation device? Questions of a nonaccounting nature are important for adding value to an audit.

▶ EXAMPLE

The auditor of a closely held family business learned that management had plans for selling stock to the public and becoming a publicly held company. The auditor recommended the termination of certain related party transactions which, while common in closely held companies, are generally considered inappropriate for public companies. A year later when the company went public, it no longer engaged in related party transactions that were inappropriate for a public company.

**Summary of Important Substantive Tests
for Equity Accounts**

- Perform analytical procedures.
- Analyze changes in equity accounts for the period and examine support for changes, such as minutes of board of directors meetings, deposit slips, and bank statements for issuance of capital stock.
- Test dividends by reference to board of director meeting minutes for dividend rate and capital stock records for number of shares.
- Examine stockbook and treasury stock or confirm with the transfer agent and registrar to determine the number of shares issued and outstanding.
- Trace description of stock, par value, and number of shares authorized to articles of incorporation.
- Review minutes, debt agreements, and other sources for restrictions on dividends and capital stock transactions that require disclosure in the financial statements.

Chapter 17 ▶ GLOSSARY OF TERMS

Broker's advice   A statement from an investment broker that reports the purchase or sale of a security, including such matters as the name, number of shares or face value, price, total amount, and other terms of the transaction.

Debt or loan agreement   A legal document that places restrictions on a debtor for as long as the related debt is outstanding.

Security count   The physical inspection of investment and other securities.

Unrecorded property retirements   The sale, scrap, or other disposition of a physical property item that has not been recorded in the accounting records.

Vouching schedule   An analysis of individual additions to a specific account that is used by the auditor to indicate the evidence examined for such additions.

Waiver by debtholder   The relinquishment by the debtholder of the right to declare a loan immediately due and payable because of a violation of the debt agreement by the debtor.

Chapter 17 ▶ REFERENCES

American Institute of Certified Public Accountants. *Professional Standards* AU Section 332–Long-Term Investments

Chapter 17 ▶ REVIEW QUESTIONS

17-1   State the objectives in the audit of property and equipment and related accumulated depreciation.

17-2   What analytical procedures may be applied to property and equipment?

17-3   State the substantive tests applied to property and equipment to determine whether additions are
a. Recorded at cost.
b. Represented by actual physical items.
c. Properly capitalizable.

17-4   What test does the auditor make to determine if property additions are complete?

17-5   List five procedures the auditor could use to detect unrecorded property retirements.

17-6   What factors should an auditor consider in evaluating the adequacy of accumulated depreciation?

17-7   What are some inquiries an auditor can make when examining the property and equipment account to add value to the audit?

17-8   State the objectives in the audit of long-term investments and intangibles.

17-9   Describe four analytical procedures that may be applied to long-term investments and intangibles.

17-10   Why are security counts often made on the audit date? Under what circumstances may they be made at other dates?

17-11   What evidence would an auditor examine for investments valued at cost? Underlying equity? Market value?

17-12   How does the CPA audit dividend and interest income?

17-13   What evidence does an auditor examine in support of purchases and sales of publicly traded securities?

17-14   What is the significance of the violation of a provision of a debt agreement?

17-15   State the objectives in the audit of long-term liabilities.

17-16   Give three analytical procedures an auditor may apply to long-term liabilities.

17-17   What audit procedures does an auditor apply to borrowings and repayments of long-term debt?

17-18   Name two factors that can determine the financial statement classification of long-term debt, other than its maturity date.

17-19   What are some inquiries an auditor can make when examining the long-term debt account to add value to the audit?

17-20   Describe the two methods that may be used to control the number of shares of stock issued and outstanding.

17-21   State the objectives in the audit of the equity accounts.

17-22 Describe two analytical procedures that may be applied to the equity accounts.

17-23 Explain how and why the audit approach to testing dividend payments would differ for companies paying their own dividends and those employing dividend-paying agents.

17-24 Why does the auditor examine the client's stockbook?

17-25 What are some inquiries an auditor can make when examining the equity accounts to add value to the audit?

Chapter 17 ▶ OBJECTIVE QUESTIONS

(* = author prepared; ** = CPA examination)

*17-26 Which of the following audit procedures provides evidence regarding the valuation assertion for the purchase of an item of equipment?
 a. Examine a canceled check made payable to the seller of the equipment.
 b. Examine the physical item of equipment that was purchased.
 c. Examine an invoice from the seller of the equipment.
 d. Examine a depreciation schedule containing the item of equipment that was purchased.

**17-27 Property acquisitions that are misclassified as maintenance expense would most likely be detected by an internal control policy that provides for
 a. Review and approval of the monthly depreciation entry by the plant supervisor.
 b. Investigation of variances within a formal budgeting system.
 c. Segregation of duties of employees in the accounts payable department.
 d. Examination by the internal auditor of vendor invoices and canceled checks for property acquisitions.

**17-28 The auditor may conclude that depreciation charges are insufficient by noting
 a. Large amounts of fully depreciated assets.
 b. Continuous trade-ins of relatively new assets.
 c. Excessive recurring losses on assets retired.
 d. Insured values greatly in excess of book values.

**17-29 An auditor analyzes repairs and maintenance accounts primarily to obtain evidence in support of the audit assertion that all
 a. Noncapitalizable expenditures for repairs and maintenance have been properly charged to expense.
 b. Noncapitalizable expenditures for repairs and maintenance have been recorded in the proper period.
 c. Expenditures for property and equipment have *not* been charged to expense.

 d. Expenditures for property and equipment have been recorded in the proper period.

**17-30 In testing for unrecorded retirements of equipment, an auditor most likely would
 a. Select items of equipment from the accounting records and then locate them during the plant tour.
 b. Compare depreciation journal entries with similar prior-year entries in search of fully depreciated equipment.
 c. Inspect items of equipment observed during the plant tour and then trace them to the equipment subsidiary ledger.
 d. Scan the general journal for unusual equipment additions and excessive debits to repairs and maintenance expense.

**17-31 Which of the following would provide the best evidential matter pertaining to the annual valuation of a long-term investment in which the independent auditor's client owns a 30 percent voting interest?
 a. Market quotations of the investee company's stock.
 b. Current fair value of the investee company's assets.
 c. Audited financial statements of the investee company.
 d. Historical cost of the investee company's assets.

**17-32 A client has a large and active investment portfolio that is kept in a bank safe deposit box. If the auditor is unable to count the securities at the balance sheet date, the auditor most likely will
 a. Request the bank to confirm to the auditor the contents of the safe deposit box at the balance sheet date.
 b. Examine supporting evidence for transactions occurring during the year.
 c. Count the securities at a subsequent date and confirm with the bank whether securi-

ties were added or removed since the balance sheet date.

d. Request the client to have the bank seal the safe deposit box until the auditor can count the securities at a subsequent date.

**17-33 In establishing the existence and ownership of a long-term investment in the form of publicly traded stock, an auditor should inspect the securities or

a. Correspond with the investee company to verify the number of shares owned.

b. Inspect the audited financial statements of the investee company.

c. Confirm the number of shares owned that are held by an independent custodian.

d. Determine that the investment is carried at the lower of cost or market.

**17-34 An auditor testing long-term investments would ordinarily use analytical procedures to ascertain the reasonableness of the

a. Existence of unrealized gains or losses in the portfolio.

b. Completeness of recorded investment income.

c. Classification between current and noncurrent portfolios.

d. Valuation of marketable equity securities.

**17-35 In auditing the amount of goodwill recorded by a client, an auditor can obtain the most convincing evidence by comparing the recorded value of assets acquired with the

a. Appraised value as evidenced by independent appraisals.

b. Insured value as evidenced by insurance policies.

c. Assessed value as evidenced by tax bills.

d. Seller's book value as evidenced by audited financial statements.

**17-36 Two months before year-end, the bookkeeper erroneously recorded the receipt of a long-term bank loan by a debit to cash and a credit to sales. Which of the following is the most effective procedure for detecting this type of error?

a. Analyze the notes payable account.

b. Prepare a year-end bank reconciliation.

c. Analyze bank confirmation information.

d. Prepare a year-end bank transfer schedule.

**17-37 An auditor's purpose in reviewing the renewal of a note payable shortly after the balance sheet date most likely is to obtain evidence concerning management's assertions about

a. Existence or occurrence.

b. Presentation and disclosure.

c. Completeness.

d. Valuation or allocation.

**17-38 Of the following, which is the most efficient audit procedure for verification of interest expense on bonds payable?

a. Tracing interest declarations to an independent record book.

b. Recomputing interest expense.

c. Confirming interest rate with the holder of the bonds.

d. Examining the canceled interest checks.

**17-39 An auditor's program to examine long-term debt most likely would include steps that require

a. Comparing the carrying amount of the debt to its year-end market value.

b. Correlating interest expense recorded for the period with outstanding debt.

c. Verifying the existence of the holders of the debt by direct confirmation.

d. Inspecting the accounts payable subsidiary ledger for unrecorded long-term debt.

**17-40 During its fiscal year, a company issued a substantial amount of first-mortgage bonds at a discount. When performing audit work in connection with the bond issue, the independent auditor should

a. Confirm the existence of the bondholders.

b. Trace the net cash received from the issuance to the bond payable account.

c. Review the minutes for authorization.

d. Inspect the records maintained by the bond trustee.

*17-41 To ascertain the number of authorized shares of stock of a corporate client, the auditor relies primarily on the

a. Corporate minutes.

b. Bylaws.

c. Transfer agent.

d. Articles of incorporation.

**17-42 When a company has treasury stock certificates on hand, a year-end count of the certificates by the auditor is

a. Not required when the treasury stock is confirmed by the corporate secretary.

b. Always required.

c. Not required if treasury stock is a deduction from stockholders' equity.

d. Required if the company had treasury stock transactions during the year.

**17-43 Which of the following is the *most* important consideration of an auditor when examining the stockholders' equity section of a client's balance sheet?

a. Changes in the capital stock account are verified by an independent stock transfer agent.

b. Entries in the capital stock account can be traced to a resolution in the minutes of the board of directors' meetings.

c. Cash dividends during the year under audit are approved by the stockholders.

d. Stock dividends are capitalized at par or stated value on the dividend declaration date.

17-44 When a client company does *not* maintain its own stock records, the auditor should obtain written confirmation from the transfer agent and registrar concerning

a. The number of shares issued and outstanding.

b. Restrictions on the payment of dividends.

c. Guarantees of preferred stock liquidation value.

d. The number of shares subject to agreements to repurchase.

17-45 Items (a) through (f) represent audit objectives for the investments and property and equipment accounts. To the right of each set of audit objectives is a listing of possible audit procedures for that account. For each audit objective, select the audit procedure that would primarily respond to the objective. Select only one procedure for each audit objective. A procedure may be selected only once, or not at all.

Audit Objectives for Investments

a. Investments are properly described and classified in the financial statements.

b. Recorded investments represent investments actually owned at the balance sheet date.

c. Investments are properly valued at the lower of cost or market at the balance sheet date.

Audit Procedures for Investments

1. Trace opening balances in the subsidiary ledger to prior year's audit working papers.

2. Determine that employees who are authorized to sell investments do not have access to cash.

3. Examine supporting documents for a sample of investment transactions to verify that prenumbered documents are used.

4. Determine that any impairments in the price of investments have been properly recorded.

5. Verify that transfers from the current to the noncurrent investment portfolio have been properly recorded.

6. Obtain positive confirmations as of the balance sheet date of investments held by independent custodians.

7. Trace investment transactions to minutes of the board of directors meetings to determine that transactions were properly authorized.

Audit Objectives for Property and Equipment

d. The entity has legal right to property and equipment acquired during the year.

e. Recorded property and equipment represent assets that actually exist at the balance sheet date.

f. Net property and equipment are properly valued at the balance sheet date.

Audit Procedures for Property and Equipment

1. Trace opening balances in the summary schedules to the prior year's audit working papers.

2. Review the provision for depreciation expense and determine that depreciable lives and methods used in the current year are consistent with those used in the prior year.

3. Determine that the responsibility for maintaining the property and equipment records is segregated from the responsibility for custody of property and equipment.

4. Examine deeds and title insurance certificates.

5. Perform cutoff tests to verify that property and equipment additions are recorded in the proper period.

6. Determine that property and equipment are adequately insured.

7. Physically examine all major property and equipment additions.

Chapter 17 ▶ DISCUSSION/CASE QUESTIONS

(* = author prepared; ** = CPA examination)

*17-46   A staff assistant who was performing work in the property section of the Theta Industries audit prepared the vouching schedule for property additions shown below. Review this schedule and make notes of any deficiencies in the schedule or audit matters that require further attention.

Theta Industries
Property Additions
12-31-Z8

Vo. no.	Vendor	Amount	Description
1-403	Midway Ford	3,500√	Down payment on truck
3-112	Computerland	3,618√	Personal computer
5-016	Dover Construction	2,947	Pave driveway
7-358	Termite-Tex	731√	Annual termite inspection
9-274	Bean Furniture	9,822√	Desk
9-501	Dover Construction	1,713√	Paint offices
9-888	Dover Construction	1,713√	Paint offices
	Total	24,080	

√ Examined canceled check.

**17-47   In connection with a recurring audit of the financial statements of Louis Manufacturing Company for the year ended December 31, 19X9, you have been assigned the audit of the manufacturing equipment, manufacturing equipment–accumulated depreciation, and repairs to manufacturing equipment accounts. Your review of Louis's internal control policies and procedures has disclosed the following pertinent information:

1. The manufacturing equipment account includes the net invoice price plus related freight and installation costs for all of the equipment in Louis's manufacturing plant.

2. The manufacturing equipment and accumulated depreciation accounts are supported by a subsidiary ledger that shows the cost and accumulated depreciation for each piece of equipment.

3. An annual budget for capital expenditures of $100,000 or more is prepared by the budget committee and approved by the board of directors. Capital expenditures over $100,000 that are not included in this budget must be approved by the board of directors, and variations of 20 percent or more must be explained to the board. Approval by the supervisor of production is required for capital expenditures under $100,000.

4. Company employees handle installation, removal, repair, and rebuilding of the machinery. Work orders are prepared for these activities and are subject to the same budgetary control as other expenditures. Work orders are not required for external expenditures.

Required:

a. Cite the major objectives of your audit of the manufacturing equipment, manufacturing equipment–accumulated depreciation, and repairs of manufacturing equipment accounts. Do not include in this listing the auditing procedures designed to accomplish these objectives.

b. Prepare the portion of your audit program applicable to the audit of 19X9 additions to the manufacturing equipment account.

**17-48   In connection with the annual audit of Johnson Corporation, a manufacturer of janitorial supplies, you have been assigned to audit property and equipment. Johnson Corporation maintains a detailed ledger for all property and equipment. You prepared an audit program for the balances of property and equipment but have yet to prepare one for accumulated depreciation and depreciation expense.

Required:

Prepare a separate comprehensive audit program for the accumulated depreciation and depreciation expense accounts.

*17-49   One procedure for determining the existence of property and equipment is physical observation, although other methods may be as effective in some cases. Discuss means of gathering evidence as to the physical existence of the following property and equipment items, other than direct observation.

   a. A producing oil well.

   b. An apartment building.

   c. An automobile.

   d. A mineral lease.

*17-50   During your audit of property and equipment, you review the following construction work order listing:

Work order no.	Description	Amount authorized	Amount expended
3103	Construct branch sales office	$38,000	$40,500
3104	Replace fence around plant	7,600	6,950
3106	Resurface parking lot	5,900	6,030
3107	Install additional boiler	18,000	38,100
3108	Construct addition to president's residence	16,000	26,500
3109	Install drapes and carpets in treasurer's office	2,700	2,800

List the items you would select for additional audit followup and give your reasons for listing them.

**17-51   You have been engaged to audit the financial statements of the Elliott Company for the year ended December 31, 19X9. You performed a similar audit as of December 31, 19X8.

Following is the trial balance for the company as of December 31, 19X9:

	Dr. (Cr.)
Cash	$128,000
Interest receivable	47,450
Dividends receivable	1,750
6½% secured note receivable	730,000
Investments at fair value:	
Bowen common stock	322,000

	Dr. (Cr.)
Investments at equity:	
Woods common stock	284,000
Land	185,000
Accounts payable	(31,000)
Interest payable	(6,500)
8% secured note payable to bank	(275,000)
Common stock	(480,000)
Paid-in capital	(800,000)
Retained earnings	(100,500)
Dividend revenue	(3,750)
Interest revenue	(47,450)
Equity in earnings of investment carried at equity	(40,000)
Interest expense	26,000
General and administrative expense	60,000

You have obtained the following data concerning certain accounts:

The 6½ percent note receivable is due from Tysinger Corporation and is secured by a first mortgage on land sold to Tysinger by Elliott on December 21, 19X8. The note was to have been paid in 20 equal quarterly payments beginning March 31, 19X9, plus interest. Tysinger, however, is in very poor financial condition and has not made any principal or interest payments to date.

The Bowen common stock was purchased on September 21, 19X8, for cash in the market where it is actively traded. It is used as security for the note payable and is held by the bank. Elliott's investment in Bowen represents approximately one percent of the total outstanding shares of Bowen.

Elliott's investment in Woods represents 40 percent of the outstanding common stock; the stock is actively traded. Woods is audited by another CPA and has a December 31 year-end.

Elliott neither purchased nor sold any stock investments during the year other than those noted above.

Required:

For the following account balances, discuss (1) the types of evidential matter you should obtain and (2) the procedures you should perform during your audit.

a. 6½ percent secured note receivable.

b. Bowen common stock.

c. Woods common stock.

d. Dividend revenue.

**17-52   Larkin, CPA, has been engaged to audit the financial statements of Vernon Distributors, Inc., a continuing audit client, for the year ended September 30, 19X1. After obtaining an understanding of Vernon's internal control, Larkin assessed control risk at the maximum level for all financial statement assertions concerning investments. Larkin determined that Vernon is unable to exercise significant influence over any investee and none are related parties.

Larkin obtained from Vernon detailed analysis of its investments in domestic securities showing

- The classification between current and noncurrent portfolios.
- A description of each security, including the interest rate and maturity date of bonds and par value and dividend rate on stocks.

- A notation of the location of each security, either in the treasurer's safe or held by an independent custodian.
- The number of shares of stock or face amount of bonds held at the beginning and end of the year.
- The beginning and ending balances at cost and at market, and the unamortized premium or discount on bonds.
- Additions to and sales from the portfolios for the year, including date, number of shares, face amount of bonds, cost, proceeds, and realized gain or loss.
- Valuation allowances at the beginning and end of the year and changes therein.
- Accrued investment income for each investment at the beginning and end of the year, and income earned and collected during the year.

Larkin then prepared the following partial audit program of substantive auditing procedures:

1. Foot and crossfoot the analyses.
2. Trace the ending totals to the general ledger and financial statements.
3. Trace the beginning balances to the prior year's working papers.
4. Obtain positive confirmation as of the balance sheet date of the investments held by any independent custodian.
5. Determine that income from investments has been properly recorded as accrued or collected by reference to published sources, by computation, and by tracing to recorded amounts.
6. For investments in nonpublic entities, compare carrying value to information in the most recently available audited financial statements.
7. Determine that all transfers between the current and noncurrent portfolios have been properly authorized and recorded.

Required:

a. Identify the primary financial statement assertion relative to investments that would be addressed by each of the procedures No. 4 through No. 7 and describe the primary audit objective of performing that procedure. Use the format illustrated below.

Primary Assertion	Objective

b. Describe three additional substantive auditing procedures Larkin should consider in auditing Vernon's investments.

**17-53 Taylor, CPA, is auditing the financial statements of Palmer Company, a continuing audit client. Taylor is about to perform substantive audit procedures on Palmer's goodwill (excess of cost over the fair value of net assets purchased) that was acquired in prior years' business combinations. An industry slowdown has occurred recently, and purchased operations have not met profit expectations.

During the planning process, Taylor determined that there is a high risk that material misstatements in the assertions related to goodwill could occur. Taylor obtained an understanding of internal control and assessed control risk at the maximum level for the assertions related to goodwill.

Required:

a. Describe the substantive audit procedures Taylor should consider performing in auditing Palmer's goodwill. Do *not* discuss Palmer's internal control.

b. Describe the two significant assertions that Taylor would be most concerned with relative to Palmer's goodwill. Do *not* describe more than two.

**17-54 Johnson, CPA, has been engaged to audit the financial statements of Broadwall Corporation for the year ended December 31, 19X1. During the year, Broadwall obtained a long-term loan from a local bank pursuant to a financing agreement, which provided that the

1. Loan was to be secured by the company's inventory and accounts receivable.

2. Company was to maintain a debt to equity ratio not to exceed 2 to 1.

3. Company was not to pay dividends without permission from the bank.

4. Monthly installment payments were to commence July 1, 19X1.

In addition, during the year the company borrowed, on a short-term basis, from the president of the company, substantial amounts just prior to the year-end.

Required:

a. What procedures should Johnson employ in examining the described loans? *Do not discuss internal control.*

b. What financial statement disclosures should Johnson expect to find with respect to the loans from the president?

*17-55 During the audit of notes payable of Mohamed Tractor Company, a CPA was reviewing the terms of a related loan agreement. She noted that the note matured within 12 months of the audit date but the loan agreement provided that the term of the note could be extended an additional 12 months at the option of the company, provided there had been "no adverse changes in its financial or operating conditions."

How can the CPA audit the classification of notes payable as a long-term liability in this case?

*17-56 Discuss the audit procedures that a CPA might use in gathering evidence of the following transactions and balances.

a. The refinancing (cancellation of old note and issuance of a new note) of a note payable to a bank.

b. Acquisition of treasury stock.

c. Year-end balance in additional paid-in capital account (assume that no transactions are shown for the current year).

d. Issuance of common stock to acquire another company.

e. Exercise of employee stock options.

f. Issuance of employee stock options.

g. Sale of treasury stock.

*17-57 Companies that have stock option plans include a footnote in their financial statements that describes the plan and states the number of options for shares authorized, granted, exercised, and expired, the option prices, and the market prices of the stock on the grant and exercise dates.

As this information is not a part of the accounting records, what is the auditor's responsibility for it? If you feel audit procedures should be employed, list those that you think should be applied.

*17-58   Kalinki Supply Company is a small, privately held corporation that manufactures and sells Christmas tree ornaments. The stock book is maintained by the corporate secretary. Treasury stock is kept in a bank safe deposit box. The equity section of the corporation's balance sheet as of December 31, 19X6, the audit date, is shown in the following statement.

Common stock, $10 par value,		
100,000 shares authorized and issued		$1,000,000
Paid-in capital		1,000,000
Retained earnings—		
Beginning of year	$5,324,816	
Add—Net income	419,605	
Less—Dividends, $10 per share	(99,000)	
End of year		5,645,421
		$7,645,421
Less—Treasury stock, 1,000 shares, at cost		87,000
		$7,558,421

There were no capital stock transactions during the year. State the objectives for auditing the equity section. Develop an audit program to audit the equity section of Kalinki Supply Company.

**17-59   Jones, CPA, the continuing auditor of Sussex, Inc., is beginning the audit of the common stock and treasury stock accounts. Jones has decided to design substantive tests with control risk assessed at maximum.

   Sussex has no par, no stated value common stock, and acts as its own registrar and transfer agent. During the past year Sussex both issued and reacquired shares of its own common stock, some of which the company still owned at year-end. Additional common stock transactions occurred among the shareholders during the year.

   Common stock transactions can be traced to individual shareholders' accounts in a subsidiary ledger and to a stock certificate book. The company has not paid any cash or stock dividends. There are no other classes of stock, stock rights, warrants, or option plans.

Required:

What substantive audit procedures should Jones apply in auditing the common stock and treasury stock accounts?

*17-60   The following misstatements could occur in the property and equipment, investments, goodwill, long-term debt, and equity accounts. Describe an audit procedure that provides reasonable assurance of detecting each misstatement.

   a. A repair expense is properly capitalized as property and equipment.

   b. Goodwill is improperly recorded in a pooling-of-interest transaction.

   c. Borrowings are made from a bank but are recorded as revenue rather than long-term debt.

   d. The president of a nonpublic company improperly issues himself 100,000 shares of the company's common stock.

   e. An item of property is improperly charged to repairs and maintenance.

f. A 20-year franchise agreement to operate a McDonalds restaurant is amortized over 30 years.

g. A company fails to accrue interest on one of its notes payable.

h. A company's financial statements fail to disclose that retained earnings are restricted as to payment of dividends because of a provision in a debt agreement.

i. A company fails to record depreciation on certain of its assets.

j. A subsidiary was purchased three years ago in a transaction that resulted in recording goodwill which is amortized over the maximum allowable period. The subsidiary has incurred losses every year since it was acquired and may not be able to continue in existence.

k. Notes payable due within one year are classified as long-term debt.

l. Dividends on treasury stock are recorded as investment income.

m. An old truck is traded in for a new truck, and the new truck is recorded at cost less trade-in value. The cost of the old truck is not removed from the property and equipment account.

n. The cost of public relations work done to create customer satisfaction is recorded as goodwill.

o. The financial statements show one million shares of common stock are authorized and outstanding when actually two million shares are authorized and outstanding.

p. The financial statements fail to disclose the existence of a stock option plan.

q. One thousand shares of $100 par value preferred stock in a nonpublic company are issued for a patent worth $50,000 and are recorded at $100,000.

r. The treasurer removes the coupons from $1 million of bearer bonds and cashes them herself.

s. Dividends of $35,000 are received on investments in common stock, but only $25,000 is deposited and recorded.

t. The dividends from an investment in a 35 percent-owned subsidiary are recorded as dividend income.

u. An investment is written off as worthless by the treasurer who then sells the securities and keeps the proceeds.

v. Securities are removed from the safe deposit box by the treasurer and misappropriated; forged securities are substituted to conceal the theft.

Auditing the Operations, Contingencies, and Subsequent Events Assertions

"To fear the worst oft cures the worst."

SHAKESPEARE, *Troilus and Cressida, III, ii*

LEARNING OBJECTIVES

After reading and studying the material in this chapter, the student should be able to

▶ Paraphrase the objectives in the audit of revenue and expense.

▶ Compare examples of (1) internal control policies and procedures and (2) substantive tests for each of the five assertions relating to revenue and expense.

▶ Describe the contents of working papers, for (1) review of operations and (2) analysis of legal expense.

▶ Describe how value can be added to the audit of revenue and expense.

▶ Paraphrase the objectives in the audit of commitments and contingencies.

▶ Describe the contents of a working paper for summary of operating leases.

▶ Describe how value can be added to the audit of contingencies.

▶ Paraphrase the objectives in the audit of subsequent events.

▶ Describe the contents of working papers for (1) management representation letters and (2) inquiry letters of a client's lawyers.

This chapter will include examples of the audit objectives, procedures, and working papers involved in the audit of revenue, expense, contingencies, and subsequent events. Important relationships exist among these elements, particularly revenue and expense; therefore, they should be examined together.

REVENUE AND EXPENSE

Investors and other users of financial statements of business enterprises rely on the statement of income as an indication of a company's performance for a given period. They often use information from this statement as a guide in projecting expected future performance. In determining the objectives for the audit of revenue and expense, the auditor should keep in mind the use made of the statement of income.

An important concept in the determination of net income is that all items of expense needed to generate a certain amount of revenue be recognized in the same period as the revenue. If net income is to be an effective criterion for gauging the performance of the company and estimating its future performance, unusual and infrequent items that are not the result of normal operations and may not recur should be segregated. Otherwise, the reader of the financial statements may be misled into anticipating the continuation of performance that was actually the result of such nonrecurring items.

Revenue and expense accounts are subject to many of the same internal control policies and procedures as are the related asset and liability accounts. In particular, they often are subject to budgetary controls. These controls can be very effective if variations between the actual and budgeted amounts are investigated carefully by management.

Audit Objectives

The objectives (assertions) in the audit of revenue and expense are as follows:

1. To determine whether all (completeness) revenues and expenses applicable to the audit period (occurrence) have been recognized and are matched properly (allocation) in accordance with generally accepted accounting principles.
2. To determine whether all material unusual and infrequent items are segregated properly in the income statement (presentation).
3. To determine whether revenues and expenses are classified properly and consistently (presentation).
4. To determine whether disclosures concerning revenue and expense are adequate and in accordance with generally accepted accounting principles (disclosure).

Audit Procedures and Working Papers

Although some detail auditing is performed, the auditor relies heavily on internal control policies and procedures and overall tests in the revenue and expense area. Tests of controls, including controls applicable to shipping, billing, cash receipts, and accounts receivable, are discussed in Chapter 10. The same controls would apply to revenue. For example, the requirement that billings not be recorded until supported by a shipping notice reduces the probability of recording *both* invalid accounts receivable *and* invalid sales. If this control does not exist, the auditor may increase the number of accounts receivable confirmations mailed *and* trace a sample of sales transactions to the related shipping notices to compensate for higher control risk. In addition, similar tests of controls would be made in the areas of (1) receiving, cash disbursements, and accounts payable, and (2) payroll. These controls would apply to expenses. For example, if cash disbursements are classified in accordance with a formal chart of accounts and the classification is reviewed by a supervisor, the probability of misclassification may be small. However, if these controls do not exist, the auditor may analyze the major expense accounts and review the propriety of any large charges included therein. The auditor also may perform other tests of controls such as tests of material issues and of the cost accounting system. Other examples of internal control policies and procedures and substantive tests related to specific assertions for revenue (note similarity to accounts receivable) and expense (note similarity to accounts payable) accounts are shown below.

Assertions	Examples of internal control policies and procedures	Examples of substantive tests
1. Occurrence	1a. Revenue—Require evidence of shipment before sales invoice is prepared and recorded.	1a. Analytical procedures (compare sales for the period with prior-year audited amounts and current-year budgeted amounts).
	b. Expense—Require evidence of receipt of goods or services (e.g., receiving report) before voucher recording the expense is prepared.	b. Analytical procedures (compare expenses for the period with prior-year audited amounts and current-year budgeted amounts).
2. Rights and obligations	2. Not applicable to revenue and expense.	2. Not applicable to revenue and expense.
3. Completeness	3a. Revenue—Require that prenumbered shipping documents be accounted for and reconciled with invoices.	3a. Analytical procedures (compare sales for the period with prior-year audited amounts and current-year budgeted amounts).
	b. Expense—Establish policy to review and investigate prenumbered purchase orders and receiving reports that are unmatched with vendor invoices at month end.	b. Analytical procedures (compare expenses for the period with prior-year audited amounts and current-year budgeted amounts).
4. Allocation	4a. Revenue—Prenumber and account for credit memos for sales returns.	4a. Analytical procedures (compare ratio of sales returns to sales for current and prior year).
	b. Expenses—Use standard monthly journal entry to calculate and record depreciation expense.	b. Analytical procedures (compare depreciation expense for the period with prior-year audited amounts and current-year budgeted amounts).

Assertions	Examples of internal control policies and procedures	Examples of substantive tests
5. Presentation	5. Revenue and expense—Control environment (require board of director approval of sales to and purchases from related parties).	5. Inquiry and review of minutes of board of directors for indications of related party transactions.

Auditors have traditionally focused their audit effort on balance sheet accounts because this is often the most efficient way to perform an audit. This focus is also logical. Balance sheets represent the results of an entity's transactions at points in time, while income statements represent cumulative transactions between balance sheets. Thus, if auditors accomplish their audit objectives for two consecutive balance sheets (at the beginning and end of the year), they have considerable evidence regarding the intervening income statement.

Also, as described in the three previous chapters, many revenue and expense accounts are audited in connection with related asset and liability accounts (e.g., depreciation expense with property and equipment, interest expense with notes payable, bad debt expense with accounts receivable). Tests of controls plus the audit work performed on the related asset and liability accounts provide the auditor with evidence regarding the revenue and expense accounts. The auditor supplements this evidence with the procedures described in the following sections.

Analytical Procedures

The auditor places heavy emphasis on analytical procedures as substantive tests in the revenue and expense area. Some of the more important procedures are discussed in the following sections.

Review of operations   In its simplest form, the *review of operations* consists of comparing amounts in the income statement for the year being audited with expected amounts (e.g., the budget for the year and the actual amounts for the prior year if no changes are anticipated) and determining the underlying reasons for significant variations or the lack thereof. Determining the variations may be simply a clerical function, but obtaining explanations of the variations and evaluating their reasonableness require an ability to work with people, as well as persistence and judgment.

Explanations for significant variations are often obtained from client personnel. The auditor should discuss a variation with the individual who is most knowledgeable in the particular area. For example, the sales manager might be the best person to explain an increase in sales, whereas the plant or maintenance supervisor should be asked to explain a material variation in maintenance expense. As discussed in Chapter 13, the explanation should come from someone outside of the accounting department, if possible.

After explanations have been obtained from client personnel, they should be corroborated. Although client explanations may save the auditor considerable time in searching for the reasons for variations, they should not be accepted as audit evidence without corroboration. As an illustration, if the auditor were informed that selling expense declined because three market researchers were terminated, this explanation could be verified by an examination of the payroll records.

A partial example of one form of documentation of a review of operations is shown in Figure 18.1. In this example, sales were analyzed by market area (they also could be analyzed by product, type of service, etc.) and compared with the budgeted and prior-year amounts. Variations were computed (percentage as well as amount variations may also be helpful), and significant variations were explained. Although the explanations were obtained from the president, the auditor examined evidence to support the explanations.

Ratio tests The ratio tests that can be applied in each audit vary by industry and by individual company. Many of these ratios have been discussed, such as the gross profit ratio, the ratio of bad debt writeoffs to revenues, and the ratio of selling expense to revenue. Another ratio usually computed in audits of corporations is income taxes as a percentage of net income before income taxes. An investigation should be made of any significant difference between this ratio and the combined federal and state corporate tax rates. The auditor should recognize important relationships between financial statement amounts and should review them to see whether any appear out of line or inconsistent.

Tests of reasonableness Although detailed audit procedures are important, the auditor should not become so engrossed with the details that he or she ignores obvious indications of problems with the financial statements. There are many overall tests of reasonableness (sometimes called predictive auditing) that an auditor can and should apply. For example, a quick overall test of revenue for a particular product may be made by calculating an average price of the product (from a review of several sales invoices throughout the year) and multiplying it by the number of units of the product sold (from sales statistics or inventory reports; also, compare sales with plant capacity). The resulting answer seldom exactly equals the recorded revenue for that product, but it should approximate it. Many companies maintain elaborate sales statistics in the sales department, which can be used to determine the reasonableness of the sales amount. In addition, budget reports can be helpful in reviewing the reasonableness of most items of expense. If any overall tests yield unreasonable results, the auditor may perform a detailed analysis of the account.

Account Analysis

The auditor usually analyzes certain expense accounts because of large unexplained variations from budgeted or prior-year amounts or to gain information about the expenditures that are included in them, as well as to document the authenticity of the expenses. Legal expense is an example of such an account that could contain significant information concerning contingent liabilities. Figure 18.2 on page 587 illustrates a working paper analysis of legal expense. Note that the auditor has examined the vouchers in payment of the legal expense as well as the invoices from the attorney and the canceled check (indicated by $\checkmark$). The first voucher was for a legal retainer that was of little interest to the auditor. The second voucher, however, was for legal representation in an antitrust complaint. The antitrust complaint, which could result in damages being assessed against the company, represents a contingent liability, which (per ①) has been evaluated by the attorney in a letter obtained in connection with the subsequent review and has been noted for disclosure in the financial statements.

FIGURE 18.1   Review of Operations

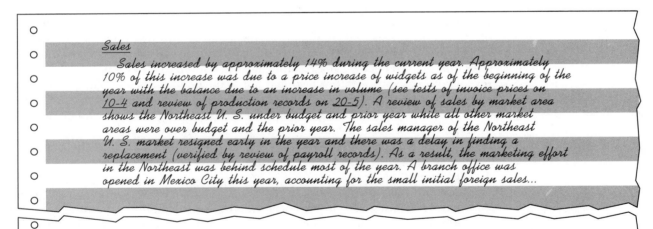

X Co.
Review of Operations
12-31-X8

J. Jones
1-20-x9

Source of explanations of variations- Mr. R J. Pender, Pres.	Actual 12-31-X8	Budget 12-31-X8	Actual Over (Under) Budget	Actual 12-31-X7	Current Year Over (Under) Prior Year
Sales by Market Area					
Southeast U. S.	627,338	600,000	27,338	512,989	114,349
Northeast U. S.	354,220	400,000	(45,780)	368,416	(14,196)
Western U. S.	411,961	400,000	11,961	366,501	45,460
Foreign	23,713	0	23,713	0	23,713
	1,417,232	1,400,000	17,232	1,247,906	169,326
Administrative Expenses					
Officer salaries	36,500	36,500	0	31,400	5,100
Office salaries	18,735	14,200	4,535	12,108	6,627
Office supplies	1,296	800	496	751	545
Legal expense	5,325	2,700	2,625	2,650	2,675
Audit fees	5,500	5,000	500	4,750	750
Computer rental	7,018	5,000	2,018	4,827	2,191
Office lease	2,400	2,400	0	2,400	0
Miscellaneous expense	232	400	(177)	429	(206)
	76,997	67,000	9,997	59,315	17,682

Sales

Sales increased by approximately 14% during the current year. Approximately 10% of this increase was due to a price increase of widgets as of the beginning of the year with the balance due to an increase in volume (see tests of invoice prices on 10-4 and review of production records on 20-5). A review of sales by market area shows the Northeast U. S. under budget and prior year while all other market areas were over budget and the prior year. The sales manager of the Northeast U. S. market resigned early in the year and there was a delay in finding a replacement (verified by review of payroll records). As a result, the marketing effort in the Northeast was behind schedule most of the year. A branch office was opened in Mexico City this year, accounting for the small initial foreign sales...

Administrative expenses

Administrative expenses for the current year were 15% over budget and 30% over the prior year. An additional employee was hired in the accounting department and considerable overtime was worked (verified by review of payroll records) in converting from a manual to a computerized inventory system and in accounting for the new foreign operations. Also, an increase in officer salaries was approved by the Board of Directors (see 1-14-X8 Board of Directors minutes at XX). Finally, legal expense increased over prior year and budget due to the filing of an antitrust action against the company (see 40-1).

FIGURE 18.2   Analysis of Legal Expense

Voucher No.	Name	Amount	Description
3-136	Wolfe & Lemann	100.00 ✓	Retainer for first quarter of 19X8
3-217	Wolfe & Lemann	3,975.00 ✓	Representation in anti-trust complaint ①

X Co.
Analysis of Legal Expense
Dec. 31, 19X8

J. Jones
1-18-x9

40-1

24,757

40

✓ *Examined properly approved voucher with supporting invoice from attorney and canceled check.*

① *Contingent liability. See letter from attorney evaluating the potential liability. Noted for disclosure in financial statements.*

Other expense accounts that usually are analyzed include repairs and maintenance (for capital items charged to expense), rents (for identification of lease liabilities), and miscellaneous expense (because it is often the repository of unusual or misclassified charges and expenses).

Review of Revenue Recognition Policies

Revenue should not be recognized until the earnings process is complete and collection of the revenue is reasonably assured. The SEC has brought a number of legal actions against accounting firms for permitting their clients to record revenue that was not subsequently realized. Provisions of sales agreements which may suggest that recognition of revenue is inappropriate include the following.

1. Products are sold to customers that are subject to a right of return arrangement (i.e., the risk of loss is not transferred to the customer).
2. Merchandise is billed but not delivered to a customer (bill and hold arrangements).
3. Products are sold to customers who make modifications, and then the products are resold to the client.
4. Products are sold to customers who do not have sufficient financial ability to demonstrate an intent or ability to pay.

The auditor should read important sales agreements and make inquiries to detect provisions that could invalidate recorded sales such as those listed above.

Review of Significant and Unusual Transactions

A number of cases of fraudulent financial reporting have arisen when management realized late in the year that publicly announced earnings projections would not be met. They then developed complex and unusual transactions in an effort to improve earnings. These transactions were recorded late in the year (often on the last day of the year). Examples of such transactions include the following.

1. Significant sales of assets outside the ordinary course of business for consideration other than cash (often involving a related party).
2. Significant increases in revenues during the last few months of the year that are inconsistent with prior trends (resulting from changes in revenue recognition policies or fictitious sales).
3. Abnormal decreases in costs and increases in gross profit percentages (resulting from changes in cost-deferral policies or overstatement of inventories).

Auditors should exercise intense professional skepticism regarding significant and unusual transactions that occur near the end of the year.

Classification and Disclosure

A number of revenue and expense transactions require special classification or disclosure, and the auditor must be alert to such transactions during the work on revenue and expense. Examples are the classification of extraordinary items and losses from discontinued operations and disclosure of certain gains and losses. The auditor should also be satisfied with the level of summarization of the revenue and expense accounts in the income statement—for example, that all significant accounts are shown separately and all insignificant accounts are aggregated.

Another important disclosure in the income statement is the earnings per share amount. For companies with complex capital structures, the auditor should prepare a worksheet to document that the appropriate factors were considered in the earnings per share calculation.

Value-Added Audit Considerations for Revenue and Expense

While performing audit procedures applicable to revenue and expense the auditor should consider such matters as: Has management established goals for increasing sales volume, decreasing product cost, and developing new products and communicated such goals throughout the organization? Does management have a plan to expand its markets? Does the entity earn an adequate return on investment compared with its industry? Does management give adequate consideration to the tax consequences of its acts? Is market research used to evaluate products? Are market share statistics developed and used in devising marketing plans? Are competitors' sales prices monitored? Do pricing policies consider research and development and other indirect costs? Has management considered other marketing channels? If the entity services its own products, is the policy cost justified? Are salespeople evaluated on both volume and profitability? Has the possibility of international sales been explored? How strong is employee morale? Has the entity been able to hire the kind of personnel it needs? Does the entity provide a good work environment? Can purchasing be simplified by establishing vendor alliances? Questions of management such as these expand the auditor's thinking beyond the attest function and add value to the audit.

▶ **EXAMPLE**

A client compensated its sales people with a fixed commission based on gross sales. The auditor noted that sales were concentrated in high-priced items with low gross margins. The auditor suggested that sales commissions be restructured to take into account both sales price and gross margin. The client accepted this suggestion, which resulted in increased gross profit.

Summary of Important Substantive Tests for Revenue and Expense

- Perform analytical procedures, including review of operations, ratio tests, and tests of reasonableness.
- Analyze selected accounts and examine supporting documentation to explain unusual variations, gain information about the accounts, and document the authenticity of the accounts.
- Review revenue recognition policies.
- Review significant and unusual transactions.
- Review the classification and disclosure of revenue and expense transactions.

MINUTES

Although minutes may contain information that is relevant to all sections of the audit, they are particularly important to operations, contingencies, and subsequent events.

As part of each audit, the auditor should extract or obtain copies of the minutes of all meetings of stockholders (or partners in the case of a partnership), board of directors, and subcommittees of the board of directors (the executive committee, audit committee, compensation committee, finance committee, etc.). The extracts or copies must be made from or compared with the original signed minutes to ensure their authenticity, and a notation should be made on them to this effect.

Because almost all important actions of a company are approved in these minutes, they should be subjected to a careful review. Matters of auditing significance that might be found in a review of the minutes and the audit disposition include the following.

1. Authorization for new bond or stock issues. Reference to long-term debt or capital stock working paper where the issue is audited.
2. Authorization of dividend payments. Reference to retained earnings analysis where dividends are audited.
3. Plans for plant expansion (which might involve significant purchase commit-

ments) or the acquisition of other companies. Reference to list of commitments.

4. Threatened or pending litigation against the client. Reference to list of contingent liabilities.

5. Adoption of pension, profit-sharing, or stock option plans. Reference to working papers supporting footnote disclosure of these plans.

6. Approval of important contracts and agreements (including employment agreements). Reference to working papers where the resulting expense or revenue is audited.

7. Approval of the purchase or sale of significant assets. Reference to property and equipment addition and retirement working papers.

The auditor should ascertain that important actions noted in the minutes have been properly reflected or disclosed in the financial statements. Important actions are cross-referenced to the sections of the working papers in which they are recorded or audited. For example, a resolution of the board of directors declaring a dividend of $0.50 a share should be cross-referenced to the retained earnings section of the working papers where a calculation such as the following is found.

Number of shares of common stock outstanding, per examination of stockbook	100,000
Dividend per share, per board of directors' authorization	$ 0.50
Total dividend paid per *TB-2*	$ 50,000

Minutes of prior years should also be reviewed during an auditor's first audit of a particular entity. In this review, the auditor is interested primarily in actions that have a continuing effect on the entity and its financial statements.

COMMITMENTS AND CONTINGENCIES

Although commitments and contingencies are generally not recorded in the financial statements, generally accepted accounting principles require their disclosure, usually in footnotes. Because these disclosures are a basic part of the financial statements, they should be subjected to audit procedures just as though they were a recorded amount.

Commitments are important to readers of financial statements because they represent future cash flow requirements. Some common commitments are those related to leases, pension plans, derivatives, and construction expenditures.

Statement of Financial Accounting Standards No. 13 specifies the accounting required for leases. From the lessee's standpoint, leases are classified as either capital or operating leases. Capital leases are reported as assets and liabilities in the balance sheet, whereas operating leases are disclosed as commitments.

Pension plan disclosures include details regarding the description of the plan, the net periodic pension cost amount, a reconciliation of balance sheet amounts with the funded status of the plan, various rates used in the calculation of pension amounts, and other information. The accounting for postretirement benefits, particularly defined benefit retiree health plans, is described in *SFAS No. 106*.

Derivatives are contracts whose values are derived from other instruments or indices, such as options, futures, forwards, and swaps. They frequently involve special risks because little or no cash outflow or inflow is required at the inception of the contract, no principal balance will be paid or received, and the potential risks and rewards are substantially greater than the amounts recognized in the balance sheet.

Disclosure of the amount of construction expenditures anticipated in the succeeding year assists the reader of the financial statements in projecting future cash flow requirements and is usually included in a footnote.

Statement of Financial Accounting Standards No. 5 provides guidance as to whether an estimated loss from a contingency should be recorded or disclosed. Examples of contingencies commonly disclosed in financial statements are pending or threatened litigation, guarantees of indebtedness, threat of expropriation of assets, and proposed assessment of additional taxes. Certain contingencies, such as those of the environmental and product liability type, relate to matters that are normally not shown in the accounting records of the entity, but may be so pervasive as to affect the viability and survival of the business. (Declaration of bankruptcy by asbestos companies is an example.)

Audit Objectives

The objectives (assertions) in the audit of commitments and contingencies are as follows.

1. To determine whether all (completeness) significant commitments and contingencies (existence and obligations) as of the balance sheet date are shown properly (valuation and presentation) in the financial statements.

2. To determine whether the disclosures of commitments and contingencies are made in accordance with generally accepted accounting principles (disclosure).

Audit Procedures and Working Papers

The auditor often finds that clients with effective internal control policies and procedures in the conventional areas, such as cash receipts and disbursements and inventories, have surprisingly ineffective procedures and controls in the areas of commitments and contingencies.

Some internal control policies and procedures that the auditor may consider include (1) formal client procedures to review each lease to determine its capital or operating characteristics, allowing the auditor to limit tests in this area, (2) board of director approval of the construction budget, reducing the auditor's time spent in evaluating this commitment, and (3) in-house legal counsel review and evaluation of pending litigation, lessening the time spent by the auditor in assessing this contingency.

Analytical Procedures

Because of the nature of commitments and contingencies, analytical procedures have limited application. However, commitments and contingencies that exist at the end of one year often are relevant at the end of the next year. For example,

1. Large construction projects often extend over several years so that related commitments would have to be disclosed at the end of each year.
2. Litigation often extends for several years, so that disclosure should be made at the end of each year it is pending.
3. Such items as pension plans and leases normally cover many years, thereby requiring continuous disclosure.

Therefore, the auditor should compare the commitments and contingencies existing at the end of the prior year with those expected for the current year and account for any differences.

Pensions

Pension plan disclosure data are audited by examining the terms of the contract between the client and the insurance company (a copy should be maintained in the permanent audit file and updated annually) and by confirming these terms with the insurance company. Using the information in the confirmation, the auditor recomputes pension expense and reviews the pension footnote to see whether the required disclosures are made.

Postretirement Benefits

Because many postretirement amounts and disclosures are actuarially determined, auditors will usually place heavy reliance on an actuary (a specialist) in the audit of these data. Examples of audit procedures that may be performed include the following.

1. Read the plan document and obtain an understanding of relevant terms and conditions.
2. Review the qualifications of the actuary and determine whether the appropriate terms and conditions of the plan are contained in the valuation report of the actuary.
3. Test the data used by the actuary for completeness and accuracy.
4. Determine whether methods used by the actuary are consistent and whether assumptions are reasonable.

Close coordination between the auditor and the actuary is important in the audit of postretirement benefits.

Leases

The accumulation of information for the disclosure of lease commitments can be very time consuming if the client does not maintain adequate records. Figure 18.3 is an example of a schedule on which lease disclosure information is accumulated and audited. The pertinent lease information has been traced to an *executed* lease agreement (indicated by ✓), and the spreading of the lease payments into time periods has been recomputed (indicated by ⋈). The classification of the leases as operating leases under *FASB No. 12* also has been evaluated. Total rental expense for the year has been cross-referenced to an expense account. The auditor should also review the applicable footnote for proper disclosure.

FIGURE 18.3 **Summary of Operating Leases**

J. Jones
1-6-x9

X Co.
Summary of Operating Leases
Dec. 31, 19X8

Period Covered	Lessor and Description of property	Type Agrees w/ FASB No 13	Annual Rental	Future Minimum Rental	Years 1-5	Years 6-10	Other Provisions
1-1-X0 1-1-XX	A. C. Head √ Carville Branch Office √	✗	1,200 √	14,400 ⌐	6,000 ⌐	6,000 ⌐	
7-1-X5 7-1-XX	Monarch Ltd. √ Manufacturing Plant √	✗	10,000 √	225,000 ⌐	50,000 ⌐	50,000 ⌐	Renewal option for additional 5 years at $60,000 per year √
			38,400	363,300 ✗	68,900 ✗	63,600 ✗	
			20				

√ Traced to executed lease agreement.
⌐ Recomputed
✗ Agrees with client totals.
✗ Checked criteria for distinguishing between capital and operating
  lease per FASB No. 13. See 9-6 for detail calculations.

Derivatives

The auditor must obtain an understanding of management's objectives in engaging in derivative transactions to determine the propriety of an entity's accounting for derivatives. The auditor also should review the contracts to understand their terms. The determination of the fair value of some complex derivatives may require the use of a specialist.

Environmental Matters

The auditor should inquire as to whether the Environmental Protection Agency has designated the entity as a "potentially responsible party." This designation subjects the entity to liabilities for cleanup costs and fines that may require disclosure in the financial statements.

Other Procedures

Auditors must be alert in every section of their work for contingent liabilities. Some of the procedures specifically designed to detect contingent liabilities include the following.

1. Review of minutes of meetings of directors and stockholders for actions indicating the existence of contingent liabilities (hiring of special legal counsel, discussion of possible asset expropriation, approval of the guarantee of third-party obligations, etc.).
2. Analysis of the legal expense account for information about litigation and claims for which legal counsel has been engaged.
3. Confirmation directly with legal counsel of the details of litigation and claims being handled for the client. This procedure is discussed further in the subsequent events section.
4. Inquiry of management. The existence of contingent liabilities is a matter that normally is included in the representation letter obtained from management.

Value-Added Considerations for Contingencies

While performing audit procedures applicable to contingencies the auditor should direct management's attention to such matters as: Does the entity have a contingency plan in the event of loss of key officers and employees, computer facilities, sources of supply, or important customers? Does the entity have a plan for succession of executive officers? Does the entity have a risk management program?

▶ EXAMPLE

The auditor noted that management made extensive use of computers in its business but did not have a contingency plan in the event of loss of its computer facilities. The auditor called this matter to the attention of management, who made arrangements with another entity with similar computer facilities to use those facilities in the event of emergency. Two months later the client's computers were damaged by fire, but there was no discontinuity in its operations because backup facilities were available.

SUBSEQUENT EVENTS

Generally, an audit is not completed and the financial statements are not issued until after the audit date, that is, the end of the client's fiscal year. The period between the audit date and the date the financial statements are issued can usually be divided into three segments: (1) time required for the client to complete, total, and balance the accounting records and otherwise prepare them for audit, (2) time required for the auditor to perform the audit procedures in the client's office (referred to as fieldwork), and (3) time after leaving the client's office required for the auditor to perform quality control reviews and reproduce and deliver the report. "Subsequent events" may occur anytime during this period (segments one, two, and three), and consist of events or transactions that have a material effect on the financial statements and therefore require adjustments or disclosure in the statements. The "subsequent period" extends through segment two. Figure 18.4 portrays the period in which subsequent events may occur.

FIGURE 18.4 **Illustration of Period During Which Subsequent Events May Occur**

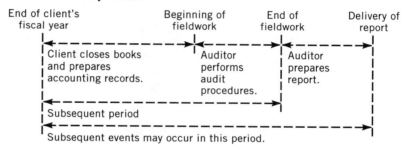

Because the auditor is in the client's office and has access to the accounting records and management to the end of fieldwork, he or she has a responsibility to search for material events through that date that might require adjustment of, or disclosure in, the financial statements. (The auditor's report is also dated as of the end of fieldwork.) From the end of fieldwork to delivery of the report the auditor has no responsibility to *search* for subsequent events. However, any that come to the auditor's attention should be reflected in the financial statements. Such events can be classified into two types.

1. Events that provide additional information about conditions that existed as of the audit date and affect estimates inherent in the preparation of financial statements.
2. Events that provide information about conditions arising after the audit date.

Information provided by the first type of event should be used to evaluate further the accounting estimates reflected in the financial statements, and the financial statements should be adjusted if changes in the estimates are necessary as a result of the additional information. An example would be the final settlement before the end of the fieldwork of a major lawsuit that arose before the audit date. The settlement would provide additional evidence on the amount of the liability as of the audit date.

Information provided by the second type of event should not result in adjustment of the financial statements (except that stock dividends and splits may be reflected retroactively) but may require disclosure. An example of this type of event is an occurrence after the audit date that results in the filing of a major lawsuit against the client. Neither the event nor the lawsuit would affect the amounts shown in the financial statement as of the audit date, and, therefore, the financial statements should not be adjusted. The event should be disclosed, however, because it could have a material effect on the client's future financial statements.

Detection and evaluation of the foregoing types of events concern the auditor in the audit of subsequent events.

Audit Objectives

The objectives (assertions) of the audit of subsequent events are as follows.

1. To determine whether the financial statements are adjusted (presentation) when necessary for all (completeness) subsequent events (occurrence) that provide additional information about accounting estimates (valuation).

2. To determine whether adequate disclosure (presentation) is made when necessary of all (completeness) subsequent events (occurrence) reflecting new conditions that may have a material future effect on the entity.

Audit Procedures and Working Papers

The audit procedures applied to the period subsequent to the audit date can be divided into four general groups, discussed in the following sections.

Review of Subsequent Financial Records

To the extent that transactions subsequent to the audit date have been summarized in interim financial statements, these statements should be read and compared with the financial statements being audited. Any unusual or unexpected variations or trends (a loss when operations previously had been profitable, significant decreases in assets or increases in liabilities, etc.) should be investigated. For the period from the date of the latest interim financial statements through the last day of fieldwork, the auditor should review the basic accounting records for unusual and significant transactions that may affect the financial statements being audited. Such records include the general ledger, general journal, cash receipts and disbursements records (the review of the cash disbursement records should be coordinated with the review of subsequent transactions as part of the accounts payable work), and sales and expense journals. The review of minutes also should be updated through the last day of fieldwork.

Inquiries of Management

Discussions should be held on the last day of fieldwork with the chief executive and financial officers as well as other company officials who may be knowledgeable about the subjects in question. Among the matters discussed would be the following.

1. The existence of any material commitments or contingencies as of the audit date or the last day of fieldwork.

2. Material changes in the equity accounts, long-term debt, or working capital subsequent to the audit date.

3. Unusual adjustments made after the audit date or subsequent changes in accounting estimates made as of the audit date.

4. Changes in trends of sales, expenses, and profit after the audit date.

5. Changes in raw material prices after the audit date and their effect on replacement cost of inventories.

6. Cancellation of sales orders or losses of important customers after the audit date.

7. Catastrophes after the audit date (expropriations, fires, explosions, etc.).

8. New contracts or agreements or renegotiation of old ones subsequent to the audit date when sales of products, wages, leases, and so on are affected.

9. Cash flow requirements for the coming year and sources of financing.

10. Effect of development of substitute products, model changes, and so forth.

11. Related party transactions.

The listing is not all-inclusive, but gives examples of the types of matters that should be covered. The inquiries should be tailored to the operations of each client. The discussions also serve as bases for management's written representations.

Management Representations

During an audit made in accordance with generally accepted auditing standards, an auditor is required by AU Section 333 to obtain certain representations from management. *Management representations* serve the dual purpose of

1. Emphasizing to the client company's management their responsibility for complete and accurate financial statements. (The representations may clarify any management misunderstandings as to required disclosures.)

2. Providing audit evidence, particularly in areas not susceptible to normal audit procedures.

The representations should not be used, however, as a substitute for customary audit procedures, and they do not relieve the auditor of the responsibility for performing the audit in accordance with generally accepted auditing standards. An example of a management representation letter is shown in Figure 18.5.

Some common representations obtained from management together with the reasons for obtaining them are as follows.

1. A representation that the financial statements being examined by the auditor are the final statements for the year, and management is responsible for determining that they are presented fairly in accordance with generally accepted accounting principles. This representation emphasizes management's responsibility for the fairness of the financial statements, and, if an error is discovered after the financial statements are issued, it prevents management from maintaining that they knew of and disclosed the error to the auditor.

2. A representation that there are no material unrecorded assets or liabilities

FIGURE 18.5   **Management Representation Letter**

X COMPANY
122 WEST AVENUE
FAYETTEVILLE, ARKANSAS 72701

February 8, 19X9

Partner & Co.
100 Main Street
Fayetteville, Arkansas 72701

Dear Sirs:

In connection with your audit of the financial statements of X Company as of December 31, 19X8, and for the year then ended, for the purpose of expressing an opinion as to whether the financial statements present fairly the financial position, results of operations, and cash flows of X Company in conformity with generally accepted accounting principles, we confirm, to the best of our knowledge and belief, the following representations made to you during your audit:

1. We are responsible for the fair presentation in the financial statements of financial position, results of operations, and cash flows in conformity with generally accepted accounting principles.
2. We have made available to you all financial records and related data and minutes of all meetings of stockholders, directors, and committees of directors.
3. There have been no:
   3.1. Frauds involving management or employees who have significant roles in the company.
   3.2. Frauds involving other employees that could have a material effect on the financial statements.
   3.3. Communications from regulatory agencies concerning noncompliance with, or deficiencies in, financial reporting practices that could have a material effect on the financial statements.
4. We have no plans or intentions that may materially affect the carrying value or classification of assets and liabilities.
5. The following have been properly recorded or disclosed in the financial statements:
   5.1. Related party transactions and related amounts receivable or payable, including sales, purchases, loans, transfers, leasing arrangements, and guarantees.
   5.2. Capital stock repurchase options or agreements or capital stock reserved for options, warrants, conversions, or other requirements.
   5.3. Arrangements with financial institutions involving restrictions on cash balances and line-of-credit or similar arrangements.
   5.4. Agreements to repurchase assets previously sold.
6. There are no:
   6.1. Violations or possible violations of laws or regulations whose effects should be considered for disclosure in the financial statements or as a basis for recording a loss contingency.
   6.2. Other material liabilities or gain or loss contingencies that are required to be accrued or disclosed by Statement of Financial Accounting Standards No. 5.
7. There are no unasserted claims or assessments that our lawyer has advised us are probable of assertion and must be disclosed in accordance with Statement of Financial Accounting Standards No. 5.

FIGURE 18.5 *(Continued)*

8. The accounting records underlying the financial statements accurately and fairly reflect, in reasonable detail, the transactions of the company.
9. Provision, when material, has been made to reduce excess or obsolete inventories to their estimated net realizable value.
10. The company has satisfactory title to all owned assets, and there are no liens or encumbrances on such assets nor has any asset been pledged.
11. Provision has been made for any material loss to be sustained in the fulfillment of, or from inability to fulfill, any sales commitments.
12. Provision has been made for any material loss to be sustained as a result of purchase commitments for inventory quantities in excess of normal requirements or at prices in excess of the prevailing market prices.
13. We have complied with all aspects of contractual agreements that would have a material effect on the financial statements in the event of noncompliance.
14. No events have occurred subsequent to the balance sheet date that would require adjustment to, or disclosure in, the financial statements.

Blair Mills
_____
Blair Mills, President

Bruce Lee
_____
Bruce Lee, Controller

and no contingent assets or liabilities that are not disclosed properly in the financial statements. Examples are unrecorded claims receivable or payable and liabilities from lawsuits or as guarantor of third-party obligations. Because transactions of this nature are difficult to detect with normal audit procedures, additional assurance is sought from management as the party most likely to be aware of such transactions.

3. A representation that all agreements relating to capital stock are disclosed properly in the financial statements. This representation concerns the disclosure of such items as stock repurchase agreements and stock option plans. Although items of this nature are usually approved by the board of directors or the stockholders and included in the minutes of their meetings, such approval is not a legal requirement in all states. Therefore, a representation covering these matters is requested from management.

4. A representation that transactions with other entities were based on arm's-length dealings. This representation is one of several audit procedures for determining the existence of related parties.

5. A representation that there have been no events or transactions subsequent to the audit date that would have a material effect on the financial statements that have not been disclosed therein. The auditor's responsibility extends beyond the audit date for material transactions that affect the financial statements; a representation is obtained to remind management that their responsibility also extends beyond the balance sheet date and to supplement the procedures performed by the auditor during this period.

6. A representation that all financial and accounting records were furnished to

the auditor and none was withheld. This representation is primarily a reminder to management of their obligation to the auditor.

7. A representation that minutes of all meetings of stockholders and directors (and any subcommittees) held during the period from the beginning of the year being audited to the date the audit is completed have been furnished the auditor. This representation, usually signed by the corporate secretary, constitutes evidence for the auditor that all minutes have been accounted for and that none has been overlooked or withheld.

8. A representation that there are no agreements to repurchase assets previously sold. This representation is intended to detect significant contingencies that may not be evident in the accounting records.

9. A representation that there have been no violations of laws or regulations, the effects of which should be considered for disclosure in the financial statements or as a basis for recording a loss contingency. This representation is intended to bring to the auditor's attention violations of environmental, product safety, or similar laws and regulations that are difficult to detect from the accounting records.

The representations are signed by the chief executive officer and the chief financial officer because these individuals should be the most knowledgeable about the subjects of the representation. Auditors should not accept the representations of lower level officers in place of those of the chief executive and financial officers. The dates of the representations should coincide with the last day of audit work in the client's office, which would make them effective through the date to which the auditor's responsibility extends.

Although auditors may be unable to corroborate all of management's representations through independent verification, consideration should be given to the *feasibility* of management's assertions and the consistency of management's expressed intent with previous transactions and current economic conditions.

Letters from Legal Counsel

The auditor should ask management to request the company's legal counsel (usually identified from an analysis of legal expense—see Figure 18.2) to confirm directly to the auditor a description and evaluation of pending or threatened litigation, claims, or other contingent liabilities as of the audit date and the end of fieldwork for which legal counsel has been engaged. The following information is requested of legal counsel:

1. Regarding pending or threatened litigation—(a) evaluation *and* (b) completeness of management's information.

2. Regarding unasserted claims—(a) evaluation *but not* completeness of management's information and (b) confirmation of legal counsel's responsibility to consult with the client concerning disclosure of unasserted claims. The American Bar Association has indicated that attorneys may be required to resign their engagement if the client disregards their advice concerning disclosures.

Figure 18.6 illustrates an audit inquiry of legal counsel with one pending lawsuit and no unasserted claims. In determining whether the financial statements are affected by a material uncertainty due to litigation, claims, and assessments, the lan-

FIGURE 18.6   Inquiry of Client's Lawyer

X COMPANY
122 WEST AVENUE
FAYETTEVILLE, ARKANSAS 72701

February 3, 19X8

Wolfe & Lemann
900 Whitney Avenue
Center City, Arkansas 72627

Gentlemen:

Our auditors, Partner & Co., are now engaged in an audit of our financial statements as of December 31, 19X8 and for the year then ended. In connection with the audit, management has furnished Partner & Co. with information concerning certain contingencies involving matters with respect to which you have been engaged and to which you have devoted substantive attention on behalf of the Company. These contingencies individually represent a maximum potential loss exposure in excess of $50,000.

Pending or Threatened Litigation,
Claims, and Assessments

We have furnished our auditors with the following information relating to the only pending or threatened litigation, claim, or assessment your firm is handling on our behalf and to which you have devoted substantive attention in the form of legal consultation or representation:

1. Description of the nature of the case—Antitrust complaint filed against the company by the U.S. Department of Justice for discriminatory pricing policies.
2. Process of case to date—Case is in the discovery phase.
3. Response to the case—Management intends to contest the case vigorously.
4. Evaluation of the likelihood of an unfavorable outcome and an estimate, if one can be made, of the amount or range of potential loss—Management believes that the probability of an unfavorable outcome is remote. No estimate of loss can be made.

Please furnish Partner & Co. such explanation, if any, that you consider necessary to supplement the foregoing information, including an explanation of those matters as to which your views may differ from those stated and an identification of the omission of any pending or threatened litigation, claim, or assessment, or a statement that the list of such matters is complete.

Unasserted Claims and Assessments

We understand that whenever, in the course of performing legal services for us with respect to a matter recognized to involve an unasserted possible claim or assessment that may call for financial statement disclosure, if you have formed a professional conclusion that we must disclose or consider disclosure concerning such possible claim or assessment, as a matter of professional responsibility to us, you will so advise us and will consult with us concerning the question of such disclosure and the applicable requirements of Statement of Financial Accounting Standards No. 5. Please specifically confirm to Partner & Co. that our understanding is correct.

FIGURE 18.6   *(Continued)*

We will be representing to Partner & Co. that there are no unasserted possible claims or assessments that you have advised are probable of assertion and must be disclosed in accordance with Statement of Financial Accounting Standards No. 5 in the financial statements currently under audit.

Other Matters

Your response should include matters that existed at December 31, 19X8 and for the period from that date to the date of your response. Please make your response effective as of February 8, 19X8, and specifically identify the nature of and reasons for any limitation on your response.

Also, please furnish Partner & Co. with the amount of any unpaid fees due you as of December 31, 19X8 for services rendered through that date.

Please mail your reply directly to Partner & Co., 100 Main Street, Fayetteville, Arkansas 72701. A stamped, addressed envelope is enclosed for your convenience. Also, please furnish us a copy of your reply.

Very truly yours,
X Company

By   *Blair Mills*

Blair Mills, President

guage used by lawyers in their responses must be considered carefully. Unequivocal statements of opinion to the effect that actions against the client have "little or no merit," that the client "will be able to successfully defend the action," or that the ultimate liability to the client "will not be material" can usually be accepted as evidence that no material uncertainties exist regarding those matters. On the other hand, vague opinions that the client has "a good chance of prevailing" or "meritorious defenses" suggest the existence of an uncertainty. It is important that the auditor not make an evaluation of the outcome of a legal matter when legal counsel is unwilling or unable to do so. The auditor's reporting problems resulting from limitations on a lawyer's response are discussed in Chapter 20.

Summary of Important Substantive Tests for Subsequent Events

- Review subsequent transactions as shown in interim financial statements, general ledger, journal entries, cash receipts and disbursements journals, minutes, and so on.
- Inquire of management regarding subsequent events and transactions.
- Obtain representation letters.
- Obtain letters from legal counsel.

Chapter 18 ▶ GLOSSARY OF TERMS

Management representations Written statements from management to the auditor confirming their responsibility for the financial statements and for representations made to the auditor.

Review of operations The application of analytical procedures to the income statement to identify and investigate unusual amounts and variations.

Subsequent events Events that provide additional information about conditions that existed as of the audit date and affect estimates in the financial statements or that provide information about conditions arising after the audit date.

Unasserted claim A potential claim against the client that has not yet been asserted by the claimant in the form of litigation or otherwise.

Chapter 18 ▶ REFERENCES

American Institute of Certified Public Accountants. *Professional Standards*
AU Section 333—*Client Representations*
AU Section 337—*Inquiry of a Client's Lawyer Concerning Litigation, Claims, and Assessments*
AU Section 560—*Subsequent Events*

Behn, Bruce K., and Pany, Kurt. "Limitations of Lawyers' Letters," *Journal of Accountancy* (February 1995), pp. 61–67.

Quinlivan, Stephen M. "Understanding Attorneys' Responses to Auditor Inquiries," *Journal of Accountancy* (November 1991), pp. 127–133.

Schwartz, Richard, and Gillmore, Michael J. "Auditing Pension Costs and Disclosures," *The CPA Journal* (June 1988), pp. 16–25.

Steinberg, Richard M., Akresh, Murray S., and Jensen, Keith F. "Auditing Postretirement Benefits: How to Deal with FASB 106," *Journal of Accountancy* (August 1992), pp. 74–78.

Zuber, George R., and Berry, Charles G. "Assessing Environmental Risk," *Journal of Accountancy* (June 1992), pp. 87–92.

Chapter 18 ▶ REVIEW QUESTIONS

18-1 Explain the importance to investors and others of the statement of income.

18-2 State the objectives of the audit of revenue and expense.

18-3 On what procedures does the auditor place heavy reliance in the audit of revenue and expense?

18-4 What are the purposes of the review of operations?

18-5 Name four ratio tests that may be applied in the audit of revenue and expense.

18-6 Describe an overall test of revenue for reasonableness.

18-7 Give two reasons for analyzing an expense account.

18-8 List four expense accounts that would usually be analyzed and indicate the reasons.

18-9 Why is an auditor concerned with a client's revenue recognition policies?

18-10 What are some inquiries an auditor can make when examining revenue and expense to add value to the audit?

18-11 List seven examples of matters of interest to an auditor that may be found in a review of minutes of meetings of stockholders and board of directors.

18-12 Why should the auditor be concerned with commitments and contingencies, since no amounts are shown for them in the financial statements?

18-13 State the objectives of the audit of commitments and contingencies.

18-14 What analytical procedures may be applied to commitments and contingencies?

18-15 List four audit procedures that are specifically designed to detect contingencies.

18-16 What are some inquiries an auditor can make when examining contingencies to add value to the audit?

18-17 What are the two types of subsequent events that may require adjustment to, or disclosure in, the financial statements? Give an example of each.

18-18 State the objectives of the audit of subsequent events.

18-19 List the four general groups of audit procedures applied to subsequent events.

18-20 Name eight documents or records that would be examined in the review of subsequent events. For what period would the review be conducted?

18-21 List eleven matters that would be discussed with management in connection with the audit of subsequent events.

18-22 What are the purposes of management representations?

18-23 List and explain nine types of representations that may be obtained from management.

18-24 Which client personnel normally sign the representation letter to the auditor?

18-25 What information is a company's legal counsel requested to confirm to the auditor?

Chapter 18 ▶ OBJECTIVE QUESTIONS

(* = author prepared; ** = CPA examination)

**18-26 An auditor compares 19X5 revenues and expenses with those of the prior year and investigates all changes exceeding 10 percent. By this procedure, the auditor would be most likely to learn that
 a. An increase in property tax rates has *not* been recognized in the client's accrual.
 b. Fourth-quarter payroll taxes were *not* paid.
 c. The client changed its capitalization policy for small tools in 19X5.
 d. The 19X5 provision for uncollectible accounts is inadequate because of worsening economic conditions.

**18-27 Auditors try to identify predictable relationships when using analytical procedures. Relationships involving transactions from which of the following accounts most likely would yield the highest level of evidence?
 a. Accounts payable.
 b. Payroll expense.
 c. Accounts receivable.
 d. Advertising expense.

*18-28 Which of the following ratios would be most useful in the audit of revenue and expense?
 a. Current ratio.
 b. Ratio of selling expense to sales.
 c. Ratio of net income to sales.
 d. Debt-to-equity ratio.

**18-29 Auditors sometimes use comparisons of ratios as audit evidence. For example, an unexplained decrease in the ratio of gross profit to sales may suggest which of the following possibilities?
 a. Merchandise purchases being charged to selling and general expense.
 b. Unrecorded purchases.
 c. Unrecorded sales.
 d. Fictitious sales.

**18-30 As a result of analytical procedures, the auditor determines that the gross profit percentage has declined from 30 percent in the preceding year to 20 percent in the current year. The auditor should
 a. Require a footnote emphasizing the decline for full disclosure.
 b. Consider the possibility of an error in property and equipment.
 c. Consider the possibility of an error in inventory.
 d. Evaluate management's performance in causing this decline.

*18-31 Legal expense is understated because legal fees related to an unexpected lawsuit brought by a minority stockholder have not been billed by the law firm or accrued by the client. Which of the following audit procedures is most likely to detect this misstatement?
 a. Analysis of charges in the legal expense account.
 b. Letter of inquiry to the law firm handling the case.
 c. Analytical procedures comparing legal expense for the current and prior years.
 d. Analytical procedures comparing legal expense for the current year to the budgeted legal expense for the current year.

**18-32 An auditor would most likely identify a contingent liability by obtaining a(an)
 a. Related party transaction confirmation.
 b. Accounts payable confirmation.
 c. Confirmation of open letters of credit from a bank.
 d. Transfer agent confirmation.

**18-33 Beta, Inc., is an affiliate of an audit client and is audited by another firm of auditors. Which of the following is *most* likely to be used by the auditor to obtain assurance that all guarantees of the affiliate's indebtedness have been detected?

a. Examine supporting documents for all entries in intercompany accounts.

b. Obtain written confirmation of indebtedness from the auditor of the affiliate.

c. Review client minutes and obtain a representation letter.

d. Send a bank confirmation request to all of the affiliate's lender banks.

*18-34 In the audit of contingent liabilities, which of the following procedures would be least effective?

a. Standard bank confirmation.

b. Analytical procedures.

c. Inquiry of management.

d. Confirmation with legal counsel.

**18-35 An auditor is concerned with completing various phases of the audit after the balance sheet date. This ''subsequent period'' extends to the date of the

a. Auditor's report.

b. Final review of the audit working papers.

c. Delivery of the auditor's report to the client.

d. Public issuance of the financial statements.

*18-36 Which of the following events occurring during the subsequent period is most likely to result in adjustment to the financial statements?

a. A worker is injured in a plant accident.

b. A large customer declares bankruptcy.

c. A significant subsidiary is sold.

d. The U.S. Justice Department brings antitrust charges.

**18-37 Which of the following procedures would an auditor most likely perform in obtaining evidence about subsequent events?

a. Determine that changes in employee pay rates after year end were properly authorized.

b. Recompute depreciation charges for plant assets sold after year end.

c. Inquire about payroll checks that were recorded before year end but cashed after year end.

d. Investigate changes in long-term debt occurring after year end.

**18-38 After an audit report containing an unqualified opinion on a nonpublic client's financial statements was issued, the client decided to sell the shares of a subsidiary that accounts for 30 percent of its revenue and 25 percent of its net income. The auditor should

a. Take *no* action because the auditor has *no* obligation to make any additional inquiries.

b. Notify the entity that the auditor's report

may *no* longer be associated with the financial statements.

c. Describe the effects of this subsequently discovered information in a communication with persons known to be relying on the financial statements.

d. Determine whether the information is reliable and, if determined to be reliable, request that revised financial statements be issued.

**18-39 A purpose of a management representation letter is to reduce

a. Audit risk to an aggregate level of misstatement that could be considered material.

b. An auditor's responsibility to detect material misstatements only to the extent that the letter is relied on.

c. The possibility of a misunderstanding concerning management's responsibility for the financial statements.

d. The scope of an auditor's procedures concerning related party transactions and subsequent events.

**18-40 Which of the following statements ordinarily is included among the written client representations obtained by the auditor?

a. Compensating balances and other arrangements involving restrictions on cash balances have been disclosed.

b. Management acknowledges responsibility for illegal actions committed by employees.

c. Sufficient evidential matter has been made available to permit the issuance of an unqualified opinion.

d. Management acknowledges that there are *no* material weaknesses in internal control.

**18-41 To which of the following matters would materiality limits *not* apply in obtaining written management representations?

a. The availability of minutes of stockholders' and directors' meetings.

b. Losses from purchase commitments at prices in excess of market value.

c. The disclosure of compensating balance arrangements involving related parties.

d. Reductions of obsolete inventory to net realizable value.

**18-42 The primary reason an auditor requests letters of inquiry be sent to a client's attorneys is to provide the auditor with

a. The probable outcome of asserted claims and pending or threatened litigation.

b. Corroboration of the information furnished

by management about litigation, claims, and assessments.

c. The attorneys' opinions of the client's historical experiences in recent similar litigation.

d. A description and evaluation of litigation, claims, and assessments that existed at the balance sheet date.

**18-43 Which of the following is *not* an audit procedure that the independent auditor would perform concerning litigation, claims, and assessments?

a. Obtain assurance from management that it has disclosed all unasserted claims that the lawyer has advised are probable of assertion and must be disclosed.

b. Confirm directly with the client's lawyer that all claims have been recorded in the financial statements.

c. Inquire of and discuss with management the policies and procedures adopted for identifying, evaluating, and accounting for litigation, claims, and assessments.

d. Obtain from management a description and evaluation of litigation, claims, and assessments existing at the balance sheet date.

**18-44 The primary source of information to be reported about litigation, claims, and assessments is the

a. Client's lawyer.
b. Court records.
c. Client's management.
d. Independent auditor.

*18-45 Match the assertion that relates to each substantive test. Each assertion may be used once, more than once, or not at all.

Substantive test	Assertion
1. Compare sales for the period with prior-year audited amounts and current-year budgeted amounts.	a. Occurrence b. Rights and obligations c. Completeness d. Allocation e. Presentation
2. Compare expenses for the period with prior-year audited amounts and current-year budgeted amounts.	
3. Review minutes of board of directors for indications of related party transactions.	
4. Compare ratio of sales returns to sales for current and prior year.	
5. Compare depreciation expense for the period with prior-year audited amounts and current-year budgeted amounts.	

Chapter 18 ▶ DISCUSSION/CASE QUESTIONS AND PROBLEMS

(* = author prepared; ** = CPA examination; *** = CMA examination)

*18-46 During your audit of Fraudulent Fabrics, you note that the company's gross profit ratio increased to 25 percent this year from 20 percent last year. List the possible causes of this increase and the audit procedures you would employ or expand to investigate each possible cause.

*18-47 In your audit of June Company, you are investigating an increase in sales during the current year and have made inquiry of the sales manager, who tells you the increase is due to a sales price increase during the year. When you ask to see a current price list to verify the increase, the sales manager becomes angry and asks if you do not trust him. How would you reply?

*18-48 As auditor of Royal Radio Broadcasting Company, you have learned from past audit experience, familiarity with broadcasting industry practice, and a review of Royal's contracts and agreements the following information regarding Royal's operations.

a. Local advertising accounts for about 70 percent and national advertising about 30 percent of Royal's revenue.

b. Salespersons receive a 15 percent commission on sales.

c. Music license fees average 10 percent of sales.

d. Fixed expenses consist of salaries of about $850,000 and depreciation of $100,000 per year.

    e. Variable operating expenses such as power and supplies approximate 10 percent of sales.

    If, on beginning the audit of Royal for the current year, you learn that total advertising revenue is $4 million, what would you expect net income to be under normal operations? Explain your answer.

*18-49   When examining documentation supporting costs and expenses, an auditor must consider its availability and its reliability. Discuss the reliability and adequacy of documentation you would expect for the following expenses.

    a. Purchase of stationery and supplies.

    b. Officer travel expenses.

    c. Rental expense on office space.

    d. Cost of taxi to send sick employee home.

    e. Purchase of hams for Christmas gift to customers.

    f. Contribution (purchase of tickets to Policemen's Ball).

    g. Payment of income taxes.

    h. Payment of directors' fees ($500 per meeting).

    i. Employee salary expense.

    j. Payment of FICA taxes withheld from employees.

    k. Payment of electric bill.

**18-50   Young, CPA, is considering the procedures to be applied concerning a client's loss contingencies relating to litigation, claims, and assessments.

    Required:

    What substantive audit procedures should Young apply when testing for loss contingencies relating to litigation, claims, and assessments?

*18-51   Commitments and contingencies can take many forms, including the following.

    a. Guarantee of the debt of an affiliated company.

    b. Contract with a builder to construct a plant.

    c. Maintenance of an unrecorded bank account for illegal political contributions.

    d. Discriminatory hiring practices.

    e. Violation of antitrust laws.

    f. Infringement on patent rights.

    g. Disputes with taxing authorities.

    State the audit procedures that could reasonably be employed to detect each of these commitments and contingencies.

*18-52   In general, a lease will be considered a capital lease if it meets any one of the following criteria.

    a. The lease transfers ownership of the property to the lessee by the end of the lease term.

    b. The lease contains an option to purchase the property at a bargain price.

    c. The lease term is equal to 75 percent or more of the estimated economic life of the property.

    d. The present value of the rentals and other minimum lease payments is equal to 90 percent or more of the fair value of the leased property.

Explain how you would audit a lease classification as capital or operating on the basis of these criteria. Indicate the specific documentation you would examine and how you would satisfy yourself as to fair value of rentals, estimated economic life, and so forth.

**18-53   Green, CPA, is auditing the financial statements of Taylor Corporation for the year ended December 31, 19X9. Green plans to complete the fieldwork and sign the auditor's report about May 10, 19X0. Green is concerned about events and transactions occurring after December 31, 19X9 that may affect the 19X9 financial statements.

Required:

a. What are the general types of subsequent events that require Green's consideration and evaluation?

b. What are the auditing procedures Green should consider performing to gather evidence concerning subsequent events?

**18-54   During the audit of the financial statements of Amis Manufacturing, Inc., the company's president, R. Alderman, and Luddy, the auditor, reviewed matters that were supposed to be included in a written representation letter. On receipt of the following client representation letter, Luddy contacted Alderman to state that it was incomplete.

To E. K. Luddy, CPA

In connection with your audit of the balance sheet of Amis Manufacturing, Inc. as of December 31, 19X2, and the related statements of income, retained earnings, and cash flows for the year then ended, for the purpose of expressing an opinion as to whether the financial statements present fairly the financial position, results of operations, and cash flows of Amis Manufacturing, Inc. in conformity with generally accepted accounting principles, we confirm, to the best of our knowledge and belief, the following representations made to you during your audit. There were no

- Plans or intentions that may materially affect the carrying value or classification of assets and liabilities.
- Communications from regulatory agencies concerning noncompliance with, or deficiencies in, financial reporting practices.
- Agreements to repurchase assets previously sold.
- Violations or possible violations of laws or regulations whose effects should be considered for disclosure in the financial statements or as a basis for recording a loss contingency.
- Unasserted claims or assessments that our lawyer has advised are probable of assertion and must be disclosed in accordance with *Statement of Financial Accounting Standards No. 5.*
- Capital stock repurchase options or agreements or capital stock reserved for options, warrants, conversions, or other requirements.
- Compensating balance or other arrangements involving restrictions on cash balances.

R. Alderman, President
Amis Manufacturing, Inc.

March 14, 19X3

Required:

Identify the other matters that Alderman's representation letter should specifically confirm.

*18-55 The fieldwork for the December 31, 19X8 audit of Bypass Manufacturing Company was completed on February 20, 19X9, and the audit report was delivered to the client on March 1, 19X9. The following material transactions and events came to the auditor's attention subsequent to December 31, 19X8. Indicate whether each transaction or event should result in (1) adjustment of, (2) disclosure in, or (3) no effect on, the December 31, 19X8 financial statements.

a. On January 10, 19X9, the company announced the sale of a product line accounting for 20 percent of its 19X8 revenues.

b. On January 18, 19X9, the company filed an antitrust suit against a major competitor.

c. On January 28, 19X9, a major customer with a large past-due year-end balance declared bankruptcy.

d. On February 10, 19X9, the company declared a two for one split of its common stock.

e. On February 24, 19X9, a serious explosion injuring dozens of workers at one of the client's plants was reported in the news media.

f. On March 4, 19X9, a lawsuit against the company that was disclosed in a footnote to the financial statements was settled for an amount substantially in excess of the estimated amount shown in the footnote.

**18-56 In connection with her audit of Flowmeter, Inc., for the year ended December 31, 19X8, Hirsch, CPA, is aware that certain events and transactions that took place after December 31, 19X8, but before she issues her report dated February 28, 19X9, may affect the company's financial statements.

The following material events or transactions have come to her attention.

a. On January 3, 19X9, Flowmeter, Inc., received a shipment of raw materials from Canada. The materials had been ordered in October 19X8 and shipped FOB shipping point in November 19X8.

b. On January 15, 19X9, the company settled and paid a personal injury claim of a former employee as the result of an accident that occurred in March 19X8. The company had not previously recorded a liability for the claim.

c. On January 25, 19X9, the company agreed to purchase for cash the outstanding stock of Porter Electrical Company. The acquisition is likely to double the sales volume of Flowmeter, Inc.

d. On February 1, 19X9, a plant owned by Flowmeter, Inc., was damaged by a flood and an uninsured loss of inventory resulted.

e. On February 5, 19X9, Flowmeter, Inc., issued and sold to the public $2 million in convertible bonds.

Required:

For each of the events or transactions above, indicate the audit procedures that should have brought the item to the attention of the auditor and the form of adjustment or disclosure in the financial statements, including the reasons. Arrange your answer in the following format:

Item No.	Audit Procedures	Adjustment or Disclosure and Reasons

*18-57 Barge Construction Company constructs large oil barges, each requiring from six to nine months to build. The company follows the percentage-of-completion method of recording construction revenue for financial statement purposes. At the audit date, two barges were under construction (one estimated as 96 percent complete and one as 41 percent complete), and there was a backlog of one barge under firm contract (although informal understandings had been reached to construct five other barges, for which materials had been ordered).

All the barges were built under fixed price contracts, including one constructed for the U.S. government during the current year. Warranty costs are recorded as incurred, and have not been significant. The completed-contract method of recording revenue is used for federal income tax purposes; the Internal Revenue Service has never examined the company's federal income tax returns.

The CPA performing the audit of the Barge Construction Company is preparing to discuss subsequent events with management. He has a standard checklist of inquiries, but he is wondering if there are not some specific additional questions he should ask in this case. What specific inquiries would you make on the basis of the preceding information?

***18-58   Caldwell and Douglas, CPA, are completing the audit of Carmel Corporation for the year ended December 31, 19X4. While performing a review of subsequent events, they note the following situations.

1. Because of political developments in the Middle East, the possibility of expropriation of one of the company's foreign facilities exists. The book value of this facility is $2.4 million.

2. Carmel manufactures a car wax. In June 19X4, Carmel changed suppliers for one of the ingredients in the car wax. Shortly thereafter, customers began complaining that the wax caused the finish on their cars to become cloudy. In January 19X5 the company recalled the products manufactured with this ingredient and changed back to the original supplier. Carmel's lawyers believe it is probable that the company will lose the $2 million class action suit that was filed by a group representing the consumers who used Carmel's car wax. However, the lawyers believe the suit will be settled for $326,000, the estimated cost to correct the problem for the cars affected.

3. Carmel initiated a lawsuit against the supplier of the defective car wax ingredient. Carmel's lawyers believe it is highly probable that the company will win the suit and recover the $375,000 lost as a result of the customer's lawsuit and other expenses associated with recalling the product.

4. Carmel also manufactures portable facsimile machines that sell for $245 each. The machines are covered by an eighteen-month warranty that includes parts and labor. Warranty cost for machines sold during the year but paid in January is $102,800.

Required:

a. Describe the audit procedures for subsequent events that are likely to have detected each of the above situations.

b. Describe how the financial statements will be affected by each of the above situations. Refer to *SFAS No. 5, Accounting for Contingencies,* for the accounting implications.

*18-59   During his review of subsequent events in connection with the audit of Jordan Match Company, Ron Gray, CPA, was informed by the corporate secretary that, although there had been two meetings of the board of directors subsequent to the audit date, no minutes had been prepared. The corporate secretary stated that he had been too busy to prepare the minutes but that the meetings had been routine and no significant matters had been discussed that would require disclosure in the financial statements. He offered to give Gray a letter to this effect.

Discuss each of the following courses of action open to Gray.

a. Accept the letter from the corporate secretary (who will be the one who subsequently prepares and signs the minutes) and issue the audit report.

b. Refuse to accept the letter of the corporate secretary and refuse to issue the audit report.

c. Attend the next board of directors' meeting and obtain oral confirmation that no significant matters had been discussed that would require disclosure in the financial statements.

What action should Gray take?

*18-60 During an audit of Miller Carpet Company, Kelley, CPA, learned that the company had been charged with discriminatory hiring policies and that lawsuits totaling $10 million had been brought against it because of this alleged practice. Kelley discussed the matter with the company's legal counsel, who pointed out that the company had a very strong defense and that few successful cases had been brought under the particular statutes involved. She was optimistic that the company would incur no liability.

When Kelley received the legal counsel's letter replying to the request for a description and evaluation of pending or threatened litigation, it contained the same optimistic evaluation of the discrimination suit but concluded by stating that no opinion could be expressed regarding the potential outcome of the suit. When Kelley contacted the legal counsel by phone to discuss the letter, he was told that the law firm had a policy against giving opinions on the outcome of future litigation but that the auditor could read between the lines and see that she considered the possibility of an adverse outcome to be very remote.

Discuss the quality of evidence represented by the letter from legal counsel and any other actions or options open to Kelley.

**18-61 Windek, CPA, is nearing the completion of an audit of the financial statements of Jubilee, Inc. Windek is currently concerned with ascertaining the occurrence of subsequent events that may require adjustment or disclosure essential to a fair presentation in conformity with generally accepted accounting principles.

Required:

a. Briefly explain what is meant by the phrase *subsequent event.*

b. How do those subsequent events that require financial statement adjustment differ from those that require financial statement disclosure?

c. What procedures should be performed to ascertain the occurrence of subsequent events?

**18-62 Cole & Cole, CPAs, are auditing the financial statements of Consolidated Industries Co. for the year ended December 31, 19X2. On April 2, 19X3, an inquiry letter to J. J. Young, Consolidated's outside attorney, was drafted to corroborate the information furnished to Cole by management concerning pending and threatened litigation, claims, and assessments and unasserted claims and assessments. On May 6, 19X3, C.R. Brown, Consolidated's Chief Financial Officer, gave Cole a draft of the inquiry letter below for Cole's review before mailing it to Young.

Required:
Describe the omissions, ambiguities, and inappropriate statements and terminology in Brown's letter below.

May 6, 19X3

J. J. Young, Attorney at Law
123 Main Street
Anytown, USA

Dear J. J. Young:

In connection with an audit of our financial statements at December 31, 19X2, and for the year then ended, management of the Company has prepared, and furnished to our auditors, Cole & Cole, CPAs, 456 Broadway, Anytown, USA, a description and evaluation of certain contingencies, including those set forth below involving matters with respect to which you have been engaged and to which you have devoted substantive attention on behalf of the Company in the form of legal consultation or representation. Your response should include matters that existed at December 31, 19X2. Because of the confidentiality of all these matters, your response may be limited.

In November 19X2, an action was brought against the Company by an outside salesman alleging breach of contract for sales commissions and pledging a second cause of action for an accounting with respect to claims for fees and commissions. The causes of action claim damages of $300,000, but the Company believes it has meritorious defenses to the claims. The possible exposure of the Company to a successful judgment on behalf of the plaintiff is slight.

In July 19W8, an action was brought against the Company by Industrial Manufacturing Co. (Industrial) alleging patent infringement and seeking damages of $20,000,000. The action in U.S. District Court resulted in a decision on October 16, 19X2, holding that the Company infringed seven Industrial patents and awarded damages of $14,000,000. The Company vigorously denies these allegations and has filed an appeal with the U.S. Court of Appeals for the Federal Circuit. The appeal process is expected to take approximately two years, but there is some chance that Industrial may ultimately prevail.

Please furnish to our auditors such explanation, if any, that you consider necessary to supplement the foregoing information, including an explanation of those matters as to which your views may differ from those stated and an identification of the omission of any pending or threatened litigation, claims, and assessments or a statement that the list of such matters is complete. Your response may be quoted or referred to in the financial statements without further correspondence with you.

You also consulted on various other matters considered pending or threatened litigation. However, you may not comment on these matters because publicizing them may alert potential plaintiffs to the strengths of their cases. In addition, various other matters probable of assertion that have some chance of an unfavorable outcome, as of December 31, 19X2, are unasserted claims and assessments.

C. R. Brown
Chief Financial Officer

*18-63   The following misstatements could affect revenue and expense, commitments and contingencies, and subsequent events. Devise one audit procedure that will provide reasonable assurance of detecting each misstatement.

a. Sales for the first few days of the subsequent year are recorded in the current year.

b. A contingent liability for damages alleged in a lawsuit is not disclosed in the client's financial statements.

c. A significant uninsured loss caused by flood damage to an important distribution center is not disclosed in the client's financial statements.

d. Sales revenue is recorded for products shipped to a customer. The customer has the right to return the products if unable to sell them.

e. Delivery expense is charged to the purchases account.

f. The details of a stock option plan are not disclosed in the client's financial statements. The plan was approved by the board of directors, but the minutes for that meeting were not furnished to the auditors.

g. The board of directors declared a 10 percent stock dividend after year-end, but before the end of fieldwork that was not reported in the financial statements.

h. A capital lease has been incorrectly recorded as an operating lease.

i. The payroll clerk paid herself for overtime that she did not work.

j. The client records revenue on the percentage-of-completion basis and has overstated revenue by understating total estimated costs.

k. Rental income received in advance of its due date is recorded as rental income.

l. The business purpose of the president's trip to Bermuda is not documented on the related expense account form.

m. The client manufactured, shipped, and recorded sales of defective products during the last month of the year. After year-end, some injuries resulted from the products, and many of the defective products were returned.

n. Expired insurance expense is understated.

o. The payroll cost of certain office employees is charged to direct labor.

p. The client is discharging pollution into a river in violation of EPA regulations.

q. The client incurred but deferred for accounting purposes routine training costs.

*18-64 Lambert Skull recently graduated from an accounting program at a local university and accepted a position on the audit staff of Look and Look, CPAs. He was assigned to the audit of Grand Toys, a manufacturer of innovative children's toys, including a plastic gun that shoots rubber arrows at other children.

Lambert's senior auditor was Christine Bore, who had extensive experience auditing Grand Toys and companies that made similar products. Christine assigned Lambert to perform analytical procedures. Lambert's first task was to compare administrative expenses for the year under audit with the previous year. Lambert secured the following schedule of comparative Administrative Expenses.

Administrative expenses	12-31-X4	12-31-X3	Over (under)
Officer salaries	$800,000	$800,000	$ 0
Office salaries	600,000	550,000	50,000
Office supplies	10,000	9,000	1,000
Legal expense	80,000	40,000	40,000
Office lease	20,000	20,000	0
Miscellaneous expense	70,000	60,000	10,000

Lambert did not wish to appear dumb in the eyes of Christine. Therefore, he went directly to the controller, who did not like the auditors and gave them as little time as possible. Lambert received these answers to the variations in administrative expenses.

1. The increase in office salaries was caused by the replacement of an unskilled worker with one who could work with the various computer software programs used in the office.

2. The increase in legal expense resulted from a retainer fee increase by the law firm retained by the company. The controller did not like the increase, but he could do nothing about it because the head of the legal firm was a friend of the chairman of the board of directors of Grand Toys.

3. The increase in miscellaneous expense was nothing the auditor should be concerned with because this category represented expenditures that could not be classified in one of the other accounts.

Lambert did not conduct any further investigation of these variances. He wrote a memo describing the controller's explanations and indicating that they appeared reasonable.

Required:

a. Describe at least one auditing procedure that Lambert could have performed to confirm the controller's explanations for each of the three variances.

Meanwhile Christine was engaged in a discussion with Grand Toys' legal counsel concerning two events.

1. The settlement of a major lawsuit filed by parents of a child whose eye was damaged severely by a rubber arrow fired from a toy gun manufactured by Grand Toys. The settlement was for an amount materially in excess of the recorded liability.

2. The filing of a lawsuit in early 19X5 by parents of another child who had suffered the same eye damage from one of Grand Toys' guns. The lawsuit was in an early stage, but the amount asked by the parents was material to the financial statements of Grand Toys.

Required:

b. Describe at least one auditing procedure Christine Bore used to discover the settlement of the first described lawsuit.

c. Describe at least one auditing procedure Christine Bore used to discover the existence of the second described lawsuit.

d. What actions should the auditor take in regard to each of the described lawsuits? Why?

The Standard Audit Report

"Trust everybody, but cut the cards."

FINLEY PETER DUNNE, *Mr. Dooley's Philosophy*

LEARNING OBJECTIVES

After reading and studying the material in this chapter, the student should be able to

▶ Paraphrase the four standards of reporting.

▶ Describe the meaning of these sections or phrases in the auditor's report: (1) title; (2) generally accepted auditing standards; (3) reasonable assurance; (4) material misstatement; (5) appropriateness of auditing procedures; (6) auditor's opinion; (7) report date; and (8) auditor's name.

▶ Give examples of report coverage of prior-year financial statements.

▶ Give an example of a report on financial sta̶   ̶ents prepared for use in other countries.

▶ Describe required supplementary inform̶   ̶   ̶   ̶   ̶information in annual reports and other documents containi̶   ̶   ̶   ̶   ̶   ̶tements.

▶ Describe how events subsequent to ̶i   ̶   ̶   ̶   ̶   ̶v affect the audited financial statements.

The next three chapters c̶
cate their opinions to ̶ȷ̶
Figure 19.1 this comȷ̶
auditor selects the ̶
the financial state̶
work for reportȷ̶

FIGURE 19.1   General Flowchart of an Audit

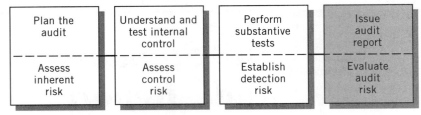

THE STANDARDS OF REPORTING

Of the ten generally accepted auditing standards, four relate to reporting.

1. *The report shall state whether the financial statements are presented in accordance with generally accepted accounting principles.*

   This standard establishes generally accepted accounting principles as the criteria against which general-purpose financial statements are to be evaluated in an audit performed in accordance with generally accepted auditing standards.

2. *The report shall identify those circumstances in which such principles have not been consistently observed in the current period in relation to the preceding period.*

   Because changes in accounting principles between periods can distort the comparison of financial statement results between the periods, auditors include reference to such changes in their audit reports. This reference alerts users of the financial statements to consider the effect of the change in accounting principles in evaluating an entity's operations.

3. *Informative disclosures in the financial statements are to be regarded as reasonably adequate unless otherwise stated in the report.*

   This standard was included at a time when generally accepted accounting principles were not well developed and many disclosures were not required then that are required by generally accepted accounting principles today. Some auditors believe that this standard and the first standard that requires reference to generally accepted accounting principles are redundant and could be combined.

4. *The report shall either contain an expression of opinion regarding the financial statements, taken as a whole, or an assertion to the effect that an opinion cannot be expressed. When an overall opinion cannot be expressed, the reasons therefor should be stated. In all cases where an auditor's name is associated with financial statements, the report should contain a clear-cut indication of the character of the auditor's work, if any, and the degree of responsibility the auditor is taking.*

   This standard requires auditors to clearly specify the degree of responsibility that they are taking for any financial statements with which they are associated. Auditors must issue some type of report when their name is associated with financial statements; they cannot remain silent.

THE STANDARD AUDIT REPORT

A standard form of audit report is issued when (1) the auditors have performed their audit in accordance with generally accepted auditing standards, (2) the financial statements are presented in conformity with generally accepted accounting principles, and (3) there are no circumstances (discussed in Chapter 20) requiring modification.

The standard audit report consists of (1) a title containing the word *independent*, (2) an opening or introductory paragraph (a description of the financial statements and a statement that they are the representations of management), (3) a scope paragraph (descriptions of the auditor's responsibility to detect material misstatements and the general nature of audit procedures and a statement as to the adequacy of the procedures), and (4) an opinion paragraph (the auditor's opinion regarding the fair presentation of the financial statements). The report form is as follows:

Independent Auditor's Report

To the Board of Directors of X Company:

(Opening paragraph)

We have audited the accompanying balance sheet of X Company as of December 31, 19XX, and the related statements of income, retained earnings, and cash flows for the year then ended. These financial statements are the responsibility of the Company's management. Our responsibility is to express an opinion on these financial statements based on our audit.

(Scope paragraph)

We conducted our audit in accordance with generally accepted auditing standards. Those standards require that we plan and perform the audit to obtain reasonable assurance about whether the financial statements are free of material misstatement. An audit includes examining, on a test basis, evidence supporting the amounts and disclosures in the financial statements. An audit also includes assessing the accounting principles used and significant estimates made by management, as well as evaluating the overall financial statement presentation. We believe that our audit provides a reasonable basis for our opinion.

(Opinion paragraph)

In our opinion, the financial statements referred to above present fairly, in all material respects, the financial position of X Company as of December 31, 19XX, and the results of its operations and its cash flows for the year then ended in conformity with generally accepted accounting principles.

(Signature)

(Date)

Modifications to this standard report form are discussed in the next chapter.

Title of the Report

Before 1934, the opinion paragraph of the standard audit report began with the phrase "we certify that in our opinion," which led to the reports being referred to as "auditor's certificates." The term *certificate* has been replaced with a title such as "independent auditor's report" to emphasize the fundamental aspect of independence of the audit function. A title that contains the word *independent* is now a required part of the report.

Addressing the Report

A survey of auditors' reports included in annual reports of public companies would find some addressed to the stockholders, some addressed to the board of directors, and some addressed to both. The audit report may be addressed to the company whose financial statements are being audited or to its board of directors or stockholders, except where the company whose financial statements the auditor is engaged to audit is not the client; in those cases, the report should be addressed to the auditor's client. In the increasing number of cases in which the auditor is elected or ratified by the stockholders, the auditor may acknowledge this by addressing the report to them.

Audit of Financial Statements

The first phrase in the report states that the auditors have audited the various financial statements (which are specifically named). The distinction between the audit of accounting records and financial statements is an important difference to the auditors. Reference to financial statements has a broad connotation in that it implies the gathering of evidence beyond that produced by the client's accounting records.

For instance, Chapter 18 explains that auditors request the client's legal counsel to confirm to them in writing the status of pending litigation. A possible result of these attorneys' letters is footnote disclosure of a contingent liability in the financial statements or an adjusting entry recording a liability. An audit of the accounting records alone might not disclose this situation.

Because the scope of the audit generally includes other procedures similar to the illustration in the preceding paragraph, auditors consider it proper to report that they have audited the *financial statements* (which include footnotes) rather than the *accounting records*. In addition, if the audit is related to the accounting records, some limiting phrase would be required in recognition of the fact that the sampling and testing procedures employed would result in fewer than 100 percent of the records being audited.

Responsibilities of Management

The opening paragraph includes a statement that the financial statements are the responsibility of management. The purpose of this statement is to prevent confusion as to who is responsible for the presentations in the financial statements. Auditors often assist their clients in preparing financial statements; nevertheless, the responsibility for those statements lies with management, not the auditors.

Generally Accepted Auditing Standards

The next important phrase is reference to generally accepted auditing standards in the scope paragraph. During the course of an audit, dozens, perhaps hundreds, of procedures are used to acquire the evidence on which the opinion is based. Reference to each of these procedures would be ponderous and repetitious, particularly since they are acts performed under the general guidelines of generally accepted auditing standards. Therefore, the report merely contains a statement that generally accepted auditing standards were followed.[1] Furthermore, there is some belief that modification of the scope paragraph might be misunderstood by the readers.

Although the three general standards are discussed throughout the text, one, in particular, warrants special attention—the standard on independence. It would be improper for auditors to issue a standard audit report if they did not adhere to the standard on independence. A special type of disclaimer, shown in Chapter 21, is applicable to the situation in which independence is impaired.

Reasonable Assurance

The scope paragraph also describes the general nature of the procedures an auditor employs to obtain *reasonable assurance* that the financial statements are free of material misstatement. These procedures are described as (1) examination of evidence, on a test basis, that supports the amounts and disclosures included in the financial statements; (2) assessment of the appropriateness of the accounting principles used and significant estimates made by management; and (3) evaluation of the appropriateness of the overall financial statement presentation.

This description emphasizes several points regarding the impreciseness of evidence-gathering techniques and financial statement presentation. First, the readers of the report are told that evidence is gathered and examined on a test basis. This implies that an item not selected for testing could be misstated and not be detected. However, the audit has been planned and performed, so that any such undetected misstatement is unlikely to result in a material misstatement. In addition, the assessment of inherent and control risks is subjective. Therefore, the audit provides reasonable, but not complete, assurance. Second, the reference to appropriateness of accounting principles and estimates suggests rather subtly that a number of subjective judgments (e.g., a choice between LIFO and FIFO inventory methods and an estimate of the allowance for doubtful accounts) are involved in the presentation of financial statements. Conclusive evidence regarding some of these judgments may not be available. This lack of conclusive evidence is further support for providing reasonable, but not complete, assurance. Finally, reference to overall presentation indicates that the auditor's opinion covers the financial statements taken as a whole and not individual elements thereof.

---

[1] Note that the auditors need not perform all *customary* audit procedures. If, for example, the auditors did not confirm accounts receivable or observe inventories because it was impracticable or impossible to do so, but satisfied themselves by means of alternative auditing procedures, they need not describe the circumstances or alternative procedures employed. What is required is that they perform all audit procedures *necessary* for them to form an opinion regarding the financial statements.

Materially Misstated

The scope paragraph explains that generally accepted auditing standards require that an audit be designed to evaluate whether financial statements are *materially misstated.* (Materiality is discussed in Chapter 7.) This phrase is an attempt to explain to users the extent of the auditor's responsibility for detecting errors and fraud. This phrase also emphasizes that an auditor does not attempt to determine whether financial statements are precise or accurate. The objective is to determine whether the financial statements are materially misstated.

Appropriateness of Auditing Procedures

The scope paragraph concludes with a statement that the auditor believes that the auditing procedures applied were appropriate to support the opinion that follows in the opinion paragraph. The auditor is stating that, notwithstanding the limitations previously discussed in this paragraph, a positive conclusion has been formed that the scope of the audit procedures is adequate.

The Auditor's Opinion

The opinion paragraph of the standard audit report begins with the words "in our opinion." This phrase is an expression of the fact that, although auditors have a special expertise in accounting and auditing, no guarantee or factual statement regarding accuracy or even fairness can be made to readers of the report for the reasons discussed in the preceding paragraphs.

Nevertheless, the readers and users of financial statements have a right to expect that the phrase "in our opinion" represents the sound judgment of professional experts, and this is the message that auditors intend to convey. Such an expression of opinion is required to meet the last standard of reporting.

A complete set of general-purpose financial statements normally consists of a balance sheet (also referred to as a statement of financial position or condition), a statement of income (or of earnings), a statement of retained earnings (sometimes combined with the statement of income), and a statement of cash flows, although other statements may be included in certain circumstances. The auditor must understand which phrase in the audit report applies to each financial statement.

The phrase "financial position" in the opinion paragraph refers to the balance sheet. Accordingly, if an auditor were expressing an opinion on a balance sheet only, an example of the opinion paragraph would be:

> In our opinion, the *balance sheet* of X Company presents fairly, in all material respects, its *financial position* as of December 31, 19X2, in conformity with. . . .

Note that this example makes no reference to results of operations or cash flows. To do so would be inappropriate, because the balance sheet does not purport to present either of these.

A statement of income and a statement of retained earnings (or a combined statement of income and retained earnings) are ordinarily considered essential for a fair presentation of "results of operations." Therefore, an audit report covering only these two statements would include the following wording in the opinion paragraph:

> In our opinion, the *statements of income and retained earnings* of X Company present fairly, in all material respects, its *results of operations* for the year ended December 31, 19X2, in conformity with. . . .

No reference is made to financial position or to cash flows in this example, because the financial statements needed to express an opinion as to those attributes of a company (the balance sheet and statement of cash flows) have not been presented.

The importance of an understanding of the relationship between the financial statements and the opinion being expressed will become apparent when qualifications of the audit report (sometimes applying to only one of several financial statements) are discussed in the next chapter.

Fair Presentation

The opinion paragraph of the standard audit report contains the phrase "present fairly, in all material respects, the financial position of X Company as of December 31, 19XX, and the results of its operations and its cash flows for the year then ended in conformity with generally accepted accounting principles."

The current report style, which includes the preceding phrase, evolved from earlier versions that contained no reference to fairness or to generally accepted accounting principles and used such words as "true" and "correct." Gradually, these terms gave way to "fairly," a word the accounting profession felt better expressed the subjective nature of financial statements. The phrase "in all material respects" was added to provide further emphasis that the auditor's report does not attest to the absolute accuracy of the financial statements.

However, there is no clear agreement within the accounting profession as to the proper relationship between the word "fairly" and the phrase "generally accepted accounting principles." Some believe that there is a general presumption that financial statements are fair *if* they are presented in accordance with generally accepted accounting principles, whereas others believe that two separate opinions are needed: one that the financial statements are fairly presented and the other that they are presented in accordance with generally accepted accounting principles.

Influential groups outside of the accounting profession have been unwilling to accept the former definition. One of the first real evidences of this reluctance appeared in the *Continental Vending* case, summarized in Chapter 4. The court made a statement to the effect that adherence to generally accepted accounting principles was only *one* determinant of fairness and was not a complete defense for the auditors.

Since then, the question of the relationship between fairness and accounting principles has gained increasing attention in the auditing literature. As a result, *SAS No. 69*, entitled *The Meaning of "Present Fairly in Conformity with Generally Accepted Accounting Principles" in the Independent Auditor's Report,* was issued. The following is one conclusion of the statement:

> The independent auditor's judgment concerning the "fairness" of the overall presentation of financial statements should be applied within the framework of generally accepted accounting principles. Without the framework, the auditor would have no uniform standard for judging the presentation of financial position, results of operations, and cash flows in financial statements.

Coupled with the preceding statement are further comments and discussions that seem to indicate that the concepts of fairness and accounting principles are broad. For example, *SAS No. 69* contains these additional comments:

> Generally accepted accounting principles recognize the importance of reporting transactions and events in accordance with their substance. The auditor should consider whether the substance of transactions or events differs materially from their form.

SAS No. 69 goes on to specify that the auditor must form a judgment as to whether

1. The accounting principles selected and applied have general acceptance,
2. The accounting principles are appropriate in the circumstances,
3. The financial statements, including the related notes, are informative of matters that may affect their use, understanding, and interpretation,
4. The information presented in the financial statements is classified and summarized in a reasonable manner; that is, it is neither too detailed nor too condensed.
5. The financial statements reflect the underlying transactions and events in a manner that presents the financial position, results of operations, and cash flows stated within a range of acceptable limits, that is, limits that are reasonable and practicable to attain in financial statements.

Some members of the profession maintain that fairness cannot be objectively measured by the auditor and recommend that the word *fairly* be deleted from the auditor's report. This recommendation has not been followed.

Generally Accepted Accounting Principles

The term *generally accepted accounting principles,* as it is understood by auditors, is set forth in *SAS No. 69* as follows:

> The phrase "generally accepted accounting principles" is a technical accounting term that encompasses the conventions, rules, and procedures necessary to define accepted accounting practice at a particular time. It includes not only broad guidelines of general application, but also detailed practices and procedures. . . .

Rule 203 of the AICPA *Code of Professional Conduct* prohibits a member of the AICPA from expressing an opinion that financial statements are presented in conformity with generally accepted accounting principles if they contain a departure from an accounting principle established by a body designated to issue such principles. An exception is provided if it can be demonstrated that owing to unusual circumstances, the principle would cause the financial statements to be misleading. *SAS No. 69* acknowledges this primary source of accounting principles and goes on to suggest and prioritize the other potential sources. These sources are summarized for nongovernment and government entities in Figure 19.2 on page 624.

Category (a) represents accounting principles issued by organizations authorized to issue such principles pursuant to Rule 203. At present, these organizations are the Financial Accounting Standards Board (FASB) and the Governmental Accounting Standards Board (GASB).

If an auditor cannot find the answer to an accounting question in the sources described in category (a), he or she next considers the sources in category (b). These are pronouncements of bodies of expert accountants that deliberate accounting issues in public forums for the purpose of establishing accounting principles or describing existing accounting practices that are generally accepted.

If the accounting question cannot be answered from sources in category (b), the auditor next considers sources in category (c). These are pronouncements of bodies organized by the FASB or GASB that deliberate accounting issues in public forums for the purpose of interpreting or establishing accounting principles or describing existing accounting principles that are generally accepted.

If category (c) sources do not contain the answer to the accounting question, the auditor next looks to category (d) sources. These are practices or pronouncements that are widely recognized as being generally accepted because they represent prevalent practice in a particular industry, or the knowledgeable application of pronouncements to specific circumstances.

In the absence of an answer to the accounting question in category (a), (b), (c), or (d) sources, the auditor considers other accounting literature. As can be seen in Figure 19.2, the other accounting literature includes a wide range of sources; this literature should be evaluated on its relevance and the general recognition of its issuer or author.

As the variety of sources listed above suggests, it may be difficult to determine that a particular accounting principle is generally accepted because there is no single reference source for all generally accepted accounting principles. If there is a conflict between accounting principles from different categories, the auditor should select the principle from the highest category or be prepared to justify that an accounting principle from a lower category best presents the substance of a transaction in the circumstances.

Although it is included as a separate standard of reporting, adequate disclosure in financial statements is often considered to be encompassed within generally accepted accounting principles. Whether adequate disclosure is considered as a separate requirement or as part of generally accepted accounting principles, there is no question but that it is essential to the fair presentation of financial statements. Examples of such disclosures include important subsequent events, restrictions on payment of dividends, guarantees of debt, commitments and contingencies, related party transactions, and depreciation and inventory methods.

Consistent Application of Accounting Principles

At one time the opinion paragraph of the auditor's report included a phrase attesting to the consistent application of accounting principles between periods. The Auditing Standards Board (ASB), although agreeing with the desirability of informing users of financial statements of changes in accounting principles, main-

FIGURE 19.2   Summary of Prioritized Sources of Generally Accepted Accounting Principles

GAAP Hierarchy Summary	
Nongovernment Entities	*State and Local Governments*

Established Accounting Principles

a. FASB Statements and Interpretations, APB Opinions, and AICPA Accounting Research Bulletins	a. GASB Statements and Interpretations, plus AICPA and FASB pronouncements if made applicable to state and local governments by a GASB Statement or Interpretation
b. FASB Technical Bulletins, AICPA Industry Audit and Accounting Guides, and AICPA Statements of Position	b. GASB Technical Bulletins, and the following pronouncements if specifically made applicable to state and local governments by the AICPA: AICPA Industry Audit and Accounting Guides and AICPA Statements of Position
c. Consensus positions of the FASB Emerging Issues Task Force and AICPA Practice Bulletins	c. Consensus positions of the GASB Emerging Issues Task Force and AICPA Practice Bulletins if specifically made applicable to state and local governments by the AICPA
d. AICPA accounting interpretations, "Questions and Answers" published by the FASB staff, as well as widely recognized and prevalent industry practices	d. "Questions and Answers" published by the GASB staff, as well as widely recognized and prevalent industry practices

Other Accounting Literature

Other accounting literature, including FASB Concepts Statements; AICPA Issues Papers; International Accounting Standards Committee Statements; GASB Statements, Interpretations, and Technical Bulletins; pronouncements of other professional associations or regulatory agencies; AICPA *Technical Practice Aids*; and accounting textbooks, handbooks, and articles	Other accounting literature, including GASB Concepts Statements; pronouncements in categories (a) through (d) of the hierarchy for nongovernmental entities when not specifically made applicable to state and local governments; FASB Concepts Statements; AICPA Issues Papers; International Accounting Standards Committee Statements; pronouncements of other professional associations or regulatory agencies; AICPA *Technical Practice Aids*; and accounting textbooks, handbooks, and articles

Source: AICPA Professional Standards

tained that this disclosure, like other financial statement disclosures, was the responsibility of management. They observed that the auditor's proper function was to consider the propriety of the change in accounting principle and the adequacy of the disclosure of the change. Thus, the ASB decided that auditors should not refer to consistency in their report unless an inconsistency in the application of accounting principles was not properly recorded or disclosed. In that case, the financial statements would not be presented in accordance with generally accepted accounting principles.

The SEC objected to the elimination of the consistency reference from the auditor's report. In a compromise between the ASB and the SEC, it was decided that no reference would be made to consistency in the auditor's standard report if the accounting principles were consistently applied. However, instances of inconsistent application of accounting principles would be noted in an explanatory paragraph. Examples of this modification of the standard audit report are presented in the next chapter.

Report Date

The date of an auditor's report has a significance that the general public does not always fully understand. This is the date to which the auditor assumes responsibility for detecting subsequent events that might have a material effect on the audited financial statements. This is normally the date on which the auditor completes his or her work in the client's office (often referred to as the end of fieldwork).

Consider the following facts. An audit is being performed as of December 31, 19X6. The auditors must allow the company time to close and balance its financial records before work on the audit can begin, so it is January 17, 19X7, before the audit work commences in the client's office. By February 3, 19X7, the audit staff has substantially completed its work, and the audit partner arrives at the client's office to review the audit work and clear any problems with the client. This review is completed on February 4, 19X7, and that evening the audit staff returns to the accounting firm's office to have a quality control review made of the audit report and audit working papers. Because February is a very busy time of year, the quality control reviews are not completed until February 8, 19X7. The completed and signed report is delivered to the client on February 9, 19X7. What should be the date of the auditor's report?

The audit report should be dated as of the last day of fieldwork, which in this case would be February 4, 19X7. The audit staff is in the client's office through this date and has access to financial records and management personnel necessary to perform a review of transactions and events subsequent to the audit date that might affect the audited financial statements. After the audit team leaves the client's office, this information is no longer readily available, and the auditor has no responsibility to make any inquiry or to perform any auditing procedure subsequent to this date (except with respect to filings under the Securities Act of 1933—see Chapter 4).

Although the auditor has no responsibility to search for subsequent events affecting the financial statements after the date of the report, material events coming to his or her attention between that date and the date the financial statements are issued should be reflected in the financial statements, or the auditor should qualify the report. In either event, the dating of the auditor's report will be affected. The auditor would have the option of *dual dating* the report, that is, using the original date for the overall report and a subsequent date for the footnote describing the subsequent event or transaction (e.g., February 4, 19X7, except for Note 8, as to which the date is February 7, 19X7), or using only the later date. In the latter case, it would be necessary for the auditor to return to the client's office and perform a subsequent review from the original date to the later date.

Dating the Auditor's Report

Assume that you are auditing a pharmaceutical company and you complete fieldwork on February 4, 19X7. On February 7, 19X7, before you have issued your report, you read in the *Wall Street Journal* that several people have died as the result of an unanticipated side effect of one of your client's drugs. You call management personnel of your client who confirm the news stories. You and client personnel agree to add a footnote (Note 10) that describes the anticipated effect of the deaths on the company's operations. How do you date your auditor's report? The efficient way would be to dual date—February 4, 19X7, except for Note 10 which is February 7, 19X7. Another less efficient alternative is to send the audit team back to the client's office to perform the subsequent review procedures from February 4, 19X7 to February 7, 19X7 and then date the report February 7, 19X7.

Auditor's Name

The audit report is signed with the accounting firm's name, not the name of the CPA who was in charge of the audit. Use of the firm name indicates that the firm as a whole accepts responsibility for the quality of the audit. In most firms, only partners are authorized to sign the firm's name to audit reports.

REPORT COVERAGE OF PRIOR-YEAR FINANCIAL STATEMENTS

The example of the audit report shown on page 617 of this chapter is applicable to financial statements covering only one year. It has become common (and is required in many SEC filings) for companies to present financial statements for two or more years. In such cases, the language of the standard audit report must be modified.

Prior Year Audited by Current Auditors

If the auditor has audited the prior-year financial statements the auditor should update the report. In an updated report the auditor reexpresses an opinion or, depending on the circumstances, expresses a different opinion from that previously expressed, on prior-year financial statements after a subsequent audit (e.g., the expression of opinions on 19X2 [prior year] and 19X3 [current year] financial statements after the 19X3 audit—the report on the 19X2 financial statements has been updated from the end of fieldwork for the 19X2 audit to the end of fieldwork for the 19X3 audit). The updating is performed by referring to both the current- and prior-year(s) financial statements in the report.

The updated report is dated as of the end of fieldwork of the most recent audit. Reports with differing opinions and the modification of previously issued reports are discussed in Chapter 20.

Prior-Year Financial Statements Not Audited

Where the prior-year financial statements have not been audited, notations to this effect should be placed above the appropriate column headings in the financial statements, and the auditor should either reissue his or her prior-period report containing a disclaimer of opinion or include a separate paragraph in the current-period report, which might be worded as follows.

> The accompanying balance sheet of X Company as of December 31, 19X1, and the related statements of income, retained earnings, and cash flows for the year then ended were not audited by us and, accordingly, we do not express an opinion on them.

AU Section 504 provides that the disclaimer of opinion may be omitted in certain SEC filings (although the applicable financial statements must still be labeled "unaudited"). There is no justification for this exception, and the authors believe it is unwarranted.

Prior-Year Financial Statements Audited by Predecessor Auditors

If prior-year financial statements are presented that were audited by predecessor auditors, the predecessor auditors may reissue their report. However, before doing so they should consider whether their original opinion is still applicable. Accordingly, they should

1. Read the financial statements of the current period.
2. Compare the prior-period financial statements that they reported on with the financial statements to be presented for comparative purposes.
3. Obtain a letter of representation from the successor auditors regarding matters that might have a material effect on, or require disclosure in, the financial statements reported on by the predecessor auditors.

The date of a reissued report should be the same date as that used in the original report to avoid the impression that the predecessor auditors' examination extended beyond the original date.[2] If the predecessor auditors' report or the applicable financial statements require revision as a result of the procedures set forth above, dual dating should be used.

---

[2] Note that the consideration of the effect on prior-year financial statements of information that the auditor obtains during his or her audit of the current-year financial statements distinguishes an updated report (current report date) from a reissued report (original report date).

If prior-year financial statements are presented, and they were audited by predecessor auditors whose report is not presented, this fact should be disclosed in the successor auditors' report. The following sentence (added to the opening paragraph) is an example of such disclosure:

> The financial statements of X Company as of December 31, 19X8 (the prior year), were audited by other auditors whose report dated March 1, 19X9, expressed an unqualified opinion on those statements.

If prior-year financial statements are presented and the predecessor auditors' report on those statements was modified, this fact should be disclosed in the successor auditors' report.

REPORTS ON FINANCIAL STATEMENTS PREPARED FOR USE IN OTHER COUNTRIES

With the growing internationalization of business, auditors may be engaged to audit and report on financial statements of a U.S. entity that have been prepared in conformity with accounting principles generally accepted in another country for use outside of the United States. For example, the financial statements of Toyota USA (a U.S. company) may be prepared for inclusion in the consolidated financial statements of Toyota International (a non–U.S. parent company). The auditor must understand the accounting principles that are generally accepted by the other country to perform this engagement and must comply with the general and fieldwork standards of the other country as well as with those of U.S. standards.

If the financial statements prepared in conformity with accounting principles generally accepted in another country are for use *only* outside the United States, the auditor may issue either (1) a U.S.-style report modified to report on the accounting principles of another country or (2) if appropriate, the report form of the other country. When option (1) is selected, the standard U.S. report is modified as follows.

> *(Opening paragraph)*
> We have audited the accompanying balance sheet of Toyota USA as of December 31, 19X3, and the related statements of income, retained earnings, and cash flows for the year then ended *which, as described in Note 1 have been prepared on the basis of accounting principles accepted in Japan.* These financial statements are the responsibility. . . .
>
> *(Scope paragraph)*
> We conducted our audit in accordance with *auditing standards generally accepted in the United States and Japan. U.S.* standards require that we plan. . . .
>
> *(Opinion paragraph)*
> In our opinion, the financial statements referred to above present fairly, in all material respects, the financial position of Toyota USA as of December 31, 19X3, and the results of its operations and its cash flows for the year then ended in conformity with *accounting principles generally accepted in Japan.*

Before using this reporting format the auditor should have a clear understanding of, and obtain written representations from management regarding, the purposes and uses of the related financial statements.

ANNUAL REPORTS AND OTHER DOCUMENTS CONTAINING AUDITED FINANCIAL STATEMENTS

Annual reports to stockholders, reports to regulatory agencies, and other documents often include (1) financial statements, together with the related auditor's report, (2) information that is supplementary to the financial statements but required by the FASB or the GASB, and (3) other information, such as a president's letter to stockholders or management's discussion and analysis of operations. The auditor has certain limited responsibilities for both the supplementary and other information.

Required Supplementary Information

The Auditing Standards Board has addressed *supplementary information* required by the FASB and the GASB by providing guidance in AU Section 558. An example of supplementary information is oil and gas reserve information for petroleum exploration companies.

If the FASB or GASB requires supplementary information, the auditor will ordinarily

1. Make inquiries about the method of preparing the information. (Written client representations are optional.)
2. Compare the information for consistency with responses to inquiries of management and knowledge gained in auditing the financial statements.
3. Apply any specific procedures prescribed for the particular FASB or GASB requirement.

Auditors report on required supplementary information by exception; that is, auditors do not refer to supplementary information in the report unless (1) the required information is omitted, (2) the required information departs materially from FASB or GASB requirements, (3) they are unable to complete the prescribed procedures, or (4) they are unable to resolve substantial doubts as to the information's adherence to FASB or GASB requirements.

Other Information

The auditor should also read the other information in documents containing audited financial statements to determine whether it is *materially inconsistent* with the information contained in the financial statements. For example, if a company's normal operations for a year produced a net loss, but an extraordinary gain more than offset the loss and resulted in net income, the text of an annual report that discussed net income for the year without stating that it resulted from an extraordinary gain could be materially inconsistent with the financial statements. AU Section

550 provides that, in the event of such a material inconsistency, the auditor should consider an explanatory paragraph in the report, the withholding of the report, or withdrawal from the audit.

In the event of a *material misstatement* in the text (e.g., the financial statements show a net loss for the year, but the president's letter says the entity had a net profit), as opposed to a material inconsistency between the text and the financial statements, AU Section 550 contains a suggestion that legal counsel be consulted.

EFFECT OF EVENTS SUBSEQUENT TO ISSUANCE OF THE AUDIT REPORT

Occasionally, events occur or are discovered after an audit report has been issued that may materially affect the financial statements being reported on. If an event *occurs* after the audit report has been issued, generally no action is required of the auditor. For example, a major lawsuit may be settled, or the client may sell or acquire a significant subsidiary. Such events occurring before the issuance of the auditor's report may have affected amounts or disclosures in the financial statements or the form of the auditor's report. However, if they occur after issuance of the auditor's report, the events will be included in the financial statements of the subsequent year.

If events are discovered after issuance of the auditor's report that *existed* at that date but were unknown to the auditor, then the auditor may be responsible for taking some action. Here we are generally referring to material errors or fraud in the financial statements that the auditor failed to detect. If an auditor becomes aware of information that indicates the possible existence of undisclosed material errors or fraud in financial statements on which he or she has issued a report, the first step is to discuss the information with the client to determine whether (1) the information is reliable, (2) the information would have affected the audit report, and (3) there are likely to be persons currently relying on the financial statements. If the answers are affirmative, the auditor should ask the client to issue corrected financial statements with a related auditor's report. Should the client refuse, the auditor should notify (1) the client, (2) appropriate regulatory agencies (for example, the Securities and Exchange Commission for public companies), and (3) any other person known to be relying on the financial statements that the audit report should not be relied on. As might be suspected, the auditor is often in deep legal difficulty at this point.

INTERNATIONAL STANDARDS ON AUDITING

International standards on auditing provide for a standard audit report that differs from the requirements for a standard U.S. audit report in the following ways.

1. The standard audit report consists of two paragraphs (compared with three paragraphs for a standard U.S. audit report). The first describes the scope of the audit, and the second expresses an opinion on the financial statements.

2. The report is signed with the name of the audit firm, the ~~~~~~~~~~~~
the auditor, or both.

3. The auditor's address must be stated. (The auditor's address is oft~
by U.S. auditors but is not required.)

4. There is no provision for dual dating a report. If a subsequent event occurs after the last day of fieldwork that results in amendment of the financial statements, the auditor should extend the review of subsequent events to the date of occurrence.

Chapter 19 ▶ GLOSSARY OF TERMS

Certificate   A term that was once used to describe the auditor's report but is no longer considered appropriate.

Dual dating   The use of the last day of fieldwork as the date for the overall audit report and a later date for a subsequent event or transaction.

Other information   Information in annual reports prepared by management and distributed to stockholders and others in addition to audited financial statements and the independent auditor's report thereon, such as the president's message or a description of operations.

Report date   The date of the auditor's report, which generally coincides with the last day of fieldwork.

Supplementary information   Information required by a pronouncement of the FASB or GASB, but presented outside of the basic financial statements.

Chapter 19 ▶ REFERENCES

American Institute of Certified Public Accountants. *Professional Standards*

AU Section 410—*Adherence to Generally Accepted Accounting Principles*

AU Section 411—*The Meaning of "Present Fairly in Conformity with Generally Accepted Accounting Principles" in the Independent Auditor's Report*

AU Section 431—*Adequacy of Disclosure in Financial Statements*

AU Section 508—*Reports on Audited Financial Statements*

AU Section 530—*Dating of the Independent Auditor's Report*

AU Section 534—*Reporting on Financial Statements Prepared for Use in Other Countries*

AU Section 550—*Other Information in Documents Containing Audited Financial Statements*

AU Section 558—*Required Supplementary Information*

AU Section 561—*Subsequent Discovery of Facts Existing at the Date of the Auditor's Report*

Geiger, Marshall A. "The New Auditor's Report," *Journal of Accountancy* (November 1994), pp. 59–64.

Hall, William D., and Renner, Arthur J. "Lessons Auditors Ignore at Their Own Risk," *Journal of Accountancy* (June 1991), pp. 63–71.

Kelly, Anne S., and Mohrweis, Lawrence C. "Bankers' and Investors' Perceptions of the Auditor's Role in Financial Statement Reporting: The Impact of SAS No. 58," *Auditing: A Journal of Practice and Theory* (Fall 1989), pp. 87–97.

Roussey, Robert S., Ten Eyck, Ernest L., and Blanco-Best, Mimi. "Three New SASs: Closing the Communications Gap," *Journal of Accountancy* (December 1988), pp. 44–52.

Chapter 19 ▶ REVIEW QUESTIONS

19-1   List the important concepts of the four standards of reporting.

19-2   State what each paragraph in the standard audit report is called and the information each conveys.

19-3   To whom should the audit report normally be addressed?

19-4   Because much of an auditor's work involves an audit of various client financial records, why does the auditor's report state that he or she has audited the financial statements rather than the financial records?

19-5   How does the auditor explain in the audit report his or her responsibility for the detection of errors and fraud?

19-6   What is the significance of the phrase "in our opinion" in the audit report?

19-7 Define the word "fairly" as used within the context of the auditor's report.

19-8 Can financial statements not be fair and yet be in conformity with generally accepted accounting principles? Explain.

19-9 List the conditions specified in *SAS No. 69* for financial statements to "present fairly."

19-10 What are the rule-making bodies whose pronouncements have been designated as generally accepted accounting principles by the AICPA?

19-11 Describe the GAAP hierarchy for nongovernment entities.

19-12 List the individual financial statements normally included in a complete set and indicate which phrase of the opinion paragraph applies to each statement.

19-13 How does the auditor determine the date of the audit report?

19-14 What is meant by the phrase "dual dating of a report," and when would an auditor use this practice?

19-15 What reporting responsibility does an auditor have for prior-year financial statements presented with current-year audited statements if (1) he or she audited the prior year, (2) the prior year was unaudited, and (3) the prior year was audited by another auditor?

19-16 Distinguish between a reissued and an updated audit report.

19-17 What types of reports may a U.S. auditor issue on financial statements prepared in conformity with accounting principles generally accepted in another country that are for use only outside the United States?

19-18 What is the auditor's responsibility for information that is supplementary to the financial statements but required by the FASB or GASB? How does the auditor report on such information?

19-19 What is the auditor's responsibility for other information in the text portion of annual reports and other documents containing audited financial statements?

19-20 What actions should an auditor take if a material error is found in the financial statements after delivery of his or her audit report?

Chapter 19 ▶ OBJECTIVE QUESTIONS

(* = author prepared; ** = CPA examination)

*19-21 The standard audit report includes all of the following except a (an)
   a. Opinion paragraph.
   b. Scope paragraph.
   c. Explanatory paragraph.
   d. Opening paragraph.

*19-22 The auditor's report may be addressed to any of the following except the client's
   a. Stockholders.
   b. Board of directors.
   c. Chief executive officer.
   d. Partners.

*19-23 In the opening paragraph of the standard audit report, auditors acknowledge their responsibility to
   a. Conduct their audit in accordance with generally accepted auditing standards.
   b. Evaluate the overall financial statement presentation.
   c. Express an opinion based on their audit.
   d. Plan and perform the audit to obtain reasonable assurance about whether the financial statements are free of material misstatement.

**19-24 The existence of audit risk is recognized by the statement in the auditor's standard report that the
   a. Auditor is responsible for expressing an opinion on the financial statements, which are the responsibility of management.
   b. Financial statements are presented fairly, in all material respects, in conformity with GAAP.
   c. Audit includes examining, on a test basis, evidence supporting the amounts and disclosures in the financial statements.
   d. Auditor obtains reasonable assurance about whether the financial statements are free of material misstatement.

**19-25 Several sources of GAAP consulted by an auditor are in conflict as to the application of an accounting principle. Which of the following should the auditor consider the most authoritative?
   a. FASB Technical Bulletins.
   b. AICPA Accounting Interpretations.
   c. FASB Statements of Financial Accounting Concepts.
   d. AICPA Technical Practice Aids.

*19-26 The auditor's standard report should be titled, and the title should include the word

    a. Standard.   **c.** Independent.

    b. Opinion.   **d.** Audit.

 *19-27 The standard audit report explains that an audit includes all of the following except

    a. Examining support for the amounts and disclosures in the financial statements.

    b. Evaluating internal control.

    c. Assessing the accounting principles used and significant estimates made by management.

    d. Evaluating the overall financial statement presentation.

**19-28 Which paragraphs of an auditor's standard report on financial statements should refer to generally accepted auditing standards (GAAS) and generally accepted accounting principles (GAAP)?

	GAAS	GAAP
a.	Opening	Scope
b.	Scope	Scope
c.	Scope	Opinion
d.	Opening	Opinion

 **19-29 An auditor issued an audit report that was dual dated for a subsequent event occurring after the completion of fieldwork but before issuance of the auditor's report. The auditor's responsibility for events occurring subsequent to the completion of fieldwork was

    a. Extended to subsequent events occurring through the date of issuance of the report.

    b. Extended to include all events occurring since the completion of fieldwork.

    c. Limited to the specific event referenced.

    d. Limited to include only events occurring up to the date of the last subsequent event referenced.

**19-30 Which of the following representations does an auditor make explicitly and which implicitly when issuing a standard report?

	Conformity with GAAP	Adequacy of disclosure
a.	Explicitly	Explicitly
b.	Implicitly	Implicitly
c.	Implicitly	Explicitly
d.	Explicitly	Implicitly

 **19-31 An auditor has been asked to report on the balance sheet of Jane Company but not on the other basic financial statements. The auditor will have access to all information underlying the basic financial statements. Under these circumstances, the auditor

    a. May accept the engagement but should disclaim an opinion because of an inability to apply the procedures considered necessary.

    b. May accept the engagement because such engagements merely involve limited reporting objectives.

    c. Should refuse the engagement because there is a client-imposed scope limitation.

    d. Should refuse the engagement because of a departure from generally accepted auditing standards.

**19-32 When unaudited financial statements of a non-public entity are presented in comparative form with audited financial statements in the subsequent year, the unaudited financial statements should be clearly marked to indicate their status and

    I. The report on the unaudited financial statements should be reissued.

    II. The report on the audited financial statements should include a separate paragraph describing the responsibility assumed for the unaudited financial statements.

        a. I only.

        b. II only.

        c. Both I and II.

        d. Either I or II.

**19-33 Comparative financial statements include the financial statements of the prior year that were audited by a predecessor auditor whose report is not presented. If the predecessor's report was qualified, the successor should

    a. Indicate the substantive reasons for the qualification in the predecessor auditor's opinion.

    b. Request the client to reissue the predecessor's report on the prior year's statements.

    c. Issue an updated comparative audit report indicating the division of responsibility.

    d. Express an opinion only on the current year's statements and make *no* reference to the prior year's statements.

**19-34 Before reporting on the financial statements of a U.S. entity that have been prepared in conformity with another country's accounting principles, an auditor practicing in the U.S. should

    a. Understand the accounting principles generally accepted in the other country.

    b. Be certified by the appropriate auditing or accountancy board of the other country.

    c. Notify management that the auditor is re-

---

quired to disclaim an opinion on the financial statements.

d. Receive a waiver from the auditor's state board of accountancy to perform the engagement.

**19-35 What is an auditor's responsibility for supplementary information that is outside the basic financial statements, but required by the FASB?

a. The auditor has *no* responsibility for required supplementary information as long as it is outside the basic financial statements.

b. The auditor's only responsibility for required supplementary information is to determine that such information has *not* been omitted.

c. The auditor should apply certain limited procedures to the required supplementary information, and report deficiencies in, or omissions of, such information.

d. The auditor should apply tests of details of transactions and balances to the required supplementary information, and report any material misstatements in such information.

**19-36 When audited financial statements are presented in a client's document containing other information, the auditor should

a. Perform inquiry and analytical procedures to ascertain whether the other information is reasonable.

b. Add an explanatory paragraph to the auditor's report without changing the opinion on the financial statements.

c. Perform the appropriate substantive auditing procedures to corroborate the other information.

d. Read the other information to determine that it is consistent with the audited financial statements.

**19-37 Which of the following events occurring after the issuance of an auditor's report most likely would cause the auditor to make further inquiries about the previously issued financial statements?

a. A technological development that could affect the entity's future ability to continue as a going concern.

b. The discovery of information regarding a contingency that existed before the financial statements were issued.

c. The entity's sale of a subsidiary that accounts for 30% of the entity's consolidated sales.

d. The final resolution of a lawsuit explained in a footnote.

**19-38 When a predecessor auditor reissues the report on the prior period's financial statements at the request of the former client, the predecessor auditor should

a. Indicate the introductory paragraph of the reissued report that the financial statements of the subsequent period were audited by another CPA.

b. Obtain an updated management representation letter and compare it to that obtained during the prior period audit.

c. Add an explanatory paragraph to the reissued report stating that the predecessor has *not* performed additional auditing procedures concerning the prior period's financial statements.

d. Compare the prior period's financial statements that the predecessor reported on with the financial statements to be presented for comparative purposes.

*19-39 The auditor's standard report states that the financial statements are presented fairly

a. With reasonable assurance.

b. Without significant error.

c. In all material respects.

d. On a consistent basis.

**19-40 Perry & Price audited Bond's consolidated financial statements for the years ended December 31, 19X4 and 19X3. These financial statements are being presented on a comparative basis and an unqualified opinion is being expressed.

Adler, an assistant on the engagement, drafted the following auditor's report on May 3, 19X5, the date of completion of the fieldwork.

Auditor's Report

We have audited the accompanying consolidated balance sheets of Bond Company and subsidiaries as of December 31, 19X4 and 19X3, and the related consolidated statements of income, retained earnings, and cash flows for the years then ended. These financial statements are the responsibility of the Company's management. Our responsibility is to express an opinion on these financial statements based on our audits.

We conducted our audits in accordance with generally accepted auditing standards. Those standards require that we plan and perform the audit to obtain reasonable assurance about whether the financial statements are free of material misstatement. An audit includes examining, on a test basis, evidence supporting the amounts and disclosures in the financial statements. An audit also includes assessing the accounting principles used, as well as evaluating the overall financial statement presentation. We believe that our audits provide a reasonable basis for our opinion.

In our opinion, the consolidated financial statements referred to above present fairly, in all material respects, the financial position of Bond Company and subsidiaries as of December 31, 19X4 and 19X3, and the results of its operations and its cash flows for the years then ended in conformity with generally accepted accounting principles.

Perry & Price, CPAs
May 3, 19X5

Required:

Smith reviewed Adler's draft and indicated in the following *Supervisor's Review Notes* that there were deficiencies in Adler's draft. Items a through i represent the deficiencies noted by Smith. For each deficiency, indicate whether Smith is correct or incorrect in the criticism of Adler's draft.

SUPERVISOR'S REVIEW NOTES

a. The report is improperly titled.
b. All the basic financial statements are *not* properly identified in the introductory paragraph.
c. There is *no* reference to the American Institute of Certified Public Accountants in the introductory paragraph.
d. The report does *not* state in the scope paragraph that generally accepted auditing standards require analytical procedures to be performed in planning an audit.
e. The report does *not* state in the scope paragraph that an audit includes assessing internal control.
f. The report does *not* state in the scope paragraph that an audit includes assessing significant estimates made by management.
g. There is no reference to the balance sheet in the opinion paragraph.
h. The second standard of reporting requires a reference to consistency in the opinion paragraph.
i. The report date is incorrect.

Chapter 19 ► DISCUSSION/CASE QUESTIONS

(* = author prepared; ** = CPA examination)

*19-41 You were recently appointed to a committee formed by the state CPA society to investigate possible substandard reporting practices. The following report was submitted to the committee, and, as the newest member of the committee, you were asked to make the initial review of the report and to give the committee your recommendations.

> We have examined the balance sheet and related statements of income and expense and surplus of Holly Corporation as of March 31, 19X9. These financial statements are the responsibility of the Company's management. Our responsibility is to express an opinion based on our audit.
> We conducted our audit in accordance with generally accepted accounting principles. These principles require that we perform the audit to obtain reasonable assurance about whether the financial statements are free of misstatement. An audit includes examining, on a test basis, evidence supporting the amounts and disclosures in the financial statements. An audit also includes assessing the accounting principles used and significant estimates made by management, as well as evaluating the overall financial statement presentation. We believe that our audit provides a reasonable basis for our opinion.
> In our opinion, the accompanying balance sheet and related statements of income and expense and surplus present fairly the financial position of Holly Corp., as of March 31, 19X9, in conformity with generally accepted accounting principles.

State whether or not you would recommend to the committee that the audit report be found to be in violation of generally accepted auditing standards of reporting, and if so, why.

*19-42   A number of years ago a large public accounting firm used a form of the opinion paragraph shown below.

> In our opinion, the financial statements referred to above present fairly (in all material respects) the financial position of X Company as of December 31, 19X2, and the results of its operations and its cash flows for the year then ended, *and were prepared* in conformity with generally accepted accounting principles.

How does this opinion differ from the one included in the present report?

What additional responsibility, if any, is the auditor assuming in the preceding opinion paragraph?

How does the concept of fairness in the above opinion compare with the concept in *SAS No. 69?*

**19-43   On completion of fieldwork on September 23, 19X5, the following standard report was rendered by Timothy Ross to the directors of The Rancho Corporation.

Report of Independent Auditors

To the Directors of
The Rancho Corporation:

We have audited the balance sheet and the related statement of income and retained earnings of The Rancho Corporation as of July 31, 19X5. In accordance with your instructions, a complete audit was conducted.

We conducted our audit in accordance with generally accepted auditing standards. These standards require that we plan and perform the audit to obtain adequate assurance about whether the financial statements are free of errors and fraud. An audit includes examining, on a test basis, evidence supporting the amounts in the financial statements. An audit also includes assessing the accounting principles used and significant estimates made by management, as well as evaluating the overall financial statement presentation. We believe that our audit provides a reasonable basis for our opinion.

In many respects, this was an unusual year for The Rancho Corporation. The weakening of the economy in the early part of the year and the strike of plant employees in the summer of 19X5 led to a decline in sales and net income. After making several tests of sales records, nothing came to our attention that would indicate that sales have not been properly recorded.

In our opinion, with the explanation given above, and with the exception of some minor errors that are considered immaterial, the aforementioned financial statements present fairly the financial position of The Rancho Corporation at July 31, 19X5, and the results of its operations for the year then ended, in conformity with pronouncements of the Financial Accounting Standards Board.

> Timothy Ross, CPA
> September 23, 19X5

Required:

List and explain deficiencies and omissions in the auditor's report. The type of opinion (unqualified, qualified, adverse, or disclaimer) is of no consequence and need not be discussed.

Organize your answer sheet by paragraph (opening, scope, explanatory, and opinion) of the auditor's report.

*19-44   Richard Adkerson, CPA, was reviewing with the president of Central Pond Shipping Company the standard audit report he intended to issue to this new client. The president had the following comments about phrases in the report that he did not understand.

a. How could Adkerson have audited the financial statements when they were not prepared until the audit was almost complete? The president suggested changing the wording to "audited the accounting records."

b. The president knew Adkerson spent considerable time examining canceled checks and suggested that this fact be included in the scope paragraph.

c. The president asked for a slightly stronger statement than "in my opinion" and suggested "in my informed opinion."

d. The president requested that some wording be included stating that the accounting records were correct, because he questioned the competency of his bookkeeper.

e. The president did not completely trust his brother, who also was associated with the company. He asked Adkerson to include in his report a statement that he had not detected any material fraud.

f. The president asked why Adkerson did not comment on consistency because there had been numerous management changes during the year.

How should Adkerson reply to each of these comments?

*19-45 Your client, Echo Software Systems, recently changed the wording of its sales contracts to permit its customers to receive software upgrades at no charge if its competitors upgrade their products. You are considering whether this change would affect revenue recognition or expense accrual for your client. What authoritative sources would you consult? Rank your sources from most authoritative to least authoritative.

*19-46 You have been engaged to audit the financial statements of Gridley Corporation for the year ended December 31, 19X7. You completed the work in the client's office on February 22, 19X8 and returned to your office to process the audit report that you drafted. On February 24, 19X8 you read in a newspaper that a major fire had occurred at the client's plant. The final audit report is to be delivered to the client that afternoon.

What date should have appeared on the original draft of the audit report? Why?

What action should you take after reading of the fire at the client's plant?

How would the final audit report be dated?

*19-47 The following audit report contains departures from the standard wording. Identify the word, phrase, or omission that departs from the standard wording and state why the word, phrase, or omission conveys an improper message to readers of the report.

Report of Independent Public Accountants

We have audited the accompanying financial statements of Hogeye Ranch Company as of December 31, 19X4. Management is responsible for maintaining the supporting accounting records. We assisted management in preparing the financial statements, and we have a responsibility to express an opinion on those financial statements based on our audit.

We conducted our audit in accordance with generally accepted auditing procedures. Those procedures require that we plan and perform the audit to obtain assurance about whether the financial statements are free of errors. An audit includes examining, on a test basis, evidence supporting the amounts in the financial statements. An audit also includes assessing the accounting principles used and significant estimates made by management, as well as evaluating the overall financial statement presentation. We believe that our procedures provide a reasonable basis for our audit.

In our opinion, the financial statements referred to above present the financial position of Hogeye Ranch Company as of December 31, 19X4, and the results of its operations and its cash flows for the year then ended in conformity with generally accepted accounting principles.

*19-48　The management of Onbeach Supply Company desires to include four years' financial statements in this year's annual report. R. Vaughn, CPA, has audited the financial statements of the current and immediately preceding year. However, another CPA audited the financial statements for the next preceding year, and the earliest year was unaudited.

Discuss and draft the audit report that Vaughn should issue, assuming that unqualified opinions were given in all of the audited years.

**19-49　The following auditor's report was drafted by a staff accountant of Jones & Jones, CPAs, at the completion of the audit engagement on the financial statements of Adams Mining, Inc., for the year ended December 31, 19X7. It was submitted to the engagement partner who reviewed the audit report and the working papers thoroughly and properly concluded that an unqualified opinion should be issued.

The financial statements for the year ended December 31, 19X6 are to be presented for comparative purposes. Jones & Jones previously audited these statements and expressed an unqualified opinion.

On January 31, 19X8, Adams acquired a new subsidiary, Harris Coal, Inc. Disclosure of this subsequent event was properly made in Note T to the consolidated financial statements.

To the Management of Adams Mining, Inc.:

We have audited the consolidated balance sheets of Adams Mining, Inc. and subsidiaries as of December 31, 19X7 and 19X6, and the related consolidated statements of income, retained earnings, and cash flows for the years then ended. These financial statements are the responsibility of the Company's management.

We conducted our audits in accordance with generally accepted auditing standards. Those standards require that we plan and perform the audit to obtain reasonable assurance about whether the financial statements are free of material misstatements. An audit includes examining, on a test basis, evidence supporting the amounts and disclosures in the financial statements. An audit also includes assessing the accounting principles used and significant estimates made by management, as well as evaluating the overall financial statement presentation. We believe that our audits provide a reasonable basis for our opinion.

In our opinion, the consolidated financial statements referred to above present fairly, in all material respects, the financial position as of December 31, 19X7, and the related consolidated statements of income and retained earnings for the year then ended, in accordance with generally accepted accounting principles.

> Jones & Jones, CPAs
> April 10, 19X8 except
> for Note T as to which
> the date is January 31, 19X8.

Required:

Identify the deficiencies contained in the auditor's report as drafted by the staff accountant. Do *not* redraft the report.

*19-50　In the current year the operating revenue of State Mountain Gas Company declined to $1.7 million from $2.2 million in the prior year. Owing to an extraordinary item, however, net income increased by $500,000 in the current year.

The audited financial statements in the annual report were properly prepared to report the effect of the extraordinary item as a separate item before net income. The president's letter, however, discussed only the increase in net income.

What responsibility does the auditor of the financial statements have for the president's letter? What action, if any, should be taken in this case?

**19-51 For the year ended December 31, 19X8, Friday & Company, CPAs (Friday), audited the financial statements of Johnson Company and expressed an unqualified opinion on the balance sheet only. Friday did not observe the taking of the physical inventory as of December 31, 19X7, because that date was prior to their appointment as auditors. Friday was unable to satisfy themselves regarding inventory by means of other auditing procedures, so they did not express an opinion on the other basic financial statements that year.

For the year ended December 31, 19X9, Friday expressed an unqualified opinion on all the basic financial statements and satisfied themselves as to the consistent application of generally accepted accounting principles. The fieldwork was completed on March 11, 19X0; the partner-in-charge reviewed the working papers and signed the auditor's report on March 18, 19X0. The report on the comparative financial statements for 19X9 and 19X8 was delivered to Johnson on March 21, 19X0.

Required:

Prepare Friday's auditor's report that was submitted to Johnson's board of directors on the 19X9 and 19X8 comparative financial statements.

*19-52 Before the present form of the standard audit report was adopted, the following form was used:

We have examined the balance sheet of X Company as of December 31, 19X7, and the related statements of income, retained earnings, and changes in financial position for the year then ended. Our examination was made in accordance with generally accepted auditing standards and, accordingly, included such tests of the accounting records and such other auditing procedures as we considered necessary in the circumstances.

In our opinion, the financial statements referred to above present fairly the financial position of X Company as of December 31, 19X7, and the results of its operations and the changes in its financial position for the year then ended, in conformity with generally accepted accounting principles applied on a basis consistent with that of the preceding year.

a. Discuss the substantive differences between the present and prior reports.

b. Which form of report best communicates the auditor's responsibility and is least likely to be misunderstood by the public? Why?

19-53 The fieldwork on Triple Steel Corporation has been completed. You were responsible for preparing the preliminary draft of the financial statements and auditors' report. You had the draft statements and report typed for presentation to the supervisor, Joan Fisher. You have worked for Joan before and know she demands the very best work. You are now reviewing the draft to make sure it is final in all respects.

Required:

a. Review the following financial statements and auditors' report. Note any changes that will have to be made to them before you submit them to the supervisor. Changes may be required because of omissions (e.g., inadequate disclosure) or carelessness in drafting the report (e.g., different amounts appearing for the same item in different places). It will not be necessary to check the clerical accuracy of the statements.

b. List any matters that you want to be sure have been investigated and discussed with management.

(*Adapted and used with permission of Ernst & Young*)

Auditors' Report

Board of Directors
Triple Steel Corporation
Detroit, Michigan

We have audited the accompanying financial statements of Triple Steel Corporation for the year ended June 30, 19X2. These financial statements are the responsibility of management. Our responsibility is to express an opinion on these financial statements based on our audit.

We conducted our audit in accordance with generally accepted auditing standards. Those standards require that we plan and perform the audit to obtain reasonable assurance about whether the financial statements are free of material misstatement. An audit includes examining, on a test basis, evidence supporting the amounts and disclosures in the financial statements. An audit also includes assessing the accounting principles used and significant estimates made by management, as well as evaluating the overall financial statement presentation. We believe that our audit provides a reasonable basis for our opinion. We previously made a similar audit of the financial statements for the preceding year.

In our opinion, the accompanying balance sheet and statements of operations and retained earnings present fairly the financial position of Triple Steel Corporation at June 30, 19X2, and the results of its operations for the year then ended in conformity with generally accepted accounting principles.

Detroit, Michigan
August 10, 19X2

Balance Sheet
Triple Steel Corporation

	June 30	
	19X2	19X1
ASSETS		
Current assets		
Cash and certificates of deposit	$ 3,548,583	$ 3,447,058
Trade receivables, less allowance of $30,000	1,465,410	2,326,510
Inventories—Notes A and C:		
Finished products	1,671,230	1,146,555
Work in process	1,068,312	1,038,238
Materials and supplies	914,173	879,668
	3,653,715	3,064,461
Prepaid taxes and insurance	340,290	420,086
Total current assets	9,007,998	9,258,115
Other assets		
Cash value of life insurance	136,298	127,618
Miscellaneous deposits and accounts	203,342	133,060
	339,640	260,678

Balance Sheet
Triple Steel Corporation

	June 30	
	19X2	19X1
Properties—at cost—Note B		
Land	815,130	721,161
Buildings	3,886,339	3,802,183
Machinery and equipment	20,965,042	19,710,505
	25,666,511	24,233,849
Less accumulated depreciation and amortization	12,595,431	11,645,132
	13,071,080	12,588,717
	$22,418,718	$22,107,510
LIABILITIES AND STOCKHOLDERS' EQUITY		
Current liabilities		
Accounts payable	$ 1,278,981	$ 1,103,641
Payrolls and amounts withheld therefrom	229,594	256,010
Taxes, other than income taxes	342,333	241,339
Pension plan contributions and other current liabilities	210,939	222,635
Federal income taxes	130,488	185,050
Current portion of long-term debt	400,000	400,000
Total current liabilities	2,592,335	2,408,675
Long-term debt		
5½% First mortgage sinking fund bonds—Note C	4,000,000	4,400,000
Deferred federal income taxes	32,000	—0—
Stockholders' equity—Notes D, E, and F		
Common stock, $2.50 par value:		
Authorized 500,000 shares		
Issued and outstanding 357,419 shares		
(19X1—357,024)	893,548	892,560
Additional paid-in capital	2,842,772	2,835,016
Retained earnings	12,058,063	11,571,259
	15,794,383	15,298,835
	$22,418,718	$22,107,510

See notes to financial statements.

Statement of Operations and Retained Earnings
Triple Steel Corporation

	Year Ended June 30	
	19X2	19X1
Net sales	$21,643,276	$24,019,044
Interest and other income	151,213	203,998
	21,794,489	24,223,042
Costs and expenses:		
Cost of products sold, exclusive of depreciation	17,467,856	18,324,089
Provision for depreciation of properties	1,397,773	1,274,509
Selling, administrative, and general expenses	777,850	763,246
Interest on long-term debt	264,000	286,000
Federal income taxes	900,000	1,780,000
	20,807,479	22,427,844
Net income for the year	987,010	1,795,198
Retained earnings at July 1	11,571,260	10,275,441
	12,558,270	12,070,639
Cash dividend paid—$1.40 a share	500,206	499,380
Retained earnings at end of year	$12,058,064	$11,571,259

Statement of Cash Flows
Triple Steel Company
June 30, 19X2

Source of funds	
From operations:	
Net income	$ 987,010
Provision for depreciation	1,397,773
Increase in deferred income taxes	32,000
Total from operations	2,416,783
Proceeds from sale of common stock	8,744
Decrease in net current assets	433,777
Total	$2,859,304
Application of funds	
Additions to property, plant, and equipment	$1,880,136
Increase in other assets	78,962
Cash dividend	500,206
Reduction in long-term debt	400,000
Total	$2,859,304

See notes to financial statements.

Notes to Financial Statements
Triple Steel Corporation
June 30, 19X2

Note A—Inventory. Inventories have been stated at the lower of cost or market prices. Cost as to raw material content of certain inventories, in the amount of $2,568,882 at June 30, 19X2, has been determined by the last-in, first-out method and, as to the remainder of the inventories, has been determined by methods that are substantially equivalent to the first-in, first-out method.

Note B—Pensions. The company has pension plans covering substantially all employees. The total pension expense for 19X2 and 19X1 was $110,000 and $115,000, respectively, including amortization of prior service cost over a period of 40 years. The company's policy is to fund pension cost accrued. Unfunded prior service cost under the plans was approximately $350,000 at June 30, 19X2.

Note C—First Mortgage Bonds. The corporation is required to pay $400,000 annually on the first mortgage bonds until retirement on June 30, 19X3.

All properties (with minor exceptions), life insurance policies, and certain inventories ($2,687,320) are pledged in connection with the bonds.

Note D—Common Stock Optioned to Officers and Employees. Certain officers and key employees have been granted options entitling them to purchase shares of common stock at $19.50 and $29.875 per share, which represented the fair market value on the dates of grant. At July 1, 19X1, options were outstanding for 941 shares. During 19X2, options for 393 shares were exercised for an aggregate option price of $8,744. At June 30, 19X2, options for 546 shares were outstanding and exercisable for an aggregate option price of $13,639. No shares were available for additional options at the beginning or end of the year.

The excess of proceeds over par value of the common stock sold during 19X2, amounting to $7,755, has been credited to additional capital and comprised the only change in that account.

Note F—Restrictions on Dividends. The indenture relating to the first mortgage bonds requires the company to maintain net current assets, as defined, of not less than $3,000,000 and otherwise restricts the declaration of dividends, other than stock dividends. At June 30, 19X2, retained earnings of $1,549,391 were free of such restrictions.

Modifications of the Standard Audit Report

"Nobody likes the bringer of bad news."

SOPHOCLES, *Antigone*

LEARNING OBJECTIVES

After reading and studying the material in this chapter, the student should be able to

► Give an example of each of these modifications to the auditor's report: (1) reference to another auditor's participation in an audit; (2) emphasis of a matter included in the financial statements; (3) Rule 203 matter; (4) inconsistent application of accounting principles; and (5) going concern.

► Give an example of each of these modifications to the auditor's report: (1) scope limitations and (2) departures from generally accepted accounting principles.

► Describe the types of opinions expressed for scope limitations and departures from generally accepted accounting principles when the effects are (1) material and (2) pervasive.

► Compare scope limitations resulting from: (1) inadequate accounting records; (2) timing of the engagement; and (3) client-imposed restrictions.

► Describe the difference between qualified and adverse opinions resulting from departures from generally accepted accounting principles.

► Give an example of an auditor's report on financial statements covering two or more years.

Although many audit reports are of the standard form discussed in Chapter 19, circumstances may arise that require the auditor to modify this form. The following circumstances can result in a modification of the standard audit report.[1]

[1] Modifications of the auditor's report, which are discussed in other sections of the text, may occur when (1) certain circumstances relating to reports on comparative financial statements exist (see page 626); (2) supplementary information required by the FASB or GASB is omitted, improperly presented, or inadequately examined (see page 629); and (3) other information in a document containing audited financial statements is materially inconsistent with those statements (see page 629).

1. The auditor's opinion is based in part on the report of another auditor.
2. The auditor wishes to emphasize a matter included in the financial statements.
3. The financial statements are fairly presented, but because of unusual circumstances contain a departure from an authoritative accounting principle promulgated by a body designated by the AICPA Council to establish such principles (Rule 203 matter).
4. Accounting principles have not been consistently applied.
5. The auditor has substantial doubt as to the ability of an entity to continue as a going concern.
6. The scope of the audit is limited with respect to one or more audit procedures considered necessary in the circumstances (qualified or disclaimer of opinion).
7. The financial statements are affected by a departure from a generally accepted accounting principle (qualified or adverse opinion).

The first five circumstances listed result in an unqualified opinion even though the report is a modification of the standard audit report.

MODIFICATIONS OTHER THAN QUALIFICATIONS, DISCLAIMERS, OR ADVERSE OPINIONS

Reference to Other Auditors' Participation in an Audit

Occasionally, more than one auditor may be involved in an audit of an entity's financial statements, particularly when numerous subsidiaries, divisions, funds, or investments are involved. This often occurs when the *principal auditor* (normally the one auditing the parent entity and at least one-half of the total enterprise in terms of revenues or total assets) does not have an office in the city or country in which the client has significant operations. In the example shown in Figure 20.1, the principal auditor audits parent Company P and two of its subsidiaries, Companies A and B. Subsidiary C is audited by other auditors. In this case, the principal auditor must

FIGURE 20.1 **Example of Entity Audited by Principal and Other Auditors**

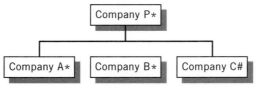

* Audited by principal auditor.
# Audited by other auditors.

determine whether he or she has performed sufficient substantive work to serve as the principal auditor. In addition to the materiality and importance of the portion of the entity audited to the total entity, the extent of the auditor's knowledge of the overall financial statements should also be considered.

On determining that he or she can serve as principal auditor, a decision must be made as to how to use the audit report of the *other auditors*. The decision may be either to assume responsibility for the other auditor's work, in which case no reference will be made to them in the report, or not to assume responsibility for their work and state the division of responsibility in the audit report. A flowchart of this decision process is shown in Figure 20.2. The following modifications would be made to the standard auditor's report if the principal auditor decides not to assume responsibility for the work of the other auditors.

(Opening paragraph)

. . . Our responsibility is to express an opinion on these financial statements based on our audit. We did not audit the financial statements of C Company, a wholly owned subsidiary, which statements reflect total assets and revenues constituting 20 percent and 22 percent, respectively, of the related consolidated totals. These statements were audited by other auditors whose report has been furnished to us, and our opinion, insofar as it relates to the amounts included for C Company, is based solely on the report of the other auditors.

(Scope paragraph)

. . . as well as evaluating the overall financial statement presentation. We believe that our audit and the report of other auditors provide a reasonable basis for our opinion.

(Opinion paragraph)

In our opinion, based on our audit and the report of the other auditors, the consolidated financial statements . . . .

The purpose of referring to another auditor is to set forth clearly the division of responsibility for the performance of the audit. Such reference is not considered a qualification of the audit report. However, if the report of the other auditor is modified, the principal auditor must determine whether the effect of the modification is material to the consolidated financial statements on which he or she is reporting. If the effect is material, the principal auditor should modify his or her report. If the effect of the other auditor's modification is judged not to be material to the consolidated financial statements, then the principal auditor need make no reference in the report to the modification. The other auditors are normally not named but may be, provided they consent and their report is included with the report of the principal auditor.

Emphasis of a Matter Included in the Financial Statements

Sometimes an auditor may wish to emphasize a matter *included in the financial statements* by using an explanatory paragraph in the audit report. This modification cannot be used to disclose a matter in the audit report that is *not* disclosed in the

FIGURE 20.2 **Using the Work and Reports of Other Auditors—An Interpretation of SAP No. 45 (Section 543 of *SAS No. 1*)**

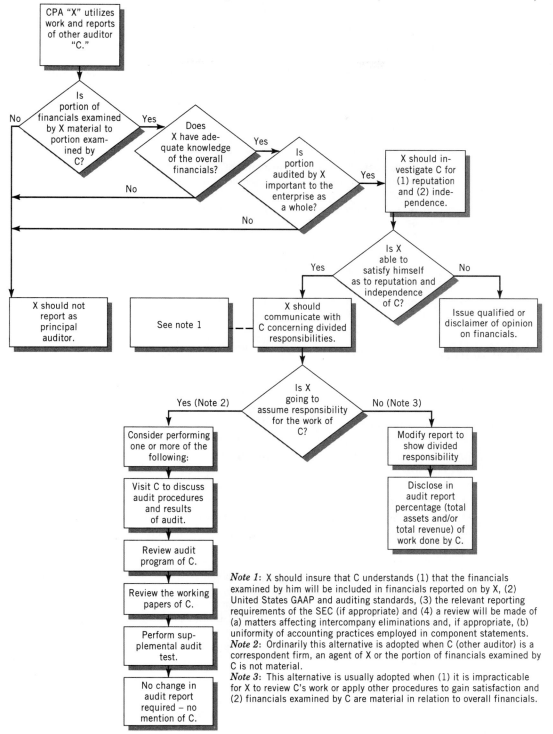

Note 1: X should insure that C understands (1) that the financials examined by him will be included in financials reported on by X, (2) United States GAAP and auditing standards, (3) the relevant reporting requirements of the SEC (if appropriate) and (4) a review will be made of (a) matters affecting intercompany eliminations and, if appropriate, (b) uniformity of accounting practices employed in component statements.
Note 2: Ordinarily this alternative is adopted when C (other auditor) is a correspondent firm, an agent of X or the portion of financials examined by C is not material.
Note 3: This alternative is usually adopted when (1) it is impracticable for X to review C's work or apply other procedures to gain satisfaction and (2) financials examined by C are material in relation to overall financials.

Source: Dan M. Guy, "SAP Flowcharts—Practitioners Forum," *Journal of Accountancy* (March 1974), p. 84.

financial statements. Auditors have found the explanatory paragraph useful to emphasize related party transactions, changes in accounting estimates, and changes in operating conditions. However, emphasis of a matter in an explanatory paragraph should not be used in place of a qualification.

The following example is an explanatory paragraph used to emphasize a change in an accounting estimate.

(Explanatory paragraph)

Effective January 1, 19XX, the Company revised its estimates of the residual values of its equipment and the obsolescence rates of inventories of material and supplies, as discussed in Note 1. This revision reflects primarily a change in conditions and not a change in accounting principles or practices. As a result of this revision, with which we concur, net income for the year ended December 31, 19X2, was increased by $500,000.

The explanatory paragraph is for the purpose of emphasis rather than disclosure; there is no intention to qualify the auditor's report. Accordingly, no reference should be made to the explanatory paragraph in the opinion paragraph. The use of a phrase such as "with the foregoing explanation" in the opinion paragraph is not appropriate, because it suggests that a qualification may be intended.

Rule 203 Matter

Chapter 3 includes a discussion of Rule 203 in the AICPA *Code of Professional Conduct*. This rule severely restricts the conditions under which an auditor may issue an unqualified audit report on financial statements containing a departure from an accounting principle published by a body designated by the AICPA Council to establish such principles (i.e., the FASB or GASB). The rule requires the auditor to demonstrate that, because of unusual circumstances, the financial statements would be misleading if the pronouncement of a designated body were followed. Professional standards require the use of an explanatory paragraph to set forth the information needed to comply with Rule 203. Circumstances involving this aspect of reporting are relatively rare. The following illustration demonstrates one such situation. Only the explanatory paragraph is shown.

In October, 19X3, the Company extinguished a substantial amount of debt through a direct exchange of new equity securities. Application of *Opinion No. 26* of the Accounting Principles Board to this exchange requires that the excess of the debt extinguished over the present value of the new securities should be recognized as a gain in the period in which the extinguishment occurred. While it is not practicable to determine the present value of the new securities issued, such value is at least $2,000,000 less than the face amount of the debt extinguished. It is the opinion of the Company's management, an opinion with which we agree, that no realization of a gain occurred in this exchange (Note 1), and therefore, no recognition of the excess of the debt extinguished over the present value of the new securities has been made in these financial statements.[2]

---

[2] Hortense Goodman and Leonard Lorensen, *Illustrations of Departures from the Auditor's Standard Report, Financial Report Survey* 7 (New York: American Institute of Certified Public Accountants), p. 97.

Note 1 states that the terms and conditions of the new equity securities are substantially similar to those of the debt securities extinguished, both on the basis of the company's continuing operations and in the event of liquidation, and that, in the opinion of management, no gain was realized as a result of the exchange.

If departures from the prescribed principles can be justified as in the foregoing case, it is appropriate for the auditor to express an unqualified opinion on the financial statements.

Inconsistent Application of Accounting Principles

Auditors modify their audit report to discuss an inconsistent application of accounting principles in an explanatory paragraph following the opinion paragraph if the effect on the financial statements is material. By pointing out inconsistent applications of accounting principles in their report, auditors alert readers to changes in financial statements between periods that are the result of changes in accounting methods rather than changes in economic conditions.

Because the continuous activity of the FASB and GASB often results in changes in existing accounting principles, modification of the auditor's report due to inconsistent application of accounting principles is not uncommon.

An example of an explanatory paragraph describing an inconsistent application of accounting principles follows:

> As discussed in Note 3, the company changed its method of computing depreciation in 19X8.

Not all factors that affect comparability of financial statements between years result in a consistency modification to the auditor's report. AU Section 420 lists the following factors that affect consistency:

1. A change in accounting principle (for example, a change from the straight-line method to the declining balance method of depreciation).
2. A change in the reporting entity (for example, changing specific subsidiaries comprising the group of companies for which consolidated financial statements are presented).
3. A failure to restate prior-year financial statements following a merger accounted for as a pooling of interests (this also results in a departure from generally accepted accounting principles when comparative financial statements are presented).
4. A correction of an error in principle (for example, a change from an accounting principle that is not generally accepted to one that is generally accepted).
5. A change in principle inseparable from a change in an estimate (for example, a change from deferring and amortizing certain costs to direct charge-off based on a new estimate that the costs no longer have value).
6. A change in presentation of cash flows (for example, a change in policy for determining which items are treated as cash equivalents).

AU Section 420 also lists the following factors that affect comparability of financial statements, but would normally not result in a modification of the standard auditor's report because they do not involve accounting principles:

1. A change in an accounting estimate (for example, a change in the estimated useful lives of depreciable assets).
2. An error correction not involving an accounting principle (for example, the correction of mathematical mistakes).
3. A change in classification or reclassification (for example, a reclassification made in previously issued financial statements to enhance comparability with current financial statements).
4. A substantially different transaction or event (for example, a change in the type of business conducted by a company).
5. A change expected to have a material future effect (for example, a change having no material effect in the current year but expected to have a material future effect).

Although the last five factors do not require modification of the auditor's report, they should be adequately disclosed in the financial statements.

It is not the task of auditors to apprise report readers of all the reasons that company operations differ from one year to another. Auditors do not serve the function of financial analysts; rather, they give financial statement users an opinion relating to generally accepted accounting principles.

Going Concern

An entity is considered to be a going concern when it has the ability to continue in operation, recover the recorded amounts of its assets, and meet its obligations. The auditor has a responsibility to evaluate whether there is substantial doubt about an entity's ability to continue as a going concern for a period of up to a year from the date of the audited financial statements. The conditions and events considered and the audit procedures employed to make this evaluation are discussed in Chapter 13.

When an auditor has substantial doubt regarding the going-concern status of a client, an explanatory paragraph is added following an unqualified opinion paragraph. (The phrases "substantial doubt" and "going concern" are required in the paragraph.)

> The accompanying financial statements have been prepared assuming that the company will continue as a going concern. As discussed in Note X to the financial statements, the company has suffered recurring losses from operations and has a net capital deficiency that raises substantial doubt about its ability to continue as a going concern. Management's plans in regard to these matters also are described in Note X. The financial statements do not include any adjustments that might result from the outcome of this uncertainty.

When an auditor is aware that an event that is likely to have implications for the going-concern status of an entity is to occur after the one-year period (e.g., the balloon payment on a note payable that will become due 13 months after the date of the financial statements), he or she may convey that information in an explanatory paragraph (emphasis of a matter).

MODIFICATIONS RESULTING IN QUALIFICATIONS, DISCLAIMERS, OR ADVERSE OPINIONS

The last two modifications listed at the beginning of this chapter (scope limitations and departures from generally accepted accounting principles) will require qualifications, disclaimers, or adverse opinions if, in the auditor's judgment, the effects are material or pervasive.[3] Before these two modifications are discussed, the forms of qualifications, disclaimers, and adverse opinions are reviewed to provide an understanding of the conclusions auditors reach and convey to the readers of their reports in each of the circumstances.

When auditors express a qualified opinion, disclaimer of opinion, or adverse opinion, they must disclose in an explanatory paragraph (immediately preceding the opinion paragraph) all substantive reasons for such an opinion, as well as the effect of the matter on the financial statements, if reasonably determinable. If the effect is not determinable, this fact should be stated. It is important that auditors clearly state in this paragraph any reservations they have about the financial statements, including differences of opinion with their client regarding accounting principles. They must avoid any temptation to use vague wording that might lessen the impact of the report modification for their client. Although it is permissible and often desirable to refer to a footnote to the financial statements for additional details and explanations of the circumstances involved (except for scope limitations), reference to a footnote explanation in lieu of an explanatory paragraph is not adequate.

Qualified Reports

The phrase "except for" is used to indicate a qualification of an auditor's opinion and means what the words imply—exception, objection, demurral. The auditor takes exception to, or objects to, some aspects of the financial statements or his or her audit of them. This qualifying phrase is used if the financial statements contain a departure from generally accepted accounting principles because the auditor would take exception to such departure. It is also used if the scope of an auditor's work has been limited in some manner; the auditor would be objecting to or taking exception to the lack of evidential matter or to restrictions imposed on the amount of evidential matter he or she has gathered. Although the following jingle uses the phrase "subject to" rather than "except for," it conveys the idea of a qualified report in a humorous and nonconventional way.

We have audited this balance sheet and say in our report
That the cash is overstated, the cashier being short;

---

[3] Modified reports due to scope limitations and departures from generally accepted accounting principles are not common occurrences because they result from factors that are often within the control of the client to correct.

That the customers' receivables are very much past due;
That if there are some good ones they are very, very few;
That the inventories are out of date and principally junk;
That the method of their pricing is very largely bunk;
That, according to our figures, the undertaking's wrecked,
But, subject to these comments, the balance sheet's correct.[4]

The auditor would issue a qualified report only if, in his or her judgment, the subject of the qualification does or could have a material effect on the financial statements, and if the subject of the qualification does not require a disclaimer or an adverse opinion. Thus, the qualifying phrases can be summarized as follows:

	Condition	
Effect	*Scope limitation*	*Departure from GAAP*
Material	Except for qualification	Except for qualification

Apply the foregoing discussion to the following example. An auditor learns that the Internal Revenue Service recently examined the income tax returns of a client and has proposed a deficiency of $2 million for additional income taxes. Management of the client states that they intend to protest the proposed deficiency and that, though they are willing to make appropriate footnote disclosure of the matter, they are unwilling to record a liability for the proposed deficiency at the present time. The auditor considers the $2 million to be material in relation to the financial statements. After reviewing the report of the Internal Revenue agent and management's protest to the deficiency, the auditor concludes that the Internal Revenue Service is correct and that it is probable that the proposed deficiency will be upheld. What type of qualification, if any, should be included in the auditor's report?

In this case, sufficient information has been obtained for the auditor to conclude that an additional liability for income taxes is probable and measurable and that, without the recording of this liability, the financial statements are not presented fairly in conformity with generally accepted accounting principles. Therefore, an "except for" qualification would be required. Note that footnote disclosure of the matter is not adequate if the financial statements require adjustment.

Assume in the foregoing example that review of the Internal Revenue agent's report and management's protest to the deficiency leaves the auditor uncertain as to the final outcome of the matter. In this case, the auditor is faced with an uncertainty that is not susceptible to reasonable estimation. Footnote disclosure of the uncertainty would be required if the auditor considers the probability of loss to be reasonably possible or probable but not measurable; however, the auditor's report would not be modified.

Assume further that the review of the Internal Revenue agent's report and management's protest of the deficiency convinces the auditor that the client would incur

---

[4] Reported by John L. Carey in *The Rise of the Accounting Profession from Technician to Professional, 1896–1936* (AICPA, New York, 1969), p. 167.

little, if any, additional income tax as a result of the examination (i.e., the likelihood of a material liability is remote). If this conclusion could be reached, the auditor could issue an unmodified report without footnote disclosure of the matter because his or her opinion would be that the financial statements are presented fairly in conformity with generally accepted accounting principles.

The Location of the Qualifying Phrase

The location of the qualifying phrase depends on which financial statement or statements are affected by the qualification. In many cases a qualification will affect all of the basic financial statements, but in other situations only individual statements are affected.

If there has been a departure from generally accepted accounting principles that affects all the basic financial statements (for example, the failure to record an adequate provision for income taxes in the current year), the qualifying phrase "except for" should be placed at the beginning of the opinion paragraph, immediately after the phrase "In our opinion." In this location, it qualifies the fair presentation in conformity with generally accepted accounting principles of (1) financial position (the balance sheet), (2) results of operations (statements of income and retained earnings), and (3) cash flows (statement of cash flows).

Assume that the client has improperly charged to retained earnings a loss on sale of securities that did not meet the criteria for a prior-period adjustment set forth in *FASB No. 16*. Obviously, net income for the year is overstated by the amount of the loss, and the financial statements presenting net income (statements of income, retained earnings, and cash flows) contain a departure from generally accepted accounting principles. But what is the effect on the balance sheet? The amount shown in the balance sheet as retained earnings is the same whether the loss is charged directly to retained earnings or indirectly through the income statement. If the auditor decides that an "except for" qualification is appropriate (rather than an adverse opinion), he or she must place the qualifying phrase in the opinion paragraph so that it applies only to results of operations and cash flows. An example of such wording follows.

In our opinion, the balance sheet referred to above presents fairly, in all material respects, the financial position of X Company as of December 31, 19X2, and except for the effect of not recording a loss on sale of securities as a reduction of net income as discussed in the preceding paragraph, the statements of income, retained earnings, and cash flows present fairly, in all material respects, the results of its operations and its cash flows for the year ended December 31, 19X2, in conformity with generally accepted accounting principles.

Disclaimers of Opinion

A *disclaimer of opinion* states that the auditor does not express an opinion on the financial statements. The auditor may use disclaimers if there have been limitations on the scope of his or her audit. Disclaimers are also used in connection with unaudited financial statements (covered in the next chapter).

In the previous section it was stated that the auditor would use a qualified opinion ("except for") in the event of a scope limitation that did not require a disclaimer of opinion. How does the auditor determine whether a disclaimer of opinion or a qualification is appropriate when he or she encounters a scope limitation? One consideration relates to the source of the limitation. Auditors view client-imposed scope limitations more seriously than scope limitations that result from the timing of the audit work. Another consideration relates to the materiality of the scope limitation and the potential effect on the financial statements. The decision of what type of audit report to issue when faced with a scope limitation is another example of when the auditor must apply judgment. Few guidelines are given in the professional standards as to how material an item must be to require a disclaimer rather than a qualification. Probably the best guidance can be provided by an illustration of the two possibilities—one situation requiring a qualification and one requiring a disclaimer. Between these two situations are less clear cases in which the auditor must rely on judgment, intuition, and experience.

Suppose an auditor is engaged to perform an audit of a company after the end of its fiscal year and therefore was not on hand to observe the taking of the year-end physical inventory. Also, the inventory records are not adequate to allow a retroactive verification of the year-end quantities. If the amount of inventories shown in the balance sheet is $10 million compared with total current assets of $50 million, total assets of $90 million, total equity of $60 million, and net income before income taxes for the year of $40 million (ignore for this purpose the problem of auditing beginning inventories), the maximum potential misstatement (overstatement) is 20 percent of current assets, 11 percent of total assets, 17 percent of total equity, and 25 percent of net income before income taxes for the year. Although the auditor would consider many other factors in evaluating materiality, such as the trend in earnings, the effect on the current ratio, and the possibility of understatement, solely on the basis of the percentages shown he or she might conclude that the effect would be material enough to require qualification but not so material to the overall financial statements as to require a disclaimer of opinion. In contrast, if the amount of inventories shown in the balance sheet is $45 million instead of $10 million, the maximum potential effect for misstatement (overstatement) is 90 percent of current assets, 50 percent of total assets, 75 percent of total equity, and 112 percent of net income before income taxes for the year. On the basis of these percentages, the auditor might conclude that the potential for misstatement pervades all the financial statements to the extent that he or she is unable to express an opinion. Thus, it would be appropriate to issue a disclaimer of opinion in this case.[5]

Form of a Disclaimer

The opinion paragraph of a report containing a disclaimer takes the following general format:

> Because of the significance of the [scope limitation] discussed in the preceding paragraph, we are unable to express, and we do not express, an opinion on the financial statements.

[5] The percentages used in these illustrations are for teaching purposes only and should not be considered applicable in all circumstances in the determination of materiality.

Every report containing a disclaimer of opinion should include an explanatory paragraph describing clearly and precisely all significant conditions that gave rise to the disclaimer. The auditor must also disclose any reservations or exceptions with regard to fairness of presentation. In other words, an auditor may not hide behind a disclaimer of opinion if he or she is aware of some deficiency in the financial statements resulting from improper application of accounting principles.

In some cases, it may be appropriate to disclaim an opinion on one or more financial statements and to express an unqualified or qualified opinion on others where scope limitations are involved. A form of report referred to as a *piecemeal opinion* (expression of opinion on specific financial statement items such as cash, accounts receivable, or accounts payable following a disclaimer of opinion on the financial statements taken as a whole or an adverse opinion) is prohibited.

Adverse Opinions

An *adverse opinion* is an opinion that the financial statements do not present fairly an entity's financial position, results of operations, or cash flows in conformity with generally accepted accounting principles. The adverse opinion is used if the financial statements being reported on contain a departure from generally accepted accounting principles so pervasive that it permeates the financial statements taken as a whole. Thus, the auditor's decision of whether an adverse opinion or "except for" qualification is appropriate in the case of a departure from a generally accepted accounting principle rests on the materiality of the amounts involved. This decision is similar to the choice between a disclaimer of opinion and an "except for" qualification in the case of a scope limitation (discussed on page 654).

Every adverse opinion requires an explanatory paragraph that clearly sets forth the subject of or reason for the adverse opinion and the amounts involved or estimated effect on the financial statements, if reasonably determinable.

The opinion paragraph of a report containing an adverse opinion takes the following form.

> In our opinion, because of the effects of [the departure from generally accepted accounting principles] discussed in the preceding paragraph, the financial statements referred to above do not present fairly, in conformity with generally accepted accounting principles, the financial position of X Company as of December 31, 19XX, or the results of its operations or its cash flows for the year then ended.

An adverse opinion is likely to have a very negative effect on the readers of the opinion and the related financial statements. Therefore, such opinions are issued only after all attempts to persuade the client to adjust the financial statements have failed.

SUMMARY OF THE FORMS OF QUALIFICATIONS, DISCLAIMERS, AND ADVERSE OPINIONS

The summary on page 652 of the types of qualifications required for material scope limitations and departures from generally accepted accounting principles can now be expanded to include circumstances so material as to require a disclaimer or adverse opinion. Although such circumstances have no specific designation in official pronouncements, they are referred to as *pervasive* in this text.

	Condition	
Effect	*Scope limitation*	*Departure from GAAP*
Material	Except for qualification	Except for qualification
Pervasive	Disclaimer	Adverse

SCOPE LIMITATIONS

Auditors should perform all the auditing procedures they consider necessary to express an unqualified opinion on the financial statements being audited, unless it is impracticable to perform certain procedures or they are instructed specifically by management to omit or limit certain procedures. Any limitation on the scope of auditors' work, whether client imposed or otherwise, constitutes a *scope limitation* unless the auditors are able to satisfy themselves by means of alternative audit procedures. If, for example, auditors are engaged by a client after the end of the client's fiscal year and do not observe the year-end physical inventory, they may be able to observe the inventory at a later date and reconcile to the audit date if there are reliable perpetual inventory records and effective internal control. If the auditors are able to satisfy themselves by this means that the inventory as of the end of the year is stated properly, they need not consider the scope of their work to be limited.

A scope limitation requires either an "except for" qualification or a disclaimer of opinion, depending on the materiality of the potential misstatement. A scope limitation also involves a modification of the scope paragraph to qualify the phrase "We conducted our audit in accordance with generally accepted auditing standards." If there has been a limitation on the scope of the auditors' work, clearly they have not conducted their audit in accordance with generally accepted auditing standards. Therefore, an exception should be indicated in both the scope and opinion paragraphs for a scope limitation. Following is an example of a modification of the scope paragraph:

> Except as discussed in the following paragraph, we conducted our audit in accordance with generally accepted auditing standards. Those standards require . . . .

A scope limitation should not be discussed in a footnote to the financial statements because the limitation applies to the work of the auditor, and the footnotes to the financial statements constitute the representations of management.

Inadequate Accounting Records

Inadequate accounting records may give rise to a scope limitation. The following example illustrates a report qualified (assume that a disclaimer is unnecessary) because of inadequate accounting records.

Except as explained in the following paragraph, we conducted our audit in accordance with generally accepted auditing standards. Those standards require . . .

Because of the inadequacy of prior-year records, we were unable to obtain sufficient evidence to form an opinion as to whether at December 31, 19XX, manufacturing equipment ($5,000,000) is stated at cost and as to the adequacy of the related accumulated depreciation ($1,500,000) and depreciation expense for the year ($400,000).

In our opinion, except for the effects of such adjustments, if any, as might have been determined to be necessary had we been able to examine evidence regarding manufacturing equipment and the related accumulated depreciation and depreciation expense, the financial statements referred to above present fairly, in all material . . . .

Note that the qualification is placed so that it applies to the statement of income as well as the balance sheet and statement of cash flows. A misstatement of manufacturing equipment also results in a misstatement of depreciation expense for the year, so the income statement should be, and is, properly covered by the qualification.

Timing of the Engagement

A scope limitation may also arise in initial audits. In some cases, auditors who are engaged during a year will be unable to satisfy themselves with regard to the quantities or consistent determination of beginning inventory because they were not present to observe it. If they are unable to satisfy themselves by other means, and if the potential effect is material, they will be unable to audit the statements of income, retained earnings, and cash flows because of the effect of beginning inventory on the determination of cost of sales and net income for the year. An example of report wording where only the balance sheet can be audited follows:

(Standard opening paragraph)

Except as explained in the following paragraph, we conducted our audit in accordance with generally accepted auditing standards. Those standards require . . .

We did not observe the taking of the physical inventory as of December 31, 19X0, because that date was prior to our appointment as auditors for the company, and we were unable to satisfy ourselves regarding inventory quantities by other auditing procedures. Inventory amounts as of December 31, 19X0, enter into the determination of net income and cash flows for the year ended December 31, 19X1.

In our opinion, the accompanying balance sheet presents fairly, in all material respects, the financial position of X Company as of December 31, 19X1 in conformity with generally accepted accounting principles. Because we were unable to make tests of inventory quantities, as noted in the preceding paragraph, the scope of our work was not sufficient to enable us to express, and we do not express, an opinion on the results of operations and cash flows for the year ended December 31, 19X1.

X Client-Imposed Restrictions

A scope limitation may also result from the specific request of a client. An example of an audit report (a disclaimer) involving a client-imposed scope limitation follows:

> We were engaged to audit the balance sheet of X Company as of December 31, 19X7, and the related statements of income, retained earnings, and cash flows for the year then ended. These financial statements are the responsibility of the company's management.
>
> As instructed, we did not request confirmation of accounts receivable balances directly from the company's customers as of December 31, 19XX, and we were unable to satisfy ourselves as to the balances by means of other auditing procedures.
>
> Because of the significance of the matter discussed in the preceding paragraph, the scope of our work was not sufficient to enable us to express, and we do not express, an opinion on these financial statements.

In the example, the words "As instructed" in the explanatory paragraph make clear that the limitation was imposed by the client and was not of the auditor's choosing. Needless to say, an auditor should consider carefully whether he or she should accept the engagement if significant scope limitations have been imposed by a client.

Note that when a scope limitation requires a disclaimer, the opening paragraph is modified ("We were engaged to audit . . ." rather than "We have audited . . ." and responsibility for expressing an opinion is omitted), the scope paragraph is omitted entirely (there was no audit to describe in the scope paragraph), an explanatory paragraph is added to describe the scope limitation, and the opinion paragraph disclaims an opinion.

Refusal by an attorney to furnish the information requested from him or her (see page 601 for an example of an audit inquiry letter to legal counsel) normally would constitute a limitation on the scope of an audit and would preclude issuance of an unqualified report. A scope limitation has occurred, because the requested information is available but is being withheld by the attorney. In contrast, the inability of an attorney to respond because the outcome of claims or litigation is uncertain and not subject to reasonable estimation is not a scope limitation, because the information requested (for example, the outcome of a lawsuit) is not available.

DEPARTURES FROM GENERALLY ACCEPTED ACCOUNTING PRINCIPLES

Departures from generally accepted accounting principles require a qualified ("except for") opinion if the effect is material and an adverse opinion if the effect is pervasive. Inadequate disclosure is considered a departure from generally accepted accounting principles. The meaning of the term *generally accepted accounting principles* within the context of the auditor's report is discussed in Chapter 19. The reader should refer to that discussion and to AU Section 411 if the meaning of the term is not understood.

An audit report on financial statements involving a departure from generally accepted accounting principles (assume that an adverse opinion is not required) might be worded as follows:

. . . provides a reasonable basis for our opinion.

As explained in Note 3, the provision for pension expense for the year ($2,000,000) was less than the amount required by generally accepted accounting principles. Had the required provision been made, pension expense would have been increased by approximately $1,500,000 and net income would have been decreased by approximately $1,000,000 ($.16 per share).

In our opinion, except for the effect of the inadequate provision for pension expense as described in the preceding paragraph, the financial statements referred to above present fairly, in all material respects, the . . . .

In the example, it must be assumed that the effect of the unrecorded pension liability is material in relation to the balance sheet, because the qualification applies to it as well as to the statements of income, retained earnings, and cash flows.

An illustration of an auditor's report containing an adverse opinion as a result of a departure from generally accepted accounting principles is shown below.

. . . provides a reasonable basis for our opinion.

As set forth in Note 2, land owned by the company is stated in the accompanying balance sheet at appraised value, which is $7,000,000 in excess of cost. Had this land been stated at cost, in accordance with generally accepted accounting principles, property and equipment and stockholders' equity would be reduced by this amount as of December 31, 19X2. The recording of appraised value has no effect on the statements of income, retained earnings, and cash flows.

In our opinion, because of the significant effect of recording appraised value as discussed in the preceding paragraph, the balance sheet referred to above does not present fairly, in conformity with generally accepted accounting principles, the financial position of X Company as of December 31, 19X2. However, in our opinion, the statements of income, retained earnings, and cash flows present fairly, in all material respects, the results of operations and cash flows for the year ended December 31, 19X2, in conformity with generally accepted accounting principles.

This example illustrates how a departure from generally accepted accounting principles can affect one rather than all of the basic financial statements.

The requirement for adequate disclosure is stated specifically in the standards of reporting; however, the auditor must not confuse long and rambling footnotes with adequate disclosure. (Such footnotes actually may make understanding more difficult for the reader.) The auditor must also understand that disclosure is not and cannot be used as a substitute for proper accounting. For example, the failure to record a significant and known liability cannot be remedied by disclosure of the unrecorded liability in a footnote; the financial statements can be corrected only by recording the proper liability.

The topic of auditors' liability in Chapter 4 included a discussion of the *Continental Vending Machine Corporation (Continental)* case. One of the most important aspects of this case involved the adequacy of the disclosure of balances and transactions

FIGURE 20.3   **Summary Flowchart of Modified Audit Reports**

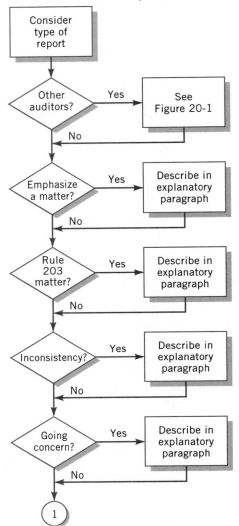

between Continental, its president, and an affiliated company. A comparison of the footnote describing these balances and transactions with the statement the prosecution successfully contended should have been made illustrates the necessity for clear and adequate disclosure. Following is the footnote as it appeared in the financial statements.

The amount receivable from Valley Commercial Corporation (an affiliated company of which Mr. Harold Roth is an officer, director, and stockholder) bears interest at 12% a year. Such amount, less the balance of the notes payable to that company, is secured by the assignment to the Company of Valley's equity in certain marketable

FIGURE 20.3 *(Continued)*

securities. As of February 15, 1963, the amount of such equity at current market quotations exceeded the net amount receivable.[6]

The government successfully contended that the footnote should have read as follows.

The amount receivable from Valley Commercial Corporation (an affiliated company of which Mr. Harold Roth is an officer, director, and stockholder), which bears interest

[6] Denzil Y. Causey, Jr., *Duties and Liabilities of the CPA* (Austin, Tex.: Bureau of Business Research, University of Texas at Austin, 1973), p. 239.

at 12% a year, was uncollectible at September 30, 1962, since Valley had loaned approximately the same amount to Mr. Roth, who was unable to pay. Since that date, Mr. Roth and others have pledged as security for the repayment of his obligations to Valley and its obligation to Continental (now $3,900,000, against which Continental's liability to Valley cannot be offset) securities which, as of February 15, 1963, had a market value of $2,978,000. Approximately 80% of such securities are stock and convertible debentures of the Company.[7]

An auditor must avoid any inclination to accept less than a necessarily harsh disclosure to pacify a client.

Adequate disclosure relates to the form, arrangement, and content of the financial statements, including related notes. If disclosures required by generally accepted accounting principles are omitted, the auditor should provide the information in the report if practicable (practicable in this context meaning that the information is reasonably obtainable and does not require the auditor to prepare basic financial information such as a statement of cash flows or segment information), unless the omission from the report is permitted by generally accepted auditing standards. A qualified or adverse opinion should also be expressed. Such a report might be worded in the following manner:

> . . . provides a reasonable basis for our opinion.
>
> The Company's financial statements do not disclose that subsequent to the end of the year the company issued $10,000,000 of 8% debentures that are due in 20X0. The debenture agreement restricts the payment of future cash dividends to earnings after December 31, 19X3.
>
> In our opinion, except for the omission of the information in the preceding paragraph, the financial statements referred to above present . . . .

In practice, qualifications and adverse opinions necessitated by inadequate disclosure are rare. Because the auditor must disclose the omitted information in an explanatory paragraph of the report, the client normally prefers to make the disclosure in the financial statements to avoid receiving an audit report that contains the omitted disclosure and takes exception to the fair presentation of the financial statements. See Figure 20.3 (pages 660–661) for a summary of the discussion to this point in the chapter.

DIFFERENT REPORTS ON DIFFERENT YEARS

If an auditor is reporting on financial statements covering two or more years, he or she may modify the report (explanatory paragraph, qualification, adverse, or disclaimer of opinion) for one or more years while issuing a standard report for others. For example, if a material departure from generally accepted accounting principles occurs in the latest year, the auditor would qualify the report for the latest year and issue an unqualified report on the previous year.

[7] Ibid., p. 240.

An example of the reporting format for such a report covering 19X6 and 19X7 is shown below:

(Standard opening and scope paragraphs)

The company has excluded from property and debt in the accompanying 19X7 balance sheet certain lease obligations that were entered into in 19X7 that, in our opinion, should be capitalized to conform with generally accepted accounting principles. If these lease obligations were capitalized, property would be increased by $6,000,000, long-term debt by $5,500,000, and retained earnings by $500,000 as of December 31, 19X7, and net income and earnings per share would be increased by $500,000 and $.50, respectively, for the year then ended.

In our opinion, except for the effects on the 19X7 financial statements of not capitalizing certain lease obligations as described in the preceding paragraph, the financial statements referred to above present fairly, in all material respects, the financial position of X Company as of December 31, 19X7 and 19X6, and the results of its operations and its cash flows for the years then ended in conformity with generally accepted accounting principles.

INTERNATIONAL STANDARDS ON AUDITING

International standards on auditing provide for modifications to the standard audit report that differ from modifications required by U.S. standards in the following ways:

1. An auditor is prohibited from accepting an audit engagement when a scope limitation imposed by a client is so material that a disclaimer of opinion would be required. (U.S. standards permit the acceptance of such an engagement provided that a disclaimer is issued.)

2. An auditor is to consider adding an explanatory paragraph describing significant uncertainties.

3. An auditor is not required to add an explanatory paragraph to identify an inconsistency in the application of accounting principles between periods, as is required by U.S. standards.

COMMENTARY

The significant effect on a company of receiving an audit report containing a qualification, a disclaimer, or an adverse opinion can be illustrated by reference to the practices of the Securities and Exchange Commission. Generally, the SEC will not accept for filing under the Securities Act of 1933 or the Securities Exchange Act of 1934 financial statements for which the related auditor's report is modified because of a scope limitation or a departure from a generally accepted accounting principle.

The failure of the management of a company to make the required filings under the securities acts may result in the suspension of trading in the company's stock and possible civil and criminal penalties. Thus, the SEC views qualifications, disclaimers, and adverse opinions as serious matters, and it has provided auditors of companies subject to SEC jurisdiction with a powerful tool to prevent limitations on the scope of their work and departures from generally accepted accounting principles. Most other users of financial statements such as bankers, other credit grantors, and stockholders share the SEC's view as to the serious nature of modifications of the auditor's report.

The disagreement between Coopers & Lybrand LLP (C&L) and its former client, CCX, Inc., reported in the *Public Accounting Report,* illustrates the difficulties auditors often have with their clients when qualifications, disclaimers, or adverse opinions are involved. C&L indicated that CCX, Inc. resisted making footnote disclosure of its deteriorating going-concern condition. CCX, Inc. also opposed a C&L request for an additional representation letter from the CCX, Inc. board of directors until C&L said, "The absence of the required representation letter would be construed to be a scope limitation on the performance of the audit, which would lead to a disclaimer of opinion." CCX, Inc. supplied the additional representation letter and subsequently changed auditors.

Chapter 20 ▶ GLOSSARY OF TERMS

Adverse opinion An audit report in which the auditor expresses an opinion that the financial statements do not present fairly the financial position, results of operations, or cash flows in conformity with generally accepted accounting principles.

Departures from generally accepted accounting principles The use of unacceptable accounting principles, the misapplication of acceptable accounting principles, or inadequate disclosure that requires a qualification or adverse opinion.

Disclaimer of opinion An audit report in which the auditor does not express an opinion on the financial statements.

Explanatory paragraph A paragraph included in an auditor's report to (1) emphasize a matter; (2) justify why a pronouncement of a standard setting body was not followed; (3) describe the subject of a qualification, a disclaimer, or an adverse opinion; (4) describe an inconsistent application of accounting principles; or (5) describe a going concern problem.

Other auditors Other independent auditors who have audited the financial statements of one or more subsidiaries, divisions, branches, components, or investments included in the financial statements on which a principal auditor expresses an opinion.

Pervasive A matter that is so significant, either quantitatively or qualitatively, that it permeates the amounts and presentations of numerous financial statement items to the extent that the overall financial statements cannot be relied on.

Piecemeal opinion Expression of opinion as to certain identified accounts in the financial statements after issuing a disclaimer or an adverse opinion; not considered appropriate.

Principal auditor The auditor who accepts responsibility for expressing an opinion on consolidated financial statements when one or more subsidiaries, divisions, branches, components, or investments are audited by other auditors.

Qualified report An auditor's report in which the opinion paragraph contains the phrase "except for" because of material scope limitations or departures from generally accepted accounting principles.

Scope limitation Restrictions on the scope of an auditor's work, whether imposed by the client or by circumstances such as the timing of the work, the inability to obtain sufficient competent evidence, or an inadequacy in the accounting records, which require a qualification or disclaimer of opinion.

Chapter 20 ▶ REFERENCES

American Institute of Certified Public Accountants. *Professional Standards*
   AU Section 341—*The Auditor's Consideration of an Entity's Ability to Continue as a Going Concern*
   AU Section 420—*Consistency of Application of Generally Accepted Accounting Principles*
   AU Section 431—*Adequacy of Disclosure in Financial Statements*
   AU Section 500—*The Fourth Standard of Reporting* (Substantially all individual statements in Section 500 are applicable to this chapter.)

Mutchler, Jane F. "Empirical Evidence Regarding the Auditor's Going-Concern Opinion Decision," *Auditing: A Journal of Practice and Theory* (Fall 1986), pp. 148–163.

Ponemon, Lawrence A. and Raghanandan, K. "What Is Substantial Doubt?" *Accounting Horizons* (June 1994), pp. 44–54.

Chapter 20 ▶ REVIEW QUESTIONS

20-1 List the modifications of the standard audit report that normally do not result in a qualification, a disclaimer, or an adverse opinion.

20-2 When more than one auditor is involved in an audit of a company's financial statements, what two decisions about reporting must the principal auditor make?

20-3 What disclosure is made in the principal auditors' report if they decide to assume responsibility for other auditors' work? If they decide not to assume responsibility for other auditors' work?

20-4 Give three examples of matters that might be emphasized in an explanatory paragraph of the audit report.

20-5 Under what conditions should the phrase "with the foregoing explanation" be used in the opinion paragraph to refer to a matter emphasized in an explanatory paragraph?

20-6 Under what condition may an auditor issue an unqualified opinion on financial statements containing a departure from an accounting principle published by a body designated by the AICPA Council to establish accounting principles? If this condition is met, what form will the auditor's report take?

20-7 What modification is made to an auditor's report if accounting principles are not applied consistently?

20-8 List the factors that affect comparability of financial statements between years and result in a modification of the standard auditor's report.

20-9 List the factors that affect comparability of financial statements between years but would normally not result in a modification of the standard auditor's report.

20-10 List two circumstances that may result in a qualification, a disclaimer, or an adverse opinion.

20-11 Explain the meaning and use of the "except for" qualification.

20-12 Where should a qualifying phrase be placed if the auditor intends to qualify all of the basic financial statements?

20-13 What is the purpose of a disclaimer of opinion and when is it used?

20-14 Under what condition would an auditor issue a disclaimer of opinion rather than an "except for" qualification?

20-15 What is a piecemeal opinion, and under what conditions is it appropriate for the auditor to use it?

20-16 What does an adverse opinion state and when is it used?

20-17 How does an auditor decide whether to use an "except for" qualification or an adverse opinion?

20-18 List three reasons for limitations on the scope of an auditor's work.

20-19 Discuss the forms an auditor's report may take as the result of a scope limitation.

20-20 How is the scope paragraph of an auditor's report modified if the auditor's scope has been limited so that a qualification is required? A disclaimer is required?

20-21 Why should a scope limitation not be discussed in a footnote?

20-22 What forms of audit report are required to describe departures from generally accepted accounting principles and when is each used?

20-23 Why are qualifications and adverse opinions because of inadequate disclosure rare in practice?

Chapter 20 ▶ OBJECTIVE QUESTIONS

(* = author prepared; ** = CPA examination)

**20-24 A principal auditor decides not to refer to the audit of another CPA who audited a subsidiary of the principal auditor's client. After making inquiries about the other CPA's professional reputation and independence, the principal auditor most likely would
  a. Add an explanatory paragraph to the auditor's report indicating that the subsidiary's financial statements are *not* material to the consolidated financial statements.
  b. Document in the engagement letter that the principal auditor assumes *no* responsibility for the other CPA's work and opinion.
  c. Obtain written permission from the other CPA to omit the reference in the principal auditor's report.
  d. Contact the other CPA and review the audit programs and working papers pertaining to the subsidiary.

**20-25 In which of the following situations would an auditor ordinarily issue an unqualified audit opinion without an explanatory paragraph?
  a. The auditor wishes to emphasize that the entity had significant related party transactions.
  b. The auditor decides to make reference to the report of another auditor as a basis, in part, for the auditor's opinion.
  c. The entity issues financial statements that present financial position and results of operations, but omits the statement of cash flows.
  d. The auditor has substantial doubt about the entity's ability to continue as a going concern, but the circumstances are fully disclosed in the financial statements.

**20-26 An auditor includes a separate paragraph in an otherwise unmodified report to emphasize that the entity being reported on had significant transactions with related parties. The inclusion of this separate paragraph
  a. Is considered an "except for" qualification of the opinion.
  b. Violates generally accepted auditing standards if this information is already disclosed in footnotes to the financial statements.
  c. Necessitates a revision of the opinion paragraph to include the phrase "with the foregoing explanation."

  d. Is appropriate and would *not* negate the unqualified opinion.

**20-27 Eagle Company's financial statements contain a departure from generally accepted accounting principles because, due to unusual circumstances, the statements would otherwise be misleading. The auditor should express an opinion that is
  a. Unqualified but *not* mention the departure in the auditor's report.
  b. Unqualified and describe the departure in a separate paragraph.
  c. Qualified and describe the departure in a separate paragraph.
  d. Qualified or adverse, depending on materiality, and describe the departure in a separate paragraph.

**20-28 When an entity changes its method of accounting for income taxes, which has a material effect on comparability, the auditor should refer to the change in an explanatory paragraph added to the auditor's report. This paragraph should identify the nature of the change and
  a. Explain why the change is justified under generally accepted accounting principles.
  b. Describe the cumulative effect of the change on the audited financial statements.
  c. State the auditor's explicit concurrence with or opposition to the change.
  d. Refer to the financial statement note that discusses the change in detail.

**20-29 Miller Company uses the first-in, first-out method of costing for its international subsidiary's inventory and the last-in, first-out method of costing for its domestic inventory. Under these circumstances, Miller should issue an auditor's report with an
  a. "Except for" qualified opinion.
  b. Unmodified opinion.
  c. Explanatory paragraph as to consistency.
  d. Opinion modified as to consistency.

**20-30 An auditor concludes that there is substantial doubt about an entity's ability to continue as a going concern for a reasonable period of time. If the entity's disclosures concerning this matter are adequate, the audit report should include a(an)

Adverse opinion	"Except for" qualified opinion
a. Yes	Yes
b. No	No
c. No	Yes
d. Yes	No

**20-31 An auditor who qualifies an opinion because of an insufficiency of evidential matter should describe the limitation in an explanatory paragraph. The auditor should also refer to the limitation in the

Scope paragraph	Opinion paragraph	Notes to the financial statements
a. Yes	No	Yes
b. Yes	Yes	No
c. No	Yes	No
d. Yes	Yes	Yes

**20-32 Restrictions imposed by a client prohibit the observation of physical inventories, which account for 35 percent of all assets. Alternative audit procedures cannot be applied, although the auditor was able to examine satisfactory evidence for all other items in the financial statements. The auditor should issue a(an)
   a. "Except for" qualified opinion.
   b. Disclaimer of opinion.
   c. Unqualified opinion with a separate explanatory paragraph.
   d. Unqualified opinion with an explanation in the scope paragraph.

**20-33 Park, CPA, was engaged to audit the financial statements of Tech Co., a new client, for the year ended December 31, 19X3. Park obtained sufficient audit evidence for all of Tech's financial statement items except Tech's opening inventory. Due to inadequate financial records, Park could not verify Tech's January 1, 19X3, inventory balances. Park's opinion on Tech's 19X3 financial statements most likely will be

Balance sheet	Income statement
a. Disclaimer	Disclaimer
b. Unqualified	Disclaimer
c. Disclaimer	Adverse
d. Unqualified	Adverse

**20-34 A limitation on the scope of an audit sufficient to preclude an unqualified opinion will usually result when management
   a. Is unable to obtain audited financial state-

ments supporting the entity's investment in a foreign subsidiary.
   b. Refuses to disclose in the notes to the financial statements related party transactions authorized by the Board of Directors.
   c. Does *not* sign an engagement letter specifying the responsibilities of both the entity and the auditor.
   d. Fails to correct a reportable condition communicated to the audit committee after the prior year's audit.

**20-35 Green, CPA, was engaged to audit the financial statements of Essex Co. after its fiscal year had ended. The timing of Green's appointment as auditor and the start of field work made confirmation of accounts receivable by direct communication with the debtors ineffective. However, Green applied other procedures and was satisfied as to the reasonableness of the account balances. Green's auditor's report most likely contained a(an)
   a. Unqualified opinion.
   b. Unqualified opinion with an explanatory paragraph.
   c. Qualified opinion due to a scope limitation.
   d. Qualified opinion due to a departure from generally accepted auditing standards.

**20-36 If a publicly held company issues financial statements that purport to present its financial position and results of operations but omits the statement of cash flows, the auditor ordinarily will express a(an)
   a. Unqualified opinion with a separate explanatory paragraph.
   b. Qualified opinion.
   c. Adverse opinion.
   d. Disclaimer of opinion.

**20-37 When an auditor qualifies an opinion because of inadequate disclosure, the auditor should describe the nature of the omission in a separate explanatory paragraph and modify the

Introductory paragraph	Scope paragraph	Opinion paragraph
a. Yes	No	No
b. Yes	Yes	No
c. No	Yes	Yes
d. No	No	Yes

**20-38 An auditor's report that refers to the use of an accounting principle at variance with generally accepted accounting principles contains the words, "In our opinion, with the foregoing ex-

planation, the financial statements referred to above present fairly. . . .'' This is considered an
  a. Adverse opinion.
  b. "Except for" qualified opinion.
  c. Unqualified opinion with an explanatory paragraph.
  d. Example of inappropriate reporting.

**20-39 In which of the following circumstances would an auditor be most likely to express an adverse opinion?
  a. Information comes to the auditor's attention that raises substantial doubt about the entity's ability to continue as a going concern.
  b. The chief executive officer refuses the auditor access to minutes of board of directors' meetings.
  c. The statements are *not* in conformity with the *FASB Statements* regarding the capitalization of leases.
  d. Tests of controls show that the entity's control risk must be assessed at the maximum level.

**20-40 Items a through h present various independent factual situations an auditor might encounter in conducting an audit. List A represents the types of opinions the auditor ordinarily would issue and List B represents the report modifications (if any) that would be necessary. For each situation, select one response from List A and one from List B. Select as the *best* answers for each item, the action the auditor normally would take. The types of opinions in List A and the report modifications in List B may be selected once, more than once, or not at all.

Assume:

- The auditor is independent.
- The auditor previously expressed an unqualified opinion on the prior year's financial statements.
- Only single-year (not comparative) statements are presented for the current year.
- The conditions for an unqualified opinion exist unless contradicted by the facts.
- The conditions stated in the factual situations are material.
- No report modifications are to be made except in response to the factual situation.

  a. An auditor hires an actuary to assist in corroborating a client's complex pension calculations concerning accrued pension liabilities that account for 35 percent of the client's total liabilities. The actuary's find-ings are reasonably close to the client's calculations and support the financial statements.
  List A _____   List B _____

  b. A client holds a note receivable consisting of principal and accrued interest receivable. The note's maker recently filed a voluntary bankruptcy petition, but the client failed to reduce the recorded value of the note to its net realizable value, which is approximately 20 percent of the recorded amount.
  List A _____   List B _____

  c. An auditor is engaged to audit a client's financial statements after the annual physical inventory count. The accounting records are not sufficiently reliable to enable the auditor to become satisfied as to the year-end inventory balances.
  List A _____   List B _____

  d. Big City is required by GASB to present supplementary information outside the basic financial statements concerning the disclosure of pension information. Big City's auditor determines that the supplementary information, which is *not* required to be part of the basic financial statements, is omitted.
  List A _____   List B _____

  e. A client's financial statements do not disclose certain long-term lease obligations. The auditor determines that the omitted disclosures are required by FASB.
  List A _____   List B _____

  f. A principal auditor decides not to take responsibility for the work of another CPA who audited a wholly owned subsidiary of the principal auditor's client. The total assets and revenues of the subsidiary represent 27 percent and 28 percent, respectively, of the related consolidated totals.
  List A _____   List B _____

  g. A client changes its method of accounting for the cost of inventories from FIFO to LIFO. The auditor concurs with the change although it has a material effect on the comparability of the financial statements.
  List A _____   List B _____

  h. Due to losses and adverse key financial ratios, an auditor has substantial doubt about a client's ability to continue as a going concern for a reasonable period of time. The client has adequately disclosed its financial difficulties in a note to its financial statements, which do *not* include any adjustments that might result from the outcome of this uncertainty.

List A	List B
Types of opinions	*Report modifications*
A. Either an "except for" qualified opinion or an adverse opinion	H. Describe the circumstances in an explanatory paragraph *without modifying* the three standard paragraphs.
B. Either a disclaimer of opinion or an "except for" qualified opinion	I. Describe the circumstances in an explanatory paragraph and *modify the opinion* paragraph.
C. Either an adverse opinion or a disclaimer of opinion	J. Describe the circumstances in an explanatory paragraph and *modify* the *scope* and *opinion* paragraphs.
D. An "except for" qualified opinion	K. Describe the circumstances in an explanatory paragraph and *modify* the *introductory, scope,* and *opinion* paragraphs.
E. An unqualified opinion	L. Describe the circumstances within the *scope* paragraph without adding an explanatory paragraph.
F. An adverse opinion	M. Describe the circumstances within the *opinion* paragraph without adding an explanatory paragraph.
G. A disclaimer of opinion	N. Describe the circumstances within the *scope* and *opinion* paragraphs without adding an explanatory paragraph.
	O. Describe the circumstances within the *introductory, scope,* and *opinion* paragraphs without adding an explanatory paragraph.
	P. Issue the *standard* auditor's report *without modification.*

Chapter 20 ▶ DISCUSSION/CASE QUESTIONS

(* = author prepared; ** = CPA examination; *** = CMA examination)

**20-41   The auditors' report below was drafted by Moore, a staff accountant of Tyler & Tyler, CPAs, at the completion of the audit of the financial statements of Park Publishing Co., Inc., for the year ended September 30, 19X2. The report was submitted to the engagement partner who reviewed the audit working papers and properly concluded that an unqualified opinion should be issued. In drafting the report, Moore considered the following:

- During fiscal year 19X2, Park changed its depreciation method. The engagement partner concurred with this change in accounting principle and its justification and Moore included an explanatory paragraph in the auditors' report.

- The financial statements for the year ended September 30, 19X1, are to be presented for comparative purposes. Tyler & Tyler previously audited these statements and expressed an unqualified opinion.

Independent Auditors' Report

To the Board of Directors of Park Publishing Co., Inc.:

We have audited the accompanying balance sheets of Park Publishing Co., Inc. as of September 30, 19X2, and 19X1, and the related statements of income and cash flows for the years then ended. These financial statements are the responsibility of the company's management.

We conducted our audits in accordance with generally accepted auditing standards. Those standards require that we plan and perform the audit to obtain reasonable assurance about whether the financial statements are fairly presented. An audit includes examining, on a test basis, evidence supporting the amounts and disclosures in the financial statements. An audit also includes assessing significant estimates made by management, as well as evaluating the overall financial statement presentation. We believe that our audits provide a basis for determining whether any material modifications should be made to the accompanying financial statements.

As discussed in Note A to the financial statements, the company changed its method of computing depreciation in fiscal 19X2.

In our opinion, except for the accounting change, with which we concur, the financial statements referred to above present fairly, in all material respects, the financial position of Park Publishing Co., Inc. as of September 30, 19X2, and the results of its operations and its cash flows for the year then ended in conformity with generally accepted accounting principles.

Tyler & Tyler, CPAs
November 5, 19X2

Required:

Identify the deficiencies in the auditors' report as drafted by Moore. Group the deficiencies by paragraph and in the order in which the deficiencies appear. Do *not* redraft the report.

*20-42   You are the auditor of X Company, and during your audit for the year ended September 30, 19X7, you note that approximately 76 percent of the company's sales were to one customer. In the prior year, no single customer accounted for more than 28 percent. You believe disclosure of this fact is significant because the loss of this customer could seriously affect future operations of X Company. Management of X Company refuses to include this information in the financial statements, maintaining that this type of information is not often found in financial statements and that it could have a negative effect on the negotiation of the renewal of a bank loan now in progress.

a. How would you reply to X Company management with regard to this disclosure?

b. Assume that you are unable to persuade X Company management to make the disclosure that you consider appropriate; draft the audit report that you would issue.

*20-43   Y Company has never been audited and is to be acquired by one of your present clients and combined on a pooling-of-interest basis. Your client includes ten years of financial statements in its annual report and has instructed you to audit Y Company for the previous ten years so that ten years of restated financial statements can be included in the annual report again this year. During this audit, you note that Y Company has substantial gains from sales of long-term investment securities in 19X7 and 19X8. However, the gains in 19X7 were presented as extraordinary items, whereas the 19X8 gains were reported as part of ordinary operations. You find that the different reporting was caused by a change in the criteria for extraordinary items contained in the professional literature that became effective in late 19X7. Thus, both transactions were reported properly in conformity with the accounting principles in effect during the respective years, and the inconsistency arose from action taken by a standard setting body, not Y Company.

a. Will you modify your audit report for lack of consistency? Explain your reasoning.

b. Draft the audit report you will issue, assuming that you have no other reservations regarding the financial statements.

*20-44   In connection with your audit of Z Company for the year ended December 31, 19XX, you find that as a result of an improper cutoff of inventory shipments at the end of the year, approximately $6,000 of sales applicable to the subsequent year were recorded in the current year. During the current year, sales totaled $5 million, and net income was $850,000. Management of Z Company refuses to adjust the financial statements for the $6,000 error.

a. What position would you take with the management of Z Company regarding the correction of this error? How would you explain your position?

b. Draft the audit report you will issue, assuming that you are satisfied with the financial statements otherwise.

*20-45 You have been engaged to audit W Company, a new company formed to explore for oil and gas. During the year, W Company acquired several large undeveloped lease holdings for $1 million and drilled several exploratory wells, all of which were dry. At December 31, 19X4, the financial statements showed total assets of $1.1 million (including the cost of the undeveloped leases) and net worth of $400,000. In your discussion with the management of W Company regarding the recoverability of the cost of the leases, they maintain that, despite the unsuccessful efforts to date, the cost of the leases could be recovered, because the geologic features underlying certain of the leases are favorable for the formation of hydrocarbons and a productive oil well recently had been drilled near their leases. They supply you with an opinion of an outside geologist and other documentary support for their position.

a. What type of audit report would you issue to W Company? Explain your reasons fully.

b. Draft the audit report you will issue, assuming that you are otherwise satisfied with the financial statements.

c. Assume that management believes that the leases probably will not be productive of oil or gas but insists that they be shown in the financial statements at cost, as this presentation would be in accordance with generally accepted accounting principles. Would this change the type of audit report you would issue? Explain why or why not.

d. Draft the audit report you would issue on the basis of the assumption in (c), if it would differ from the report you drafted in (b).

*20-46 During the current year, your client, U Company, acquired B Company in a business combination accounted for as a pooling-of-interest. B Company previously had reported on a fiscal year ending on June 30, whereas U Company used a year ending December 31. Considerable time and cost would be involved in restating and auditing the prior-year financial statements of B Company on a December 31 year-end for combination with U Company on a pooling-of-interest basis. The management of U Company decides to combine B Company for the current year, which they believe is most important to readers of the financial statements, but not for prior years, because they do not consider the extra cost justified. You think the financial statements of B Company are significant in relation to those of U Company in the current and prior years, and that failure to combine them for the prior year would make the financial statements of that year misleading. Current and one-year-prior financial statements are to be included in the annual report.

a. Discuss the propriety of management's position regarding the restatement of current and prior-year financial statements.

b. Explain the reporting problems, if any, in the case.

c. Draft an appropriate audit report.

*20-47 As a normal procedure in your audits, you request management of your clients to furnish you a management representation letter including, among other things, representations that the financial statements are presented fairly in all material respects, that there are no material unrecorded liabilities, and so on. One of your clients, T Company, has had a recent change in management soon after the end of the company's fiscal year, December 31. As you are concluding your audit for the year, you ask the new management to sign the normal management representation letter. They respond that they are unwilling to do so because they do not have full knowledge of the company's affairs for the year being audited.

    a. Discuss the reasonableness of the new management's position.

    b. Under these particular circumstances, would failure to obtain a management representation letter be considered a scope limitation?

    c. Draft the audit report you would issue.

*20-48   During 19X7, R Company, your client, changed its method, effective January 1, 19X7, of computing inventory cost from the average cost method to the last-in, first-out method. This change had the effect of reducing net income for the year ended December 31, 19X7 by $300,000 ($0.26 per share), a material amount.

    a. How can the company justify the change in inventory pricing as required by *APB Opinion No. 20*?

    b. Draft the audit report that you will issue, assuming that you are otherwise satisfied with the financial statements.

*20-49   You recently were engaged to audit the financial statements of P Company, a company that previously has not been audited. During your work, you learn that three years ago a serious fire destroyed most of the company's accounting records, including those substantiating the cost of its property and equipment. You physically observe the major items of property and equipment included in the financial statements, but you are unable to determine when and at what price most of it had been acquired. Property and equipment is a material item in the balance sheet.

    a. Describe the reporting problem in the case.

    b. Draft an audit report covering the matter, assuming that you have no other reservations about the financial statements.

    c. If your report is qualified, how long do you anticipate the same qualification will continue?

**20-50   The auditor's report below was drafted by Miller, a staff accountant of Pell & Pell, CPAs, at the completion of the audit of the consolidated financial statements of Bond Co. for the year ended July 31, 19X3. The report was submitted to the engagement partner who reviewed the audit working papers and properly concluded that an unqualified opinion should be issued. In drafting the report, Miller considered the following:

- Bond's consolidated financial statements for the year ended July 31, 19X2, are to be presented for comparative purposes. Pell previously audited these statements and appropriately rendered an unmodified report.

- Bond has suffered recurring losses from operations and has adequately disclosed these losses and management's plans concerning the losses in a note to the financial statements. Although Bond has prepared the financial statements assuming it will continue as a going concern, Miller has substantial doubt about Bond's ability to continue as a going concern.

- Smith & Smith, CPAs, audited the financial statements of BC Services, Inc., a consolidated subsidiary of Bond, for the year ended July 31, 19X3. The subsidiary's financial statements reflected total assets and revenues of 15 percent and 18 percent, respectively, of the consolidated totals. Smith expressed an unqualified opinion and furnished Miller with a copy of the auditor's report. Smith also granted permission to present the report together with the principal auditor's report. Miller decided not to present Smith's report with that of Pell, but instead to make reference to Smith.

Independent Auditor's Report

We have audited the consolidated balance sheets of Bond Co. and subsidiaries as of July 31, 19X3, and 19X2, and the related consolidated statements of income and retained earnings for the years then ended. Our responsibility is to express an opinion on these financial statements based on our audits. We did not audit the financial statements of BC Services, Inc., a wholly owned subsidiary. Those statements were audited by Smith & Smith, CPAs, whose report has been furnished to us, and our opinion, insofar as it relates to the amounts included for BC Services, Inc., is based solely on the report of Smith & Smith.

We conducted our audits in accordance with generally accepted auditing standards. Those standards require that we plan and perform the audit to obtain reasonable assurance about whether the financial statements are free of material misstatement. An audit includes assessing control risk, the accounting principles used, and significant estimates made by management, as well as evaluating the overall financial statement presentation. We believe that our audits provide a reasonable basis for our opinion.

In our opinion, based on our audits and the report of Smith & Smith, CPAs, the consolidated financial statements referred to above present fairly, in all material respects except for the matter discussed below, the financial position of Bond Co. as of July 31, 19X3, and 19X2, and the results of its operations for the years then ended.

The accompanying consolidated financial statements have been prepared with the disclosure in Note 13 that the company has suffered recurring losses from operations. Management's plans in regard to those matters are also discussed in Note 13. The financial statements do not include any adjustments that might result from the outcome of this uncertainty.

Pell & Pell, CPAs
November 4, 19X3

Required:

Identify the deficiencies in the auditor's report as drafted by Miller. Group the deficiencies by paragraph and in the order in which the deficiencies appear. Do *not* redraft the report.

*20-51 The partner in charge of the audit of Weishar Inc. began to draft the audit report for the year ended June 30, 19X2. She completed the first paragraph, which is shown below, before being called to another client.

Independent Auditors' Report

To the stockholders and board of directors of Weishar, Inc.:

We have audited the consolidated balance sheet of Weishar, Inc. as of June 30, 19X2 and the related consolidated statements of income, retained earnings, and cash flows for the year then ended. These financial statements are the responsibility of the company's management. Our responsibility is to express an opinion on these financial statements based on our audit. We did not audit the financial statements of Markham Co., a wholly owned subsidiary, which financial statements reflect total assets and revenues constituting 40 and 44 percent, respectively, of the related consolidated totals. Those statements were audited by other auditors whose report, which contained an explanatory paragraph expressing substantial doubt as to the ability of Markham Co. to continue as a going concern, has been furnished to us, and our opinion, insofar as it relates to amounts included for Markham Co., is based solely on the report of the other auditors.

You are aware that Markham Co. constitutes 40 percent of Weishar's total assets. The going concern issue of Markham Co. is disclosed in Note Y of Weishar's financial statements.

Required:

Your assignment is to draft the remaining paragraphs of the auditor's report.

*20-52   The following circumstances affect the comparability of financial statements between periods. The effect is material unless otherwise indicated. For each circumstance, state whether the auditor's report should be modified and why.

a. The client changes from the cost to the equity method of accounting for a significant subsidiary.

b. The client changes its estimate of warranty costs from one percent of sales to two percent of sales.

c. A retail merchandise client changes from charging store opening cost to expense to deferring those costs. The change had an immaterial effect in the current year but is reasonably certain to have a substantial effect in future years.

d. The client changes from a FIFO to a LIFO basis of pricing inventory.

e. The client merged with another company on a pooling-of-interests basis but did not restate prior periods that were presented on a comparative basis with the present period.

f. The client changed from a direct costing basis to a full absorption basis of accounting for inventory.

g. The client reclassified certain items in the prior-year financial statements to make them comparable with the current year. Significant amounts such as net current assets, total assets, gross profit, and net income were not affected.

h. In 19X2 the client operated a fleet of buses as a bus company. At the beginning of 19X3 the client sold all of its bus assets and purchased a chain of bookstores, which it operated in 19X3.

i. In 19X2 the client capitalized overhead costs associated with the construction of new facilities. In 19X3 these costs were expensed because capitalization resulted in the cost of the new facilities exceeding their market value.

j. In 19X2 the client treated certificates of deposits of four months' maturity or less as cash equivalents in the statement of cash flows, while in 19X3 only certificates of deposits of three months or less were treated as cash equivalents.

k. In 19X2 the client made a material mathematical mistake in computing prepaid expenses. In 19X3 the computation was made correctly.

Other Types of Reports

"Modest doubt is called the beacon of the wise."

SHAKESPEARE, *Troilus and Cressida*, II, ii

LEARNING OBJECTIVES

After reading and studying the material in this chapter, the student should be able to

▶ Write a brief summary of CPA financial statement services to both public and nonpublic companies.

▶ Compare the three levels of assurance that a CPA may provide on financial information by describing and giving examples of the various reports at each of these levels.

▶ Describe reports on accompanying information in auditor-submitted documents and give an example of such a report.

▶ Describe the purpose of pro forma financial information.

The form of audit report applicable to general-purpose financial statements is recognized by readers of published annual reports and applies to all financial statements that purport to show financial position, results of operations, and cash flows in conformity with generally accepted accounting principles. CPAs issue other types of reports, however, that are less familiar to the general public. This chapter contains discussions of some of these types of reports, including reports on unaudited, compiled, and reviewed financial statements, special reports, letters for underwriters, and reports on prospective financial statements and accompanying information in auditor-submitted documents.

When auditors issue a standard audit report, they express the type of opinion that constitutes positive assurance on the related financial statements. In contrast, some of the reports discussed in this chapter express a form of *negative (limited) assurance*. An example of negative assurance is *"nothing* came to our attention to indicate that the financial statements are *not* fairly presented." To appreciate the implications of negative assurance, one must remember that the less work CPAs perform, the stronger negative assurance (that they know of nothing wrong with the financial statements) they can give. In other words, the more ignorant they are of the financial statements, the surer they are that they know of no reason why the statements are not fairly presented. Because many within the accounting profession believe that negative assurance reports might result in a decline in the quality of work performed by CPAs, their use was restricted for many years to reports that were not publicly distributed, such as letters for underwriters and certain special reports. However, owing to pressures to expand its responsibilities, the accounting profession has authorized the use of negative assurance in reports on reviews of general-purpose financial statements.

The concept of differential reporting for public and nonpublic companies is also introduced in this chapter. The *Accounting and Review Services Committee* of the American Institute of Certified Public Accountants (with standing equal to that of the Auditing Standards Board) is designated to issue pronouncements in connection with unaudited financial statements of nonpublic entities.[1] Its pronouncements take the form of *Statements on Standards for Accounting and Review Services (SSARS),* and it has established the concept of compilation and review that are discussed later in this chapter. A summary of certain services CPAs may provide, classified by type of company, is provided in Figure 21.1. Note that reviews are not appropriate for prospective financial statements.

FIGURE 21.1   Summary of CPA Financial Statement Services

Historical financial statements		Prospective financial statements
Public companies	Nonpublic companies	
Audits, including special reports[a]	Audits, including special reports[a]	Examinations[c]
Reviews of interim financial information[a]	Reviews of financial statements[b]	
————————————Independence Cutoff[d]————————————		
Preparation of unaudited financial statements[a]	Compilations[b]	Compilations[c]

[a]Standards are established by the Auditing Standards Board through Statements on Auditing Standards.

[b]Standards are established by the Accounting and Review Services Committee through Statements on Standards for Accounting and Review Services.

[c]Standards are established by the Auditing Standards Board through Statements on Standards for Attestation Engagements.

[d]Independence is required to perform the services above this line, but not for the services below the line.

The three general levels of assurance that a CPA may provide on financial information, together with examples of each, are shown in Figure 21.2. The descriptions of the levels of assurance may be subject to question. For example, even though a

---

[1] *SSARS No. 2* defines a nonpublic entity as any other than (a) one whose securities are publicly traded either internationally, nationally, regionally, or locally, (b) one that files with a regulatory agency in preparation for the sale of securities in a public market, or (c) a subsidiary, joint venture, or other entity controlled by an entity covered by (a) or (b). Although reviews of annual financial statements apply primarily to nonpublic entities, a public entity that does not have its annual financial statements audited may engage an accountant to review its annual or interim financial statements.

FIGURE 21.2   **Levels of Assurance that a CPA May Provide on Financial Information**

Levels of assurance	Example	Type of assurance
Maximum^a	Standard audit report	Positive
	Special reports on	Positive
	Financial statements that are prepared in conformity with a comprehensive basis of accounting other than generally accepted accounting principles	
	Specified elements, accounts, or items of a financial statement	
	Financial presentations that comply with contractual agreements or regulatory provisions	
	Examination of financial forecasts and projections	Positive
Limited	Review of financial statements of a nonpublic entity	Negative
	Review of interim financial information of a public entity	Negative
	Letter for underwriter covering unaudited financial statements and certain subsequent changes therein	Negative
	Special reports on compliance with aspects of contractual agreements or regulatory requirements related to audited financial statements	Negative
	Application of agreed-upon procedures	Findings
Minimum	Compiled financial statements of a nonpublic entity	None
	Compiled financial forecasts and projections	None
	Unaudited financial statements of a public entity	None

^aMaximum assurance is defined by the profession as reasonable, as opposed to absolute, assurance.

CPA provides no assurance in reports on unaudited or compiled financial statements, surely one would expect him or her to detect obvious errors and omissions, such as failure to record depreciation or income taxes. A more uncertain question is the level of limited assurance provided by a review. Is it slightly below an audit, slightly above unaudited, halfway between audited and unaudited, or at some other level? These questions are still to be addressed by the accounting profession.

REPORTS PROVIDING MAXIMUM LEVELS OF ASSURANCE

Because the standard audit report is discussed in the two preceding chapters, this section will be devoted to a discussion of other types of reports that provide a maximum level of assurance.

AU Section 623 defines *special reports* as those issued in connection with (1) financial statements that are prepared in conformity with a comprehensive basis of accounting other than generally accepted accounting principles, (2) specified elements, accounts, or items of a financial statement, (3) compliance with aspects of contractual agreements or regulatory requirements related to audited financial statements, (4) financial presentations to comply with contractual agreements or regulatory provisions, and (5) financial statements presented in prescribed form or schedules that require a prescribed form of auditor's report. Discussions of the first two types of special reports follow.

Reports on Financial Statements Prepared in Conformity with a Comprehensive Basis of Accounting Other Than Generally Accepted Accounting Principles

A comprehensive basis of accounting other than generally accepted accounting principles is defined in AU Section 623 (*SAS No. 62*) as one with at least one of the following characteristics:

1. A basis of accounting required to comply with the regulations of a government regulatory agency having jurisdiction over an entity (e.g., the statutes of many states require insurance companies operating within a state to file audited financial statements with the state insurance commission; these financial statements are used for regulatory purposes and are prepared on a basis that differs substantially from generally accepted accounting principles).
2. A basis of accounting used for income tax reporting purposes.
3. The cash receipts and disbursements basis of accounting (and certain modifications thereof such as recording depreciation).
4. A basis of accounting having "substantial support" (the term *substantial support* is not defined) that is applied to all material items, such as the price-level basis of accounting.

If the financial statements being reported on have one of these characteristics, an additional paragraph should be added to the audit report. The additional paragraph should state the basis of accounting employed, refer to a note to the financial statements, and state that the basis of accounting differs from generally accepted accounting principles (the monetary effect need not be stated). The opinion paragraph should state the auditor's opinion as to whether or not the financial statements are presented fairly in conformity with the basis of accounting described in the additional paragraph and footnote.[2]

The cash receipts and disbursements basis of accounting will be considered as an example. These statements are prepared on the basis of cash receipts and disbursements without adjustment for uncollected assets (e.g., accounts receivable) or unpaid liabilities (e.g., accounts payable). If the omitted assets or liabilities are material, financial statements prepared on a cash receipts and disbursements basis would not be in conformity with generally accepted accounting principles. In certain situations, however, cash-basis financial statements are necessary, such as when a company uses the cash basis for income tax purposes or when a partnership is required by its articles of partnership to compute and distribute income to its partners on a cash basis.

Cash basis financial statements should be referred to as statements of assets and liabilities arising from cash transactions (rather than balance sheets) and statements of revenue collected and expenses paid (rather than statements of income). Disclosure should be made of the basis on which the financial statements were prepared. A report on such statements might be worded as follows:

[2] If the financial statements are prepared to comply with regulations of a government regulatory agency, another paragraph may be added to the auditor's report restricting its use.

Independent Auditor's Report

We have audited the accompanying statement of assets, liabilities, and capital arising from cash transactions of A Company as of December 31, 19XX, and the related statements of revenues collected and expenses paid and cash changes in partners' capital accounts for the year then ended. These financial statements are the responsibility of the Company's management. Our responsibility is to express an opinion on these financial statements based on our audit.

We conducted our audit in accordance with generally accepted auditing standards. Those standards require that we plan and perform the audit to obtain reasonable assurance about whether the financial statements are free of material misstatement. An audit includes examining, on a test basis, evidence supporting the amounts and disclosures in the financial statements. An audit also includes assessing the accounting principles used and significant estimates made by management, as well as evaluating the overall financial statement presentation. We believe that our audit provides a reasonable basis for our opinion.

As described in Note 1, these financial statements were prepared on the basis of cash receipts and disbursements, which is a comprehensive basis of accounting other than generally accepted accounting principles.

In our opinion, the financial statements referred to above present fairly, in all material respects, the assets, liabilities, and capital arising from cash transactions of A Company as of December 31, 19XX, and its cash revenues collected and expenses paid and cash changes in the partners' capital accounts for the year then ended, on the basis of accounting described in Note 1.

Government agencies sometimes prescribe the form of auditor's report that is to be associated with financial information filed with those agencies. The form of these reports may be unacceptable to independent auditors because they require statements by the auditors that are inconsistent with the auditor's function and responsibility. In these cases, the auditor should reword the report or attach a standard auditor's report.

Reports on Specified Elements, Accounts, or Items of a Financial Statement

The need for an audit report on specific elements of a financial statement could arise from provisions of franchise, lease, and royalty agreements (where payments are based on sales, production, etc.), or provisions of agreements for business combinations (where the value of the acquired company may be based in part on its net current assets).

Auditors must approach such audits with care, because materiality must be considered within the context of the individual element or account being reported on and not the financial statements as a whole. If the engagement is not performed in connection with an audit of the financial statements, the auditors should also be aware that it may be necessary to audit several or even most of the accounts to express an opinion on only one. For example, a report on inventories might require the auditors to examine cash, cost of sales, accounts payable, and perhaps other accounts because of their potential effect on inventories. The auditors also must be certain that they are not placed in the position of interpreting rather than reporting compliance with legal agreements or contracts (e.g., a royalty agreement may not specify whether sales are to be adjusted for returns and allowances, bad debts, other income, etc.). An opinion of legal counsel should be requested for any ambiguous provisions.

A report relating to a specific account should identify the account that was audited in an opening paragraph, include a standard scope paragraph, and express an opinion as to whether the account is fairly presented.

Examination of Financial Forecasts and Projections

The examination of financial forecasts and financial projections is an attest function, and the general attestation standards described in Chapter 2 apply. Additional specific attestation standards for financial forecasts and projections are presented in AT Section 200. Whereas an audit is performed on *historical* financial statements, an examination of a financial forecast or projection is performed on *prospective* financial statements.

In an examination of prospective financial statements, the accountant is concerned with restricting attestation risk to a low level. Attestation risk is the risk that the accountant will unknowingly fail to modify his or her examination report on prospective financial statements that are materially misstated. Like audit risk, it consists of inherent risk (inherent susceptibility of the prospective financial statements to misstatement), control risk (risk that the client's controls over the preparation of prospective financial statements do not prevent or detect the misstatement), and detection risk (risk that the accountant will not detect the misstatement). A similar approach to assessing inherent and control risks and establishing detection risk is used in an examination of prospective financial statements as in an audit of historical financial statements.

Financial Forecasts

The AICPA has provided guidance to the CPA who is associated with the preparation and issuance of financial forecasts by describing the applicable examination procedures and reporting format.

A *financial forecast* is defined as a set of prospective financial statements that presents, to the best of the responsible party's[3] knowledge and belief, an entity's expected financial position, results of operations, and cash flows. A financial forecast reflects conditions as they are *expected* to exist.

A reasonably objective basis must exist for the preparation of a forecast; that is, the preparer must be able to develop sufficiently objective assumptions on which to base the forecast. Financial forecasts may be for "general" or "limited" use, that is, for use by the public or restricted to use by the responsible party and others with whom direct negotiations are held.

The CPA's purpose in examining a financial forecast is to determine whether

---

[3] The responsible party is the person responsible for the assumptions underlying the prospective financial statements, usually management, but could be someone such as a party considering acquiring the entity.

1. The underlying assumptions are reasonable as a basis for management's forecast.

2. The forecast is properly prepared based on the stated assumptions, and the presentation conforms with the recommendations in the AICPA *Guide for Prospective Financial Statements.*

The CPA is required to evaluate the client's procedures for preparing the forecast. The CPA should also identify and evaluate the important assumptions by analyzing prior periods' financial results and forecasts of similar businesses, reviewing contracts, agreements, and minutes, and using business knowledge to identify market trends, competitive conditions, pending laws and regulations, macroeconomic and political conditions, technological influences, and dependence on major customers and suppliers. The CPA must then determine that the computations made to translate the assumptions into the forecasted amounts are mathematically accurate, the accounting principles used in the forecast are consistent with generally accepted accounting principles, the assumptions are identified in the forecast and are internally consistent, and the presentation follows the guidelines in *Guide for Prospective Financial Statements.*

The CPA's standard report on a financial forecast describes the forecasted statements, describes the CPA's examination, and expresses positive assurances as to the presentation of the forecast in conformity with AICPA guidelines and the reasonableness of the underlying assumptions. The following is an illustration of the form of such a report:

> We have examined the accompanying forecasted balance sheet, statements of income, retained earnings, and cash flows of XYZ Company as of December 31, 19X8, and for the year then ending. Our examination was made in accordance with standards for an examination of a forecast established by the American Institute of Certified Public Accountants and, accordingly, included such procedures as we considered necessary to evaluate both the assumptions used by management and the preparation and presentation of the forecast.
>
> In our opinion, the accompanying forecast is presented in conformity with guidelines for presentation of a forecast established by the American Institute of Certified Public Accountants, and the underlying assumptions provide a reasonable basis for management's forecast. However, there will usually be differences between the forecasted and actual results, because events and circumstances frequently do not occur as expected, and those differences may be material. We have no responsibility to update this report for events and circumstances occurring after the date of this report.

CPAs should issue an "except for" qualification or an adverse opinion if they believe the forecast departs from AICPA presentation guidelines. An adverse opinion should be issued if one or more significant assumptions are not disclosed or are not reasonable. A significant scope limitation should result in a disclaimer of opinion. The report may also be modified for reference to other accountants, inclusion of comparative historical information, emphasis of a matter, or description of a larger engagement. When CPAs are not independent they may compile, but not examine, a financial forecast. A flowchart for reporting on an examination of a financial forecast is shown in Figure 21.3.

Financial Projections

Projections differ from forecasts in that they present expected results *given one or more hypothetical assumptions.* This allows the reader to evaluate the effect on the statements of the occurrence of the assumptions. For example, projected financial statements may be prepared to show the effect of the construction of a new manufacturing plant. The projections may be based on assumptions about one or more production or interest rates. A reader could then evaluate the effect of the rates or his or her decision to grant a loan to construct the plant.

The guidelines for preparation, presentation, and examination of financial forecasts are generally applicable to financial projections, except that the CPA need not obtain evidence to support the hypothetical assumptions. A form of report for the examination of a financial projection is as follows:

We have examined the accompanying projected balance sheet and statements of income, retained earnings, and cash flows of X Company as of December 31, 19X8, and for the year then ending. Our examination was made in accordance with standards for an examination of a projection established by the American Institute of Certified Public Accountants and, accordingly, included such procedures as we considered necessary to evaluate both the assumptions used by management and the preparation and presentation of the projection.

The accompanying projection and this report were prepared for the D Bank for the purpose of negotiating a loan to expand X Company's plant and should not be used for any other purpose.

In our opinion, the accompanying projection is presented in conformity with guidelines for presentation of a projection established by the American Institute of Certified Public Accountants, and the underlying assumptions provide a reasonable basis for management's projection assuming the granting of the requested loan for the purpose of expanding X Company's plant as described in the summary of significant assumptions. However, even if the loan is granted and the plant is expanded, there will usually be differences between the projected and actual results, because events and circumstances frequently do not occur as expected, and those differences may be material. We have no responsibility to update this report for events and circumstances occurring after the date of this report.

Financial projections should be for "limited" use only, that is, for use only by the responsible party and others with whom negotiations are being held (D Bank in the foregoing example). This restriction is imposed because the general public cannot discuss or inquire about the hypothetical assumptions as can parties directly involved in the negotiations.

The report modifications previously discussed for a financial forecast also apply to a financial projection.

FIGURE 21.3   Flowchart for Reporting on the Examination of Prospective Financial Statements

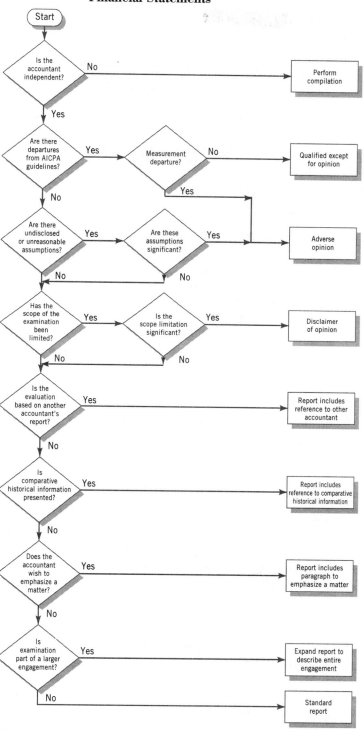

Note: An example of a measurement departure is the failure to capitalize a capital lease.

REPORTS PROVIDING LIMITED LEVELS OF ASSURANCE

Limited levels of assurance may be provided when a CPA performs a review of financial statements, prepares a letter for underwriters, evaluates compliance with aspects of contractual agreements or regulatory requirements related to audited financial statements, or applies agreed-upon procedures. The term *review* has a technical meaning to CPAs, and the minimum review procedures to be performed are described in the applicable professional standards.

Review of Financial Statements of a Nonpublic Company

AR Section 100 (*SSARS No. 1*) defines a review as

> performing inquiry and analytical procedures that provide the accountant with a reasonable basis for expressing limited assurance that there are no material modifications that should be made to the statements in order for them to be in conformity with generally accepted accounting principles or, if applicable, with another comprehensive basis of accounting.

To perform a review, a CPA must understand (1) the accounting principles and practices of the industry in which the client operates, and (2) the client's organization, operating characteristics, and the nature of its assets, liabilities, revenues, and expenses.

The CPA should make *inquiries* of management regarding the accounting principles and practices in use, the procedures used for recording transactions, and the procedures for accumulating financial statement information. Additional inquiries should cover actions taken at meetings of stockholders and boards of directors, changes in accounting principles, and subsequent events.

Examples of Inquiries That May Be Made Regarding Inventories During a Review of the Financial Statements of a Nonpublic Company

1. Have physical inventories been counted? If not, how have inventories been determined?
2. Have general ledger control accounts been adjusted to agree with physical inventories?
3. If physical inventories were taken at a date other than the balance sheet date, what procedures were used to record changes in inventories between the date of the physical inventory and the balance sheet date?
4. Were consignments in or out considered in taking physical inventories?
5. What is the basis of inventory valuation?
6. Does inventory cost include material, labor, and overhead where applicable?
7. Have writedowns for obsolescence or cost in excess of net realizable value been made?
8. Have proper cutoffs of purchases, goods in transit, and returned goods been made?
9. Are there any inventory encumbrances?

Source: Appendix A to AR Section 100 (*SSARS No. 1*).

The *analytical procedures* are similar to those performed in an audit and include comparisons of current financial results with prior years' and budgeted results and evaluation of the relationships of the elements of the financial statements that would be expected to conform to a predictable pattern.

There is no requirement for the CPA to assess control risk or to gather any evidence to corroborate the inquiries and analytical procedures unless he or she becomes aware that the information may be incorrect, incomplete, or otherwise unsatisfactory; however, the CPA should obtain a client representation letter that is similar but less extensive than a client representation obtained in an audit. Each page of the financial statements should include a reference such as "See Accountant's Review Report."

A report on a review consists of three paragraphs (assuming no exceptions) that describe the scope of the review, disclaim an opinion on the financial statements, and provide limited (negative) assurance as to conformity with generally accepted accounting principles. An illustration follows:

We have reviewed the accompanying balance sheet of Guy Company as of December 31, 19X3, and the related statements of income, retained earnings, and cash flows for the year then ended, in accordance with Statements on Standards for Accounting and Review Services issued by the American Institute of Certified Public Accountants. All information included in these financial statements is the representation of the management of Guy Company.

A review consists principally of inquiries of company personnel and analytical procedures applied to financial data. It is substantially less in scope than an audit in accordance with generally accepted auditing standards, the objective of which is the expression of an opinion regarding the financial statements taken as a whole. Accordingly, we do not express such an opinion.

Based on our review, we are not aware of any material modifications that should be made to the accompanying financial statements in order for them to be in conformity with generally accepted accounting principles.

The CPA should modify the limited assurance paragraph ("Except as noted in the following paragraph . . .") and describe in a separate paragraph of the report any departures from generally accepted accounting principles, including omission of any required disclosures, which come to his or her attention as a result of performing the review. The reporting of an uncertainty about an entity's ability to continue as a going concern and inconsistencies in the application of generally accepted accounting principles is optional. CPAs may not issue a review report on financial statements of an entity of which they are not independent or for which all necessary procedures have not been performed. A flowchart of *SSARS No. 1* is presented in the appendix to this chapter.

If a CPA is engaged to perform an audit of a nonpublic entity and the client subsequently requests that the engagement be changed to a review (or a compilation), the CPA should consider the reason for the request and the additional effort and cost to complete the audit. If the audit is substantially complete and the reason for the request is to prohibit the CPA from performing audit procedures such as corresponding with legal counsel or obtaining a management representation letter, the CPA should not consent to a change in the engagement.

Review of Interim Financial Information of a Public Company

CPAs may also perform reviews of interim (but not annual) financial information of public companies. The SEC requires disclosure of unaudited quarterly data in a note to the annual financial statements and a review of these data by an independent public accountant. The SEC encourages, but does not require, companies to have their unaudited interim statements reviewed quarterly by their auditor rather than at the end of the year.

AU Section 722 (*SAS No. 71*) applies to reviews of interim financial information (1) that is presented alone by a public entity and purports to conform with the provisions of *APB Opinion No. 28* (Interim Financial Reporting) and (2) that accompanies or is included in a note to audited financial statements of a public or nonpublic entity.[4] The statement implies that the CPA will normally have audited the company's financial statements for one or more annual periods and that such audits will provide a basis for the review procedures. To perform a review of interim financial information, the accountant should have a sufficient understanding of internal control to (1) identify types of potential misstatements and consider the likelihood of their occurrence and (2) select the appropriate inquiries and analytical procedures. This understanding may be acquired while performing a recent audit; otherwise, the accountant should perform procedures to obtain this understanding.

The procedures consist primarily of inquiries and analytical procedures. Examples include

1. Inquiries concerning (a) internal control, (b) significant changes in internal control, and (c) subsequent events.
2. Analytical procedures consisting of comparison of the financial information with prior interim periods, industry data, nonfinancial information, and anticipated results, and evaluation of the relationships of the elements of the financial information that would be expected to conform to a predictable pattern.
3. Reading of minutes and the interim financial information.
4. Obtaining written representations from management.

All pages of the financial information should be clearly marked as "unaudited." If, while performing the review, the accountants become aware of reportable conditions (see Chapter 10), fraud, illegal acts, or material misstatements in the interim financial information that management refuses to correct, the audit committee should be notified.

For interim financial information presented alone, the form of report consists of three paragraphs (assuming no departures from generally accepted accounting principles are noted in the review; no reporting is required of going-concern uncertainties or lack of consistency in the application of accounting principles) describing the scope of the review, disclaiming an opinion on the financial statements taken as a whole, and expressing negative assurance that the CPA is not aware of

---

[4] The SEC requires footnote disclosure in audited financial statements of certain larger companies of selected interim financial information. This section would have limited applicability to nonpublic entities, for few would have reason to make such disclosures.

any departures from generally accepted accounting principles. An example of such a report follows:

Independent Accountant's Report

We have reviewed the accompanying interim financial information of Granger Company as of March 31, 19X4, and for the three-month period then ended. This financial information is the responsibility of the company's management.

We conducted our review in accordance with standards established by the American Institute of Certified Public Accountants. A review of interim financial information consists principally of applying analytical procedures to financial data and making inquiries of persons responsible for financial and accounting matters. It is substantially less in scope than an audit conducted in accordance with generally accepted auditing standards, the objective of which is the expression of an opinion regarding the financial statements taken as a whole. Accordingly, we do not express such an opinion.

Based on our review, we are not aware of any material modifications that should be made to the accompanying financial information for it to be in conformity with generally accepted accounting principles.

Departures from generally accepted accounting principles, including inadequate disclosure (but note that disclosure requirements under *APB Opinion No. 28* are considerably less extensive than those necessary for annual general-purpose financial statements), should be described in an additional paragraph.

When the interim financial information accompanies or is included in a note to audited financial statements, the review procedures set forth above may be performed. If the results of the review are satisfactory and if the information is designated as unaudited, CPAs ordinarily need not modify their report on the audited financial statements to make reference to their review or the interim financial information.

Letter for Underwriter Covering Unaudited Financial Statements and Certain Subsequent Changes Therein

Before considering the form of letters for underwriters (also commonly referred to as *comfort letters*), we must understand their purpose. They are *not* required by any of the federal securities acts, and copies are *not* filed with the SEC. They usually are requested by underwriters (normally, investment bankers assisting a company in the sale of securities) as one means of meeting their responsibilities under the Securities Act of 1933, which was discussed in Chapter 4. In general, this act provides that certain persons (including underwriters) may limit or avoid liability under the act if, *after reasonable investigation,* they had *reasonable grounds to believe* and did believe that the registration statement (a document filed with the SEC containing a detailed description of a company and its operations, including audited financial statements) was true and no material facts were omitted. A comfort letter is considered one element of a reasonable investigation by the underwriters.

A comfort letter may cover all or some of the following topics:

1. Independence of the auditor.
2. Compliance of the audited financial statements included in the registration statement with SEC accounting requirements.
3. Negative assurance regarding unaudited financial statements and interim financial information included in the registration statement.
4. Negative assurance regarding changes in certain financial statement items subsequent to the date of the latest financial statements included in the registration statement.
5. Negative assurance regarding financial data included in the text section (as opposed to the financial statement section) of the registration statement.

The topic of independence is not controversial. The auditor must be able to state that he or she is independent to have audited the necessary financial statements for inclusion in the registration statement. The representation concerning independence is a statement of fact rather than of opinion.

In contrast, the representation regarding compliance with SEC accounting requirements is the auditor's opinion and is presented as such. The SEC accounting requirements include those within the 1933 act, Regulation S-X, and the *Financial Reporting Releases.*

If the audited financial statements included in the registration statement are not current, unaudited financial statements as of a current date must be included. It is on these unaudited financial statements that the auditor may give negative assurance. Auditors must include in the letter the specific steps performed as a basis for their findings.

The fourth topic included in comfort letters is negative assurance about changes in certain financial statement items subsequent to the date of the latest financial statements included in the registration statement. The purpose of this section is to alert the underwriter at the latest practicable time to changes in important financial statement items (such as declines in sales, net income, and net assets) that the underwriters may consider adverse. Thus, the underwriters have an opportunity to cancel the offering or at least delay it until all material adverse conditions are properly disclosed in the registration statement. The auditor searches for changes in important financial statement items by reviewing minutes and any financial statements prepared after those included in the registration statement, and by inquiring of certain company officials as to significant transactions during the period subsequent to the date of the latest financial statements. If changes have occurred, they must be disclosed in the letter.

The final comfort letter topic is negative assurance about financial data included in the text section of the registration statement. AU Section 634 recommends that auditors limit their procedures and comments to information that is expressed in dollars and has been obtained from accounting records subject to internal control or has been computed from such records.

Comfort letters are never distributed beyond the client and the underwriter, and the general public is unaware that they exist.

Reports on Compliance with Contractual Agreements or Regulatory Requirements Related to Audited Financial Statements

An auditor sometimes encounters provisions in a client's loan agreement that requests assurance from the auditor that, as a result of the audit, he or she acquired no knowledge of defaults under the loan agreement pertaining to accounting matters. The auditor's report takes the form of negative assurance and is worded as follows:

Independent Auditor's Report

We have audited, in accordance with generally accepted auditing standards, the balance sheet of Irwin International as of December 31, 19X2, and the related statements of income, retained earnings, and cash flows for the year then ended, and have issued our report thereon dated February 5, 19X3.

In connection with our audit, nothing came to our attention that caused us to believe that the company failed to comply with the terms, covenants, provisions, or conditions of sections 2.03 to 2.10, inclusive, of the indenture dated July 16, 19X0, with McIlroy National Bank insofar as they relate to accounting matters. However, our audit was not directed primarily toward obtaining knowledge of such noncompliance.

This report is intended solely for the information and use of the boards of directors and managements of Irwin International and McIlroy National Bank and should not be used for any other purpose.

This example of negative assurance supplements an audit of the financial statements made in accordance with generally accepted auditing standards and may be given only in conjunction with an audit.

Application of Agreed-upon Procedures

Clients sometimes ask CPAs to apply one or more audit procedures to an account (or group of accounts) without performing all procedures necessary to audit that account. *SAS No. 75* permits an accountant to perform such an engagement in which the scope is limited to applying agreed-upon procedures that are not sufficient for expressing an opinion on one or more specified elements, accounts, or items of a financial statement, provided (1) the users take responsibility for the procedures to be performed and (2) distribution of the report is restricted to the parties involved. The CPA should report the procedures performed and his or her findings. An example of such a report follows:

Independent Accountant's Report on Applying Agreed-upon Procedures

To the Trustee of Gentry Ironworks:

We have performed the procedures described below, which were agreed to by the Trustee of Gentry Ironworks, with respect to the claims of creditors to determine the validity of claims of Gentry Ironworks as of May 31, 19X9, as set forth in accompanying Schedule A. This engagement to apply agreed-upon procedures was performed in accordance with standards established by the American Institute of Certified Public Accountants. The sufficiency of these procedures is solely the responsibility of the Trustee of

Gentry Ironworks. Consequently, we make no representation regarding the sufficiency of the procedures described below either for the purpose for which this report has been requested or for any other purpose. The procedures and associated findings are as follows:

a. Compare the total of the trial balance of accounts payable at May 31, 19X9, prepared by the company, to the balance in the related general ledger account.

The total of the accounts payable trial balance agreed with the balance in the related general ledger account.

b. Compare the amounts for claims received from creditors to the respective amounts on the trial balance of accounts payable.

All differences noted are presented in column 3 of Schedule A and were satisfactorily reconciled.

c. Examine documentation submitted by creditors in support of their claims and compare it to documentation in the company's files, including invoices, receiving reports, and other evidence of receipt of goods or services.

No exceptions were found as a result of these comparisons.

We were not engaged to and did not perform an audit, the objective of which would be the expression of an opinion on the specified elements, accounts, or items. Accordingly, we do not express such an opinion. Had we performed additional procedures, other matters might have come to our attention that would have been reported to you.

Agreed-upon procedures may be applied to both historical and prospective financial statements.

REPORTS PROVIDING A MINIMUM LEVEL OF ASSURANCE

Many small nonpublic companies are unable to employ a high level of accounting talent and need outside assistance in preparing both historical and prospective financial statements. CPAs provide a useful service by rendering such assistance. They may also be associated[5] with unaudited financial statements of public companies. This section covers the CPA's responsibilities in these instances.

Compiled Financial Statements of a Nonpublic Company

AR Section 100 (*SSARS No. 1*) defines a compilation as

presenting in the form of financial statements information that is the representation of management (owners) without undertaking to express any assurance on the statements.

---

[5] CPAs are associated with financial statements that they prepare or assist in preparing or when they consent to the use of their name in a report or document (excluding tax returns) containing the financial statements.

To compile financial statements, CPAs should understand the industry and nature of the business in which the client is engaged, including the form of its accounting records, the qualifications of its accounting personnel, the accounting basis on which the financial statements are to be presented, and the form and content of the financial statements. However, CPAs are not required to make inquiries or to perform any procedures to validate the information provided to them unless it appears to be incomplete or incorrect. Each page of the financial statements should contain a reference such as "See Accountant's Compilation Report."

Standard Compilation Report

A report on a compilation of financial statements containing all disclosures required by generally accepted accounting principles follows:

> I have compiled the accompanying balance sheet of Clay Company as of December 31, 19X4, and the related statements of income, retained earnings, and cash flows for the year then ended, in accordance with Statements on Standards for Accounting and Review Services issued by the American Institute of Certified Public Accountants.
>
> A compilation is limited to presenting in the form of financial statements information that is the representation of management. I have not audited or reviewed the accompanying financial statements and, accordingly, do not express an opinion or any other form of assurance on them.

Compilation Report on Financial Statements That Omit Substantially All Disclosures Required by Generally Accepted Accounting Principles

CPAs may also compile financial statements that omit substantially all disclosures required by generally accepted accounting principles if this fact is clearly stated in the report and is not, to their knowledge, done to mislead the users of the statements. In such a case, a third paragraph in the following form would be added to the report.

> Management has elected to omit substantially all of the disclosures required by generally accepted accounting principles. If the omitted disclosures were included in the financial statements, they might influence the user's conclusions about the company's financial position, results of operations, and cash flows. Accordingly, these financial statements are not designed for those who are not informed about such matters.

Compilation Report on Financial Statements Presented on a Prescribed Form

A third paragraph also should be added if the financial statements are compiled on the prescribed form of a bank, trade association, government agency, and so forth, and the form contains departures from generally accepted accounting principles, including inadequate disclosure. As the form is presumed to meet the needs of the entity requesting it, a paragraph in the following form is added:

> These financial statements (including related disclosures) are presented in accordance with the requirements of (name of body), which differ from generally accepted accounting principles. Accordingly, these financial statements are not designed for those who are not informed about such differences.

Other Departures from the Standard Compilation Report

If CPAs become aware of a departure from generally accepted accounting principles other than under the aforementioned circumstances, they should include a separate paragraph that discusses the departure. As in the case of a review, disclosure in the report of inconsistencies in the application of accounting principles is optional if adequately disclosed in the financial statements. CPAs may issue a compilation on financial statements even though they are not independent, provided the lack of independence is disclosed in the last paragraph of the report (but not the reason therefor). A flowchart of *SSARS No. 1* is presented in the appendix to this chapter.

If a CPA prepares personal financial statements that are included only in a written personal financial plan, the CPA is not required to perform a compilation.

Compilation of Financial Forecasts and Projections

CPAs may compile financial forecasts and projections and should look to *Statements on Standards for Attestation Engagements* (AT Section 200) for guidance. A compilation consists of (1) assembling the forecast or projection based on the client's assumptions, (2) considering whether the underlying assumptions appear to be not obviously inappropriate, and (3) reading the forecast or projection for presentation in conformity with AICPA guidelines. A form of report for the compilation of a financial forecast is as follows:

> We have compiled the accompanying forecasted balance sheet and statements of income, retained earnings, and cash flows of XYZ Company as of December 31, 19XX, and for the year then ending, in accordance with standards established by the American Institute of Certified Public Accountants.
>
> A compilation is limited to presenting in the form of a forecast information that is the representation of management and does not include evaluation of the support for the assumptions underlying the forecast. We have not examined the forecast and, accordingly, do not express an opinion or any other form of assurance on the accompanying statements or assumptions. Furthermore, there will usually be differences between the forecasted and actual results, because events and circumstances frequently do not occur as expected, and those differences may be material. We have no responsibility to update this report for events and circumstances occurring after the date of this report.

A report on the compilation of a financial projection would contain two paragraphs similar to those shown above plus an additional paragraph limiting the use of the report to its intended purpose.

Similar modifications may be made to reports based on compiled financial forecasts and projections as are made to reports based on compiled historical financial statements (e.g., an additional paragraph may be added to describe lack of indepen-dence).

Unaudited Financial Statements of a Public Company

When CPAs are associated with financial statements of a public company that have not been audited or reviewed, they must disclaim an opinion on the statements. Note that because of the requirements for audits of the annual financial statements by the federal securities acts (see Chapter 4), this is a relatively rare occurrence. An example of the form of such a report follows.[6]

> The accompanying balance sheet of Wilson Company as of December 31, 19X4, and the related statements of income, retained earnings, and cash flows for the year then ended were not audited by us and, accordingly, we do not express an opinion on them.

In addition to attaching a disclaimer to the financial statements, the CPA should make sure that each page of the financial statements is marked clearly as unaudited.

CPAs have no responsibility to apply any procedures beyond reading the finan-cial statements for obvious material misstatements. In some cases, for their own satisfaction, CPAs may wish to perform certain steps in connection with the prepara-tion of unaudited financial statements that might be considered auditing proce-dures. For example, they may wish to review bank reconciliations, tax returns, and other documents supporting amounts shown in the financial statements. However, they should make no reference to these steps in the report. To describe any proce-dures performed might cause the reader to believe that an audit was performed.

CPAs may detect errors in the data used to prepare financial statements, even though they do not perform an audit. For example, they may note that incorrect prices were used to compute inventory or that certain necessary accrued liabilities for such items as payroll or income taxes have been omitted. In this situation, they should suggest that the accounting records and financial statements be corrected. If the client refuses to make the necessary corrections, the CPAs must either state their reservations regarding the financial statements in their disclaimer or withdraw from the engagement. An example of the wording that might be added to a dis-claimer follows:

> The accompanying financial statements do not include $250,000 of income tax expense and liability in the statement of income and balance sheet, respectively, as required by generally accepted accounting principles.

It would not be appropriate to issue a qualified or adverse opinion, because no audit has been performed and without an audit, no opinion—unqualified, quali-fied, or adverse—can be expressed.

---

[6] Note that the wording of this type of disclaimer is different from that used in the case of a scope limitation on an audit in Chapter 20.

REPORTS ON ACCOMPANYING INFORMATION IN AUDITOR-SUBMITTED DOCUMENTS

Reports on *accompanying information* in auditor-submitted documents may provide either limited or minimum assurance. Accompanying information (as opposed to "other information" and "supplemental information" discussed in Chapter 20) is any information submitted by the CPA to his or her client in a document containing the basic financial statements and the auditor's report thereon. It is presented outside of the basic financial statements and is not considered necessary for their presentation in accordance with generally accepted accounting principles. Accompanying information includes details or explanations of amounts shown in the basic financial statements, consolidating information, historical summaries of the basic financial statements, statistical data derived from the basic financial statements, as well as nonaccounting information. For example, such a report might contain a section for accounts receivable, including analyses of receivables by type, age, and major customers compared by amount and percentage with those of the prior year, and analyses of the allowance for doubtful accounts for the year including ratios of total amount written off to total revenues, total amount over 90 days old to the balance in the allowance account, and so forth. Similar comments and analyses could be included for all significant balance sheet and income statement accounts. A description of significant audit procedures performed may also be included as a separate section of the report.

In commenting on individual accounts, auditors must be careful that the wording does not convey more assurance than they are prepared to give. It is also important to remember that, although auditors may assist in preparing the accompanying information, it consists basically of representations of management.

The report normally begins with the standard audit report to establish the auditor's responsibility for the basic financial statements. To comply with the fourth standard of reporting, the report should include another paragraph indicating the degree of responsibility taken for the accompanying information. This paragraph might be worded as follows:

Our audit was conducted for the purpose of forming an opinion on the basic financial statements taken as a whole. The accompanying information is presented for purposes of additional analysis and is not a required part of the basic financial statements. Such information has been subjected to the auditing procedures applied in the audit of the basic financial statements and, in our opinion, is fairly stated in all material respects in relation to the basic financial statements taken as a whole.[7]

Reports on accompanying information are not as common today as they were several years ago. At one time, the annual auditor's report, including accompanying information, was the only reliable financial information available to many managers and stockholders, because internal financial statements were not prepared. Today,

[7] The last sentence could be "Such information has not been subjected to the auditing procedures applied in the audit of the basic financial statements, and, accordingly, we express no opinion on it."

however, few companies attempt to operate without periodic, timely, and reliable financial information.

PRO FORMA FINANCIAL INFORMATION

Occasionally because material transactions such as business combinations, changes in capitalization, and disposition of a significant portion of a business occur near or after an entity's year-end, management will present pro forma financial statements to show the effects of such transactions on historical financial statements had the transactions occurred at an earlier date. This is accomplished by applying pro forma adjustments (based on management's assumptions as to the effect of the transactions) to the historical financial statements.

A CPA is guided by *Statements on Standards for Attestation Engagements* (AT Section 300) and may perform either an examination or a review of pro forma financial information. However, the document containing the pro forma information should include the latest historical financial statements, and those statements should have been audited or reviewed by the CPA. The goals of the CPA are to obtain assurance (positive for an examination and negative for a review) about whether

1. Management's assumptions provide a reasonable basis for attributing the effects on the financial statements to the material transaction.
2. The pro forma adjustments give appropriate effect to the assumptions.
3. The pro forma financial information reflects the proper application of these adjustments to the historical financial statements.

Restrictions on the scope of the engagement, significant uncertainties about the assumptions, and other reservations may require the CPA to issue a qualified, adverse, or disclaimer of opinion or withdraw from the engagement.

APPENDIX: FLOWCHART OF STATEMENT ON STANDARDS FOR ACCOUNTING AND REVIEW SERVICES NO. 1, COMPILATION AND REVIEW OF FINANCIAL STATEMENTS

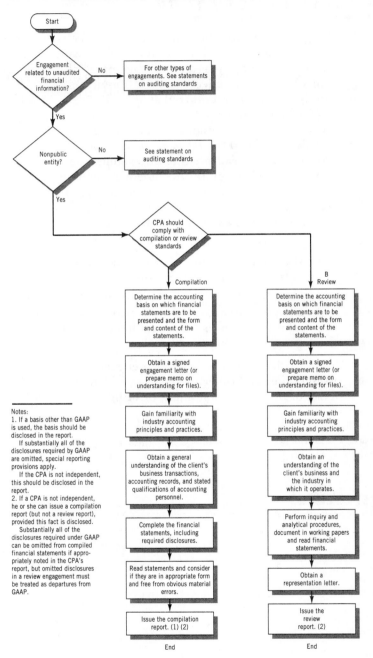

Notes:
1. If a basis other than GAAP is used, the basis should be disclosed in the report.

If substantially all of the disclosures required by GAAP are omitted, special reporting provisions apply.

If the CPA is not independent, this should be disclosed in the report.

2. If a CPA is not independent, he or she can issue a compilation report (but not a review report), provided this fact is disclosed.

Substantially all of the disclosures required under GAAP can be omitted from compiled financial statements if appropriately noted in the CPA's report, but omitted disclosures in a review engagement must be treated as departures from GAAP.

Source: T. R. Weirich and G. M. Pintar, "Interpretation and Flowchart of SSARS No. 1," *Journal of Accountancy* (November 1979), p. 61.

Chapter 21 ► GLOSSARY OF TERMS

Accompanying information Information in addition to the basic financial statements submitted by a CPA to a client in a document prepared by the CPA.

Accounting and Review Services Committee A senior technical committee of the AICPA with authority to issue pronouncements (*Statements on Standards for Accounting and Review Services*) dealing with unaudited financial statements of nonpublic companies.

Agreed-upon procedures Limited (less than required by generally accepted auditing standards) audit procedures that are agreed on between the client and the auditor to be applied to an account or group of accounts.

Attestation risk on prospective financial statements The risk that the accountant will unknowingly fail to modify his or her examination report on prospective financial statements that are materially misstated.

Comfort letters Letters requested from auditors by underwriters as one means of meeting their responsibility to exercise due diligence to ensure that information included in a registration statement filed under the Securities Act of 1933 is not misleading.

Compilation of historical financial statements Presentation in the form of financial statements of information that is management's (owner's) representation without expressing any assurance on the statements.

Compilation of prospective financial statements Assembling prospective financial statements based on client assumptions; considering whether the assumptions are obviously inappropriate; and comparing the statements with AICPA guidelines.

Examination of prospective financial statements Evaluation of the (1) preparation of the statements, (2) support underlying the assumptions, and (3) presentation of the statements for conformity with AICPA guidelines.

Financial forecast Prospective financial statements that present, to the best of the responsible party's knowledge and belief, an entity's expected financial position, results of operations, and cash flows.

Financial projection Prospective financial statements that present, to the best of the responsible party's knowledge and belief, given one or more hypothetical assumptions, an entity's expected financial position, results of operations, and cash flows.

Negative (limited) assurance A type of assurance provided by a CPA that he or she is not aware of material misstatements (but not that the information is fairly presented).

Pro forma financial information Historical financial statements that have been adjusted to reflect the effects of significant transactions as if the transactions had occurred at an earlier date.

Review (interim financial information of a public company) Application of knowledge of financial reporting practices to significant accounting matters of which the accountant becomes aware through inquiries and analytical procedures, to form a basis for reporting whether material modifications should be made for such information to conform with generally accepted accounting principles.

Review (nonpublic company) Performance of inquiry and analytical procedures that provide the accountant with a reasonable basis for expressing negative (limited) assurance that there are no material modifications that should be made to accompanying financial statements for them to conform with generally accepted accounting principles or, if applicable, with another comprehensive basis of accounting.

Special reports Audit reports on financial statements (and portions thereof) that do not purport to present financial position, results of operations, or cash flows in conformity with generally accepted accounting principles.

Chapter 21 ► REFERENCES

American Institute of Certified Public Accountants, *Professional Standards*

AR Section 100—*Compilation and Review of Financial Statements*

AR Section 200—*Reporting on Comparative Financial Statements*

AR Section 300—*Compilation Reports on Financial Statements Included in Certain Prescribed Forms*

AR Section 600—*Reporting on Personal Financial Statements Included in Written Personal Financial Plans*

AU Section 504—*Association with Financial Statements*

AU Section 551—*Reporting on Information Accompanying the Basic Financial Statements in Auditor-Submitted Documents*

AU Section 622—*Engagements to Apply Agreed-Upon Procedures to Specified Elements Accounts, or Items of a Financial Statement*

AU Section 623—*Special Reports*

AU Section 634—*Letters for Underwriters and Certain Other Requesting Parties*

AU Section 722—*Interim Financial Information*

AT Section 200—*Financial Forecasts and Projections*

AT Section 300—*Reporting on Pro Forma Financial Information*

Jones, Wm. Jarell, and Ward, Catherine C. "Forecasts and Projections for Third Party Use," *Journal of Accountancy* (April 1986), pp. 100–102.

Pallais, Don, and Guy, Dan M. "Prospective Financial Statements," *Journal of Accountancy* (April 1986), pp. 90–99.

Reed, Ronald, Murray, Dennis, and Murray, Lucy. "Compilations and Reviews Gaining Acceptance," *The CPA Journal* (February 1989), pp. 10–15.

Rosenberg, Rita F. J. "SSARS in Action," *The CPA Journal* (February 1985), pp. 10–18.

Serlin, Jerry, and Blanco-Best, Mimi. "What's So Special About Special Reports?" *Journal of Accountancy* (October 1989), pp. 60–74.

Stilwell, Martin C. "Prospective Reporting and Small Business Clients," *Journal of Accountancy* (May 1986), pp. 68–84.

Sullivan, John B., and Mancino, Jane M. "Comfort Letters: How Does SAS 72 Affect Them?" *Journal of Accountancy* (December 1993), pp. 61–64.

Chapter 21 ▶ REVIEW QUESTIONS

21-1 What is negative assurance within the context of an auditor's report? How does it differ from positive assurance?

21-2 What body establishes standards for
a. All audits and for reviews of interim financial information and preparation of unaudited financial statements of public companies?
b. Reviews and compilations of financial statements of nonpublic companies?
c. Prospective financial statements?

21-3 Define a special report according to AU Section 623.

21-4 What is the general reporting format on financial statements prepared in accordance with a comprehensive basis of accounting other than generally accepted accounting principles?

21-5 Define a financial forecast.

21-6 How does a financial projection differ from a financial forecast?

21-7 What is the CPA's purpose in examining a financial forecast or projection?

21-8 Describe the reporting format for reports on examinations of financial forecasts and projections. What type of assurance is given?

21-9 When reporting on an examination of prospective financial statements, what is the CPA's responsibility should he or she determine that
a. The forecast departs from AICPA guidelines?
b. One or more significant assumptions are not reasonable?
c. There is a significant scope limitation?
d. Other accountants performed part of the examination?
e. Historical financial information is included?
f. He or she wants to emphasize a matter?
g. He or she is not independent?

21-10 Define a review of the financial statements of a nonpublic entity.

21-11 Describe the reporting format for a review of the financial statements of a nonpublic entity. What type of assurance is expressed?

21-12 When performing a review of the financial statements of a nonpublic entity, what is the CPA's reporting obligation if he or she determines that the statements are materially affected by (a) a departure from generally accepted accounting principles and (b) an inconsistency in the application of generally accepted accounting principles?

21-13 What procedures would a CPA perform in a review of interim financial information of a public company?

21-14 Describe the reporting format for a report on a review of interim financial information of a public company. What type of assurance is given?

21-15 List the five topics that may be covered in a letter for underwriters.

21-16 What are agreed-upon procedures?

21-17 When is a CPA associated with financial statements?

21-18 Define a compilation of financial statements.

21-19 Describe the reporting format for a report on a compilation. What type of assurance is given?

21-20 Under what conditions may a CPA compile financial statements that omit substantially all disclosures required by generally accepted accounting principles? How would this affect the form of his or her report?

21-21 How do the following matters affect a CPA's reporting responsibilities in performing a compilation?
a. A departure from generally accepted accounting principles.
b. Inconsistent application of accounting principles.
c. Lack of independence.

21-22 Describe the compilation of a financial forecast or projection and the form of report that may be issued.

21-23 What is a CPA's reporting responsibility when associated with unaudited financial statements of a public company?

21-24 Define *accompanying information* in an auditing context and give an example. What is a CPA's responsibility for this information?

21-25 What levels of service may a CPA provide on pro forma financial information?

Chapter 21 ▶ OBJECTIVE QUESTIONS

(* = author prepared; ** = CPA examination)

**21-26 Statements on Standards for Accounting and Review Services (SSARS) require an accountant to report when the accountant has
   a. Typed client-prepared financial statements, without modification, as an accommodation to the client.
   b. Provided a client with a financial statement format that does *not* include dollar amounts, to be used by the client in preparing financial statements.
   c. Proposed correcting journal entries to be recorded by the client that change client-prepared financial statements.
   d. Generated, through the use of computer software, financial statements prepared in accordance with a comprehensive basis of accounting other than GAAP.

**21-27 An auditor's report would be designated a special report when it is issued in connection with
   a. Interim financial information of a publicly held company that is subject to a limited review.
   b. Compliance with aspects of regulatory requirements related to audited financial statements.
   c. Application of accounting principles to specified transactions.
   d. Limited use prospective financial statements such as a financial projection.

**21-28 An auditor's report on financial statements prepared on the cash receipts and disbursements basis of accounting should include all of the following *except*
   a. A reference to the note to the financial statements that describes the cash receipts and disbursements basis of accounting.
   b. A statement that the cash receipts and disbursements basis of accounting is *not* a comprehensive basis of accounting.
   c. An opinion as to whether the financial statements are presented fairly in conformity with the cash receipts and disbursements basis of accounting.

   d. A statement that the audit was conducted in accordance with generally accepted auditing standards.

**21-29 When an auditor reports on financial statements prepared on an entity's income tax basis, the auditor's report should
   a. Disclaim an opinion on whether the statements were examined in accordance with generally accepted auditing standards.
   b. Not express an opinion on whether the statements are presented in conformity with the comprehensive basis of accounting used.
   c. Include an explanation of how the results of operations differ from the cash receipts and disbursements basis of accounting.
   d. State that the basis of presentation is a comprehensive basis of accounting other than GAAP.

**21-30 Helpful Company, a nonprofit entity, prepared its financial statements on an accounting basis prescribed by a regulatory agency solely for filing with that agency. Greer audited the financial statements in accordance with generally accepted auditing standards and concluded that the financial statements were fairly presented on the prescribed basis. Green should issue a
   a. Qualified opinion.
   b. Standard three paragraph report with reference to footnote disclosure.
   c. Disclaimer of opinion.
   d. Special report.

**21-31 Which of the following statements concerning prospective financial statements is correct?
   a. Only a financial forecast would normally be appropriate for limited use.
   b. Only a financial projection would normally be appropriate for general use.
   c. Any type of prospective financial statements would normally be appropriate for limited use.
   d. Any type of prospective financial statements would normally be appropriate for general use.

**21-32   An examination of a financial forecast is a professional service that involves
   a. Compiling or assembling a financial forecast that is based on management's assumptions.
   b. Limiting the distribution of the accountant's report to management and the board of directors.
   c. Assuming responsibility to update management on key events for one year after the report's date.
   d. Evaluating the preparation of a financial forecast and the support underlying management's assumptions.

**21-33   When an accountant examines a financial forecast that fails to disclose several significant assumptions used to prepare the forecast, the accountant should describe the assumptions in the accountant's report and issue a(an)
   a. "Except for" qualified opinion.
   b. Disclaimer of opinion.
   c. Unqualified opinion with a separate explanatory paragraph.
   d. Adverse opinion.

**21-34   Accepting an engagement to examine an entity's financial projection most likely would be appropriate if the projection were to be distributed to
   a. All employees who work for the entity.
   b. Potential stockholders who request a prospectus or a registration statement.
   c. A bank with which the entity is negotiating for a loan.
   d. All stockholders of record as of the report date.

**21-35   An accountant's compilation report on a financial forecast should include a statement that the
   a. Compilation does *not* include evaluation of the support of the assumptions underlying the forecast.
   b. Hypothetical assumptions used in the forecast are reasonable.
   c. Range of assumptions selected is one in which one end of the range is less likely to occur than the other.
   d. Prospective statements are limited to presenting, in the form of a forecast, information that is the accountant's representation.

**21-36   The objective of a review of interim financial information of a public entity is to provide an accountant with a basis for reporting whether
   a. Material modifications should be made to conform with generally accepted accounting principles.

   b. A reasonable basis exists for expressing an updated opinion regarding the financial statements that were previously audited.
   c. Condensed financial statements or pro forma financial information should be included in a registration statement.
   d. The financial statements are presented fairly in accordance with generally accepted accounting principles.

**21-37   An accountant's standard report on a review of the financial statements of a nonpublic entity should state that the accountant
   a. Does *not* express an opinion or any form of limited assurance on the financial statements.
   b. Is *not* aware of any material modifications that should be made to the financial statements for them to conform with GAAP.
   c. Obtained reasonable assurance about whether the financial statements are free of material misstatement.
   d. Examined evidence, on a test basis, supporting the amounts and disclosures in the financial statements.

**21-38   Baker, CPA, was engaged to review the financial statements of Hall Company, a nonpublic entity. Evidence came to Baker's attention that indicated substantial doubt as to Hall's ability to continue as a going concern. The principal conditions and events that caused the substantial doubt have been fully disclosed in the notes to Hall's financial statements. Which of the following statements best describes Baker's reporting responsibility concerning this matter?
   a. Baker is *not* required to modify the accountant's review report.
   b. Baker is *not* permitted to modify the accountant's review report.
   c. Baker should issue an accountant's compilation report instead of a review report.
   d. Baker should express a qualified opinion in the accountant's review report.

**21-39   Which of the following statements is correct concerning letters for underwriters, commonly referred to as comfort letters?
   a. Letters for underwriters are required by the Securities Act of 1933 for the initial public sale of registered securities.
   b. Letters for underwriters typically give negative assurance on unaudited interim financial information.
   c. Letters for underwriters usually are included in the registration statement accompanying a prospectus.

d. Letters for underwriters ordinarily update auditors' opinions on the prior year's financial statements.

**21-40 Which of the following statements is correct concerning both an engagement to compile and an engagement to review a nonpublic entity's financial statements?

    a. The accountant does *not* contemplate obtaining and documenting an understanding of internal control.

    b. The accountant must be independent in fact and appearance.

    c. The accountant expresses *no* assurance on the financial statements.

    d. The accountant should obtain a written management representation letter.

**21-41 Which of the following procedures is ordinarily performed by an accountant in a compilation engagement of a nonpublic entity?

    a. Reading the financial statements to consider whether they are free of obvious mistakes in the application of accounting principles.

    b. Obtaining written representations from management indicating that the compiled financial statements will *not* be used to obtain credit.

    c. Making inquiries of management concerning actions taken at meetings of the stockholders and the board of directors.

    d. Applying analytical procedures designed to corroborate management's assertions that are embodied in the financial statement components.

**21-42 An accountant may compile a nonpublic entity's financial statements that omit all of the disclosures required by GAAP only if the omission is

    I. Clearly indicated in the accountant's report.

    II. Not undertaken with the intention of misleading the financial statement users.

    a. I only.

    b. II only.

    c. Both I and II.

    d. Either I or II.

**21-43 Which of the following statements should be included in an accountant's standard report based on the compilation of a nonpublic entity's financial statements?

    a. A compilation consists principally of inquiries of company personnel and analytical procedures applied to financial data.

    b. A compilation is limited to presenting in the form of financial statements information that is the representation of management.

    c. A compilation is *not* designed to detect material modifications that should be made to the financial statements.

    d. A compilation is substantially less in scope than an audit in accordance with generally accepted auditing standards.

**21-44 When an independent CPA assists in preparing the financial statements of a publicly held entity, but has *not* audited or reviewed them, the CPA should issue a disclaimer of opinion. In such situations, the CPA has *no* responsibility to apply any procedures beyond

    a. Documenting that internal control is *not* being relied on.

    b. Reading the financial statements for obvious material misstatements.

    c. Ascertaining whether the financial statements are in conformity with GAAP.

    d. Determining whether management has elected to omit substantially all required disclosures.

**21-45 Jordan & Stone, CPAs, audited the financial statements of Tech Co., a nonpublic entity, for the year ended December 31, 19X1, and expressed an unqualified opinion. For the year ended December 31, 19X2, Tech issued comparative financial statements. Jordan & Stone reviewed Tech's 19X2 financial statements and Kent, an assistant on the engagement, drafted the accountants' review report below. Land, the engagement supervisor, decided not to reissue the prior year's auditors' report, but instructed Kent to include a separate paragraph in the current year's review report describing the responsibility assumed for the prior year's audited financial statements. This is an appropriate reporting procedure.

Land reviewed Kent's draft and indicated in the *Supervisor's Review Notes* below that there were several deficiencies in Kent's draft.

Accountant's Review Report

We have reviewed and audited the accompanying balance sheets of Tech Co. as of December 31, 19X2 and 19X1, and the related statements of income, retained earnings, and cash flows for the years then ended, in accordance with Statements on Standards for Accounting and Review Services issued by the American Institute of Certified Public Accountants and generally accepted auditing standards. All information included in these financial statements is the representation of the management of Tech Co.

A review consists principally of inquiries of company personnel and analytical procedures applied to financial data. It is substantially less in scope than an audit in accordance with generally accepted auditing standards, the objective of which is the expression of an opinion regarding the financial statements taken as a whole.

Based on our review, we are not aware of any material modifications that should be made to the accompanying financial statements. Because of the inherent limitations of a review engagement, this report is intended for the information of management and should not be used for any other purpose.

The financial statements for the year ended December 31, 19X1, were audited by us and our report was dated March 2, 19X2. We have no responsibility for updating that report for events and circumstances occurring after that date.

Jordan and Stone, CPAs
March 1, 19X3

Required:

Items **a** through **m** represent deficiencies noted by Land. For each deficiency, indicate whether Land is correct or incorrect in the criticism of Kent's draft.

Supervisor's Review Notes

a. There should be *no* reference to the prior year's audited financial statements in the first (introductory) paragraph.
b. All the current-year basic financial statements are *not* properly identified in the first (introductory) paragraph.
c. There should be *no* reference to the American Institute of Certified Public Accountants in the first (introductory) paragraph.
d. The accountant's review and audit responsibilities should follow management's responsibilities in the first (introductory) paragraph.
e. There should be *no* comparison of the scope of a review to an audit in the second (scope) paragraph.
f. Negative assurance should be expressed on the current year's reviewed financial statements in the second (scope) paragraph.
g. There should be a statement that *no* opinion is expressed on the current year's financial statements in the second (scope) paragraph.
h. There should be a reference to "conformity with generally accepted accounting principles" in the third paragraph.
i. There should be *no* restriction on the distribution of the accountant's review report in the third paragraph.
j. There should be *no* reference to "material modifications" in the third paragraph.
k. There should be an indication of the type of opinion expressed on the prior year's audited financial statements in the fourth (separate) paragraph.
l. There should be an indication that *no* auditing procedures were performed after the date of the report on the prior year's financial statements in the fourth (separate) paragraph.
m. There should be *no* reference to "updating the prior year's auditor's report for events and circumstances occurring after that date" in the fourth (separate) paragraph.

Chapter 21 ▶ DISCUSSION/CASE QUESTIONS

(* = author prepared; ** = CPA examination; *** = CMA examination)

*21-46   You have been engaged by the trustees of Roger Trust to audit the trust as of December 31, 19XX. The audit is for the purpose of assuring the trustees and beneficiaries that trust assets, distributions, and income and expenses have been accounted for in accordance with the terms of the trust instrument. The trust instrument provides that financial statements are to be prepared on the cash basis.

   a. State the type of audit report you consider most appropriate in this circumstance and explain why.

   b. Draft the report you would issue if, after your audit, you had no reservations about the financial statements.

*21-47   Steam Clean, Inc., produces unique washing machines under a license agreement with Tom Nessinger, who invented the unique process. Nessinger has engaged you to audit the sales of Steam Clean, Inc., which are the basis for royalty payments to him. (He is to be paid $10 for each washing machine sold.)

During your audit, you find that the sales amount on which Nessinger was paid excludes (1) 15 units for which the sales prices were never collected (written off as bad debts), (2) 17 units that were returned because of defects, (3) 21 units sold at a reduced price as demonstrators, (4) 106 units manufactured and sold by a foreign subsidiary, and (5) 57 units that were modified slightly from the original design. Nessinger disputes the exclusion of all of these units from sales on which royalty payments were made.

Discuss and draft the form of audit report you would issue in this case.

**21-48   The auditors' report below was drafted by a staff accountant of Baker and Baker, CPAs, at the completion of the audit of the comparative financial statements of Ocean Shore Partnership for the years ended December 31, 19X1 and 19X0. Ocean Shore prepares its financial statements on the income tax basis of accounting. The report was submitted to the engagement partner, who reviewed matters thoroughly and properly concluded that an unqualified opinion should be expressed.

Auditor's Report

We have audited the accompanying statements of assets, liabilities, and capital—income tax basis of Ocean Shore Partnership as of December 31, 19X1 and 19X0, and the related statements of revenue and expenses—income tax basis and changes in partners' capital accounts—income tax basis for the years then ended.

We conducted our audits in accordance with standards established by the American Institute of Certified Public Accountants. Those standards require that we plan and perform the audit to obtain reasonable assurance about whether the financial statements are free of material misstatement. An audit includes examining, on a test basis, evidence supporting the amounts and disclosures in the financial statements. An audit also includes assessing the accounting principles used as well as evaluating the overall financial statement presentation.

As described in Note A, these financial statements were prepared on the basis of accounting the Partnership uses for income tax purposes. Accordingly, these financial statements are not designed for those who do not have access to the Partnership's tax returns.

In our opinion, the financial statements referred to above present fairly, in all material respects, the assets, liabilities, and capital of Ocean Shore Partnership as of December 31, 19X1 and 19X0, and its revenue and expenses and changes in partners' capital accounts for the years then ended, in conformity with generally accepted accounting principles applied on a consistent basis.

Baker and Baker, CPAs
April 3, 19X2

Required:

Identify the deficiencies contained in the auditors' report as drafted by the staff accountant. Group the deficiencies by paragraph, where applicable. Do *not* redraft the report.

*21-49   Sam Sheppard, CPA, has been asked by the management of his client, Indian Togs, Inc., to examine the financial forecast of the company for the coming year.

a. What is a financial forecast, and how does it differ from a financial projection?

b. What is the objective of Sheppard's examination of the company's financial forecast?

    c. What procedures might Sheppard use to evaluate (1) the assumptions and (2) the preparation and presentation of the forecast?

    d. Assuming that Sheppard's examination is satisfactory, draft a report on the examination of the financial forecast.

*21-50   Your client, Byrd and Byrd, Inc., a regional trucking company, has prepared a financial forecast for the coming year and has asked you to examine it and issue a report to accompany it. Management's assumptions, on which the forecast is based, are as follows.

    1. Inflation will average 2 percent next year.

    2. There will be no change in accounting principles or tax rates.

    3. The company will acquire a new route between Tulsa and Kansas City.

    4. Motor fuel will be in adequate supply, although at a slightly higher cost.

    5. There will be no net expansion of the company's truck fleet; a few new trucks will be purchased to replace older models.

    6. Real GNP growth will moderate in the coming year to a real rate of two percent.

    7. Industrywide, truck shipment miles will increase 5 percent.

    8. The union agreement with the Teamsters will be renegotiated without a strike and for no pay increase.

    9. Interest rates will average 10 percent next year.

    Evaluate these assumptions for reasonableness and consistency. In addition, state the procedures you would use to determine whether the assumptions are adequately supported.

*21-51   John Wilguess, CPA, has been engaged to review the financial statements of Lucky Oil Company, a nonpublic company, for the year ended June 30, 19X4. The previous year's financial statements of Lucky Oil Company were compiled by another CPA. Wilguess has no experience with this company or the oil industry.

    a. Discuss the knowledge Wilguess should acquire to perform a review of Lucky Oil Company. What sources could Wilguess consult to obtain this knowledge?

    b. Describe the procedures Wilguess would perform in a review of the financial statements of Lucky Oil Company. Be specific as to procedures for Lucky Oil Company, not just procedures in general.

    c. The owner of Lucky Oil Company has requested that the financial statements of both the current and prior year be presented. Assuming that Wilguess is satisfied with the current year and that the predecessor's compilation report dated July 30, 19X3, is not presented, draft the report that Wilguess may issue.

*21-52   In connection with a review of the December 31, 19X5, financial statements of Quick Profits Real Estate, a nonpublic company, Hilton and Hilton, CPAs, noted that certain parcels of land were recorded at appraised value that exceeded cost by $1,200,000. Management of the company refused to change the financial statements to show the land at cost.

    a. What courses of action should Hilton and Hilton consider?

    b. If it is concluded that modification of their standard review report is appropriate for the land recorded at appraised value and the review is otherwise satisfactory, draft the report that Hilton and Hilton should issue.

    c. If the company, in addition to recording land at appraised value, also changed the method of computing depreciation on its buildings from the double-declining balance method to the straight-line method, how would the review report of Hilton and Hilton be affected?

**21-53   The following report was drafted by a staff assistant at the completion of the review engagement of GLM Company, a continuing client, for the year ended September 30, 19X8. The financial statements for the year ended September 30, 19X7, which were also reviewed, contained a departure from generally accepted accounting principles that was properly referred to in the 19X7 review report dated October 26, 19X7. The 19X7 financial statements have been restated.

> To the Board of Directors of GLM Company:
>
> We have reviewed the accompanying balance sheets of GLM Company as of September 30, 19X8 and 19X7, and the related statements of income and retained earnings for the years then ended, in accordance with generally accepted auditing standards. All information included in these financial statements is the representation of the management of GLM Company.
>
> A review consists principally of inquiries of company personnel. It is substantially less in scope than an audit, but more in scope than a compilation. Accordingly, we express only limited assurance on the accompanying financial statements.
>
> Based on our reviews, with the exception of the matter described in the following paragraph, we are not aware of any material modifications that should be made to the accompanying financial statements in order for them to be in conformity with generally accepted accounting principles applied on a consistent basis.
>
> In its 19X7 financial statements the company stated its land at appraised values. However, as disclosed in note X, the company has restated its 19X7 financial statements to reflect land at cost.
>
> November 2, 19X8

Required:

Identify the deficiencies in the draft of the proposed report on the comparative financial statements. Group the deficiencies by paragraph. Do *not* redraft the report.

*21-54   John Alvis, CPA, has completed his review of the interim financial information of Wilson and Love, a public company, for the six months ended June 30, 19X5.

a. Discuss the form of report that Alvis may issue.

b. What should be the date of the report and to whom should it be addressed?

c. Discuss the form of the modification, if any, that should be made to Alvis's report as the result of (1) departures from generally accepted accounting principles, (2) inadequate disclosures, and (3) lack of consistency in the application of accounting principles.

d. If the management of Wilson and Love state in an interim report to stockholders that Alvis has reviewed the financial information but will not agree to include his report, what action should Alvis take?

*21-55   As a condition for a public offering of securities by your largest and most important audit client, the underwriter requires a comfort letter containing the following items.

1. An unequivocal statement that you are independent with respect to your client within the meaning of the Securities Act of 1933.

2. Negative assurance regarding the audited financial statements included in the registration statement.

3. Negative assurance about decreases in certain financial statement items during a period subsequent to the date of the latest financial statements in the registration statement.

4. Negative assurance about certain financial information in the text section of the registration statement, including the percentage of capacity at which the client's plant operated during the year.

A meeting is to be held for the underwriter, your client, and you to review the procedures for the public offering. Before the meeting gets under way, the underwriter shows you a copy of a comfort letter issued by another office of your firm in connection with a previous public offering that exactly conforms with the underwriter's requirements, and the client states that the comfort letter is so standard that it is not worth discussing at this meeting. What matters, if any, would you wish to discuss concerning the comfort letter?

*21-56   Keith Sellers, a new CPA, is establishing an accounting practice and has decided to specialize in performing compilations. He stated, "Because CPAs provide no assurance in compilation reports, they have no legal liability." Evaluate his position.

*21-57   Becky Maupin, CPA, has been asked to compile the financial statements of George's Diner, a nonpublic company, for the year ended April 30, 19X5.

    a. What understanding should Maupin establish with George before accepting the engagement? Must this understanding be in writing?

    b. Under what conditions could Maupin accept the engagement if she is not familiar with the diner industry?

    c. What procedures must Maupin perform before issuing her compilation report?

**21-58   The following report was drafted on October 25, 19X0, by Major, CPA, at the completion of the engagement to compile the financial statements of Ajax Company for the year ended September 30, 19X0. Ajax is a nonpublic entity in which Major's child has an immaterial direct financial interest. Ajax decided to omit substantially all the disclosures required by generally accepted accounting principles because the financial statements will be for management's use only. The statement of cash flows also was omitted because management does not believe it to be a useful financial statement.

> To the Board of Directors of Ajax Company:
>
>   I have compiled the accompanying financial statements of Ajax Company as of September 30, 19X0, and for the year then ended. I planned and performed the compilation to obtain limited assurance about whether the financial statements are free of material misstatements.
>
>   A compilation is limited to presenting information in the form of financial statements. It is substantially less in scope than an audit in accordance with generally accepted auditing standards, the objective of which is the expression of an opinion regarding the financial statements taken as a whole. I have not audited the accompanying financial statements and, accordingly, do not express any opinion on them.
>
>   Management has elected to omit substantially all of the disclosures required by generally accepted accounting principles. If the omitted disclosures were included in the financial statements, they might influence the user's conclusions about the Company's financial position, results of operations, and changes in financial position.
>
>   I am not independent with respect to Ajax Company. This lack of independence is due to my child's ownership of an immaterial direct financial interest in Ajax Company.
>
>   This report is intended solely for the information and use of the Board of Directors and management of Ajax Company and should not be used for any other purpose.
>
> Major, CPA

Required:
Identify the deficiencies contained in Major's report on the compiled financial statements. Group the deficiencies by paragraph where applicable. Do *not* redraft the report.

*21-59   Steve White, CPA, has completed the compilation of the financial statements of the Elbow Macaroni Factory, a nonpublic entity, and is now considering the form of report that he should issue.

a. Discuss the general form of a compilation report.

b. If White performed additional procedures such as a review of the bank reconciliations and tax returns and a test of inventory pricing, how would the general form of the compilation report be modified? Why?

c. What factors should White consider before issuing his compilation report if the owner of the Elbow Macaroni Factory requests that substantially all disclosures required by generally accepted accounting principles be omitted?

d. How would White's compilation report be affected if he has not yet been paid for compiling the prior year financial statements of the Elbow Macaroni Factory?

e. How would White's compilation report be affected if he determines that the macaroni tax credit was not considered in computing the company's tax liability and that the effect on the financial statements is material?

f. What action should White take if he believes that modification of his report is not adequate to indicate the deficiencies in the financial statements taken as a whole?

***21-60   Easecom Company is a manufacturer of highly specialized products for networking videoconferencing equipment. Production of specialized units is, to a large extent, performed under contract, with standard units manufactured to marketing projections. With the recent downturn in the computer industry, the videoconferencing equipment segment has suffered, causing a slide in Easecom's performance. Easecom's Income Statement for the fiscal year ended October 31, 19X1, is presented below.

Easecom Company
Income Statement
For the Year Ended October 31, 19X1
($000 omitted)

Net Sales	
Equipment	$6,000
Maintenance contracts	1,800
Total net sales	7,800
Expenses	
Cost of goods sold	4,600
Customer maintenance	1,000
Selling expense	600
Administrative expense	900
Interest expense	150
Total expenses	7,250
Income before income taxes	550
Income taxes	220
Net income	$ 330

Easecom's return on sales before interest and taxes was 9 percent in fiscal 19X1, while the industry average was 12 percent. Easecom's total asset turnover was three times, and its return on average assets before interest and taxes was 27 percent, both well below the industry average. In order to improve performance and raise these ratios nearer to, or above, industry averages, Bill Hunt, Easecom's president, established the following goals for fiscal 19X2.

- Return on sales before interest and taxes   11 percent
- Total asset turnover   4 times
- Return on average assets before interest and taxes   35 percent

To achieve Hunt's goals, Easecom's management team took into consideration the growing international videoconferencing market and proposed the following actions for fiscal 19X2.

- Increase equipment sales prices by 10 percent.
- Increase the cost of each unit sold by 3 percent for needed technology and quality improvements, and increased variable costs.
- Increase maintenance inventory by $250,000 at the beginning of the year and add two maintenance technicians at a total cost of $136,000 to cover wages and related travel expenses. These revisions are intended to improve customer service and response time. The increased inventory will be financed at an annual interest rate of 12 percent, no other borrowings or loan reductions are contemplated during fiscal 19X2. All other assets will be held to fiscal 19X1 levels.
- Increase selling expenses by $250,000 but hold administrative expenses at 19X1 levels.
- The effective rate for 19X2 federal and state taxes is expected to be 40 percent, the same as 19X1.

It is expected that these actions will increase equipment unit sales by 6 percent, with a corresponding 6 percent growth in maintenance contracts.

Required:

a. Compile a financial forecast of an income statement for Easecom Company for the fiscal year ending October 31, 19X2, on the assumption that the proposed actions are implemented as planned and that the increased sales objectives will be met. (All numbers should be rounded to the nearest thousand.)

b. Draft an accountant's compilation report to accompany the financial forecast.

c. Calculate the following ratios for Easecom Company for fiscal year 19X2 and determine whether Bill Hunt's goals will be achieved.

1. Return on sales before interest and taxes.
2. Total asset turnover.
3. Return on average assets before interest and taxes.

d. Discuss the limitations and difficulties that can be encountered in using ratio analysis, particularly when making comparisons to industry averages.

*21-61   Slow Burn Candle, Inc., a public company, asked its CPA, Parker Granger, to assist it in preparing footnotes for unaudited financial statements as of June 30, 19X5. Granger has previously audited the company's annual financial statements as of December 31, 19X4.

a. If Granger assisted in drafting footnotes for the unaudited financial statements, but did not append his name to them, would he be deemed to be associated with them?

b. If Granger did *no* work on the unaudited financial statements and only consented to a statement in a transmittal letter that he was the company's auditor, would he be deemed to be associated with them?

c. If Granger is deemed to be associated with the unaudited financial statements, what is his reporting responsibility?

d. What is Granger's reporting responsibility if the unaudited financial statements are presented in comparative form with audited financial statements?

*21-62 Atlas Company is a small refinery owned by several individuals who are not active in its management. To supply them with reliable information about the company's operations for the year, you are requested to prepare a report on accompanying information in connection with this year's audit. You are asked specifically to include the following items in your report.

a. An aged trial balance of accounts receivable as of the end of the year.

b. An analysis of the allowance for doubtful accounts for the year and your conclusion as to its adequacy.

c. An analysis of insurance coverage at the end of the year and your recommendation for any changes.

d. An analysis of the major additions to property and equipment for the year and a description of the procedures you used to audit the additions.

e. An analysis of accrued liabilities at the end of the year and a comment regarding the income tax returns subject to review by the IRS.

f. A schedule showing the percentage of the total outstanding common stock owned by each stockholder of record as shown in the stockbook.

g. Your comments as to why revenues increased during the year.

Discuss the appropriateness of including each of these matters in your report on accompanying information.

Operational and Compliance Auditing

"He is well paid that is well satisfied."

SHAKESPEARE, *The Merchant of Venice, IV, i*

LEARNING OBJECTIVES

After reading and studying the material in this chapter, the student should be able to

▶ Describe the differences between operational and financial auditing and explain why there is a demand for operational auditing.

▶ Write a brief paragraph describing the importance of internal auditing and the work done by internal auditors.

▶ Describe how operational audits are planned.

▶ Describe how evidence of performance is gathered in an operational audit.

▶ Describe how deviations are analyzed and investigated in an operational audit.

▶ Describe how corrective action is determined in an operational audit.

▶ Describe how the results of an operational audit are reported.

▶ Give examples of operational audits of specific activities.

▶ Give examples of efficiencies resulting from operational audits.

▶ Describe compliance auditing and give examples of audits of government entities.

▶ Give an example of an auditor's report on compliance that is required by *Government Auditing Standards*.

▶ Compare generally accepted auditing standards with government auditing standards.

Operational and compliance audits are defined and briefly described in Chapter 1. This chapter provides a more detailed discussion of these two types of audits, including some aspects of government auditing standards and the Single Audit Act. Although operational and compliance audits are often prescribed for government audits, they are applicable in a broad range of settings, as is illustrated throughout the chapter.

OPERATIONAL AUDITING

Because operational auditing is not as common as financial auditing, it has not been as well defined. Operational auditing is often used interchangeably with "management auditing," "performance auditing," and "program results auditing." Internal auditors and government auditors are often associated with operational auditing although they may perform financial auditing functions as well.

As discussed and illustrated in earlier chapters, auditors often provide business advice to their clients while performing financial statement audits. Although there is a similarity between providing business advice and operational auditing, in this chapter we describe operational auditing as a specific engagement apart from a financial statement audit.

Definition of Operational Auditing

Most definitions of *operational auditing* include some reference to efficiency (minimum expenditure of resources), effectiveness (accomplishment of the desired results), economy, or performance of an entity. Operational auditors ask such questions as: Have specific policies and objectives been defined? Are established policies being followed and are established objectives being met? Are desired results being obtained? Thus, operational auditing is concerned with why transactions occur in the first place and whether there are economical alternatives. Here is a simple, straightforward definition of operational auditing:

> An operational audit is an organized search for ways of improving efficiency and effectiveness. It can be considered a form of constructive criticism.[1]

Differences Between Operational and Financial Audits

An important difference between an operational audit and a financial audit is the unit of measure. Most financial audits concentrate on attesting to the fairness of the financial statements in accordance with generally accepted accounting principles as defined by authoritative bodies and accepted practice. Thus, the criteria for evaluating the amounts and disclosures contained in financial statements are fairly well defined. On the other hand, the measurement or evaluation of effectiveness, efficiency, economy, or performance in an operational audit is more difficult. There are no generally accepted standards. Some surrogates for effectiveness, efficiency, and economy must be used. Some examples will be provided later in the chapter.

Other differences between financial and operational auditing include:

1. Financial audit results are often reported to parties outside of the entity (e.g., stockholders, regulatory agencies, and the general public), whereas operational audit results are usually reported to management.

2. Operational audits may be directed toward many nonfinancial areas such as personnel and engineering.

[1] Dale L. Flesher and Stewart Siewert, *Independent Auditor's Guide to Operational Auditing* (New York: John Wiley & Sons, 1982).

Demand for Operational Audits

In today's highly competitive business environment, the demand for operational audits can be attributed to management's desire to increase revenues, increase productivity, and reduce costs. Operational auditors search for ways to reduce waste and inefficiency. Many corporate restructurings reported in the business press are the result of operational audits.

> ▶ **EXAMPLE**
>
> Waste occurs when there is insufficient work to keep employees busy and when there are unused or unnecessarily expensive supplies and idle equipment. Inefficiency may be caused by cumbersome or unnecessary policies and procedures, excess paperwork that serves no useful purpose, poor arrangement of the work area, and overspecialization. Indications of low productivity include poor worker morale, high absenteeism, low-quality products, high rejection rates, and excessive downtime of machines.

A properly conducted operational audit should provide management with a number of benefits, including (1) increased profitability, (2) more efficient allocation of resources, (3) identification of problems at an early stage, and (4) improved communications. Management is responsible for all these functions. In a small enterprise, management can perform them by direct personal supervision, and there may be little need for an operational audit. As enterprises grow and add levels of authority between management and the operating functions, the needs for operational audits increase, and we see the development of internal audit departments.

Although internal, external, and government auditors perform operational audits, the emphasis in this chapter will be on operational audits performed by internal auditors. They are especially qualified to perform these audits because of their skills in audit planning and the gathering and evaluating of audit evidence, as well as their special perspectives and insights into the business operations of their employer.

INTERNAL AUDITORS

Internal auditing has evolved from a simple clerical function into a highly professional operation. At one time, internal auditing consisted primarily of the audit of compliance with internal financial procedures; now it extends to the appraisal of efficiency and effectiveness in nonfinancial as well as financial matters. The importance of the internal audit function increases as organizations grow larger and more geographically dispersed. Today it is not unusual to find internal auditors reporting directly to the audit committee of the board of directors and using the latest electronic data processing and statistical techniques in their work. The *Institute of Internal Auditors (IIA)* emphasizes that internal auditing serves the organization as a whole and not merely the management of the organization.

IIA was formed in 1941 as an international association dedicated to the continuing professional development of the individual internal auditor and the internal auditing profession. Over the years it has adopted a *Code of Ethics,* approved a *Standards for the Professional Practice of Internal Auditing,* established a program of continuing education, developed a *Common Body of Knowledge,* and instituted a certification program leading to an individual's designation as a certified internal auditor (CIA). The *Code of Ethics* emphasizes honesty and objectivity. The *Standards for the Professional Practice of Internal Auditing* are to internal auditors what generally accepted auditing standards are to external auditors. They establish general levels of performance against which internal audit departments may be evaluated and cover such areas as independence, professional proficiency, scope and performance of work, and management of the internal audit department. The CIA examination lasts two days and covers (1) the internal audit process, (2) internal audit skills, (3) management control and information technology, and (4) the audit environment.

It is an oversimplification to say that external auditors are independent and internal auditors are not. Independence is a continuous rather than a discrete concept. The fact that the external auditor is selected and paid by management could be perceived to affect his or her independence, but this situation is not considered so serious that it invalidates the independent audit function. Internal auditors should increase the degree of their independence to the maximum practical extent. One method used in some companies is to have the internal auditor report to the board of directors or its audit committee. This assures that the internal audit findings will be considered at the highest corporate level and reduces the influence of management on the work of the internal auditor.

The internal auditor usually has opportunities to (1) see many aspects of the company very quickly, (2) get broad exposure to management, and (3) apply a variety of accounting, auditing, and personal skills. Because of the broad understanding of company operations obtained, internal auditors are often promoted to key management positions.

AN APPROACH TO AN OPERATIONAL AUDIT

Because of the many areas of coverage, no single approach can be taken to operational audits. However, some general functions are usually applicable to most operational audits:

1. Plan the work to be performed, including the establishment of standards by which the audited operation is to be evaluated.
2. Gather evidence with which to measure the performance of the operation.
3. Analyze and investigate deviations from the standards.
4. Determine corrective action, where needed.
5. Report the results to the appropriate level of authority.

Each of these general functions is discussed further in the following sections.

PLANNING THE OPERATIONAL AUDIT

Often the subject area and objectives of an operational audit are designated by top management. The internal auditor must then prepare and document a plan to accomplish the designated objectives.

Risk assessment is a major part of the planning process. This risk assessment is for the purpose of determining areas to emphasize in an operational audit, as opposed to risk assessment in an external financial audit (discussed in earlier chapters) that is for the purpose of determining the nature, timing, and extent of audit procedures to be performed. Areas of high risk should be identified for audit emphasis. The areas where the greatest risks exist and the greatest benefits can be realized should be chosen to be audited. Operational audits are not mandatory, and cost-benefit decisions must be employed to justify their use.

A *preliminary survey* is a common procedure for the operational auditor to use to become familiar with the history, objectives, organizational structure, management style, programs, and products of the operation to be audited. The auditor may use questionnaires, flowcharts, inquiries, management reports, policy manuals, and observations in the performance of the preliminary survey. Note that the term *preliminary survey* is unique to operational audits.

The questionnaire contains questions regarding matters affecting effectiveness, efficiency, and performance of the operation. The auditor will then evaluate the answers obtained. Later, he or she will gather evidence to substantiate the answers received. Some examples of the types of questions that might be included are as follows:

1. How is the performance of this operation evaluated by top management?
2. What authority has been delegated to meet the performance criteria?
3. Has performance of this operation been satisfactory?
4. What areas need the most managerial attention?
5. What methods are used to safeguard assets?
6. Are sufficient but not excessive personnel assigned to the operation?
7. Is there a program to control excessive or duplicate paperwork?

To aid in understanding the flow of goods, services, and transactions to, from, and within the operation, the auditor may review or prepare flowcharts. When studying a flowchart, the auditor will be looking for inefficiencies and lack of controls, such as duplicate operations, unnecessary forms and operations, and lack of approvals.

While an auditor will make inquiries throughout the audit, many inquiries will be made at a preliminary meeting with the supervisors of the operation being audited. At this meeting, the auditor should attempt to establish rapport and promote a cooperative attitude with the personnel of the operation being audited. Their cooperation is important to the efficient completion of the operational audit. At this meeting the auditor may ask such questions as:

1. What reports and other information do you need to manage the operation?
2. How do you use each report?
3. What operating problems are you experiencing?
4. Describe your training programs.
5. How do you set priorities for the operation?

The auditor will also review such management reports as interim financial statements, budgets, and sales and production reports. Of particular interest to the auditor are such things as budget variances, cost increases, inventory shortages, and production spoilage. All of these may indicate lack of efficiency. While performing other parts of the preliminary survey, the auditor should observe his or her surroundings. Idle personnel or equipment, unsafe operations, unsecured assets such as cash or inventory, or inefficient plant or office layout may suggest areas for potential increases in efficiency and effectiveness.

Based on the information obtained from these sources, the auditor may establish some objective criteria to evaluate the operation. Data from internal company records or from statistics of the industry in which the company operates also may be useful. Usually there are no perfect criteria, and the auditor must develop the best he or she can under the circumstances. What criteria, for example, would be used to evaluate the effectiveness of a purchasing department? One could look at the dollar volume of purchases compared to the number of personnel in the department, but this criterion does not take into account whether or not the purchases were made at the lowest price. To take this factor into account, one might determine the percentage of purchases subjected to competitive bidding, but this does not take into account the timeliness of the delivery of the purchased product or the quality of the product. As this example illustrates, multiple criteria often will be required.

In arriving at evaluative criteria, the operational auditor takes into account such factors as

1. *Historical results.* Current-period operations can be compared with those of one or more periods. This implicitly assumes that the prior periods represent acceptable goals, which may not always be the case.
2. *Results of similar entities.* If entities with similar operations can be identified and if information regarding their operations is available, this information can be used to evaluate performance. However, operations of entities with similar characteristics are often not comparable, and even when they are, the information (e.g., from competitors) may not be available.
3. *Management-established standards.* In some entities, management has established production quotas, sales goals, and other criteria that are likely to be useful in evaluating performance. Often these standards are based on Total Quality Management approaches to continuously improving products and services and to such programs as ISO (International Organization for Standardization) 9000 standards for assessing potential suppliers' quality control systems.

With this information, the auditor will design an audit program to use as a guide to gathering the evidence for a final evaluation of the operations. The written audit program lists the steps to be performed in the operational audit and provides documentation of audit planning. Each operational audit requires a uniquely designed audit program because each operational audit has its own environment, objectives, and risk considerations.

GATHERING EVIDENCE OF PERFORMANCE

The purpose of gathering evidence is to obtain a factual basis for evaluating the performance criteria previously identified. Examples of evidence that might be examined to evaluate performance follow.

Performance Criteria	*Evidence of Performance*
1. Employees receive 40 hours of training per year.	1. Examine personnel files or training records to verify 40 hours of training per year.
2. Budget reports are received by the tenth of the subsequent month.	2. Interview department head to determine time of receipt of budget reports.
3. Budget variances are investigated and corrective action is taken where necessary.	3. Review budget reports for variances and examine documentation of corrective action taken (e.g., reallocation of personnel, equipment adjustments, changes in production scheduling).
4. Computer equipment is not used by the operator for personal purposes.	4. Review console log of computer operations.
5. Excess funds are invested in interest-bearing obligations.	5. Review cash flow budget and minimum daily cash balances.
6. Customer orders are to be shipped within 24 hours of receipt.	6. Compare quantities, dates, and times on order forms and shipping records.

The interview is an important means of obtaining evidence during an operational audit (an example of the importance of communication skills). The better the interviewer, the more evidence that will be obtained. A good interview involves more than merely asking questions. The interview should be planned and as much information obtained in advance as possible. The interviewee should be made to feel as comfortable as possible. The interviewer should be tactful and avoid implying an expected answer to a question. For example, the question, ''You do use this report, don't you?'' will usually result in a positive response. A better question would be, ''What use do you make of this report?'' After the interview is completed, a memorandum should be prepared of the important points covered in the interview. This memorandum will constitute the evidence of information obtained in the interview.

The auditor will accumulate the evidence obtained in a file. The evidence may take the form of schedules listing information examined (e.g., a list of employees and the number of hours of training received per year), memoranda of discussions held (e.g., interview with department head to determine time of receipt of budget reports), and copies of documents (e.g., budget reports and console logs). Regardless of the form it takes, the auditor must have documentary evidence to support his or her findings and recommendations.

This documentary evidence, referred to as working papers, is compiled primarily from sources internal to the company. Operational audits seldom include external verification of internal data, although external information such as industry statistics may be useful in evaluating the efficiency of some operations.

ANALYSIS AND INVESTIGATION OF DEVIATIONS

While gathering evidence, the auditor should be alert for deviations from company policy and ineffective or inefficient performance. He or she should learn to distinguish between insignificant deviations (one minor supply order slightly in excess of the economic order quantity) and significant ones (numerous large supply orders for which competitive bids were not requested). Past deviations may or may not be correctable, but the auditor's main concern is with the potential effect on the company if the deviations continue in the future.

For example, in the operational audit of a research and development division, the auditor may note that security is lax because the area is not separately locked during nonbusiness hours and research results are not protected. Investigation might lead him or her to the following conclusions:

1. This is a significant deviation because of the possible loss of potential new or improved products to competitors or others.
2. These were not isolated deviations but regular occurrences.
3. The deviation is caused by the need for employees of this division to check and monitor experiments during nonbusiness hours.
4. There are no formal security controls for this division.

The analyses and investigations of deviations should be documented in the auditor's file because they are the basis for determining corrective action.

DETERMINING CORRECTIVE ACTION

After analyzing and investigating a deviation the auditor must answer two questions: What corrective actions can be taken? Are the corrective actions practicable? The second question is often the most difficult to answer because the auditor must consider such factors as cost-benefit relationships, effect on employee morale, and consistency with other company policies.

In the example of lax security in the research and development division, one possible corrective action would be to allow no admittance to the area during nonbusiness hours, but this would be self-defeating because admittance is required to monitor experiments. Another possible corrective action would be to hire 24-hour guards for the area. This would be a costly action, but it might be considered in some cases. A third possible corrective action would be to lock the area and provide selected employees with keys and identification badges that would allow them admittance.

All proposed corrective actions should be discussed with the personnel involved to obtain their ideas and cooperation.

REPORTING THE RESULTS OF AN OPERATIONAL AUDIT

Although formal reporting may be considered the final step in the operational audit, informal interim reports should be made throughout the audit. For example, if the auditor notes a serious inefficiency during the preliminary survey, it should be investigated, evaluated, and reported immediately rather than waiting for the entire audit to be completed. Benefits of interim reporting include fewer surprises for the auditee, more time to resolve disagreements, and earlier implementation of recommended procedures.

FIGURE 22.1   Illustrative Operational Audit Report

Mr. D. Z. Williams
General Manager
California Products, Inc.
Pearson, California 98641

Dear Mr. Williams:

As you requested, we have reviewed the operations of the company's computer information systems department. Our review was conducted during the period from April 16, 19X8 to June 3, 19X8, and consisted of (1) interviews with key personnel in the department, (2) review of operational guidelines including organizational charts, job descriptions, procedures, forms, and system and program documentation, (3) observation of activities within the department, and (4) review of productivity reports including equipment utilization reports and budgets. The computer information systems department utilizes 20 employees and has a budget for the current year of $5,100,000.

We are pleased to report to you our findings and recommendations.

General Evaluation

We found the overall operation of the department to be efficient and effective. Employees exhibited good technical expertise and expressed a desire to be of service to the other departments of the company. Some additional coordination with user departments would be useful in meeting future hardware demands at the lowest cost.

Summary of Major Findings

1. Lack of a long-range plan for computer utilization.

2. Lack of periodic review of computer-generated reports that might be discontinued.

Discussion of Major Findings

1. Lack of a long-range plan for computer utilization.

Findings

The utilization rate of the present computer equipment will approach the maximum sustainable rate within a year. Additionally, certain user departments are considering the acquisition of additional microcomputers to process special information needs. While department personnel have discussed their future needs with various computer equipment manufacturers, no long-range plan that considers the total company computer needs for future years has been developed.

Recommendation

We recommend that the computer information systems department, in consultation with the user departments, prepare a detailed projection of computer needs for the next five years. This projection should include estimates of increases in the data presently processed as well as expected new applications. Top management also should be consulted for information that might affect future computer needs such as mergers, acquisitions, dispositions, etc. Based on this projection, plans may be made to obtain both the equipment and personnel to supply the company's computer needs at the lowest cost.

FIGURE 22.1 *(Continued)*

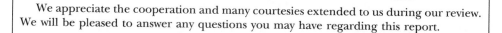

We appreciate the cooperation and many courtesies extended to us during our review. We will be pleased to answer any questions you may have regarding this report.

Sincerely,

Susan Davis
Chief Internal Auditor

Formal reporting is likely to include:

1. A conference with department or division supervisors at the completion of the audit.
2. A written audit report to the department or division that includes detailed audit findings and recommendations.
3. A written audit report to top management or the audit committee of the board of directors that summarizes only the more significant audit findings and recommendations.

Because economy and efficiency are relative terms, an auditor does not express an opinion as to whether an operation was performed at maximum levels of economy or efficiency. Instead, the auditor should report specific findings and conclusions. There is no standard form for reporting on an operational audit (the report may include such things as photographs, charts, graphs, and schedules), but several matters would be covered in most such reports. An opening or scope paragraph should describe the operation that was audited, the time period covered, and so forth. Any limitations placed on the scope of the auditor's work also should be noted. Another paragraph should give an overall evaluation of the operation and an assessment of its performance. This may be followed by a section presenting detailed findings on individual issues. Here it is important to report both favorable and unfavorable findings. Giving proper credit for good performance promotes an objective image of the auditor and encourages cooperation with the auditor in future audits. Unfavorable findings should include a description of the deviation, suggested corrective action, and comments by department or division personnel. A final paragraph may express the auditor's appreciation for the cooperation and assistance received during the audit.

Determinations of the actual corrective actions to be taken on the findings included in the report are management responsibilities and are normally beyond the scope of the operational audit.

A partial illustration of a report on an operational audit is shown in Figure 22.1.

Internal auditors must keep in mind that, although their reports are not intended for use outside their companies, there is no assurance that they will not be seen by outsiders. The Internal Revenue Service, for example, has obtained copies of reports of internal auditors by court action. The reports should not contain speculations or assumptions that could be misconstrued by adverse parties.

OPERATIONAL AUDITS OF SPECIFIC ACTIVITIES

Although it is beyond the scope of this chapter to present detailed programs for the audit of specific departments, the following partial examples were taken from *Modern Internal Auditing*[2] to illustrate the types of matters that might be investigated.

Production
1. To what extent does the production department study new manufacturing approaches for current products?
2. How much waste or spoilage occurs in the processing of materials?
3. How much idle time or overtime is incurred? What are the causes?
4. What is the program for preventive maintenance?
5. Describe the safety program. Is it based on existing hazards and past experience?

Marketing
1. What provision is made for periodic reappraisal of major product market strategy?
2. What is the procedure for the formal presentation of new product proposals and the overall product planning and development program?
3. How are sales promotion budgets developed, approved, and used as a basis of project control?
4. Are advertising agency billings supported as to company authorization, actual rendering of services, and best available rates?
5. Are customers being adequately serviced?

Personnel
1. How does each manager evaluate the personnel for whom he or she is directly responsible?
2. What records and files relating to recruitment are maintained?
3. Are personnel satisfied with their training? If not, why not?
4. How are work specifications developed for individual jobs?
5. Are individual personnel files kept up to date and available for current reference?

Computer Operations
1. Has a long-range plan for computer utilization been prepared, and, if so, is it adequate?

[2] Victor Z. Brink and Herbert Witt, *Modern Internal Auditing,* 4th ed. (New York: Wiley, 1982).

2. Is the computer department staff adequate but not excessive in terms of numbers, types of expertise, and personal qualifications?

3. Are computer processing activities consolidated adequately as a basis for reasonable achievement of potential operational economies, such as (a) purchase of equipment of more efficient size and with most advanced operational features, (b) best possible equipment utilization, and (c) uniform programming and operational practices?

4. What provisions are made for controlling access to operational areas?

5. Are priority policies clearly stated and periodically reviewed?

EXAMPLES OF EFFICIENCIES RESULTING FROM OPERATIONAL AUDITS

Each issue of *The Internal Auditor* publishes examples of audit findings reported by its members. The following cases are examples of the results of actual operational audits that were reported.[3]

During a recent branch bank audit, internal auditors discovered that tellers routinely kept up to $50,000 in cash at the window. The auditors recommended that tellers keep only enough cash on hand to service the customers—around $5,000, depending on the specific situation for the particular teller. Shortly after the auditors' recommendation was implemented, the branch was robbed. The robber escaped with $6,000, primarily because a commercial customer had just made a large cash deposit. If the branch had not implemented the auditors' recommendation, the robber could have gotten away with $56,000.

For numerous years, the internal auditors found that the company's insurance department was not inviting competitive bids for fire, boiler, and machinery insurance. Management's responses to the auditors' recommendations for competitive bidding were always the same: "The present carrier . . . provides excellent service . . . has an outstanding relationship with us . . . provides numerous intangible services . . . et al." Management was also aware of what other carriers were quoting on similar coverage. As a result of the auditors' continued perseverance on the subject, the insurance department finally solicited competitive bids for the insurance coverage. The leverage obtained from the competitive bidding caused the current carrier to restructure premium deposit requirements and premium amounts which reduced the company's insurance costs by more than $500,000 a year.

A consumer goods company used to require each of its manufacturing plants to submit monthly samples of raw materials and finished product to a company-owned laboratory for quality control testing. The internal auditor found that management, due to quality improvements, had phased out the testing over a period of years. However, the plants were still faithfully sending the samples month after month. Why was this, wondered the auditor—who found it was because no one had told the plants to stop sending the samples. Management had only told the lab to stop making the tests. When informed of the auditor's findings, management notified the plants to stop sending the samples for an estimated savings of about $60,000 a year.

---

[3] The examples from *The Internal Auditor,* copyright © by The Institute of Internal Auditors, Inc., are reprinted with permission.

During an operational audit of the advertising department, the internal auditor was compiling costs for the printing of advertising inserts which are distributed inside newspapers. The auditor found that a high percentage of the cost was for the ink alone and questioned its validity. Research determined that the higher the density of the ink, the more costly the insert. Samples of inserts printed with ink that had a lesser density convinced management that using a less costly ink would change the appearance of the insert so insignificantly that customers would not notice. About $2.5 million a year will be saved.

SUMMARY OF OPERATIONAL AUDITING

The benefits top management may receive from an operational audit may easily be seen from the foregoing illustrations. If problems are identified at an early stage, profitability should be enhanced. Department and division personnel also should benefit by having their good performance recognized and by receiving suggestions for further improvement. Finally, the nonroutine nature of the work would provide internal (and other) auditors with challenging engagements and increasing recognition.

COMPLIANCE AUDITING

All audits are, in a sense, a form of compliance auditing. In financial audits, a determination is made of whether financial statements comply with generally accepted accounting principles. In operational audits, a determination is made of whether an entity's performance complies with standards of efficiency developed by management or the operational auditor. In the auditing literature, however, compliance auditing has a narrower definition. It refers to the determination of whether transactions and events conform with laws and regulations. Compliance auditing has added significance in audits of government entities because generally there are more compliance requirements than in audits of nongovernment entities.

Audits of Government Entities

Audits of government entities may be performed by government auditors at federal, state, and local levels or by independent public accountants. The professional standards and guidance applicable to audits of government entities go beyond those found in other types of audits. In addition to *generally accepted auditing standards* (GAAS) prescribed by the AICPA Auditing Standards Board in *Statements on Auditing Standards* (see Chapter 2), government audits also are subject to government auditing standards (GAS), which are prescribed in *Government Auditing Standards* (often referred to as the Yellow Book) that is issued by the General Accounting Office (GAO). GAS pronouncements are broader in scope than those prescribed by GAAS and include reporting on compliance with laws and regulations and on internal control. GAS pronouncements also cover performance (operational) au-

FIGURE 22.2   **Types of Government Audits**

*Financial
Audits*

1. Financial statement audits provide reasonable assurance about whether the financial statements of an audited entity present fairly the financial position, results of operations, and cash flows in conformity with generally accepted accounting principles or other comprehensive basis of accounting.

2. Financial related audits include determining whether (a) financial information is presented in accordance with established or stated criteria, (b) the entity has adhered to specific financial compliance requirements, and (c) the entity's internal control over financial reporting and/or safeguarding assets is suitably designed and implemented to achieve the control objectives.

*Performance
(Operational) Audits*

1. Economy and efficiency audits include determining (a) whether the entity is acquiring, protecting, and using its resources (such as personnel, property, and space) economically and efficiently, (b) the causes of inefficiencies or uneconomical practices, and (c) whether the entity has complied with laws and regulations on matters of economy and efficiency.

2. Program audits include determining (a) the extent to which the desired results or benefits established by the legislature or other authorizing body are being achieved, (b) the effectiveness of organizations, programs, activities, or functions, and (c) whether the entity has complied with significant laws and regulations applicable to the program.

Source: GAO, Government Auditing Standards (1994 revision), pp. 12–14.

dits as well as financial statement audits. Figure 22.2 describes GAS audits applicable to government organizations, programs, activities, and functions. GAS audits may also be performed for contractors, nonprofit organizations, and other nongovernment organizations that receive financial assistance from the federal government.

GAS requirements applicable to financial audits are similar to GAAS, but two requirements merit discussion. The first is the qualifications requirement for continuing professional education. It requires that auditors performing government audits complete at least 80 hours of continuing professional education every two years and that 24 of the 80 hours relate directly to government auditing. The second is the quality control requirement. It requires that accounting firms and individual practitioners that conduct government audits have an external quality review of their accounting practice by an unaffiliated organization at least once every three years. This generally involves having another accounting firm examine the policies and procedures that are instituted to assure that audit quality is maintained. These requirements are intended to raise the quality of government auditing.

In addition to AICPA and GAO standards, the federal Office of Management and Budget (OMB) sets auditing standards for audits of federally funded programs. Some of these standards are contained in the following publications:

- The Single Audit Act and Circular A-128, which provides audit requirements for state and local governments that receive federal aid.

- Circular A-133, which provides audit requirements for institutions of higher education and other nonprofit institutions.

In addition to the auditing standards set by the AICPA, GAO, and OMB, government audits may also be subject to the provisions of federal, state, and local audit program guides and contractual terms contained in programs and grants being audited. As these examples suggest, government audits are often subject to numerous complex requirements.

The Single Audit Act

Because of a diversity of federal government funding sources, state and local governments often receive funds from several programs administered by various federal agencies, each of which has its own audit requirements. For example, a city might receive funds from different federal agencies for its transportation needs, poverty programs, educational assistance, and health care facilities. The same payroll system may be used to pay the personnel costs for all four programs. If the four programs are audited by four different auditors, portions of the same payroll system may be audited four separate times, but no auditor may audit the entire system.

Rather than continue the inefficient, and often ineffective, audits of each of the federal programs, the government decided to replace the audits of individual programs with a single entitywide audit. The emphasis has shifted from individual programs to the entity's overall financial management policies and practices. State and local governments that receive $300,000 or more in federal financial assistance in a single year must be audited in accordance with the Single Audit Act. This act and OMB Circular A-128 require that auditors perform sufficient work to report on an entity's internal controls and on its compliance with laws and regulations that have a material effect on each of its major federal financial assistance programs.

COMPLIANCE AUDITING RESPONSIBILITIES IN GOVERNMENT AUDITS

Auditors of government entities and other recipients of federal financial assistance have the following compliance auditing responsibilities:

1. Compliance auditing in audits conducted in accordance with generally accepted auditing standards.
2. Reporting under *Government Auditing Standards.*
3. Responsibilities under the Single Audit Act.

Compliance Auditing in Audits Conducted in Accordance with Generally Accepted Auditing Standards

Noncompliance with laws and regulations constitute illegal acts. Recall from Chapter 5 that, under generally accepted auditing standards, the auditor's responsibility for illegal acts having a direct and material effect on the financial statements is the same as that for errors and fraud. This responsibility is to assess the risk of material errors and fraud and, based on that assessment, to design the audit to provide reasonable assurance of detecting errors and fraud that are material to the financial statements.

When auditing a government entity, the auditor should obtain an understanding of laws and regulations recognized to have a direct and material effect on the amounts in a government entity's financial statements. Examples include:

1. Legal provisions that require the establishment of funds for designated purposes.
2. Appropriations bills that establish budgetary reporting.
3. Grants that require matching contributions by the grantee.
4. Constitutional and other legal restrictions on the purpose for which the proceeds of certain government revenues may be expended.
5. Laws that place limits on local government taxing authority and ceiling limits on debt.

Audit procedures that auditors use to evaluate compliance with laws and regulations include: (1) consideration of knowledge about laws and regulations obtained in prior-year audits, (2) inquiry regarding laws and regulations with the entity's management and oversight officials, (3) review of grant and loan agreements, (4) review of minutes of meetings of legislative bodies, and (5) review of written representations from management regarding compliance with laws and regulations. Unless an instance of noncompliance is detected that is so significant as to affect the fair presentation of the financial statements, no reference to compliance is made in the auditor's report.

Reporting under Government Auditing Standards

Government Auditing Standards impose additional responsibilities on auditors to specifically report on compliance with laws and regulations and on internal control.

Reporting on Compliance
The auditor's report on compliance is based on the results of procedures performed as part of the audit of the financial statements. No additional procedures need be performed. An example of an auditor's report on compliance when the auditor's procedures disclosed no material instances of noncompliance is shown in Figure 22.3.

If material instances of noncompliance are found, the auditor should modify the report to include a definition of material instances of noncompliance, a description of the material instances of noncompliance found, and a statement that the noncompliance was considered by the auditor in forming his or her opinion on the financial statements. If any instance of noncompliance can result in criminal prosecution, separate reporting of these matters is appropriate.

Reporting on Internal Control
As discussed in Chapter 10, auditors are required to communicate to the audit committee any reportable conditions noted during any audit performed in accor-

FIGURE 22.3   Auditor's Report on Compliance that Is Required by *Government Auditing Standards*

We have audited the financial statements of the City of Winslow as of and for the year ended June 30, 19X8, and have issued our report thereon dated August 15, 19X8.

We conducted our audit in accordance with generally accepted auditing standards and *Government Auditing Standards*, issued by the Comptroller General of the United States. Those standards require that we plan and perform the audit to obtain reasonable assurance about whether the financial statements are free of material misstatement.

Compliance with laws, regulations, contracts, and grants applicable to the City of Winslow is the responsibility of the City of Winslow's management. As part of obtaining reasonable assurance about whether the financial statements are free of material misstatement, we performed tests of the City of Winslow's compliance with certain provisions of laws, regulations, contracts, and grants. However, the objective of our audit of the financial statements was not to provide an opinion on overall compliance with such provisions. Accordingly, we do not express such an opinion.

The results of our tests disclosed no instances of noncompliance that are required to be reported under *Government Auditing Standards*.

The results of our tests disclosed immaterial instances of noncompliance with the above requirements which we have communicated to the management of the City of Winslow in a separate letter dated August 15, 19X8.

This report is intended for the information of the audit committee, management, and the state legislative auditor. However, this report is a matter of public record and its distribution is not limited.

August 15, 19X8   Williams & Weishar

---

dance with generally accepted auditing standards. There are, however, differences between this requirement and the requirements under *Government Auditing Standards*. These differences are as follows.

Generally Accepted Auditing Standards	*Government Auditing Standards*
• Requires communication—oral or written—only when reportable conditions are noted.	• Requires a written report on internal control in all audits.
• Permits, but does not require, the auditor to identify material weaknesses.	• Requires identification of material weaknesses.
• Does not require a description of deficiencies not considered significant enough to be reportable conditions.	• Requires a description of deficiencies not considered significant enough to be reportable conditions.

An example of an auditor's report on a government entity's internal control is shown in Figure 22.4.

FIGURE 22.4   Report on Internal Control Required by *Government Auditing Standards*

We have audited the financial statements of the City of Winslow as of and for the year ended June 30, 19X8, and have issued our report thereon dated August 15, 19X8.

We conducted our audit in accordance with generally accepted auditing standards and *Government Auditing Standards,* issued by the Comptroller General of the United States. Those standards require that we plan and perform the audit to obtain reasonable assurance about whether the financial statements are free of material misstatement.

The management of the City of Winslow is responsible for establishing and maintaining internal control. In fulfilling this responsibility, estimates and judgments by management are required to assess the expected benefits and related costs of internal control policies and procedures. The objectives of internal control are to provide management with reasonable, but not absolute, assurance that assets are safeguarded against loss from unauthorized use or disposition and that transactions are executed in accordance with management's authorization and recorded properly to permit the preparation of financial statements in accordance with generally accepted accounting principles. Because of inherent limitations in internal control, errors or fraud may nevertheless occur and not be detected. Also, projection of any evaluation of internal control to future periods is subject to the risk that procedures may become inadequate because of changes in conditions or that the effectiveness of the design and operation of policies and procedures may deteriorate.

In planning and performing our audit of the financial statements of the City of Winslow for the year ended June 30, 19X8, we obtained an understanding of internal control. With respect to internal control, we obtained an understanding of the design of relevant policies and procedures and whether they have been placed in operation, and we assessed control risk in order to determine our auditing procedures for the purpose of expressing our opinion on the financial statements and not to provide an opinion on internal control. Accordingly, we do not express such an opinion.

We noted certain matters involving internal control and its operation that we consider to be reportable conditions under standards established by the American Institute of Certified Public Accountants. Reportable conditions involve matters coming to our attention relating to significant deficiencies in the design or operation of internal control that, in our judgment, could adversely affect the entity's ability to record, process, summarize, and report financial data in a manner that is consistent with the assertions of management in the financial statements.

[*Include paragraphs to describe the reportable conditions noted.*]

A material weakness is a reportable condition in which the design or operation of one or more of the internal control components does not reduce to a relatively low level the risk that errors or fraud in amounts that would be material in relation to the financial statements being audited may occur and not be detected within a timely period by employees in the normal course of performing their assigned functions.

FIGURE 22.4   *(Continued)*

Our consideration of internal control would not necessarily disclose all internal control matters that might be reportable conditions and, accordingly, would not necessarily disclose all reportable conditions that are also considered to be material weaknesses as defined above. However, we believe none of the reportable conditions described above is a material weakness.

We also noted other matters involving internal control and its operation that we have reported to the management of the City of Winslow in a separate letter dated August 15, 19X8.

This report is intended for the information of the audit committee, management, and the state legislative auditor. However, this report is a matter of public record and its distribution is not limited.

As noted in Chapter 10, an auditor is prohibited from issuing a written report stating that no reportable conditions were noted during an audit. When an auditor finds no reportable conditions during an audit of a government entity, he or she may satisfy the *Government Auditing Standards* requirement to report on internal control by issuing a report stating that the auditor found no material weaknesses.

Responsibilities under the Single Audit Act

In addition to the audit procedures and reports issued under GAAS and GAS, the Single Audit Act requires auditors to test and report on compliance with

1. General requirements applicable to federal financial assistance.
2. Specific requirements that may have a material effect on each major federal financial assistance program.
3. Certain laws and regulations applicable to nonmajor federal financial assistance programs.

Compliance with General Requirements
Applicable to Federal Financial Assistance

Nine general compliance requirements have been identified that "involve significant national policy and for which failure to comply could have a material impact on an organization's financial statements." These requirements are summarized in Figure 22.5. Auditors use such procedures as inquiry, observation, and inspection of documents to test compliance with the general requirements and issue a report on the results of applying the procedures.

Compliance with Specific Requirements That
May Have a Material Effect on Major Programs

Management is responsible for preparing a schedule of federal financial assistance (i.e., a schedule of all programs for which funds were received from the federal government and the amounts expended under each). Major programs are defined as those for which total expenditures during a year exceed the larger of three percent of federal funds expended or $300,000, when expenditures for all federal pro-

FIGURE 22.5   General Requirements for Compliance with Laws and Regulations

1. *Davis-Bacon Act*—Requires that laborers working on federally financed construction contracts be paid a wage established by the Secretary of Labor.

2. *Political Activity*—Prohibits the use of federal funds for partisan political activity.

3. *Civil Rights*—Prohibits violation of anyone's civil rights in a program funded by the federal government.

4. *Cash Management*—Requires that recipients of federal assistance minimize the time elapsed between receipt and disbursement of that assistance.

5. *Relocation Assistance and Real Property Acquisition*—Prescribes how real property should be acquired with federal financial assistance and how recipients must help relocate people displaced when that property is acquired.

6. *Federal Financial Reports*—Prescribes federal financial reports that must be filed.

7. *Allowable Costs/Costs Principles*—Prescribes the direct and indirect costs allowable for federal reimbursement.

8. *Drug-Free Workplace*—Prescribes that grantees certify that they provide a drug-free workplace.

9. *Administrative Requirements*—Prescribes administrative requirements that should be followed.

grams are equal to or less than $100 million. A sliding scale applies when expenditures for all programs exceed $100 million.

To evaluate the effect of noncompliance on a major program the auditor considers materiality in relation to expenditures under that program, not the financial statements as a whole. Specific requirements applicable to major programs pertain to the following matters:

1. *Types of services allowed or not allowed,* which specifies the types of goods or services that may be purchased with federal funds.
2. *Eligibility,* which specifies the characteristics of individuals or groups who may receive federal assistance.
3. *Matching,* which specifies the amounts of matching resources that must be contributed.
4. *Reporting,* which specifies reports that must be filed.
5. *Special tests and provisions,* such as requirements to hold public hearings and deadlines for making expenditures.

Auditors use the risk assessment approach embodied in the audit risk model when auditing compliance with specific requirements applicable to major programs. Inherent risk (that material noncompliance could occur) and control risk (that internal control would not prevent or detect material noncompliance) are assessed, and detection risk (that the auditor will fail to detect material noncompliance) is restricted to an appropriate level by varying substantive tests (often referred to as compliance tests).

In evaluating the results of applying audit procedures the auditor should consider the frequency of any noncompliance identified and whether any identified

noncompliance resulted in *questioned costs.* Generally, the following costs are classified as questioned costs.

1. *Unallowable costs.* Costs specifically not allowed under the general and specific
requirements or conditions of the program.
2. *Undocumented costs.* Costs charged to a program for which documentation
(e.g., vendor invoice, purchase order, or receiving report) does not exist.
3. *Unapproved costs.* Costs not approved for payment by an authorized person or
not provided for in an approved budget.
4. *Unreasonable costs.* Costs incurred that do not reflect the actions of a prudent
person.

The auditor should relate the number of instances of noncompliance that resulted in questioned costs to the number of transactions examined. The auditor
may issue an unqualified opinion, a qualified or disclaimer of opinion because of
a material or pervasive scope limitation, or a qualified or adverse opinion because
of material or pervasive noncompliance.

Compliance with Certain Laws and Regulations Applicable to Nonmajor Federal Financial Assistance Programs

In connection with the audit of the financial statements, the auditor may select for
testing transactions from federal financial assistance programs other than major
programs. If so, they should be tested for compliance with all applicable requirements. For example, if in the audit of the financial statements the auditor examines
a payroll transaction that was charged to a nonmajor program, the auditor should
determine whether the position could reasonably be charged to that program and
whether the individual's salary was correctly charged to that program.

SUMMARY OF REPORTING IN A GOVERNMENT AUDIT

In addition to the standard audit report on the financial statements of a government
entity, GAS requires the auditor to report on an entity's internal control and compliance with applicable laws and regulations. Further, additional reports are required
for entities subject to the Single Audit Act. Illustration 22.1 shows how the reports
relate to the various reporting standards.

ILLUSTRATION 22.1 **The Relationship of Reports under GAAS, GAS, and Single Audit Act**

GAAS vs. GAS vs. Single Audit

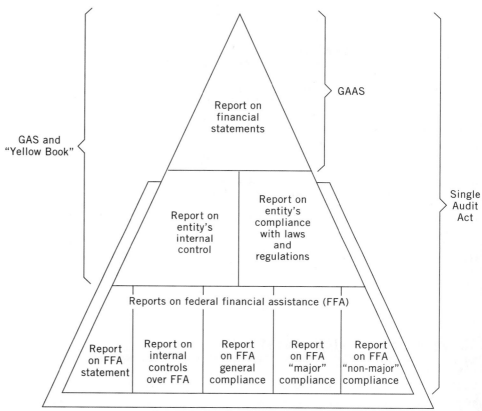

Chapter 22 ▶ GLOSSARY OF TERMS

Compliance auditing A determination of whether transactions and events conform with laws and regulations.

Effectiveness Accomplishment of the desired results.

Efficiency Accomplishment of goals with a minimum expenditure of resources.

General requirements Laws and regulations involving significant national policy issues that are tested for compliance when an audit is performed under the Single Audit Act.

Government auditing standards Standards prescribed by the General Accounting Office, often referred to as the Yellow Book.

Institute of Internal Auditors (IIA) An international association of internal auditors dedicated to the continuing professional development of the individual internal auditor and the internal auditing profession.

Major programs Federal financial assistance programs for which expenditures during a year exceed the larger of three percent of federal funds expended or $300,000 when expenditures for all programs are equal to or less than $100 million.

Operational auditing An organized search for ways of improving efficiency and effectiveness. It can be considered a form of constructive criticism.

Preliminary survey A process in an operational audit for gaining familiarity with the operation to be audited.

Questioned costs Costs paid with federal financial assistance that are unallowable, undocumented, unapproved, or unreasonable.

Single Audit Act A federal law that provides guidelines for auditing state and local governments and other entities that receive $300,000 or more in federal financial assistance.

Chapter 22 ▶ REFERENCES

American Institute of Certified Public Accountants. *Professional Standards:* SAS No. 74—Compliance Auditing Considerations in Audits of Governmental Entities and Recipients of Governmental Financial Assistance.

Blessing, Linda J. "New Opportunities: A CPA's Primer on Performance Auditing." *Journal of Accountancy* (May 1991), pp. 58–68.

Bogan, Walter, R., and Conn, Walton T. "The Meaning of Compliance Attestation," *Journal of Accountancy* (April 1994), pp. 59–64.

Buchanan, Marcia, and Koebele, Deborah A. "What the 1994 Yellow Book Means for Auditors," *Journal of Accountancy* (April 1995), pp. 53–61.

Forrester, Robert. "Are Your Not-For-Profit Clients Ready for Compliance Auditing?" *Journal of Accountancy* (July 1990), pp. 70–76.

Hepp, Gerald W., and Mengel, Jeffrey F. "Improving the Quality of Government Audits," *Journal of Accountancy* (June 1992), pp. 87–92.

McNamee, Patrick. "The New Yellow Book: Focus on Internal Controls," *Journal of Accountancy* (October 1993), pp. 83–86.

Neebes, Donald L., and Broadus, William A. "GAAS vs. GAGAS: How to Report on Internal Controls," *Journal of Accountancy* (February 1990), pp. 58–64.

Raman, K. K., and Van Daniker, Relmond P. "Materiality in Government Accounting," *Journal of Accountancy* (February 1994), pp. 71–76.

Ramsey, Terrill W., and Rippey, George A. "Change the Single Audit Requirements," *Journal of Accountancy* (June 1994), pp. 83–88.

Chapter 22 ▶ REVIEW QUESTIONS

22-1 Describe operational auditing.

22-2 Why is the unit of measure difficult to establish in an operational audit?

22-3 Differentiate between financial and operational auditing.

22-4 List four potential benefits of an operational audit.

22-5 Discuss the activities of the Institute of Internal Auditors.

22-6 What general functions are usually applicable in an operational audit?

22-7 What is the purpose of a preliminary survey and how is it performed?

22-8 Why does the auditor gather evidence of performance?

22-9 What forms may the auditor's evidence take?

22-10 What investigation does an auditor make of deviations?

22-11 List three forms of formal reporting of an operational audit's results.

22-12 What is the purpose of a compliance audit?

22-13 What publication provides guidance to auditors who perform audits of government entities?

22-14 How do government auditing standards differ from generally accepted auditing standards?

22-15 What two federal agencies publish auditing standards for audits of programs for federal financial assistance?

22-16 If an auditor finds no reportable conditions during an audit of a government entity, how is this reported under *Government Auditing Standards*?

22-17 What governmental entities are subject to the Single Audit Act?

22-18 Name and describe the general requirements that are tested for compliance in a single audit.

22-19 What specific requirements applicable to major programs are tested for compliance in a single audit?

22-20 What types of expenditures are classified as questioned costs in a compliance audit?

Chapter 22 ▶ OBJECTIVE QUESTIONS

(* = author prepared; ** = CPA examination; *** = CIA examination) [4]

*22-21 An operational auditor is most likely to be concerned with whether a transaction was
   a. Necessary.
   b. Reasonable.
   c. Properly approved.
   d. Properly supported with documentation.

*22-22 When planning an operational audit, the auditor should consider the risk of
   a. Misleading financial statements.
   b. Inadequate internal controls.
   c. Inefficient operations.
   d. Lawsuits for inadequate auditing.

*22-23 When performing an operational audit, the auditor would normally be concerned with all of the following except
   a. Calculation of earnings per share.
   b. Investigation of budget variances.
   c. Followup on inventory shortages.
   d. Reasons for idle equipment.

*22-24 When performing a preliminary survey an auditor would
   a. Assess control risk.
   b. Review flowcharts of operations.
   c. Compute sample sizes for tests of operations.
   d. Prepare a draft of the audit report.

***22-25 If the objective of the audit is to determine that adequate environmental protection and alarm devices are installed and operating, the auditor should
   a. Review the architect's alarm specification documents.
   b. Examine invoices for alarm devices.
   c. Observe and test the operation of the units.
   d. Interview the plant safety officer and plant management.

*22-26 Which of the following deviations from company policy would an operational auditor consider to be the most critical?
   a. Several late payments to vendors resulted in loss of discounts.
   b. The sales manager bribed customers to obtain their business.
   c. An employee was found to have been paid at the wrong pay rate.

   d. The personnel manager used a company car for personal purposes.

*22-27 The benefits of an operational audit generally include all of the following except
   a. Increased revenue.
   b. Increased reliability of the financial statements.
   c. Increased productivity.
   d. Decreased costs.

*22-28 An operational audit report is not likely to be addressed to the
   a. Department supervisors.
   b. Audit committee.
   c. Stockholders.
   d. Top management.

***22-29 When the operational auditor and the auditee reviewed the draft audit report, they found they had different interpretations of the facts. The auditor should
   a. Eliminate the item from the audit report.
   b. State only the auditor's position in the report.
   c. Refer the matter to the auditee's supervisor for review and resolution.
   d. Report both interpretations.

***22-30 In an operational audit of the tax department, you found that certain officers were abusing some of their executive perquisites and that this abuse may have a tax effect for the company. The tax department manager took strong exception to this finding, stating that these matters were of minor importance and their inclusion in an audit report would be embarrassing to the officers. Which of the following reporting practices would be unacceptable?
   a. Do not report the findings.
   b. Omit the findings but report the details in a confidential communication to the company president.
   c. State the findings and include comments by the tax department manager.
   d. State the findings without the comments by the tax department manager.

---

[4] Material from the Certified Internal Auditor Examination—Questions and Suggested Solutions, copyright © by The Institute of Internal Auditors, Inc., is reprinted with permission.

*22-31 In a compliance audit, an auditor is concerned with whether an entity's transactions are in conformance with
 a. Management objectives.
 b. Board of director directives.
 c. Laws and regulations.
 d. Accepted business practices.

*22-32 Organizations that issue standards affecting government audits include all of the following except the
 a. OMB.
 b. AICPA.
 c. SEC.
 d. GAO.

*22-33 Government auditing standards require external quality reviews to
 a. Demonstrate independence.
 b. Assure investors of audit competence.
 c. Increase competition among accounting firms.
 d. Assure that audit quality is maintained.

**22-34 When engaged to audit a government entity in accordance with *Government Auditing Standards,* an auditor prepares a written report on internal control
 a. In all audits, regardless of circumstances.
 b. Only when the auditor has noted reportable conditions.
 c. Only when requested by the government entity being audited.
 d. Only when requested by the federal government funding agency.

**22-35 Reporting on internal control under *Government Auditing Standards* differs from reporting under generally accepted auditing standards in that *Government Auditing Standards* requires a
 a. Written report describing the entity's internal control procedures specifically designed to prevent fraud, abuse, and illegal acts.
 b. Written report describing each reportable condition observed including identification of those considered material weaknesses.
 c. Statement of negative assurance that the internal control procedures *not* tested have an immaterial effect on the entity's financial statements.
 d. Statement of positive assurance that internal control procedures designed to detect material errors and fraud were tested.

*22-36 All of the following are general requirements for compliance with laws and regulations except
 a. Civil rights.
 b. Political activity.
 c. Freedom of information.
 d. Cash management.

**22-37 When auditing an entity's financial statements in accordance with *Government Auditing Standards,* an auditor should prepare a written report on the auditor's
 a. Identification of the causes of performance problems and recommendations for actions to improve operations.
 b. Understanding of internal control and assessment of control risk.
 c. Fieldwork and procedures that substantiated the auditor's specific findings and conclusions.
 d. Opinion on the entity's attainment of the goals and objectives specified by applicable laws and regulations.

*22-38 In auditing expenditures for compliance under a federal grant program, an auditor would be least likely to question an expenditure for supplies that is not
 a. Supported by a receiving report.
 b. Paid within the discount period.
 c. Initialed as approved for payment by an authorized official.
 d. Used in connection with the program.

**22-39 Wolf is auditing an entity's compliance with requirements governing a major federal financial assistance program in accordance with *Government Auditing Standards.* Wolf detected noncompliance with requirements that have a material effect on the program. Wolf's report on compliance should express
 a. No assurance on the compliance tests.
 b. Reasonable assurance on the compliance tests.
 c. A qualified or adverse opinion.
 d. An adverse or disclaimer of opinion.

*22-40 An auditor performing a single audit would issue all the following reports except
 a. Opinion on the financial statements.
 b. Report on management objectives.
 c. Report on internal controls over federal financial assistance.
 d. Opinion on compliance with specific requirements applicable to major federal financial assistance programs.

Chapter 22 ▶ DISCUSSION/CASE QUESTIONS

(* = author prepared; ** = CPA examination; *** = CIA examination; **** = CMA examination)

****22-41 Operational auditors use measures to evaluate performance, to identify and correct problems, and to discover opportunities. To assist in measuring achievement, a number of performance measures are available. To present a more complete picture of performance, it is strongly recommended that several of these performance measures be utilized and that they be combined with nonfinancial measures such as market share, new product development, and human resource utilization. Five commonly used performance measures that are derived from the traditional historical accounting system are

- Gross profit margin (percent).
- Cash flows.
- Return on investment in assets.
- Residual income.
- Total asset turnover.

Required:

For each of the five performance measures identified above,

a. Describe how the measure is calculated.

b. Describe the information provided by the measure.

c. Explain the limitations of this information.

***22-42 Risk assessment can be useful to an internal audit director in setting audit priorities.

Required:

Explain how the audit director should employ risk assessment in developing audit work priorities. Be specific and identify the risk indicators that would be included in the analysis.

****22-43 Brock Company is a manufacturer of children's toys and games. The company has been experiencing declining profit margins and is looking for ways to increase operating income. Because of the competitive nature of the industry, Brock is unable to raise its selling prices and must either cut costs or increase productivity. The following departments have made recommendations for improving worker efficiency and reducing costs. As an operational auditor, you have been assigned to evaluate the recommendations.

Accounts Payable Department

As the company purchases a variety of raw materials, the volume of paperwork in the accounts payable department is very large, and several accounting clerks are involved in processing and paying the invoices. The repetitive nature of this work leads to errors because of inattention to details such as part numbers and unit prices. These errors have led to double payments, payments for goods not yet received, and delays in the receipt of raw materials because suppliers that should have been paid have not been paid. These situations often require a great deal of supervisory time to resolve. The department manager has recommended that increased emphasis be placed on quality control. This would be achieved by increased monitoring of daily output, curtailing talking among staff members, and strict adherence to work hours. All errors would be discussed with the employee, and the staff would be informed that performance evaluations will be negative if errors are not reduced.

Assembly Department

Brock uses a standard cost system to monitor performance and investigates negative variances at the end of each month. The production manager has noticed that the assembly department seldom exceeds the established standards and occasionally requires less than the standard time to accomplish some of its operations. Reasoning that the application of lower standard costs to the products manufactured will result in improved profit margins, the production manager has recommended that all standard times for assembly operations be lowered. The production manager will inform the assembly personnel that the standards have been lowered and relay the company expectations that these new standards will be met.

Creative Department

Because of quickly changing consumer tastes in the toy market, demands on the creative department are increasing; however, Brock's management believes there is a need to trim departmental expenses and set priorities for the staff. Traditionally, the staff members have been given a large degree of latitude in deciding which projects are most important, but management does not believe that the projects deemed most important are always the most profitable. The manager of the creative department has recommended that the staff be allowed to participate in all budget discussions and make suggestions as to how the monies could be most effectively spent. This would afford the management team the benefit of the staff's professional expertise and allow the staff members to better understand the objectives of management.

Required:

Discuss whether the above proposals will improve productivity.

****22-44 Avery Research is a department of Northern Valley Hospital that is affiliated with a leading university. Avery operates on a project basis and consists of a pool of highly respected scientists and technicians who can be called upon to participate in a given project. Assignments are made for the duration of the project, and a project manager is given responsibility for the work.

All major projects undertaken by Avery must be approved by the hospital's board of directors. Each project requires a proposal outlining the scope, cost, expected amount of time required to complete the work, and anticipated benefits. The board must also be informed of any major projects that are terminated before completion. The status of all open projects is reviewed by the board each quarter.

Avery performs preliminary research work on potential major projects prior to requesting the board to approve the project and commit large amounts of time and money. The department also assesses the potential for grants and estimates future revenues from the project. Expenditures on preliminary research must not exceed $5,000 for any one project or $25,000 for any given quarter. Financial reports for the department and each project are prepared quarterly and reviewed with the board.

Over 75 percent of Avery's operating cost is for labor; the remaining costs are for materials utilized during research. Materials used for experimentation are purchased by the hospital's centralized purchasing department. Once delivered, Avery is accountable for storage, utilization, and assignment of cost to the projects. To protect the hospital's rights to discoveries, staff members are required to sign waiver agreements at the time of hire. These agreements relinquish the employees' rights to patent and royalty fees relating to hospital work.

Because of its desire to ensure the continued solid reputation of Avery, the board of directors has requested that the hospital's internal auditors perform an operational audit of the Avery research department. In its request, the board outlined the following set of objectives for the audit. The audit should provide assurances that

• Avery has properly assessed the revenues and costs of each project. Revenue potential should be equal to or greater than estimated costs.

- Appropriate controls exist to provide a measure of how projects are progressing and to identify, on a timely basis, if corrective actions are required.
- Financial reports prepared by Avery for presentation to the board properly reflect all revenues and all costs.

Required:

a. Evaluate the objectives presented by the board of directors in terms of their appropriateness as objectives for an operational audit. Include in your discussion

  (1) The strengths of the objectives.

  (2) Modifications and/or additions needed to improve the objectives.

b. Outline, in general terms, the basic procedures that would be suitable for performing the audit of the Avery research department.

c. Identify three documents that members of the internal auditing staff would be expected to review during the audit of the Avery research department, and describe the purpose that the review of each document serves in carrying out the audit.

***22-45** You are asked to plan and prepare for an operational audit of customer service and inventory levels of a wholesaling division that handles various types of small electric motors and parts.

Required:

a. Specify in detail the type of information the auditor should gather in the preliminary survey and identify the source of the information.

b. The division operates in a dynamic environment. Your primary audit thrust will be to determine the effectiveness of the division to (1) meet customer delivery demand so that 95 percent of all orders are delivered on time and 99 percent are delivered on time or within two weeks of specified delivery, and (2) determine that inventory levels are not excessive. Write a general audit program to accomplish the two objectives.

****22-46** You have been assigned to perform an operational audit of the Palmer Division. The division management had recently been told to implement a management by objectives (MBO) system and to increase profits by 15 percent. However, profits have actually declined, and you have been assigned to determine the reasons. While interviewing various division managers, you were told the following:

SALES MANAGER: I realized that to reach the objective, we would need a sizable increase in sales. To achieve this increase, I instituted quantity discounts on several products, and sales of these products have increased dramatically. I don't understand why we have a problem.

PRODUCTION MANAGER: We have been able to increase production to keep up with the increased sales. In addition, we have been able to make on-time deliveries for all orders by enlarging the second shift crew and having some key employees work additional hours. Production has kept pace; we're not the problem.

DIVISION CONTROLLER: Unfortunately, the products selected for the discounts already had relatively low contribution margins. With the addition of increased production costs caused by overtime payments and shift premiums, these products are scarcely at the break-even point. To make matters worse, the attention given to these discounted products diverted promotion efforts away from products with higher contribution margins.

What recommendations will you make to improve performance?

***22-47** You have just received the following draft audit report that was prepared by one of your staff auditors.

1 Audit of the purchasing department

2   Introduction

3 The purchasing department is responsible for
4 all procurements except those involving
5 executive approval. During the past months,
6 purchasing issued 19,736 purchase orders for
7 a variety of products. Our audit covered
8 only 4 of the 12 separate product classifications for which purchasing is done.

9   Purpose and Scope

10 We made our audit to determine whether
11 a. Competitive bidding was employed.
12 b. Purchase orders were being approved at
13   an appropriate level.
14 c. Buyers were following up appropriately.

15   Findings and Opinion

16 a. New procurement procedures prescribe an
17   adequate control system which is designed to
18   require supervisory review of all bidders'
19   lists to see that all qualified suppliers
20   are permitted to bid.
21 b. We found that 43 purchase orders for
22   more than $25,000 had been approved only by
23   the buyer. We reported this to the
      purchasing agent.
24 c. Followup action on late shipments has
25   been ineffective because shipments continue
26   to be received late.
27 d. Based on a random sample of 200 items,
28   there shouldn't be more than a 2% error rate
29   in the purchase orders issued.

30   _____
                                               (Signed)   Auditor

Required:
Evaluate the quality of the report and recommend improvements therein. Please use the
following format.

Line Number	Weakness in Report	Improvement Suggested

*22-48   You have been assigned to perform an operational audit of the vehicle maintenance department of a large university. What factors will you consider in determining if the department
is operating efficiently and effectively?

*22-49   Your audit of a United Fund agency that received a grant of federal funds included tests of transactions for compliance with applicable laws and regulations. Indicate whether or not and why you would question the following grant expenditures.

   a. Cost of newspaper ad for secretarial assistance.

   b. Cost of medical insurance for employees.

   c. A $500 contribution to the governor's campaign fund.

   d. Cost of having lunch with the auditors.

   e. Cost of first-class airfare to attend a meeting that was necessary for the proper administration of the grant.

   f. Cost of a monthly retainer paid to an attorney.

   g. Cost of penalty for late filing of a payroll tax return.

**22-50   Toxic Waste Disposal Company, Inc. (TWD) is a not-for-profit organization that receives grants and fees from various state and municipal governments as well as grants from several federal government agencies.

   TWD engaged Hall & Hall, CPAs, to audit its financial statements for the year ended July 31, 19X1, in accordance with *Government Auditing Standards*. Accordingly, the auditors' reports are to be submitted by TWD to the granting government agencies, which make the reports available for public inspection.

   The auditors' separate report on compliance with laws and regulations that was drafted by a staff accountant of Hall & Hall at the completion of the engagement contained the statements below. It was submitted to the engagement partner who reviewed matters thoroughly and properly concluded that no material instances of noncompliance were identified.

   1. A statement that the audit was conducted in accordance with generally accepted auditing standards and with *Government Auditing Standards* issued by the comptroller general of the United States.

   2. A statement that the auditor's procedures included tests of compliance.

   3. A statement that the standards require the auditors to plan and perform the audit to detect all instances of noncompliance with applicable laws and regulations.

   4. A statement that management is responsible for compliance with laws, regulations, contracts, and grants.

   5. A statement that the auditors' objective was to provide an opinion on compliance with the provisions of laws and regulations equivalent to that to be expressed on the financial statements.

   6. A statement that the results of the tests disclosed no instances of noncompliance that are required to be reported under *Government Auditing Standards*.

   7. A statement that the report is intended only for the information of the specific legislative or regulatory bodies, and that this restriction is intended to limit the distribution of the report.

Required:

For each of the above statements indicate whether each is an appropriate or inappropriate element within the report on compliance with laws and regulations. If a statement is not appropriate, explain why.

*22-51   You have completed your audit of State College. As required by GAS, you tested compliance with laws and regulations that could have a material effect on the financial statements. You found no material instances of noncompliance, but you did find some immaterial instances of noncompliance. Draft the report you would issue on compliance with laws and regulations.

*22-52   Modern Widgets, Inc. manufactures various types of widgets in its Ames, Iowa, plant. Management recently completed an expansion that will permit the manufacture of superwidgets, for which a large demand is anticipated.

Recently, top management has become concerned about problems in the purchasing department. The following symptoms have been noted.

1. Delays in manufacturing were caused by out-of-stock conditions for certain parts.
2. Other parts were slow-moving and in danger of becoming obsolete.
3. A large number of parts were returned to vendors, often because they did not meet specifications.
4. Unfavorable material cost variances have appeared on recent budget reports.

Management was concerned that, while these problems were important for the manufacture of widgets, they would become critical when production of the superwidgets began. The internal auditor, Diane Green, was asked to perform an operational audit of the purchasing department to identify the sources of the problems.

Required:

a. What is the purpose of the purchasing department?
b. Describe the typical document flow in a purchasing department.
c. What are some of the potential sources of the problems outside of the purchasing department?

Diane performed a preliminary survey by reviewing flowcharts of transactions and documents in the purchasing department, making general inquiries of personnel, and reviewing departmental policy manuals.

Required:

d. Prepare a list of documents that Diane would want to examine.
e. Prepare a list of questions that Diane would want to ask.

Based on these procedures Diane identified the following sources of the problems:

1. There was no policy for prioritizing requisitions from the production department. Requisitions were processed in the order in which they were received by the purchasing department. This lack of priority resulted in emergency orders being processed after routine orders. This, in turn, sometimes caused production delays.
2. Large orders were placed for certain parts when discounts became available, but no consideration was given to the cost of long-term storage or possible obsolescence of these parts.
3. Part specifications were not always clearly set forth on the purchase order. In fact, written purchase orders were not always prepared for recurring purchases from established vendors.
4. Competitive bids were seldom requested. Purchasing department personnel had done business with most of the regular vendors over a long period of time and believed they were getting a fair price.
5. Purchase order forms were not prenumbered and accounted for, which sometimes resulted in duplicate purchases that had to be returned.

Diane reviewed these matters with purchasing department personnel, who said they would be receptive to any recommendations she wished to make.

Required:

f. What specific recommendations should Diane make?
g. To whom should these recommendations be reported?
h. Who should be responsible for implementing the recommendations?